THE ALMANAC OF HIGHER EDUCATION

1992

THE ALMANAC OF HIGHER EDUCATION 1992

The Editors of
The Chronicle of Higher Education

The University of Chicago Press
Chicago and London

The University of Chicago Press, Chicago 60637
The University of Chicago Press, Ltd., London

© 1992 by The Chronicle of Higher Education, Inc.
All rights reserved. Published 1992
Printed in the United States of America

International Standard Serial Number 1044-3096
International Standard Book Number 0-226-18457-9

∞ The paper used in this publication meets the minimum requirements of the American National Standard for Information Sciences–Permanence of Paper for Printed Library Materials, ANSI Z39.48-1984.

CONTENTS

The Nation

INTRODUCTION 1-5

SUMMARY STATISTICS 6-14

MAPS

    Proportion of Adults With Four or More Years of College **15**
    Projected Change in the Number of High-School Graduates **15**
    High-School Dropout Rates **16**
    Number of Colleges and Universities **16**
    Proportion of College Students Who Are Minority-Group Members **17**
    Proportion of College Students Who Are Enrolled Full-Time **17**
    Proportion of First-Time College Freshmen Enrolled
       on Campuses in Their Home States **18**
    States' Share of Total U.S. College Enrollment **18**
    Percentage Change in College Enrollment **19**
    Percentage Change in State Appropriations for Higher Education **19**

8 ISSUES AFFECTING COLLEGES 20-21

STUDENTS

    Average SAT Scores by Sex and Racial and Ethnic Group **22**
    Average ACT Scores by Sex and Racial and Ethnic Group **22**
    Student Financial Aid **23**
    College Enrollment by Racial and Ethnic Group **24-25**
    College and University Enrollment by Level and Age of Student **26-27**
    Projections of College Enrollment and Degrees
       to be Awarded **28-29**
    Earned Degrees Conferred **30-31**
    Professional Degrees Conferred **30**
    Degrees Conferred by Racial and Ethnic Group **32**
    Proportion of 18-to-24-Year-Olds Enrolled in College **32**
    Educational Attainment of 1980 High-School Seniors by 1986 **33**
    Characteristics of Recipients of Doctorates **34-35**
    Financial Aid to Undergraduates **36**
    Attitudes and Characteristics of Freshmen **37-39**
    Foreign Students' Countries of Origin **40**
    Educational Attainment of the U.S. Population **40**
    Institutions Enrolling the Most Foreign Students **41**
    Campuses With the Largest Enrollments **42-43**
    Colleges With the Most Freshman National Merit Scholars **44**
    Number of Colleges by Enrollment **45**

FACULTY AND STAFF

    Average Faculty Salaries **46-47**
    Median Salaries of Chief Executive and Academic Officers **48**
    Employment Status of Faculty Members **48**
    Median Salaries of Administrators **49-51**
    Average Faculty Salaries by Rank in Selected Fields **52-53**
    Colleges' Experience in Faculty Recruiting **54**
    Employment Policies and Perquisites for College Presidents **55**
    Faculty Attitudes and Activities **56-59**
    Full-Time Employees in Colleges and Universities by Race **60**
    Faculty Workloads **60**
    Distribution of Full-Time Faculty Members by Rank **61**
    Distribution of Full-Time Faculty Members by
        Age and Discipline at Four-Year Institutions **61**

RESOURCES

    Total Return on College Endowments **62**
    Top Institutions in Voluntary Support **62**
    College and University Endowments Over $75-Million **63-65**
    Top Institutions in Research-and-Development Spending **66-67**
    Revenues and Expenditures of Colleges and Universities **68**
    Non-Profit Institutions Receiving the Largest Contracts
        From the Defense Department **69**
    Range of Tuition at Four-Year Institutions **70**
    Voluntary Support for Higher Education **70**
    Average College Costs **71**
    Changes in Campus Operating Budgets **71**

INSTITUTIONS

    Administrators' Views on Campus Issues **72**
    Administrators' Views of Challenges Facing Institutions
        in the Next Five Years **72**
    Holdings of University Research Libraries **73-75**

The States

Alabama 77	Kentucky 143	North Dakota 208
Alaska 81	Louisiana 146	Ohio 211
Arizona 84	Maine 151	Oklahoma 215
Arkansas 88	Maryland 154	Oregon 219
California 92	Massachusetts 158	Pennsylvania 223
Colorado 97	Michigan 163	Rhode Island 227
Connecticut 101	Minnesota 167	South Carolina 230
Delaware 105	Mississippi 170	South Dakota 234
D.C. 108	Missouri 174	Tennessee 238
Florida 112	Montana 178	Texas 242
Georgia 117	Nebraska 181	Utah 247
Hawaii 120	Nevada 185	Vermont 250
Idaho 124	New Hampshire 188	Virginia 254
Illinois 127	New Jersey 192	Washington 258
Indiana 131	New Mexico 195	West Virginia 261
Iowa 135	New York 199	Wisconsin 265
Kansas 139	North Carolina 204	Wyoming 269

SOURCES AND NOTES 272-276

Enrollment by Race 277-342

The Nation

BUFFETED BY FINANCIAL PRESSURES and inundated by scandals ranging from athletics to research, American higher education entered 1991-92 bruised and beleaguered.

The nation's 3,500 colleges and universities have been showered with negative publicity in recent years. Among the troubles in academe:
- Accusations that universities have billed the U.S. government for improper overhead charges in connection with federally sponsored research.
- Incidents of scientific fraud and misconduct.
- An investigation by the Justice Department of what it perceives to be antitrust violations by colleges in awarding financial aid and in setting tuition and admissions policies.
- Accusations of "political correctness" in the way colleges recruit, hire, and reward their professors—and in the way many professors teach.
- Criticism from minority groups that colleges are moving too slowly in diversifying the student population and faculty.

Certainly this is not the first time that colleges have been on the defensive. What is different now is the conjunction of so many strains on higher education. Educators could probably deal with any one of the strains, taken separately, but the fact that they are occurring simultaneously has made managing them all the more difficult.

College presidents, administrators, scholars, and trustees sense that the good will they once enjoyed from the American public has ebbed. Many academics are frustrated by the bad publicity, and some complain that the news media have exaggerated or oversimplified the problems.

Whether or not the perception is fair, the reality is that higher education is increasingly viewed as a business, with some of the same basic concerns as any company: namely, money and image.

And money and image will indeed be major concerns for colleges in 1991-92.

Across the nation, the news about state budgets is almost uniformly bad. The recession has led to short-term cuts for higher education, but it has also inspired long-term thinking about the need for colleges to become leaner—and better managed.

The recession's consequences have been dire for many public institutions. Tuition is rising faster than expected. Pay raises that faculty members were anticipating may fall through or be reduced. Some states are limiting enrollment.

Many private colleges are faring no better. Rising costs and dwindling resources are forcing many of them to reduce their work forces. Some institutions are going one step further: setting priorities and looking for ways to restructure their operations dramatically.

Fiscal constraints will also prevail at the federal level, limiting the amount of new money provided for student-aid programs or for improving campus facilities.

Congress has started the process of reauthorizing the Higher Education Act. Proposals under consideration include the elimination of banks from the student-loan program and a substantial increase in the maximum Pell Grant. Any such changes would take effect in 1994-95, but there is no guarantee that money will be available to pay for them.

The federal government is also reallocating funds, robbing some programs to finance others. Many scientists are concerned, for example, that too much government money is going into such "big science" projects as the Superconducting Supercollider and the space station, at the expense of smaller projects that they see as equally important to science—or more so.

Furthermore, colleges and universities can expect a brighter spotlight on the way they spend money.

The national scandal over questionable or improper overhead costs that universities have billed to the federal government has resulted in some of the country's most prominent institutions' being mocked as greedy. Overhead costs are indirect expenses that universities incur in conducting federally sponsored research. Congress and the Office of Management and Budget are now pushing for new limits on the rate at which institutions will be reimbursed for overhead costs.

EDUCATORS MAY HAVE HOPED that the Justice Department's antitrust investigation of a number of colleges would end after eight Ivy League institutions agreed to stop comparing the aid packages of students. However, the inquiry is expected to go on, since the department has requested detailed admissions information from at least 15 colleges and universities.

Sports programs also can expect to undergo more government scrutiny. A House subcommittee is in the midst of a series of hearings on college-athletics issues, and a half-dozen bills are under consideration. Meanwhile, the skyrocketing costs of athletics programs have led some institutions to eliminate teams in certain sports.

Ethnicity is at the root of a broad set of concerns that will continue to stir controversy on campuses. In the past, the federal government pushed colleges to open their doors to minority students. Now, many campus officials feel their attempts to increase racial and ethnic diversity on their campuses are at odds with the conservative notions of the Bush Administration.

The government can be expected to weigh in on several of these matters. The Education Department has been examining the legality of scholarships that are reserved for members of certain minority groups. Another debate concerns whether accrediting agencies should hold institutions accountable when they profess a commitment to increasing ethnic diversity on their campuses. Education Secretary Lamar Alexander contends that accrediting bodies should stay out of such issues.

Dramatic changes occurred on campuses as colleges sought to recruit more minority students and professors and to make the climate more hospitable to them. Colleges are facing competing pressures—both to slow down and to move faster, as they make changes in the name of "multiculturalism."

During the 1990-91 academic year, a backlash erupted against affirmative action and other policies that critics felt went too far, as well as against the efforts to broaden the curriculum to include new perspectives. Critics accused academe of operating under a "politically correct" mentality, while educators hurled counterclaims of misrepresentation and right-wing posturing.

Amid the shouting, efforts to broaden the curriculum did take place—with and without rancor—on some campuses. The debate in the humanities remains lively, pitting those who look at issues of race, class, and gender in whatever they are studying against those who opt for a more traditional literary and historical outlook.

Colleges also have been attracting attention for the misbehavior of their students. Drug raids at fraternities, instances of date rape, and other such excesses have prompted calls for colleges to take more control over their students.

As colleges struggle to deal with a full plate of problems in 1991-92, one thing is clear: Optimism is in short supply.

DEMOGRAPHICS

Population: 248,709,873

Age distribution:
Up to 17 .... 25.6%
18 to 24 .... 10.8%
25 to 44 .... 32.5%
45 and older 31.1%

Racial and ethnic distribution:
American Indian 0.8%
Asian 2.9%
Black 12.1%
White 80.3%
Other and unknown 3.9%
Hispanic (may be any race) .. 9.0%

Educational attainment of adults:
At least 4 years of high school 66.5%
At least 1 to 3 years of college 31.9%
At least 4 years of college ... 16.2%

Per-capita personal income: $18,691

Poverty rate: 13.5%

New high-school graduates in:
1991-92 (estimate) 2,441,054
2001-02 (estimate) 2,823,872

New GED diploma recipients: 409,898

High-school dropout rate: 28.9%

POLITICAL LEADERSHIP

President:
George Bush (R), term ends 1993

Vice-President:
Dan Quayle (R), term ends 1993

Secretary of Education:
Lamar Alexander

COLLEGES AND UNIVERSITIES

Higher education:
Public 4-year institutions 595
Public 2-year institutions 968
Private 4-year institutions 1,532
Private 2-year institutions 440
Total 3,535

Vocational institutions: 7,071

FACULTY MEMBERS

Full-time faculty members by rank:
Professor 112,892
Associate professor 90,342
Assistant professor 88,455
Instructor 21,896
Lecturer 7,400
No rank 48,127
Total 369,112

Average pay of full-time professors:
At public 4-year institutions $42,355
At public 2-year institutions $34,404
At private 4-year institutions $39,860
At private 2-year institutions $24,601
At all institutions $39,965
Men (all institutions) $42,629
Women (all institutions) $33,936

STUDENTS

Enrollment:
Total 13,457,855
At public 4-year
  institutions 5,694,202
At public 2-year
  institutions 4,820,771
At private 4-year
  institutions 2,680,192
At private 2-year institutions 262,690
Undergraduate 11,665,643
  First-time freshmen ... 2,353,236
Graduate 1,518,484
Professional 273,728
American Indian 92,534
Asian 496,688
Black 1,129,580
Hispanic 679,962
White 10,283,176
Foreign 361,178

Enrollment highlights:
Women 54.3%
Full-time 56.7%
Minority 18.9%
Foreign 2.8%
10-year change in total
  enrollment .... Up 15.0%

Proportion of enrollment made up of minority students:
At public 4-year institutions . 16.9%
At public 2-year institutions . 23.0%
At private 4-year institutions 15.3%
At private 2-year institutions 23.7%

Degrees awarded:
Associate 435,210
Bachelor's 1,017,667
Master's 309,762
Doctorate 35,759
Professional 70,758

Residence of new students: 81% of all freshmen attended colleges in their home states.

Test scores: Students averaged 18.6 on the A.C.T. and 896 on the S.A.T.

MONEY

Average tuition and fees:
At public 4-year institutions . $1,781
At public 2-year institutions .. $758
At private 4-year institutions $8,446
At private 2-year institutions $5,324

Expenditures:
Public institutions . $63,193,853,000
Private institutions $34,341,889,000

State funds for higher-education operating expenses: $40,096,613,000

Two-year change: Up 3%

State spending on student aid:
Need-based: $1,695,384,000; 1,423,610 awards
Non–need-based: $233,682,000; 256,946 awards
Other: $221,966,000

Total spending on research and development by doctorate-granting universities: $16,057,003,000

Sources:
Federal government 58.9%
State and local governments .. 8.1%
Industry 6.9%
The institution itself 18.6%
Other 7.5%

Federal spending on education and student aid (selected programs):
Vocational and
  adult education .. $1,287,089,000
GI Bill $342,750,000
Pell Grants $4,323,651,000

Total federal spending on college- and university-based research and development: $8,516,849,000

Selected programs:
Department of Health and
  Human Services . $4,512,022,000
National Science
  Foundation $1,206,568,000
Department
  of Defense $1,220,606,000
Department
  of Agriculture $336,036,000
Department of Energy $444,499,000

The Nation: SUMMARY STATISTICS

	1990 population	Rank	Educational attainment of adults in 1980 4 years of high school	1-3 years of college	4 years of college	1991-92 high-school graduates	High-school dropout rate in 1988
Alabama	4,040,587	22	56.5%	24.7%	12.2%	39,939	25.1%
Alaska	550,043	50	82.5%	43.7%	21.1%	6,197	34.5%
Arizona	3,665,228	24	72.4%	38.0%	17.4%	31,096	38.9%
Arkansas	2,350,725	33	55.5%	22.3%	10.8%	26,725	22.8%
California	29,760,021	1	73.5%	42.0%	19.6%	251,306	34.1%
Colorado	3,294,394	26	78.6%	44.1%	23.0%	32,598	25.3%
Connecticut	3,287,116	27	70.3%	35.9%	20.7%	29,719	15.1%
Delaware	666,168	46	68.6%	32.4%	17.5%	6,937	28.3%
D.C.	606,900	48	67.1%	41.5%	27.5%	3,976	41.8%
Florida	12,937,926	4	66.7%	31.6%	14.9%	96,709	42.0%
Georgia	6,478,216	11	56.4%	27.9%	14.6%	63,625	39.0%
Hawaii	1,108,229	41	73.8%	38.8%	20.3%	11,686	30.9%
Idaho	1,006,749	42	73.7%	37.2%	15.8%	11,825	24.6%
Illinois	11,430,602	6	66.5%	31.4%	16.2%	114,923	24.4%
Indiana	5,544,159	14	66.4%	24.6%	12.5%	61,219	23.7%
Iowa	2,776,755	30	71.5%	28.6%	13.9%	30,788	14.2%
Kansas	2,477,574	32	73.3%	34.2%	17.0%	25,671	19.8%
Kentucky	3,685,296	23	53.1%	21.8%	11.1%	36,692	31.0%
Louisiana	4,219,973	21	57.7%	26.7%	13.9%	41,494	38.6%
Maine	1,227,928	38	68.7%	29.4%	14.4%	13,533	25.6%
Maryland	4,781,468	19	67.4%	34.9%	20.4%	43,539	25.9%
Massachusetts	6,016,425	13	72.2%	35.8%	20.0%	55,444	30.0%
Michigan	9,295,297	8	68.0%	30.0%	14.3%	102,695	26.4%
Minnesota	4,375,099	20	73.1%	34.5%	17.4%	49,837	9.1%
Mississippi	2,573,216	31	54.8%	25.6%	12.3%	25,072	33.1%
Missouri	5,117,073	15	63.5%	27.2%	13.9%	52,082	26.0%
Montana	799,065	44	74.4%	36.5%	17.5%	9,086	12.7%
Nebraska	1,578,385	36	73.4%	32.8%	15.5%	18,210	14.6%
Nevada	1,201,833	39	75.5%	35.1%	14.4%	9,886	24.2%
New Hampshire	1,109,252	40	72.3%	35.1%	18.2%	11,359	25.9%
New Jersey	7,730,188	9	67.4%	31.5%	18.3%	78,401	22.6%
New Mexico	1,515,069	37	68.9%	34.7%	17.6%	16,709	28.1%
New York	17,990,455	2	66.3%	32.2%	17.9%	158,845	37.7%
North Carolina	6,628,637	10	54.8%	27.0%	13.2%	63,676	33.3%
North Dakota	638,800	47	66.4%	35.1%	14.8%	7,669	11.7%
Ohio	10,847,115	7	67.0%	26.5%	13.7%	121,401	20.4%
Oklahoma	3,145,585	28	66.0%	31.2%	15.1%	33,668	28.3%
Oregon	2,842,321	29	75.6%	38.5%	17.9%	24,968	27.0%
Pennsylvania	11,881,643	5	64.7%	24.3%	13.6%	119,577	21.6%
Rhode Island	1,003,464	43	61.1%	28.3%	15.4%	8,702	30.2%
South Carolina	3,486,703	25	53.7%	26.7%	13.4%	36,111	35.4%
South Dakota	696,004	45	67.9%	31.7%	14.0%	7,659	20.4%
Tennessee	4,877,185	17	56.2%	24.5%	12.6%	46,305	30.7%
Texas	16,986,510	3	62.6%	33.8%	16.9%	181,144	34.7%
Utah	1,722,850	35	80.0%	44.1%	19.9%	25,369	20.6%
Vermont	562,758	49	71.0%	34.7%	19.0%	6,147	21.3%
Virginia	6,187,358	12	62.4%	34.0%	19.1%	64,289	28.4%
Washington	4,866,692	18	77.6%	40.2%	19.0%	45,846	22.9%
West Virginia	1,793,477	34	56.0%	20.4%	10.4%	20,982	22.7%
Wisconsin	4,891,769	16	69.6%	29.2%	14.8%	53,930	15.1%
Wyoming	453,588	51	77.9%	37.9%	17.2%	5,783	11.7%
U.S.	248,709,873		66.5%	31.9%	16.2%	2,441,054	28.9%

Note: Totals may include data for service schools and outlying areas. Sources and additional notes begin on Page 272.

	Number of colleges and universities, fall 1989					Vocational institutions fall 1989	Faculty members, 1989-90
	Public 4-year	Public 2-year	Private 4-year	Private 2-year	Total		
Alabama	18	37	18	14	87	72	5,807
Alaska	3	0	4	1	8	40	669
Arizona	3	17	14	3	37	176	4,737
Arkansas	10	10	10	7	37	109	2,777
California	31	107	140	32	310	916	33,792
Colorado	13	15	17	9	54	119	5,255
Connecticut	7	17	21	3	48	122	5,597
Delaware	2	3	5	0	10	21	1,257
D.C.	2	0	15	0	17	31	3,383
Florida	10	28	43	14	95	320	11,181
Georgia	19	28	32	16	95	137	7,414
Hawaii	3	6	5	0	14	35	1,604
Idaho	4	2	3	2	11	39	1,532
Illinois	12	47	91	16	166	359	17,634
Indiana	14	14	41	9	78	135	8,876
Iowa	3	15	34	6	58	77	5,107
Kansas	8	21	22	3	54	76	4,729
Kentucky	8	14	24	13	59	131	5,030
Louisiana	14	6	10	4	34	196	5,821
Maine	8	5	13	5	31	22	1,935
Maryland	14	19	21	3	57	180	6,478
Massachusetts	14	16	71	16	117	177	15,167
Michigan	15	29	48	5	97	314	13,328
Minnesota	10	26	34	11	81	122	7,137
Mississippi	9	20	12	6	47	48	3,994
Missouri	13	14	52	10	89	203	7,234
Montana	6	7	3	3	19	45	1,409
Nebraska	7	13	14	2	36	48	2,656
Nevada	2	4	1	1	8	55	1,056
New Hampshire	5	7	12	5	29	28	1,907
New Jersey	14	19	25	4	62	192	8,534
New Mexico	6	16	4	0	26	39	2,123
New York	42	48	186	50	326	356	36,015
North Carolina	16	58	37	15	126	72	9,627
North Dakota	6	9	4	1	20	21	1,366
Ohio	25	36	65	26	152	310	15,232
Oklahoma	14	14	13	6	47	90	4,463
Oregon	8	13	24	1	46	113	4,550
Pennsylvania	43	18	103	53	217	366	20,219
Rhode Island	2	1	8	0	11	28	2,269
South Carolina	12	21	20	11	64	62	5,079
South Dakota	7	0	10	2	19	21	1,234
Tennessee	10	14	42	20	86	127	7,216
Texas	40	67	56	11	174	397	21,091
Utah	4	5	2	3	14	40	3,759
Vermont	4	2	13	3	22	11	1,438
Virginia	15	24	33	6	78	165	10,188
Washington	6	27	20	2	55	143	6,756
West Virginia	12	4	9	3	28	52	2,444
Wisconsin	13	17	28	3	61	99	10,016
Wyoming	1	7	0	1	9	14	990
U. S.	595	968	1,532	440	3,535	7,071	369,112

The Nation: SUMMARY STATISTICS

	Average pay of full-time faculty, 1989-90				Enrollment, fall 1989	
	Public 4-year	Public 2-year	Private 4-year	Private 2-year	Public 4-year	Public 2-year
Alabama	$35,386	$30,644	$29,760	$23,961	121,155	66,420
Alaska	$45,280	n/a	$37,976	n/a	26,274	0
Arizona	$43,465	$37,413	$32,987	n/a	96,276	143,038
Arkansas	$33,369	$25,471	$28,116	$23,969	58,662	17,754
California	$52,765	$35,482	$44,071	$33,148	494,099	1,040,110
Colorado	$41,043	$27,701	$40,380	n/a	107,324	68,526
Connecticut	$49,930	$41,081	$46,894	$27,639	65,427	44,270
Delaware	$42,074	$35,401	$36,537	n/a	23,080	9,957
D.C.	$42,195	n/a	$45,186	n/a	12,439	0
Florida	$41,741	$34,100	$36,225	$22,834	168,576	312,293
Georgia	$38,118	$30,925	$35,198	$23,326	136,239	50,537
Hawaii	$43,535	$35,317	$25,466	n/a	23,111	20,533
Idaho	$34,430	$29,090	$26,893	$24,436	33,093	5,354
Illinois	$41,181	$38,201	$41,728	$24,667	194,913	341,730
Indiana	$39,556	$25,442	$37,668	$28,825	181,286	35,147
Iowa	$45,619	$29,047	$32,499	$26,936	68,221	48,668
Kansas	$39,129	$29,453	$24,238	$19,878	89,180	55,954
Kentucky	$35,739	$26,596	$28,287	$17,797	102,332	34,965
Louisiana	$32,579	$26,641	$38,664	n/a	133,856	17,877
Maine	$38,389	$28,683	$36,923	$27,740	34,233	6,278
Maryland	$43,686	$38,560	$41,126	$20,076	110,167	107,395
Massachusetts	$47,079	$36,110	$48,138	$25,912	112,222	75,550
Michigan	$44,081	$39,648	$33,757	$23,095	255,555	224,159
Minnesota	$42,342	$38,119	$35,303	$25,670	134,896	63,714
Mississippi	$33,602	$26,972	$30,290	$17,156	56,716	46,319
Missouri	$37,006	$33,514	$34,573	$23,706	121,045	71,277
Montana	$31,305	$26,029	$25,871	$24,048	28,461	4,736
Nebraska	$38,069	$24,603	$31,514	$19,936	59,221	32,116
Nevada	$41,104	$33,411	$27,454	$33,250	27,085	29,099
New Hampshire	$39,166	$28,982	$41,379	$16,851	24,688	8,201
New Jersey	$46,741	$39,293	$46,510	n/a	135,101	118,443
New Mexico	$37,099	$27,328	$29,226	$21,911	47,591	31,768
New York	$49,452	$41,741	$42,631	$25,709	358,538	242,049
North Carolina	$40,473	$24,915	$34,592	$17,948	144,413	132,649
North Dakota	$32,768	$27,642	$24,897	$32,177	29,718	7,783
Ohio	$44,721	$33,091	$34,799	$20,775	284,356	127,717
Oklahoma	$35,665	$29,554	$36,182	n/a	94,688	56,722
Oregon	$35,504	$32,887	$34,257	$24,894	66,775	74,536
Pennsylvania	$42,983	$36,545	$40,832	n/a	234,784	100,317
Rhode Island	$44,559	$36,018	$45,566	n/a	25,204	15,400
South Carolina	$38,343	$26,117	$29,755	$24,209	79,252	39,387
South Dakota	$31,351	n/a	$24,928	$21,000	25,075	0
Tennessee	$39,158	$29,094	$34,157	$21,337	107,780	59,276
Texas	$40,233	$32,469	$38,444	$22,529	410,392	372,103
Utah	$36,404	$27,109	$43,684	$33,596	54,444	25,179
Vermont	$39,891	$28,138	$34,828	$23,680	16,127	4,798
Virginia	$46,232	$34,370	$33,861	$24,068	158,260	129,364
Washington	$41,097	$31,435	$35,120	n/a	78,387	142,975
West Virginia	$30,975	$24,471	$26,583	$21,295	62,227	10,251
Wisconsin	$40,920	$35,501	$36,133	n/a	151,146	94,822
Wyoming	$39,468	$28,961	n/a	n/a	12,335	16,218
U.S.	**$42,355**	**$34,404**	**$39,860**	**$24,601**	**5,694,202**	**4,820,771**

Enrollment, fall 1989

	Private 4-year	Private 2-year	All undergraduate	First-time freshmen	Graduate	Professional	Total
Alabama	17,526	3,461	185,592	44,003	19,921	3,049	208,562
Alaska	2,064	289	27,518	2,397	1,109	0	28,627
Arizona	11,371	1,929	226,120	61,241	25,059	1,435	252,614
Arkansas	9,916	2,240	80,962	18,398	6,195	1,415	88,572
California	201,938	8,732	1,546,687	273,783	166,676	31,516	1,744,879
Colorado	19,756	5,508	178,680	35,002	19,448	2,986	201,114
Connecticut	58,068	1,673	134,354	28,393	31,811	3,273	169,438
Delaware	7,525	0	35,757	8,227	3,277	1,528	40,562
D.C.	67,361	0	49,611	9,030	21,994	8,195	79,800
Florida	87,818	5,025	515,560	69,357	50,718	7,434	573,712
Georgia	42,284	10,148	202,793	50,914	28,288	8,127	239,208
Hawaii	10,544	0	47,361	8,675	6,389	438	54,188
Idaho	2,315	8,207	42,489	10,360	6,014	466	48,969
Illinois	164,985	8,309	607,274	125,519	85,452	17,211	709,937
Indiana	56,433	2,955	239,557	54,891	30,934	5,330	275,821
Iowa	50,955	2,057	142,936	37,583	21,218	5,747	169,901
Kansas	12,461	902	137,164	26,915	19,134	2,199	158,497
Kentucky	22,261	6,456	145,315	30,242	17,307	3,392	166,014
Louisiana	25,859	2,335	154,376	29,415	19,879	5,672	179,927
Maine	16,277	1,442	53,275	9,484	4,326	629	58,230
Maryland	37,043	721	216,118	31,486	34,829	4,379	255,326
Massachusetts	225,041	13,663	341,563	70,780	71,901	13,012	426,476
Michigan	75,567	5,039	492,910	93,725	56,358	11,052	560,320
Minnesota	49,381	5,106	222,852	49,123	24,674	5,571	253,097
Mississippi	10,329	3,006	104,352	27,244	9,848	2,170	116,370
Missouri	83,468	2,715	236,742	41,544	33,129	8,634	278,505
Montana	3,231	1,232	34,008	6,365	3,441	211	37,660
Nebraska	16,824	683	95,189	21,786	11,026	2,629	108,844
Nevada	264	23	51,610	8,455	4,666	195	56,471
New Hampshire	24,432	1,279	50,714	10,425	7,236	650	58,600
New Jersey	56,648	3,899	266,876	48,241	41,075	6,140	314,091
New Mexico	1,991	0	70,425	11,378	10,310	615	81,350
New York	394,521	23,022	828,344	162,398	163,025	26,761	1,018,130
North Carolina	63,205	5,134	307,980	66,320	30,622	6,799	345,401
North Dakota	2,672	177	36,334	8,558	2,871	1,145	40,350
Ohio	108,132	30,524	478,698	108,393	60,189	11,842	550,729
Oklahoma	18,497	5,948	151,543	30,031	20,810	3,502	175,855
Oregon	20,225	286	143,093	27,233	15,105	3,624	161,822
Pennsylvania	214,270	60,986	523,380	148,334	73,158	13,819	610,357
Rhode Island	35,899	0	66,920	13,308	9,286	297	76,503
South Carolina	22,490	4,601	125,407	33,752	17,892	2,431	145,730
South Dakota	7,232	359	28,851	6,390	3,320	495	32,666
Tennessee	45,666	6,144	192,321	37,846	21,308	5,237	218,866
Texas	90,771	4,593	766,863	132,051	95,487	15,509	877,859
Utah	34,164	1,028	104,394	20,374	9,191	1,230	114,815
Vermont	12,921	2,100	31,510	6,642	3,834	602	35,946
Virginia	54,389	2,271	297,369	47,098	40,818	6,097	344,284
Washington	32,455	1,943	234,974	66,853	17,864	2,922	255,760
West Virginia	7,196	2,781	72,115	18,318	8,891	1,449	82,455
Wisconsin	43,551	1,153	261,620	54,348	25,463	3,589	290,672
Wyoming	0	606	26,148	5,890	2,807	204	29,159
U.S.	2,680,192	262,690	11,665,643	2,353,236	1,518,484	273,728	13,457,855

The Nation: SUMMARY STATISTICS

	Degrees awarded, 1988-89					Test Scores	
	Associate	Bachelor's	Master's	Doctorate	Professional	1989 A.C.T., 1991 S.A.T.	Score
Alabama	5,877	16,508	4,233	341	787	A.C.T.	17.9
Alaska	606	1,011	286	14	0	A.C.T.	17.9
Arizona	6,167	13,767	4,884	559	420	A.C.T.	19.0
Arkansas	2,432	7,300	1,801	96	343	A.C.T.	17.6
California	48,018	91,508	33,060	4,209	7,651	S.A.T.	897
Colorado	5,943	15,561	4,574	665	873	A.C.T.	19.6
Connecticut	4,703	13,525	6,022	553	920	S.A.T.	897
Delaware	1,138	3,414	691	114	317	S.A.T.	892
D.C.	407	7,482	5,123	503	2,467	S.A.T.	840
Florida	32,244	34,244	10,563	1,201	2,051	S.A.T.	882
Georgia	7,126	19,883	6,099	800	1,846	S.A.T.	844
Hawaii	2,120	3,628	1,017	172	119	S.A.T.	883
Idaho	2,589	3,017	706	60	67	A.C.T.	19.1
Illinois	23,141	48,865	18,666	2,176	4,404	A.C.T.	18.8
Indiana	8,902	26,874	7,514	962	1,442	S.A.T.	865
Iowa	8,145	16,859	3,218	574	1,489	A.C.T.	20.1
Kansas	5,171	12,189	3,132	379	590	A.C.T.	19.1
Kentucky	4,938	12,337	3,491	332	1,167	A.C.T.	17.8
Louisiana	2,542	16,210	3,859	384	1,505	A.C.T.	17.1
Maine	1,884	5,173	633	36	139	S.A.T.	879
Maryland	6,938	17,928	5,970	711	1,124	S.A.T.	904
Massachusetts	13,016	42,500	16,967	1,986	3,605	S.A.T.	896
Michigan	20,168	40,767	12,720	1,333	2,212	A.C.T.	18.6
Minnesota	6,947	21,901	4,114	568	1,486	A.C.T.	19.7
Mississippi	4,810	8,227	2,108	245	414	A.C.T.	15.9
Missouri	6,891	23,700	8,569	621	2,300	A.C.T.	19.0
Montana	683	3,887	674	57	59	A.C.T.	19.8
Nebraska	2,734	8,406	1,776	248	727	A.C.T.	19.6
Nevada	885	2,023	502	35	46	A.C.T.	19.0
New Hampshire	2,334	6,797	1,754	87	154	S.A.T.	921
New Jersey	9,337	22,898	7,024	747	1,613	S.A.T.	886
New Mexico	1,698	4,959	1,868	217	181	A.C.T.	17.8
New York	45,465	87,719	34,442	3,579	7,046	S.A.T.	881
North Carolina	9,894	26,981	5,872	724	1,632	S.A.T.	844
North Dakota	1,797	4,287	579	61	115	A.C.T.	18.7
Ohio	18,827	45,141	12,791	1,652	3,225	A.C.T.	19.1
Oklahoma	6,172	13,617	4,112	358	950	A.C.T.	17.7
Oregon	4,456	11,823	3,120	414	906	S.A.T.	922
Pennsylvania	16,823	58,890	14,587	2,027	3,575	S.A.T.	876
Rhode Island	3,663	8,493	1,774	222	80	S.A.T.	880
South Carolina	4,949	12,524	3,269	266	738	S.A.T.	832
South Dakota	783	3,698	793	48	130	A.C.T.	19.4
Tennessee	5,605	17,398	4,840	582	1,343	A.C.T.	17.9
Texas	22,595	56,987	17,163	2,113	4,146	S.A.T.	874
Utah	3,572	10,682	2,345	367	376	A.C.T.	18.9
Vermont	1,136	4,193	991	49	85	S.A.T.	890
Virginia	7,438	26,028	6,545	764	1,695	S.A.T.	890
Washington	12,284	18,118	4,275	583	809	S.A.T.	913
West Virginia	2,640	7,033	1,691	112	315	A.C.T.	17.4
Wisconsin	8,658	25,604	5,398	771	1,017	A.C.T.	20.1
Wyoming	1,507	1,647	335	73	57	A.C.T.	19.4
U.S.	435,210	1,017,667	309,762	35,759	70,758	A.C.T./S.A.T.	18.6/896

	Minority enrollment, fall 1988				Average tuition and fees, 1989-90			
	Public 4-year	Public 2-year	Private 4-year	Private 2-year	Public 4-year	Public 2-year	Private 4-year	Private 2-year
Alabama	18.3%	19.8%	41.8%	42.2%	$1,522	$662	$5,484	$3,703
Alaska	16.2%	14.1%	25.8%	n/a	$1,280	n/a	$5,078	n/a
Arizona	13.0%	22.0%	18.9%	28.1%	$1,362	$519	$4,127	$11,007
Arkansas	15.3%	13.9%	12.9%	34.8%	$1,376	$644	$3,715	$6,102
California	33.0%	34.7%	22.8%	37.2%	$1,123	$112	$9,489	$7,664
Colorado	11.4%	15.6%	13.6%	24.1%	$1,830	$792	$9,188	$8,036
Connecticut	8.2%	15.7%	10.3%	16.0%	$2,017	$915	$11,268	$7,906
Delaware	13.0%	17.8%	12.3%	n/a	$2,768	$882	$5,388	n/a
D.C.	94.6%	n/a	30.8%	n/a	$664	n/a	$9,489	n/a
Florida	20.2%	23.3%	24.6%	40.1%	n/a	$729	$7,153	$5,519
Georgia	17.2%	20.7%	33.5%	36.6%	$1,631	$852	$7,076	$3,194
Hawaii	70.9%	74.3%	42.7%	n/a	$1,293	$410	$4,008	n/a
Idaho	4.7%	3.5%	3.6%	2.7%	$1,119	$779	$6,669	$1,400
Illinois	17.9%	27.0%	17.6%	53.4%	$2,370	$871	$8,281	$5,505
Indiana	8.1%	10.4%	7.9%	21.2%	$1,975	$1,374	$8,267	$7,412
Iowa	5.0%	4.6%	4.6%	5.4%	$1,823	$1,225	$7,945	$6,423
Kansas	7.4%	10.1%	11.6%	31.9%	$1,467	$711	$5,460	$3,962
Kentucky	7.5%	8.0%	4.0%	11.4%	$1,316	$693	$4,689	$4,669
Louisiana	27.0%	31.7%	29.1%	38.4%	$1,768	$837	$9,257	$5,648
Maine	1.5%	1.2%	3.5%	1.1%	$1,980	$1,134	$10,425	$3,787
Maryland	25.1%	22.8%	13.0%	12.9%	$2,120	$1,172	$9,914	$8,393
Massachusetts	7.3%	13.4%	11.6%	14.5%	$2,052	$1,332	$11,450	$7,186
Michigan	11.4%	14.3%	16.4%	28.5%	$2,484	$1,047	$6,520	$6,400
Minnesota	4.3%	4.1%	4.4%	8.7%	$2,063	$1,499	$8,776	$5,181
Mississippi	31.1%	25.1%	27.0%	42.4%	$1,858	$680	$4,828	$3,602
Missouri	8.9%	13.4%	10.9%	20.7%	$1,532	$815	$7,170	$5,554
Montana	4.3%	9.8%	5.7%	77.0%	$1,535	$877	$5,034	$1,144
Nebraska	4.1%	6.1%	7.1%	4.6%	$1,519	$919	$6,442	$3,410
Nevada	12.1%	16.5%	n/a	8.0%	$1,100	$522	$5,400	n/a
New Hampshire	1.6%	1.6%	6.4%	3.1%	$2,196	$1,608	$10,299	$4,050
New Jersey	20.6%	21.8%	16.0%	23.4%	$2,511	$1,130	$9,398	$6,748
New Mexico	30.7%	41.9%	33.4%	n/a	$1,326	$496	$7,335	n/a
New York	29.2%	24.3%	17.0%	37.1%	$1,460	$1,412	$9,517	$5,544
North Carolina	21.1%	20.1%	19.3%	31.0%	$1,015	$288	$7,373	$4,880
North Dakota	3.0%	14.0%	6.2%	n/a	$1,604	$1,286	$5,149	$2,100
Ohio	8.5%	11.9%	10.5%	5.6%	$2,432	$1,636	$8,019	$5,690
Oklahoma	14.5%	14.1%	13.2%	27.9%	$1,309	$840	$5,133	$5,382
Oregon	8.9%	7.3%	8.2%	7.0%	$1,738	$753	$8,656	$5,250
Pennsylvania	9.7%	13.0%	7.4%	18.4%	$3,210	$1,419	$9,430	$5,497
Rhode Island	5.1%	9.3%	6.9%	n/a	$2,281	$1,004	$10,143	n/a
South Carolina	16.7%	24.5%	30.1%	39.5%	$2,162	$807	$5,914	$4,898
South Dakota	5.7%	n/a	11.8%	33.8%	$1,718	n/a	$6,224	$2,447
Tennessee	14.6%	15.6%	17.5%	22.9%	$1,406	$803	$6,530	$3,395
Texas	25.1%	32.0%	19.8%	33.5%	$959	$455	$6,047	$5,112
Utah	5.5%	7.7%	2.0%	15.1%	$1,429	$1,136	$1,975	$2,768
Vermont	3.2%	1.3%	3.6%	1.6%	$3,641	$2,210	$10,928	$5,979
Virginia	18.1%	16.9%	21.0%	36.4%	$2,532	$813	$7,238	$4,409
Washington	12.6%	11.3%	9.3%	9.2%	$1,710	$802	$8,096	$7,045
West Virginia	5.2%	2.5%	5.9%	6.3%	$1,591	$803	$7,197	$2,554
Wisconsin	5.4%	7.7%	8.2%	18.6%	$1,861	$1,160	$7,615	$4,001
Wyoming	4.8%	5.5%	n/a	6.8%	$1,003	$613	n/a	$6,900
U.S.	16.9%	23.0%	15.3%	23.7%	$1,781	$758	$8,446	$5,324

The Nation: SUMMARY STATISTICS

	Expenditures, 1985-86		State appropriations 1991-92
	Public institutions	Private institutions	
Alabama	$1,324,774,000	$186,596,000	$791,587,000
Alaska	$224,042,000	$10,171,000	$179,981,000
Arizona	$1,017,203,000	$52,887,000	$607,819,000
Arkansas	$528,831,000	$72,321,000	$384,814,000
California	$8,515,440,000	$3,641,630,000	$5,662,752,000
Colorado	$1,057,558,000	$160,193,000	$523,785,000
Connecticut	$562,696,000	$836,949,000	$503,748,000
Delaware	$229,377,000	$15,855,000	$121,011,000
D.C.	$88,462,000	$1,307,377,000	n/a
Florida	$1,782,180,000	$723,270,000	$1,486,480,000
Georgia	$1,255,964,000	$696,734,000	$874,320,000
Hawaii	$312,248,000	$20,964,000	$321,201,000
Idaho	$238,438,000	$49,768,000	$195,881,000
Illinois	$2,571,409,000	$2,722,294,000	$1,734,761,000
Indiana	$1,602,203,000	$530,163,000	$899,643,000
Iowa	$1,092,542,000	$353,753,000	$563,570,000
Kansas	$848,602,000	$105,193,000	$446,517,000
Kentucky	$898,718,000	$194,873,000	$674,327,000
Louisiana	$1,039,177,000	$353,433,000	$574,336,000
Maine	$216,737,000	$133,778,000	$186,664,000
Maryland	$1,064,430,000	$901,948,000	$804,886,000
Massachusetts	$980,585,000	$3,544,867,000	$583,569,000
Michigan	$2,946,336,000	$447,436,000	$1,541,648,000
Minnesota	$1,324,691,000	$521,441,000	$995,429,000
Mississippi	$706,380,000	$64,054,000	$412,311,000
Missouri	$999,869,000	$911,951,000	$569,257,000
Montana	$182,102,000	$22,349,000	$131,910,000
Nebraska	$537,858,000	$161,066,000	$340,106,000
Nevada	$180,107,000	$2,448,000	$191,773,000
New Hampshire	$183,959,000	$264,440,000	$75,175,000
New Jersey	$1,406,490,000	$714,733,000	$1,132,432,000
New Mexico	$456,600,000	$16,500,000	$349,378,000
New York	$3,802,602,000	$5,594,159,000	$2,760,719,000
North Carolina	$1,799,173,000	$837,291,000	$1,445,790,000
North Dakota	$288,214,000	$18,853,000	$145,535,000
Ohio	$2,718,408,000	$980,801,000	$1,460,068,000
Oklahoma	$844,829,000	$178,905,000	$542,277,000
Oregon	$880,696,000	$171,604,000	$466,322,000
Pennsylvania	$2,392,145,000	$3,169,219,000	$1,483,233,000
Rhode Island	$213,253,000	$315,651,000	$116,128,000
South Carolina	$951,848,000	$196,271,000	$634,226,000
South Dakota	$149,092,000	$51,675,000	$97,273,000
Tennessee	$1,081,052,000	$684,948,000	$692,402,000
Texas	$4,375,082,000	$993,824,000	$2,821,810,000
Utah	$669,714,000	$194,649,000	$319,561,000
Vermont	$188,112,000	$150,689,000	$55,742,000
Virginia	$1,825,156,000	$387,455,000	$1,030,112,000
Washington	$1,399,780,000	$227,211,000	$898,184,000
West Virginia	$376,293,000	$73,716,000	$277,921,000
Wisconsin	$1,754,395,000	$373,533,000	$863,337,000
Wyoming	$203,307,000	n/a	$124,902,000
U.S.	**$63,193,853,000**	**$34,341,889,000**	**$40,096,613,000**

	State spending on student aid, 1990-91	Research spending by universities fiscal 1990	Federal funds for college-and-university-based research, fiscal 1989
Alabama	$15,881,000	$239,556,000	$123,373,000
Alaska	$2,575,000	$65,571,000	$15,111,000
Arizona	$3,427,000	$260,187,000	$103,319,000
Arkansas	$5,107,000	$48,861,000	$19,643,000
California	$164,747,000	$2,007,361,000	$1,258,964,000
Colorado	$24,279,000	$249,958,000	$147,301,000
Connecticut	$36,167,000	$298,076,000	$188,744,000
Delaware	$1,848,000	$40,119,000	$16,333,000
D.C.	$974,000	$112,146,000	$69,206,000
Florida	$69,060,000	$433,413,000	$196,397,000
Georgia	$23,058,000	$445,011,000	$183,001,000
Hawaii	$611,000	$76,525,000	$47,913,000
Idaho	$730,000	$36,570,000	$10,424,000
Illinois	$203,083,000	$647,863,000	$324,405,000
Indiana	$47,454,000	$240,696,000	$131,315,000
Iowa	$40,169,000	$232,147,000	$103,214,000
Kansas	$6,666,000	$114,651,000	$39,105,000
Kentucky	$19,393,000	$90,880,000	$36,140,000
Louisiana	$4,966,000	$207,038,000	$100,418,000
Maine	$5,100,000	$23,605,000	$9,090,000
Maryland	$20,914,000	$977,593,000	$514,747,000
Massachusetts	$71,967,000	$898,808,000	$629,070,000
Michigan	$74,878,000	$527,070,000	$259,265,000
Minnesota	$77,794,000	$292,046,000	$133,439,000
Mississippi	$1,841,000	$85,229,000	$36,227,000
Missouri	$21,495,000	$281,133,000	$150,269,000
Montana	$383,000	$34,980,000	$10,414,000
Nebraska	$2,196,000	$105,373,000	$27,462,000
Nevada	$400,000	$38,301,000	$14,113,000
New Hampshire	$1,479,000	$69,731,000	$37,007,000
New Jersey	$102,080,000	$319,797,000	$120,772,000
New Mexico	$13,424,000	$151,927,000	$74,134,000
New York	$439,124,000	$1,410,700,000	$843,497,000
North Carolina	$58,425,000	$441,860,000	$287,838,000
North Dakota	$1,492,000	$29,966,000	$11,715,000
Ohio	$80,041,000	$457,189,000	$238,131,000
Oklahoma	$35,124,000	$130,650,000	$30,968,000
Oregon	$11,748,000	$171,550,000	$90,171,000
Pennsylvania	$145,576,000	$829,518,000	$484,619,000
Rhode Island	$10,615,000	$82,634,000	$49,525,000
South Carolina	$19,447,000	$137,269,000	$38,927,000
South Dakota	$558,000	$14,342,000	$6,861,000
Tennessee	$18,002,000	$232,121,000	$115,369,000
Texas	$118,368,000	$1,123,816,000	$439,820,000
Utah	$11,486,000	$187,076,000	$108,117,000
Vermont	$11,177,000	$45,162,000	$29,630,000
Virginia	$25,514,000	$321,547,000	$155,454,000
Washington	$22,040,000	$312,169,000	$224,465,000
West Virginia	$12,953,000	$46,946,000	$15,092,000
Wisconsin	$44,757,000	$363,364,000	$186,093,000
Wyoming	$241,000	$22,831,000	$10,349,000
U.S.	$2,151,032,000	$16,057,003,000	$8,516,849,000

The Nation: SUMMARY STATISTICS

	Federal spending on selected programs, fiscal 1990		
	Vocational education	GI Bill	Pell Grants
Alabama	$25,582,000	$10,281,000	$91,096,000
Alaska	$6,056,000	$1,056,000	$7,548,000
Arizona	$17,173,000	$7,569,000	$78,363,000
Arkansas	$14,810,000	$3,948,000	$55,903,000
California	$110,652,000	$35,564,000	$392,463,000
Colorado	$26,800,000	$7,481,000	$69,308,000
Connecticut	$2,407,000	$2,485,000	$25,366,000
Delaware	$6,348,000	$619,000	$7,418,000
D.C.	$6,422,000	$666,000	$11,367,000
Florida	$53,810,000	$18,547,000	$168,987,000
Georgia	$35,754,000	$11,603,000	$80,340,000
Hawaii	$6,479,000	$2,062,000	$6,930,000
Idaho	$6,476,000	$2,065,000	$21,839,000
Illinois	$54,620,000	$12,713,000	$169,398,000
Indiana	$31,138,000	$6,222,000	$89,366,000
Iowa	$15,100,000	$4,253,000	$63,462,000
Kansas	$11,877,000	$4,504,000	$56,490,000
Kentucky	$23,678,000	$5,240,000	$71,405,000
Louisiana	$27,528,000	$8,389,000	$118,124,000
Maine	$7,037,000	$1,709,000	$13,336,000
Maryland	$20,696,000	$6,080,000	$42,774,000
Massachusetts	$26,988,000	$6,018,000	$60,299,000
Michigan	$48,288,000	$10,803,000	$165,822,000
Minnesota	$20,691,000	$7,999,000	$100,501,000
Mississippi	$17,118,000	$4,308,000	$71,312,000
Missouri	$26,648,000	$7,421,000	$97,934,000
Montana	$6,395,000	$1,790,000	$21,701,000
Nebraska	$8,420,000	$3,992,000	$35,317,000
Nevada	$6,405,000	$1,539,000	$13,135,000
New Hampshire	$6,500,000	$1,340,000	$6,299,000
New Jersey	$31,763,000	$3,769,000	$66,839,000
New Mexico	$9,171,000	$3,605,000	$36,614,000
New York	$81,216,000	$11,469,000	$372,653,000
North Carolina	$38,765,000	$9,484,000	$71,865,000
North Dakota	$6,382,000	$2,054,000	$23,799,000
Ohio	$56,926,000	$14,413,000	$189,475,000
Oklahoma	$18,612,000	$5,589,000	$80,169,000
Oregon	$13,859,000	$4,869,000	$50,767,000
Pennsylvania	$60,402,000	$11,509,000	$192,796,000
Rhode Island	$6,697,000	$1,262,000	$13,977,000
South Carolina	$21,954,000	$6,473,000	$49,459,000
South Dakota	$6,403,000	$1,990,000	$20,272,000
Tennessee	$29,411,000	$6,414,000	$75,723,000
Texas	$89,586,000	$23,268,000	$287,782,000
Utah	$9,928,000	$3,169,000	$54,196,000
Vermont	$6,829,000	$511,000	$6,771,000
Virginia	$29,378,000	$11,050,000	$75,088,000
Washington	$21,233,000	$10,516,000	$72,746,000
West Virginia	$12,095,000	$1,955,000	$34,050,000
Wisconsin	$25,229,000	$6,923,000	$81,790,000
Wyoming	$6,141,000	$859,000	$10,567,000
U. S.	**$1,287,089,000**	**$342,750,000**	**$4,323,651,000**

The Nation

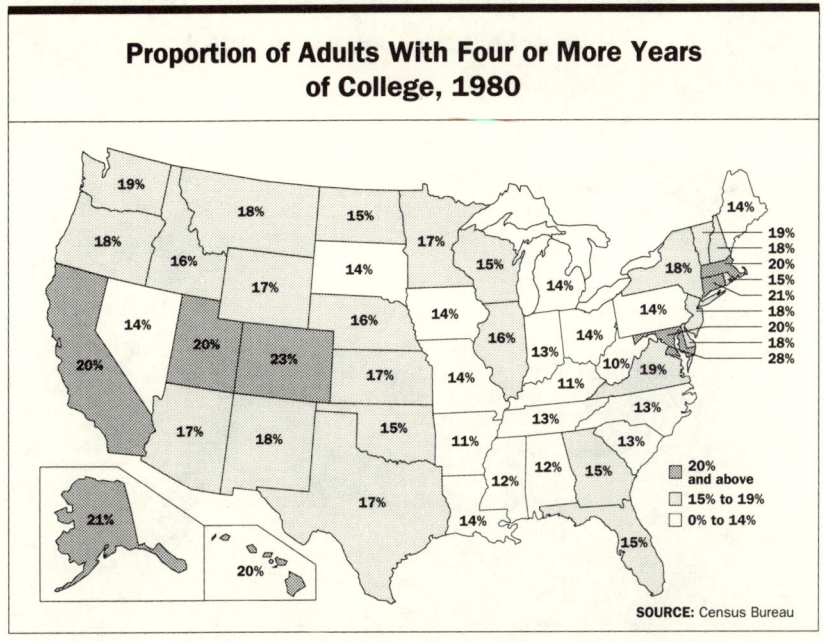

Proportion of Adults With Four or More Years of College, 1980

SOURCE: Census Bureau

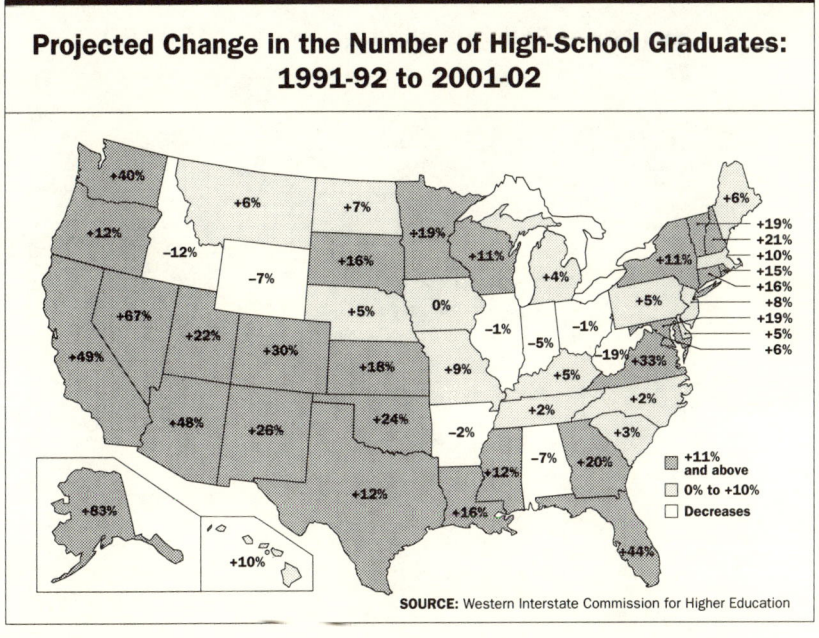

Projected Change in the Number of High-School Graduates: 1991-92 to 2001-02

SOURCE: Western Interstate Commission for Higher Education

The Nation

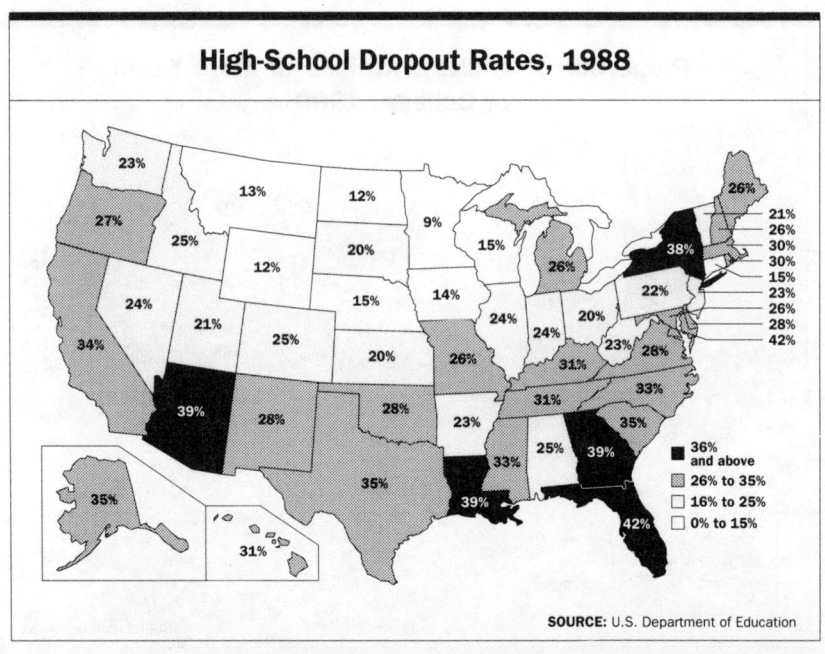

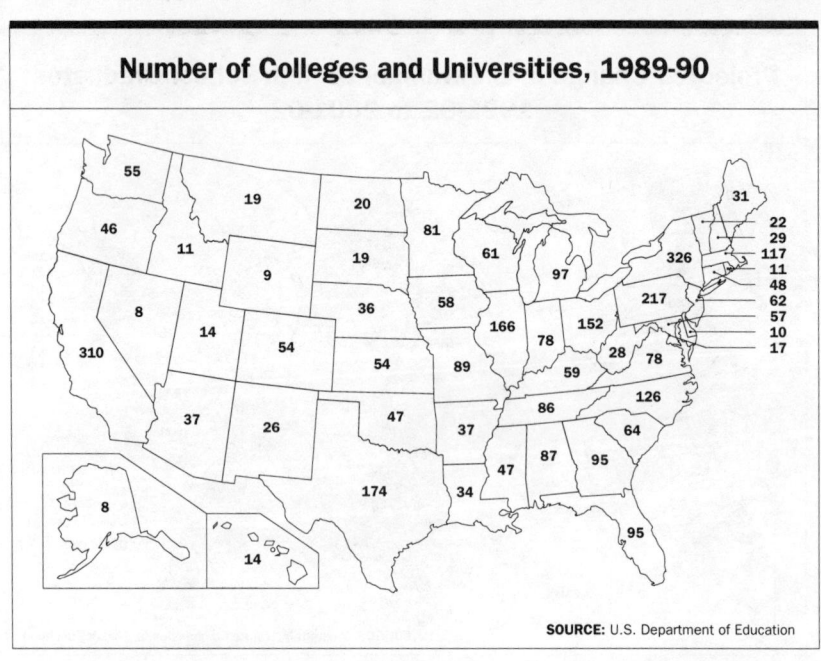

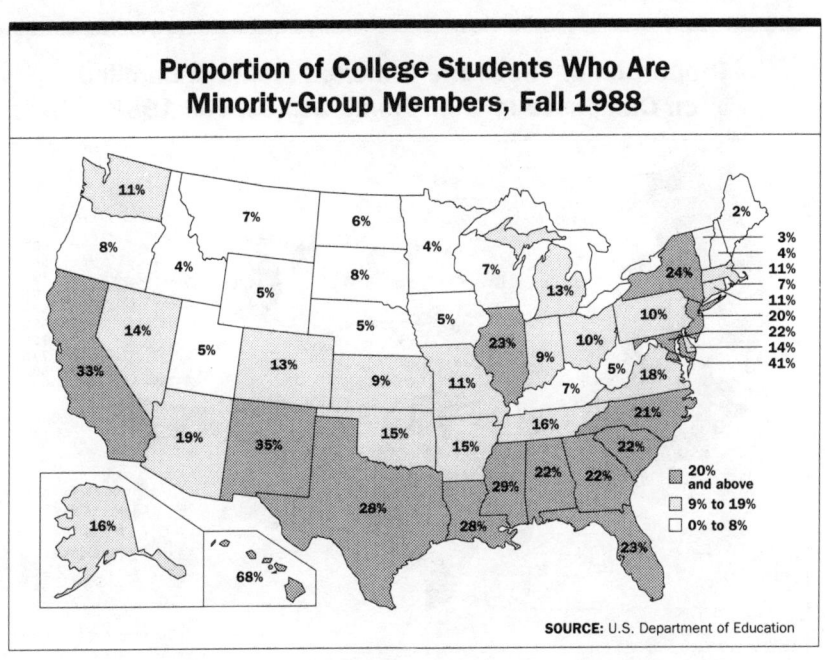

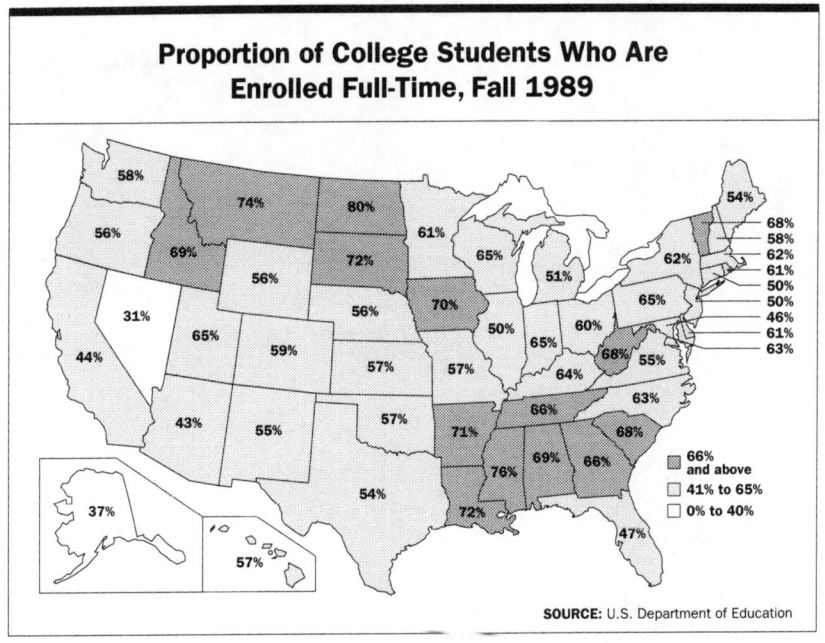

The Nation

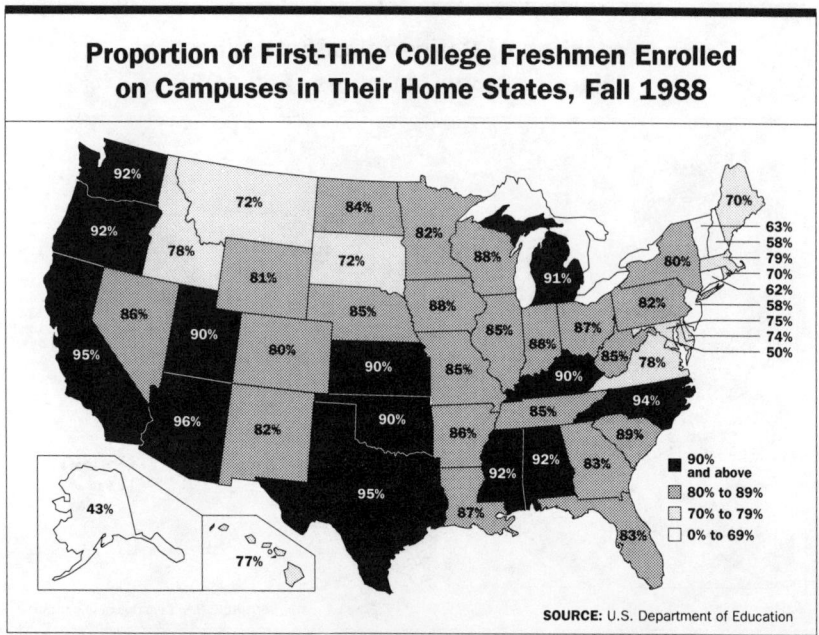

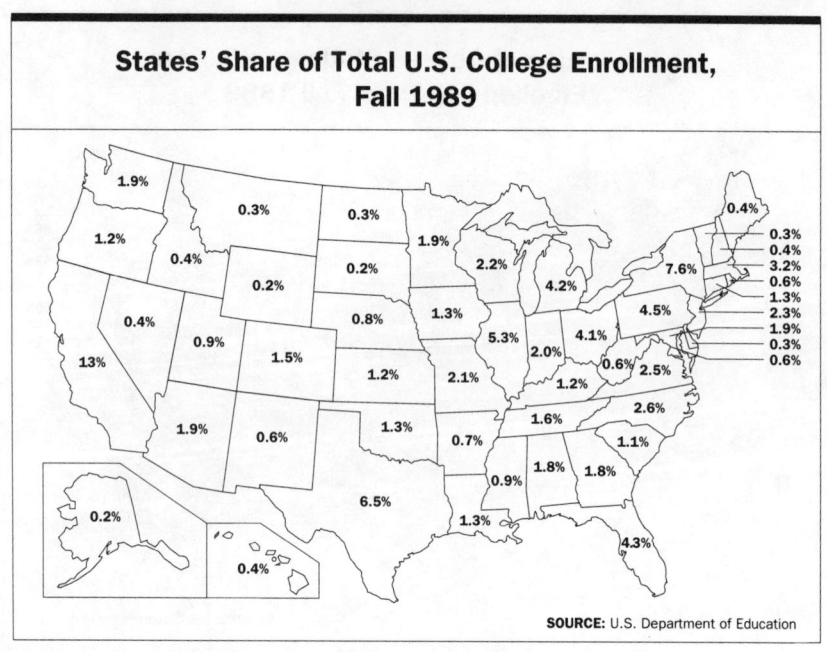

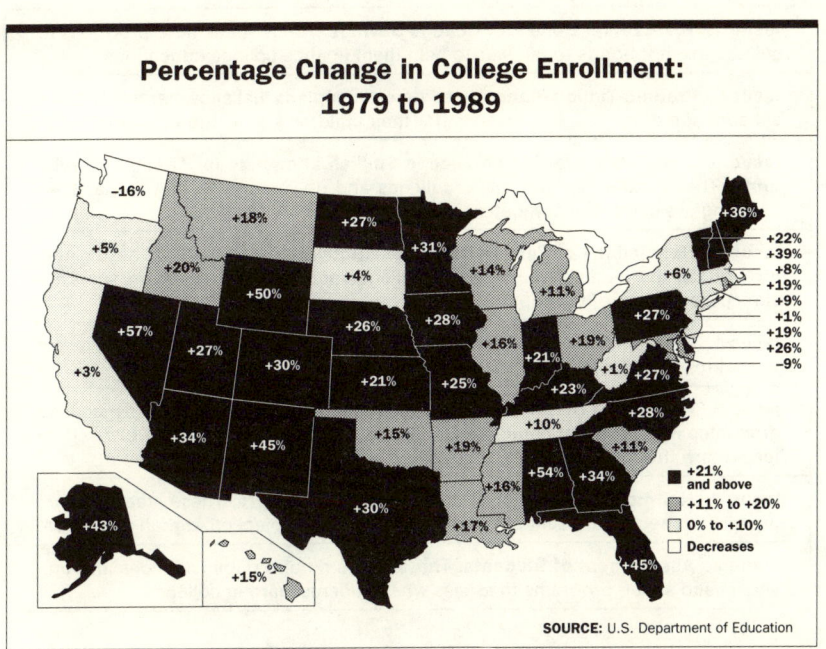

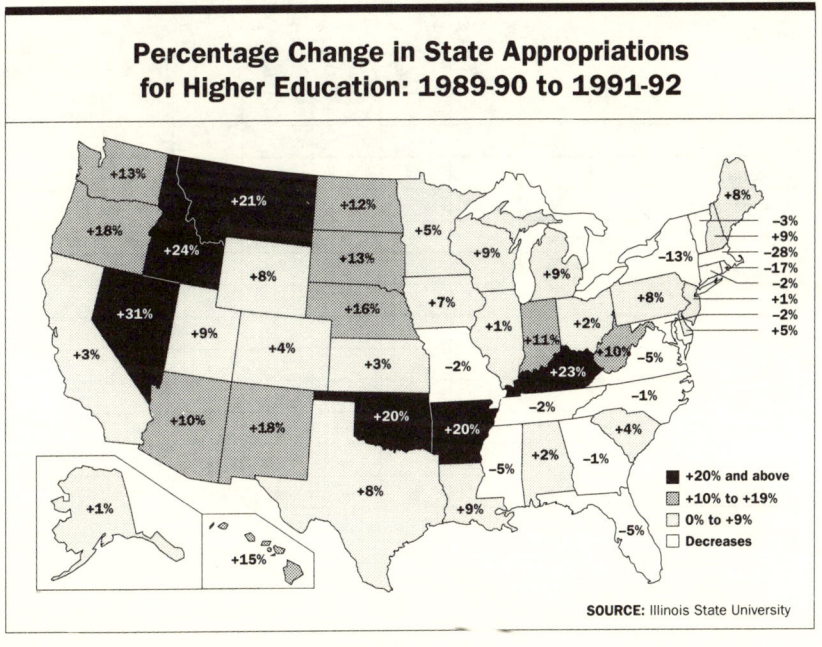

THE ALMANAC OF HIGHER EDUCATION • THE NATION

8 Issues Affecting Colleges: Roll Call of the States

Issue 1. Tax-Exempt Bonds for College Savings. These states have programs to sell tax-exempt bonds to families to help them finance college educations.

Issue 2. Prepaid-Tuition Plans. These states offer plans that allow parents to pay a set sum of money, years in advance, for their children's education.

Issue 3. Certification of Competence in English Language for Teaching Assistants. These states require public colleges and universities to certify that their teaching assistants are competent in English.

Issue 4. Restrictions or Taxes on Business Activities of Colleges. These states limit or tax the business activities of colleges and universities (or, in some instances, all non-profit groups).

Issue 5. Vandalism of Animal-Research Facilities. These states treat vandalism of animal-research facilities as a specific crime.

Issue 6. Alternative Certification for Schoolteachers. These states allow college graduates who have not completed an education major to become public-school teachers without completing a traditional course of study in education.

Issue 7. Non-Education Majors for High-School Teachers. These states require prospective secondary-school teachers to major in a subject other than education.

Issue 8. Assessment of Students. These states require public colleges and universities to set up programs to assess what students learn in college.

	Issue 1	Issue 2	Issue 3	Issue 4	Issue 5	Issue 6	Issue 7	Issue 8
Alabama		★				★		★
Alaska		★				★		
Arizona			★	★	★	★		
Arkansas	★				★	★	★	★
California	★					★	★	
Colorado	★			★			★	★
Connecticut	★					★	★	★
Delaware	★					★	★	
Florida		★	★			★	★	★
Georgia		★			★	★		★
Hawaii						★	★	
Idaho				★	★	★		★
Illinois	★		★	★	★			

	Issue 1	Issue 2	Issue 3	Issue 4	Issue 5	Issue 6	Issue 7	Issue 8
Indiana	★				★			
Iowa	★	★	★	★	★			★
Kansas			★	★	★			
Kentucky	★				★	★	★	
Louisiana	★		★	★	★	★		
Maine								
Maryland					★			★
Massachusetts	★	★			★	★	★	
Michigan		★				★	★	
Minnesota					★	★	★	
Mississippi						★		
Missouri			★	★		★	★	
Montana					★			
Nebraska								
Nevada							★	★
New Hampshire	★					★	★	
New Jersey	★					★	★	★
New Mexico						★		
New York					★	★	★	
North Carolina	★				★	★	★	
North Dakota	★		★		★		★	
Ohio	★	★	★					
Oklahoma		★	★		★	★	★	
Oregon	★				★			
Pennsylvania	★		★			★	★	
Rhode Island	★						★	
South Carolina			★			★		★
South Dakota	★			★				★
Tennessee	★		★				★	★
Texas	★		★		★	★	★	★
Utah				★	★	★	★	★
Vermont								
Virginia	★					★	★	★
Washington	★				★		★	★
West Virginia	★	★				★		★
Wisconsin	★				★		★	★
Wyoming		★						

A STAR INDICATES AN ACTION EITHER BY A STATE LEGISLATURE OR BY A STATEWIDE COORDINATING BOARD OR GOVERNING BOARD, AS OF NOVEMBER 1, 1991. SOURCE: CHRONICLE REPORTING

Average SAT Scores by Sex and Racial and Ethnic Group, 1991

	Verbal section		Mathematical section	
	Score	1-year change	Score	1-year change
Men	426	− 3	497	− 2
Women	418	− 1	453	− 2
American Indian	393	+ 5	437	0
Asian	411	+ 1	530	+ 2
Black	351	− 1	385	0
Mexican-American	377	− 3	427	− 2
Puerto Rican	361	+ 2	406	+ 1
Other Hispanic	382	− 1	431	− 3
White	441	− 1	489	− 2
Other	411	+ 1	466	− 1
All	422	− 2	474	− 2

Note: Each section of the Scholastic Aptitude Test is scored on a scale from 200 to 800.

SOURCE: THE COLLEGE BOARD

Average ACT Scores by Sex and Racial and Ethnic Group, 1991

	Score	1-year change
Men	20.9	−0.1
Women	20.4	+0.1
American Indian	18.2	+0.2
Asian	21.6	−0.1
Black	17.0	0.0
Mexican-American	18.4	+0.1
Other Hispanic	19.3	0.0
White	21.3	+0.1
All	20.6	0.0

Note: The American College Testing Program's ACT Assessment is scored on a scale from 1 to 36.

SOURCE: AMERICAN COLLEGE TESTING PROGRAM

Student Financial Aid, 1990-91

Total spending, by source

Federal programs
Generally available aid
Pell Grants	$4,915,000,000
Supplemental Educational Opportunity Grants	439,000,000
State Student Incentive Grants	59,000,000
College Work-Study	823,000,000
Perkins Loans	860,000,000
Income Contingent Loans	6,000,000
Stafford Student Loans	9,844,000,000
Supplemental Loans for Students	1,630,000,000
Parent Loans for Undergraduate Students	942,000,000
Subtotal	19,517,000,000

Specially directed aid
Veterans	701,000,000
Military	378,000,000
Other grants	119,000,000
Other loans	349,000,000
Subtotal	1,547,000,000
Total federal aid	21,065,000,000
State grant programs	1,870,000,000
Institutional and other grants	4,915,000,000
Total federal, state, and institutional aid	$27,850,000,000

Number of recipients and amount of aid per recipient, selected programs

Program	Recipients	Amount
Pell Grants	3,300,000	$1,489
Supplemental Educational Opportunity Grants	678,000	648
College Work-Study	876,000	940
Perkins Loans	804,000	1,070
Stafford Student Loans	3,633,000	2,709
Supplemental Loans for Students	576,000	2,828
Parent Loans for Undergraduate Students	293,000	3,213
State Grants and State Student Incentive Grants	1,681,000	1,148

Note: Figures are estimates and include assistance to undergraduate and graduate students.
 Several of the federal programs include small amounts of money from sources other than the federal government. For example, College Work-Study includes some contributions by institutions, although most of the funds in the program are federal.
 Federal spending for State Student Incentive Grants is reported under federal programs; state spending for those grants is reported in the "state grants" category.
 Funds for Stafford Student Loans, Supplemental Loans for Students, and Parent Loans for Undergraduate Students come mostly from private sources. The federal government subsidizes interest payments and repays defaults. Amounts reported represent loan commitments rather than amounts loaned, but the difference between the two is insignificant.
 Veterans' benefits are payments for postsecondary education and training to veterans and their dependents.
 Military aid covers the Armed Forces Health Professions Scholarship program; Reserve Officers Training Corps programs for the Air Force, Army, and Navy; and tuition assistance for military personnel on active duty.
 Because of rounding, details may not add to totals.

SOURCE: THE COLLEGE BOARD

College Enrollment by Racial and Ethnic Group, Selected Years

American Indian	1978	1980	1982	1984	1986	1988
All	78,000	84,000	88,000	84,000	90,000	93,000
Men	37,000	38,000	40,000	38,000	39,000	39,000
Women	41,000	46,000	48,000	46,000	51,000	53,000
Public	68,000	74,000	77,000	72,000	79,000	81,000
Private	9,000	10,000	10,000	11,000	11,000	11,000
4-year	35,000	37,000	39,000	38,000	40,000	42,000
2-year	43,000	47,000	49,000	46,000	51,000	50,000
Undergraduate	72,000	79,000	82,000	78,000	83,000	86,000
Graduate	4,000	4,000	5,000	5,000	5,000	6,000
Professional	1,000	1,000	1,000	1,000	1,000	1,000
Asian						
All	235,000	286,000	351,000	390,000	448,000	497,000
Men	126,000	151,000	189,000	210,000	239,000	259,000
Women	109,000	135,000	162,000	180,000	209,000	237,000
Public	195,000	240,000	296,000	323,000	371,000	406,000
Private	40,000	47,000	55,000	67,000	77,000	91,000
4-year	138,000	162,000	193,000	223,000	262,000	297,000
2-year	97,000	124,000	158,000	167,000	186,000	199,000
Undergraduate	206,000	253,000	313,000	343,000	393,000	437,000
Graduate	24,000	28,000	30,000	37,000	43,000	46,000
Professional	5,000	6,000	8,000	9,000	11,000	14,000
Black						
All	1,054,000	1,107,000	1,101,000	1,076,000	1,082,000	1,130,000
Men	453,000	464,000	458,000	437,000	436,000	443,000
Women	601,000	643,000	644,000	639,000	646,000	687,000
Public	840,000	876,000	873,000	844,000	854,000	881,000
Private	215,000	231,000	228,000	232,000	228,000	248,000
4-year	612,000	634,000	612,000	617,000	615,000	656,000
2-year	443,000	472,000	489,000	459,000	467,000	473,000
Undergraduate	975,000	1,028,000	1,028,000	995,000	996,000	1,039,000
Graduate	68,000	66,000	61,000	67,000	72,000	76,000
Professional	11,000	13,000	13,000	13,000	14,000	14,000
Hispanic						
All	417,000	472,000	519,000	535,000	618,000	680,000
Men	213,000	232,000	252,000	254,000	290,000	310,000
Women	205,000	240,000	267,000	281,000	328,000	370,000
Public	363,000	406,000	446,000	456,000	532,000	587,000
Private	55,000	66,000	74,000	79,000	86,000	93,000
4-year	190,000	217,000	229,000	246,000	278,000	296,000
2-year	227,000	255,000	291,000	289,000	340,000	384,000
Undergraduate	388,000	438,000	485,000	495,000	563,000	631,000
Graduate	24,000	27,000	27,000	32,000	46,000	39,000
Professional	5,000	7,000	7,000	8,000	9,000	9,000

Note: Because of rounding, details may not add to totals. The federal government compiles data on the race of students every two years; the latest report covers 1988.

White	1978	1980	1982	1984	1986	1988
All	9,194,000	9,833,000	9,997,000	9,815,000	9,921,000	10,283,000
Men	4,613,000	4,773,000	4,830,000	4,690,000	4,647,000	4,712,000
Women	4,581,000	5,060,000	5,167,000	5,125,000	5,273,000	5,572,000
Public	7,136,000	7,656,000	7,785,000	7,543,000	7,654,000	7,964,000
Private	2,058,000	2,177,000	2,212,000	2,272,000	2,267,000	2,319,000
4-year	6,027,000	6,275,000	6,306,000	6,301,000	6,337,000	6,582,000
2-year	3,167,000	3,558,000	3,692,000	3,514,000	3,584,000	3,702,000
Undergraduate	7,946,000	8,556,000	8,749,000	8,484,000	8,558,000	8,907,000
Graduate	1,019,000	1,030,000	1,002,000	1,087,000	1,133,000	1,153,000
Professional	229,000	248,000	246,000	243,000	231,000	223,000
Foreign						
All	253,000	305,000	331,000	335,000	345,000	361,000
Men	180,000	211,000	230,000	231,000	233,000	235,000
Women	73,000	94,000	101,000	104,000	112,000	126,000
Public	167,000	204,000	219,000	219,000	224,000	238,000
Private	85,000	101,000	113,000	116,000	120,000	123,000
4-year	201,000	241,000	270,000	282,000	292,000	302,000
2-year	52,000	64,000	61,000	53,000	53,000	60,000
Undergraduate	169,000	208,000	220,000	216,000	205,000	205,000
Graduate	80,000	94,000	108,000	115,000	136,000	151,000
Professional	3,000	3,000	3,000	3,000	4,000	5,000
All						
Total	11,231,000	12,087,000	12,388,000	12,235,000	12,504,000	13,043,000
Men	5,621,000	5,868,000	5,999,000	5,859,000	5,885,000	5,998,000
Women	5,609,000	6,219,000	6,389,000	6,376,000	6,619,000	7,045,000
Public	8,770,000	9,456,000	9,695,000	9,458,000	9,714,000	10,156,000
Private	2,461,000	2,630,000	2,693,000	2,777,000	2,790,000	2,887,000
4-year	7,203,000	7,565,000	7,648,000	7,708,000	7,824,000	8,175,000
2-year	4,028,000	4,521,000	4,740,000	4,527,000	4,680,000	4,868,000
Undergraduate	9,757,000	10,560,000	10,875,000	10,610,000	10,798,000	11,304,000
Graduate	1,219,000	1,250,000	1,235,000	1,344,000	1,435,000	1,472,000
Professional	255,000	277,000	278,000	278,000	270,000	267,000

SOURCE: U. S. DEPARTMENT OF EDUCATION

College and University Enrollment by Level and Age of Student, Fall 1987

	Undergraduate			First-professional		
	Men	Women	Total	Men	Women	Total
Full-time students						
Under 18	1.5%	2.0%	1.8%	0.0%	0.0%	0.0%
18 to 19	34.4	37.6	36.1	0.1	0.1	0.1
20 to 21	29.8	29.2	29.5	2.6	3.6	3.0
22 to 24	18.7	13.5	16.0	40.0	40.2	40.1
25 to 29	7.8	6.5	7.2	37.6	32.4	35.7
30 to 34	3.4	4.3	3.8	10.9	11.5	11.1
35 to 39	1.7	2.9	2.3	4.5	5.9	5.0
40 to 49	1.3	2.4	1.8	2.1	3.9	2.8
50 to 64	0.3	0.5	0.4	0.4	0.7	0.5
65 and over	0.1	0.1	0.1	0.1	0.1	0.1
Age unknown	1.0	1.0	1.0	1.6	1.7	1.7
Number of full-time students	3,163,754	3,299,312	6,463,066	153,661	88,143	241,804
Part-time students						
Under 18	2.0%	2.0%	2.0%	0.0%	0.0%	0.0%
18 to 19	8.7	7.5	8.0	0.0	0.0	0.0
20 to 21	11.5	9.3	10.2	0.4	0.3	0.4
22 to 24	17.1	13.6	15.1	10.5	10.0	10.3
25 to 29	20.6	17.6	18.9	35.8	30.4	33.7
30 to 34	14.6	14.7	14.7	24.3	22.3	23.6
35 to 39	9.3	12.0	10.9	14.6	16.0	15.1
40 to 49	8.8	13.7	11.7	10.1	14.7	11.9
50 to 64	3.7	5.3	4.6	2.6	3.8	3.1
65 and over	1.6	2.1	1.9	0.3	0.3	0.3
Age unknown	2.1	2.1	2.1	1.4	2.1	1.7
Number of part-time students	1,904,930	2,679,906	4,584,836	16,472	10,191	26,663
All students						
Under 18	1.7%	2.0%	1.9%	0.0%	0.0%	0.0%
18 to 19	24.7	24.1	24.4	0.1	0.1	0.1
20 to 21	22.9	20.3	21.5	2.4	3.2	2.7
22 to 24	18.1	13.5	15.6	37.1	37.1	37.1
25 to 29	12.6	11.5	12.0	37.4	32.2	35.5
30 to 34	7.6	8.9	8.3	12.2	12.6	12.3
35 to 39	4.6	7.0	5.9	5.5	6.9	6.0
40 to 49	4.1	7.4	5.9	2.9	5.0	3.7
50 to 64	1.6	2.6	2.2	0.7	1.0	0.8
65 and over	0.7	1.0	0.9	0.1	0.1	0.1
Age unknown	1.4	1.5	1.5	1.6	1.8	1.7
Total number of students	5,068,684	5,979,218	11,047,902	170,133	98,334	268,467

Note: The federal government compiles data on the age of students every two years; the latest published report covers 1987.

| | Graduate | | | All levels | |
Men	Women	Total	Men	Women	Total
0.0%	0.0%	0.0%	1.3%	1.8%	1.6%
0.1	0.1	0.1	30.2	34.3	32.2
1.1	1.3	1.2	26.3	26.8	26.5
22.0	24.0	22.9	19.8	14.8	17.3
36.8	30.3	33.9	11.4	8.7	10.1
19.7	16.5	18.3	5.0	5.2	5.1
10.3	11.7	10.9	2.5	3.5	3.0
6.0	11.3	8.3	1.7	3.0	2.4
1.3	2.6	1.9	0.4	0.7	0.5
0.7	0.2	0.5	0.2	0.1	0.1
2.1	1.9	2.0	1.1	1.1	1.1
293,503	233,133	526,636	3,610,918	3,620,588	7,231,506
0.1%	0.1%	0.1%	1.7%	1.7%	1.7%
0.0	0.0	0.0	7.1	6.2	6.6
0.3	0.3	0.3	9.5	7.8	8.5
8.9	8.6	8.7	15.6	12.8	14.0
28.9	23.3	25.7	22.2	18.6	20.1
23.4	18.7	20.7	16.2	15.4	15.7
16.7	18.0	17.5	10.6	13.0	12.0
14.2	20.5	17.8	9.7	14.8	12.7
3.3	5.4	4.5	3.6	5.3	4.6
0.6	0.5	0.5	1.4	1.9	1.7
3.6	4.5	4.1	2.4	2.5	2.4
399,811	525,491	925,302	2,321,213	3,215,588	5,536,801
0.1%	0.0%	0.1%	1.5%	1.8%	1.6%
0.0	0.0	0.0	21.1	21.1	21.1
0.6	0.7	0.6	19.7	17.9	18.7
14.4	13.4	13.9	18.2	13.9	15.9
32.2	25.5	28.7	15.6	13.4	14.4
21.8	18.0	19.8	9.4	10.0	9.7
14.0	16.1	15.1	5.7	8.0	6.9
10.7	17.7	14.3	4.9	8.5	6.8
2.5	4.6	3.6	1.7	2.8	2.3
0.6	0.4	0.5	0.6	0.9	0.8
3.0	3.7	3.3	1.6	1.7	1.7
693,314	758,624	1,451,938	5,932,131	6,836,176	12,768,307

SOURCE: U. S. DEPARTMENT OF EDUCATION

Projections of College Enrollment and Degrees to Be Awarded, 1991-2001

	1991	1992	1993	1994	1995
Enrollment	13,643,000	13,613,000	13,597,000	13,579,000	13,657,000
Men	6,309,000	6,276,000	6,254,000	6,228,000	6,247,000
Women	7,334,000	7,337,000	7,343,000	7,351,000	7,410,000
Public institutions	10,608,000	10,587,000	10,579,000	10,571,000	10,637,000
Private institutions	3,035,000	3,026,000	3,018,000	3,008,000	3,020,000
Full-time students	7,627,000	7,569,000	7,508,000	7,456,000	7,490,000
Part-time students	6,016,000	6,044,000	6,089,000	6,123,000	6,167,000
Four-year institutions					
Total	8,599,000	8,572,000	8,540,000	8,507,000	8,542,000
Public	5,826,000	5,806,000	5,783,000	5,760,000	5,785,000
Private	2,773,000	2,766,000	2,757,000	2,747,000	2,757,000
Two-year institutions					
Total	5,044,000	5,041,000	5,057,000	5,072,000	5,115,000
Public	4,782,000	4,781,000	4,796,000	4,811,000	4,852,000
Private	262,000	260,000	261,000	261,000	263,000
Undergraduate	11,706,000	11,661,000	11,625,000	11,598,000	11,668,000
Graduate	1,644,000	1,657,000	1,674,000	1,684,000	1,691,000
First-professional	293,000	295,000	298,000	297,000	298,000
Degrees					
Associate	463,000	465,000	461,000	459,000	458,000
Bachelor's	1,024,000	1,060,000	1,063,000	1,058,000	1,047,000
Master's	321,000	322,000	323,000	323,000	324,000
Doctorate	35,900	35,900	36,100	36,200	36,300
First-professional	74,600	75,800	76,800	77,900	77,300

1996	1997	1998	1999	2000	2001
13,747,000	13,906,000	14,089,000	14,165,000	14,326,000	14,447,000
6,271,000	6,331,000	6,412,000	6,395,000	6,468,000	6,522,000
7,476,000	7,575,000	7,677,000	7,770,000	7,858,000	7,925,000
10,710,000	10,834,000	10,977,000	11,047,000	11,171,000	11,264,000
3,037,000	3,072,000	3,112,000	3,118,000	3,155,000	3,183,000
7,542,000	7,654,000	7,801,000	7,841,000	7,970,000	8,067,000
6,205,000	6,252,000	6,288,000	6,324,000	6,356,000	6,380,000
8,588,000	8,685,000	8,803,000	8,837,000	8,945,000	9,026,000
5,816,000	5,883,000	5,965,000	5,994,000	6,070,000	6,126,000
2,772,000	2,802,000	2,838,000	2,843,000	2,875,000	2,900,000
5,159,000	5,221,000	5,286,000	5,328,000	5,381,000	5,421,000
4,894,000	4,951,000	5,012,000	5,053,000	5,101,000	5,138,000
265,000	270,000	274,000	275,000	280,000	283,000
11,753,000	11,903,000	12,084,000	12,208,000	12,365,000	12,487,000
1,696,000	1,704,000	1,706,000	1,675,000	1,679,000	1,678,000
298,000	299,000	299,000	282,000	282,000	282,000
459,000	463,000	469,000	477,000	482,000	489,000
1,031,000	1,015,000	1,012,000	1,010,000	1,019,000	1,037,000
324,000	324,000	324,000	325,000	326,000	327,000
36,400	36,400	36,400	36,400	36,300	36,200
77,300	77,300	77,800	77,800	71,300	71,300

SOURCE: U. S. DEPARTMENT OF EDUCATION

Earned Degrees Conferred, 1988-89

	Bachelor's degrees		
	Total	Men	Women
Agriculture and natural resources	13,488	9,295	4,193
Architecture and environmental design	9,191	5,580	3,611
Area and ethnic studies	3,949	1,613	2,336
Business and management	246,659	131,419	115,240
Communications	47,385	18,567	28,818
Communications technologies	1,240	696	544
Computer and information sciences	30,637	21,221	9,416
Education	96,988	21,662	75,326
Engineering	66,296	56,234	10,062
Engineering technologies	18,977	17,417	1,560
Foreign languages	10,774	2,879	7,895
Health sciences	59,111	8,926	50,185
Home economics	14,717	1,380	13,337
Law	1,976	785	1,191
Letters	43,323	14,237	29,086
Liberal/general studies	23,459	10,051	13,408
Library and archival sciences	122	16	106
Life sciences	36,079	17,970	18,109
Mathematics	15,237	8,221	7,016
Military sciences	419	378	41
Multi/interdisciplinary studies	18,213	8,419	9,794
Parks and recreation	4,171	1,709	2,462
Philosophy and religion	6,411	4,122	2,289
Physical sciences	17,204	12,097	5,107
Protective services	14,626	9,074	5,552
Psychology	48,516	14,181	34,335
Public affairs and social work	15,254	4,948	10,306
Social sciences	107,714	59,924	47,790
Theology	5,322	4,108	1,214
Visual and performing arts	37,781	14,558	23,223
Not classified by field of study	2,428	1,410	1,018
All fields	1,017,667	483,097	534,570

Professional Degrees Conferred, 1988-89

	Total	Men	Women
Chiropractic	2,890	2,159	731
Dentistry	4,247	3,139	1,108
Law	35,567	21,048	14,519
Medicine	15,454	10,326	5,128
Optometry	1,093	683	410
Osteopathic medicine	1,635	1,183	452
Pharmacy	1,074	422	652
Podiatry, podiatric medicine	636	487	149
Theological professions	6,005	4,639	1,366
Veterinary medicine	2,157	981	1,176
All fields	70,758	45,067	25,691

SOURCE: U.S. DEPARTMENT OF EDUCATION

	Master's degrees			Doctoral degrees	
Total	Men	Women	Total	Men	Women
3,245	2,231	1,014	1,184	952	232
3,378	2,191	1,187	86	63	23
978	497	481	110	57	53
73,154	48,557	24,597	1,150	844	306
3,926	1,540	2,386	242	135	107
307	170	137	6	2	4
9,392	6,769	2,623	538	457	81
82,238	20,286	61,952	6,783	2,894	3,889
23,713	20,633	3,080	4,521	4,121	400
828	722	106	12	12	0
1,911	602	1,309	422	169	253
19,255	4,210	15,045	1,439	612	827
2,174	311	1,863	263	59	204
2,098	1,491	607	76	46	30
6,608	2,272	4,336	1,238	559	679
1,408	495	913	32	16	16
3,940	816	3,124	61	27	34
4,933	2,484	2,449	3,533	2,235	1,298
3,424	2,058	1,366	882	711	171
0	0	0	0	0	0
3,225	1,966	1,259	257	158	99
460	213	247	36	28	8
1,274	755	519	464	341	123
5,737	4,204	1,533	3,852	3,093	759
1,046	722	324	27	19	8
8,579	2,799	5,780	3,263	1,429	1,834
17,928	6,398	11,530	417	208	209
10,854	6,493	4,361	2,878	1,939	939
4,625	3,003	1,622	1,165	1,022	143
8,234	3,598	4,636	755	443	312
890	496	394	67	54	13
309,762	148,982	160,780	35,759	22,705	13,054

SOURCE: U.S. DEPARTMENT OF EDUCATION

Degrees Conferred by Racial and Ethnic Group, 1988-89

	American Indian	Asian	Black	Hispanic	White	Foreign
Associate						
Men	1,315	6,320	12,826	9,172	150,073	3,203
Women	2,003	6,113	21,585	11,122	203,049	3,165
Total	3,318	12,433	34,411	20,294	353,122	6,368
Bachelor's						
Men	1,768	19,537	22,365	13,920	406,656	17,441
Women	2,278	18,682	35,651	15,880	451,530	9,531
Total	4,046	38,219	58,016	29,800	858,186	26,972
Master's						
Men	500	6,247	5,200	3,360	109,184	23,995
Women	633	4,467	8,876	3,910	132,423	10,077
Total	1,133	10,714	14,076	7,270	241,607	34,072
Doctorate						
Men	49	954	497	352	14,568	6,231
Women	35	383	574	273	10,327	1,449
Total	84	1,337	1,071	625	24,895	7,680
Professional						
Men	149	1,811	1,608	1,367	39,448	684
Women	119	1,156	1,493	887	21,740	296
Total	268	2,967	3,101	2,254	61,188	980

SOURCE: U. S. DEPARTMENT OF EDUCATION

Proportion of 18-to-24-Year-Olds Enrolled in College, by High-School-Graduation Status and Race

	White All	White High-school graduates	Black All	Black High-school graduates	Hispanic All	Hispanic High-school graduates
1979	25.6%	31.2%	19.8%	29.5%	16.6%	30.2%
1980	26.2	31.8	19.2	27.6	16.1	29.8
1981	26.7	32.5	19.9	28.0	16.7	29.9
1982	27.2	33.1	19.8	28.0	16.8	29.2
1983	27.0	32.9	19.2	27.0	17.2	31.4
1984	28.0	33.7	20.4	27.2	17.9	29.9
1985	28.7	34.4	19.8	26.1	16.9	26.9
1986	28.6	34.5	22.2	29.1	18.2	30.4
1987	30.2	36.6	22.8	30.0	17.6	28.5
1988	31.3	38.1	21.1	28.1	17.0	30.9
1989	31.8	38.8	23.5	30.8	16.1	28.7

Note: The figures are based on annual Census Bureau surveys of 60,000 households. The survey defined high-school graduates as those who had completed four years of high school or more. Hispanics may be of any race.

SOURCE: CENSUS BUREAU

Educational Attainment of 1980 High-School Seniors by 1986

	No high-school diploma	High-school diploma	License	Associate degree	Bachelor's degree	Professional/ graduate degree
Sex						
Men	1.0%	64.0%	10.5%	5.9%	17.6%	0.9%
Women	0.8	59.6	13.3	7.0	18.8	0.6
Racial and ethnic group						
American Indian	—	61.3	18.6	9.3	10.8	—
Asian	—	49.6	12.6	8.7	27.3	1.7
Black, non-Hispanic	1.2	69.4	13.9	5.3	9.9	0.2
Hispanic	1.7	70.2	13.8	7.3	6.8	0.1
White, non-Hispanic	0.8	60.0	11.5	6.6	20.2	0.9
Socioeconomic status						
Low	1.2	74.1	12.3	5.5	6.6	0.2
Low-middle	0.5	66.7	13.6	8.0	11.1	0.2
High-middle	0.1	58.4	12.9	7.7	20.4	0.6
High	—	45.7	8.7	6.3	37.1	2.2
High-school program						
General	0.8	69.7	12.6	6.5	10.2	0.2
Academic	0.1	45.6	8.8	7.2	36.6	1.8
Vocational	0.6	72.8	16.2	6.9	3.6	0.0
Type of high school						
Public	1.0	63.2	12.1	6.6	16.4	0.7
Catholic	—	47.4	11.9	6.4	32.8	1.6
Other private	—	52.3	7.0	3.9	36.7	0.1
Postsecondary education plans						
No plans	1.4	83.5	12.7	2.1	0.2	—
Attend voc/tech school	0.3	72.5	17.7	8.4	1.1	—
Attend college less than 4 years	0.2	65.5	14.4	13.1	6.8	—
Earn bachelor's degree	—	48.3	8.2	6.9	35.8	0.7
Earn advanced degree	0.1	43.5	7.9	4.9	40.6	3.0
1980 enrollment status						
Part-time 2-year public college	0.7	66.4	17.7	8.8	6.5	—
Part-time 4-year public college	2.7	57.1	15.4	1.6	22.6	0.6
Full-time 2-year public college	—	49.5	11.7	20.7	17.6	0.5
Full-time 4-year public college	—	41.7	7.6	4.5	44.9	1.3
Full-time 4-year private college	—	31.1	8.8	5.1	51.9	3.0
Not a student	1.8	78.2	12.8	3.6	3.5	0.2
Total	0.9%	61.8%	11.9%	6.5%	18.2%	0.7%

Note: Figures are based on data from "High School and Beyond," a longitudinal study of more than 10,500 students who were high-school seniors in 1980. They show students' highest level of education achieved by the spring of 1986.
Because of rounding, figures may not add to 100 per cent. A dash indicates less than 0.1 per cent.
Socioeconomic status was determined by parental education, family income, father's occupation, and household characteristics in 1980.

SOURCE: U.S. DEPARTMENT OF EDUCATION

Characteristics of Recipients of Doctorates, 1990

	All fields [1]	Arts and humanities	Business and management
Doctoral degrees conferred	36,027	3,820	1,038
Median age at conferral	33.9	35.7	34.9
Median number of years from bachelor's degree to doctorate	10.5	12.2	11.8
Median number of years registered as a graduate student	7.0	8.3	7.1
Proportion with bachelor's degree in same field as doctorate	55.4%	57.1%	35.8%
Sex			
Male	63.7%	54.4%	74.4%
Female	36.3	45.6	25.6
Citizenship			
United States	67.1	78.3	55.7
Non-U.S., permanent visa	4.6	5.0	7.5
Non-U.S., temporary visa	21.5	10.2	29.8
Unknown	6.8	6.5	7.0
Racial and ethnic group [3]			
American Indian	0.4	0.3	0.3
Asian	2.6	1.2	2.3
Black	3.5	2.3	1.7
Hispanic	2.9	3.6	1.6
White	90.6	92.6	94.1
Planned postdoctoral study			
Fellowship	11.8%	3.9%	0.6%
Research associateship	9.8	1.1	1.6
Traineeship	1.1	0.4	0.5
Other	1.6	1.3	0.5
Planned postdoctoral employment			
Educational institution	39.5	69.3	75.6
Industry or business	14.0	4.6	8.0
Government	5.7	1.9	1.5
Non-profit organization	3.9	4.1	0.9
Other or unknown	3.6	3.8	2.1
Postdoctoral status unknown	9.0	9.6	8.7
Primary postdoctoral employment activity			
Research and development	28.6%	8.3%	34.4%
Teaching	32.5	65.6	46.1
Administration	11.5	4.4	3.5
Professional services	12.5	4.8	2.5
Other	1.0	1.0	0.1
Unknown	14.0	16.0	13.8

[1] Includes degree categories not listed separately
[2] Excludes business and management, which is listed separately
[3] Figures cover only U.S. citizens

Education	Engineering	Life sciences	Physical sciences	Social sciences	Professional fields [2]
6,484	4,892	6,613	5,859	6,076	1,178
41.6	31.2	32.3	30.5	34.2	37.9
17.9	8.2	9.1	7.6	10.6	14.5
8.1	6.0	6.7	6.2	7.5	7.9
37.5%	76.9%	53.8%	67.5%	55.4%	26.3%
42.4%	91.5%	62.6%	81.8%	53.7%	56.8%
57.6	8.5	37.4	18.2	46.3	43.2
84.4	39.4	68.0	56.5	73.8	75.0
2.3	7.7	4.2	4.9	3.9	4.1
7.4	44.8	22.1	31.9	14.1	14.4
5.8	8.1	5.6	6.7	8.2	6.5
0.7	0.2	0.2	0.2	0.5	0.8
1.1	8.0	3.4	3.3	1.8	1.8
7.7	1.5	1.4	0.7	3.9	4.2
3.2	2.1	2.3	2.6	3.7	2.4
87.3	88.2	92.7	93.2	90.1	90.7
1.7%	6.2%	31.2%	17.8%	9.1%	1.7%
1.4	11.9	19.1	22.8	3.2	1.2
0.6	1.3	1.5	1.1	1.8	0.5
1.3	0.8	3.8	0.8	1.2	1.4
66.8	22.2	17.9	20.0	38.6	55.5
5.4	35.5	8.0	21.8	12.8	7.9
6.0	7.0	6.1	4.0	8.8	5.3
4.3	1.4	2.1	0.6	9.1	14.0
4.5	2.8	2.9	˙2.2	5.7	4.3
8.1	10.9	7.4	9.1	9.7	8.1
5.8%	65.2%	44.9%	56.6%	23.1%	9.5%
32.6	15.4	24.2	22.7	26.9	43.1
33.1	1.9	5.9	1.8	5.6	10.8
10.8	5.9	12.0	4.9	31.0	17.0
0.7	0.8	1.5	1.3	0.9	2.7
17.1	10.9	11.5	12.7	12.5	16.7

SOURCE: NATIONAL RESEARCH COUNCIL

Financial Aid to Undergraduates, Fall 1986

	Proportion of students receiving financial assistance, by source			Type of assistance		
By type of institution	Total	Federal	Other	Grants	Loans	Work-study
Public						
Doctoral	46.8%	35.5%	28.5%	36.4%	27.6%	5.8%
Other 4-year	47.3	38.4	30.0	38.1	24.9	8.1
2-year	28.5	19.9	18.1	25.4	7.8	2.4
Less-than-2-year	51.8	41.9	22.9	46.1	19.6	3.4
All	38.0	28.5	23.7	31.5	17.3	4.6
Private, not-for-profit						
Doctoral	61.8	45.7	50.8	52.2	39.5	13.0
Other 4-year	67.9	50.1	57.7	60.1	42.1	16.4
2-year	63.9	47.9	44.7	53.6	35.7	5.7
Less-than-2-year	66.2	59.4	35.5	55.5	40.4	5.0
All	65.3	48.4	54.1	56.7	40.7	14.3
Private, for-profit						
2-year and above	82.7	79.2	24.2	54.9	69.3	1.2
Less-than-2-year	84.8	81.4	13.0	63.5	71.5	0.5
All	84.0	80.6	17.2	60.3	70.7	0.8
By student characteristics						
Sex						
Men	44.5%	34.1%	27.8%	36.5%	23.9%	5.6%
Women	46.3	35.6	29.7	38.6	24.9	6.6
Racial and ethnic group						
American Indian	48.9	40.3	28.7	41.2	19.7	6.8
Asian	40.5	33.3	28.5	36.2	18.4	7.6
Black, non-Hispanic	63.8	55.7	33.2	56.6	35.0	9.8
Hispanic	47.8	40.9	27.2	41.1	24.0	5.8
White, non-Hispanic	43.3	32.0	28.4	35.1	23.6	5.6
Age						
23 or younger	50.0	39.0	33.5	41.2	28.7	8.4
24 to 29	42.8	34.2	21.9	34.4	22.5	3.6
30 and older	35.4	24.8	21.7	30.6	14.4	2.0
Attendance status						
Full-time	58.3	47.4	37.3	48.2	34.2	9.2
Part-time	24.4	14.4	15.0	20.3	8.4	1.1
All	45.5%	34.9%	28.8%	37.6%	24.4%	6.1%

Note: Figures are based on a survey of 59,886 students enrolled at 1,074 colleges, universities, and proprietary institutions in the fall of 1986. Details may add up to more than the total because some students received multiple types and sources of aid.
The total includes students who reported that they received aid but did not specify its source.

SOURCE: U.S. DEPARTMENT OF EDUCATION

Attitudes and Characteristics of Freshmen, Fall 1990

	Total	Men	Women
Racial and ethnic background:			
American Indian	1.3%	1.2%	1.4%
Asian-American	2.9	3.1	2.8
Black	9.6	8.5	10.6
Mexican-American	1.5	1.4	1.5
Puerto-Rican American	0.5	0.5	0.6
White	84.3	85.2	83.5
Other	1.8	1.8	1.7
Estimated parental income:			
Less than $6,000	3.0	2.4	3.6
$6,000 — $9,999	3.0	2.3	3.6
$10,000 — $14,999	4.9	3.9	5.8
$15,000 — $19,999	5.3	4.7	5.8
$20,000 — $24,999	6.8	6.5	7.2
$25,000 — $29,999	6.4	6.1	6.7
$30,000 — $34,999	8.8	8.2	9.4
$35,000 — $39,999	8.7	8.7	8.7
$40,000 — $49,999	12.6	13.4	12.0
$50,000 — $59,999	11.6	12.1	11.2
$60,000 — $74,999	11.4	12.2	10.7
$75,000 — $99,999	7.7	8.7	6.8
$100,000 — $149,999	5.0	5.8	4.4
$150,000 or more	4.6	5.1	4.2
Number of other colleges applied to for admission this year:			
None	31.9	30.3	33.3
One	15.7	14.9	16.3
Two	16.7	16.5	16.8
Three	14.9	15.6	14.3
Four	8.9	9.6	8.2
Five	5.5	5.8	5.1
Six or more	6.6	7.2	6.0
College attended is student's:			
First choice	70.7	70.4	71.0
Second choice	22.2	22.0	22.3
Third choice	4.7	4.9	4.5
Other	2.4	2.7	2.2
Highest degree planned:			
None	1.5	1.7	1.3
Vocational certificate	1.3	1.9	0.7
Associate (or equivalent)	5.5	4.7	6.3
Bachelor's	29.0	30.7	27.6
Master's	37.2	36.1	38.1
Ph.D. or Ed.D.	12.4	12.3	12.5
M.D., D.O., D.D.S., or D.V.M.	6.3	5.9	6.6
LL.B. or J.D.	4.8	4.7	4.9
B.D. or M.Div.	0.4	0.5	0.2
Other	1.7	1.5	1.8

Note: The statistics are based on a survey of 194,182 freshmen entering 382 two-year and four-year institutions in the fall of 1990. The figures were statistically adjusted to represent the total population of approximately 1.6 million first-time, full-time freshmen. Because of rounding or multiple responses, figures may add to more than 100 per cent.

Continued on Following Page

THE ALMANAC OF HIGHER EDUCATION • STUDENTS

Attitudes and Characteristics of Freshmen, continued

	Total	Men	Women
Political views:			
Far left	1.8%	2.3%	1.4%
Liberal	22.6	20.3	24.7
Middle of the road	54.7	51.7	57.3
Conservative	19.7	24.0	16.0
Far right	1.2	1.8	0.6
Reasons noted as very important in deciding to go to college:			
Parents wanted me to go	35.2	33.0	37.1
Could not find job	7.1	6.5	7.6
To get away from home	16.0	15.8	16.2
To be able to get a better job	78.3	77.9	78.6
To gain a general education and appreciation of ideas	63.1	56.0	69.1
To improve reading and study skills	43.0	38.4	46.9
Nothing better to do	2.3	3.0	1.8
To become a more cultured person	39.8	33.0	45.7
To be able to make more money	73.2	77.0	70.0
To learn more about things that interest me	73.1	68.4	77.0
To prepare for graduate or professional school	53.1	48.5	57.1
Students estimate chances are very good that they will:			
Change major field	12.4	12.0	12.7
Graduate with honors	13.5	14.8	12.3
Be elected to student office	3.5	3.6	3.4
Get a job to pay college expenses	36.0	32.9	38.6
Work full-time while attending college	4.0	3.8	4.1
Join a social fraternity or sorority	17.2	15.2	18.9
Play varsity athletics	15.4	20.8	10.8
Be elected to an honor society	8.1	8.2	8.0
Make at least a B average	41.3	41.8	40.9
Need extra time to complete degree	8.2	8.0	8.4
Get tutoring in some courses	15.9	13.3	18.1
Seek vocational counseling	5.1	4.5	5.6
Seek individual counseling	3.7	3.5	3.9
Participate in student protests	7.1	5.9	8.1
Transfer to another college	12.8	13.3	12.4
Drop out permanently	1.0	1.3	0.7
Drop out temporarily	1.1	1.3	0.8
Get bachelor's degree	66.1	64.5	67.4
Be satisfied with college	50.9	45.3	55.5
Find job in preferred field	70.6	66.9	73.8
Participate in volunteer or community-service work	14.2	9.7	18.1
Agree strongly or somewhat that:			
Government is not doing enough to protect the consumer	68.4	64.7	71.6
Government is not doing enough to control pollution	87.9	87.0	88.7
Taxes should be raised to reduce the federal deficit	28.6	33.8	24.2
There is too much concern in the courts for the rights of criminals	66.3	69.8	63.2
Military spending should be increased	25.1	29.0	21.8
Abortion should be legal	64.9	65.0	64.8
Married women's activities are best confined to home and family	25.2	30.6	20.5

	Total	Men	Women
Agree strongly or somewhat that:			
The death penalty should be abolished	21.5%	18.5%	24.1%
It is all right for two people who really like each other to have sex even if they've known each other for a very short time	51.0	66.3	37.9
Marijuana should be legalized	18.6	21.7	16.0
Busing to achieve racial balance in schools is all right	56.7	56.4	57.1
It is important to have laws prohibiting homosexual relationships	44.4	56.0	34.5
The chief benefit of college is that it increases one's earning power	70.7	76.0	66.2
Employers should be allowed to require employees or job applicants to take drug tests	80.4	78.5	82.1
The best way to control AIDS is through widespread, mandatory testing	66.4	66.5	66.3
Just because a man thinks that a woman has "led him on" does not entitle him to have sex with her	86.9	79.2	93.3
The government should do more to control the sale of handguns	77.1	65.5	87.0
A national health-care plan is needed to cover everybody's medical costs	73.7	69.7	77.0
Colleges would be improved if organized sports were de-emphasized	35.8	34.9	36.5
Nuclear disarmament is attainable	60.9	61.4	60.4
Scientists should publish their findings regardless of the possible consequences	53.1	57.1	49.7
Faculty promotions should be based in part on student evaluations	74.9	74.9	75.0
Racial discrimination is no longer a major problem in America	20.6	23.2	18.5
Objectives considered essential or very important:			
Becoming accomplished in a performing art	10.8	10.3	11.2
Becoming an authority in own field	65.4	67.4	63.6
Obtaining recognition from colleagues for contributions to field	54.9	56.0	54.0
Influencing the political structure	20.6	22.9	18.6
Influencing social values	42.9	36.3	48.4
Raising a family	69.5	68.2	70.6
Having administrative responsibility for the work of others	42.9	44.2	41.8
Being very well-off financially	73.7	77.7	70.3
Helping others who are in difficulty	62.0	50.9	71.4
Making a theoretical contribution to science	17.1	20.3	14.5
Writing original works	12.2	11.8	12.5
Creating artistic work	12.2	12.3	12.2
Becoming successful in own business	43.3	49.5	38.0
Becoming involved in programs to clean up environment	33.9	33.5	34.3
Developing a meaningful philosophy of life	43.2	41.8	44.3
Participating in a community-action program	25.9	22.1	29.1
Helping to promote racial understanding	38.0	34.1	41.2
Keeping up to date with political affairs	42.4	46.5	38.9

SOURCE: "THE AMERICAN FRESHMAN: NATIONAL NORMS FOR FALL 1990," BY ALEXANDER W. ASTIN, PUBLISHED BY AMERICAN COUNCIL ON EDUCATION AND UNIVERSITY OF CALIFORNIA AT LOS ANGELES

Foreign Students' Countries of Origin, 1990-91

Country or territory	Students	Country or territory	Students
China	39,600	Norway	2,350
Japan	36,610	Sri Lanka	2,320
Taiwan	33,530	Nicaragua	2,290
India	28,860	Trinidad & Tobago	2,240
Republic of Korea	23,360	South Africa	2,170
Canada	18,350	Netherlands	2,030
Malaysia	13,610	Sweden	2,030
Hong Kong	12,630	Panama	2,010
Indonesia	9,520	Ethiopia	2,000
Pakistan	7,730	Argentina	1,910
United Kingdom	7,300	Australia	1,910
Thailand	7,090	Bahamas	1,850
Germany	7,000	Egypt	1,780
Mexico	6,740	Cyprus	1,710
Iran	6,260	Kuwait	1,620
France	5,630	Haiti	1,450
Singapore	4,500	Vietnam	1,400
Greece	4,360	United Arab Emirates	1,350
Jordan	4,320	Switzerland	1,340
Spain	4,300	Honduras	1,310
Philippines	4,270	Syria	1,280
Turkey	4,080	Ireland	1,240
Brazil	3,900	Poland	1,240
Lebanon	3,900	El Salvador	1,210
Nigeria	3,710	U.S.S.R.	1,210
Saudi Arabia	3,590	Yugoslavia	1,200
Colombia	3,180	Ecuador	1,130
Israel	2,980	Chile	1,100
Venezuela	2,890	Costa Rica	1,100
Peru	2,800	Ghana	1,100
Bangladesh	2,530	Cuba	1,080
Jamaica	2,450	Morocco	1,070
Italy	2,390	Cameroon	1,020
Kenya	2,360		

Note: Includes only countries with over 1,000 students in U.S. institutions.

SOURCE: INSTITUTE OF INTERNATIONAL EDUCATION

Educational Attainment of the U.S. Population

Highest level reached	Total	Men	Women
Doctorate	0.6%	0.9%	0.2%
Professional	1.0	1.6	0.4
Master's	3.5	4.1	3.0
Bachelor's	11.9	13.0	11.0
Associate	4.2	4.0	4.4
Vocational	2.1	1.5	2.7
Some college, no degree	17.6	18.0	17.2
High-school diploma	36.6	33.9	39.2
No high-school diploma	22.5	23.0	22.0

Note: The figures are based on a 1987 survey of 11,100 households. They cover the civilian, resident population of adults age 18 and older.

SOURCE: CENSUS BUREAU

Institutions Enrolling the Most Foreign Students, 1990-91

Miami-Dade Community College	5,757
University of Southern California	3,886
University of Texas at Austin	3,867
Boston University	3,633
University of Wisconsin at Madison	3,565
University of Pennsylvania	3,122
Columbia University	3,077
Ohio State University main campus	3,021
University of Illinois at Urbana-Champaign	2,967
University of California at Los Angeles	2,921
University of Minnesota–Twin Cities	2,636
Southern Illinois University at Carbondale	2,627
Texas A&M University main campus	2,497
University of Maryland at College Park	2,462
Harvard University	2,409
University of Houston at University Park	2,406
Northeastern University	2,385
George Washington University	2,378
Purdue University main campus	2,317
University of Michigan at Ann Arbor	2,308
Michigan State University	2,281
New York University	2,279
Arizona State University	2,215
University of California at Berkeley	2,200
State University of New York at Buffalo	2,195
Rutgers University	2,192
Cornell University	2,178
Iowa State University	2,171
Indiana University at Bloomington	2,131
California State University at Los Angeles	2,123
Massachusetts Institute of Technology	2,103
Pennsylvania State University main campus	2,095
University of Florida	2,053
University of Hawaii at Manoa	2,017
Stanford University	2,000
University of Arizona	1,997
Temple University	1,960
University of Iowa	1,925
University of Missouri at Columbia	1,873
University of Kansas	1,870
University of Washington	1,776
University of Illinois at Chicago	1,743
Wayne State University	1,740
University of Massachusetts at Amherst	1,701
City University of New York Baruch College	1,681
New Jersey Institute of Technology	1,669
University of Miami	1,665
Oklahoma State University main campus	1,664
Northern Virginia Community College	1,645
Brigham Young University	1,621

SOURCE: INSTITUTE OF INTERNATIONAL EDUCATION

Campuses With the Largest Enrollments, Fall 1989

University of Minnesota–Twin Cities	58,815
Ohio State University main campus	52,895
University of Texas at Austin	50,245
Miami-Dade Community College	47,330
Michigan State University	44,423
Arizona State University	43,550
University of Wisconsin at Madison	43,364
Texas A&M University	40,492
Pennsylvania State University main campus	37,718
University of Illinois at Urbana-Champaign	37,481
Purdue University main campus	37,459
Community College of the Air Force	37,037
University of Arizona	36,676
University of Michigan at Ann Arbor	36,474
University of Maryland at College Park	35,825
University of California at Los Angeles	34,993
Indiana University at Bloomington	34,863
Northern Virginia Community College	34,539
University of Florida	34,098
San Diego State University	33,406
University of Washington	33,238
Rutgers University at New Brunswick	33,020
Northeastern University	32,809
Temple University	32,713
Houston Community College	32,536
Wayne State University	32,477
University of Houston–University Park	32,289
Brigham Young University main campus	32,213
St. Louis Community College	31,847
Macomb Community College	31,670
University of South Florida	31,566
New York University	31,083
University of Cincinnati main campus	30,787
California State University at Long Beach	30,665
University of Iowa	29,674
University of California at Berkeley	29,674
University of Southern California	29,657
University of Akron main campus	28,967
California State University at Northridge	28,604
Boston University	28,529
University of Pittsburgh main campus	28,362
College of Du Page	28,037
Florida State University	27,975
San Jose State University	27,650
Oakland Community College	27,504
University of Georgia	27,448
State University of New York at Buffalo	27,406
University of Massachusetts at Amherst	27,298
Tarrant County Junior College District	27,109
North Carolina State University	26,870

Louisiana State University	26,750
Pima Community College	26,747
Indiana University–Purdue University at Indianapolis	26,649
University of North Texas	26,523
University of South Carolina at Columbia	26,435
University of Kansas main campus	26,320
Western Michigan University	26,315
Iowa State University	26,038
El Camino College	25,789
San Francisco State University	25,656
University of Connecticut	25,634
University of Tennessee at Knoxville	25,512
University of Wisconsin at Milwaukee	25,212
Texas Tech University	25,027
Virginia Polytechnic Institute and State University	24,926
University of New Mexico main campus	24,645
Southern Illinois University at Carbondale	24,596
University of Colorado at Boulder	24,589
Harvard University	24,509
Northern Illinois University	24,443
City College of San Francisco	24,408
University of Missouri at Columbia	24,344
University of Illinois at Chicago	24,050
University of Toledo	23,928
University of Nebraska at Lincoln	23,926
University of Utah	23,883
University of Texas at Arlington	23,871
Kent State University main campus	23,746
University of North Carolina at Chapel Hill	23,619
California State University at Fullerton	23,588
Broward Community College	23,547
San Diego Mesa College	23,410
Cleveland Institute of Electronics	23,373
California State University at Sacramento	23,337
Eastern Michigan University	23,288
Illinois State University	23,107
Austin Community College	23,067
Georgia State University	23,004
ICS Center for Degree Studies	22,669
University of Louisville	22,555
Cuyahoga Community College District	22,548
University of Kentucky	22,407
Orange Coast College	22,365
University of Oklahoma at Norman	22,225
Syracuse University	22,196
University of Pennsylvania	22,016
De Anza College	21,948
Lansing Community College	21,716
Auburn University main campus	21,701
Portland Community College	21,578

SOURCE: U. S. DEPARTMENT OF EDUCATION

Colleges With the Most Freshman National Merit Scholars, 1990

	Number of scholars	Number sponsored by institution
Harvard and Radcliffe Colleges	321	0
Rice University	225	141
University of Texas at Austin	209	160
Stanford University	169	0
Yale University	167	0
Princeton University	152	0
Texas A&M University	131	100
University of Florida	124	106
Massachusetts Institute of Technology	113	0
Carleton College	108	83
Duke University	95	10
University of Chicago	95	74
University of Oklahoma	94	77
Brigham Young University	84	61
Georgia Institute of Technology	83	62
University of California at Berkeley	83	4
Northwestern University	78	42
University of Houston	70	52
Cornell University	68	0
Brown University	66	0
University of Michigan	63	0
Michigan State University	61	53
Virginia Polytechnic Institute and State University	61	51
Harvey Mudd College	60	53
University of California at Los Angeles	60	47
University of Toledo	59	51
Washington University (Mo.)	53	31
Bowling Green State University	52	46
University of California at San Diego	51	39
University of New Orleans	51	45
Baylor University	49	36
University of Kansas	49	35
Trinity University	49	39
Vanderbilt University	47	23
University of Arizona	45	35
University of Iowa	45	31
University of Southern California	45	31

Note: The table shows the total number of Merit Scholarship winners and the number whose scholarships were paid for by the institution, not by the National Merit Scholarship Corporation or other corporate sponsors. The rankings were determined by The Chronicle from an alphabetical listing appearing in the 1990 annual report of the National Merit Scholarship Corporation.

SOURCE: NATIONAL MERIT SCHOLARSHIP CORPORATION

Number of Colleges by Enrollment, Fall 1989

	All institutions	Universities	Other 4-year institutions	2-year institutions
Public institutions				
Under 200	7	0	0	7
200 to 499	33	0	9	24
500 to 999	114	0	26	88
1,000 to 2,499	390	0	103	287
2,500 to 4,999	332	0	104	228
5,000 to 9,999	330	6	137	187
10,000 to 19,999	228	29	97	102
20,000 to 29,999	78	37	18	23
30,000 or more	31	22	3	6
All	1,543	94	497	952
Private institutions				
Under 200	427	0	289	138
200 to 499	394	0	237	157
500 to 999	346	0	266	80
1,000 to 2,499	500	0	456	44
2,500 to 4,999	157	5	149	3
5,000 to 9,999	78	25	52	1
10,000 to 19,999	32	24	7	1
20,000 to 29,999	7	5	0	2
30,000 or more	3	3	0	0
All	1,944	62	1,456	426
All institutions				
Under 200	434	0	289	145
200 to 499	427	0	246	181
500 to 999	460	0	292	168
1,000 to 2,499	890	0	559	331
2,500 to 4,999	489	5	253	231
5,000 to 9,999	408	31	189	188
10,000 to 19,999	260	53	104	103
20,000 to 29,999	85	42	18	25
30,000 or more	34	25	3	6
All	3,487	156	1,953	1,378

Note: Figures exclude approximately 50 institutions that did not report enrollment.

SOURCE: U. S. DEPARTMENT OF EDUCATION

Average Faculty Salaries, 1990-91

	All Salary	All 1-year increase	Public Salary	Public 1-year increase
Doctoral institutions				
Professor	$62,910	5.5%	$60,450	5.2%
Associate professor	44,870	5.1	44,000	4.9
Assistant professor	37,820	5.2	36,980	4.8
Instructor	26,840	4.9	25,910	5.3
Lecturer	31,810	—	31,290	—
All ranks	49,320	5.4	47,650	5.1
Comprehensive institutions				
Professor	52,180	5.4	52,190	5.3
Associate professor	41,390	5.5	41,570	5.2
Assistant professor	34,160	5.7	34,460	5.4
Instructor	25,980	4.8	26,170	4.6
Lecturer	26,920	—	26,500	—
All ranks	41,830	5.5	42,170	5.3
Baccalaureate institutions				
Professor	44,570	5.9	44,900	5.5
Associate professor	35,980	5.8	37,550	5.6
Assistant professor	29,980	6.1	31,390	5.7
Instructor	24,760	6.2	26,510	6.1
Lecturer	28,030	—	27,110	—
All ranks	35,480	6.0	36,410	5.6
2-year institutions with academic ranks				
Professor	44,620	4.4	45,050	4.3
Associate professor	37,680	4.3	38,070	4.3
Assistant professor	31,470	4.5	31,870	4.5
Instructor	26,740	4.2	27,060	4.1
Lecturer	22,370	—	22,490	—
All ranks	35,960	4.4	36,420	4.3
2-year institutions without academic ranks				
All	37,030	5.4	37,200	5.4
All institutions except institutions without academic ranks				
Professor	56,210	5.5	55,830	5.2
Associate professor	41,780	5.3	42,210	5.0
Assistant professor	34,640	5.5	35,200	5.1
Instructor	26,090	5.0	26,330	4.8
Lecturer	29,930	—	29,310	—
All ranks	43,720	5.4	44,020	5.1

— No data reported

Note: Figures cover full-time members of the instructional staff except those in medical schools. The salaries are adjusted to a standard nine-month work year. The salary figures are based on 2,215 institutions; percentage increases are based on 1,754 institutions.

| Private, independent || Church-related ||
Salary	1-year increase	Salary	1-year increase
$72,950	6.5%	$60,790	5.3%
49,420	5.9	44,980	5.4
41,640	6.4	38,030	6.6
32,340	3.9	30,000	1.9
34,460	—	28,080	—
57,320	6.3	47,520	5.6
52,820	5.5	51,180	6.4
41,050	6.1	40,700	6.9
33,020	6.3	33,950	6.6
24,520	4.7	27,310	7.6
28,380	—	33,560	—
40,730	5.9	41,010	6.6
49,610	6.1	40,040	6.0
38,200	6.0	33,080	5.8
31,570	6.3	28,020	6.2
25,470	5.8	23,600	6.5
32,840	—	22,470	—
38,620	6.1	32,440	6.0
35,080	6.6	30,460	9.6
29,950	5.6	26,320	4.8
27,150	6.1	23,300	4.3
21,530	5.8	20,520	9.2
—	—	—	—
28,280	5.1	25,320	6.4
28,660	5.2	24,800	3.2
61,620	6.2	47,240	6.0
43,280	6.0	37,540	6.0
35,540	6.4	31,050	6.4
26,240	4.9	24,800	6.4
33,190	—	27,690	—
47,010	6.2	37,270	6.1

SOURCE: AMERICAN ASSOCIATION OF UNIVERSITY PROFESSORS

Median Salaries of Chief Executive and Academic Officers, 1990-91

Type of institution by size of budget	Chief executive officer	Chief academic officer
Doctoral		
Up to $93-million	$116,200	$90,000
$93-million to $191.8-million	129,400	101,500
$191.8-million to $330.8-million	147,600	118,700
$330.8-million or more	142,700	131,900
All	132,000	111,300
Comprehensive		
Up to $24-million	$89,600	$70,000
$24-million to $37.8-million	99,200	80,200
$37.8-million to $62-million	99,800	84,000
$62-million or more	118,100	100,000
All	99,300	82,500
Baccalaureate		
Up to $8-million	$70,500	$50,100
$8-million to $12-million	85,000	58,100
$12-million to $20-million	95,500	69,500
$20-million or more	118,500	77,400
All	90,500	63,600
2-year		
Up to $6.4-million	$70,200	$50,800
$6.4-million to $11-million	76,200	58,000
$11-million to $20-million	83,400	63,200
$20-million or more	91,500	71,700
All	78,300	60,500

Note: The figures are based on reports of 1,402 colleges and universities.

SOURCE: COLLEGE AND UNIVERSITY PERSONNEL ASSOCIATION

Employment Status of Faculty Members, 1987

	All	Public 4-year	Private 4-year	Public 2-year	Other
Number of faculty members	825,000	319,000	218,000	218,000	70,000
Regular full-time	60%	72%	58%	41%	63%
Regular part-time	22	14	21	35	20
Temporary full-time	3	4	3	1	1
Temporary part-time	16	9	19	23	16

Note: The figures are based on a 1988 survey of administrators at 480 colleges and universities. The response rate was 88 per cent. The figures are adjusted to represent the distribution of all professors whose regular assignment includes instruction. The category of "Other" institutions includes private two-year colleges and specialized institutions. "Temporary" faculty members include visiting, acting, and adjunct professors. Because of rounding, figures may not add to 100 per cent.

SOURCE: U.S. DEPARTMENT OF EDUCATION

Median Salaries of Administrators, 1990-91

	All institutions
Executive	
Chief executive of a system	$98,666
Assistant to chief executive of a system	60,000
Chief executive of a single institution	93,000
Assistant to chief executive of a single institution	46,465
Executive vice-president	76,740
Academic	
Chief academic officer	$70,721
Chief health-professions officer	89,444
Director, library services	46,480
Circulation librarian	28,000
Acquisitions librarian	31,922
Technical-services librarian	32,700
Public-services librarian	34,080
Reference librarian	30,428
Director, institutional research	47,290
Associate director, institutional research	38,292
Director, educational-media services	35,900
Director, learning-resources center	38,500
Director, international studies	48,438
Director, academic computer center	47,100
Administrator, grants and contracts	46,027
Dean, architecture	87,255
Dean, agriculture	84,700
Dean, arts and letters	61,250
Dean, arts and sciences	70,000
Dean, business	70,000
Dean, communications	57,600
Dean, continuing education	53,400
Dean, dentistry	115,000
Dean, education	68,300
Dean, engineering	88,564
Dean, extension	60,862
Dean, fine arts	60,765
Dean, graduate programs	68,784
Dean, health-related professions	62,205
Dean, home economics	77,425
Dean, humanities	52,384
Dean, instruction	56,476
Dean, law	120,338
Dean, library and information sciences	68,000
Dean, mathematics	52,164
Dean, medicine	160,172
Dean, music	66,000
Dean, nursing	60,000
Dean, pharmacy	93,445
Dean, public health	110,750
Dean, sciences	58,314
Dean, social sciences	53,273
Dean, social work	78,981
Dean, special programs	47,000
Dean, undergraduate programs	61,392
Dean, veterinary medicine	106,963
Dean, vocational education	54,600

Continued on Following Page

Median Salaries of Administrators, continued

Administrative	All institutions
Chief business officer	$67,760
Chief administration officer	65,150
Chief financial officer	62,000
Director, health and safety	46,720
Director, telecommunications	45,000
Chief planning officer	62,250
Chief budget officer	52,838
Chief planning and budget officer	68,709
General counsel	71,175
Staff attorney	52,084
Chief personnel officer	49,429
Manager, benefits	32,000
Manager, training and development	35,767
Manager, employee relations	38,925
Manager, labor relations	52,521
Manager, employment	32,500
Manager, wage and salary	35,977
Manager, personnel information systems	34,041
Director, affirmative action and equal employment	49,737
Director, personnel and affirmative action	40,500
Chief computer officer	53,500
Data base administrator	43,270
Systems analyst, highest level	38,410
Systems analyst, lowest level	30,782
Programmer analyst, highest level	32,427
Programmer analyst, lowest level	25,737
Director, administrative computer center	46,503
Director, information systems	54,994
Chief physical-plant officer	48,200
Manager, landscape and grounds	30,898
Manager, building maintenance trades	34,405
Manager, technical trades	34,920
Manager, custodial services	29,946
Manager, power plant	37,615
Comptroller	48,240
Manager, payroll	30,484
Director, accounting	40,432
Staff accountant, highest level	29,258
Staff accountant, lowest level	23,820
Bursar	36,206
Director, purchasing	38,326
Director, bookstore	29,862
Director, internal audit	46,640
Director, auxiliary services	46,980
Manager, mail services	22,725
Director, campus security	36,764
Director, risk management and insurance	48,300
Administrator, hospital medical center	125,035
External affairs	
Chief development officer	$61,175

	All institutions
Director, annual giving	$35,265
Director, corporate and foundation relations	41,354
Coordinator, resource development	30,500
Director, estate planning	45,150
Chief public-relations officer	42,298
Director, governmental relations	64,685
Chief development and public-relations officer	67,980
Director, alumni affairs	35,175
Director, development and alumni affairs	46,195
Director, special and deferred gifts	44,335
Director, church relations	36,169
Director, community services	42,443
Director, publications	35,989
Associate director, publications	28,920
Manager, printing services	30,500
Director, information office	36,136
Director, news bureau	31,745
Student services	
Chief student-affairs officer	$59,934
Dean, students	47,621
Chief admissions officer	45,000
Associate director, admissions	31,400
Admissions counselor	21,523
Academic advisor	27,040
Director, admissions and registrar	45,893
Registrar	39,400
Associate registrar	34,247
Director, admissions and financial aid	47,567
Director, student financial aid	38,256
Director, food services	39,445
Director, student housing	35,900
Associate director, student housing	30,451
Housing officer, administrative operations	31,903
Housing officer, residential life	26,453
Director, foreign students	32,945
Director, student union and student activities	37,623
Director, student union	39,900
Director, student activities	30,609
Director, student placement	35,880
Director, student counseling	41,556
Director, student health services, physician	74,262
Director, student health services, nurse	28,248
Director, campus ministries	31,540
Director, athletics	48,810
Men's	50,700
Women's	39,141
Director, sports information	27,055
Director, campus recreation	31,500
Chief, enrollment management	52,505
Director, minority affairs	37,012
Director, conferences	36,268

Note: The figures are based on a survey sent to 3,400 colleges and universities in the fall of 1990. The response rate was 41 per cent. The figures are meant to provide a broad overview of salaries in higher education.

SOURCE: COLLEGE AND UNIVERSITY PERSONNEL ASSOCIATION

Average Faculty Salaries by Rank in Selected Fields at Public and Private Institutions, 1990-91

	Professor	Associate professor	Assistant professor*	New assistant professor	Instructor	All ranks
Accounting						
Public	$58,680	$49,198	$42,635	$42,799	$28,343	$47,341
Private	57,303	46,298	39,025	40,491	30,475	43,997
Agribusiness and agricultural production						
Public	44,028	37,772	33,611	29,495	36,650	38,947
Private	41,203	30,706	29,188	—	—	32,760
Anthropology						
Public	50,005	38,965	31,694	29,123	—	42,628
Private	51,213	39,168	31,766	29,702	—	40,660
Architecture and environmental design						
Public	49,831	41,540	34,341	31,834	30,115	41,454
Private	54,329	42,484	35,930	—	—	43,883
Business						
Public	56,309	46,963	41,873	43,896	28,429	46,364
Private	59,787	48,627	42,361	40,545	29,702	47,947
Chemistry						
Public	50,301	39,355	32,171	30,720	25,131	43,116
Private	50,342	37,226	30,995	29,312	24,701	41,957
Communications						
Public	48,407	38,976	31,627	30,393	25,833	36,863
Private	46,734	38,412	30,258	29,161	24,974	35,466
Computer and information science						
Public	55,229	46,270	40,456	41,417	29,091	44,043
Private	56,047	43,283	35,772	35,120	28,197	41,290
Economics						
Public	53,447	42,574	36,452	37,174	29,901	44,654
Private	64,690	41,734	36,542	32,609	29,901	47,077
Education						
Public	48,349	39,781	32,515	32,602	25,833	39,620
Private	47,162	36,755	30,085	30,100	24,895	37,308
Engineering						
Public	57,756	47,171	40,799	41,365	31,856	49,087
Private	66,465	50,424	43,867	40,737	30,294	55,260
Foreign languages						
Public	49,163	38,415	30,964	29,134	24,046	37,649
Private	46,925	37,456	30,511	28,582	24,084	36,387
Geography						
Public	50,249	39,688	32,243	31,114	28,201	41,944
Private	50,840	37,813	31,574	—	—	40,848
History						
Public	49,033	38,862	30,108	27,764	25,126	42,236
Private	47,208	37,044	29,564	27,531	24,756	39,220
Letters						
Public	47,697	38,268	30,246	28,296	22,746	36,868
Private	46,401	36,087	29,210	27,882	25,179	36,620

Note: The figures are based on reports from 282 public institutions that are members of the American Association of State Colleges and Universities and from 494 private colleges and universities.
* Includes data for new assistant professors
— Indicates fewer than 10 positions in a rank

	Professor	Associate professor	Assistant professor*	New assistant professor	Instructor	All ranks
Library sciences						
Public	$49,104	$39,037	$32,282	$28,060	$26,205	$36,971
Private	45,695	36,230	29,550	26,862	24,622	33,736
Life sciences						
Public	49,247	39,918	32,287	30,553	24,321	42,299
Private	46,594	36,651	30,169	28,968	22,908	39,059
Mathematics						
Public	50,379	40,386	33,327	33,029	24,776	39,657
Private	51,622	38,802	31,949	31,299	24,646	39,523
Nursing						
Public	49,137	39,425	32,380	31,044	27,391	34,801
Private	43,461	35,176	29,740	29,553	25,367	31,637
Philosophy and religion						
Public	49,922	39,169	31,007	28,740	26,679	41,607
Private	45,808	36,407	30,159	28,866	24,396	38,496
Physical education						
Public	48,190	39,808	33,017	30,538	27,419	37,479
Private	43,042	36,111	28,989	26,996	24,339	33,106
Physical science						
Public	48,108	38,822	32,324	34,813	23,615	40,913
Private	54,318	41,428	33,064	31,042	23,382	44,863
Physics						
Public	51,117	40,408	34,042	32,586	27,452	44,046
Private	55,801	41,083	36,168	33,894	29,734	46,788
Political science						
Public	50,105	39,122	31,145	29,835	26,561	41,428
Private	50,466	38,640	31,203	29,584	26,735	40,707
Psychology						
Public	49,892	39,597	31,863	30,607	26,904	41,963
Private	47,857	36,959	30,331	29,244	24,881	38,648
Social sciences						
Public	46,296	37,360	30,506	30,487	24,376	37,515
Private	51,564	36,148	31,525	30,703	25,364	39,544
Sociology						
Public	49,428	39,175	31,543	29,799	25,773	40,951
Private	47,125	36,807	30,018	28,229	23,566	37,517
Special education						
Public	49,300	39,348	32,392	30,070	26,287	40,451
Private	48,042	35,624	28,967	28,264	21,656	35,602
Teacher education, general programs						
Public	48,754	38,788	32,062	31,035	26,005	39,379
Private	39,284	33,850	28,370	28,091	22,902	32,648
Visual and performing arts						
Public	46,326	36,935	30,097	29,443	25,296	37,144
Private	46,347	36,396	29,640	28,189	24,896	36,018

SOURCE: COLLEGE AND UNIVERSITY PERSONNEL ASSOCIATION

Colleges' Experience in Faculty Recruiting, 1990-91

	Total	Doctoral	Bacca-laureate	Compre-hensive	2-year
Compared to five years ago, the number of faculty members who received job offers from other institutions has increased					
Yes	34%	55%	37%	43%	24%
No	66	45	63	57	76
The quality of applicants has declined					
Yes, generally	7	3	6	0	10
Yes, in a few fields	30	10	29	39	31
No	63	87	66	61	59
It has taken longer to find qualified people					
Yes, generally	22	5	17	19	30
Yes, in a few fields	38	38	35	53	35
No	39	56	48	28	35
Institution has had greater difficulty in getting top applicants to accept positions					
Yes, generally	19	9	13	17	24
Yes, in a few fields	36	35	35	58	28
No	45	56	52	25	47
A lower percentage of offers is being accepted					
Yes, generally	8	3	5	7	12
Yes, in a few fields	28	27	21	39	28
No	64	70	74	54	60
Institution has hired some faculty members at salaries above the salary scale					
Yes, generally	7	9	7	11	5
Yes, in a few fields	41	57	51	61	23
No	53	34	42	28	72
Institution has hired new junior faculty members at a salary above that of some senior faculty members in the same department					
Yes, generally	3	7	3	9	1
Yes, in a few fields	24	61	30	40	9
No	72	32	67	52	90
Institution has moved some part-time faculty members into full-time positions					
Yes, generally	6	0	0	6	11
Yes, in a few fields	49	23	51	40	55
No	45	77	49	54	34
Institution is concerned about predicted faculty shortages as they might affect					
Institution generally					
Yes	44	53	38	57	42
No	56	47	62	43	58
A few departments					
Yes	82	80	74	87	85
No	18	20	26	13	15

Note: The figures are based on responses to a survey sent to senior administrators at 444 colleges and universities in the spring of 1991 and describe experiences in recruiting full-time professors in 1990-91. The response rate was 81 per cent. Because of rounding, figures may not add to 100 per cent.

SOURCE: AMERICAN COUNCIL ON EDUCATION

Employment Policies and Perquisites for College Presidents, 1990-91

Housing
Residence provided on campus .. 47.7%
Allowances for housing provided
by institution:
  Maintenance 91.5
  Utilities 91.0
  Household staff 70.0
  Remodeling 54.8
Assistance where residence
not provided:
  Home-purchase allowance 59.8
  Mortgage-interest subsidy 24.5
  Property-tax allowance 8.8
  Rental allowance 33.3
  Rent paid in full 5.9

Relocation
Household moving expenses:
  Paid in full 79.9%
  Paid in part 12.0
Travel expenses for family:
  Paid in full 50.1
  Paid in part 10.7

Car
Personal car provided 67.4%
Pool car:
  Assigned to chief executive 18.6
  Available as needed 6.9
Operating expenses:
  Paid 65.3
  Allowance provided 12.1
Option to purchase car 3.0
Driver provided as needed 11.3
No provision 14.8

Business travel, entertainment
Reimbursement 89.4%
Per-diem allowance 25.9
Unrestricted expense account ... 10.6
Reimbursement for spouse's
  expenses 27.1
Airline V.I.P. club 8.3
First-class air travel 4.8
Use of institution-owned aircraft 3.5

Local entertainment
Reimbursement 76.1%
Fixed allowance 23.8
Unrestricted expense account ... 13.3
Use of campus facilities 57.3
Use of institution staff 53.8
No provision 15.0

Tuition assistance for children
Full tuition at own institution 77.8%
Full tuition at other institution ... 48.0
50% or more at own institution .. 19.9
50% or more at other institution . 29.5
Up to 50% at own institution 2.3
Up to 50% at other institution 11.6

Assistance to spouse
Staff and facilities for entertaining 17.5%
Secretarial staff 8.8
Remuneration for involvement
  at institution 3.4
No provision 78.8

Employment contracts
Provided 76.9%
  Formal written contract 57.6
  Letter of agreement 33.8
  Oral agreement 5.4
Term of agreement specified 63.4
Time period:
  One year 31.3
  Two years 10.4
  Three years 31.8
  Four years 10.4
  Five years 11.6
  Six or more years 2.7

Performance review
Formal performance review 77.9%
Frequency of review:
  End of contract term 5.1
  Annually 69.1
  Every two years 5.0
  Every three years 5.8
  Other 12.7
Responsibility for review:
  Chairman of the board 12.7
  Committee of the board 28.2
  Entire governing board 37.8
  Special review committee 7.2
  Other 14.1

Involuntary departure
Involuntary departure policy 25.8%
Departure pay 76.0
Amount:
  Less than 6 months' pay 23.3
  6-12 months' pay 35.0
  Over 12 months' pay 11.6
  Negotiable at time of departure 30.1

Note: The figures are based on the reports of chief executive officers at 874 colleges and universities.

SOURCES: AMERICAN COUNCIL ON EDUCATION
ASSOCIATION OF GOVERNING BOARDS OF UNIVERSITIES AND COLLEGES
COLLEGE AND UNIVERSITY PERSONNEL ASSOCIATION

Faculty Attitudes and Activities, 1989-90

Political orientation:
Far left
Liberal
Moderate
Conservative
Far right

Professional writings accepted for publication or published in last two years:
None
1-2
3-4
5-10
11-20
21-50
50 or more

Professional goals noted as essential or very important:
Engage in research
Engage in outside activities
Provide services to the community
Participate in committee or other administrative work
Be a good colleague
Be a good teacher

Aspects of job noted as very satisfactory or satisfactory:
Salary and fringe benefits
Opportunity for scholarly pursuits
Teaching load
Quality of students
Working conditions

Autonomy and independence
Relationships with other faculty
Competency of colleagues
Visibility for jobs at other institutions and organizations
Job security

Undergraduate course assignments
Graduate course assignments
Relationship with administration
Overall job satisfaction

Attributes noted as being very descriptive of own institution:
It is easy for students to see faculty outside of regular office hours
There is a great deal of conformity among students
Most students are very bright
The administration is open about its policies
There is keen competition among most students for high grades

Faculty are rewarded for their advising skills
The faculty are typically at odds with the campus administration
Intercollegiate sports are overemphasized
Faculty here respect each other
Most students are treated like "numbers in a book"

	All institutions		Universities		Other 4-year colleges		2-year colleges
Total	Men	Women	Public	Private	Public	Private	Public
4.9%	4.9%	5.1%	6.5%	8.2%	4.3%	5.3%	2.3%
36.8	35.6	39.7	42.1	48.0	35.7	37.0	27.1
40.2	39.8	40.9	37.9	30.8	42.1	39.2	45.0
17.8	19.2	14.2	13.1	12.5	17.5	18.3	25.2
0.4	0.5	0.1	0.3	0.5	0.4	0.2	0.4
45.3%	40.9%	56.3%	21.6%	15.8%	42.8%	51.9%	81.9%
25.7	26.1	24.5	27.6	26.1	31.2	29.5	13.9
15.8	17.4	11.7	25.1	28.4	15.8	12.1	2.8
10.8	12.4	6.7	21.0	23.9	8.5	5.4	0.9
1.9	2.4	0.6	3.8	4.4	1.4	0.7	0.2
0.4	0.6	0.2	0.9	1.3	0.2	0.2	0.1
0.1	0.1	0.1	0.1	0.1	0.1	0.1	0.1
58.5%	61.1%	52.3%	78.6%	85.2%	61.0%	54.2%	25.1%
52.5	49.8	59.1	48.7	48.3	54.4	53.9	54.9
43.4	39.9	52.0	35.8	33.6	45.7	44.8	52.4
29.2	25.7	37.9	23.0	19.3	30.7	32.1	36.3
80.0	77.4	86.4	75.9	74.8	79.7	83.4	84.5
98.2	98.1	98.4	97.6	95.5	98.3	99.0	99.2
44.5%	44.3%	44.9%	44.3%	51.3%	39.0%	40.2%	52.1%
45.4	48.4	37.8	53.3	62.4	38.1	38.8	43.6
50.3	51.3	47.7	58.3	63.5	42.2	45.2	49.3
37.5	35.5	42.5	38.0	58.6	32.2	43.3	30.2
64.6	65.7	62.0	66.4	74.8	58.9	66.2	63.9
82.9	83.3	81.9	85.0	89.1	80.0	83.8	80.6
75.1	74.5	76.5	69.0	74.3	73.9	79.7	80.0
68.4	68.1	69.0	64.6	75.0	63.3	74.4	71.2
43.1	43.7	41.7	45.5	58.8	38.3	39.5	42.0
74.6	77.7	66.9	73.5	73.8	75.4	69.9	79.4
77.5	77.8	76.8	76.8	79.5	75.4	79.7	78.2
72.3	73.9	66.0	75.1	78.0	71.0	68.2	41.3
51.8	50.7	54.4	48.4	53.1	49.0	58.2	52.8
69.2	69.0	69.8	65.6	74.8	64.9	71.4	74.4
33.6%	33.6%	33.7%	20.6%	27.6%	30.5%	53.6%	38.2%
24.6	25.1	23.3	26.2	24.9	22.7	35.7	15.8
8.9	9.0	8.6	7.0	35.5	4.0	13.6	2.3
11.9	11.5	13.0	7.9	8.8	10.1	17.3	15.8
20.1	20.5	19.0	25.4	48.9	13.9	20.6	9.4
2.0	1.9	2.2	1.3	2.0	1.6	4.1	1.4
18.6	19.1	17.5	19.8	14.9	21.0	14.7	19.1
16.1	17.1	13.5	33.0	6.8	15.6	10.0	5.5
31.7	30.1	35.7	23.3	35.0	24.4	44.1	38.2
5.9	6.3	4.8	12.1	4.5	6.2	1.5	2.8

Continued on Following Page

Faculty Attitudes and Activities, continued

Attributes noted as being very descriptive of own institution, continued:
There is little or no contact between students and faculty ....
The student body is apathetic and has little "school spirit" ....
Faculty are rewarded for being good teachers ....
Student services are well supported ....

Agree strongly or somewhat that at own institution:
Faculty here are interested in students' personal problems ....
Most faculty are sensitive to the issues of minorities ....
The curriculum has suffered from faculty overspecialization ....
Faculty are committed to the welfare of institution ....
Many courses include minority-group perspectives ....
Administrators consider student concerns when making policy ....
Faculty here are strongly interested in the academic problems of undergraduates ....
There is a lot of campus racial conflict ....
Students of different racial or ethnic origins communicate well with one another ....
Campus administrators care little about what happens to students ....
There is little trust between minority-student groups and campus administrators ....
Many courses include feminist perspectives ....
There are many opportunities for faculty and students to socialize with one another ....
Administrators consider faculty concerns when making policy ....
Faculty feel that students are well prepared academically ....
Institutional demands for doing research interfere with my effectiveness as a teacher ....

Issues noted as being of highest or high priority at own institution:
Promoting the intellectual development of students ....
Helping students examine and understand their personal values ....
Increasing the representation of minorities in the faculty and administration ....
Developing a sense of community among students and faculty ....
Developing leadership ability among students ....

Conducting basic and applied research ....
Raising money for the institution ....
Developing leadership ability among faculty ....
Increasing the representation of women in the faculty and administration ....
Facilitating student involvement in community-service projects ....

Helping students learn how to bring about change in American society ....
Helping solve major social and environmental problems ....
Maintaining a campus climate where differences of opinion can be aired openly ....
Increasing or maintaining institutional prestige ....
Developing among students and faculty an appreciation for a multicultural society ....

Hiring faculty "stars" ....
Economizing and cutting costs ....
Recruiting more minority students ....
Enhancing the institution's national image ....
Creating a positive undergraduate experience ....
Creating a diverse multicultural environment on campus ....

Note: The figures are based on survey responses of 35,478 faculty members at 392 colleges and universities. The survey was conducted in the fall and winter of 1989-90 and was limited to full-time professors who spent at least part of their time teaching undergraduates. The response rate was 55 per cent. The figures were statistically adjusted to represent the total population of full-time faculty members. Because of rounding or multiple responses, figures may add to more than 100 per cent. The total includes figures for private two-year colleges, which are not shown separately.

	All institutions		Universities		Other 4-year colleges		2-year colleges
Total	Men	Women	Public	Private	Public	Private	Public
5.1%	5.5%	4.3%	7.5%	5.9%	5.9%	2.0%	3.9%
17.0	18.3	13.7	12.9	7.6	21.4	8.6	27.3
9.8	9.6	10.2	6.2	10.8	8.1	19.2	8.0
18.8	18.6	19.4	15.9	18.1	15.4	25.9	20.5
73.8%	71.9%	78.5%	58.4%	60.8%	72.7%	89.3%	84.9%
69.1	69.5	68.0	64.8	67.0	67.6	73.4	73.0
28.3	29.8	24.5	42.3	37.4	27.2	21.0	16.1
76.1	75.2	78.2	67.5	76.3	71.9	87.1	81.5
36.0	34.6	39.6	33.2	29.7	37.3	37.3	40.0
59.7	59.3	61.0	51.7	55.9	58.2	71.2	62.6
76.4	75.3	79.0	61.6	67.6	77.2	90.4	84.2
11.8	11.0	13.8	20.8	11.1	10.4	9.4	5.4
59.0	59.3	58.4	50.2	51.4	58.4	62.2	69.7
23.8	24.8	21.4	30.8	21.2	26.5	13.2	22.5
27.5	28.2	25.7	41.0	34.7	26.6	19.3	17.5
28.8	29.8	26.3	28.4	30.1	25.0	32.4	31.1
38.4	39.3	36.1	28.0	39.6	34.7	58.6	36.8
50.0	50.3	49.1	45.9	52.7	45.7	61.5	49.5
27.4	26.6	29.5	23.7	50.5	22.1	37.7	20.3
26.7	26.9	26.2	44.4	34.7	31.9	15.7	6.1
76.1%	75.5%	77.6%	70.6%	83.7%	72.4%	85.5%	75.8%
47.4	45.6	51.7	32.3	47.2	43.0	71.9	48.8
46.9	46.1	49.0	52.3	40.5	52.2	39.0	44.4
41.0	38.7	46.5	25.5	34.8	38.4	60.6	47.9
37.6	35.5	43.0	25.8	32.0	37.6	53.9	39.7
44.5	47.0	38.4	80.5	74.0	41.9	24.4	10.9
58.3	57.2	61.2	63.7	77.7	53.1	71.5	39.1
24.0	22.0	28.9	20.2	20.6	23.1	25.9	29.0
39.2	40.9	34.8	45.2	36.7	42.1	35.2	33.6
23.3	21.2	28.4	13.3	25.1	21.6	40.0	22.6
21.1	19.4	25.3	14.7	15.7	21.5	31.0	22.2
26.3	25.9	27.2	26.4	25.8	25.1	31.1	24.2
52.0	53.4	48.5	53.0	54.9	48.1	56.5	51.1
75.3	75.0	76.2	80.4	87.0	71.0	77.9	67.6
46.5	44.5	51.5	45.6	40.0	46.6	54.3	44.2
26.8	26.9	26.4	49.8	47.4	20.5	12.7	10.8
54.5	53.0	58.3	58.9	57.4	53.9	50.1	52.4
46.9	45.8	49.7	50.7	44.0	52.1	43.7	40.5
61.7	62.6	59.6	78.0	84.9	56.7	64.3	37.2
69.2	68.0	72.1	52.3	71.8	69.1	85.7	73.9
40.0	38.2	44.3	38.9	35.0	42.4	43.4	37.9

SOURCE: "THE AMERICAN COLLEGE TEACHER: NATIONAL NORMS FOR THE 1989-90 H.E.R.I. FACULTY SURVEY," PUBLISHED BY UNIVERSITY OF CALIFORNIA AT LOS ANGELES HIGHER EDUCATION RESEARCH INSTITUTE

Full-Time Employees in Colleges and Universities by Racial and Ethnic Group, 1989-90

	Total	American Indian	Asian	Black	Hispanic	White
Professional						
Faculty............	514,662	1,498	24,252	23,225	10,087	455,600
Executive, administrative, managerial......	137,561	491	1,980	11,796	3,183	120,111
Other professionals	343,699	1,398	17,193	29,045	9,510	286,553
Non-professional						
Clerical, secretarial	370,336	1,969	8,928	58,966	18,798	281,675
Technical, paraprofessional	147,569	735	6,657	23,126	7,484	109,567
Skilled crafts......	63,728	441	702	7,094	3,410	52,081
Service, maintenance	201,973	1,317	4,348	67,025	16,766	112,517
Total..............	1,779,528	7,849	64,060	220,277	69,238	1,418,104

Note: Figures are based on reports of 3,156 colleges.

SOURCE: U. S. EQUAL EMPLOYMENT OPPORTUNITY COMMISSION

Faculty Workloads, 1989-90

Proportion reporting number of hours per week

	0	1-4	5-8	9-12	13-16	17-20	21-34	35-44	45+
Teaching	0.3%	7.2%	26.2%	32.0%	17.6%	10.1%	5.9%	0.5%	0.1%
Preparing for teaching ...	0.3	8.4	22.9	25.2	17.3	13.8	9.4	2.0	0.7
Research and scholarly writing	20.2	27.9	16.4	12.4	7.3	6.7	6.3	1.8	1.0
Advising or counseling students	2.6	56.6	29.5	8.0	2.0	0.9	0.4	0.1	0.0
Committee work / meetings	4.6	68.8	20.6	4.3	1.1	0.3	0.1	0.0	0.0
Other administration	36.5	38.6	11.5	5.8	3.0	2.3	1.7	0.4	0.2
Consultation with clients or patients	68.8	20.7	6.3	2.2	0.8	0.6	0.4	0.1	0.1

Note: The figures are based on survey responses of 35,478 faculty members at 392 colleges and universities. The survey was conducted in the fall and winter of 1989-90 and was limited to full-time professors who spent at least part of their time teaching undergraduates. The response rate was 55 per cent. The figures were statistically adjusted to represent the total population of full-time faculty members. Because of rounding or multiple responses, figures may add to more than 100 per cent.

SOURCE: "THE AMERICAN COLLEGE TEACHER: NATIONAL NORMS FOR THE 1989-90 H.E.R.I. FACULTY SURVEY," PUBLISHED BY UNIVERSITY OF CALIFORNIA AT LOS ANGELES HIGHER EDUCATION RESEARCH INSTITUTE

Distribution of Full-Time Faculty Members by Rank, 1987

	All	Public 4-year	Private 4-year	Public 2-year	Other
Full professor	30%	38%	31%	12%	23%
Associate professor	24	27	27	11	22
Assistant professor	24	24	29	11	31
Instructor	11	5	7	33	13
Other	11	5	6	34	10

Note: The figures are based on a 1988 survey of administrators at 480 colleges and universities. The response rate was 88 per cent. The category of "Other" institutions includes private two-year colleges and specialized institutions. Because of rounding, figures may not add to 100 per cent.

SOURCE: U.S. DEPARTMENT OF EDUCATION

Distribution of Full-Time Faculty Members by Age and Discipline at Four-Year Institutions, 1987

	Under 30	30 to 44	45 to 54	55 to 64	65 and over	Average age
Agriculture and home economics	2%	47%	32%	19%	1%	45
Business	2	50	28	17	2	45
Education	2	30	35	30	3	49
Engineering	1	35	31	31	3	48
Fine arts	4	40	35	17	4	46
Health sciences	1	46	28	20	5	46
Humanities	1	32	35	27	5	49
Natural sciences	1	41	39	17	2	47
Social sciences	1	43	34	17	5	47
Other	2	38	31	23	5	48
All	1	40	33	21	4	47

Note: The figures are based on a 1988 survey of 11,013 faculty members at 480 colleges and universities. The response rate was 76 per cent. Figures may not add to 100 per cent because of rounding.

SOURCE: U.S. DEPARTMENT OF EDUCATION

Total Return on College Endowments

	Periods ending June 30, 1990			
	1 year	3 years	5 years	10 years
All investment pools	+9.6%	+8.1%	+14.6%	+13.4%
By size				
$25-million and under	+8.7%	+8.0%	+13.8%	+12.6%
$25-million to $100-million	+9.6	+7.7	+14.0	+12.9
$100-million to $400-million	+10.3	+8.7	+15.5	+14.1
$400-million or more	+11.3	+8.9	+15.9	+14.4
By type of institution				
Public	+8.5%	+7.8%	+14.3%	+13.0%
Private	+10.1	+8.3	+14.8	+12.6
Comparative measurements				
Standard & Poor's 500 Index	+16.5%	+9.3%	+17.2%	+16.8%
Lehman Brothers Government/Corporate Bond Index	+7.1	+9.0	+10.3	+11.6
Lehman Brothers Government Bond Index	+6.9	+8.7	+10.0	+11.4
Consumer Price Index	+4.4	+4.5	+3.7	+4.4

Note: Total-return rates represent change in market value, plus dividends and interest, for periods ending June 30, 1990, based on data for investment pools at 367 colleges and universities.

SOURCE: NATIONAL ASSOCIATION OF COLLEGE AND UNIVERSITY BUSINESS OFFICERS

Top Institutions in Voluntary Support, 1989-90

Harvard University	$213,451,868
Stanford University	202,165,961
Cornell University	161,338,332
University of Pennsylvania	140,045,350
Yale University	130,000,100
University of Southern California	126,136,395
University of Wisconsin at Madison	124,399,972
Columbia University	123,225,490
Massachusetts Institute of Technology	117,603,798
Johns Hopkins University	111,814,058
Duke University	108,011,121
University of Minnesota	105,298,301
University of California at Berkeley	97,397,641
University of California at Los Angeles	96,454,560
University of Washington	89,426,938
University of Illinois	86,607,414
University of Michigan	83,608,567
Indiana University	79,118,891
Princeton University	75,163,623
New York University	74,675,955

SOURCE: COUNCIL FOR AID TO EDUCATION

College and University Endowments Over $75-Million, 1990

	Market value June 30, 1990
Harvard University	$4,653,229,000
University of Texas System	3,256,192,000
Yale University	2,570,892,000
Princeton University	2,527,140,000
Stanford University [1]	2,053,128,000
Columbia University	1,494,938,000
Massachusetts Institute of Technology	1,404,588,000
Texas A&M University	1,369,000,000
Washington University	1,365,854,000
Emory University	1,153,875,000
University of Chicago	1,074,505,000
Rice University	1,068,633,000
Northwestern University	983,556,000
Cornell University	926,900,000
University of Pennsylvania	808,409,000
University of Notre Dame	605,630,000
Vanderbilt University	603,708,000
Dartmouth College	593,952,000
University of Rochester	589,007,000
Johns Hopkins University	560,478,000
Rockefeller University	544,274,000
New York University	542,672,000
California Institute of Technology	523,729,000
University of Southern California	495,595,000
University of Virginia	487,007,000
Duke University	472,923,000
University of Michigan	448,209,000
Brown University	425,750,000
Case Western Reserve University	421,820,000
Wellesley College	374,127,000
University of Delaware	360,278,000
Southern Methodist University	355,322,000
Smith College	341,927,000
Swarthmore College	336,014,000
Ohio State University	321,880,000
Macalester College [2]	320,127,000
Wake Forest University	318,511,000
Williams College	314,679,000
University of Cincinnati	314,461,000
University of Tulsa [2]	309,769,000
Loyola University of Chicago	309,459,000
Carnegie Mellon University	299,168,000
George Washington University	296,677,000
Pomona College	295,982,000
Texas Christian University [2]	290,816,000
Grinnell College	286,770,000
Trinity University [2]	285,933,000
Indiana University and Foundation	285,929,000
University of Richmond	280,567,000
University of Pittsburgh	279,641,000

Continued on Following Page

College and University Endowments Over $75-Million, continued

	Market value June 30, 1990
Boston College [2]	$276,314,000
University of Minnesota	275,255,000
Berea College	271,114,000
Wesleyan University	270,958,000
Amherst College	269,441,000
Baylor University [2]	250,377,000
Lehigh University	244,043,000
Georgetown University	242,255,000
Vassar College	240,670,000
Rensselaer Polytechnic Institute	240,078,000
Tulane University	233,417,000
Oberlin College	229,515,000
Middlebury College	227,488,000
Kansas University Endowment Association	226,008,000
University of Florida Foundation	218,559,000
Lafayette College	206,081,000
Georgia Institute of Technology	200,446,000
Thomas Jefferson University	196,033,000
Saint Louis University	188,134,000
Pennsylvania State University	180,457,000
Boston University	180,272,000
Mount Holyoke College	180,000,000
University of Nebraska	178,213,000
Carleton College	175,793,000
Texas A&M Development Foundation	175,000,000
University of Minnesota Foundation	173,899,000
University of Miami [2]	170,978,000
Purdue University	170,760,000
University of Washington	170,071,000
University of North Carolina at Chapel Hill	169,082,000
Rochester Institute of Technology	165,807,000
Washington State University	165,386,000
Syracuse University	165,042,000
Principia College	160,922,000
Northeastern University	157,237,000
Tufts University	155,615,000
University of Alabama System [1]	155,000,000
Bryn Mawr College	154,602,000
Rush University	154,410,000
Brandeis University	153,137,000
Bowdoin College	151,744,000
State University of New York at Buffalo and Foundation	149,632,000
Occidental College	147,278,000
University of Missouri	146,545,000
University of Illinois Foundation	143,348,000
Agnes Scott College	142,747,000
Academy of the New Church	141,843,000
Colorado College	137,694,000
Trinity College (Conn.)	137,348,000

	Market value June 30, 1990
Colgate University	$137,153,000
Earlham College	132,790,000
Wabash College	129,621,000
University of Wisconsin Foundation	127,271,000
Southwestern University	126,673,000
University of Oklahoma and Foundation	122,741,000
Virginia Tech Foundation	117,400,000
Hamilton College	114,519,000
Rutgers University	114,002,000
Cranbrook Educational Community	111,213,000
Santa Clara University	110,562,000
Washington and Lee University	109,484,000
University of Tennessee System	107,145,000
Loyola Marymount University	106,353,000
Cooper Union	106,053,000
Claremont McKenna College	103,078,000
University of Wisconsin System	101,373,000
Radcliffe College	99,986,000
Whitman College	99,935,000
Worcester Polytechnic Institute	98,236,000
Bucknell University	98,193,000
Union College (N.Y.)	97,684,000
Mercer University	97,486,000
University of the South	97,085,000
University of Louisville Foundation	95,021,000
College of Saint Thomas	94,179,000
University of Georgia and Foundation	93,128,000
De Pauw University	92,422,000
Reed College	89,662,000
College of William and Mary	87,591,000
Wheaton College (Ill.)	86,906,000
University of Houston System	86,589,000
University of California at Los Angeles Foundation	85,403,000
Franklin and Marshall College	85,356,000
Davidson College	85,092,000
Haverford College	83,876,000
Marquette University	83,085,000
College of the Holy Cross	81,055,000
University of Iowa Foundation	80,741,000
Rhodes College	80,156,000
Drew University	80,064,000
St. Lawrence University	80,058,000
Furman University [2]	79,748,000
Hampton University	78,221,000
Colby College	77,682,000
University of Kentucky	76,046,000
Denison University	75,071,000

Note: Table includes institutions participating in the comparative-performance study by the National Association of College and University Business Officers.

[1] As of September 30   [2] As of May 31

SOURCE: NATIONAL ASSOCIATION OF COLLEGE AND UNIVERSITY BUSINESS OFFICERS

Top Institutions in Research-and-Development Spending, Fiscal Year 1990

	Total funds for research & development
Johns Hopkins University *	$668,915,000
Massachusetts Institute of Technology	311,767,000
University of Michigan	310,578,000
University of Wisconsin at Madison	309,841,000
Stanford University	305,700,000
Cornell University	300,144,000
University of Minnesota	292,046,000
Texas A&M University	272,800,000
Pennsylvania State University	256,926,000
University of California at Los Angeles	246,795,000
University of Washington	245,313,000
University of California at San Francisco	238,278,000
University of California at San Diego	237,032,000
University of California at Berkeley	231,061,000
University of Texas at Austin	228,203,000
University of Illinois at Urbana-Champaign	227,742,000
Harvard University	220,812,000
University of California at Davis	198,075,000
University of Arizona	195,633,000
University of Pennsylvania	189,390,000
Columbia University	182,769,000
Yale University	180,706,000
Ohio State University	178,569,000
University of Southern California	169,102,000
Georgia Institute of Technology	168,193,000
University of Maryland at College Park	166,022,000
University of Georgia	156,742,000
Baylor College of Medicine	155,122,000
University of Colorado	154,723,000
Washington University	151,249,000
Duke University	140,708,000
University of Florida	139,678,000
Rutgers University	137,985,000
Louisiana State University	135,849,000
Northwestern University	131,979,000
North Carolina State University	131,133,000
Purdue University	130,379,000
University of Rochester	129,011,000
Michigan State University	126,987,000
University of Tennessee System	126,790,000
University of North Carolina at Chapel Hill	123,113,000
Virginia Polytechnic Institute and State University	121,423,000
University of Chicago	117,955,000
University of Pittsburgh	117,716,000
Iowa State University	115,945,000

Note: Figures cover only research-and-development expenditures in science and engineering, and exclude spending in such disciplines as the arts, education, the humanities, law, and physical education.

* Includes the Applied Physics Laboratory with $416-million in total research-and-development expenditures.

	Total funds for research & development
University of Iowa	$115,778,000
University of Connecticut	113,349,000
University of Alabama at Birmingham	110,603,000
State University of New York at Buffalo	109,190,000
New York University	108,511,000
California Institute of Technology	105,730,000
University of Massachusetts	101,812,000
Carnegie Mellon University	100,201,000
University of Virginia	96,815,000
University of Miami	94,344,000
Case Western Reserve University	93,384,000
Princeton University	91,514,000
University of Texas Anderson Cancer Center	91,283,000
Oregon State University	90,688,000
Indiana University	89,191,000
University of Utah	89,018,000
Utah State University	86,450,000
University of Texas Southwestern Medical Center Dallas	85,919,000
University of Illinois at Chicago	85,268,000
University of Missouri at Columbia	84,311,000
Yeshiva University	83,968,000
University of Maryland at Baltimore	83,689,000
Emory University	82,774,000
State University of New York at Stony Brook	82,236,000
University of California at Irvine	78,074,000
University of Nebraska at Lincoln	77,598,000
University of Hawaii at Manoa	76,525,000
University of South Florida	76,404,000
Rockefeller University	75,245,000
Vanderbilt University	75,062,000
University of Kentucky	74,959,000
University of Cincinnati	74,461,000
Colorado State University	73,967,000
Boston University	73,655,000
Woods Hole Oceanographic Institute	71,747,000
New Mexico State University	71,288,000
Washington State University	66,856,000
Auburn University	66,795,000
Clemson University	66,664,000
Oklahoma State University	65,685,000
University of Alaska at Fairbanks	65,571,000
University of Medicine and Dentistry of New Jersey	64,229,000
City University of New York Mount Sinai School of Medicine	63,752,000

SOURCE: NATIONAL SCIENCE FOUNDATION

Revenues and Expenditures of Colleges and Universities, 1987-88

	Public institutions 1987-88	Per cent of total	Private institutions 1987-88	Per cent of total
Revenues				
Tuition and fees	$11,184,657,000	15.0%	$16,615,523,000	39.1%
Appropriations				
Federal	1,434,906,000	1.9	229,148,000	0.5
State	30,917,354,000	41.3	381,183,000	0.9
Local	2,465,172,000	3.3	5,267,000	—
Government grants and contracts				
Federal	6,279,355,000	8.4	6,828,485,000	16.1
State	1,520,150,000	2.1	698,328,000	1.6
Local	266,691,000	0.4	269,133,000	0.7
Private gifts, grants, and contracts	2,517,422,000	3.4	3,841,860,000	9.0
Endowment income	361,545,000	0.5	2,224,896,000	5.2
Sales and services				
Educational activities	1,948,679,000	2.6	969,411,000	2.3
Auxiliary enterprises	7,306,302,000	9.8	4,639,539,000	10.9
Hospitals	6,596,733,000	8.8	4,029,833,000	9.5
Other	1,972,290,000	2.6	1,797,280,000	4.2
Total current-fund revenues	$74,771,255,000	100.0%	$42,529,887,000	100.0%
Expenditures				
Instruction	$24,954,204,000	34.4%	$10,865,480,000	26.4%
Research	6,976,925,000	9.6	3,374,006,000	8.2
Public service	2,986,164,000	4.1	800,198,000	1.9
Academic support	5,436,156,000	7.5	2,705,019,000	6.6
Student services	3,482,112,000	4.8	1,908,708,000	4.6
Institutional support	6,470,163,000	8.9	4,301,497,000	10.5
Plant operation and maintenance	5,601,733,000	7.7	2,627,873,000	6.4
Scholarships and fellowships	1,941,390,000	2.7	3,383,543,000	8.2
Mandatory transfers	790,624,000	1.1	527,009,000	1.3
Auxiliary enterprises	7,237,867,000	10.0	4,160,454,000	10.1
Hospitals	6,532,906,000	9.0	3,873,557,000	9.4
Other	231,063,000	0.3	2,591,570,000	6.3
Total current-fund expenditures	$72,641,305,000	100.0%	$41,118,914,000	100.0%

Note: A dash indicates less than 0.1 per cent. Because of rounding, details may not add up to totals.

SOURCE: U.S. DEPARTMENT OF EDUCATION

Non-Profit Institutions Receiving the Largest Contracts From the Defense Department, Fiscal Year 1990

	Amount
Massachusetts Institute of Technology	$455,149,000
Aerospace Corporation	416,217,000
Mitre Corporation	407,283,000
Johns Hopkins University	373,946,000
Rand Corporation	79,348,000
IIT Research Institute	63,424,000
Institute for Defense Analyses	60,081,000
Pennsylvania State University	61,621,000
Charles S. Draper Laboratory	58,489,000
Carnegie Mellon University	57,229,000
University of Texas System	49,047,000
Utah State University	44,562,000
University of California	39,259,000
SRI International	37,067,000
Analytic Services Inc.	34,751,000
University of Southern California	30,953,000
Georgia Tech Research Corporation	27,593,000
Battelle Memorial Institute	26,199,000
University of Washington	26,796,000
Stanford University	23,317,000
University of Dayton	22,216,000
Trident Technical College	21,022,000
Logistics Management Institute	20,311,000
Environmental Research Institute of Michigan	13,724,000
New Mexico State University	13,507,000
University of Illinois	10,908,000
University of Pittsburgh	9,619,000
University of Maryland	9,145,000
Georgia Institute of Technology	9,032,000
Cornell University	8,946,000
Riverside Research Institute	8,559,000
National Academy of Sciences	8,233,000
Woods Hole Oceanographic Institution	8,207,000

Note: The list includes those colleges, universities, and other non-profit organizations that received a total of $8-million or more in contracts from the Department of Defense. The figures cover only contracts of more than $25,000 for research, development, testing, and evaluation for military projects and for civilian water-resource projects. Other types of funding are not included in this table.

SOURCE: U.S. DEPARTMENT OF DEFENSE

Range of 1991-92 Tuition at Four-Year Institutions

	Number of colleges	Average tuition and fees	Proportion of total enrollment
Private institutions			
$15,000 or more	73	$16,141	12.9%
14,000 — 14,999	30	14,404	3.2
13,000 — 13,999	25	13,522	2.8
12,000 — 12,999	44	12,459	4.4
11,000 — 11,999	63	11,431	6.0
10,000 — 10,999	96	10,448	9.2
9,000 — 9,999	120	9,462	13.7
8,000 — 8,999	130	8,438	9.7
7,000 — 7,999	132	7,482	8.7
6,000 — 6,999	129	6,474	9.1
5,000 — 5,999	99	5,449	6.3
4,000 — 4,999	94	4,467	4.4
3,000 — 3,999	90	3,479	3.0
2,000 — 2,999	55	2,512	6.0
1,000 — 1,999	12	1,602	0.3
Less than $1,000	6	440	0.3
Total	1,198	—	100.0%
Public institutions			
$3,000 or more	60	$3,672	11.1%
2,500 — 2,999	54	2,738	10.9
2,000 — 2,499	113	2,283	23.8
1,500 — 1,999	148	1,754	26.6
1,000 — 1,499	128	1,275	25.0
Less than $1,000	18	753	2.6
Total	521	—	100.0%

Note: Includes only those institutions that provided final or estimated 1991-92 tuition and fees by September 10, 1991.

SOURCE: THE COLLEGE BOARD

Voluntary Support for Higher Education, 1989-90

			Percentage change	
Sources	Amount	Per cent	1-year	5-year
Alumni	$2,540,000,000	25.9%	+10.8%	+74.0%
Other individuals	2,230,000,000	22.8	+ 7.4	+57.5
Corporations	2,170,000,000	22.1	+11.5	+37.9
Foundations	1,920,000,000	19.6	+10.2	+63.4
Religious organizations	240,000,000	2.4	+ 1.3	+15.4
Other	700,000,000	7.1	+10.8	+43.7
Total	$9,800,000,000	100%	+ 9.8%	+55.1%

SOURCE: COUNCIL FOR AID TO EDUCATION

Average College Costs, 1991-92

	Public colleges		Private colleges	
	Resident	Commuter	Resident	Commuter
4-year colleges				
Tuition and fees	$2,137	$2,137	$10,017	$10,017
Books and supplies	485	485	508	508
Room and board*	3,351	1,468	4,386	1,634
Transportation	464	793	470	795
Other	1,147	1,153	911	1,029
Total	$7,584	$6,036	$16,292	$13,983
2-year colleges				
Tuition and fees	$1,022	$1,022	$5,290	$5,290
Books and supplies	480	480	476	476
Room and board*	—	1,543	3,734	1,529
Transportation	—	902	519	786
Other	—	966	895	925
Total	—	$4,913	$10,914	$9,006

Note: The figures are weighted by enrollment to reflect the charges incurred by the average undergraduate enrolled at each type of institution.
* Room not included for commuter students
— Insufficient data

SOURCE: THE COLLEGE BOARD

Changes in Campus Operating Budgets, 1989-90 to 1990-91

	Total	Doctoral	Compre-hensive	Bacca-laureate	2-year
Percentage reporting each change:					
Increase of 11% or more	14%	17%	16%	16%	12%
Increase of 7% to 10%	27	15	18	41	23
Increase of 5% to 6%	22	16	26	15	26
Increase of 1% to 4%	16	18	13	13	18
No change	12	18	10	13	11
Decrease of 11% or more	2	0	2	1	2
Decrease of 7% to 10%	3	5	4	0	4
Decrease of 5% to 6%	1	2	2	0	2
Decrease of 1% to 4%	3	10	10	1	1

Note: The figures are based on responses to a survey sent to senior administrators at 444 colleges and universities in the spring of 1991. The response rate was 81 per cent. Because of rounding, figures may not add to 100 per cent.

SOURCE: AMERICAN COUNCIL ON EDUCATION

Administrators' Views on Campus Issues

	Total	Doctoral	Compre-hensive	Bacca-laureate	2-year
Percentage agreeing:					
Collaboration with high schools is a high priority for this institution	75%	71%	74%	56%	88%
Federal law permitting mandatory retirement of faculty at age 70 should be retained	57	59	64	54	57
It is appropriate for regional accrediting bodies to review college performance on ethnic and cultural diversity	55	59	68	48	54
In the past year, this institution:					
Had incidents of intolerance	36	74	53	38	24
Had an increased frequency of incidents of intolerance	8	17	12	6	7
Experienced significant controversy over the political or cultural content of:					
Course tests	3	5	1	6	0
Information presented in the classroom	4	10	5	6	1
Invited speakers or lecturers	10	20	15	11	5
Received complaints from faculty of pressure to alter the political or cultural content of their courses	5	12	10	5	3

Note: The figures are based on responses to a survey sent to senior administrators at 444 colleges and universities in the spring of 1991. The response rate was 81 per cent. Because of rounding, figures may not add to 100 per cent.

SOURCE: AMERICAN COUNCIL ON EDUCATION

Administrators' Views of Challenges Facing Institutions in the Next Five Years

	Total	Doctoral	Compre-hensive	Bacca-laureate	2-year
Percentage of administrators citing each challenge:					
Adequate finances	71%	91%	57%	53%	87%
Fund raising	13	9	12	25	5
Maintain enrollment	30	28	31	40	22
Enrollment growth	11	7	11	8	15
Assessment	16	5	7	22	16
Maintain quality	27	32	48	21	23
Strengthen curriculum	21	18	16	25	20
Serve new needs and populations	5	5	12	4	4
Effective faculty	14	18	13	14	14
Recruitment and retention of faculty members	3	2	0	7	2
Other faculty issues	28	18	41	26	26
Diversity	17	32	21	19	13
Facilities and technology	27	18	17	29	30

Note: The figures are based on responses to a survey sent to senior administrators at 444 colleges and universities in the spring of 1991. The response rate was 81 per cent.

SOURCE: AMERICAN COUNCIL ON EDUCATION

Holdings of University Research Libraries in U.S. and Canada, 1989-90

	Rank[1]	Volumes in library	Volumes added	Current serials	Total staff	Total expenditures[2]
Harvard University	1	11,874,148	261,846	103,075	1,095	$45,703,359
University of California at Los Angeles	2	6,156,761	246,737	96,676	686	32,653,412
University of California at Berkeley	3	7,540,234	202,202	92,978	788	31,399,069
Yale University	4	8,862,768	147,841	51,985	704	28,709,200
University of Illinois at Urbana-Champaign	5	7,748,736	187,489	92,077	532	18,520,182
University of Toronto	6	5,951,752	174,598	38,063	701	27,138,651
Stanford University	7	5,871,063	144,450	49,673	596	31,326,296
University of Texas	8	6,265,236	202,338	50,506	608	19,191,606
Columbia University	9	6,032,545	148,872	59,044	644	23,417,989
University of Michigan	10	6,369,490	141,606	69,937	583	22,394,006
Cornell University[3]	11	5,216,501	189,070	59,801	551	21,055,340
University of Wisconsin	12	5,036,144	139,194	49,553	528	21,844,945
University of Minnesota	13	4,651,111	105,357	47,491	484	21,836,149
University of Washington	14	4,908,988	102,887	50,215	486	18,111,845
University of Chicago	15	5,191,998	132,437	48,925	370	14,922,568
Indiana University	16	4,133,331	103,279	38,430	475	18,376,165
Rutgers University[3]	17	3,219,823	102,635	30,097	519	21,880,472
Princeton University	18	4,276,086	105,659	32,037	396	17,038,820
Ohio State University	19	4,430,132	101,714	32,870	473	16,813,196
University of North Carolina	20	3,751,660	123,899	39,998	405	14,402,816
Arizona State University[3]	21	2,599,701	138,242	34,844	388	14,948,385
University of Florida	22	2,892,301	127,167	27,999	441	16,122,500
University of Pennsylvania	23	3,665,786	98,659	31,887	372	16,495,798
University of Arizona	24	3,549,281	128,634	28,620	390	13,662,887
University of Georgia[3]	25	2,889,108	101,285	55,954	351	12,883,133
University of British Columbia	26	2,918,279	106,091	22,151	407	17,120,088
Pennsylvania State University	27	3,095,863	64,286	31,846	472	17,243,989
University of Virginia	28	3,193,260	106,577	26,268	370	15,921,187
Duke University	29	3,846,295	95,633	30,364	312	14,523,509
University of California at Davis	30	2,376,157	80,900	51,604	335	16,203,556
Northwestern University	31	3,474,423	80,284	36,696	342	13,586,594
University of Alberta[3]	32	2,956,553	99,331	18,823	396	14,841,362
New York University	33	3,092,620	73,877	23,474	408	17,045,841
Michigan State University	34	3,417,388	114,116	28,910	329	12,481,402
University of Pittsburgh	35	2,878,713	96,693	22,403	358	13,026,194
University of California at San Diego	36	1,949,397	72,815	32,551	364	16,735,467
University of Kansas[3]	37	2,868,223	80,443	28,431	333	14,767,353
Johns Hopkins University	38	2,835,664	77,339	20,531	339	15,214,302

Continued on Following Page

Holdings of University Research Libraries in U.S. and Canada, continued

	Rank[1]	Volumes in library	Volumes added	Current serials	Total staff	Total expenditures[2]
University of Southern California[3]	39	2,626,271	54,528	33,805	350	$14,892,419
University of Iowa	40	3,104,621	91,083	24,176	273	11,613,626
University of Maryland	41	2,055,403	67,348	23,018	345	15,121,610
McGill University	42	2,509,979	64,930	17,516	326	13,667,722
State University of New York at Buffalo	43	2,591,006	64,787	23,507	289	12,113,946
University of Hawaii	44	2,385,601	74,381	32,265	232	9,754,608
University of California at Santa Barbara	45	1,996,662	77,487	21,242	250	11,680,964
Wayne State University	46	2,374,831	66,286	24,173	238	11,457,301
Georgetown University	47	1,802,242	64,921	22,799	295	12,070,953
University of Western Ontario	48	1,961,386	68,930	17,995	287	11,557,572
University of Connecticut	49	2,271,849	79,837	17,620	230	11,968,917
University of Laval	50	1,793,368	72,682	15,847	267	11,246,268
Texas A&M University	51	1,892,454	55,037	25,378	309	11,008,870
Boston University	52	1,761,954	58,075	29,540	274	10,054,921
Washington University	53	2,277,203	59,093	18,387	258	11,403,738
Vanderbilt University	54	1,873,598	68,622	16,448	303	11,476,698
Howard University	55	1,783,876	55,294	26,300	283	10,618,060
Massachusetts Institute of Technology	56	2,180,873	55,710	21,313	245	9,718,298
Purdue University	57	1,924,982	61,606	21,505	266	9,691,456
Emory University	58	1,872,313	59,399	16,623	264	11,969,585
York University (Ontario)[3]	59	1,845,478	64,633	19,641	250	10,385,556
University of Illinois at Chicago	60	1,656,307	52,924	17,652	298	11,365,864
University of New Mexico	61	1,711,771	56,303	16,169	337	11,241,022
Florida State University[3]	62	1,829,826	68,447	18,843	249	10,234,935
University of Cincinnati	63	1,746,857	59,686	19,642	302	10,718,338
Syracuse University	64	2,332,676	50,126	18,044	267	9,457,422
University of South Carolina	65	2,431,129	64,735	20,552	198	8,170,685
University of Delaware	66	1,953,028	55,097	24,202	225	9,228,202
Brown University	67	2,227,301	55,392	13,510	277	10,603,303
University of Colorado	68	2,286,736	60,149	15,588	223	10,225,273
Louisiana State University	69	2,460,219	52,689	19,573	252	8,263,718
University of Rochester	70	2,686,996	54,792	14,214	244	8,908,321
Brigham Young University	71	2,063,384	70,162	18,582	335	9,533,011
University of Massachusetts	72	2,409,946	67,670	15,267	202	8,311,979
University of Notre Dame	73	1,996,606	76,518	17,513	191	7,183,272
University of Missouri	74	2,486,014	43,872	17,766	235	8,388,702
University of Tennessee	75	1,874,535	42,491	21,606	259	8,249,066
University of Kentucky	76	2,154,837	39,591	19,819	250	8,908,340
University of California at Irvine	77	1,449,246	54,097	16,346	250	11,266,455

	Rank[1]	Volumes in library	Volumes added	Current serials	Total staff	Total expenditures[2]
University of Miami	78	1,697,581	48,714	16,717	249	$9,628,243
Southern Illinois University	79	2,082,358	50,074	19,842	245	8,796,210
Queen's University (Kingston)	80	1,796,893	48,481	15,982	227	8,849,728
University of Nebraska	81	2,013,548	51,485	18,041	214	8,131,992
Virginia Polytechnic Institute and State University	82	1,710,202	53,286	17,746	204	8,730,428
Temple University	83	2,071,461	44,852	15,474	226	8,396,512
Iowa State University	84	1,830,214	43,204	18,557	222	9,218,296
Dartmouth College	85	1,824,377	51,846	20,788	175	7,838,950
Washington State University	86	1,606,851	47,300	22,573	211	8,136,463
University of Oregon	87	1,844,996	41,880	21,187	217	8,394,719
North Carolina State University	88	1,375,049	48,917	18,401	217	8,414,798
Tulane University [3]	89	1,802,910	47,767	17,091	187	7,585,533
State University of New York at Stony Brook	90	1,701,101	47,355	11,239	220	9,800,376
University of Utah	91	1,813,560	58,137	12,144	230	7,429,915
University of Guelph	92	1,900,416	63,252	13,600	159	6,456,800
University of Manitoba	93	1,520,920	38,260	12,578	228	9,140,214
McMaster University	94	1,377,237	47,111	11,549	203	9,336,427
University of Alabama	95	1,814,178	48,149	17,603	178	7,070,586
University of Oklahoma	96	2,297,087	39,412	17,783	185	7,082,575
University of Saskatchewan	97	1,404,391	60,519	10,689	179	7,847,548
Kent State University [3]	98	2,041,567	35,321	10,692	238	9,278,896
University of Waterloo [3]	99	1,566,042	24,941	15,150	206	8,437,553
University of California at Riverside	100	1,461,147	47,604	13,901	177	7,422,888
Georgia Institute of Technology	101	1,648,178	52,015	23,438	113	5,196,995
State University of New York at Albany	102	1,278,657	38,231	14,534	174	7,697,389
Case Western Reserve University	103	1,584,782	31,990	13,033	175	7,305,047
University of Houston	104	1,622,189	28,681	15,103	192	6,723,883
Oklahoma State University	105	1,543,356	31,284	11,482	177	6,942,329
Colorado State University	106	1,220,897	39,596	11,720	143	6,856,673
Rice University	107	1,441,470	39,034	12,413	145	5,098,528

Note: Institutions are asked to report figures for their main campuses only, unless a branch campus is indicated.

[1] Based on an index developed by the Association of Research Libraries to measure the relative size of university libraries. The index takes into account the number of volumes held, number of volumes added during the previous fiscal year, number of current serials, total operating expenditures, and size of staff, excluding student assistants. It does not measure a library's services, the quality of its collections, or its success in meeting the needs of users.

[2] Figures for Canadian libraries are expressed in U.S. dollars.

[3] Includes branches as well as the main institution.

ASSOCIATION OF RESEARCH LIBRARIES

The States

ALABAMA

KNOWN as one of the most regressive tax systems in the nation, Alabama's revenue structure is considered by higher-education officials to be woefully inadequate to provide the money needed to improve public services—including the state's colleges and universities.

The revenue system relies heavily on a sales tax and other levies that hit low-income residents the hardest. In addition, Alabama lawmakers face strong pressure to limit state spending. Consequently, the Legislature and government agencies tend to rely on a budget strategy of robbing Peter to pay Paul.

In November 1990, for instance, the Alabama Commission on Higher Education was criticized by leaders at state institutions for proposing to change the college-financing formula in a way that favored research universities. State legislators, in turn, came under fire from college officials for shifting money from higher education to public schools. The Legislature resolved the dispute by reducing the state's scheduled payment to the Alabama pension fund and putting the money that would have gone to pensions into the budget for higher-education institutions.

The commission, which is the state coordinating board, recommended a budget for fiscal 1992 that would have brought the level of state support for Alabama's public colleges up to the Southern regional average in about five years. Instead, budget cuts in fiscal 1991 brought layoffs, salary reductions, and tuition increases.

Adding to the state's financial troubles is the propensity of legislators to promote pork-barrel projects. Gov. Guy Hunt, a Republican serving his second term, has tried to curb the legislators' interference with academic missions and the financing of the state's colleges, but has had limited success.

An unwelcome legacy of Alabama's past is visible in a continuing legal battle over desegregation. In 1991 a federal district court heard arguments on whether or not Alabama's public colleges remain illegally segregated.

State leaders and university officials say they fully support the concept of racial integration in higher education. But civil-rights activists, the federal government, and black-college officials say the state has not done enough to attract black students to predominantly white colleges or to improve the programs and facilities of public black colleges.

No ruling has been handed down in the case. Even if a decision comes, it may be appealed on the basis of an expected U.S. Supreme Court ruling

ALABAMA
Continued

in a Mississippi desegregation case that the Court is considering.

Black colleges have a long history in Alabama. Along with two public black universities and two black community colleges, the state is home to Tuskegee University, a private institution that receives some financial support from the state.

Alabama A&M University and its administration have come under fire from Governor Hunt. Its former president, Carl Marbury, resigned amid allegations that he had given jobs in return for sex, fired employees arbitrarily, and bribed legislators. The interim president, Alan L. Keyes, a prominent black Republican and an opponent of affirmative action, has the support of the board. But his critics fear he is "conspiring" with Governor Hunt either to close the institution or to merge it with the University of Alabama System.

The two universities with the most political clout are arch-rivals Auburn University and the University of Alabama. But recently, the University of Alabama faced competition from other institutions: A joint application by Troy State and Alabama State Universities to operate a public radio station in Selma conflicts with a similar venture proposed by the University of Alabama. The institutions have been trying to negotiate a joint operating agreement, but if that effort fails the issue will have to be resolved by the Federal Communications Commission.

DEMOGRAPHICS

Population: 4,040,587   (Rank: 22)

Age distribution:
Up to 17 .... 26.2%
18 to 24 .... 11.0%
25 to 44 .... 30.5%
45 and older 32.3%

Racial and ethnic distribution:
American Indian 0.4%
Asian 0.5%
Black 25.3%
White 73.6%
Other and unknown 0.1%
Hispanic (may be any race) .. 0.6%

Educational attainment of adults:
At least 4 years of high school 56.5%
At least 1 to 3 years of college 24.7%
At least 4 years of college ... 12.2%

Per-capita personal income: $15,021

Poverty rate: 19.1%

New high-school graduates in:
1991-92 (estimate) 39,939
2001-02 (estimate) 37,093

New GED diploma recipients: 7,549

High-school dropout rate: 25.1%

POLITICAL LEADERSHIP

Governor: Guy Hunt (R), term ends 1995

Governor's higher-education aide: Anita Buckley-Commander, 11 South Union Street, State House, Montgomery 36130; (205) 242-7130

U.S. Senators: Howell Heflin (D), term ends 1997; Richard C. Shelby (D), term ends 1993

U.S. Representatives:
5 Democrats, 2 Republicans
Tom Bevill (D), Glen Browder (D),

Sonny Callahan (R), Robert E. (Bud) Cramer, Jr. (D), William L. Dickinson (R), Ben Erdreich (D), Claude Harris (D)

Legislature: Senate, 28 Democrats, 7 Republicans; House, 81 Democrats, 23 Republicans, 1 vacancy

COLLEGES AND UNIVERSITIES

Higher education:
Public 4-year institutions 18
Public 2-year institutions 37
Private 4-year institutions 18
Private 2-year institutions 14
Total 87

Vocational institutions: 72

Statewide coordinating board:
Commission on Higher Education
One Court Square, Suite 221
Montgomery 36104
(205) 269-2700
Henry J. Hector, executive director

Private-college association:
Council for the Advancement
 of Private Colleges in Alabama
6 Office Park Circle, Suite 112
Birmingham 35223
(205) 879-1673
Position of president vacant

Institutions censured by the AAUP:
Alabama State University,
Auburn University, Talladega College

Institutions under NCAA sanctions:
Alabama A&M University,
Auburn University

FACULTY MEMBERS

Full-time faculty members by rank:
Professor 1,127
Associate professor 1,226
Assistant professor 1,543
Instructor 538
Lecturer 51
No rank 1,322
Total 5,807

Average pay of full-time professors:
At public 4-year institutions $35,386
At public 2-year institutions $30,644
At private 4-year institutions $29,760
At private 2-year institutions $23,961
At all institutions $33,308
Men (all institutions) $35,564
Women (all institutions) $29,130

STUDENTS

Enrollment:
Total 208,562
At public 4-year institutions   121,155
At public 2-year institutions . 66,420
At private 4-year institutions 17,526
At private 2-year institutions . 3,461
Undergraduate 185,592
 First-time freshmen 44,003
Graduate 19,921
Professional 3,049
American Indian 438
Asian 1,596
Black 38,978
Hispanic 1,121
White 153,884
Foreign 3,796

Enrollment highlights:
Women 48.3%
Full-time 69.0%
Minority 21.5%
Foreign 1.9%
10-year change in total
 enrollment .... Up 53.7%

Proportion of enrollment made up of minority students:
At public 4-year institutions . 18.3%
At public 2-year institutions . 19.8%

ALABAMA
Continued

At private 4-year institutions   41.8%
At private 2-year institutions   42.2%

Degrees awarded:
Associate 5,877
Bachelor's 16,508
Master's 4,233
Doctorate 341
Professional 787

Residence of new students: State residents made up 79% of all freshmen enrolled in Alabama; 92% of all Alabama residents who were freshmen attended college in their home state.

Test scores: Students averaged 17.9 on the A.C.T., which was taken by 53% of Alabama's high-school seniors.

MONEY

Average tuition and fees:
At public 4-year institutions . $1,522
At public 2-year institutions .. $662
At private 4-year institutions $5,484
At private 2-year institutions $3,703

Expenditures:
Public institutions .. $1,324,774,000
Private institutions ... $186,596,000

State funds for higher-education operating expenses: $791,587,000

Two-year change: Up 2%

State spending on student aid:
Need-based: $4,353,000; 4,783 awards
Non–need-based: $6,637,000; 7,446 awards
Other: $4,891,000

Salary of chief executive of largest public 4-year campus: James E. Martin, Auburn University main campus: $137,500

Total spending on research and development by doctorate-granting universities: $239,556,000
Sources:
Federal government 52.0%
State and local governments . 10.7%
Industry 7.8%
The institution itself 21.2%
Other 8.2%

Federal spending on education and student aid (selected programs):
Vocational and
  adult education $25,582,000
GI Bill $10,281,000
Pell Grants $91,096,000

Total federal spending on college- and university-based research and development: $123,373,000
Selected programs:
Department of Health
  and Human Services $72,285,000
National Science
  Foundation $6,793,000
Department of Defense . $12,477,000
Department
  of Agriculture $8,102,000
Department of Energy .. $1,970,000

Largest endowment:
University of Alabama
  System $155,000,000

Top fund raisers:
University of Alabama
  at Birmingham $16,455,000
Auburn University $15,389,000
University of Alabama
  at Tuscaloosa $14,340,000

MISCELLANY

■ Auburn University researchers

developed AU Lean, a reduced-fat hamburger meat that is the basis for McDonald's McLean DeLuxe.

■ Stillman College, a historically black institution, and the University of Alabama offer dual-degree programs in engineering, nursing, and social work. Students must complete a three-year program at Stillman and then spend two years at the university. Upon completion of the program, students receive a bachelor's degree from each institution. In addition, the president of the private college, Cordell Wynn, sits on the university's Board of Trustees.

■ Some dispute exists as to which college in Alabama is the oldest. The state's first constitution, in 1819, required the establishment of the University of Alabama; its doors swung open in 1831. It had been beaten to the punch, however, by Athens Academy (now Athens State College), whose first class was held in 1822.

ALASKA

UNTIL VOTERS returned Walter J. Hickel to the Governor's mansion in 1990 after a 20-year absence, the fluctuating price of oil had been the single most important factor driving the fortunes of higher education in Alaska. Now the university system has the fiscal conservatism of its new Governor to deal with, too.

The oil boom of the early 1980's financed the development of several new community colleges, and the drop in oil prices a few years later drove the University of Alaska System to absorb the colleges as a money-saving move. As a consequence of that, and of the vastness of the state itself, the university is responsible for a lot of territory—from vocational courses in food science to doctoral programs in the ecological and climatic issues of the Arctic.

The university has also been a pioneer in distance learning, using telecommunications to bring higher education to such isolated "bush" communities as Barrow and Bethel. Jerome Komisar, the system's new president, has said he plans to make rural education a priority of his administration.

The university has been criticized for failing to attract and retain Native Alaskans, but it has been trying to develop "bridge" programs with high schools in Eskimo and Aleut villages to familiarize them with higher education.

The state has also taken other steps to increase participation in higher education. It expanded its student-loan program in 1991 to include part-time students, and has created an unusual prepaid-tuition program in which families can use the yearly dividend that each resident receives from the state's oil profits.

But Governor Hickel, an independent, is looking to the day when the state's Prudhoe Bay oil supplies are depleted. In his first year in office, he pledged to cut state spending by 5 per cent in each year of his term. However, the university has built strong alliances with the Legislature in the past few years, and lawmakers have been able so far to protect the system's far-flung enterprises from the budget cuts Mr. Hickel has sought.

In matters other than money, Mr. Hickel—who was also Governor from 1966 to 1969—has been a strong supporter of the university. He was in-

ALASKA
Continued

strumental, for example, in the creation of a public corporation that will explore commercial opportunities for the university's Poker Flat Research Range.

But the Governor's role in the abrupt dismissal in the summer of 1991 of the executive director of the Commission on Postsecondary Education has raised some eyebrows. With no public discussion, the former director, Jane Byers Maynard, was asked to resign by members of the commission appointed by Mr. Hickel. She was replaced by Allan Barnes, a former school superintendent and education consultant.

DEMOGRAPHICS

Population: 550,043 (Rank: 50)

Age distribution:
Up to 17 .... 31.3%
18 to 24 .... 10.2%
25 to 44 .... 39.3%
45 and older 19.2%

Racial and ethnic distribution:
American Indian 15.6%
Asian 3.6%
Black 4.1%
White 75.5%
Other and unknown 1.2%
Hispanic (may be any race) .. 3.2%

Educational attainment of adults:
At least 4 years of high school 82.5%
At least 1 to 3 years of college 43.7%
At least 4 years of college ... 21.1%

Per-capita personal income: $21,688

Poverty rate: 11.0%

New high-school graduates in:
1991-92 (estimate) 6,197
2001-02 (estimate) 11,341

New GED diploma recipients: 1,367

High-school dropout rate: 34.5%

POLITICAL LEADERSHIP

Governor: Walter J. Hickel (Ind), term ends 1994

Governor's higher-education aide: Jerry Covey, Department of Education, P.O. Box F, Juneau 99811; (907) 465-2800

U.S. Senators: Frank H. Murkowski (R), term ends 1993; Ted Stevens (R), term ends 1997

U.S. Representative:
1 Republican
Don Young (R)

Legislature: Senate, 10 Democrats, 10 Republicans; House, 23 Democrats, 17 Republicans

COLLEGES AND UNIVERSITIES

Higher education:
Public 4-year institutions 3
Public 2-year institutions 0
Private 4-year institutions 4
Private 2-year institutions 1
Total 8

Vocational institutions: 40

Statewide coordinating board:
Alaska Commission on
   Postsecondary Education
400 Willoughby Avenue
Box FP
Juneau 99811

(907) 465-2854
Allan Barnes, executive director

Private-college association:
None

Institutions censured by the AAUP:
None

Institutions under NCAA sanctions:
None

FACULTY MEMBERS

Full-time faculty members by rank:
Professor 128
Associate professor 258
Assistant professor 164
Instructor 63
Lecturer 0
No rank 56
Total 669

Average pay of full-time professors:
At public 4-year institutions $45,280
At public 2-year institutions .... n/a
At private 4-year institutions $37,976
At private 2-year institutions ... n/a
At all institutions $44,789
Men (all institutions) $45,979
Women (all institutions) $42,471

STUDENTS

Enrollment:
Total 28,627
At public 4-year institutions . 26,274
At public 2-year institutions 0
At private 4-year institutions . 2,064
At private 2-year institutions .. 289
Undergraduate 27,518
   First-time freshmen 2,397
Graduate 1,109
Professional 0
American Indian 2,233
Asian 784
Black 1,048
Hispanic 522
White 23,613
Foreign 161

Enrollment highlights:
Women 59.6%
Full-time 36.8%
Minority 16.3%
Foreign 0.6%
10-year change in total
   enrollment .... Up 42.8%

Proportion of enrollment made up of minority students:
At public 4-year institutions . 16.2%
At public 2-year institutions . 14.1%
At private 4-year institutions   25.8%
At private 2-year institutions ... n/a

Degrees awarded:
Associate 606
Bachelor's 1,011
Master's 286
Doctorate 14
Professional 0

Residence of new students: State residents made up 78% of all freshmen enrolled in Alaska; 43% of all Alaska residents who were freshmen attended college in their home state.

Test scores: Students averaged 17.9 on the A.C.T., which was taken by 36% of Alaska's high-school seniors.

MONEY

Average tuition and fees:
At public 4-year institutions . $1,280
At public 2-year institutions .... n/a
At private 4-year institutions $5,078
At private 2-year institutions ... n/a

Expenditures:
Public institutions $224,042,000
Private institutions $10,171,000

ALASKA
Continued

State funds for higher-education operating expenses: $179,981,000

Two-year change: Up 1%

State spending on student aid:
Need-based: $464,000; 307 awards
Non–need-based: $2,111,000; number of awards n/a
Other: None

Salary of chief executive of largest public 4-year campus:
Donald F. Behrend, University of Alaska at Anchorage: $111,940

Total spending on research and development by doctorate-granting universities: $65,571,000

Sources:
Federal government 48.6%
State and local governments .. 3.4%
Industry 6.3%
The institution itself 36.0%
Other 5.7%

Federal spending on education and student aid (selected programs):
Vocational and
 adult education $6,056,000
GI Bill $1,056,000
Pell Grants $7,548,000

Total federal spending on college- and university-based research and development: $15,111,000

Selected programs:
Department of Health
 and Human Services ... $721,000
National Science
 Foundation $6,597,000
Department of Defense ... $533,000
Department
 of Agriculture $1,264,000
Department of Energy $704,000

Largest endowment:
University of Alaska .. $31,855,000

Top fund raisers:
data not reported

MISCELLANY

■ The name of the northernmost campus in the country, formerly the North Slope Higher Education Center, was changed in September 1990 by local officials, who preferred an Eskimo name. It is now Arctic Sivunmum Ilisagvik College.

■ The television show "Northern Exposure" is built around a doctor who came to Alaska to repay his obligation to the state for sending him to medical school. The state has no such program, but does send its medical students to the University of Washington's medical school for three years at a cost of more than $100,000 per student. Students are encouraged, but not required, to return to Alaska to practice when they graduate, and there have been attempts to make returning mandatory. (Idaho and Montana have similar programs.)

■ The oldest higher-education institution in Alaska is Sheldon Jackson College, founded in 1878.

ARIZONA

For the first few months of 1991, solving the budget problems of the Grand Canyon State took a back seat to an extended gubernatorial campaign and a headline-grabbing bribery investigation of leading state legislators.

In February 1991, a 16-month inquiry by local law-enforcement officials led to the indictment of seven legislators for accepting payments from an undercover agent posing as a Las Vegas gaming consultant trying to build support for legalized casino gambling in Arizona.

The vote tally in the November 1990 governor's race was so close that a run-off election had to be held. Arizona's voters finally elected Republican Fife Symington on February 26, 1991—just two months before the legislative session was to end.

One of his first acts as Governor was to appoint a committee to develop legislative recommendations for education reform and financing.

Although the financing plan does not specifically address higher education, college officials say the final committee report could include a tax increase for public schools. At this point, any measure that would generate more state revenue—even if it were not earmarked for higher education—would be welcomed by college officials.

In the past, the Legislature has opted for politically expedient taxes that could be paid by tourists. But that approach no longer provides adequate revenues to serve the state's rapidly growing population. A series of budget deficits and a growing need for public services are putting new pressure on Arizona's legislators to act decisively.

In seven of the last 10 years, budget increases for the universities were followed by mid-year cutbacks. No mid-year cuts were made in higher education's 1990-91 appropriation, but the 1991-92 appropriation for the Arizona Board of Regents contained no money for salary increases or to offset inflation.

The state's ability to finance higher education is not the board's only concern in 1992. Governor Symington has said that the Board of Regents should be eliminated and replaced by individual governing boards for the state's three universities. That recommendation will be among his proposals for the 1992 legislation session.

Some of the board's legislative opponents have embraced the idea and have a report by the state Auditor General's Office as proof that there are problems with the Board of Regents. The auditor's report criticized the board for spending too much time on routine matters, such as leases, research contracts, and the use of skateboards on campuses, and not enough on long-range planning.

The Arizona Board of Regents, however, has appointed a task force of legislators and community-college and university officials to review the financing formula for higher education. The Board is also reviewing recommendations for enrollment management. The state's three universities now enroll about 96,000 students. By 2010, the system is expected to grow by 55,000 students.

Arizona's large Hispanic and American Indian populations are a growing proportion of the citizenry. Consequently, the state's colleges and universities are developing a variety of programs to recruit and retain minority students.

Two boards, both with governing and coordinating responsibilities, oversee the state's public colleges and universities: the Board of Regents for the three universities, and the state Board of Directors for community colleges.

ARIZONA
Continued

DEMOGRAPHICS

Population: 3,665,228 (Rank: 24)

Age distribution:
Up to 17 .... 26.8%
18 to 24 .... 10.7%
25 to 44 .... 31.7%
45 and older 30.8%

Racial and ethnic distribution:
American Indian 5.6%
Asian 1.5%
Black 3.0%
White 80.8%
Other and unknown 9.1%
Hispanic (may be any race) . 18.8%

Educational attainment of adults:
At least 4 years of high school 72.4%
At least 1 to 3 years of college 38.0%
At least 4 years of college ... 17.4%

Per-capita personal income: $16,012

Poverty rate: 14.0%

New high-school graduates in:
1991-92 (estimate) 31,096
2001-02 (estimate) 46,128

New GED diploma recipients: 8,512

High-school dropout rate: 38.9%

POLITICAL LEADERSHIP

Governor: Fife Symington (R), term ends 1994

Governor's higher-education aide:
Nancy Mendoza, 1700 West Washington Street, Phoenix 85007; (602) 542-4331

U.S. Senators: Dennis DeConcini (D), term ends 1995; John S. McCain (R), term ends 1993

U.S. Representatives:
1 Democrat, 4 Republicans
Jim Kolbe (R), Jon Kyl (R), Ed Pastor (D), John J. Rhodes, III (R), Bob Stump (R)

Legislature: Senate, 17 Democrats, 13 Republicans; House, 27 Democrats, 33 Republicans

COLLEGES AND UNIVERSITIES

Higher education:
Public 4-year institutions 3
Public 2-year institutions 17
Private 4-year institutions 14
Private 2-year institutions 3
Total 37

Vocational institutions: 176

Statewide coordinating board:
Arizona Board of Regents
2020 North Central Avenue
Suite 230
Phoenix 85004
(602) 255-4082
Molly C. Broad, executive director

Private-college association:
None

Institutions censured by the AAUP:
None

Institutions under NCAA sanctions:
None

FACULTY MEMBERS

Full-time faculty members by rank:
Professor 1,145

Associate professor 974
Assistant professor 827
Instructor 89
Lecturer 157
No rank 1,545
Total 4,737

Average pay of full-time professors:
At public 4-year institutions $43,465
At public 2-year institutions $37,413
At private 4-year institutions $32,987
At private 2-year institutions ... n/a
At all institutions $40,903
Men (all institutions) $43,289
Women (all institutions) $35,612

STUDENTS

Enrollment:
Total 252,614
At public 4-year institutions . 96,276
At public 2-year institutions 143,038
At private 4-year institutions 11,371
At private 2-year institutions . 1,929
Undergraduate 226,120
    First-time freshmen 61,241
Graduate 25,059
Professional 1,435
American Indian 8,301
Asian 5,340
Black 7,263
Hispanic 26,082
White 203,748
Foreign 7,052

Enrollment highlights:
Women 52.8%
Full-time 43.0%
Minority 18.7%
Foreign 2.7%
10-year change in total
    enrollment .... Up 33.7%

Proportion of enrollment made up of minority students:
At public 4-year institutions . 13.0%
At public 2-year institutions . 22.0%
At private 4-year institutions 18.9%
At private 2-year institutions 28.1%

Degrees awarded:
Associate 6,167
Bachelor's 13,767
Master's 4,884
Doctorate 559
Professional 420

Residence of new students: State residents made up 87% of all freshmen enrolled in Arizona; 96% of all Arizona residents who were freshmen attended college in their home state.

Test scores: Students averaged 19.0 on the A.C.T., which was taken by 36% of Arizona's high-school seniors.

MONEY

Average tuition and fees:
At public 4-year institutions . $1,362
At public 2-year institutions .. $519
At private 4-year institutions $4,127
At private 2-year institutions $11,007

Expenditures:
Public institutions .. $1,017,203,000
Private institutions $52,887,000

State funds for higher-education operating expenses: $607,819,000
Two-year change: Up 10%

State spending on student aid:
Need-based: $3,427,000; 5,000 awards
Non–need-based: None
Other: None

Salary of chief executive of largest public 4-year campus:
Lattie F. Coor, Arizona State
    University: $151,003

ARIZONA
Continued

Total spending on research and development by doctorate-granting universities: $260,187,000

Sources:
Federal government 47.0%
State and local governments .. 2.8%
Industry 6.9%
The institution itself 37.3%
Other 6.0%

Federal spending on education and student aid (selected programs):
Vocational and
  adult education $17,173,000
GI Bill $7,569,000
Pell Grants $78,363,000

Total federal spending on college- and university-based research and development: $103,319,000

Selected programs:
Department of Health
  and Human Services $41,792,000
National Science
  Foundation $20,206,000
Department of Defense $11,387,000
Department
  of Agriculture $3,973,000
Department of Energy .. $3,043,000

Largest endowment:
University of Arizona . $55,790,000

Top fund raisers:
University of Arizona . $33,396,000
Arizona State University $25,712,000
Northern Arizona
  University $3,550,000

MISCELLANY

■ Northern Arizona University is the site each summer of the Arizona Honors Academy, which draws college students from around the country for a three-week program in which they study and discuss issues of national security, foreign policy, and international relations.

■ Phoenix is the site of the next annual convention of the American Association of Community and Junior Colleges. The AACJC had considered moving its annual meeting to another state because Arizona voters had chosen not to recognize the birthday of the Rev. Martin Luther King, Jr., a holiday in the rest of the nation. The association's board of directors later voted overwhelmingly to hold the 1992 convention in Phoenix after all, since the city and state colleges and universities in the area recognize the King holiday.

■ Prescott College, which declared bankruptcy in 1974 and lost its 600-acre campus, is experiencing new popularity. College officials attribute its regeneration to an emphasis on experiential learning and a commitment to the environment. Environmental issues are woven into the curriculum, and new students are required to complete a three-week wilderness orientation in the Grand Canyon.

■ The oldest institution of higher education in the state is Arizona State University, founded in 1886.

ARKANSAS

GOV. BILL CLINTON has made education reform a keystone of his administration for more than a decade. But until recently, Arkansas's colleges and universities were left out of the picture—mostly for lack of money.

In 1991 all that changed.

The General Assembly approved a tax increase that will provide the institutions with more money for salaries and new equipment. The increase was a coup for Governor Clinton, a Democrat who had been rebuffed in three previous attempts to win legislative support for his tax proposals. Mr. Clinton, who decided to seek the Democratic nomination for President, is regarded as one of the nation's most knowledgeable "education governors" and has been active in the effort to establish national education goals.

The new money for higher education is especially welcome at the state's four-year colleges and universities, which have seen many faculty members flee to better-paying states.

Arkansas will also use some of the tax money to create new scholarship programs to attract more students to college—an important goal for the state that is second only to West Virginia in having the lowest proportion of citizens with four or more years of college education. Some of the new money will be used to create a special scholarship program to encourage more minority students to become teachers.

Business and political leaders in the state have also been concerned about the quality and availability of postsecondary technical education, and lawmakers passed legislation in 1991 to address those concerns.

Under the new law, 12 of the state's 24 vocational-technical schools will be upgraded to technical colleges and required to develop and offer college-level courses and associate degrees. Lawmakers approved another tax increase to finance those changes, which are designed to bring technical education within driving distance of all residents.

The changes in technical colleges also brought some changes to the State Board of Higher Education, the coordinating board for all postsecondary education. Under the law, the board is made up of two bodies: the College Panel, which oversees the programs and budgets of technical and community colleges; and the University Panel, which handles the same duties for the state's 10 four-year public institutions.

Arkansas has three private historically black institutions and one public one, the University of Arkansas at Pine Bluff.

DEMOGRAPHICS

Population: 2,350,725 (Rank: 33)

Age distribution:
Up to 17 .... 26.4%
18 to 24 .... 10.1%
25 to 44 .... 29.2%
45 and older 34.3%

Racial and ethnic distribution:
American Indian 0.5%
Asian 0.5%
Black 15.9%
White 82.7%
Other and unknown 0.3%
Hispanic (may be any race) .. 0.8%

Educational attainment of adults:
At least 4 years of high school 55.5%
At least 1 to 3 years of college 22.3%
At least 4 years of college ... 10.8%

Per-capita personal income: $14,188

Poverty rate: 19.8%

New high-school graduates in:
1991-92 (estimate) 26,725
2001-02 (estimate) 26,329

ARKANSAS
Continued

New GED diploma recipients: 7,013

High-school dropout rate: 22.8%

POLITICAL LEADERSHIP

Governor: Bill Clinton (D), term ends 1995

Governor's higher-education aide: Kathy VanLaningham, State Capitol, Little Rock 72201; (501) 682-2345

U.S. Senators: Dale Bumpers (D), term ends 1993; David Pryor (D), term ends 1997

U.S. Representatives:
3 Democrats, 1 Republican
Bill Alexander (D), Beryl Anthony, Jr. (D), John Paul Hammerschmidt (R), Ray Thornton (D)

General Assembly: Senate, 31 Democrats, 4 Republicans; House, 91 Democrats, 9 Republicans

COLLEGES AND UNIVERSITIES

Higher education:
Public 4-year institutions 10
Public 2-year institutions 10
Private 4-year institutions 10
Private 2-year institutions 7
Total 37

Vocational institutions: 109

Statewide coordinating board:
State Board of Higher Education
114 East Capitol
Little Rock 72201
(501) 324-9300
Diane Gilleland, director

Private-college association:
Independent Colleges of Arkansas
One Riverfront Place, Suite 610
North Little Rock 72114
(501) 378-0843
E. Kearney Dietz, president

Institutions censured by the AAUP:
Phillips County Community College, Southern Arkansas University, University of the Ozarks (governing board)

Institutions under NCAA sanctions: None

FACULTY MEMBERS

Full-time faculty members by rank:
Professor 665
Associate professor 660
Assistant professor 720
Instructor 381
Lecturer 32
No rank 319
Total 2,777

Average pay of full-time professors:
At public 4-year institutions $33,369
At public 2-year institutions $25,471
At private 4-year institutions $28,116
At private 2-year institutions $23,969
At all institutions $31,588
Men (all institutions) $34,061
Women (all institutions) $27,111

STUDENTS

Enrollment:
Total 88,572
At public 4-year institutions . 58,662
At public 2-year institutions . 17,754
At private 4-year institutions . 9,916
At private 2-year institutions . 2,240
Undergraduate 80,962
　First-time freshmen 18,398
Graduate 6,195

Professional 1,415
American Indian 380
Asian 668
Black 11,361
Hispanic 366
White 70,180
Foreign 1,595

Enrollment highlights:
Women 57.0%
Full-time 71.4%
Minority 15.4%
Foreign 1.9%
10-year change in total
  enrollment .... Up 18.6%

Proportion of enrollment made up of minority students:
At public 4-year institutions . 15.3%
At public 2-year institutions . 13.9%
At private 4-year institutions 12.9%
At private 2-year institutions 34.8%

Degrees awarded:
Associate 2,432
Bachelor's 7,300
Master's 1,801
Doctorate 96
Professional 343

Residence of new students: State residents made up 85% of all freshmen enrolled in Arkansas; 86% of all Arkansas residents who were freshmen attended college in their home state.

Test scores: Students averaged 17.6 on the A.C.T., which was taken by 59% of Arkansas's high-school seniors.

MONEY

Average tuition and fees:
At public 4-year institutions . $1,376
At public 2-year institutions .. $644
At private 4-year institutions $3,175
At private 2-year institutions $6,102

Expenditures:
Public institutions $528,831,000
Private institutions $72,321,000

State funds for higher-education operating expenses: $384,814,000
Two-year change: Up 20%

State spending on student aid:
Need-based: $4,137,000;
  10,307 awards
Non–need-based: $790,000;
  388 awards
Other: $180,000

Salary of chief executive of largest public 4-year campus:
Daniel E. Ferritor, University
  of Arkansas main campus: $120,000

Total spending on research and development by doctorate-granting universities: $48,861,000
Sources:
Federal government 35.8%
State and local governments . 24.2%
Industry 8.3%
The institution itself 25.5%
Other 6.2%

Federal spending on education and student aid (selected programs):
Vocational and
  adult education $14,810,000
GI Bill $3,948,000
Pell Grants $55,903,000

Total federal spending on college- and university-based research and development: $19,643,000
Selected programs:
Department of Health
  and Human Services . $6,996,000
National Science
  Foundation $1,420,000
Department of Defense ... $593,000
Department
  of Agriculture $7,308,000

ARKANSAS
Continued

Department of Energy .. $1,177,000

Largest endowment:
Hendrix College $51,983,000

Top fund raisers:
Arkansas College $7,035,000
Harding University $4,992,000
Ouachita Baptist
 University $4,473,000

MISCELLANY

■ Former Sen. J. William Fulbright, the creator of the international scholarly and student exchanges that bear his name, served as president of the University of Arkansas from 1939 to 1941.

■ On September 21, 1991, the University of Arkansas at Fayetteville rededicated Old Main, a building that was started in 1873 and for many years housed all of the university's offices and classrooms. The building houses administrative offices and several academic departments of the university's Fulbright College of Arts and Sciences.

■ The oldest institution of higher education in Arkansas is the University of the Ozarks, founded in 1834. It is affiliated with the United Presbyterian Church, USA.

CALIFORNIA

BETWEEN the day Republican Gov. Pete Wilson took office in January 1991 and July, when the state budget was finally signed, estimates of California's deficit doubled—to $14.3-billion. And while the deficit spiraled out of control, higher-education officials saw their budgets for 1991-92 slashed to below the allocations for academic 1990-91—despite bigger enrollments.

The solution to the budget crisis pleased no one: The gap was closed by raising taxes and slashing support of social programs and public services.

For higher-education officials, the solution included reducing their work forces by thousands of employees, freezing salaries, and raising tuition by 20 per cent for students in the California State University System and community colleges. Students at the University of California saw their tuition jump by 40 per cent.

Private colleges suffered, as well. For the third year in a row, no increase was made in the maximum state grant for students attending private institutions. The current maximum is about $5,200.

The budget crisis of 1991 has led many college officials to question whether the state can continue its historic commitment to insuring that all California residents have a chance to go to college. They say California's revenue system must be revised radically to pay for the mammoth enrollment increases that are projected for the next 15 years. By 2005, according to predictions, California's college enrollment will increase by 700,000—pushing the public-college population to 2.6 million—and a large proportion will be minority and non-traditional students.

To serve all those students, the California Postsecondary Education Commission—the state's coordinating board—estimates that the state will need at least one more University of California campus and about two dozen new community colleges.

But in November 1990, voters rejected a $450-million bond issue to finance construction projects that higher-education officials had called essential. And in April 1991, Los Angeles voters rejected a $200-million bond issue to finance construction and repairs throughout the Los Angeles Community College District.

In 1963, higher education in California was divided into three separately governed systems: the University of California, the California State University System, and the community colleges.

The University of California, the only doctorate-granting system, offers admission to the top eighth of the state's high-school graduates. Cal State offers bachelor's- and master's-degree programs to students from the top third of their high-school classes. The community colleges have an open-admissions policy.

By limiting expensive doctoral and research programs to the UC system, California has avoided some of the costly competition between systems that is found in other states. But some say the emphasis on research and graduate programs at UC has hurt the quality of undergraduate programs.

In recent years, the university system has also been under intense pressure to admit more minority students. Black and Hispanic leaders say the system hasn't done enough to recruit black and Hispanic students and faculty members. And Asian-American leaders contend that informal quotas have limited the enrollment of Asian students. The university has promised to do more for all minority students and has repeatedly denied that it uses quotas. The naming of Chang-Lin Tien as chancellor of the university's Berkeley campus has won rave reviews from Asian Americans.

David P. Gardner, the system's president, announced that he would step down in October 1992, citing the death of his wife.

The management of the CSU System has repeatedly come under fire by legislators. In 1990 the criticism lead to the resignation of the system's chancellor, W. Ann Reynolds. Her successor, Barry Munitz, a former businessman and chancellor of the University of Houston's central campus, has many challenges ahead. He must restore the Legislature's confidence in the system, contend with tight budgets, and try to improve the graduation rate. The Legislature has complained that too few students seem able to complete undergraduate studies in four or five years.

The California Community Colleges have a challenge of their own: to reduce the rate at which students default on education loans. Nine of the system's 107 colleges could lose their eligibility to take part in the federal student-loan program because they have had default rates in excess of 35 per cent for three consecutive years.

The state is also home to such well-known private research universities as the California Institute of Technology, Stanford University, and the University of Southern California. Liberal-arts colleges include Claremont McKenna, Mills, and Pomona Colleges. There are also specialized institutions, such as the California Institute of the Arts and the Monterey Institute of International Studies.

Stanford has been at the center of a national controversy over its use of federal research funds. The government provides money to institutions to cover the overhead costs associated with research—expenses that sup-

CALIFORNIA
Continued

port federally financed research, but are not directly related to a specific research award—such as the cost of utilities and the maintenance of campus facilities.

Stanford and other universities have broadly interpreted the regulations on overhead costs. Among the things Stanford charged partly to the government were flowers, silverware, depreciation on a yacht, and increasing the size of the president's bed. Ultimately the controversy led to the resignation of Donald Kennedy, Stanford's president, effective in August 1992.

With all that, Stanford has good news on at least one front. In June 1991 it exceeded its $1.1-billion fund-raising goal—eight months before the campaign's scheduled end.

DEMOGRAPHICS

Population: 29,760,021   (Rank: 1)

Age distribution:
Up to 17 .... 26.0%
18 to 24 .... 11.5%
25 to 44 .... 34.7%
45 and older 27.8%

Racial and ethnic distribution:
American Indian 0.8%
Asian 9.6%
Black 7.4%
White 69.0%
Other and unknown 13.2%
Hispanic (may be any race) . 25.8%

Educational attainment of adults:
At least 4 years of high school 73.5%
At least 1 to 3 years of college 42.0%
At least 4 years of college ... 19.6%

Per-capita personal income: $20,677

Poverty rate: 13.3%

New high-school graduates in:
1991-92 (estimate) 251,306
2001-02 (estimate) 375,160

New GED diploma recipients: 16,800

High-school dropout rate: 34.1%

POLITICAL LEADERSHIP

Governor: Pete Wilson (R), term ends 1995

Governor's higher-education aide: Maureen DiMarco, 1121 L Street, Suite 502, Sacramento 95814; (916) 323-0611

U.S. Senators: Alan Cranston (D), term ends 1993; John Seymour (R), term ends 1992

U.S. Representatives:
26 Democrats, 19 Republicans
Glenn M. Anderson (D), Anthony C. Beilenson (D), Howard L. Berman (D), Barbara Boxer (D), George E. Brown, Jr. (D), Tom Campbell (R), Gary Condit (D), C. Christopher Cox (R), Randy "Duke" Cunningham (R), William E. Dannemeyer (R), Ronald V. Dellums (D), Julian C. Dixon (D), Calvin M. Dooley (D), John T. Doolittle (R), Robert K. Dornan (R), David Dreier (R), Mervyn M. Dymally (D), Don Edwards (D), Vic Fazio (D), Elton Gallegly (R), Wally Herger (R), Duncan Hunter (R), Robert J. Lagomarsino (R), Tom Lantos (D), Richard H. Lehman (D), Mel Levine (D), Jerry Lewis (R), Bill Lowery (R), Matthew G. Martinez (D), Robert T. Matsui (D), Alfred A. (Al) McCandless (R), George Miller (D), Norman Y. Mineta

(D), Carlos J. Moorhead (R), Ron Packard (R), Leon E. Panetta (D), Nancy Pelosi (D), Frank D. Riggs (R), Dana Rohrabacher (R), Edward R. Roybal (D), Fortney Pete Stark (D), William M. Thomas (R), Esteban Edward Torres (D), Maxine Waters (D), Henry A. Waxman (D)

Legislature: Senate, 25 Democrats, 13 Republicans, 2 Independents; House, 47 Democrats, 33 Republicans

COLLEGES AND UNIVERSITIES

Higher education:
Public 4-year institutions 31
Public 2-year institutions 107
Private 4-year institutions 140
Private 2-year institutions 32
Total 310

Vocational institutions: 916

Statewide coordinating board:
California Postsecondary Education Commission
1020 12th Street, 3rd Floor
Sacramento 95814
(916) 445-1000
Warren H. Fox, executive director

Private-college association:
Association of Independent California Colleges and Universities
1100 11th Street, Suite 315
Sacramento 95814
(916) 446-7626
Jonathan A. Brown, president

Institutions censured by the AAUP:
Sonoma State University,
University of Judaism

Institution under NCAA sanctions:
University of the Pacific

FACULTY MEMBERS

Full-time faculty members by rank:
Professor 13,633
Associate professor 5,451
Assistant professor 4,878
Instructor 638
Lecturer 747
No rank 8,445
Total 33,792

Average pay of full-time professors:
At public 4-year institutions $52,765
At public 2-year institutions $35,482
At private 4-year institutions $44,071
At private 2-year institutions $33,148
At all institutions $46,476
Men (all institutions) $49,224
Women (all institutions) $39,628

STUDENTS

Enrollment:
Total 1,744,879
At public 4-year institutions   494,099
At public 2-year institutions 1,040,110
At private 4-year institutions 201,938
At private 2-year institutions . 8,732
Undergraduate 1,546,687
   First-time freshmen 273,783
Graduate 166,676
Professional 31,516
American Indian 20,600
Asian 205,929
Black 114,388
Hispanic 215,397
White 1,131,731
Foreign 65,519

Enrollment highlights:
Women 53.9%
Full-time 44.3%
Minority 33.0%
Foreign 3.7%
10-year change in total
   enrollment .... Up 2.8%

CALIFORNIA
Continued

Proportion of enrollment made up of minority students:
At public 4-year institutions . 33.0%
At public 2-year institutions . 34.7%
At private 4-year institutions   22.8%
At private 2-year institutions   37.2%

Degrees awarded:
Associate 48,018
Bachelor's 91,508
Master's 33,060
Doctorate 4,209
Professional 7,651

Residence of new students: State residents made up 90% of all freshmen enrolled in California; 95% of all California residents who were freshmen attended college in their home state.

Test scores: Students averaged 897 on the S.A.T., which was taken by 47% of California's high-school seniors.

MONEY

Average tuition and fees:
At public 4-year institutions . $1,123
At public 2-year institutions .. $112
At private 4-year institutions $9,489
At private 2-year institutions $7,664

Expenditures:
Public institutions .. $8,515,440,000
Private institutions . $3,641,630,000

State funds for higher-education operating expenses: $5,662,752,000
Two-year change: Up 3%

State spending on student aid:
Need-based: $164,747,000; 76,968 awards
Non–need-based: None
Other: None

Salary of chief executive of largest public 4-year campus:
Charles E. Young, University of California at Los Angeles: $175,000

Total spending on research and development by doctorate-granting universities: $2,007,361,000
Sources:
Federal government 68.2%
State and local governments .. 2.6%
Industry 4.5%
The institution itself 17.7%
Other 7.0%

Federal spending on education and student aid (selected programs):
Vocational and
  adult education $110,652,000
GI Bill $35,564,000
Pell Grants $392,463,000

Total federal spending on college- and university-based research and development: $1,258,964,000
Selected programs:
Department of Health
  and Human Services $671,546,000
National Science
  Foundation $193,512,000
Department of Defense $167,992,000
Department
  of Agriculture $15,101,000
Department of Energy . $73,289,000

Largest endowment:
Stanford University $2,053,128,000

Top fund raisers:
Stanford University .. $202,166,000
University of Southern
  California $126,136,000
University of California
  at Berkeley $97,398,000

MISCELLANY

■ Stanford University fired Stuart Reges, a lecturer in computer science, after he claimed to have carried illegal drugs on the campus in violation of federal anti-drug laws and the university's anti-drug regulations.

■ Thirty students from California State University at Hayward are serving as consultants to companies on the Pacific Rim. As part of a class called "Asian International Marketing," the students are helping companies explore options for exporting their goods to the United States.

■ In a class that could just as well be called "Spying 101," law students at the University of San Francisco learn the tricks of the trade—surveillance, forgery, bugging, and snapping clandestine photographs. Taught by Robert Talbot, a law professor, and Harold K. Lipset, a private investigator, "The Fundamentals of Investigation" may be the only course of its kind in the country.

■ The oldest institutions of higher education in California are the University of the Pacific (an independent institution) and Santa Clara University (a Roman Catholic institution), both founded in 1851.

COLORADO

IT HAS BEEN a difficult year for higher education in Colorado. Gov. Roy Romer, a Democrat with a strong record of supporting education, told college officials that he would be able to allocate only $15-million in new money for their campuses in the 1991-92 fiscal year—a 4-per-cent increase.

To the dismay of many on the campuses, the Republican-controlled General Assembly concurred. But lawmakers also recognized that tuition would have to be raised to compensate for the shortage of state support, so they increased need-based financial aid by 11 per cent and allocated $500,000 for the state's first need-based grants for part-time students.

Despite the state's financial woes, lawmakers still place a high priority on higher education. But for many years they have believed that an increase in financial support and an increase in accountability go hand-in-hand.

In 1985, when the General Assembly adopted a plan to increase financial support for higher education, it also approved the "Colorado Higher Education Accountability Act," which required institutions to develop strategies to improve retention and graduation rates and to monitor students' performance. In 1991 the Colorado Commission on Higher Education, the state coordinating board, issued its first "ScoreCard" on how the state's public colleges were performing.

The commission found that the average national test scores of first-time freshmen attending Colorado's public institutions were higher than the national figures. It also found that the rate at which white and Hispanic high-school graduates enrolled in postsecondary institutions from 1986 to 1989 had increased. The enrollment rate of black students decreased slightly in that same period.

Higher education in Colorado is decentralized, and the state's public universities are among the most active in

COLORADO
Continued

the country in pursuing federal and private research dollars and in recruiting high-technology businesses. A chemist at the University of Colorado at Boulder shared the Nobel Prize for chemistry with a Yale researcher in 1989.

University officials hope to build on that success as they work to earn the university a place among the nation's premier research institutions.

The university system also received approval to expand and improve the University of Colorado at Colorado Springs. As state money becomes available, the number of graduate programs will be increased, and housing for 800 students will be built either by the state or in partnership with local developers.

The state's 15 community colleges are highly regarded for their innovative worker-training programs, developed in cooperation with businesses. But their popularity with Colorado residents has proved to be a mixed blessing.

Even though state support for two-year institutions has increased by 44 per cent in the last five years, enrollment has grown by 67 per cent in the same period. And in recent years, community colleges have been aggressively lobbying state legislators for a larger share of the higher-education budget.

Concern over the growing "tuition gap" between Colorado's public institutions and the state's private, non-profit colleges also has been a political issue in recent years.

Private-college leaders were able to persuade lawmakers in 1988 to enact a program to provide direct payments to the institutions, based on their enrollment, but so far the colleges have been unable to get the legislature to come up with the money.

DEMOGRAPHICS

Population: 3,294,394   (Rank: 26)

Age distribution:
Up to 17 .... 26.1%
18 to 24 .... 10.2%
25 to 44 .... 35.8%
45 and older 27.9%

Racial and ethnic distribution:
American Indian 0.8%
Asian 1.8%
Black 4.0%
White 88.2%
Other and unknown 5.1%
Hispanic (may be any race) . 12.9%

Educational attainment of adults:
At least 4 years of high school 78.6%
At least 1 to 3 years of college 44.1%
At least 4 years of college ... 23.0%

Per-capita personal income: $18,890

Poverty rate: 12.8%

New high-school graduates in:
1991-92 (estimate) 32,598
2001-02 (estimate) 42,257

New GED diploma recipients: 7,633

High-school dropout rate: 25.3%

POLITICAL LEADERSHIP

Governor: Roy Romer (D), term ends 1995

Governor's higher-education aide: Karen Sandstead, 136 State Capitol, Denver 80203; (303) 866-2471

U.S. Senators: Hank Brown (R), term ends 1997; Timothy E. Wirth (D), term ends 1993

U.S. Representatives:
3 Democrats, 3 Republicans
Wayne Allard (R), Ben Nighthorse Campbell (D), Joel Hefley (R), Dan Schaefer (R), Patricia Schroeder (D), David E. Skaggs (D)

General Assembly: Senate, 12 Democrats, 23 Republicans; House, 27 Democrats, 38 Republicans

COLLEGES AND UNIVERSITIES

Higher education:
Public 4-year institutions	13
Public 2-year institutions	15
Private 4-year institutions	17
Private 2-year institutions	9
Total	54

Vocational institutions: 119

Statewide coordinating board:
Commission on Higher Education
1300 Broadway, 2nd Floor
Denver 80203
(303) 866-2723
David A. Longanecker,
executive director

Private-college association:
Independent Higher Education
  of Colorado
387 Denver Club Building
518 17th Street
Denver 80202
(303) 571-5559
Toni Worcester, executive director

Institutions censured by the AAUP:
Colorado School of Mines,
University of Northern Colorado

Institutions under NCAA sanctions:
None

FACULTY MEMBERS

Full-time faculty members by rank:
Professor	1,832
Associate professor	1,277
Assistant professor	1,041
Instructor	205
Lecturer	36
No rank	864
Total	5,255

Average pay of full-time professors:
At public 4-year institutions	$41,043
At public 2-year institutions	$27,701
At private 4-year institutions	$40,380
At private 2-year institutions	n/a
At all institutions	$38,450
Men (all institutions)	$40,612
Women (all institutions)	$32,177

STUDENTS

Enrollment:
Total	201,114
At public 4-year institutions	107,324
At public 2-year institutions	68,526
At private 4-year institutions	19,756
At private 2-year institutions	5,508
Undergraduate	178,680
First-time freshmen	35,002
Graduate	19,448
Professional	2,986
American Indian	1,654
Asian	4,050
Black	5,078
Hispanic	13,452
White	157,982
Foreign	4,072

Enrollment highlights:
Women	52.9%
Full-time	59.1%
Minority	13.3%
Foreign	2.2%

COLORADO
Continued

10-year change in total
  enrollment .... Up 29.9%

Proportion of enrollment made up of minority students:
At public 4-year institutions . 11.4%
At public 2-year institutions . 15.6%
At private 4-year institutions   13.6%
At private 2-year institutions   24.1%

Degrees awarded:
Associate 5,943
Bachelor's 15,561
Master's 4,574
Doctorate 665
Professional 873

Residence of new students: State residents made up 78% of all freshmen enrolled in Colorado; 80% of all Colorado residents who were freshmen attended college in their home state.

Test scores: Students averaged 19.6 on the A.C.T., which was taken by 60% of Colorado's high-school seniors.

MONEY

Average tuition and fees:
At public 4-year institutions . $1,830
At public 2-year institutions .. $792
At private 4-year institutions $9,188
At private 2-year institutions $8,036

Expenditures:
Public institutions .. $1,057,558,000
Private institutions ... $160,193,000

State funds for higher-education operating expenses: $523,785,000
Two-year change: Up 4%

State spending on student aid:
Need-based: $12,087,000;
  15,280 awards
Non–need-based: $10,911,000;
  12,821 awards
Other: $1,281,000

Salary of chief executive of largest public 4-year campus:
James N. Corbridge, Jr., University of Colorado at Boulder: $123,900

Total spending on research and development by doctorate-granting universities: $249,958,000
Sources:
Federal government 72.0%
State and local governments .. 4.7%
Industry 6.4%
The institution itself 9.0%
Other 8.0%

Federal spending on education and student aid (selected programs):
Vocational and
  adult education $26,800,000
GI Bill $7,481,000
Pell Grants $69,308,000

Total federal spending on college- and university-based research and development: $147,301,000
Selected programs:
Department of Health
  and Human Services $71,113,000
National Science
  Foundation $30,098,000
Department of Defense $12,261,000
Department
  of Agriculture $6,232,000
Department of Energy .. $6,538,000

Largest endowment:
Colorado College $137,694,000

Top fund raisers:
University of Colorado $37,657,000

University of Denver .. $15,126,000
Colorado College $7,057,000

MISCELLANY

■ Students at Metropolitan State College of Denver cover the legislature and put out a free weekly newspaper that is read by legislators, lobbyists, state employees, and other reporters. The students work as full-time interns for *The Capitol Reporter*, which is published by the college.

■ High-school students applying to Colorado State University can learn quickly how much money they can expect to receive in financial-aid awards through a new computer program called FAST, which stands for "financial-aid service team." University financial-aid officers run aid and tax forms through a computer that provides estimates for awards.

■ The oldest institution of higher education in Colorado is the University of Denver, an independent institution founded in 1864.

CONNECTICUT

Long overshadowed by traditionally strong private colleges, public higher education in Connecticut flourished in the 1980's as the state's economy boomed. But the recession is now taking its toll.

For most of the past decade, public-college enrollments grew appreciably, particularly among adult and minority students, and spending on financial aid increased steadily.

Trouble surfaced as the recession hit Connecticut in 1990, and college budgets were cut in response. Then came 1991 and the worst deficit in Connecticut's history—a $1-billion gap in an overall state budget of about $8.8-billion.

While a new governor, Lowell P. Weicker, Jr., and the General Assembly battled over tax proposals and spending cuts well past the deadline for adopting a 1991-92 budget, anxious college leaders prepared contingency plans for massive layoffs and cancellations of hundreds of course sections.

Ultimately, lawmakers bowed to Mr. Weicker's will and enacted a personal income tax.

The budget crisis has put unusual burdens on the labor unions that represent most of the public-college faculty and staff members and are unusually active in state politics. At first the faculty and staff members and other state workers were the targets of layoffs planned by Governor Weicker, but later their unions were taken on as allies as he campaigned for the income tax. But even after the tax passed, the unions and the Weicker Administration remained at odds over his call for further layoffs. Mr. Weicker says the job cuts were always part of his budget package; the unions say the layoffs are a sellout.

Advocates for the state's 12 community and five technical colleges fear the budget problems will intensify interest in proposals to merge or close some of those institutions, some of which are close to each other and offer similar programs. Since 1990 the two-year institutions have been governed by a single Board of Trustees of Technical and Community Colleges. The technical colleges in particular have been criticized for teaching skills that are out of touch with the state's changing industrial base.

The five-campus University of Connecticut, with its base in Storrs, is

CONNECTICUT
Continued

governed by its own board, as are the four universities that make up the Connecticut State University System. The Board of Governors for Higher Education is a coordinating board that has been influential in pushing colleges to make minority students feel more welcome on campuses, and to assess what students have learned.

Private colleges have not been immune to the state's budget problems—particularly colleges that enroll large numbers of state residents. Institutions award state financial aid in Connecticut, and for private colleges the amount of aid is determined by the number of residents enrolled. State money for that program could be in short supply in 1991-92.

That may not hurt places like Yale University, which since its founding in 1701 has developed an international student body and a huge endowment. (Yale was especially lucky in 1990 and 1991, receiving four gifts totaling $80-million from members of the Bass family of Texas). Other elite institutions, like Wesleyan University and Connecticut College, which draw many students from out of state, also will not be badly hurt. But the loss of funds could prove painful for institutions like Sacred Heart University, which depends heavily on state money.

The private sector has also seen its share of union activism, notably at the University of Bridgeport, where about 70 of the 170 faculty members remain on strike a more than a year after the outbreak of a dispute over wage concessions.

The strike and declining enrollments have injured the university's financial stability. But in October 1991 the trustees rejected a $50-million offer from an organization affiliated with the Rev. Sun Myung Moon's Unification Church that would have brought the college an injection of cash and more students. They said the plan would have given the organization too much control over the campus.

DEMOGRAPHICS

Population: 3,287,116 (Rank: 27)

Age distribution:
Up to 17 .... 22.8%
18 to 24 .... 10.5%
25 to 44 .... 33.3%
45 and older 33.4%

Racial and ethnic distribution:
American Indian 0.2%
Asian 1.5%
Black 8.3%
White 87.0%
Other and unknown 2.9%
Hispanic (may be any race) .. 6.5%

Educational attainment of adults:
At least 4 years of high school 70.3%
At least 1 to 3 years of college 35.9%
At least 4 years of college ... 20.7%

Per-capita personal income: $25,484

Poverty rate: 4.3%

New high-school graduates in:
1991-92 (estimate) 29,719
2001-02 (estimate) 34,499

New GED diploma recipients: 4,811

High-school dropout rate: 15.1%

POLITICAL LEADERSHIP

Governor: Lowell P. Weicker, Jr. (Ind), term ends 1995

Governor's higher-education aide:
Emily V. Melendez, State Capitol, Hartford 06106; (203) 566-4840

U.S. Senators: Christopher J. Dodd (D), term ends 1993; Joseph I. Lieberman (D), term ends 1995

U.S. Representatives:
3 Democrats, 3 Republicans
Rosa L. DeLauro (D), Gary A. Franks (R), Sam Gejdenson (D), Nancy L. Johnson (R), Barbara B. Kennelly (D), Christopher Shays (R)

General Assembly: Senate, 20 Democrats, 16 Republicans; House, 88 Democrats, 63 Republicans

COLLEGES AND UNIVERSITIES

Higher education:
Public 4-year institutions 7
Public 2-year institutions 17
Private 4-year institutions 21
Private 2-year institutions 3
Total 48

Vocational institutions: 122

Statewide coordinating board:
Board of Governors for
  Higher Education
61 Woodland Street
Hartford 06105
(203) 566-5766
Valerie F. Lewis, interim commissioner of higher education

Private-college association:
Connecticut Conference of
  Independent Colleges
36 Gillett Street
Hartford 06105
(203) 522-0271
Michael A. Gerber, president

Institutions censured by the AAUP:
None

Institutions under NCAA sanctions:
None

FACULTY MEMBERS

Full-time faculty members by rank:
Professor 2,297
Associate professor 1,526
Assistant professor 1,382
Instructor 253
Lecturer 115
No rank 24
Total 5,597

Average pay of full-time professors:
At public 4-year institutions $49,930
At public 2-year institutions $41,081
At private 4-year institutions $46,894
At private 2-year institutions $27,639
At all institutions $47,230
Men (all institutions) $50,080
Women (all institutions) $39,847

STUDENTS

Enrollment:
Total 169,438
At public 4-year institutions . 65,427
At public 2-year institutions . 44,270
At private 4-year institutions 58,068
At private 2-year institutions . 1,673
Undergraduate 134,354
    First-time freshmen 28,393
Graduate 31,811
Professional 3,273
American Indian 398
Asian 3,528
Black 8,930
Hispanic 4,824
White 143,934
Foreign 4,063

Enrollment highlights:
Women 56.3%

CONNECTICUT
Continued

Full-time 50.3%
Minority 10.9%
Foreign 2.5%
10-year change in total
  enrollment .... Up 9.1%

Proportion of enrollment made up of minority students:
At public 4-year institutions .. 8.2%
At public 2-year institutions . 15.7%
At private 4-year institutions 10.3%
At private 2-year institutions 16.0%

Degrees awarded:
Associate 4,703
Bachelor's 13,525
Master's 6,022
Doctorate 553
Professional 920

Residence of new students: State residents made up 78% of all freshmen enrolled in Connecticut; 62% of all Connecticut residents who were freshmen attended college in their home state.

Test scores: Students averaged 897 on the S.A.T., which was taken by 81% of Connecticut's high-school seniors.

MONEY

Average tuition and fees:
At public 4-year institutions . $2,017
At public 2-year institutions .. $915
At private 4-year institutions $11,268
At private 2-year institutions $7,906

Expenditures:
Public institutions $562,696,000
Private institutions ... $836,949,000

State funds for higher-education operating expenses: $503,748,000
Two-year change: Down 2%

State spending on student aid:
Need-based: $20,803,000;
  15,500 awards
Non–need-based: $200,000; 20 awards
Other: $15,164,000

Salary of chief executive of largest public 4-year campus:
Harry J. Hartley, Jr., University of Connecticut: $140,000

Total spending on research and development by doctorate-granting universities: $298,076,000
Sources:
Federal government 63.9%
State and local governments .. 1.8%
Industry 4.5%
The institution itself 21.6%
Other 8.3%

Federal spending on education and student aid (selected programs):
Vocational and
  adult education $2,407,000
GI Bill $2,485,000
Pell Grants $25,366,000

Total federal spending on college- and university-based research and development: $188,744,000
Selected programs:
Department of Health
  and Human Services $144,981,000
National Science
  Foundation $15,321,000
Department of Defense $11,078,000
Department
  of Agriculture $1,584,000
Department of Energy . $10,100,000

Largest endowment:
Yale University $2,570,892,000

Top fund raisers:
Yale University $130,000,000
Wesleyan University .. $12,310,000
Trinity College $9,247,000

MISCELLANY

■ Daniel Yergin's acclaimed 1991 history of the oil industry, *The Prize*, credits a 19th-century Yale chemistry professor, Benjamin Silliman, Jr., with the research that started the modern oil industry. In 1854, Silliman did a study for a group of potential investors and found that oil could be used in lamps for illumination. He was paid $526.08 for his work.

■ As part of a consent decree with the U.S. Justice Department, Yale University, along with the other Ivy League institutions, agreed in 1991 to stop setting financial-aid policies in collaboration with other institutions and to stop comparing its student-aid packages with other institutions'.

■ Hartford College for Women became part of the University of Hartford in 1991. The women's college, founded as an independent institution in 1933, will still have separate academic programs, but will now be administered by the larger university.

■ The University of Bridgeport is allowing parents of full-time students to take one free course each semester.

■ Yale University, founded in 1701, is the oldest institution of higher education in Connecticut. In 1831, it had the distinction of running the nation's first endowment drive, which raised $107,000.

DELAWARE

SINCE Gov. Michael N. Castle, a Republican, took office in 1989, most of the talk and movement in Delaware education have centered on elementary and secondary schools, not higher education. Since the recession extended its grip on Delaware this year, money for new college and university programs has been even scarcer than attention.

It should come as no surprise, then, that most of the new higher-education activity in recent years has focused on programs that assist public schools and their students—and that such programs depend heavily on private funds.

They include one at Delaware State College, "Saturday Academy," designed to expose middle-school students to the college experience, and one sponsored by the Delaware Postsecondary Education Commission that encourages minority and female students to pursue careers in engineering.

Delaware State, a historically black institution, lacks the resources and prestige of the more established University of Delaware, but in recent years it has taken steps to raise its profile in the General Assembly and the business community.

Although the slump in the national economy has reverberated through Delaware—home to several giant chemical companies, bank credit-card operations, and food companies—Delaware State hopes to tap into the same stream of corporate benefactors that helped make the University of Delaware one of the best-endowed public institutions in the nation.

In addition to the two public four-

DELAWARE
Continued

year institutions, the state operates the Delaware Technical and Community College, a four-campus system. The college is unusual in that it does not offer its own undergraduate courses in liberal arts, but does make such courses available to students on each of its campuses through the university. The arrangement is one legacy of the university's clout: When Delaware Tech was created in 1969, the university blocked its plans to offer undergraduate transfer courses.

A more cooperative attitude prevails today, as seen in the state's development of a new, as yet unnamed higher-education facility on the campus of Delaware Tech's Southern campus. The facility, in a rural part of the state, will be available to public and private universities offering undergraduate and graduate programs. The university, state college, and community college are governed by separate boards.

Delaware is also home to a few private colleges, but their presence will shrink a little with the planned May 1992 closing of Brandywine College, a two-year institution that is part of Widener University in Pennsylvania.

DEMOGRAPHICS

Population: 666,168 (Rank: 46)

Age distribution:
Up to 17 .... 24.5%
18 to 24 .... 11.4%
25 to 44 .... 32.7%
45 and older 31.4%

Racial and ethnic distribution:
American Indian 0.3%
Asian 1.4%
Black 16.9%
White 80.3%
Other and unknown 1.1%
Hispanic (may be any race) .. 2.4%

Educational attainment of adults:
At least 4 years of high school 68.6%
At least 1 to 3 years of college 32.4%
At least 4 years of college ... 17.5%

Per-capita personal income: $20,022

Poverty rate: 8.5%

New high-school graduates in:
1991-92 (estimate) 6,937
2001-02 (estimate) 7,298

New GED diploma recipients: 1,050

High-school dropout rate: 28.3%

POLITICAL LEADERSHIP

Governor: Michael N. Castle (R), term ends 1993

Governor's higher-education aide: Helen Foss, 820 North French Street, 12th Floor, Wilmington 19801; (302) 577-3210

U.S. Senators: Joseph R. Biden, Jr. (D), term ends 1997; William V. Roth, Jr. (R), term ends 1995

U.S. Representative:
1 Democrat
Thomas R. Carper (D)

General Assembly: Senate, 15 Democrats, 6 Republicans; House, 17 Democrats, 24 Republicans

COLLEGES AND UNIVERSITIES

Higher education:
Public 4-year institutions 2

Public 2-year institutions 3
Private 4-year institutions 5
Private 2-year institutions 0
Total 10

Vocational institutions: 21

Statewide coordinating board:
Delaware Higher Education
  Commission
820 North French Street
Wilmington 19801
(302) 577-3240
John F. Corrozi, executive director

Private-college association:
None

Institutions censured by the AAUP:
None

Institutions under NCAA sanctions:
None

FACULTY MEMBERS

Full-time faculty members by rank:
Professor 311
Associate professor 354
Assistant professor 337
Instructor 89
Lecturer 29
No rank 137
Total 1,257

Average pay of full-time professors:
At public 4-year institutions $42,074
At public 2-year institutions $35,401
At private 4-year institutions $36,537
At private 2-year institutions ... n/a
At all institutions $40,682
Men (all institutions) $44,556
Women (all institutions) $34,150

STUDENTS

Enrollment:
Total 40,562
At public 4-year institutions . 23,080
At public 2-year institutions .. 9,957
At private 4-year institutions . 7,525
At private 2-year institutions 0
Undergraduate 35,757
  First-time freshmen 8,227
Graduate 3,277
Professional 1,528
American Indian 68
Asian 545
Black 4,313
Hispanic 356
White 32,315
Foreign 663

Enrollment highlights:
Women 56.7%
Full-time 61.2%
Minority 14.0%
Foreign 1.7%
10-year change in total
  enrollment .... Up 25.5%

Proportion of enrollment made up of minority students:
At public 4-year institutions . 13.0%
At public 2-year institutions . 17.8%
At private 4-year institutions 12.3%
At private 2-year institutions ... n/a

Degrees awarded:
Associate 1,138
Bachelor's 3,414
Master's 691
Doctorate 114
Professional 317

Residence of new students: State residents made up 57% of all freshmen enrolled in Delaware; 74% of all Delaware residents who were freshmen attended college in their home state.

Test scores: Students averaged 892 on the S.A.T., which was taken by 61% of Delaware's high-school seniors.

DELAWARE
Continued

MONEY

Average tuition and fees:
At public 4-year institutions . $2,768
At public 2-year institutions .. $882
At private 4-year institutions $5,388
At private 2-year institutions ... n/a

Expenditures:
Public institutions $229,377,000
Private institutions $15,855,000

State funds for higher-education operating expenses: $121,011,000
Two-year change: Up 5%

State spending on student aid:
Need-based: $1,462,000; 1,734 awards
Non–need-based: $197,000; 188 awards
Other: $189,000

Salary of chief executive of largest public 4-year campus:
David P. Roselle, University of Delaware: salary n/a

Total spending on research and development by doctorate-granting universities: $40,119,000
Sources:
Federal government 43.8%
State and local governments .. 7.8%
Industry 11.0%
The institution itself 29.3%
Other 8.1%

Federal spending on education and student aid (selected programs):
Vocational and
  adult education $6,348,000
GI Bill $619,000
Pell Grants $7,418,000

Total federal spending on college- and university-based research and development: $16,333,000
Selected programs:
Department of Health
  and Human Services . $2,927,000
National Science
  Foundation $4,890,000
Department of Defense . $2,836,000
Department
  of Agriculture $1,928,000
Department of Energy $585,000

Largest endowment:
University of Delaware $360,278,000

Top fund raisers:
Wesley College $392,000
Delaware State College ... $229,000

MISCELLANY

■ Goldey Beacom College is the result of a merger arranged by two Wilmington proprietary-school owners: H. S. Goldey and W. H. Beacom. The two men ran separate and competing secretarial schools until 1951, when they merged. The college became a four-year, non-profit institution in 1974.

■ The oldest higher-education institution in the state is the University of Delaware, founded in 1833.

DISTRICT OF COLUMBIA

THE board of trustees of the University of the District of Columbia selected Tilden J. LeMelle as the institution's new president in 1991, largely because he had gained experience dealing with student and faculty protests when he served as vice-chancellor for student affairs at the City University of New York system.

The experience may well come in handy in his new job. UDC's students and faculty members have become increasingly frustrated because of tight budgets, bitter fighting with the administration, and uncertainty about the institution's mission.

Even with the new leadership, Washington's only public university is expected to face difficulties. The city's public-school system, where most UDC students receive their pre-college education, has serious financial and academic problems.

University officials predict that they will continue to enroll students who are not prepared for college-level work.

Transition is also in the works for private institutions in Washington. The president of the Catholic University of America, the Rev. William J. Byron, announced in 1991 that he would retire in 1992. A new president, Joseph Duffey, took office in 1991 at the American University, succeeding Richard Berendzen, who resigned in 1990 after revelations that he had made obscene telephone calls from his office.

The last three years have seen new presidents named at Gallaudet University (I. King Jordan), Georgetown University (the Rev. Leo J. O'Donovan), George Washington University (Stephen Joel Trachtenberg), and Howard University (Franklyn G. Jenifer).

The new executives have received generally good reviews on their campuses, but race relations have prompted controversy at several institutions. The most widely publicized incident in 1991 erupted when a Georgetown law student published an article saying that affirmative action had led the law school to admit unqualified students.

The article, based on confidential admissions materials, angered many minority students. But university officials said that it was misleading, and that the university's affirmative-action policy had helped the institution.

DEMOGRAPHICS

Population: 606,900   (Rank: 48)

Age distribution:
Up to 17 .... 19.3%
18 to 24 .... 13.6%
25 to 44 .... 35.7%
45 and older 31.4%

Racial and ethnic distribution:
American Indian 0.2%
Asian 1.8%
Black 65.8%
White 29.6%
Other and unknown 2.5%
Hispanic (may be any race) .. 5.4%

Educational attainment of adults:
At least 4 years of high school 67.1%
At least 1 to 3 years of college 41.5%
At least 4 years of college ... 27.5%

Per-capita personal income: $23,243

Poverty rate: 18.1%

New high-school graduates in:
1991-92 (estimate) 3,976
2001-02 (estimate) 4,227

New GED diploma recipients: 650

High-school dropout rate: 41.8%

DISTRICT OF COLUMBIA
Continued

POLITICAL LEADERSHIP

Mayor: Sharon Pratt Dixon (D), term ends 1994

Mayor's higher-education aide: Janette Hoston Harris, District Building, Room 212, Washington 20004; (202) 727-0248

U.S. Senators: None

U.S. Representative: Delegate Eleanor Holmes Norton (D); non-voting

Legislature: n/a

COLLEGES AND UNIVERSITIES

Higher education:
Public 4-year institutions 2
Public 2-year institutions 0
Private 4-year institutions 15
Private 2-year institutions 0
Total 17

Vocational institutions: 31

Statewide coordinating board:
Office of Postsecondary Education Research and Assistance
2100 Martin Luther King Avenue S.E.
Suite 401
Washington 20020
(202) 727-3685
Sheila Drews, acting chief

Private-college association:
Consortium of Universities of the Washington Metropolitan Area
1717 Massachusetts Avenue, N.W.
Suite 101
Washington 20036
(202) 265-1313
Monte P. Shepler, president

Institution censured by the AAUP: Catholic University of America

Institution under NCAA sanctions: University of the District of Columbia

FACULTY MEMBERS

Full-time faculty members by rank:
Professor 1,168
Associate professor 1,006
Assistant professor 926
Instructor 186
Lecturer 77
No rank 20
Total 3,383

Average pay of full-time professors:
At public 4-year institutions $42,195
At public 2-year institutions .... n/a
At private 4-year institutions $45,186
At private 2-year institutions ... n/a
At all institutions $44,708
Men (all institutions) $47,773
Women (all institutions) $38,225

STUDENTS

Enrollment:
Total 79,800
At public 4-year institutions . 12,439
At public 2-year institutions 0
At private 4-year institutions 67,361
At private 2-year institutions 0
Undergraduate 49,611
 First-time freshmen 9,030
Graduate 21,994
Professional 8,195
American Indian 134
Asian 2,494
Black 23,926

Hispanic 2,114
White 41,348
Foreign 9,073

Enrollment highlights:
Women 53.8%
Full-time 62.8%
Minority 40.9%
Foreign 11.5%
10-year change in total
  enrollment .... Down 9.2%

Proportion of enrollment made up of minority students:
At public 4-year institutions . 94.6%
At public 2-year institutions .... n/a
At private 4-year institutions   30.8%
At private 2-year institutions ... n/a

Degrees awarded:
Associate 407
Bachelor's 7,482
Master's 5,123
Doctorate 503
Professional 2,467

Residence of new students: Residents made up 18% of all freshmen enrolled in the District of Columbia; 50% of all District of Columbia residents who were freshmen attended college in the District.

Test scores: Students averaged 840 on the S.A.T., which was taken by 71% of the District of Columbia's high-school seniors.

MONEY

Average tuition and fees:
At public 4-year institutions .. $664
At public 2-year institutions .... n/a
At private 4-year institutions $9,489
At private 2-year institutions ... n/a

Expenditures:
Public institutions $88,462,000
Private institutions . $1,307,377,000

State funds for higher-education operating expenses: n/a
Two-year change: n/a

State spending on student aid:
Need-based: $974,000; 829 awards
Non–need-based: None
Other: None

Salary of chief executive of largest public 4-year campus:
Tilden J. LeMelle, University of the
  District of Columbia: $90,700

Total spending on research and development by doctorate-granting universities: $112,146,000
Sources:
Federal government 76.9%
Local government 0.4%
Industry 7.1%
The institution itself 9.4%
Other 6.1%

Federal spending on education and student aid (selected programs):
Vocational and
  adult education $6,422,000
GI Bill $666,000
Pell Grants $11,367,000

Total federal spending on college- and university-based research and development: $69,206,000
Selected programs:
Department of Health
  and Human Services $40,929,000
National Science
  Foundation $5,742,000
Department of Defense . $5,693,000
Department
  of Agriculture $1,053,000
Department of Energy .. $1,695,000

Largest endowment:
George Washington
  University $296,677,000

DISTRICT OF COLUMBIA
Continued

Top fund raisers:
Georgetown University $28,555,000
George Washington
  University $15,549,000
American University ... $6,575,000

MISCELLANY

■ Two undergraduates taught a course at George Washington University in 1991 called "Confrontation and the Development of the Individual Mind." The students said they were frustrated because they rarely were encouraged to discuss their views in class. They wanted to replace lectures and exams with discussions and "free expression" projects.

■ An American University faculty member became immersed in the national debate over "political correctness" when, in the women's rest room during an academic conference, she was told by another conferee that her pale-pink nail polish was politically incorrect.

■ In the spring of 1991, two George Washington professors with opposing views on abortion taught a course that examined the debate.

■ The oldest institution of higher education in the District of Columbia is Georgetown University, a Roman Catholic institution founded in 1789. First called Georgetown College, it became a university in 1815 when it received the first university charter granted by the federal government. Georgetown's colors are blue and gray, representing the reunification of the North and South after the Civil War.

FLORIDA

FLORIDA'S GROWTH shows little sign of slowing, and the tax structure is still inadequate to meet the ever-expanding cost of public services. Public colleges and universities are being forced to accommodate thousands of additional students with budgets that are actually smaller than in years past.

Nonetheless, university leaders found some things to celebrate in 1991.

The major source of their happiness is a new law that gives the Board of Regents, the governing board for the university system, greater freedom to raise tuition and spend money. In return for the new authority, the institutions must report annually on such indicators as their graduation rates, the availability of class sections, and how well students perform on professional licensing examinations and graduate-school admission tests.

The law is especially significant because Florida legislators have a strong tradition of getting involved in education issues and of using the budget to influence—some would say interfere with—education policies.

Under the new law, legislators will have little opportunity to use the budget as leverage, although many legislators maintain an interest in higher education because they are employed at public or private colleges. (Such relationships have raised questions about conflicts of interest.)

Although some still question whether Florida provides enough money to support its nine existing public universities, the Legislature and Gov. Lawton Chiles, a Democrat who is in his first term, have approved the development of a 10th university.

The same budget constraints that led state officials to consider rescinding more than 5 per cent of the financing for colleges and universities in the fall of 1991 are expected to delay actual construction of the new campus.

The new institution will be located somewhere in southwest Florida, a region that has seen explosive population growth but has no public university of its own. This is the first expansion of the state university system since the early 1960's, when Florida opened five new institutions—in its central, southern, and Panhandle regions.

The University of Florida and Florida State University drew national attention with an aggressive—and successful—bid to attract the National High Field Magnetic Laboratory to north Florida. The institutions beat out the Massachusetts Institute of Technology, the site of an existing national magnet laboratory, in winning the competition. The magnet lab will be housed at Florida State in Tallahassee.

Even when the new university opens at the end of the decade, officials in Florida say the enrollment pressures will require that admissions standards for the state university system continue to rise. For a growing number of Floridians, that means that the first entry point into higher education will be through one of the state's 28 community colleges, already strained by their own surge in enrollments.

The community colleges, governed by their own boards of trustees under auspices of the state Board of Community Colleges, have also borne the brunt of remedial-education costs as a result of the state's controversial college-competency test, instituted in 1989. All students must pass the test before they receive an associate degree or are permitted to enroll in junior- or senior-level courses.

Community-college leaders argued against the imposition of higher passing grades, contending that the test is flawed and a disproportionate number of black and Hispanic students fail it. Although the state has given community colleges additional money to help their students prepare for the state test, college officials say it is not enough.

Money battles have also affected the state's private colleges, several of which receive state funds to provide programs that public institutions do not. The University of Miami and the Florida Institute of Technology are among those that work under such academic contracts.

Florida is home to four historically black institutions. One of them, Florida A&M University, is a land-grant institution known for its business school.

Following the state's college athletic teams is a popular pastime in Florida, but the sports news often centers on the latest violation of recruiting rules in major sports like basketball and football.

More serious matters also drew Florida into the headlines, first with the unsolved murders of five college students in Gainesville at the start of the 1990-91 academic year, and again in June 1991 when two University of Florida students were strangled in their apartments, apparently by a man who had cleaned their carpet. The first murders prompted about 100 students to withdraw and the university to start

FLORIDA
Continued

escort services and other safety programs.

Although most higher-education policies are set by the Board of Regents and the community-college trustees, the Governor and elected Cabinet are the chief education policy makers in the state. As the state coordinating board, the Postsecondary Education Planning Commission conducts many studies on education.

DEMOGRAPHICS

Population: 12,937,926 (Rank: 4)

Age distribution:
Up to 17 .... 22.2%
18 to 24 .... 9.4%
25 to 44 .... 30.4%
45 and older 38.0%

Racial and ethnic distribution:
American Indian 0.3%
Asian 1.2%
Black 13.6%
White 83.1%
Other and unknown 1.8%
Hispanic (may be any race) . 12.2%

Educational attainment of adults:
At least 4 years of high school 66.7%
At least 1 to 3 years of college 31.6%
At least 4 years of college ... 14.9%

Per-capita personal income: $18,530

Poverty rate: 13.5%

New high-school graduates in:
1991-92 (estimate) 96,709
2001-02 (estimate) 139,321

New GED diploma recipients: 32,734

High-school dropout rate: 42.0%

POLITICAL LEADERSHIP

Governor: Lawton Chiles (D), term ends 1995

Governor's higher-education aide: Barbara Cohen, The Capitol, Room 209, Tallahassee 32399; (904) 922-4642

U.S. Senators: Bob Graham (D), term ends 1993; Connie Mack (R), term ends 1995

U.S. Representatives:
9 Democrats, 10 Republicans
Jim Bacchus (D), Charles E. Bennett (D), Michael Bilirakis (R), Dante B. Fascell (D), Sam Gibbons (D), Porter J. Goss (R), Earl Hutto (D), Andy Ireland (R), Craig T. James (R), Harry Johnston (D), William Lehman (D), Tom Lewis (R), Bill McCollum (R), Douglas "Pete" Peterson (D), Ileana Ros-Lehtinen (R), E. Clay Shaw, Jr. (R), Lawrence J. Smith (D), Cliff Stearns (R), C.W. Bill Young (R)

Legislature: Senate, 22 Democrats, 18 Republicans; House, 74 Democrats, 46 Republicans

COLLEGES AND UNIVERSITIES

Higher education:
Public 4-year institutions 10
Public 2-year institutions 28
Private 4-year institutions 43
Private 2-year institutions 14
Total 95

Vocational institutions: 320

Statewide coordinating board:
Postsecondary Education
  Planning Commission
Florida Education Center

Tallahassee 32399
(904) 488-7894
William Proctor, executive director

Private-college association:
Independent Colleges
  and Universities of Florida
123 South Calhoun Street
Tallahassee 32301
(904) 681-3188
T. K. Wetherell, president

Institution censured by the AAUP:
Saint Leo College

Institutions under NCAA sanctions:
Florida A&M University,
University of Florida

FACULTY MEMBERS

Full-time faculty members by rank:
Professor 2,985
Associate professor 2,762
Assistant professor 2,316
Instructor 851
Lecturer 106
No rank 2,161
Total 11,181

Average pay of full-time professors:
At public 4-year institutions $41,741
At public 2-year institutions $34,100
At private 4-year institutions $36,225
At private 2-year institutions $22,834
At all institutions $38,027
Men (all institutions) $40,193
Women (all institutions) $33,076

STUDENTS

Enrollment:
Total 573,712
At public 4-year institutions   168,576
At public 2-year institutions   312,293
At private 4-year institutions   87,818
At private 2-year institutions . 5,025

Undergraduate 515,560
  First-time freshmen 69,357
Graduate 50,718
Professional 7,434
American Indian 1,509
Asian 9,331
Black 48,396
Hispanic 54,513
White 386,687
Foreign 15,154

Enrollment highlights:
Women 54.8%
Full-time 46.8%
Minority 22.7%
Foreign 2.9%
10-year change in total
  enrollment .... Up 45.2%

Proportion of enrollment made up of minority students:
At public 4-year institutions . 20.2%
At public 2-year institutions . 23.3%
At private 4-year institutions   24.6%
At private 2-year institutions   40.1%

Degrees awarded:
Associate 32,244
Bachelor's 34,244
Master's 10,563
Doctorate 1,201
Professional 2,051

Residence of new students: State residents made up 78% of all freshmen enrolled in Florida; 83% of all Florida residents who were freshmen attended college in their home state.

Test scores: Students averaged 882 on the S.A.T., which was taken by 48% of Florida's high-school seniors.

MONEY

Average tuition and fees:
At public 4-year institutions .... n/a
At public 2-year institutions .. $729

FLORIDA
Continued

At private 4-year institutions $7,153
At private 2-year institutions $5,519

Expenditures:
Public institutions .. $1,782,180,000
Private institutions ... $723,270,000

State funds for higher-education operating expenses: $1,486,480,000

Two-year change: Down 5%

State spending on student aid:
Need-based: $27,132,000;
  25,116 awards
Non–need-based: $41,928,000;
  26,767 awards
Other: None

Salary of chief executive of largest public 4-year campus:
John V. Lombardi, University
  of Florida: $190,000

Total spending on research and development by doctorate-granting universities: $433,413,000

Sources:
Federal government 51.5%
State and local governments .. 7.7%
Industry 6.6%
The institution itself 28.2%
Other 6.1%

Federal spending on education and student aid (selected programs):
Vocational and
  adult education $53,810,000
GI Bill $18,547,000
Pell Grants $168,987,000

Total federal spending on college- and university-based research and development: $196,397,000

Selected programs:
Department of Health
  and Human Services $86,946,000
National Science
  Foundation $26,710,000
Department of Defense $43,122,000
Department
  of Agriculture $9,136,000
Department of Energy . $17,545,000

Largest endowment:
University of Florida
  Foundation $218,559,000

Top fund raisers:
University of Miami ... $65,891,000
University of Florida .. $54,793,000
Florida State University $31,626,000

MISCELLANY

■ The University of Miami's medical school has the highest percentage of minority students of any Southern medical school, excluding historically black institutions, the Southern Regional Education Board reports. At Miami, 22.8 per cent of the students are members of minority groups.

■ Gatorade, one of higher education's biggest money makers, was developed by a team of scientists at the University of Florida in 1965. The beverage has earned about $17-million for the university since 1972.

■ The oldest institution of higher education in the state is, depending on whom you ask, either Florida State University, founded in 1851 as Seminary West of the Suwannee, or the University of Florida, founded in 1853. The seminary underwent dramatic changes in 1857, when it became Florida State and held its first college-level classes.

GEORGIA

FOR A STATE that boasts that its university system is insulated from legislative maneuvering or gubernatorial whim because it is governed by a powerful Board of Regents, Georgia higher education seems never too far from politics.

The regents may set the budgets and approve the programs, but they are acutely sensitive to the wishes of the Governor and of legislators—who keep a tight hold on the purse strings.

The delicate relationship has been apparent in several recent developments, including the regents' decision in the late 1980's to upgrade Georgia Southern College into a university, as lawmakers had been urging. The General Assembly also controls where and when campus construction takes place.

The University System of Georgia encompasses a wide array of institutions, including four-year technical colleges, four-year comprehensive colleges, and junior colleges.

The state also has four public research institutions. And while universities like the Georgia Institute of Technology and the University of Georgia are attracting an increasing amount of federal and private research support—and prestige—higher-education leaders say the state's financing formulas do not provide enough money to cover the added expenses the institutions must incur.

Georgia has been less affected by the recession than other states, but it did impose budget cuts in 1991-92. Gov. Zell Miller's veto of a pay raise for all non-faculty employees so angered workers at the University of Georgia that they planned to protest his commencement address. The Democratic Governor canceled his appearance. Faculty members were further unnerved by the Board of Regents' declaration of financial exigency in the fall of 1991—a move that would allow layoffs of tenured faculty members. The regents took the action after Governor Miller said he might order a 5-per-cent reduction in the state government's workforce.

The lesser-known research university, Georgia State, hit a lull in 1991 when its gregarious president, John Palms, left to become president of the University of South Carolina after just 18 months in Georgia. Nonetheless, the institution, in downtown Atlanta, will reap big benefits once dormitories and other facilities built for the 1996 Olympics are converted to university use.

Black colleges in Georgia present a picture of contrasts. While the state's three public black colleges have been struggling in recent years, some of the nation's best-known and wealthiest private black colleges are here, including Spelman and Morehouse Colleges in Atlanta.

Another prominent Atlanta private institution is Emory University, known for its research, for its medical school, and as the site of the Carter Presidential library.

Georgia also supports 15 junior colleges. While many say that is too many, no one suggests that some be closed because of the political fight such efforts would provoke.

A foray by lawmakers into the "war on drugs" has also affected public colleges. Georgia briefly had a law on the books in 1990 that would have required all new state employees, including those at public colleges, to be tested for illegal drug use. Faculty unions were among the groups that suc-

GEORGIA
Continued

cessfully challenged the law's constitutionality, and state officials decided in late 1990 not to pursue the policy.

DEMOGRAPHICS

Population: 6,478,216 (Rank: 11)

Age distribution:
Up to 17 .... 26.7%
18 to 24 .... 11.4%
25 to 44 .... 33.8%
45 and older 28.1%

Racial and ethnic distribution:
American Indian 0.2%
Asian 1.2%
Black 27.0%
White 71.0%
Other and unknown 0.7%
Hispanic (may be any race) .. 1.7%

Educational attainment of adults:
At least 4 years of high school 56.4%
At least 1 to 3 years of college 27.9%
At least 4 years of college ... 14.6%

Per-capita personal income: $17,049

Poverty rate: 14.9%

New high-school graduates in:
1991-92 (estimate) 63,625
2001-02 (estimate) 76,496

New GED diploma recipients: 13,174

High-school dropout rate: 39.0%

POLITICAL LEADERSHIP

Governor: Zell Miller (D), term ends 1995

Governor's higher-education aide: Steve Wrigley, State Capitol, Room 201, Atlanta 30334; (404) 656-1731

U.S. Senators: Wyche Fowler, Jr. (D), term ends 1993; Sam Nunn (D), term ends 1997

U.S. Representatives:
9 Democrats, 1 Republican
Doug Barnard, Jr. (D), George (Buddy) Darden (D), Newt Gingrich (R), Charles Hatcher (D), Ed Jenkins (D), Ben Jones (D), John Lewis (D), Richard Ray (D), J. Roy Rowland (D), Lindsay Thomas (D)

General Assembly: Senate, 45 Democrats, 11 Republicans; House, 145 Democrats, 35 Republicans

COLLEGES AND UNIVERSITIES

Higher education:
Public 4-year institutions 19
Public 2-year institutions 28
Private 4-year institutions 32
Private 2-year institutions 16
Total 95

Vocational institutions: 137

Statewide coordinating board:
Board of Regents
University System of Georgia
244 Washington Street, S.W.
Atlanta 30334
(404) 656-2203
H. Dean Propst, chancellor

Private-college association:
Association of Private Colleges and Universities in Georgia
945 East Paces Ferry Road
Resurgens Plaza, Suite 1730
Atlanta 30326
(404) 233-5434
William W. Kelly, president

Institutions censured by the AAUP:
None

Institutions under NCAA sanctions:
None

FACULTY MEMBERS

Full-time faculty members by rank:
Professor 1,893
Associate professor 2,160
Assistant professor 2,384
Instructor 748
Lecturer 50
No rank 179
Total 7,414

Average pay of full-time professors:
At public 4-year institutions $38,118
At public 2-year institutions $30,925
At private 4-year institutions $35,198
At private 2-year institutions $23,326
At all institutions $36,261
Men (all institutions) $38,976
Women (all institutions) $31,081

STUDENTS

Enrollment:
Total 239,208
At public 4-year institutions 136,239
At public 2-year institutions . 50,537
At private 4-year institutions 42,284
At private 2-year institutions 10,148
Undergraduate 202,793
   First-time freshmen 50,914
Graduate 28,288
Professional 8,127
American Indian 428
Asian 3,237
Black 43,029
Hispanic 2,336
White 176,235
Foreign 5,497

Enrollment highlights:
Women 54.0%
Full-time 66.3%
Minority 21.8%
Foreign 2.4%
10-year change in total
   enrollment .... Up 34.4%

Proportion of enrollment made up of minority students:
At public 4-year institutions . 17.2%
At public 2-year institutions . 20.7%
At private 4-year institutions 33.5%
At private 2-year institutions 36.6%

Degrees awarded:
Associate 7,126
Bachelor's 19,883
Master's 6,099
Doctorate 800
Professional 1,846

Residence of new students: State residents made up 80% of all freshmen enrolled in Georgia; 83% of all Georgia residents who were freshmen attended college in their home state.

Test scores: Students averaged 844 on the S.A.T., which was taken by 62% of Georgia's high-school seniors.

MONEY

Average tuition and fees:
At public 4-year institutions . $1,631
At public 2-year institutions .. $852
At private 4-year institutions $7,076
At private 2-year institutions $3,194

Expenditures:
Public institutions .. $1,255,964,000
Private institutions ... $696,734,000

State funds for higher-education operating expenses: $874,320,000
Two-year change: Down 1%

GEORGIA
Continued

State spending on student aid:
Need-based: $5,174,000;
  14,141 awards
Non–need-based: $16,316,000;
  17,298 awards
Other: $1,568,000

**Salary of chief executive
of largest public 4-year campus:**
Charles B. Knapp, University
  of Georgia: $132,000 from state
  plus $16,000 from private sources

**Total spending on research and
development by doctorate-granting
universities:** $445,011,000

Sources:
Federal government 47.7%
State and local governments .. 9.6%
Industry 8.3%
The institution itself 32.0%
Other 2.4%

**Federal spending on education
and student aid (selected programs):**
Vocational and
  adult education $35,754,000
GI Bill $11,603,000
Pell Grants $80,340,000

**Total federal spending on college-
and university-based research
and development:** $183,001,000

Selected programs:
Department of Health
  and Human Services $72,652,000
National Science
  Foundation $16,707,000
Department of Defense $53,923,000
Department
  of Agriculture $8,586,000
Department of Energy . $18,355,000

Largest endowment:
Emory University .. $1,153,875,000

Top fund raisers:
Emory University $38,789,000
Georgia Institute
  of Technology $28,531,000
University of Georgia . $28,151,000

MISCELLANY

■ Oglethorpe University is the home of the International Time Capsule Society, which maintains a registry of time capsules and studies them.

■ The University of Georgia library holds nearly 60,000 pieces of material about Margaret Mitchell, the author of *Gone With the Wind.*

■ Just a mile from the campus of Valdosta State College lies a wealth of artifacts waiting to be uncovered—beneath the rubble of a turn-of-the-century dump. Every year, archaeology students from Valdosta use the dump as a site for their digs. They have unearthed cooking utensils, inkwells, and parts of porcelain dolls.

■ The oldest institution of higher education in the state is the University of Georgia, founded in 1785.

HAWAII

ON July 11, 1991 the University of Hawaii and its Institute for Astronomy were the envy of astronomers around the world.

The university operates four telescopes at the Mauna Kea Observatories, the world's largest and most powerful concentration of astronomical telescopes and instruments. On that day, the path of a total solar eclipse passed directly over the observatories, providing scientists a once-in-a-lifetime opportunity to obtain calibration measurements for future research.

The research on the eclipse is only one example of how higher education in Hawaii takes advantage of its location. In June 1991 the University of Hawaii, a leader in Pacific Rim studies, announced a joint project with the University of Miami to sponsor environmental, oceanographic, and geologic research in the Southern Hemisphere. Initially, the work will focus on South America.

The university has strong ties with Asian nations on the Pacific Rim, and its location has helped it attract students and scholars from many Asian countries, adding to the islands' rich ethnic mix. But the isolation of the 1,500-mile archipelago can also be a burden.

The University of Hawaii System is governed by a single Board of Regents and includes six community colleges. The system is called upon to satisfy a wide variety of educational demands for the many students who cannot travel to the mainland for higher education.

Occasionally, the system's attempts to balance community demands for a full range of educational services at each of the university's three main campuses conflict with the Legislature's calls for savings by reducing duplicative programs.

There also has been increased concern about the underrepresentation of Native Hawaiians and Filipinos at the University of Hawaii at Manoa. Manoa, the system's flagship campus, has developed several programs to increase their representation, including a community-college transfer project and recruitment campaigns to attract and support them.

Gov. John D. Waihee, III, a Democrat who was re-elected in November 1990 to a second term, has been a strong supporter of the university's science programs and its efforts to recruit more minority and disadvantaged students.

DEMOGRAPHICS

Population: 1,108,229   (Rank: 41)

Age distribution:
Up to 17 .... 25.3%
18 to 24 .... 10.9%
25 to 44 .... 34.2%
45 and older 29.6%

Racial and ethnic distribution:
American Indian 0.5%
Asian 61.8%
Black 2.5%
White 33.4%
Other and unknown 1.9%
Hispanic (may be any race) .. 7.3%

Educational attainment of adults:
At least 4 years of high school 73.8%
At least 1 to 3 years of college 38.8%
At least 4 years of college ... 20.3%

Per-capita personal income: $20,356

Poverty rate: 11.1%

New high-school graduates in:
1991-92 (estimate) 11,686
2001-02 (estimate) 12,853

New GED diploma recipients: 1,318

High-school dropout rate: 30.9%

POLITICAL LEADERSHIP

Governor: John D. Waihee, III (D), term ends 1994

HAWAII
Continued

Governor's higher-education aide:
Patricia Brandt, State Capitol, Honolulu 96813; (808) 548-3031

U.S. Senators: Daniel K. Akaka (D), term ends 1995; Daniel K. Inouye (D), term ends 1993

U.S. Representatives:
2 Democrats, 0 Republicans
Neil Abercrombie (D), Patsy T. Mink (D)

Legislature: Senate, 22 Democrats, 3 Republicans; House, 45 Democrats, 6 Republicans

COLLEGES AND UNIVERSITIES

Higher education:
Public 4-year institutions	3
Public 2-year institutions	6
Private 4-year institutions	5
Private 2-year institutions	0
Total	14

Vocational institutions: 35

Statewide coordinating board:
University of Hawaii Board
 of Regents
Bachman Hall, Room 209
2444 Dole Street
Honolulu 96822
(808) 956-8213
Albert J. Simone, president

Private-college association:
None

Institutions censured by the AAUP:
None

Institutions under NCAA sanctions:
None

FACULTY MEMBERS

Full-time faculty members by rank:
Professor	368
Associate professor	309
Assistant professor	305
Instructor	64
Lecturer	0
No rank	558
Total	1,604

Average pay of full-time professors:
At public 4-year institutions	$43,535
At public 2-year institutions	$35,317
At private 4-year institutions	$25,466
At private 2-year institutions	n/a
At all institutions	$39,917
Men (all institutions)	$42,346
Women (all institutions)	$35,156

STUDENTS

Enrollment:
Total	54,188
At public 4-year institutions	23,111
At public 2-year institutions	20,533
At private 4-year institutions	10,544
At private 2-year institutions	0
Undergraduate	47,361
First-time freshmen	8,675
Graduate	6,389
Professional	438
American Indian	194
Asian	31,008
Black	957
Hispanic	844
White	15,700
Foreign	3,594

Enrollment highlights:
Women	53.8%
Full-time	56.8%
Minority	67.8%
Foreign	6.9%

10-year change in total
  enrollment .... Up 14.8%

Proportion of enrollment made up of minority students:
At public 4-year institutions . 70.9%
At public 2-year institutions . 74.3%
At private 4-year institutions   42.7%
At private 2-year institutions ... n/a

Degrees awarded:
Associate 2,120
Bachelor's 3,628
Master's 1,017
Doctorate 172
Professional 119

Residence of new students: State residents made up 88% of all freshmen enrolled in Hawaii; 77% of all Hawaii residents who were freshmen attended college in their home state.

Test scores: Students averaged 883 on the S.A.T., which was taken by 55% of Hawaii's high-school seniors.

MONEY

Average tuition and fees:
At public 4-year institutions . $1,293
At public 2-year institutions .. $410
At private 4-year institutions $4,008
At private 2-year institutions ... n/a

Expenditures:
Public institutions $312,248,000
Private institutions $20,964,000

State funds for higher-education operating expenses: $321,201,000

Two-year change: Up 15%

State spending on student aid:
Need-based: $611,000; 700 awards
Non–need-based: None
Other: None

Salary of chief executive of largest public 4-year campus:
Albert J. Simone, University of Hawaii at Manoa: $95,000

Total spending on research and development by doctorate-granting universities: $76,525,000
Sources:
Federal government 55.8%
State and local governments . 35.9%
Industry 2.1%
The institution itself 4.7%
Other 1.6%

Federal spending on education and student aid (selected programs):
Vocational and
  adult education $6,479,000
GI Bill $2,062,000
Pell Grants $6,930,000

Total federal spending on college- and university-based research and development: $47,913,000
Selected programs:
Department of Health
  and Human Services . $9,136,000
National Science
  Foundation $12,390,000
Department of Defense . $2,666,000
Department
  of Agriculture $4,282,000
Department of Energy .. $1,659,000

Largest endowment:
University of Hawaii .. $55,216,000

Top fund raisers:
University of Hawaii ... $9,734,000
Chaminade University
  of Honolulu $914,000

MISCELLANY

■ The East-West Center, adjacent to the University of Hawaii's Manoa campus, was established by Congress

HAWAII
Continued

in 1960 "to promote better relations and understanding between the United States and the nations of Asia and the Pacific through cooperative study, training, and research."

■ The Polynesian Cultural Center in Oahu, a showcase for the traditional arts and crafts and songs and dances of the Pacific region, was started by the Church of Jesus Christ of Latter-day Saints to preserve the cultural heritage of Polynesia and to provide jobs for students from Brigham Young University's Hawaii campus.

■ The world's largest and most powerful optical telescope, the 10-meter W. M. Keck Telescope, is expected to be completed by the end of 1991 on Mauna Kea. The California Institute of Technology and the University of California, which are constructing the telescope, have announced plans to build a second, identical instrument next to the Keck telescope.

■ The oldest institution of higher education in Hawaii is the University of Hawaii at Manoa, founded in 1907.

IDAHO

IDAHO'S ECONOMY is gradually expanding beyond its traditional base of mining, timber, and agriculture, and higher education is beginning to see some benefits from new jobs in manufacturing, technology, and tourism.

But while state spending for higher education is on the upswing—Idaho ranked second nationwide in the rate of increase in state support from 1989-90 to 1991-92—public colleges and universities are still struggling to overcome the effects of slim budgets that prevailed in the early 1980's.

In particular, higher-education leaders say, campus facilities are badly in need of repair and maintenance, and the state lacks the resources to help pay for new buildings and laboratories. College officials say the state also lags in faculty salaries, and that has put Idaho at a disadvantage in attracting professors.

The Board of Regents is the coordinating and governing board for all colleges and universities. The same board also oversees the state's elementary and secondary schools. (It is known as the Board of Education when acting in that capacity.)

Gov. Cecil D. Andrus, a Democrat in his third term, has supported higher education, although he was among several politicians who took the regents to task in May 1991 for granting big pay raises to college presidents. Mr. Andrus was also instrumental in the state's decision to create a new $100,000 Minority and At-Risk Scholarship Program, which will provide up to $2,500 to qualified students.

A persistent issue is whether the state should shift some of its spending from the flagship University of Idaho, in Moscow, to some of the other four-year institutions. Pressure for new programs is particularly strong in Boise, the state's capital and population center. But Idaho's Board of Regents has held institutions firmly to their missions. Rather than let Boise State University expand from its specialties in the arts, business, and public affairs, the regents have pushed the other institutions with their own specialties to provide advanced programs in Boise. Now graduate engineering courses are available through the University of Idaho and graduate classes in health sciences are provided by Idaho State University. The regents are also overseeing a program that requires institutions to report on how well their students are being taught.

Idaho has two public community colleges. Some legislators had hoped to win their colleagues' support for developing new community colleges in 1991. But the legislative effort failed, and in October 1991 voters in the Idaho Falls region resoundingly rejected a measure to create a taxing district to support a new community college to serve them. State higher-education officials now say they will try to provide educational opportunities to that region with a consortium of existing state institutions.

The state has few private colleges; most of them have religious affiliations.

DEMOGRAPHICS

Population: 1,006,749   (Rank: 42)

Age distribution:
Up to 17 .... 30.6%
18 to 24 .... 9.8%
25 to 44 .... 30.0%
45 and older 29.6%

Racial and ethnic distribution:
American Indian 1.4%
Asian 0.9%
Black 0.3%
White 94.4%
Other and unknown 3.0%
Hispanic (may be any race) .. 5.3%

Educational attainment of adults:
At least 4 years of high school 73.7%
At least 1 to 3 years of college 37.2%
At least 4 years of college ... 15.8%

Per-capita personal income: $15,249

Poverty rate: 13.3%

New high-school graduates in:
1991-92 (estimate) 11,825
2001-02 (estimate) 10,448

New GED diploma recipients: 790

High-school dropout rate: 24.6%

POLITICAL LEADERSHIP

Governor: Cecil D. Andrus (D), term ends 1995

Governor's higher-education aide: Julie M. Cheever, Statehouse, Boise 83720; (208) 334-2100

U.S. Senators: Larry E. Craig (R), term ends 1997; Steve Symms (R), term ends 1993

U.S. Representatives:
2 Democrats, 0 Republicans
Larry LaRocco (D), Richard H. Stallings (D)

Legislature: Senate, 21 Democrats, 21 Republicans; House, 28 Democrats, 56 Republicans

COLLEGES AND UNIVERSITIES

Higher education:
Public 4-year institutions 4
Public 2-year institutions 2
Private 4-year institutions 3
Private 2-year institutions 2
Total 11

Vocational institutions: 39

IDAHO
Continued

Statewide coordinating board:
Board of Regents
650 West State Street, Room 307
Boise 83720
(208) 334-2270
Rayburn Barton, executive director for higher education

Private-college association:
None

Institutions censured by the AAUP:
None

Institutions under NCAA sanctions:
None

FACULTY MEMBERS

Full-time faculty members by rank:
Professor 408
Associate professor 343
Assistant professor 317
Instructor 62
Lecturer 0
No rank 402
Total 1,532

Average pay of full-time professors:
At public 4-year institutions $34,430
At public 2-year institutions $29,090
At private 4-year institutions $26,893
At private 2-year institutions $24,436
At all institutions $32,118
Men (all institutions) $33,345
Women (all institutions) $29,102

STUDENTS

Enrollment:
Total 48,969
At public 4-year institutions . 33,093
At public 2-year institutions .. 5,354
At private 4-year institutions . 2,315
At private 2-year institutions . 8,207
Undergraduate 42,489
 First-time freshmen 10,360
Graduate 6,014
Professional 466
American Indian 373
Asian 541
Black 280
Hispanic 653
White 42,695
Foreign 1,175

Enrollment highlights:
Women 53.9%
Full-time 68.6%
Minority 4.1%
Foreign 2.6%
10-year change in total
 enrollment .... Up 20.4%

Proportion of enrollment made up of minority students:
At public 4-year institutions .. 4.7%
At public 2-year institutions .. 3.5%
At private 4-year institutions . 3.6%
At private 2-year institutions . 2.7%

Degrees awarded:
Associate 2,589
Bachelor's 3,017
Master's 706
Doctorate 60
Professional 67

Residence of new students: State residents made up 59% of all freshmen enrolled in Idaho; 78% of all Idaho residents who were freshmen attended college in their home state.

Test scores: Students averaged 19.1 on the A.C.T., which was taken by 58% of Idaho's high-school seniors.

MONEY

Average tuition and fees:
At public 4-year institutions . $1,119

At public 2-year institutions .. $779
At private 4-year institutions $6,669
At private 2-year institutions $1,400

Expenditures:
Public institutions $238,438,000
Private institutions $49,768,000

State funds for higher-education operating expenses: $195,881,000
Two-year change: Up 24%

State spending on student aid:
Need-based: $485,000; 800 awards
Non–need-based: $245,000; 98 awards
Other: None

Salary of chief executive of largest public 4-year campus:
Larry Selland (interim), Boise State University: $93,712

Total spending on research and development by doctorate-granting universities: $36,570,000
Sources:
Federal government 39.3%
State and local governments . 22.3%
Industry 11.5%
The institution itself 26.2%
Other 0.7%

Federal spending on education and student aid (selected programs):
Vocational and
  adult education $6,476,000
GI Bill $2,065,000
Pell Grants $21,839,000

Total federal spending on college- and university-based research and development: $10,424,000
Selected programs:
Department of Health
  and Human Services ... $939,000
National Science
  Foundation $1,585,000

Department of Defense ... $152,000
Department
  of Agriculture $3,397,000
Department of Energy $271,000

Largest endowment:
University of Idaho ... $36,326,000

Top fund raisers:
College of Idaho $3,583,000
Boise State University .. $2,192,000

MISCELLANY

■ Boise State University, located near a canyon that contains one of the country's largest populations of birds of prey, offers a highly specialized master's-degree program in raptor biology.

■ Idaho State University attracts thousands of rodeo fans every spring when it holds the Dodge National Circuit Finals Rodeo in its Minidome. The event—sponsored by the Professional Rodeo Circuit Association—draws rodeo performers from across the country.

■ The oldest institution of higher education in Idaho is Ricks College, a Mormon institution founded in 1888.

ILLINOIS

UNCHARACTERISTIC unity characterized higher education in Illinois in 1991. Colleges and universities put aside their political and regional rivalries and lobbied the General Assembly to make permanent a two-year surcharge on the state income tax.
While the lobbying was successful—and vital to the institutions,

ILLINOIS
Continued

which otherwise could have faced devastating budget cuts in the 1991 academic year—it's unclear whether the effort marks a new era of cooperation.

Tradition and recent history, in fact, suggest otherwise. Public colleges are governed by five separate boards, and the five systems, along with several aggressive private colleges, compete for money and students.

The competition is especially fierce in the "collar counties"—the wealthy and growing suburbs that ring Chicago and are home to many high-technology companies and the Argonne and Fermi National Laboratories.

The state's Board of Higher Education is charged with refereeing many of those battles, but its powers, as a coordinating board, are limited. Occasionally its policies actually fuel the rivalries, as when the board agreed to let Northern Illinois University build a new classroom building 15 miles from Roosevelt University, a private institution, or when it agreed to subsidize the tuition of Peoria-area students attending Bradley University, a private institution, despite protests from public-college leaders.

What chafes many public institutions the most, however, is the political clout of the University of Illinois at Urbana-Champaign, one of the nation's leading research universities.

The City Colleges of Chicago system—eight community colleges that serve some of the neediest students in the country—is also enjoying political popularity with its efforts to cut spending and increase the number of students taking college-level, not remedial, courses.

As the tax surcharge shows, the General Assembly supports higher education. The new Governor, Republican Jim Edgar, campaigned on a promise to make the surcharge permanent.

Lawmakers also agreed in 1991 to spend the next year re-evaluating university governance—a move prompted in part by the controversy that arose in the selection of a new chancellor for the Chicago campus of the University of Illinois. Faculty members had complained that politicians were interfering in the search. But the legislature's interest may be more parochial: the desire to give the Chicago campus, and other branches of university systems, their own boards of trustees.

Student concerns about racism on the campuses also prompted lawmakers in 1991 to require all colleges to include "human relations" study in their general-education curricula.

Private institutions in Illinois are diverse and politically active, and their activism reaps results. The state's generous student-aid program is open to private-college students, and the institutions receive direct state aid as well. The state is home to the University of Chicago and Northwestern University—two major research institutions—and small liberal-arts colleges like Rockford and Knox Colleges.

Chicago is a center for Catholic higher education, with such institutions as DePaul and Loyola Universities.

DEMOGRAPHICS

Population: 11,430,602   (Rank: 6)

Age distribution:
Up to 17 .... 25.8%
18 to 24 .... 10.6%
25 to 44 .... 32.3%
45 and older 31.3%

Racial and ethnic distribution:
American Indian 0.2%
Asian 2.5%
Black 14.8%
White 78.3%
Other and unknown 4.2%
Hispanic (may be any race) .. 7.9%

Educational attainment of adults:
At least 4 years of high school 66.5%
At least 1 to 3 years of college 31.4%
At least 4 years of college ... 16.2%

Per-capita personal income: $20,419

Poverty rate: 13.0%

New high-school graduates in:
1991-92 (estimate) 114,923
2001-02 (estimate) 113,634

New GED diploma recipients: 15,137

High-school dropout rate: 24.4%

POLITICAL LEADERSHIP

Governor: Jim Edgar (R), term ends 1995

Governor's higher-education aide:
Mary Ann Louderback, State House, Floor 2½, Springfield 62706; (217) 782-2654

U.S. Senators: Alan J. Dixon (D), term ends 1993; Paul Simon (D), term ends 1997

U.S. Representatives:
15 Democrats, 7 Republicans
Frank Annunzio (D), Terry L. Bruce (D), Cardiss Collins (D), Jerry F. Costello (D), John W. Cox, Jr. (D), Philip M. Crane (R), Richard J. Durbin (D), Lane Evans (D), Thomas W. Ewing (R), Harris W. Fawell (R), J. Dennis Hastert (R), Charles A. Hayes (D), Henry J. Hyde (R), William O. Lipinski (D), Robert H. Michel (R), John Edward Porter (R), Glenn Poshard (D), Dan Rostenkowski (D), Marty Russo (D), George E. Sangmeister (D), Gus Savage (D), Sidney R. Yates (D)

General Assembly: Senate, 31 Democrats, 28 Republicans; House, 72 Democrats, 46 Republicans

COLLEGES AND UNIVERSITIES

Higher education:
Public 4-year institutions 12
Public 2-year institutions 47
Private 4-year institutions 91
Private 2-year institutions 16
Total 166

Vocational institutions: 359

Statewide coordinating board:
Board of Higher Education
500 Reisch Building
4 West Old Capitol Square
Springfield 62701
(217) 782-2551
Richard D. Wagner,
executive director

Private-college association:
Federation of Independent Illinois
  Colleges and Universities
944 South 2nd Street
Springfield 62704
(217) 789-1400
Donald E. Fouts, president

Institution censured by the AAUP:
Illinois College of Optometry

ILLINOIS
Continued

Institution under NCAA sanctions:
University of Illinois
at Urbana-Champaign

FACULTY MEMBERS

Full-time faculty members by rank:
Professor 4,760
Associate professor 3,639
Assistant professor 3,572
Instructor 712
Lecturer 302
No rank 4,649
Total 17,634

Average pay of full-time professors:
At public 4-year institutions $41,181
At public 2-year institutions $38,201
At private 4-year institutions $41,728
At private 2-year institutions $24,667
At all institutions $40,546
Men (all institutions) $43,212
Women (all institutions) $34,117

STUDENTS

Enrollment:
Total 709,937
At public 4-year institutions   194,913
At public 2-year institutions   341,730
At private 4-year institutions 164,985
At private 2-year institutions . 8,309
Undergraduate 607,274
   First-time freshmen 125,519
Graduate 85,452
Professional 17,211
American Indian 1,972
Asian 27,798
Black 83,090
Hispanic 40,784
White 521,510
Foreign 13,820

Enrollment highlights:
Women 54.3%
Full-time 50.2%
Minority 22.8%
Foreign 2.0%
10-year change in total
   enrollment .... Up 15.8%

Proportion of enrollment made up of minority students:
At public 4-year institutions . 17.9%
At public 2-year institutions . 27.0%
At private 4-year institutions 17.6%
At private 2-year institutions 53.4%

Degrees awarded:
Associate 23,141
Bachelor's 48,865
Master's 18,666
Doctorate 2,176
Professional 4,404

Residence of new students: State residents made up 92% of all freshmen enrolled in Illinois; 85% of all Illinois residents who were freshmen attended college in their home state.

Test scores: Students averaged 18.8 on the A.C.T., which was taken by 61% of Illinois's high-school seniors.

MONEY

Average tuition and fees:
At public 4-year institutions . $2,370
At public 2-year institutions .. $871
At private 4-year institutions $8,281
At private 2-year institutions $5,505

Expenditures:
Public institutions .. $2,571,409,000
Private institutions . $2,722,294,000

State funds for higher-education operating expenses: $1,734,761,000
Two-year change: Up 1%

State spending on student aid:
Need-based: $180,650,000;
  112,000 awards
Non–need-based: $18,285,000;
  20,842 awards
Other: $4,148,000

**Salary of chief executive
of largest public 4-year campus:**
Morton W. Weir, University of
  Illinois at Urbana-Champaign:
  $133,600

**Total spending on research and
development by doctorate-granting
universities:** $647,863,000
Sources:
Federal government 54.4%
State and local governments .. 5.9%
Industry 6.8%
The institution itself 25.3%
Other 7.6%

**Federal spending on education
and student aid (selected programs):**
Vocational and
  adult education $54,620,000
GI Bill $12,713,000
Pell Grants $169,398,000

**Total federal spending on college-
and university-based research
and development:** $324,405,000
Selected programs:
Department of Health
  and Human Services $161,519,000
National Science
  Foundation $79,383,000
Department of Defense $32,119,000
Department
  of Agriculture $8,134,000
Department of Energy . $20,964,000

Largest endowment:
University of Chicago $1,074,505,000

Top fund raisers:
Northwestern
  University $68,076,000
University of Chicago . $67,118,000
University of Illinois
  at Urbana-Champaign $56,590,000

MISCELLANY

■ Mundelein College, the only Catholic women's liberal-arts college in Illinois, merged in the summer of 1991 with Loyola University of Chicago. Under the merger agreement, Loyola's undergraduate college for part-time students will be called Mundelein College.

■ The University of Chicago will start celebrations of its 100th anniversary during the 1991-92 academic year. The university was founded by John D. Rockefeller, who called it "the best investment I ever made." It started classes on October 1, 1892.

■ The oldest higher-education institution in Illinois is McKendree College, which was founded in 1828 and is affiliated with the United Methodist Church.

INDIANA

MORE THAN 93,000 Indiana students applied for state financial aid in 1991—an all-time high.

College and university officials point to the recession as one cause of the increase. But the rise in applications can also be attributed to a campaign by the State Student Assistance Commission to encourage students to apply for aid.

Increasing Indiana's low college-

INDIANA
Continued

going rates has been a top priority for the aid commission, for legislators, and for Gov. Evan Bayh, a Democrat. In 1986, 27 per cent of Indiana residents between 18 and 24 were enrolled in postsecondary institutions. By 1990-91, state officials said the proportion had climbed to 35 per cent.

In northern Indiana in particular, where the economy has been dominated by automobile-related industries, residents traditionally have not needed a college degree to find well-paying jobs. But declines in the industry have changed that picture in recent years.

Institutions are designing recruitment programs for ninth-graders and are working with secondary-school systems to help students get any remedial help they may need.

In 1990, Governor Bayh signed a bill that established an early-intervention program in which participants are called 21st-Century Scholars.

To join the program, students must pledge that they will not use illegal drugs, engage in criminal activity, or drink alcohol. If they graduate from high school and apply for state and federal financial aid, the state makes up the difference between the aid they receive and the full tuition at a state university or at Indiana Vocational Technical College.

Because the state is also home to many private colleges, students who attend private institutions are eligible for the program. If a student decides to attend a private college or university in Indiana, the program will provide a grant equal to the average grant awarded to a student attending a public university in Indiana.

The Commission for Higher Education, the statewide coordinating board, is responsible for planning and reviewing budgets and academic programs. The seven public systems are governed by individual boards.

One of the nation's premier Roman Catholic institutions is in Indiana. The University of Notre Dame is influential around the state and throughout the nation. Several small liberal-arts institutions are also affiliated with religious organizations. Among them are Bethel, Earlham, Franklin, Goshen, and Saint Mary-of-the-Woods Colleges.

College sports—especially Notre Dame football and Indiana University basketball—are taken seriously in Indiana. Bob Knight, the IU basketball coach, is extremely popular, but some higher-education officials worry that his tremendous influence distorts the university's priorities.

DEMOGRAPHICS

Population: 5,544,159 (Rank: 14)

Age distribution:
Up to 17 .... 26.3%
18 to 24 .... 10.9%
25 to 44 .... 31.3%
45 and older 31.5%

Racial and ethnic distribution:
American Indian 0.2%
Asian 0.7%
Black 7.8%
White 90.6%
Other and unknown 0.7%
Hispanic (may be any race) .. 1.8%

Educational attainment of adults:
At least 4 years of high school 66.4%
At least 1 to 3 years of college 24.6%
At least 4 years of college ... 12.5%

Per-capita personal income: $16,890

Poverty rate: 12.3%

New high-school graduates in:
1991-92 (estimate) 61,219
2001-02 (estimate) 58,205

New GED diploma recipients: 10,581

High-school dropout rate: 23.7%

POLITICAL LEADERSHIP

Governor: Evan Bayh (D), term ends 1993

Governor's higher-education aide: Stanley G. Jones, State House, Room 206, Indianapolis 46204; (317) 233-3723

U.S. Senators: Dan Coats (R), term ends 1993; Richard G. Lugar (R), term ends 1995

U.S. Representatives:
8 Democrats, 2 Republicans
Dan Burton (R), Lee H. Hamilton (D), Andrew Jacobs, Jr. (D), Jim Jontz (D), Jill L. Long (D), Frank McCloskey (D), John T. Myers (R), Tim Roemer (D), Philip R. Sharp (D), Peter J. Visclosky (D)

General Assembly: Senate, 24 Democrats, 26 Republicans; House, 52 Democrats, 48 Republicans

COLLEGES AND UNIVERSITIES

Higher education:
Public 4-year institutions 14
Public 2-year institutions 14
Private 4-year institutions 41
Private 2-year institutions 9
Total 78

Vocational institutions: 135

Statewide coordinating board:
Commission for Higher Education
101 West Ohio Street, Suite 550
Indianapolis 46204
(317) 232-1900
Clyde Ingle, commissioner for higher education

Private-college association:
Independent Colleges and Universities of Indiana
200 South Meridian Street, Suite 220
Indianapolis 46225
(317) 635-2655
T. K. Olson, president

Institution censured by the AAUP:
Concordia Theological Seminary

Institutions under NCAA sanctions:
None

FACULTY MEMBERS

Full-time faculty members by rank:
Professor 2,655
Associate professor 2,347
Assistant professor 2,451
Instructor 495
Lecturer 253
No rank 675
Total 8,876

Average pay of full-time professors:
At public 4-year institutions $39,556
At public 2-year institutions $25,442
At private 4-year institutions $37,668
At private 2-year institutions $28,825
At all institutions $37,442
Men (all institutions) $40,632
Women (all institutions) $29,947

STUDENTS

Enrollment:
Total 275,821
At public 4-year institutions   181,286

INDIANA
Continued

At public 2-year institutions . 35,147
At private 4-year institutions   56,433
At private 2-year institutions . 2,955
Undergraduate 239,557
  First-time freshmen 54,891
Graduate 30,934
Professional 5,330
American Indian 604
Asian 3,329
Black 14,723
Hispanic 3,686
White 239,057
Foreign 6,503

Enrollment highlights:
Women 52.5%
Full-time 65.1%
Minority 8.5%
Foreign 2.4%
10-year change in total
  enrollment .... Up 20.8%

Proportion of enrollment made up of minority students:
At public 4-year institutions .. 8.1%
At public 2-year institutions . 10.4%
At private 4-year institutions . 7.9%
At private 2-year institutions   21.2%

Degrees awarded:
Associate 8,902
Bachelor's 26,874
Master's 7,514
Doctorate 962
Professional 1,442

Residence of new students: State residents made up 75% of all freshmen enrolled in Indiana; 88% of all Indiana residents who were freshmen attended college in their home state.

Test scores: Students averaged 865 on the S.A.T., which was taken by 57% of Indiana's high-school seniors.

MONEY

Average tuition and fees:
At public 4-year institutions . $1,975
At public 2-year institutions . $1,374
At private 4-year institutions $8,267
At private 2-year institutions $7,412

Expenditures:
Public institutions .. $1,602,203,000
Private institutions ... $530,163,000

State funds for higher-education operating expenses: $899,643,000
Two-year change: Up 11%

State spending on student aid:
Need-based: $46,488,000;
  34,500 awards
Non–need-based: $966,000;
  808 awards
Other: None

Salary of chief executive of largest public 4-year campus:
Steven C. Beering, Purdue University main campus: $160,000

Total spending on research and development by doctorate-granting universities: $240,696,000
Sources:
Federal government 56.1%
State and local governments .. 8.1%
Industry 7.5%
The institution itself 21.6%
Other 6.7%

Federal spending on education and student aid (selected programs):
Vocational and
  adult education $31,138,000
GI Bill $6,222,000
Pell Grants $89,366,000

Total federal spending on college- and university-based research and development: $131,315,000

Selected programs:
Department of Health
  and Human Services $55,905,000
National Science
  Foundation $37,486,000
Department of Defense . $9,258,000
Department
  of Agriculture $7,770,000
Department of Energy . $11,243,000

Largest endowment:
University of
  Notre Dame $605,630,000

Top fund raisers:
Indiana University $79,119,000
University of
  Notre Dame $53,781,000
Hanover College $31,331,000

MISCELLANY

■ Students at DePauw University racked up more than 150,000 hours of volunteer service in the 1990-91 academic year. That was almost three times the goal of 55,000 hours the students set at the beginning of the year and added up to about 65 hours of community service for each student at the university.

■ The oldest institution of higher education in Indiana is Vincennes University, a two-year college founded in 1801 as the Jefferson Academy and renamed in 1806.

IOWA

Iowans pride themselves on their support for education and the quality of their schools, colleges, and universities. But fulfilling their expectations is becoming increasingly difficult. Iowa was on the rebound from an economic slump that cut into state revenues in the mid-1980's—but then the recession struck.

The budget passed in 1991 by the General Assembly would have given higher education a standstill budget for 1991-92. But Gov. Terry E. Branstad, a Republican in his third term, warned lawmakers before they adjourned in May 1991 that state revenues were not meeting projections.

He said he would slash millions of dollars from the appropriations if legislators did not provide enough to finance federally mandated social programs. On July 1, 1991, he announced across-the-board budget cuts of 3.25 per cent.

Higher-education institutions face even bigger cuts if the Governor loses a court battle over his vetoes of allocations for pay increases for both union and non-union state employees. Losing the case could be financially devastating.

The executive director of the Board of Regents, which runs the three public universities, says a decision against the Governor could cost his system $49-million. Faculty members at the University of Northern Iowa are under a union contract, as are support staff and other non-faculty personnel throughout the system.

The state Board of Education governs the community colleges, which in Iowa are called "area colleges." In contrast to the difficulties facing the four-year institutions, the two-year institutions received an increase of 6 per cent, before the across-the-board cuts, to support enrollment growth. Even with the Governor's budget rescission, some two-year institutions saw a slight increase in their allocation

IOWA
Continued

from the state.

Lawmakers did not cut the Iowa Tuition Grant program, which provides need-based grants to students at private institutions. The state will enforce the deadline for applications strictly, however, and private-college officials fear that could leave many needy students without aid.

Despite his tough stance on the budget, Governor Branstad was generous to higher education when state revenues were more plentiful. He increased faculty salaries and expanded tuition-assistance programs. He also spearheaded the National Governors' Association study of education.

During his re-election campaign in 1990, he promised to increase schoolteachers' salaries significantly. Some higher-education officials are afraid that keeping that promise may limit the Governor's ability to increase state spending for colleges and universities.

Although research on agriculture is well financed and a priority of lobbyists for state agricultural groups, higher education in Iowa belies many of the other stereotypes of farm states.

The Iowa Writers' Workshop, for example, is a nationally known program at the University of Iowa that competes with New York City as a mecca for aspiring authors. High-technology research is also prominent at that university and at Iowa State University.

Private higher education is important in Iowa. Coe, Cornell, and Grinnell Colleges are typical of the small private institutions throughout the state.

DEMOGRAPHICS

Population: 2,776,755   (Rank: 30)

Age distribution:
Up to 17 .... 25.9%
18 to 24 .... 10.2%
25 to 44 .... 29.7%
45 and older 34.2%

Racial and ethnic distribution:
American Indian 0.3%
Asian 0.9%
Black 1.7%
White 96.6%
Other and unknown 0.5%
Hispanic (may be any race) .. 1.2%

Educational attainment of adults:
At least 4 years of high school 71.5%
At least 1 to 3 years of college 28.6%
At least 4 years of college ... 13.9%

Per-capita personal income: $17,218

Poverty rate: 10.0%

New high-school graduates in:
1991-92 (estimate) 30,788
2001-02 (estimate) 30,865

New GED diploma recipients: 5,027

High-school dropout rate: 14.2%

POLITICAL LEADERSHIP

Governor: Terry E. Branstad (R), term ends 1995

Governor's higher-education aide: Phillip Dunshee, State House, Des Moines 50319; (515) 281-5211

U.S. Senators: Charles E. Grassley

(R), term ends 1993; Tom Harkin (D), term ends 1997

U.S. Representatives:
2 Democrats, 4 Republicans
Fred Grandy (R), Jim Leach (R), Jim Lightfoot (R), David R. Nagle (D), Jim Nussle (R), Neal Smith (D)

General Assembly: Senate, 28 Democrats, 22 Republicans; House, 55 Democrats, 45 Republicans

COLLEGES AND UNIVERSITIES

Higher education:
Public 4-year institutions 3
Public 2-year institutions 15
Private 4-year institutions 34
Private 2-year institutions 6
Total 58

Vocational institutions: 77

Statewide coordinating boards:
State Board of Regents
East 12th Street and Grand Avenue
Old State Historical Building
Des Moines 50319
(515) 281-3934
R. Wayne Richey, executive director

Board of Education
Division of Community Colleges
East 14th Street and Grand Avenue
Grimes State Office Building
Des Moines 50319
(515) 281-8260
Joann Horton, administrator

Private-college association:
Iowa Association of Independent Colleges and Universities
307 Equitable Building
604 Locust Street

Des Moines 50309
(515) 282-3175
John V. Hartung, president

Institution censured by the AAUP:
University of Osteopathic Medicine and Health Sciences

Institutions under NCAA sanctions:
None

FACULTY MEMBERS

Full-time faculty members by rank:
Professor 1,558
Associate professor 1,109
Assistant professor 1,312
Instructor 553
Lecturer 6
No rank 569
Total 5,107

Average pay of full-time professors:
At public 4-year institutions $45,619
At public 2-year institutions $29,047
At private 4-year institutions $32,499
At private 2-year institutions $26,936
At all institutions $38,028
Men (all institutions) $40,818
Women (all institutions) $31,388

STUDENTS

Enrollment:
Total 169,901
At public 4-year institutions . 68,221
At public 2-year institutions . 48,668
At private 4-year institutions 50,955
At private 2-year institutions . 2,057
Undergraduate 142,936
 First-time freshmen 37,583
Graduate 21,218
Professional 5,747
American Indian 457
Asian 2,056
Black 3,511
Hispanic 1,402

IOWA
Continued

White 147,933
Foreign 5,815

Enrollment highlights:
Women 53.0%
Full-time 70.1%
Minority 4.8%
Foreign 3.6%
10-year change in total
  enrollment .... Up 28.1%

Proportion of enrollment made up of minority students:
At public 4-year institutions .. 5.0%
At public 2-year institutions .. 4.6%
At private 4-year institutions . 4.6%
At private 2-year institutions . 5.4%

Degrees awarded:
Associate 8,145
Bachelor's 16,859
Master's 3,218
Doctorate 574
Professional 1,489

Residence of new students: State residents made up 83% of all freshmen enrolled in Iowa; 88% of all Iowa residents who were freshmen attended college in their home state.

Test scores: Students averaged 20.1 on the A.C.T., which was taken by 60% of Iowa's high-school seniors.

MONEY

Average tuition and fees:
At public 4-year institutions . $1,823
At public 2-year institutions . $1,225
At private 4-year institutions $7,945
At private 2-year institutions $6,423

Expenditures:
Public institutions .. $1,092,542,000
Private institutions ... $353,753,000

State funds for higher-education operating expenses: $563,570,000
Two-year change: Up 7%

State spending on student aid:
Need-based: $37,748,000;
  22,442 awards
Non–need-based: $904,000;
  1,308 awards
Other: $1,517,000

Salary of chief executive of largest public 4-year campus:
Hunter R. Rawlings III, University of Iowa: $164,000

Total spending on research and development by doctorate-granting universities: $232,147,000
Sources:
Federal government 48.8%
State and local governments . 12.7%
Industry 5.3%
The institution itself 29.0%
Other 4.2%

Federal spending on education and student aid (selected programs):
Vocational and
  adult education $15,100,000
GI Bill $4,253,000
Pell Grants $63,462,000

Total federal spending on college- and university-based research and development: $103,214,000
Selected programs:
Department of Health
  and Human Services $60,763,000
National Science
  Foundation $8,028,000
Department of Defense . $3,630,000
Department
  of Agriculture $11,510,000

Department of Energy .. $1,208,000

Largest endowment:
Grinnell College $286,770,000

Top fund raisers:
University of Iowa $32,251,000
Iowa State University . $21,046,000
Drake University $10,214,000

MISCELLANY

■ Four Japanese manufacturers of facsimile machines have agreed to pay royalties to Iowa State University after the institution's research foundation notified some 30 manufacturers and distributors of the machines that it held the patent on an essential part of the devices. Foundation officials have not said how much the four companies agreed to pay.

■ Grinnell College has established an academic program to prepare students for volunteer service in developing countries. The Peace Corps Preparatory Program is designed to enhance student involvement in the corps and other international programs after graduation. In addition to the courses, students participate in a variety of activities such as teaching English as a second language.

■ The Iowa Women's Archives will be established at the University of Iowa with proceeds of the sale of "Self-Portrait with Loose Hair," a painting by the Mexican artist Frida Kahlo. The painting's former owner, Louise R. Noun, gave the university $1.5-million from the sale.

■ The oldest higher-education institution in Iowa is Loras College, a Roman Catholic institution founded in 1839.

KANSAS

KANSAS'S NEW GOVERNOR, Joan Finney, a Democrat, seems determined to keep her pledge not to increase taxes—even though many college officials would be happy to see her break it.

She vetoed a package of sales- and income-tax increases passed by legislators in 1991. Many in higher education fear that when those tax proposals died, so did the momentum the state was building in its drive to improve postsecondary education.

Kansas embarked on a three-year plan in 1987 to raise faculty salaries and improve facilities and the quality of instruction. The plan, "Margin of Excellence," had broad support. During her 1990 campaign, Ms. Finney promised to back the effort.

But she has been unwilling to change her tax policies to find more money for the program. Furthermore, some lawmakers in 1991 began to question how the public institutions were spending the additional allocations they had already received.

As a result, the Board of Regents is now back where it was in the mid-1980's, when the colleges were complaining of inadequate funds after the state's farm economy went into decline.

Eliminating programs and duplication is a difficult task. The president of Kansas State University dropped a plan to cancel several programs in the College of Human Ecology and the College of Architecture and Design after protests by as many as 2,000 students and professors.

While the regents have raised the hopes of many in Kansas for a high-quality university system, they have

KANSAS
Continued

failed to meet their goal of setting admission standards for the state's public institutions. Legislators cite the state's strong populist traditions each time they reject proposals to end the policy of admitting all high-school graduates.

The Board of Regents serves as the coordinating board for all higher education in Kansas and as the governing board for the six state universities.

In 1991 the Legislature approved the merger of the Kansas College of Technology, a two-year technical institute, with Kansas State University. The college was renamed Kansas State University at Salina. Students will be able to complete two-year and four-year degree programs in engineering technology at the former technical institute.

The community colleges are governed by local boards under the supervision of the state's Board of Education.

DEMOGRAPHICS

Population: 2,477,574   (Rank: 32)

Age distribution:
Up to 17 .... 26.7%
18 to 24 .... 10.3%
25 to 44 .... 31.3%
45 and older 31.7%

Racial and ethnic distribution:
American Indian 0.9%
Asian 1.3%
Black 5.8%
White 90.1%
Other and unknown 2.0%
Hispanic (may be any race) .. 3.8%

Educational attainment of adults:
At least 4 years of high school   73.3%
At least 1 to 3 years of college   34.2%
At least 4 years of college ...   17.0%

Per-capita personal income: $18,162

Poverty rate: 9.7%

New high-school graduates in:
1991-92 (estimate) 25,671
2001-02 (estimate) 30,376

New GED diploma recipients: 5,489

High-school dropout rate: 19.8%

POLITICAL LEADERSHIP

Governor: Joan Finney (D), term ends 1995

Governor's higher-education aide: Ladislado M. Hernandez, Capitol Building, Room 252 East, Topeka 66612; (913) 296-1773

U.S. Senators: Bob Dole (R), term ends 1993; Nancy Landon Kassebaum (R), term ends 1997

U.S. Representatives:
2 Democrats, 3 Republicans
Dan Glickman (D), Jan Meyers (R), Dick Nichols (R), Pat Roberts (R), Jim Slattery (D)

Legislature: Senate, 18 Democrats, 22 Republicans; House, 63 Democrats, 62 Republicans

COLLEGES AND UNIVERSITIES

Higher education:
Public 4-year institutions 8
Public 2-year institutions 21
Private 4-year institutions 22
Private 2-year institutions 3

Total 54

Vocational institutions: 76

Statewide coordinating board:
Kansas Board of Regents
Capitol Tower
Suite 609
Topeka 66603
(913) 296-3421
Stanley Z. Koplik, executive director

Private-college association:
Kansas Independent
 College Association
Capitol Federal Building, Room 515
700 Kansas Avenue
Topeka 66603
(913) 235-9877
Robert N. Kelly, executive director

Institutions censured by the AAUP:
None

Institutions under NCAA sanctions:
None

FACULTY MEMBERS

Full-time faculty members by rank:
Professor 1,263
Associate professor 1,027
Assistant professor 1,055
Instructor 264
Lecturer 16
No rank 1,104
Total 4,729

Average pay of full-time professors:
At public 4-year institutions $39,129
At public 2-year institutions $29,453
At private 4-year institutions $24,238
At private 2-year institutions $19,878
At all institutions $34,629
Men (all institutions) $37,057
Women (all institutions) $28,814

STUDENTS

Enrollment:
Total 158,497
At public 4-year institutions . 89,180
At public 2-year institutions . 55,954
At private 4-year institutions 12,461
At private 2-year institutions .. 902
Undergraduate 137,164
 First-time freshmen 26,915
Graduate 19,134
Professional 2,199
American Indian 1,826
Asian 2,089
Black 6,300
Hispanic 2,910
White 134,878
Foreign 4,844

Enrollment highlights:
Women 55.0%
Full-time 56.9%
Minority 8.9%
Foreign 3.2%
10-year change in total
 enrollment .... Up 21.2%

Proportion of enrollment made up of minority students:
At public 4-year institutions .. 7.4%
At public 2-year institutions . 10.1%
At private 4-year institutions 11.6%
At private 2-year institutions 31.9%

Degrees awarded:
Associate 5,171
Bachelor's 12,189
Master's 3,132
Doctorate 379
Professional 590

Residence of new students: State residents made up 82% of all freshmen enrolled in Kansas; 90% of all Kansas residents who were freshmen attended college in their home state.

KANSAS
Continued

Test scores: Students averaged 19.1 on the A.C.T., which was taken by 66% of Kansas' high-school seniors.

MONEY

Average tuition and fees:
At public 4-year institutions . $1,467
At public 2-year institutions .. $711
At private 4-year institutions $5,460
At private 2-year institutions $3,962

Expenditures:
Public institutions $848,602,000
Private institutions ... $105,193,000

State funds for higher-education operating expenses: $446,517,000

Two-year change: Up 3%

State spending on student aid:
Need-based: $6,585,000; 4,492 awards
Non–need-based: $31,000; 78 awards
Other: $50,000

Salary of chief executive of largest public 4-year campus:
Gene A. Budig, University of Kansas: $135,000

Total spending on research and development by doctorate-granting universities: $114,651,000
Sources:
Federal government 37.9%
State and local governments . 22.3%
Industry 6.6%
The institution itself 29.2%
Other 4.0%

Federal spending on education and student aid (selected programs):
Vocational and
 adult education $11,877,000
GI Bill $4,504,000
Pell Grants $56,490,000

Total federal spending on college- and university-based research and development: $39,105,000
Selected programs:
Department of Health
 and Human Services $17,835,000
National Science
 Foundation $5,306,000
Department of Defense . $1,668,000
Department
 of Agriculture $4,837,000
Department of Energy .. $2,346,000

Largest endowment:
Kansas University Endowment
 Association $226,008,000

Top fund raisers:
University of Kansas .. $23,670,000
Kansas State University $13,177,000
Pittsburg State University $3,138,000

MISCELLANY

■ The One-Room Rural Schoolhouse on Emporia State University's campus is the temporary site of the National Teachers Hall of Fame. The permanent facility, which will also be at Emporia State, is scheduled to be completed in 1993. The first members of the hall of fame were inducted in November 1991.

■ The oldest higher-education institution in Kansas is Highland Community College, which was chartered in 1857. The oldest four-year university in the state is Baker University, a United Methodist institution, which received its charter just three days after Highland did.

KENTUCKY

KENTUCKY LAW gives the Governor ultimate control of the purse strings and a great deal of power over the rest of the state's political process, and under the stewardship of Wallace G. Wilkinson, that has been a mixed blessing for higher education.

Mr. Wilkinson, a Democrat who by law was required to leave office in December 1991, has drawn national praise for his 1990 program to improve public-school teaching and make financing for school districts across the state more equitable.

For higher education, the plan and the accompanying tax increase have meant more money for new buildings and general operations—and new attention. The General Assembly has asked all colleges and universities in the state to work with the schools in developing new curricula and management practices.

Already, the University of Kentucky and Western Kentucky University have responded by creating institutes for school reform, and Murray State University has announced it will create special incentives to encourage faculty members to work in the public schools.

Private colleges in the state, which are mostly small, church-related institutions, have also been invited to assist the public schools.

Colleges have a lot at stake in the success of the school-reform plan. According to the latest available figures, only about 21 per cent of all 18- to 24-year-olds in Kentucky attended college in 1987—a figure among the lowest for Southern states and well below the national figure of 26.5 per cent.

Mr. Wilkinson has also been a supporter of Kentucky Educational Television, and on the national scene he is championing the idea of using telecommunications for distance learning.

But back home in the Bluegrass State, the former Governor's reputation suffered from charges of political favoritism in his appointments to college governing boards. Many of those he has named have contributed to his political campaign (and to that of his wife, Martha, who was briefly a candidate in the spring 1991 Democratic gubernatorial primary).

Mr. Wilkinson was also criticized for his overt efforts in getting his friend Charles T. Wethington, Jr., named to the UK presidency in the fall of 1990. Mr. Wethington was then chancellor of the community-college system, which consists of 14 colleges and is under the auspices of the University of Kentucky.

Mr. Wilkinson's successor, Brereton Jones, has endorsed the idea of having appointees to the governing board screened by a nominating commission. A single board governs the University of Kentucky and its community-college system, and seven other public colleges are governed by their own boards.

Mr. Jones was previously the Lieutenant Governor. During his campaign, he pledged that he would create a state council to bring business and education leaders together to share ideas for improving both the economy and colleges and universities.

Regional and racial politics have been a tradition in Kentucky higher education. Kentucky State University, the historically black institution, has long complained that it does not receive enough money from the state. Backers of the University of Louisville, in the state's major urban center,

KENTUCKY
Continued

say their institution has the same problem.

The Kentucky Council on Higher Education is the statewide coordinating board.

DEMOGRAPHICS

Population: 3,685,296 (Rank: 23)

Age distribution:
Up to 17 .... 25.9%
18 to 24 .... 10.9%
25 to 44 .... 31.5%
45 and older 31.7%

Racial and ethnic distribution:
American Indian 0.2%
Asian 0.5%
Black 7.1%
White 92.0%
Other and unknown 0.2%
Hispanic (may be any race) .. 0.6%

Educational attainment of adults:
At least 4 years of high school 53.1%
At least 1 to 3 years of college 21.8%
At least 4 years of college ... 11.1%

Per-capita personal income: $15,001

Poverty rate: 17.0%

New high-school graduates in:
1991-92 (estimate) 36,692
2001-02 (estimate) 38,352

New GED diploma recipients: 11,822

High-school dropout rate: 31.0%

POLITICAL LEADERSHIP

Governor: Brereton C. Jones (D), term ends 1995

Governor's higher-education aide: n/a

U.S. Senators: Wendell H. Ford (D), term ends 1993; Mitch McConnell (R), term ends 1997

U.S. Representatives:
4 Democrats, 3 Republicans
Jim Bunning (R), Larry J. Hopkins (R), Carroll Hubbard, Jr. (D), Romano L. Mazzoli (D), William H. Natcher (D), Carl C. Perkins (D), Harold Rogers (R)

General Assembly: Senate, 27 Democrats, 11 Republicans; House, 68 Democrats, 32 Republicans

COLLEGES AND UNIVERSITIES

Higher education:
Public 4-year institutions 8
Public 2-year institutions 14
Private 4-year institutions 24
Private 2-year institutions 13
Total 59

Vocational institutions: 131

Statewide coordinating board:
Council on Higher Education
1050 U.S. 127 South, Suite 101
Frankfort 40601
(502) 564-3553
Gary S. Cox, executive director

Private-college association:
Council of Independent Kentucky Colleges and Universities
P.O. Box 668
Danville 40423
(606) 236-3533
John W. Frazer, executive director

Institution censured by the AAUP:
Murray State University

Institution under NCAA sanctions:
University of Kentucky

FACULTY MEMBERS

Full-time faculty members by rank:
Professor 1,504
Associate professor 1,455
Assistant professor 1,445
Instructor 531
Lecturer 50
No rank 45
Total 5,030

Average pay of full-time professors:
At public 4-year institutions $35,739
At public 2-year institutions $26,596
At private 4-year institutions $28,287
At private 2-year institutions $17,797
At all institutions $32,714
Men (all institutions) $35,052
Women (all institutions) $28,339

STUDENTS

Enrollment:
Total 166,014
At public 4-year institutions 102,332
At public 2-year institutions . 34,965
At private 4-year institutions 22,261
At private 2-year institutions . 6,456
Undergraduate 145,315
   First-time freshmen 30,242
Graduate 17,307
Professional 3,392
American Indian 427
Asian 1,078
Black 9,296
Hispanic 683
White 146,703
Foreign 1,681

Enrollment highlights:
Women 57.6%
Full-time 63.9%
Minority 7.3%
Foreign 1.1%

10-year change in total
  enrollment .... Up 22.8%

Proportion of enrollment made up of minority students:
At public 4-year institutions .. 7.5%
At public 2-year institutions .. 8.0%
At private 4-year institutions . 4.0%
At private 2-year institutions 11.4%

Degrees awarded:
Associate 4,938
Bachelor's 12,337
Master's 3,491
Doctorate 332
Professional 1,167

Residence of new students: State residents made up 88% of all freshmen enrolled in Kentucky; 90% of all Kentucky residents who were freshmen attended college in their home state.

Test scores: Students averaged 17.8 on the A.C.T., which was taken by 58% of Kentucky's high-school seniors.

MONEY

Average tuition and fees:
At public 4-year institutions . $1,316
At public 2-year institutions .. $693
At private 4-year institutions $4,689
At private 2-year institutions $4,669

Expenditures:
Public institutions $898,718,000
Private institutions ... $194,873,000

State funds for higher-education operating expenses: $674,327,000

Two-year change: Up 23%

State spending on student aid:
Need-based: $19,393,000;
  27,400 awards

KENTUCKY
Continued

Non–need-based: None
Other: None

Salary of chief executive of largest public 4-year campus:
Donald C. Swain, University of Louisville: $137,461

Total spending on research and development by doctorate-granting universities: $90,880,000
Sources:
Federal government 42.1%
State and local governments .. 7.4%
Industry 8.9%
The institution itself 36.6%
Other 5.0%

Federal spending on education and student aid (selected programs):
Vocational and
  adult education $23,678,000
GI Bill $5,240,000
Pell Grants $71,405,000

Total federal spending on college- and university-based research and development: $36,140,000
Selected programs:
Department of Health
  and Human Services $19,811,000
National Science
  Foundation $3,496,000
Department of Defense . $1,000,000
Department
  of Agriculture $8,255,000
Department of Energy .. $2,220,000

Largest endowment:
Berea College $271,114,000

Top fund raisers:
University of Kentucky $19,600,000
Berea College $14,645,000
University of Louisville $10,433,000

MISCELLANY

■ Spalding University holds the "Running of the Rodents" each year in the week before the Kentucky Derby. Students painstakingly train eight rats to run around a miniature version of Churchill Downs.

■ Graduating seniors at the University of Kentucky dedicated a book-buying campaign to the Chinese students who died in Tiananmen Square in 1989. The campaign was also part of the students' graduation gift to the university. The students bought library books inscribed with the names of donors as part of the university's $55-million campaign to build a new collection on its Lexington campus.

■ The oldest higher-education institution in the state is Transylvania University, founded in 1780. Kentucky's 1857-58 legislature repealed the bill establishing Transylvania as a university, and it operated until 1865 as a high school. Since then it has been a liberal-arts college.

LOUISIANA

IN 1990 the Louisiana Board of Regents adopted a three-year plan to bring faculty salaries up to the regional average. The Governor and legislators applauded the proposal and gave faculty members their first substantial raise in years.

But if 1990 was a year for rejoicing,

1991 made higher-education officials cringe.

Higher-education officials said the 1990 appropriations bill spelled out a commitment to give faculty members three consecutive annual raises of 12 per cent. But the Legislature only financed a 5-per-cent increase in 1991.

Furthermore, the 1991 Governor's race was one of the most heated battles in Louisiana history. Gov. Buddy Roemer, a long-time Democrat who turned Republican, was ousted in the primary. That left voters to choose between Republican David Duke, a former Ku Klux Klan leader, and Democrat Edwin W. Edwards, who had served three previous terms as Governor.

The prospect that a former Klan leader could be the next Governor sent a chill through many college officials, who said the state would have difficulty attracting outstanding scholars, especially ones from minority groups, if Mr. Duke won. Officials at several historically black institutions used buses to transport students to the polls on Election Day.

In the end, Mr. Edwards won by a large margin. He served as Governor from 1972 to 1980 and from 1984 to 1988. During those terms he was a strong supporter of historically black colleges, and he has pledged to continue that backing. In addition, he says he will call a state Constitutional Convention to study state financing and the need for tax reform.

Former Governor Roemer saw several of his tax-reform proposals defeated by the voters. And his efforts to reorganize higher education were repeatedly rejected by legislators.

Mr. Roemer was thwarted in his attempts to deal with two long-standing problems: the segregation of Louisiana's public institutions and the debate about the structure of higher education.

In 1990 a federal judge threw out a court order directing the state to desegregate its colleges. The order, issued in 1989, mirrored a proposal supported by Mr. Roemer. The order required the state to eliminate its coordinating board and its three boards for college and university systems. The boards would have been replaced with a single governing body. Both Mr. Roemer's plan and the court order were opposed by Southern University, the nation's only historically black university system.

Although the order was withdrawn, Mr. Roemer continued his fight in the Legislature for a single board. And Southern University continued its campaign against the idea, arguing that the new board would ignore the interests of black students.

Another major higher-education issue in Louisiana is admission standards. The state's strong populist tradition has led most public institutions to operate on an open-admission basis that critics say has filled the campuses with people who are not prepared to do college-level work.

Louisiana State University adopted admission standards in 1988. Now, fewer students need remedial courses and more students are graduating. But the size of the freshman class is shrinking. The enrollment decline is cutting into the institution's budget and its board is trying to decide whether to lower the standards.

Although the vast majority of Louisiana's students attend public colleges, the state also has private institutions that exert considerable political influence. Tulane University has long been regarded as a leader, and Dillard and Xavier Universities are respected black institutions.

LOUISIANA
Continued

DEMOGRAPHICS

Population: 4,219,973 (Rank: 21)

Age distribution:
Up to 17 .... 29.1%
18 to 24 .... 11.0%
25 to 44 .... 31.0%
45 and older 28.9%

Racial and ethnic distribution:
American Indian 0.4%
Asian 1.0%
Black 30.8%
White 67.3%
Other and unknown 0.5%
Hispanic (may be any race) .. 2.2%

Educational attainment of adults:
At least 4 years of high school 57.7%
At least 1 to 3 years of college 26.7%
At least 4 years of college ... 13.9%

Per-capita personal income: $14,542

Poverty rate: 23.2%

New high-school graduates in:
1991-92 (estimate) 41,494
2001-02 (estimate) 48,138

New GED diploma recipients: 6,874

High-school dropout rate: 38.6%

POLITICAL LEADERSHIP

Governor: Edwin W. Edwards (D), term ends 1996

Governor's higher-education aide: n/a

U.S. Senators: John B. Breaux (D), term ends 1993; J. Bennett Johnston (D), term ends 1997

U.S. Representatives:
4 Democrats, 4 Republicans
Richard H. Baker (R), James A. Hayes (D), Clyde C. Holloway (R), Jerry Huckaby (D), William J. Jefferson (D), Bob Livingston (R), Jim McCrery (R), W.J. (Billy) Tauzin (D)

Legislature: Senate, 34 Democrats, 5 Republicans; House, 88 Democrats, 16 Republicans, 1 Independent

COLLEGES AND UNIVERSITIES

Higher education:
Public 4-year institutions 14
Public 2-year institutions 6
Private 4-year institutions 10
Private 2-year institutions 4
Total 34

Vocational institutions: 196

Statewide coordinating board:
Louisiana Board of Regents
150 Riverside Mall
Suite 129
Baton Rouge 70801
(504) 342-4253
Sammie W. Cosper, commissioner of higher education

Private-college association:
Louisiana Association of Independent Colleges and Universities
320 Riverside Mall, Suite 104
Baton Rouge 70801
(504) 389-9885
William Arceneaux, president

Institutions censured by the AAUP: None

Institutions under NCAA sanctions:
Louisiana State University,
Northwestern State University,
Southeastern Louisiana University

FACULTY MEMBERS

Full-time faculty members by rank:
Professor 1,451
Associate professor 1,570
Assistant professor 1,883
Instructor 846
Lecturer 11
No rank 60
Total 5,821

Average pay of full-time professors:
At public 4-year institutions $32,579
At public 2-year institutions $26,641
At private 4-year institutions $38,664
At private 2-year institutions ... n/a
At all institutions $33,275
Men (all institutions) $36,194
Women (all institutions) $27,837

STUDENTS

Enrollment:
Total 179,927
At public 4-year institutions 133,856
At public 2-year institutions . 17,877
At private 4-year institutions 25,859
At private 2-year institutions . 2,335
Undergraduate 154,376
   First-time freshmen 29,415
Graduate 19,879
Professional 5,672
American Indian 624
Asian 2,507
Black 41,213
Hispanic 3,283
White 123,362
Foreign 5,042

Enrollment highlights:
Women 56.0%
Full-time 72.4%
Minority 27.9%
Foreign 2.9%
10-year change in total
   enrollment .... Up 17.0%

Proportion of enrollment made up of minority students:
At public 4-year institutions . 27.0%
At public 2-year institutions . 31.7%
At private 4-year institutions 29.1%
At private 2-year institutions 38.4%

Degrees awarded:
Associate 2,542
Bachelor's 16,210
Master's 3,859
Doctorate 384
Professional 1,505

Residence of new students: State residents made up 83% of all freshmen enrolled in Louisiana; 87% of all Louisiana residents who were freshmen attended college in their home state.

Test scores: Students averaged 17.1 on the A.C.T., which was taken by 62% of Louisiana's high-school seniors.

MONEY

Average tuition and fees:
At public 4-year institutions . $1,768
At public 2-year institutions .. $837
At private 4-year institutions $9,257
At private 2-year institutions $5,648

Expenditures:
Public institutions .. $1,039,177,000
Private institutions ... $353,433,000

State funds for higher-education operating expenses: $574,336,000
Two-year change: Up 9%

State spending on student aid:
Need-based: $4,196,000; 4,292 awards

LOUISIANA
Continued

Non–need-based: $770,000;
1,833 awards
Other: None

Salary of chief executive of largest public 4-year campus:
William E. Davis, Louisiana State University: $121,500

Total spending on research and development by doctorate-granting universities: $207,038,000
Sources:
Federal government 40.0%
State and local governments . 21.1%
Industry 4.9%
The institution itself 26.6%
Other 7.4%

Federal spending on education and student aid (selected programs):
Vocational and
  adult education $27,528,000
GI Bill $8,389,000
Pell Grants $118,124,000

Total federal spending on college- and university-based research and development: $100,418,000
Selected programs:
Department of Health
  and Human Services $42,121,000
National Science
  Foundation $7,157,000
Department of Defense $36,373,000
Department
  of Agriculture $5,501,000
Department of Energy .. $3,136,000

Largest endowment:
Tulane University $233,417,000

Top fund raisers:
Tulane University $22,845,000

Centenary College
  of Louisiana $4,835,000
Xavier University
  of Louisiana $4,815,000

MISCELLANY

■ Tulane University's Center for Bioenvironmental Research has received $1-million from Freeport-McMoRan, a New Orleans–based petroleum and mining company. The money is being used to establish an endowed professorship in environmental policy, finance a series of lectures on environmental-policy formulation, and sponsor an international conference on environmental policy that is tentatively scheduled for fall 1992.

■ Xavier University was second in the nation in placing black students in medical school, according to the Association of American Medical Colleges. Only Howard University, with an undergraduate enrollment four times as large, produced more.

■ In spring 1991, for the first time, students at predominantly white Louisiana State University and historically black Southern University published a joint issue of the institutions' student newspapers.

■ Dillard University, a historically black institution, offers a program each summer in which Japanese high-school students learn English and study issues related to cultural and ethnic diversity in the United States.

■ The oldest higher-education institution in the state is Centenary College of Louisiana. It is affiliated with the United Methodist Church and was founded in 1825.

MAINE

IN THE 1980'S, with generous budget increases, Maine lawmakers fueled a campaign to improve public higher education.

In the most recent analysis of state support for higher education, conducted by the Center for Higher Education at Illinois State University, Maine ranked second in the percentage increase in appropriations over the last 10 years.

But now the state's economy is in a recession and an official of the University of Maine System says, "Everyone realizes we have to batten down the hatches and ride out this storm."

Gov. John R. McKernan, Jr., a Republican serving his second term, was one of many governors around the nation who decided in 1991 that a tax increase was the only way to balance the budget and avoid debilitating cuts in services.

The University of Maine System includes almost all public institutions, and its governing board also functions as the state's coordinating board for higher education. Despite the recent economic troubles, officials of the system remain optimistic about efforts to attract more Maine residents to higher education.

They also hope some of the university's research projects could lead to new business for the state. For example, engineers at the University of Maine are making advances in preserving wood fibers and in structural engineering that could lead to the development of timber bridges to replace thousands of old and unsafe rural bridges across the country.

Maine lawmakers will have a difficult time, however, balancing the financial needs of various programs until the state's revenues improve.

The cost of higher education in Maine is a long-standing concern. The strength of the state's private institutions has led Maine to offer generous student-aid programs. Maine is among the New England states in which the private institutions of higher education are older and more prestigious than the public colleges and universities. Bates, Bowdoin, and Colby Colleges, for instance, all have national reputations and predate the University of Maine.

Meanwhile, competition between the system's flagship campus in Orono and the University of Southern Maine continues to be a problem for lawmakers and higher-education officials alike. Orono faculty members fear the growth at Southern Maine will come at the expense of their own programs, while there is pressure at Southern Maine for new programs to serve Portland, the state's largest city.

DEMOGRAPHICS

Population: 1,227,928   (Rank: 38)

Age distribution:
Up to 17	25.2%
18 to 24	10.1%
25 to 44	32.5%
45 and older	32.2%

Racial and ethnic distribution:
American Indian	0.5%
Asian	0.5%
Black	0.4%
White	98.4%
Other and unknown	0.1%
Hispanic (may be any race)	0.6%

Educational attainment of adults:
At least 4 years of high school 68.7%

MAINE
Continued

At least 1 to 3 years of college 29.4%
At least 4 years of college ... 14.4%

Per-capita personal income: $17,175

Poverty rate: 12.2%

New high-school graduates in:
1991-92 (estimate) 13,533
2001-02 (estimate) 14,381

New GED diploma recipients: 3,415

High-school dropout rate: 25.6%

POLITICAL LEADERSHIP

Governor: John R. McKernan, Jr. (R), term ends 1995

Governor's higher-education aide:
Fred Douglas, State House, Station 23, Augusta 04333; (207) 289-5800

U.S. Senators: William S. Cohen (R), term ends 1997; George J. Mitchell (D), term ends 1995

U.S. Representatives:
1 Democrat, 1 Republican
Thomas H. Andrews (D), Olympia J. Snowe (R)

Legislature: Senate, 22 Democrats, 13 Republicans; House, 97 Democrats, 54 Republicans

COLLEGES AND UNIVERSITIES

Higher education:
Public 4-year institutions 8
Public 2-year institutions 5
Private 4-year institutions 13
Private 2-year institutions 5
Total 31

Vocational institutions: 22

Statewide coordinating board:
University of Maine System
Board of Trustees
107 Maine Avenue
Bangor 04401
(207) 947-0336
Robert L. Woodbury, chancellor

Private-college association:
Maine Independent College and University Association
Thomas College
West River Road
Waterville 04901
(207) 873-0771
George R. Spann, president

Institution censured by the AAUP:
Husson College

Institutions under NCAA sanctions:
None

FACULTY MEMBERS

Full-time faculty members by rank:
Professor 478
Associate professor 533
Assistant professor 588
Instructor 67
Lecturer 27
No rank 242
Total 1,935

Average pay of full-time professors:
At public 4-year institutions $38,389
At public 2-year institutions $28,683
At private 4-year institutions $36,923
At private 2-year institutions $27,740
At all institutions $36,794
Men (all institutions) $39,021
Women (all institutions) $31,618

STUDENTS

Enrollment:
Total 58,230
At public 4-year institutions . 34,233
At public 2-year institutions .. 6,278
At private 4-year institutions 16,277
At private 2-year institutions . 1,442
Undergraduate 53,275
  First-time freshmen 9,484
Graduate 4,326
Professional 629
American Indian 235
Asian 260
Black 263
Hispanic 135
White 46,748
Foreign 262

Enrollment highlights:
Women 59.0%
Full-time 54.2%
Minority 1.9%
Foreign 0.5%
10-year change in total
  enrollment .... Up 35.7%

Proportion of enrollment made up of minority students:
At public 4-year institutions .. 1.5%
At public 2-year institutions .. 1.2%
At private 4-year institutions . 3.5%
At private 2-year institutions . 1.1%

Degrees awarded:
Associate 1,884
Bachelor's 5,173
Master's 633
Doctorate 36
Professional 139

Residence of new students: State residents made up 71% of all freshmen enrolled in Maine; 70% of all Maine residents who were freshmen attended college in their home state.

Test scores: Students averaged 879 on the S.A.T., which was taken by 64% of Maine's high-school seniors.

MONEY

Average tuition and fees:
At public 4-year institutions . $1,980
At public 2-year institutions . $1,134
At private 4-year institutions $10,425
At private 2-year institutions $3,787

Expenditures:
Public institutions $216,737,000
Private institutions ... $133,778,000

State funds for higher-education operating expenses: $186,664,000
Two-year change: Up 8%

State spending on student aid:
Need-based: $5,100,000; 8,000 awards
Non–need-based: None
Other: None

Salary of chief executive of largest public 4-year campus:
John C. Hitt (interim), University
  of Maine at Orono: $115,000

Total spending on research and development by doctorate-granting universities: $23,605,000
Sources:
Federal government 38.3%
State and local governments .. 3.8%
Industry 19.8%
The institution itself 35.0%
Other 3.1%

Federal spending on education and student aid (selected programs):
Vocational and
  adult education $7,037,000
GI Bill $1,709,000
Pell Grants $13,336,000

MAINE
Continued

Total federal spending on college- and university-based research and development: $9,090,000

Selected programs:
Department of Health
　and Human Services ... $902,000
National Science
　Foundation $1,656,000
Department of Defense ... $176,000
Department
　of Agriculture $2,843,000
Department of Energy 0

Largest endowment:
Bowdoin College $151,744,000

Top fund raisers:
Bowdoin College $14,466,000
University of Maine
　at Orono $11,716,000
Bates College $5,388,000

MISCELLANY

■ The University of Maine is helping to set up the first American university in Eastern Europe, the American University of Blagoevgrad in Bulgaria. The first classes started in fall 1991.

■ The student center at Unity College has been fitted with the solar-energy panels that heated the White House dining room during the Presidency of Jimmy Carter and were later warehoused. Unity, which focuses on environmental studies, also heats a campus building with the experimental Dover Stove, which burns waste for fuel.

■ Bowdoin is the oldest higher-education institution in Maine. It was founded in 1794.

MARYLAND

SINCE William Donald Schaefer became Governor in 1987, change has been the only constant in Maryland higher education.

Starting with a major reorganization of public colleges that brought all but two of the state's four-year institutions under the University of Maryland System, Governor Schaefer seems intent on shaking up every corner of the education establishment.

His hand-picked Secretary of Higher Education, Shaila R. Aery, and an activist Commission on Higher Education have been instrumental in many of the changes. Included in the reforms are the adoption of a new formula to increase financing of the state's 19 community colleges and a new financial-aid program that eventually will shift more resources to the state's neediest students. The program includes financial aid for part-time students, who now account for 53 per cent of Maryland's student body.

In 1992, a proposal to revamp the training of teachers by eliminating education as an undergraduate major and requiring a fifth year in an internship—is expected to be debated throughout the state.

All the activity has not, however, obscured some of Maryland's most persistent higher-education concerns. If anything, reaction to the commission's recent proposals, calling for mergers of institutions in Baltimore, only highlights the complexities.

For example, some black legislators—and others who want to improve the educational attainment of black Marylanders—questioned the idea of merging Morgan State University and Coppin State College, two of the state's four historically black institutions. Although the merger proposal was quickly dismissed, black-college supporters said it showed the state's readiness to retreat from its promise to redress the effects of past illegal segregation. Maryland officials are still under a federal court order to desegregate their higher-education system, but want to be released from it.

The other proposed merger—of two University of Maryland institutions that would then focus on science, health, and technology—worries partisans of the flagship campus at College Park, who fear the political clout of a stronger, research-oriented institution in Baltimore.

While the commission, college presidents, and legislators thrash out those issues, an even bigger challenge remains: finding the money to pay for the new financing formulas, scholarships, and enhanced programs. Higher-education leaders have estimated they will need an additional $550-million over the next five years to carry out plans that already have been approved.

Lawmakers were very generous to education when the economy was flourishing, but times have changed in recent years. When revenues fell in 1991-92 and in the previous academic year, Governor Schaefer ordered midyear cuts in college budgets. Although there is talk of new taxes, the prospects for major increases in state support are uncertain.

Maryland is one of the few states that provide direct aid to private colleges. The amount of money that goes to private colleges is based in part on the level of state financing for public institutions in the previous year, and private colleges often join public institutions in lobbying the General Assembly for state funds.

The private institutions are well organized politically and wield considerable clout in the legislature as a group, and in some cases independently. This is especially true for the Johns Hopkins University, a nationally respected research institution. Other private colleges include Capitol College and St. John's College, with the latter known for its "great books" curriculum.

All four-year public institutions, except for Morgan State and St. Mary's College of Maryland, are governed by the University of Maryland System Board of Regents and its new chancellor, Donald N. Langenberg. Community colleges are run by their own boards of trustees. The 1991-92 academic year is the last in which their oversight will be handled by the State Board for Community Colleges. On July 1, 1992, that board will go out of business, and oversight duties will shift to the Higher Education Commission.

DEMOGRAPHICS

Population: 4,781,468   (Rank: 19)

Age distribution:
Up to 17	24.3%
18 to 24	10.6%
25 to 44	35.1%
45 and older	30.0%

Racial and ethnic distribution:
American Indian	0.3%
Asian	2.9%
Black	24.9%
White	71.0%
Other and unknown	0.9%
Hispanic (may be any race)	2.6%

Educational attainment of adults:
At least 4 years of high school   67.4%

MARYLAND
Continued

At least 1 to 3 years of college 34.9%
At least 4 years of college ... 20.4%

Per-capita personal income: $21,789

Poverty rate: 9.6%

New high-school graduates in:
1991-92 (estimate) 43,539
2001-02 (estimate) 51,783

New GED diploma recipients: 5,782

High-school dropout rate: 25.9%

POLITICAL LEADERSHIP

Governor: William Donald Schaefer (D), term ends 1995

Governor's higher-education aide: Judy Sachwald, State House, Annapolis 21401; (301) 974-3004

U.S. Senators: Barbara A. Mikulski (D), term ends 1993; Paul S. Sarbanes (D), term ends 1995

U.S. Representatives:
5 Democrats, 3 Republicans
Helen Delich Bentley (R), Beverly B. Byron (D), Benjamin L. Cardin (D), Wayne T. Gilchrest (R), Steny H. Hoyer (D), C. Thomas McMillen (D), Kweisi Mfume (D), Constance A. Morella (R)

General Assembly: Senate, 38 Democrats, 9 Republicans; House, 116 Democrats, 25 Republicans

COLLEGES AND UNIVERSITIES

Higher education:
Public 4-year institutions 14
Public 2-year institutions 19
Private 4-year institutions 21
Private 2-year institutions 3
Total 57

Vocational institutions: 180

Statewide coordinating board:
Maryland Higher Education Commission
Jeffrey Building
16 Francis Street
Annapolis 21401
(301) 974-2971
Shaila R. Aery, secretary of higher education

Private-college association:
Maryland Independent College and University Association
208 Duke of Gloucester Street
Annapolis 21401
(301) 269-0306
J. Elizabeth Garraway, president

Institutions censured by the AAUP:
Maryland Institute College of Art, Morgan State University

Institution under NCAA sanctions:
University of Maryland at College Park

FACULTY MEMBERS

Full-time faculty members by rank:
Professor 2,031
Associate professor 1,804
Assistant professor 1,804
Instructor 455
Lecturer 200
No rank 184
Total 6,478

Average pay of full-time professors:
At public 4-year institutions $43,686
At public 2-year institutions $38,560

At private 4-year institutions $41,126
At private 2-year institutions $20,076
At all institutions $41,806
Men (all institutions) $44,744
Women (all institutions) $36,189

STUDENTS

Enrollment:
Total 255,326
At public 4-year institutions 110,167
At public 2-year institutions 107,395
At private 4-year institutions 37,043
At private 2-year institutions .. 721
Undergraduate 216,118
  First-time freshmen 31,486
Graduate 34,829
Professional 4,379
American Indian 688
Asian 9,962
Black 39,530
Hispanic 4,327
White 188,900
Foreign 5,672

Enrollment highlights:
Women 55.6%
Full-time 45.9%
Minority 22.4%
Foreign 2.3%
10-year change in total
  enrollment .... Up 18.8%

Proportion of enrollment made up of minority students:
At public 4-year institutions . 25.1%
At public 2-year institutions . 22.8%
At private 4-year institutions 13.0%
At private 2-year institutions 12.9%

Degrees awarded:
Associate 6,938
Bachelor's 17,928
Master's 5,970
Doctorate 711
Professional 1,124

Residence of new students: State residents made up 83% of all freshmen enrolled in Maryland; 75% of all Maryland residents who were freshmen attended college in their home state.

Test scores: Students averaged 904 on the S.A.T., which was taken by 64% of Maryland's high-school seniors.

MONEY

Average tuition and fees:
At public 4-year institutions . $2,120
At public 2-year institutions . $1,172
At private 4-year institutions $9,914
At private 2-year institutions $8,393

Expenditures:
Public institutions .. $1,064,430,000
Private institutions ... $901,948,000

State funds for higher-education operating expenses: $804,886,000
Two-year change: Down 2%

State spending on student aid:
Need-based: $15,669,000;
  19,096 awards
Non–need-based: $5,110,000;
  3,371 awards
Other: $135,000

Salary of chief executive of largest public 4-year campus:
William E. Kirwan, University
  of Maryland at College Park:
  $143,377

Total spending on research and development by doctorate-granting universities: $977,593,000
Sources:
Federal government 74.1%
State and local governments .. 7.3%
Industry 4.3%

MARYLAND
Continued

The institution itself 11.1%
Other 3.1%

Federal spending on education and student aid (selected programs):
Vocational and
  adult education $20,696,000
GI Bill $6,080,000
Pell Grants $42,774,000

Total federal spending on college- and university-based research and development: $514,747,000
Selected programs:
Department of Health
  and Human Services $218,504,000
National Science
  Foundation $27,766,000
Department of Defense $217,668,000
Department
  of Agriculture $4,825,000
Department of Energy .. $8,442,000

Largest endowment:
Johns Hopkins
  University $560,478,000

Top fund raisers:
Johns Hopkins
  University $111,814,000
University of Maryland $27,319,000
Goucher College $6,197,000

MISCELLANY

■ The Peabody Institute, now a division of the Johns Hopkins University, is the oldest music school in the country. Western Maryland College is the oldest coeducational institution south of the Mason-Dixon Line.

■ The Johns Hopkins University Press, established in 1878, is the oldest university press in continuous operation in the United States.

■ The oldest institution of higher education in Maryland is Washington College, founded in 1782 and said to be the only institution of higher education to which George Washington gave his express consent for the use of his name.

MASSACHUSETTS

AFTER THREE YEARS of devastating budget cuts, threats of college closings, and shakeups at the highest levels of higher education, the real "Massachusetts Miracle" may well be that public colleges are operating at all.

Not only the public sector has been jolted. While Massachusetts still enjoys its stature as home of many of the nation's elite liberal-arts colleges and research universities, some of those institutions have been shaken by charges of plagiarism, of improper use of federal funds, and of illegal collusion in admissions and financial aid.

For the public institutions, 1991 brought enormous and, in many cases, unsettling changes. They included the resignation of the interim state chancellor of higher education, in protest over early reorganization proposals and budget cuts by the new Governor, William F. Weld; the replacement of the state Board of Regents of Higher Education with a new Higher Education Coordinating Commission; the naming of Bunker Hill Community College President Piedad Robertson as the new Secretary of Education, with authority over elementary, secondary, and higher education; and the expansion of the University of Massachusetts into a five-campus system with the addition of the University of Lowell and Southeastern Massachusetts University.

Massachusetts has also established a new commission to evaluate the future of four-year and community colleges.

Leaders of the state colleges hope the commission's work will lead to new laws giving them the same authority over tuition, spending, and academic affairs that was accorded to the new University of Massachusetts system.

Community-college officials hope the commission will develop new financing formulas that reflect the expenses those two-year institutions incur in offering technical-training programs to displaced workers and remedial education to ill-prepared students.

Backers of the University of Massachusetts expansion said the new system could better compete for federal and private research grants. The university was founded with the Amherst campus as the state land-grant institution. The campus has been the scene of several racial incidents and, partly in response, it instituted a revamped freshman writing course in 1991 that focuses on issues of racial and social diversity.

The one thing that didn't change in 1991, however, was the state's grim financial situation. Once again state appropriations for higher education were slashed. Since 1988, annual state financing for public colleges and financial-aid programs has plunged to $485-million, from $750-million. As a result, courses have been eliminated, enrollments have been cut back, and tuition and fees have careered skyward.

Governor Weld, a Republican, has said he will give higher education more money once the state's crippled economy improves.

While public colleges in Massachusetts have always had difficulty gaining state support, the ties of private colleges and the Bay State have been strong since 1636, with the founding of what is now Harvard University. Since then, private higher education has flourished. The roster includes elite liberal-arts colleges like Amherst, Smith, Wellesley, and Williams, and world-renowned musical institutions like the Boston and New England Conservatories.

But it is the state's major private research universities—Harvard, Boston University, and the Massachusetts Institute of Technology—that draw most of the acclaim—and, in 1991, notoriety as well.

BU, the youngest of the three, has been praised for its initiative in running the school system of the City of Chelsea. But the institution was embarrassed in June 1991 when it was forced to demote the dean of the School of Communications after it was learned that he had plagiarized a commencement address.

MIT also came in for its share of bad press when Congressional investigations revealed that it had included ineligible expenses in calculating how much federal money it was entitled to receive to cover the indirect costs of research. It promised to return $731,000.

MIT has also been in the center of the storm over the U.S. Justice Department's inquiry into possible antitrust violations in the way Ivy League colleges and other prestigious institutions award financial aid. The institute decided to fight the department's charges in federal court. Many of the other colleges involved in the depart-

MASSACHUSETTS
Continued

ment's inquiry are also in Massachusetts.

While MIT is fighting the Justice Department's charges, Harvard University, along with the other Ivy League institutions, agreed in 1991 to stop setting financial-aid policies with other institutions and to stop comparing its student-aid packages with other institutions'.

In 1991 Harvard named Neil L. Rudenstine as its 26th president, one of the most visible posts in American higher education. Transition is also in store for another prominent educator: Jean Mayer, the president of Tufts University, has announced that he will retire in mid-1993.

DEMOGRAPHICS

Population: 6,016,425 (Rank: 13)

Age distribution:
Up to 17 .... 22.5%
18 to 24 .... 11.8%
25 to 44 .... 33.6%
45 and older 32.1%

Racial and ethnic distribution:
American Indian 0.2%
Asian 2.4%
Black 5.0%
White 89.8%
Other and unknown 2.6%
Hispanic (may be any race) .. 4.8%

Educational attainment of adults:
At least 4 years of high school 72.2%
At least 1 to 3 years of college 35.8%
At least 4 years of college ... 20.0%

Per-capita personal income: $22,569

Poverty rate: 9.3%

New high-school graduates in:
1991-92 (estimate) 55,444
2001-02 (estimate) 60,974

New GED diploma recipients: 9,389

High-school dropout rate: 30.0%

POLITICAL LEADERSHIP

Governor: William F. Weld (R), term ends 1995

Governor's higher-education aide: Piedad Robertson, Higher Education Coordinating Council, One Ashburton Place, Boston 02108; (617) 727-7785

U.S. Senators: Edward M. Kennedy (D), term ends 1995; John F. Kerry (D), term ends 1997

U.S. Representatives:
11 Democrats, 0 Republicans
Chester G. Atkins (D) Brian J. Donnelly (D), Joseph D. Early (D), Barney Frank (D), Joseph P. Kennedy, II (D), Edward J. Markey (D), Nicholas Mavroules (D), John Joseph Moakley (D), Richard E. Neal (D), John W. Olver (D), Gerry E. Studds (D)

General Court: Senate, 24 Democrats, 15 Republicans, 1 vacancy; House, 118 Democrats, 37 Republicans, 1 Independent, 4 vacancies

COLLEGES AND UNIVERSITIES

Higher education:
Public 4-year institutions 14
Public 2-year institutions 16
Private 4-year institutions 71
Private 2-year institutions 16
Total 117

Vocational institutions: 177

Statewide coordinating board:
Higher Education Coordinating
  Council
One Ashburton Place
Boston 02108
(617) 727-7785
Paul G. Marks, chancellor for higher education

Private-college association:
Association of Independent Colleges
  and Universities in Massachusetts
11 Beacon Street, Suite 1224
Boston 02108
(617) 742-5147
Clare M. Cotton, president

Institutions censured by the AAUP:
American International College,
Bridgewater State College,
Nichols College

Institution under NCAA sanctions:
University of Lowell

FACULTY MEMBERS

Full-time faculty members by rank:
Professor	5,962
Associate professor	4,039
Assistant professor	3,883
Instructor	499
Lecturer	458
No rank	326
Total	15,167

Average pay of full-time professors:
At public 4-year institutions	$47,079
At public 2-year institutions	$36,110
At private 4-year institutions	$48,138
At private 2-year institutions	$25,912
At all institutions	$46,113
Men (all institutions)	$49,415
Women (all institutions)	$38,588

STUDENTS

Enrollment:
Total	426,476
At public 4-year institutions	112,222
At public 2-year institutions	75,550
At private 4-year institutions	225,041
At private 2-year institutions	13,663
Undergraduate	341,563
First-time freshmen	70,780
Graduate	71,901
Professional	13,012
American Indian	1,157
Asian	13,731
Black	17,777
Hispanic	11,628
White	362,797
Foreign	19,530

Enrollment highlights:
Women	55.1%
Full-time	62.1%
Minority	10.9%
Foreign	4.6%
10-year change in total enrollment	Up 7.6%

Proportion of enrollment made up of minority students:
At public 4-year institutions	7.3%
At public 2-year institutions	13.4%
At private 4-year institutions	11.6%
At private 2-year institutions	14.5%

Degrees awarded:
Associate	13,016
Bachelor's	42,500
Master's	16,967
Doctorate	1,986
Professional	3,605

Residence of new students: State residents made up 68% of all freshmen enrolled in Massachusetts; 79% of all Massachusetts residents who were freshmen attended college in their home state.

MASSACHUSETTS
Continued

Test scores: Students averaged 896 on the S.A.T., which was taken by 79% of Massachusetts' high-school seniors.

MONEY

Average tuition and fees:
At public 4-year institutions . $2,052
At public 2-year institutions . $1,132
At private 4-year institutions $11,450
At private 2-year institutions $7,186

Expenditures:
Public institutions $980,585,000
Private institutions . $3,544,867,000

State funds for higher-education operating expenses: $583,569,000
Two-year change: Down 28%

State spending on student aid:
Need-based: $53,283,000; 39,400 awards
Non–need-based: $48,000; 50 awards
Other: $18,636,000

Salary of chief executive of largest public 4-year campus:
Richard D. O'Brien, University of Massachusetts at Amherst: $123,500

Total spending on research and development by doctorate-granting universities: $898,808,000
Sources:
Federal government 72.2%
State and local governments .. 1.6%
Industry 9.6%
The institution itself 6.0%
Other 10.7%

Federal spending on education and student aid (selected programs):
Vocational and adult education $26,988,000
GI Bill $6,018,000
Pell Grants $60,299,000

Total federal spending on college- and university-based research and development: $629,070,000
Selected programs:
Department of Health and Human Services $271,872,000
National Science Foundation $117,285,000
Department of Defense $115,298,000
Department of Agriculture $15,251,000
Department of Energy . $59,970,000

Largest endowment:
Harvard University $4,653,229,000

Top fund raisers:
Harvard University .. $213,452,000
Massachusetts Institute of Technology $117,604,000
Tufts University $39,129,000

MISCELLANY

- Drawing on a 70-year tradition of research on the links between nature and society, Clark University's graduate school of geography established the George Perkins Marsh Institute. The interdisciplinary institute will focus on analyzing the human dimensions of global environmental change.

- Supreme Court Justice Clarence Thomas is a member of the Board of Trustees of the College of the Holy Cross, his alma mater.

- Harvard University is the country's oldest institution of higher education.

MICHIGAN

Michigan lawmakers gave education a top priority in 1991, despite shortfalls in state revenues.

While other Michigan agencies saw their budgets slashed by as much as 9 per cent in the middle of the 1991 budget year, higher education was trimmed a mere 1 per cent. Higher-education officials are quick to thank the Legislature and Gov. John M. Engler.

Furthermore, Governor Engler, a Republican who was elected in 1990, and the Legislature increased support for higher education by about 4 per cent for the 1991-92 fiscal year.

Higher education's non-combative relationship with the new Governor is in sharp contrast with its experience with his predecessor, James J. Blanchard, a Democrat who threatened to cut state appropriations to colleges that did not adhere to his policy of limiting tuition increases to slightly more than the rate of inflation.

Governor Engler differs from Mr. Blanchard on at least one other higher-education issue—the Michigan Education Trust. In 1986, then-Governor Blanchard created the nation's first prepaid-tuition program. But during his 1990 gubernatorial campaign Mr. Engler criticized the program.

Michigan's new State Treasurer has questioned the financial soundness of the program and is seeking to determine whether it should be discontinued or closed to new participants. While the fate of the program is in doubt, the treasurer decided to halt sales of new prepaid-tuition contracts beginning in fall 1991.

Michigan has no statewide governing or coordinating board. Public colleges and universities are run by their own independent boards, three of which—those at the University of Michigan and Michigan State and Wayne State Universities—are selected in statewide, partisan elections. The boards enjoy considerable autonomy, although their decisions are frequently influenced by the Governor and the fiscal committees in the Legislature. Community colleges are run by local boards.

Most of the private institutions in the state are small, liberal-arts colleges. Their students are eligible for state aid.

Competition among public institutions for state financing has often been intense. But in recent years, the Presidents Council of the State Universities of Michigan has persuaded the institutions to work together in lobbying campaigns designed to increase public support for higher education.

Michigan has been in the vanguard of efforts to improve the racial climate on its campuses. The University of Michigan made national headlines when a proposal on racist speech and activities was declared unconstitutional by a federal judge. A modified version of the policy, now in place, allows the "broadest range of speech and expression" in public areas and forums on campus, but prohibits physical acts or threats that are not made as part of a discussion or an exchange of ideas in academic and educational centers.

The University of Michigan Board of Regents is considering a report from a campus committee on alcohol and drug abuse that recommends, among other things, that advertisements for alcoholic beverages be banned from university publications

MICHIGAN
Continued

and that alcohol be limited or prohibited at university functions.

DEMOGRAPHICS

Population: 9,295,297   (Rank: 8)

Age distribution:
Up to 17 .... 26.5%
18 to 24 .... 10.8%
25 to 44 .... 32.1%
45 and older 30.6%

Racial and ethnic distribution:
American Indian 0.6%
Asian 1.1%
Black 13.9%
White 83.4%
Other and unknown 0.9%
Hispanic (may be any race) .. 2.2%

Educational attainment of adults:
At least 4 years of high school 68.0%
At least 1 to 3 years of college 30.0%
At least 4 years of college ... 14.3%

Per-capita personal income: $18,360

Poverty rate: 13.2%

New high-school graduates in:
1991-92 (estimate) 102,695
2001-02 (estimate) 106,587

New GED diploma recipients: 12,687

High-school dropout rate: 26.4%

POLITICAL LEADERSHIP

Governor: John Engler (R), term ends 1995

Governor's higher-education aide:
Mike Addonizio, Governor's Office, Box 30013, Lansing 48909; (517) 335-7839

U.S. Senators: Carl Levin (D), term ends 1997; Donald W. Riegle, Jr. (D), term ends 1995

U.S. Representatives:
11 Democrats, 7 Republicans
David E. Bonior (D), Wm. S. Broomfield (R), Dave Camp (R), Bob Carr (D), Barbara-Rose Collins (D), John Conyers, Jr. (D), Robert W. Davis (R), John D. Dingell (D), William D. Ford (D), Paul B. Henry (R), Dennis M. Hertel (D), Dale E. Kildee (D), Sander M. Levin (D), Carl D. Pursell (R), Bob Traxler (D), Frederick S. Upton (R), Guy Vander Jagt (R), Howard Wolpe (D)

Legislature: Senate, 18 Democrats, 20 Republicans; House, 61 Democrats, 48 Republicans, 1 vacancy

COLLEGES AND UNIVERSITIES

Higher education:
Public 4-year institutions 15
Public 2-year institutions 29
Private 4-year institutions 48
Private 2-year institutions 5
Total 97

Vocational institutions: 314

Statewide coordinating board:
State Department of Education
P.O. Box 30008
Lansing 48909
(517) 373-3357
Gary D. Hawks, interim superintendent of public instruction

Private-college association:
Association of Independent Colleges and Universities of Michigan

650 Michigan National Tower
Lansing 48933
(517) 372-9160
Edward O. Blews, Jr., president

Institutions censured by the AAUP:
Hillsdale College, Olivet College, University of Detroit Mercy

Institution under NCAA sanctions:
University of Michigan

FACULTY MEMBERS

Full-time faculty members by rank:
Professor 3,831
Associate professor 2,890
Assistant professor 2,759
Instructor 536
Lecturer 334
No rank 2,978
Total 13,328

Average pay of full-time professors:
At public 4-year institutions $44,081
At public 2-year institutions $39,648
At private 4-year institutions $33,757
At private 2-year institutions $23,095
At all institutions $41,270
Men (all institutions) $43,907
Women (all institutions) $34,973

STUDENTS

Enrollment:
Total 560,320
At public 4-year institutions 255,555
At public 2-year institutions 224,159
At private 4-year institutions 75,567
At private 2-year institutions . 5,039
Undergraduate 492,910
  First-time freshmen 93,725
Graduate 56,358
Professional 11,052
American Indian 3,122
Asian 8,607
Black 51,494
Hispanic 7,718
White 458,194
Foreign 13,445

Enrollment highlights:
Women 54.6%
Full-time 50.8%
Minority 13.4%
Foreign 2.5%
10-year change in total
  enrollment .... Up 11.2%

Proportion of enrollment made up of minority students:
At public 4-year institutions . 11.4%
At public 2-year institutions . 14.3%
At private 4-year institutions 16.4%
At private 2-year institutions 28.5%

Degrees awarded:
Associate 20,168
Bachelor's 40,767
Master's 12,720
Doctorate 1,333
Professional 2,212

Residence of new students: State residents made up 85% of all freshmen enrolled in Michigan; 91% of all Michigan residents who were freshmen attended college in their home state.

Test scores: Students averaged 18.6 on the A.C.T., which was taken by 57% of Michigan's high-school seniors.

MONEY

Average tuition and fees:
At public 4-year institutions . $2,484
At public 2-year institutions . $1,047
At private 4-year institutions $6,520
At private 2-year institutions $6,400

Expenditures:
Public institutions .. $2,946,336,000
Private institutions ... $447,436,000

MICHIGAN
Continued

State funds for higher-education operating expenses: $1,541,648,000
Two-year change: Up 9%

State spending on student aid:
Need-based: $73,160,000; 58,500 awards
Non–need-based: None
Other: $1,718,000

Salary of chief executive of largest public 4-year campus:
John A. DiBiaggio, Michigan State University: $157,000

Total spending on research and development by doctorate-granting universities: $527,070,000
Sources:
Federal government 52.4%
State and local governments .. 7.0%
Industry 8.5%
The institution itself 24.3%
Other 7.8%

Federal spending on education and student aid (selected programs):
Vocational and
  adult education $48,288,000
GI Bill $10,803,000
Pell Grants $165,822,000

Total federal spending on college- and university-based research and development: $259,265,000
Selected programs:
Department of Health
  and Human Services $146,496,000
National Science
  Foundation $43,825,000
Department of Defense $16,292,000
Department
  of Agriculture $12,036,000
Department of Energy . $12,470,000

Largest endowment:
University of Michigan $448,209,000

Top fund raisers:
University of Michigan $83,609,000
Michigan State
  University $50,077,000
Wayne State University $12,020,000

MISCELLANY

- President Bush used a 1991 commencement address at the University of Michigan to denounce the "political correctness" movement on college campuses.

- On the last day of classes each year, students at the University of Michigan make a mad dash in the buff from one end of the campus to the other. Many don ski masks for the "Nude Run," which winds past campus monuments.

- An increasing number of students are registering to live in "substance-free" dorm rooms at 13 public institutions in Michigan. The students sign pledges that they will not drink, smoke, or use drugs in their residence halls. The institutions agreed to offer the housing option after a Michigan legislator introduced a bill that would have required them to do so.

- A group of students in the Michigan Collegiate Coalition is researching the effect of tuition increases and stagnant financial-aid budgets on students. The group is compiling a report for the Michigan Legislature about students' problems in paying for college.

- The oldest institution of higher education in the state is the University of Michigan, founded in 1817.

MINNESOTA

MINNESOTA'S TRADITION of making college accessible to anyone who wants to attend has led to the development of an extensive, 64-campus system of public higher education and a college-going rate that is the envy of most other states. But increasingly, legislators are questioning whether the state has more institutions and programs than it needs—or can afford.

That sentiment was evident in the 1991 legislative session, when lawmakers voted to merge the state's four-year, community, and technical colleges into a single system by 1995. The merger is an attempt to reduce expensive duplication, such as that which exists in the city of Rochester, where a community college and technical college are just a half-mile apart.

The merger plan, approved in the closing seconds of the legislative session, may be undone in 1992, since some legislators felt pressured to adopt it before adjourning. Also, some fear that the unique mission of technical colleges would be lost in a giant system.

But the concerns that drove the merger legislation remain. And the budget crisis that hit the state in 1991—it averted a potential deficit of $1.2-billion in its biennial budget by raising taxes and making deep cuts in spending—has only heightened interest in ideas that could save money in the future.

While state leaders are looking at public colleges, the institutions themselves have been through a period of self-examination and change. For the University of Minnesota, which is constitutionally chartered and was not included in the merger proposal, the new president, Nils Hasselmo, recently pushed through a "reallocation" plan to help the university focus its resources. The plan included the controversial closing of the two-year agriculture campus in Waseca.

Meanwhile, the State University System announced that in 1994 it would impose tougher admissions standards and cap its enrollment at 1992 levels. University officials said the plan would slow a financing crisis that has evolved because state support has not kept pace with enrollment growth. In the 1980's, enrollment in the seven-campus university system grew by 30 per cent, while state support increased by only 17 per cent.

The renewed emphasis on standards at the four-year institutions is also creating new pressures for the state's 20-campus Community College System, which expects to see even greater enrollment demands once the state-university system's admissions rules go into effect.

Although public institutions dominate the higher-education hierarchy, private institutions like Carleton College have a long and influential history in Minnesota. One sign of that influence is the state's generous financial-aid programs, which are open to private-college students. Another is the state's willingness to allow private colleges to participate in an offshoot of "school choice." The program allows 11th- and 12th-graders to receive high-school credit for courses they take at colleges. Participating colleges are reimbursed by school districts. Under recent federal court decisions, most of Minnesota's many small, religiously affiliated colleges are also eligible to participate in the program.

The Minnesota Private College Council is active in legislative issues

MINNESOTA
Continued

and has been urging the state to spend more of its higher-education funds on financial aid, rather than subsidizing students from richer families who attend public institutions.

DEMOGRAPHICS

Population: 4,375,099 (Rank: 20)

Age distribution:
Up to 17 .... 26.7%
18 to 24 .... 10.1%
25 to 44 .... 33.0%
45 and older 30.2%

Racial and ethnic distribution:
American Indian 1.1%
Asian 1.8%
Black 2.2%
White 94.4%
Other and unknown 0.5%
Hispanic (may be any race) .. 1.2%

Educational attainment of adults:
At least 4 years of high school 73.1%
At least 1 to 3 years of college 34.5%
At least 4 years of college ... 17.4%

Per-capita personal income: $18,731

Poverty rate: 11.6%

New high-school graduates in:
1991-92 (estimate) 49,837
2001-02 (estimate) 59,252

New GED diploma recipients: 5,757

High-school dropout rate: 9.1%

POLITICAL LEADERSHIP

Governor: Arne H. Carlson (R), term ends 1995

Governor's higher-education aide: Peder Larson, Governor's Office, 130 Capitol Building, St. Paul 55155; (612) 296-3391

U.S. Senators: Dave Durenberger (R), term ends 1995; Paul D. Wellstone (D), term ends 1997

U.S. Representatives:
6 Democrats, 2 Republicans
James L. Oberstar (D), Timothy J. Penny (D), Collin C. Peterson (D), Jim Ramstad (R), Martin Olav Sabo (D), Gerry Sikorski (D), Bruce F. Vento (D), Vin Weber (R)

Legislature: Senate, 46 Democrats, 21 Republicans; House, 78 Democrats, 55 Republicans, 1 vacancy

COLLEGES AND UNIVERSITIES

Higher education:
Public 4-year institutions 10
Public 2-year institutions 26
Private 4-year institutions 34
Private 2-year institutions 11
Total 81

Vocational institutions: 122

Statewide coordinating board:
Minnesota Higher Education
   Coordinating Board
400 Capitol Square Building
550 Cedar Street
St. Paul 55101
(612) 296-9665
David R. Powers, executive director

Private-college association:
Minnesota Private College Council
401 Galtier Plaza
Box 40
175 East Fifth Street
St. Paul 55101

(612) 228-9061
David B. Laird, Jr., president

Institutions censured by the AAUP:
None

Institution under NCAA sanctions:
University of Minnesota–Twin Cities

FACULTY MEMBERS

Full-time faculty members by rank:
Professor	2,117
Associate professor	1,611
Assistant professor	1,667
Instructor	437
Lecturer	15
No rank	1,290
Total	7,137

Average pay of full-time professors:
At public 4-year institutions	$42,342
At public 2-year institutions	$38,119
At private 4-year institutions	$35,303
At private 2-year institutions	$25,670
At all institutions	$39,376
Men (all institutions)	$41,598
Women (all institutions)	$34,221

STUDENTS

Enrollment:
Total	253,097
At public 4-year institutions	134,896
At public 2-year institutions	63,714
At private 4-year institutions	49,381
At private 2-year institutions	5,106
Undergraduate	222,852
First-time freshmen	49,123
Graduate	24,674
Professional	5,571
American Indian	1,731
Asian	3,929
Black	3,274
Hispanic	1,507
White	229,422
Foreign	4,843

Enrollment highlights:
Women	55.0%
Full-time	60.5%
Minority	4.4%
Foreign	2.0%
10-year change in total enrollment	Up 30.6%

Proportion of enrollment made up of minority students:
At public 4-year institutions	4.3%
At public 2-year institutions	4.1%
At private 4-year institutions	4.4%
At private 2-year institutions	8.7%

Degrees awarded:
Associate	6,947
Bachelor's	21,901
Master's	4,114
Doctorate	568
Professional	1,486

Residence of new students: State residents made up 80% of all freshmen enrolled in Minnesota; 82% of all Minnesota residents who were freshmen attended college in their home state.

Test scores: Students averaged 19.7 on the A.C.T., which was taken by 46% of Minnesota's high-school seniors.

MONEY

Average tuition and fees:
At public 4-year institutions	$2,063
At public 2-year institutions	$1,499
At private 4-year institutions	$8,776
At private 2-year institutions	$5,181

Expenditures:
Public institutions	$1,324,691,000
Private institutions	$521,441,000

State funds for higher-education operating expenses: $995,429,000

Two-year change: Up 5%

MINNESOTA
Continued

State spending on student aid:
Need-based: $76,074,000;
66,527 awards
Non–need-based: None
Other: $1,720,000

Salary of chief executive of largest public 4-year campus:
Nils Hasselmo, University of Minnesota–Twin Cities: $152,300

Total spending on research and development by doctorate-granting universities: $292,046,000
Sources:
Federal government 49.2%
State and local governments . 16.2%
Industry 6.2%
The institution itself 18.3%
Other 10.0%

Federal spending on education and student aid (selected programs):
Vocational and
  adult education $20,691,000
GI Bill $7,999,000
Pell Grants $100,501,000

Total federal spending on college- and university-based research and development: $133,439,000
Selected programs:
Department of Health
  and Human Services $91,271,000
National Science
  Foundation $20,117,000
Department of Defense . $5,068,000
Department
  of Agriculture $6,764,000
Department of Energy .. $5,202,000

Largest endowment:
Macalester College ... $320,127,000

Top fund raisers:
University
  of Minnesota $105,298,000
Gustavus Adolphus
  College $9,214,000
St. Olaf College $8,843,000

MISCELLANY

■ Carleton College reached an out-of-court settlement in 1991 with four women who had sued the institution, charging that it had been negligent in dealing with their allegations of date rape.

■ Law students at the University of Minnesota used most of the $125,000 they discovered in an old bank account to help pay off loans to students who want to practice public-interest law. The money came from earnings at the student Law Council's bookstore.

■ Minnesotans battle over which institution of higher education is the oldest in the state. The University of Minnesota–Twin Cities was chartered in 1851 but did not admit a freshman class until 1869. Hamline University slipped in with its charter in 1854, and commenced classes that same year.

MISSISSIPPI

MISSISSIPPI'S LEGACY of segregated higher education was reviewed by the U.S. Supreme Court in 1991 in a case that will probably affect all of the Southern and border states that have been covered by desegregation court orders. A decision is expected in 1992.

At issue is a 1990 ruling by the U.S. Court of Appeals for the Fifth Circuit.

The court, in finding that Mississippi's colleges were desegregated, said that state officials were "discontinuing prior discriminatory practices and adopting and implementing good-faith, race-neutral policies and procedures."

The U.S. Justice Department and civil-rights groups appealed the decision, saying it went against past federal-court rulings that required states to demonstrate that they had taken specific steps not only to remedy past discrimination, but also to promote equal opportunity in higher education.

Mississippi citizens are divided on the case, generally along racial lines. But black and white leaders agree that predominantly white colleges need to attract more black students and faculty members, and that black colleges face serious difficulties. Black leaders say the problems of the latter were caused by inadequate financial support from the state. Many white officials, however, say the problems at one of those institutions, Jackson State University, are the result of mismanagement.

Against that emotionally charged backdrop, Mississippi's higher-education leaders are trying to improve the quality of all their colleges and universities despite continuing shortfalls in state revenues. Higher education's budget was cut 5 per cent in the middle of the 1991 fiscal year. The final budget for fiscal 1992 will reduce support by an additional 2 per cent.

Officials at the Board of Trustees of State Institutions of Higher Learning—the governing and coordinating board for the state's eight public, four-year institutions—say the only way they will be able to improve their institutions is to restructure, eliminate unnecessary or duplicative programs, set new priorities, and raise tuition.

Meanwhile, officials at the State Board for Community and Junior Colleges are frustrated. Their institutions have seen an enrollment growth of about 6 per cent a year since 1988. But state officials now are talking about capping enrollment and terminating programs.

1991 was a year of political surprise in Mississippi. Kirk Fordice, a Republican business executive, won an upset victory in the governor's race, defeating a bid by Gov. Ray Mabus, a Democrat, to win a second term. During the campaign, Mr. Fordice criticized government spending on education and called for the elimination of many academic programs at public colleges and universities.

Toward the end of the campaign, Mr. Mabus accused Mr. Fordice of having a secret plan to close some of the state's black colleges. Mr. Fordice denied the charges.

DEMOGRAPHICS

Population: 2,573,216 (Rank: 31)

Age distribution:
Up to 17 .... 29.0%
18 to 24 .... 11.4%
25 to 44 .... 29.1%
45 and older 30.5%

Racial and ethnic distribution:
American Indian 0.3%
Asian 0.5%
Black 35.6%
White 63.5%
Other and unknown 0.1%
Hispanic (may be any race) .. 0.6%

Educational attainment of adults:
At least 4 years of high school 54.8%
At least 1 to 3 years of college 25.6%
At least 4 years of college ... 12.3%

MISSISSIPPI
Continued

Per-capita personal income: $12,823

Poverty rate: 25.0%

New high-school graduates in:
1991-92 (estimate) 25,072
2001-02 (estimate) 28,146

New GED diploma recipients: 5,751

High-school dropout rate: 33.1%

POLITICAL LEADERSHIP

Governor: Kirk Fordice (R), term ends 1996

Governor's higher-education aide: n/a

U.S. Senators: Thad Cochran (R), term ends 1997; Trent Lott (R), term ends 1995

U.S. Representatives:
5 Democrats, 0 Republicans
Mike Espy (D), G.V. (Sonny) Montgomery (D), Mike Parker (D), Gene Taylor (D), Jamie L. Whitten (D)

Legislature: Senate, 43 Democrats, 9 Republicans; House, 98 Democrats, 23 Republicans, 1 Independent

COLLEGES AND UNIVERSITIES

Higher education:
Public 4-year institutions 9
Public 2-year institutions 20
Private 4-year institutions 12
Private 2-year institutions 6
Total 47

Vocational institutions: 48

Statewide coordinating boards:
Board of Trustees of State Institutions of Higher Learning
3825 Ridgewood Road
Jackson 39211
(601) 982-6611
W. Ray Cleere, commissioner

State Board for Community and Junior Colleges
3825 Ridgewood Road
Jackson 39211
(601) 982-6518
Olon E. Ray, executive director

Private-college association:
Mississippi Association of Independent Colleges
P.O. Drawer 1198
Clinton 39060
(601) 925-3400
Johnnie Ruth Hudson, executive director

Institutions censured by the AAUP: None

Institutions under NCAA sanctions: None

FACULTY MEMBERS

Full-time faculty members by rank:
Professor 641
Associate professor 647
Assistant professor 794
Instructor 364
Lecturer 9
No rank 1,539
Total 3,994

Average pay of full-time professors:
At public 4-year institutions $33,602
At public 2-year institutions $26,972
At private 4-year institutions $30,290
At private 2-year institutions $17,156
At all institutions $30,595

Men (all institutions) $33,054
Women (all institutions) $27,138

STUDENTS

Enrollment:
Total 116,370
At public 4-year institutions . 56,716
At public 2-year institutions . 46,319
At private 4-year institutions 10,329
At private 2-year institutions . 3,006
Undergraduate 104,352
  First-time freshmen 27,244
Graduate 9,848
Professional 2,170
American Indian 337
Asian 604
Black 30,367
Hispanic 316
White 79,451
Foreign 1,797

Enrollment highlights:
Women 56.4%
Full-time 75.7%
Minority 28.5%
Foreign 1.6%
10-year change in total
  enrollment .... Up 16.1%

Proportion of enrollment made up of minority students:
At public 4-year institutions . 31.1%
At public 2-year institutions . 25.1%
At private 4-year institutions 27.0%
At private 2-year institutions 42.4%

Degrees awarded:
Associate 4,810
Bachelor's 8,227
Master's 2,108
Doctorate 245
Professional 414

Residence of new students: State residents made up 87% of all freshmen enrolled in Mississippi; 92% of all Mississippi residents who were freshmen attended college in their home state.

Test scores: Students averaged 15.9 on the A.C.T., which was taken by 64% of Mississippi's high-school seniors.

MONEY

Average tuition and fees:
At public 4-year institutions . $1,858
At public 2-year institutions .. $680
At private 4-year institutions $4,826
At private 2-year institutions $3,602

Expenditures:
Public institutions $706,380,000
Private institutions $64,054,000

State funds for higher-education operating expenses: $412,311,000
Two-year change: Down 5%

State spending on student aid:
Need-based: $1,136,000; 2,200 awards
Non–need-based: $705,000;
  130 awards
Other: None

Salary of chief executive of largest public 4-year campus:
Donald W. Zacharias,
  Mississippi State University:
  $97,500

Total spending on research and development by doctorate-granting universities: $85,229,000
Sources:
Federal government 47.3%
State and local governments . 24.3%
Industry 9.6%
The institution itself 11.1%
Other 7.6%

MISSISSIPPI
Continued

Federal spending on education and student aid (selected programs):
Vocational and
  adult education $17,118,000
GI Bill $4,308,000
Pell Grants $71,312,000

Total federal spending on college- and university-based research and development: $36,227,000
Selected programs:
Department of Health
  and Human Services . $8,536,000
National Science
  Foundation $3,085,000
Department of Defense . $4,002,000
Department
  of Agriculture $11,357,000
Department of Energy .. $4,251,000

Largest endowment:
University of Mississippi $44,059,000

Top fund raisers:
University of Mississippi $15,444,000
Mississippi State
  University $11,185,000
Millsaps College $4,732,000

MISCELLANY

■ The University of Mississippi is the home of the Center for the Study of Southern Culture, a leading institute in the growing field of regional studies. The center recently commissioned an operatic version of William Faulkner's *As I Lay Dying,* which was performed during the university's 1991 Faulkner and Yoknapatawpha Conference.

■ When Berkshire Cottage, a building constructed in 1894 on the campus of Tougaloo College, was destroyed by a fire in 1991, the college decided to raise money by selling the building's bricks for $100 each.

■ The Mississippi University for Women is one of two state-supported institutions in the country whose primary mission is the education of women. The other is Texas Woman's University

■ The faculty senate at the University of Mississippi has endorsed a resolution by the institution's alumni association asking fans to refrain from waving Confederate flags at campus events. Officials of the university have been trying to eliminate the flag waving, which many say inflames racial tensions.

■ The oldest institution of higher education in the state is Mississippi College, a Southern Baptist institution founded in 1826.

MISSOURI

PUBLIC higher-education officials in Missouri have complained for years that the state's aversion to taxes and government spending has created an environment in which colleges are starved for money, faculty members are underpaid, and students are shut out of the financial-aid programs they need.

So in 1990, when college boosters started their most recent campaign for more state support, they acknowledged the state's tradition of skepticism by calling their effort "Show Me the Future—The Needs of Missouri Higher Education."

The effort won over the General Assembly. But in November 1991, voters soundly rejected legislators' plans for a $385-million tax increase for education. About half of the money would have gone for competitive research grants, student aid, and colleges and universities. The tax package was defeated despite support from Gov. John Ashcroft, a Republican who had fought tax increases for higher education in previous years, effectively killing them in the legislature.

He signed on this time, he says, because the tax law would have also required colleges to eliminate programs that are not part of their missions and to assess what students have learned—ideas that Mr. Ashcroft has pushed in the state and nationally since taking office in 1985. The Governor has said he will continue to press for those reforms, despite the defeat of the tax increase.

Another issue that will continue to dog public higher education is the long-held criticism that the state spends too much on its public institutions in sparsely populated regions and too little on those in metropolitan areas, where many of the students attend part time. The conflict is particularly strong in the University of Missouri system, where influential business interests in St. Louis and Kansas City have been trying to wrest resources for the campuses in their cities from the flagship campus in rural Columbia.

A Board of Curators oversees the University of Missouri system, which includes a fourth campus (at Rolla, for engineering), while each of the nine other four-year institutions and 10 community colleges is governed by its own board. Two of the public four-year campuses—Harris-Stowe State College and Lincoln University—are historically black institutions.

The state also has a Coordinating Board for Higher Education, which in recent years has been given greater authority to prevent duplication of programs.

Many of Missouri's private colleges are small, religiously affiliated institutions with regional appeal, but two private institutions are well-known for their research: Saint Louis University and Washington University.

Washington University made headlines in 1990 when it eliminated its department of sociology in a money-saving move. William H. Danforth, the university's president, has been a prominent player in Missourians for Higher Education, a coalition of nearly 50 chancellors and presidents from public and private colleges that has been working to increase state spending on higher education.

Another prominent player in that organization, President C. Peter Magrath of the University of Missouri system, departed at the end of 1991 for Washington, D. C. He became president of the National Association of State Universities and Land-Grant Colleges.

DEMOGRAPHICS

Population: 5,117,073   (Rank: 15)

Age distribution:
Up to 17	25.7%
18 to 24	10.1%
25 to 44	31.0%
45 and older	33.2%

Racial and ethnic distribution:
American Indian	0.4%
Asian	0.8%
Black	10.7%
White	87.7%
Other and unknown	0.4%
Hispanic (may be any race)	1.2%

MISSOURI
Continued

Educational attainment of adults:
At least 4 years of high school 63.5%
At least 1 to 3 years of college 27.2%
At least 4 years of college ... 13.9%

Per-capita personal income: $17,472

Poverty rate: 12.9%

New high-school graduates in:
1991-92 (estimate) 52,082
2001-02 (estimate) 56,606

New GED diploma recipients: 8,174

High-school dropout rate: 26.0%

POLITICAL LEADERSHIP

Governor: John Ashcroft (R), term ends 1993

Governor's higher-education aide: Karen Gallagher, State Capitol, P.O. Box 720, Jefferson City 65102; (314) 751-3283

U.S. Senators: Christopher S. Bond (R), term ends 1993; John C. Danforth (R), term ends 1995

U.S. Representatives:
6 Democrats, 3 Republicans
William (Bill) Clay (D), E. Thomas Coleman (R), Bill Emerson (R), Richard A. Gephardt (D), Mel Hancock (R), Joan Kelly Horn (D), Ike Skelton (D), Harold L. Volkmer (D), Alan Wheat (D)

General Assembly: Senate, 22 Democrats, 12 Republicans; House, 98 Democrats, 64 Republicans, 1 vacancy

COLLEGES AND UNIVERSITIES

Higher education:
Public 4-year institutions 13
Public 2-year institutions 14
Private 4-year institutions 52
Private 2-year institutions 10

Total 89

Vocational institutions: 203

Statewide coordinating board:
Coordinating Board for
  Higher Education
101 Adams Street
Jefferson City 65101
(314) 751-2361
Charles J. McClain, commissioner of higher education

Private-college association:
Independent Colleges and
  Universities of Missouri
514 Earth City Expressway, Suite 244
Earth City 63045
(314) 739-4770
Charles V. Gallagher, president

Institutions censured by the AAUP:
Concordia Seminary,
Metropolitan Community Colleges

Institution under NCAA sanctions:
University of Missouri at Columbia

FACULTY MEMBERS

Full-time faculty members by rank:
Professor 2,106
Associate professor 1,778
Assistant professor 1,988
Instructor 578
Lecturer 84
No rank 700

Total 7,234

Average pay of full-time professors:
At public 4-year institutions $37,006
At public 2-year institutions $33,514
At private 4-year institutions $34,573
At private 2-year institutions $23,706
At all institutions $35,621
Men (all institutions) $37,836
Women (all institutions) $30,400

STUDENTS

Enrollment:
Total 278,505
At public 4-year institutions 121,045
At public 2-year institutions . 71,277
At private 4-year institutions 83,468
At private 2-year institutions . 2,715
Undergraduate 236,742
  First-time freshmen 41,544
Graduate 33,129
Professional 8,634
American Indian 840
Asian 3,922
Black 20,110
Hispanic 2,610
White 228,721
Foreign 5,464

Enrollment highlights:
Women 54.3%
Full-time 57.0%
Minority 10.7%
Foreign 2.1%
10-year change in total
  enrollment .... Up 25.4%

Proportion of enrollment made up of minority students:
At public 4-year institutions .. 8.9%
At public 2-year institutions . 13.4%
At private 4-year institutions 10.9%
At private 2-year institutions 20.7%

Degrees awarded:
Associate 6,891
Bachelor's 23,700
Master's 8,569
Doctorate 621
Professional 2,300

Residence of new students: State residents made up 79% of all freshmen enrolled in Missouri; 85% of all Missouri residents who were freshmen attended college in their home state.

Test scores: Students averaged 19.0 on the A.C.T., which was taken by 60% of Missouri's high-school seniors.

MONEY

Average tuition and fees:
At public 4-year institutions . $1,532
At public 2-year institutions .. $815
At private 4-year institutions $7,170
At private 2-year institutions $5,554

Expenditures:
Public institutions $999,869,000
Private institutions ... $911,951,000

State funds for higher-education operating expenses: $569,257,000
Two-year change: Down 2%

State spending on student aid:
Need-based: $11,144,000;
  8,950 awards
Non–need-based: $10,091,000;
  4,513 awards
Other: $260,000

Salary of chief executive of largest public 4-year campus:
Haskell M. Monroe, University
  of Missouri at Columbia: $120,500

Total spending on research and development by doctorate-granting universities: $281,133,000
Sources:
Federal government 54.2%

THE ALMANAC OF HIGHER EDUCATION • THE STATES

MISSOURI
Continued

State and local governments .. 6.6%
Industry 10.0%
The institution itself 21.2%
Other 8.1%

Federal spending on education and student aid (selected programs):
Vocational and
  adult education $26,648,000
GI Bill $7,421,000
Pell Grants $97,934,000

Total federal spending on college- and university-based research and development: $150,269,000

Selected programs:
Department of Health
  and Human Services $116,891,000
National Science
  Foundation $11,529,000
Department of Defense . $2,782,000
Department
  of Agriculture $7,838,000
Department of Energy .. $3,077,000

Largest endowment:
Washington
  University $1,365,854,000

Top fund raisers:
Washington University $49,603,000
University of Missouri . $45,724,000
Saint Louis University . $29,475,000

MISCELLANY

■ Traci Bauer, a student at Southwest Missouri State University, won what may become a landmark legal victory in 1991 when a federal judge ruled that campus crime reports are not covered by federal privacy-protection laws and ordered the university to show them to Ms. Bauer.

■ Harris-Stowe State College is the only college in the nation not attached to a larger university where all of the students are enrolled in teacher-education programs.

■ The oldest higher-education institution in Missouri is Saint Louis University, a Roman Catholic institution founded in 1818.

MONTANA

AFTER YEARS of dealing with chronic financing problems, officials of the Montana University System say they have two options: Either the state's colleges and universities must get much-needed catch-up money, or they must reduce their services and programs. Proposals for streamlining higher education will be reviewed and debated in 1992.

Although the Legislature gave the system a 14-per-cent increase in its biennial budget for 1991-93, university officials say they still lack the support given to peer institutions in other states. So John M. Hutchinson, the Commissioner of Higher Education, has asked college and university presidents to submit plans for reducing enrollments, programs, and faculty and staff positions. He has asked for comment on future tuition increases and the possibility of tougher admission standards.

The commissioner is acting upon recommendations from a citizens' committee appointed by Gov. Stan Stephens, a Republican. The colleges had hoped the committee's call for more money for higher education would lead to a push for tax reform. But the committee and higher-education officials may find it difficult to convince lawmakers and voters that a tax increase is needed.

Montana is one of five states with no sales tax, and politicians aggressively avoid any appearance of supporting one. Voters reminded legislators of their opposition to tax increases in November 1990, when they rejected a proposal to increase tobacco taxes.

The Board of Regents of Higher Education is the governing board for all public institutions in the state. Montana also has several small, private colleges.

The Montana University System is financing the development of a computer data base to track the participation and performance of American Indians at every educational level. It also is developing a strategy to improve their involvement and achievement in postsecondary institutions.

DEMOGRAPHICS

Population: 799,065 (Rank: 44)

Age distribution:
Up to 17 .... 27.8%
18 to 24 .... 8.8%
25 to 44 .... 31.3%
45 and older 32.1%

Racial and ethnic distribution:
American Indian 6.0%
Asian 0.5%
Black 0.3%
White 92.7%
Other and unknown 0.5%
Hispanic (may be any race) .. 1.5%

Educational attainment of adults:
At least 4 years of high school 74.4%
At least 1 to 3 years of college 36.5%
At least 4 years of college ... 17.5%

Per-capita personal income: $15,270

Poverty rate: 15.5%

New high-school graduates in:
1991-92 (estimate) 9,086
2001-02 (estimate) 9,660

New GED diploma recipients: 1,649

High-school dropout rate: 12.7%

POLITICAL LEADERSHIP

Governor: Stan Stephens (R), term ends 1993

Governor's higher-education aide: Marilyn Miller, Governor's Office, State Capitol, Helena 59620; (406) 444-3111

U.S. Senators: Max Baucus (D), term ends 1997; Conrad R. Burns (R), term ends 1995

U.S. Representatives:
1 Democrat, 1 Republican
Ron Marlenee (R), Pat Williams (D)

Legislature: Senate, 29 Democrats, 21 Republicans; House, 61 Democrats, 39 Republicans

COLLEGES AND UNIVERSITIES

Higher education:
Public 4-year institutions 6
Public 2-year institutions 7
Private 4-year institutions 3
Private 2-year institutions 3
Total 19

Vocational institutions: 45

Statewide coordinating board: Montana University System

MONTANA
Continued

33 South Last Chance Gulch
Helena 59620
(406) 444-6570
John M. Hutchinson,
commissioner of higher education

Private-college association:
None

Institutions censured by the AAUP:
None

Institutions under NCAA sanctions:
None

FACULTY MEMBERS

Full-time faculty members by rank:
Professor	414
Associate professor	329
Assistant professor	349
Instructor	73
Lecturer	11
No rank	233
Total	1,409

Average pay of full-time professors:
At public 4-year institutions	$31,305
At public 2-year institutions	$26,029
At private 4-year institutions	$25,871
At private 2-year institutions	$24,048
At all institutions	$29,780
Men (all institutions)	$30,992
Women (all institutions)	$26,613

STUDENTS

Enrollment:
Total	37,660
At public 4-year institutions	28,461
At public 2-year institutions	4,736
At private 4-year institutions	3,231
At private 2-year institutions	1,232
Undergraduate	34,008
First-time freshmen	6,365
Graduate	3,441
Professional	211
American Indian	2,068
Asian	135
Black	141
Hispanic	269
White	32,472
Foreign	687

Enrollment highlights:
Women	52.7%
Full-time	73.9%
Minority	7.4%
Foreign	1.9%
10-year change in total enrollment	Up 18.0%

Proportion of enrollment made up of minority students:
At public 4-year institutions	4.3%
At public 2-year institutions	9.8%
At private 4-year institutions	5.7%
At private 2-year institutions	77.0%

Degrees awarded:
Associate	683
Bachelor's	3,887
Master's	674
Doctorate	57
Professional	59

Residence of new students: State residents made up 86% of all freshmen enrolled in Montana; 72% of all Montana residents who were freshmen attended college in their home state.

Test scores: Students averaged 19.8 on the A.C.T., which was taken by 54% of Montana's high-school seniors.

MONEY

Average tuition and fees:
At public 4-year institutions . $1,535

At public 2-year institutions .. $877
At private 4-year institutions $5,034
At private 2-year institutions $1,144

Expenditures:
Public institutions $182,102,000
Private institutions $22,349,000

State funds for higher-education operating expenses: $131,910,000
Two-year change: Up 21%

State spending on student aid:
Need-based: $383,000; 1,100 awards
Non–need-based: None
Other: None

Salary of chief executive of largest public 4-year campus:
Michael P. Malone, Montana State University: $89,000

Total spending on research and development by doctorate-granting universities: $34,980,000
Sources:
Federal government 35.8%
State and local governments . 22.5%
Industry 12.2%
The institution itself 29.0%
Other 0.5%

Federal spending on education and student aid (selected programs):
Vocational and
  adult education $6,395,000
GI Bill $1,790,000
Pell Grants $21,701,000

Total federal spending on college- and university-based research and development: $10,414,000
Selected programs:
Department of Health
  and Human Services . $2,217,000
National Science
  Foundation $3,034,000

Department of Defense ... $259,000
Department
  of Agriculture $2,739,000
Department of Energy $44,000

Largest endowment:
University of Montana
  Foundation $17,576,000

Top fund raisers:
Eastern Montana College . $953,000
College of Great Falls $403,000

MISCELLANY

■ American Indians are the largest minority group in Montana. Seven colleges in the state are controlled by American Indian tribal councils.

■ Montana State University is the site of the Center for Interfacial Microbial Process Engineering, described by a public-relations officer as the only National Science Foundation engineering research center that studies "scum."

■ The oldest institution of higher education in Montana is Rocky Mountain College, an interdenominational institution founded in 1878.

NEBRASKA

IN A 1990 REFERENDUM, Nebraska's voters asked for a new state agency to help set higher-education policy. State legislators responded in 1991 by endowing the state's once-enervated Coordinating Commission for Postsecondary Education with broad new powers.

On July 1, 1991, the commission became responsible for directing how public-college budget requests are

NEBRASKA
Continued

presented to the legislature, determining whether new academic programs should be created or existing ones continued, and setting priorities for new campus construction projects.

The newly powerful commission is just one sign of the state's continuing effort to strengthen many regional colleges and universities, which have suffered from a lack of state support and political clout because of the hegemony of the University of Nebraska at Lincoln.

Influential members of the one-house legislature, the Unicameral, are behind the plan.

The Unicameral also took steps to bolster the state's community technical colleges, enacting a new financing equalization formula that uses state funds to supplement budgets in the poorer college districts. Six college districts operate 14 campuses throughout the state.

Even with the new commission and strengthened community colleges, the University of Nebraska remains the pre-eminent player. The state is still heavily dependent on agriculture, and the university has taken steps to upgrade its College of Technical Agriculture to reflect the growth of agribusiness. In recent years, the university has also devoted new resources to other fields, such as genetics and biomedicine.

When Kay A. Orr, a Republican, was Governor, the state pledged that it would spend $60-million over five years to build new laboratories and centers. In 1991 the new Governor, Democrat Ben Nelson, was unable to meet the $16-million target for that year because of budget problems, but lawmakers did provide $12-million for the research effort. University officials hope the planned increases will be forthcoming in future years.

Financing for the university system's general operations also will become a bigger issue, now that Kearney State College has been merged into the university system. Enrollment at the University of Nebraska–Kearney, as it is now called, has been increasing faster than its state support. While some lawmakers say the growth reflects a pent-up demand for higher education in central and western Nebraska, the situation will also create some financial pressures for the University of Nebraska Board of Regents, the university's governing board.

The Board of Trustees of State Colleges governs the three other four-year institutions. The technical colleges are run by their own boards of trustees, but as part of the 1991 reorganization, the Unicameral has established the Nebraska Technical Community College Association as the coordinating board for community colleges.

DEMOGRAPHICS

Population: 1,578,385   (Rank: 36)

Age distribution:
Up to 17	27.2%
18 to 24	9.9%
25 to 44	30.8%
45 and older	32.1%

Racial and ethnic distribution:
American Indian	0.8%
Asian	0.8%
Black	3.6%
White	93.8%
Other and unknown	1.0%
Hispanic (may be any race)	2.3%

Educational attainment of adults:
At least 4 years of high school 73.4%
At least 1 to 3 years of college 32.8%
At least 4 years of college ... 15.5%

Per-capita personal income: $17,549

Poverty rate: 11.1%

New high-school graduates in:
1991-92 (estimate) 18,210
2001-02 (estimate) 19,095

New GED diploma recipients: 2,300

High-school dropout rate: 14.6%

POLITICAL LEADERSHIP

Governor: Ben Nelson (D), term ends 1995

Governor's higher-education aide:
Andrew Cunningham, State Capitol, Room 1319, P.O. Box 94601, Lincoln 68509; (402) 471-2742

U.S. Senators: J. James Exon (D), term ends 1997; J. Robert Kerrey (D), term ends 1995

U.S. Representatives:
1 Democrat, 2 Republicans
Bill Barrett (R), Doug Bereuter (R), Peter Hoagland (D)

Unicameral: Nonpartisan legislature

COLLEGES AND UNIVERSITIES

Higher education:
Public 4-year institutions 7
Public 2-year institutions 13
Private 4-year institutions 14
Private 2-year institutions 2
Total 36

Vocational institutions: 48

Statewide coordinating board:
Coordinating Commission for
 Postsecondary Education
State Capitol, 6th Floor
P.O. Box 95005
Lincoln 68509
(402) 471-2847
Bruce G. Stahl, executive director

Private-college association:
Association of Independent Colleges
 and Universities of Nebraska
521 South 14th Street, Suite 302
Lincoln 68508
(402) 434-2818
Thomas J. O'Neill, Jr., president

Institutions censured by the AAUP:
None

Institutions under NCAA sanctions:
None

FACULTY MEMBERS

Full-time faculty members by rank:
Professor 713
Associate professor 627
Assistant professor 772
Instructor 194
Lecturer 6
No rank 344
Total 2,656

Average pay of full-time professors:
At public 4-year institutions $38,069
At public 2-year institutions $24,603
At private 4-year institutions $31,514
At private 2-year institutions $19,936
At all institutions $34,745
Men (all institutions) $36,852
Women (all institutions) $29,237

STUDENTS

Enrollment:
Total 108,844

NEBRASKA
Continued

At public 4-year institutions . 59,221
At public 2-year institutions . 32,116
At private 4-year institutions   16,824
At private 2-year institutions . . 683
Undergraduate 95,189
  First-time freshmen 21,786
Graduate 11,026
Professional 2,629
American Indian 625
Asian 948
Black 2,520
Hispanic 1,220
White 97,630
Foreign 1,674

Enrollment highlights:
Women 54.7%
Full-time 55.8%
Minority 5.2%
Foreign 1.6%
10-year change in total
  enrollment . . . . Up 25.9%

Proportion of enrollment made up of minority students:
At public 4-year institutions . . 4.1%
At public 2-year institutions . . 6.1%
At private 4-year institutions . 7.1%
At private 2-year institutions . 4.6%

Degrees awarded:
Associate 2,734
Bachelor's 8,406
Master's 1,776
Doctorate 248
Professional 727

Residence of new students: State residents made up 86% of all freshmen enrolled in Nebraska; 85% of all Nebraska residents who were freshmen attended college in their home state.

Test scores: Students averaged 19.6 on the A.C.T., which was taken by 69% of Nebraska's high-school seniors.

MONEY

Average tuition and fees:
At public 4-year institutions . $1,519
At public 2-year institutions . . $919
At private 4-year institutions $6,442
At private 2-year institutions $3,410

Expenditures:
Public institutions $537,858,000
Private institutions . . . $161,066,000

State funds for higher-education operating expenses: $340,106,000

Two-year change: Up 16%

State spending on student aid:
Need-based: $2,196,000; 3,328 awards
Non–need-based: None
Other: None

Salary of chief executive of largest public 4-year campus:
Graham B. Spanier, University
  of Nebraska at Lincoln: $140,000

Total spending on research and development by doctorate-granting universities: $105,373,000
Sources:
Federal government 32.6%
State and local governments . 26.5%
Industry 10.5%
The institution itself 26.7%
Other 3.6%

Federal spending on education and student aid (selected programs):
Vocational and
  adult education $8,420,000
GI Bill $3,992,000
Pell Grants $35,317,000

THE STATES • THE ALMANAC OF HIGHER EDUCATION

Total federal spending on college- and university-based research and development: $27,462,000

Selected programs:
Department of Health
  and Human Services $13,968,000
National Science
  Foundation $2,612,000
Department of Defense . $1,334,000
Department
  of Agriculture $5,390,000
Department of Energy $412,000

Largest endowment:
University of Nebraska $178,213,000

Top fund raisers:
University of Nebraska $37,792,000
Creighton University ... $9,728,000
Nebraska Wesleyan
  University $3,864,000

MISCELLANY

■ Nebraska was the first state to adopt a law that requires the National Collegiate Athletic Association to meet certain due-process standards when it investigates public colleges in the state.

■ The oldest institution of higher education in Nebraska is Peru State College, founded in 1867.

NEVADA

THE UNIVERSITY OF NEVADA has ambitions that go beyond the basketball court.

The system has long been known for the successful men's basketball team at its Las Vegas campus and the seemingly endless fights between Jerry Tarkanian and the National Collegiate Athletic Association over allegations of rules violations.

Now the university is trying to build a record of achievement in academe to rival its winning record in college basketball. It has been lobbying legislators for extra money for salaries so it will be able to offer competitive packages to prospective faculty members. The university also is trying to lay the groundwork for a law school. But it faces a formidable obstacle—a shortage of state funds.

Enrollment in the University of Nevada, an aggressive system with four-year campuses in Reno and Las Vegas, is outpacing growth in the general population. Enrollment growth is also outstripping the state's ability to finance the system.

Higher-education and civic leaders are urging Nevada's lawmakers to look beyond the traditional sources of state income—tourism and gambling—to increase financing for higher education and other public services. If the state's ability to finance its colleges does not improve substantially, the Board of Regents of the University of Nevada system has warned it may have no choice but to limit enrollment.

The university system has made a concerted push in recent years to enhance its scientific and research facilities. In 1990 the University of Nevada at Reno began a six-year, $105-million fund-raising drive. The Las Vegas campus has shown an aptitude for attracting federal funds, including $10-million for a National Supercomputing Center for Energy and the Environment.

The Board of Regents, an elected body, governs the state's two universities and four community colleges. It also oversees the state's Desert Research Institute, which is devoted to

NEVADA
Continued

scientific and social studies on topics related to water, energy, and geology.

Sports fans on and off the Las Vegas campus are expected to follow closely Mr. Tarkanian's final season and the selection of his successor. Mr. Tarkanian announced in June 1991 that he would serve for one more season before retiring as men's basketball coach.

DEMOGRAPHICS

Population: 1,201,833 (Rank: 39)

Age distribution:
Up to 17 .... 24.7%
18 to 24 .... 9.9%
25 to 44 .... 34.5%
45 and older 30.9%

Racial and ethnic distribution:
American Indian 1.6%
Asian 3.2%
Black 6.6%
White 84.3%
Other and unknown 4.4%
Hispanic (may be any race) . 10.4%

Educational attainment of adults:
At least 4 years of high school 75.5%
At least 1 to 3 years of college 35.1%
At least 4 years of college ... 14.4%

Per-capita personal income: $19,035

Poverty rate: 9.7%

New high-school graduates in:
1991-92 (estimate) 9,886
2001-02 (estimate) 16,534

New GED diploma recipients: 2,453

High-school dropout rate: 24.2%

POLITICAL LEADERSHIP

Governor: Bob Miller (D), term ends 1995

Governor's higher-education aide: Scott M. Craigie, Executive Chambers, Capitol Complex, Carson City 89710; (702) 687-5670

U.S. Senators: Richard H. Bryan (D), term ends 1995; Harry Reid (D), term ends 1993

U.S. Representatives:
1 Democrat, 1 Republican
James H. Bilbray (D), Barbara F. Vucanovich (R)

Legislature: Senate, 11 Democrats, 10 Republicans; House, 22 Democrats, 19 Republicans, 1 vacancy

COLLEGES AND UNIVERSITIES

Higher education:
Public 4-year institutions 2
Public 2-year institutions 4
Private 4-year institutions 1
Private 2-year institutions 1
Total 8

Vocational institutions: 55

Statewide coordinating board:
University of Nevada System
2601 Enterprise Road
Reno 89512
(702) 784-4901
Mark H. Dawson, chancellor

Private-college association:
None

Institutions censured by the AAUP:
None

Institution under NCAA sanctions:
University of Nevada at Las Vegas

FACULTY MEMBERS

Full-time faculty members by rank:
Professor 217
Associate professor 248
Assistant professor 244
Instructor 91
Lecturer 29
No rank 227
Total 1,056

Average pay of full-time professors:
At public 4-year institutions $41,104
At public 2-year institutions $33,411
At private 4-year institutions $27,454
At private 2-year institutions $33,250
At all institutions $39,414
Men (all institutions) $41,574
Women (all institutions) $33,945

STUDENTS

Enrollment:
Total 56,471
At public 4-year institutions . 27,085
At public 2-year institutions . 29,099
At private 4-year institutions .. 264
At private 2-year institutions ... 23
Undergraduate 51,610
  First-time freshmen 8,455
Graduate 4,666
Professional 195
American Indian 667
Asian 1,603
Black 2,242
Hispanic 2,324
White 41,304
Foreign 692

Enrollment highlights:
Women 56.2%
Full-time 30.6%
Minority 14.2%
Foreign 1.4%

10-year change in total
  enrollment .... Up 57.1%

Proportion of enrollment made up of minority students:
At public 4-year institutions . 12.1%
At public 2-year institutions . 16.5%
At private 4-year institutions ... n/a
At private 2-year institutions . 8.0%

Degrees awarded:
Associate 885
Bachelor's 2,023
Master's 502
Doctorate 35
Professional 46

Residence of new students: State residents made up 89% of all freshmen enrolled in Nevada; 86% of all Nevada residents who were freshmen attended college in their home state.

Test scores: Students averaged 19.0 on the A.C.T., which was taken by 42% of Nevada's high-school seniors.

MONEY

Average tuition and fees:
At public 4-year institutions . $1,100
At public 2-year institutions .. $522
At private 4-year institutions $5,400
At private 2-year institutions ... n/a

Expenditures:
Public institutions $180,107,000
Private institutions $2,448,000

State funds for higher-education operating expenses: $191,773,000

Two-year change: Up 31%

State spending on student aid:
Need-based: $400,000; 400 awards
Non–need-based: None
Other: None

NEVADA
Continued

Salary of chief executive of largest public 4-year campus:
Robert C. Maxson, University of Nevada at Las Vegas: $149,997

Total spending on research and development by doctorate-granting universities: $38,301,000
Sources:
Federal government 54.0%
State and local governments .. 6.3%
Industry 11.9%
The institution itself 24.0%
Other 3.8%

Federal spending on education and student aid (selected programs):
Vocational and
 adult education $6,405,000
GI Bill $1,539,000
Pell Grants $13,135,000

Total federal spending on college- and university-based research and development: $14,113,000
Selected programs:
Department of Health
 and Human Services . $3,644,000
National Science
 Foundation $2,831,000
Department of Defense ... $128,000
Department
 of Agriculture $1,429,000
Department of Energy $123,000

Largest endowment:
University of Nevada
 System $62,546,000

Top fund raisers:
data not reported

MISCELLANY

■ A small group of students at the University of Nevada at Las Vegas won formal recognition from the student government for their openly gay fraternity called Delta Lambda Phi. The fraternity has chapters on 16 other campuses around the country.

■ The oldest institution of higher education in the state is the University of Nevada at Reno, founded in 1874.

NEW HAMPSHIRE

IT WAS unfortunate timing when the trustees of the University of New Hampshire system chose 1991 as the year they would ask for a huge increase in state money to raise faculty salaries.

With the economy in a slump and Republican Gov. Judd Gregg demanding cutbacks from all state agencies, it was also probably clumsy politics.

The university's request prompted a spate of harangues by Governor Gregg, who accused the system of "ivory-tower budgeting" and said universities were havens for overpaid and underworked administrators and faculty members. Ultimately, the legislature approved a modest increase that requires institutions to lay off some employees and hold other positions vacant.

Later the Governor called for the ouster of the president of Keene State College because Mr. Gregg disagreed with a decision to hold the college's baccalaureate ceremony off campus to avoid mixing church and state.

Whether Mr. Gregg's rhetoric was heartfelt or expedient, higher-education officials found the criticism ironic. They have contended for years that the state shortchanges its public colleges because of its fiscal conservatism and its philosophy of looking to the private sector, rather than government, to meet as many needs as possible.

New Hampshire has no sales tax or personal income tax and ranks last in the nation in the level of state and local support for higher education on a per-capita basis. About half of all four-year students in the state are enrolled in private colleges, although some of those institutions, like Dartmouth College, draw many of their students from out of state.

Increasingly, however, the state is looking to its public colleges to help expand economic opportunities. One sign of that came in 1991 when the legislature created the University of New Hampshire Industrial Research Center, which is designed to help local businesses collaborate with university scientists in developing new products and techniques.

Public-college officials also see some hope in the legislature's recent decision to study a personal income tax.

But even if the politicians drop their long-time resistance to such a levy, it's not likely to produce a windfall for higher education. Lawmakers said they would use the revenues to help local governments reduce property taxes.

The state also has a system of vocational-technical colleges run by its own governing board. But unlike two-year college systems in some other, more-industrialized states in the Northeast, New Hampshire's system lacks the university's political clout, particularly in the legislature.

DEMOGRAPHICS

Population: 1,109,252 (Rank: 40)

Age distribution:
Up to 17 .... 25.1%
18 to 24 .... 10.6%
25 to 44 .... 34.9%
45 and older 29.4%

Racial and ethnic distribution:
American Indian 0.2%
Asian 0.8%
Black 0.6%
White 98.0%
Other and unknown 0.3%
Hispanic (may be any race) .. 1.0%

Educational attainment of adults:
At least 4 years of high school 72.3%
At least 1 to 3 years of college 35.1%
At least 4 years of college ... 18.2%

Per-capita personal income: $20,827

Poverty rate: 6.9%

New high-school graduates in:
1991-92 (estimate) 11,359
2001-02 (estimate) 13,714

New GED diploma recipients: 2,177

High-school dropout rate: 25.9%

POLITICAL LEADERSHIP

Governor: Judd Gregg (R), term ends 1993

Governor's higher-education aide: Darcy Bryant, State House, Concord 03301; (603) 271-2121

U.S. Senators: Warren Rudman (R), term ends 1993; Bob Smith (R), term ends 1997

U.S. Representatives:
1 Democrat, 1 Republican
Dick Swett (D), William H. Zeliff, Jr. (R)

NEW HAMPSHIRE
Continued

General Court: Senate, 11 Democrats, 13 Republicans; House, 125 Democrats, 268 Republicans, 2 Independents, 5 vacancies

COLLEGES AND UNIVERSITIES

Higher education:
Public 4-year institutions 5
Public 2-year institutions 7
Private 4-year institutions 12
Private 2-year institutions 5
Total 29

Vocational institutions: 28

Statewide coordinating board:
New Hampshire Postsecondary
 Education Commission
Two Industrial Park Drive
Concord 03301
(603) 271-2555
James A. Busselle, executive director

Private-college association:
None

Institutions censured by the AAUP:
None

Institutions under NCAA sanctions:
None

FACULTY MEMBERS

Full-time faculty members by rank:
Professor 676
Associate professor 587
Assistant professor 545
Instructor 65
Lecturer 14
No rank 20
Total 1,907

Average pay of full-time professors:
At public 4-year institutions $39,166
At public 2-year institutions $28,982
At private 4-year institutions $41,379
At private 2-year institutions $16,851
At all institutions $38,783
Men (all institutions) $41,240
Women (all institutions) $32,750

STUDENTS

Enrollment:
Total 58,600
At public 4-year institutions . 24,688
At public 2-year institutions .. 8,201
At private 4-year institutions 24,432
At private 2-year institutions . 1,279
Undergraduate 50,714
 First-time freshmen 10,425
Graduate 7,236
Professional 650
American Indian 190
Asian 541
Black 611
Hispanic 647
White 52,433
Foreign 912

Enrollment highlights:
Women 53.3%
Full-time 57.7%
Minority 3.7%
Foreign 1.6%
10-year change in total
 enrollment .... Up 39.2%

Proportion of enrollment made up of minority students:
At public 4-year institutions .. 1.6%
At public 2-year institutions .. 1.6%
At private 4-year institutions . 6.4%
At private 2-year institutions . 3.1%

Degrees awarded:
Associate 2,334
Bachelor's 6,797

Master's 1,754
Doctorate 87
Professional 154

Residence of new students: State residents made up 49% of all freshmen enrolled in New Hampshire; 58% of all New Hampshire residents who were freshmen attended college in their home state.

Test scores: Students averaged 921 on the S.A.T., which was taken by 75% of New Hampshire's high-school seniors.

MONEY

Average tuition and fees:
At public 4-year institutions . $2,196
At public 2-year institutions . $1,608
At private 4-year institutions $10,299
At private 2-year institutions $4,050

Expenditures:
Public institutions $183,959,000
Private institutions ... $264,440,000

State funds for higher-education operating expenses: $75,175,000
Two-year change: Up 9%

State spending on student aid:
Need-based: $775,000; 1,544 awards
Non–need-based: $10,000; 10 awards
Other: $694,000

Salary of chief executive of largest public 4-year campus:
Dale F. Nitzschke, University of New Hampshire: $120,000

Total spending on research and development by doctorate-granting universities: $69,731,000
Sources:
Federal government 63.9%
State and local governments .. 5.7%
Industry 5.3%
The institution itself 16.5%
Other 8.5%

Federal spending on education and student aid (selected programs):
Vocational and
  adult education $6,500,000
GI Bill $1,340,000
Pell Grants $6,299,000

Total federal spending on college- and university-based research and development: $37,007,000
Selected programs:
Department of Health
  and Human Services $20,106,000
National Science
  Foundation $5,560,000
Department of Defense . $2,436,000
Department
  of Agriculture $1,815,000
Department of Energy $977,000

Largest endowment:
Dartmouth College ... $593,952,000

Top fund raisers:
Dartmouth College $51,145,000
Colby-Sawyer College .. $2,158,000
St. Anselm College $1,647,000

MISCELLANY

■ Alexander Solzhenitsyn made a rare public appearance in 1991 to accept an honorary degree from Dartmouth.

■ Randy Olson, an assistant professor of zoology at the University of New Hampshire, is trying to popularize marine biology through such projects as a film on how to eat lobsters and a music video about barnacles.

■ Dartmouth College, founded in 1769, is the oldest higher-education institution in New Hampshire.

NEW JERSEY

THE 1980's will go down in New Jersey's history as the decade in which college officials and lawmakers dramatically improved the state's public institutions.

But so far it appears that the 1990's may be remembered as a time in which college officials and lawmakers battled a recession and struggled not to lose ground in academic quality or student access to higher education.

Gov. Jim Florio's first two years in office have been tumultuous. Faced with a $3-billion revenue shortfall in 1990, the Democratic Governor cut state spending and raised taxes—much to the outrage of the public-employee unions and faculty associations that had backed his gubernatorial campaign. The spending cuts led to steep tuition increases in a state where the cost of attending a public institution was already above the national average.

The Governor was not able to restore financing for fiscal 1992. But he dropped his initial proposal for an 8-per-cent cut in postsecondary-education funds and left higher education with a budget that was just slightly lower than the one for fiscal 1991. The budget also increased student aid to compensate for tuition increases.

The state Board of Higher Education has been trying to balance institutional needs for more revenue through tuition increases against complaints from students and others that more and more New Jersey residents are being priced out of a public-college education.

On the one hand, the board revised a 13-year policy that had limited total tuition revenue to 30 per cent of an institution's operating costs. Under the new policy, colleges may temporarily exceed the limit, but they must submit reports to the board on how the extra money is being spent. The colleges must also outline a plan for reducing tuition to 30 per cent or less of their operating costs.

On the other hand, the board imposed an informal tuition cap. It announced that the Governor's budget increase for the state's student-aid program would provide enough new aid money to pay for the needs of students only if tuition increases were limited to 9 per cent during the 1991-92 academic year at public institutions.

The board said that institutions that increased their 1991-92 tuition charges by more than 9 per cent must provide any additional financial aid required for needy students from other sources, such as institutional or federal funds. As a result, many colleges are keeping their tuition increases near or below the board's informal cap.

New Jersey has had a strong tradition of private higher education since the founding of Princeton University in 1746. Under the leadership of a former Governor, Thomas H. Kean, Drew University is becoming more prominent. Other important private institutions include Rider College and Fairleigh Dickinson and Seton Hall Universities.

But like New Jersey's public institutions, some of the private colleges are experiencing financial difficulties. Fairleigh Dickinson is trimming its faculty by 15 per cent, reducing its enrollment, and reorganizing its three campuses as part of a plan to reduce a $31-million deficit. Financially ailing Westminster Choir College is merging with Rider College. In addition, falling real-estate prices have prompted many institutions in the Northeast, including Princeton, to reduce estimates of the value of their investments.

The state also has a long political tradition of strong local governments, which has led state leaders to eschew a statewide community-college system in favor of one that is controlled and financed largely by localities.

The Board of Higher Education coordinates postsecondary education. Its staff is the Department of Higher Education, headed by a chancellor who is a member of the Governor's cabinet. There are 31 governing boards for public institutions.

DEMOGRAPHICS

Population: 7,730,188   (Rank: 9)

Age distribution:
Up to 17 .... 23.3%
18 to 24 .... 10.1%
25 to 44 .... 33.1%
45 and older 33.5%

Racial and ethnic distribution:
American Indian 0.2%
Asian 3.5%
Black 13.4%
White 79.3%
Other and unknown 3.6%
Hispanic (may be any race) .. 9.6%

Educational attainment of adults:
At least 4 years of high school 67.4%
At least 1 to 3 years of college 31.5%
At least 4 years of college ... 18.3%

Per-capita personal income: $24,936

Poverty rate: 7.9%

New high-school graduates in:
1991-92 (estimate) 78,401
2001-02 (estimate) 84,875

New GED diploma recipients: 8,146

High-school dropout rate: 22.6%

POLITICAL LEADERSHIP

Governor: Jim Florio (D), term ends 1994

Governor's higher-education aide: Elizabeth Garlatti, State House, CN-001, Trenton 08625; (609) 777-1243

U.S. Senators: Bill Bradley (D), term ends 1997; Frank R. Lautenberg (D), term ends 1995

U.S. Representatives:
8 Democrats, 6 Republicans
Robert E. Andrews (D), Bernard J. Dwyer (D), Dean A. Gallo (R), Frank J. Guarini (D), William J. Hughes (D), Frank Pallone, Jr. (D), Donald M. Payne (D), Matthew J. Rinaldo (R), Robert A. Roe (D), Marge Roukema (R), Jim Saxton (R), Christopher H. Smith (R), Robert G. Torricelli (D), Dick Zimmer (R)

Legislature: Senate, 13 Democrats, 27 Republicans; House, 22 Democrats, 58 Republicans

COLLEGES AND UNIVERSITIES

Higher education:
Public 4-year institutions 14
Public 2-year institutions 19
Private 4-year institutions 25
Private 2-year institutions 4
Total 62

Vocational institutions: 192

Statewide coordinating board:
Board of Higher Education
20 West State Street, CN 542

NEW JERSEY
Continued

Trenton 08625
(609) 292-4310
Edward D. Goldberg, chancellor

Private-college association:
Association of Independent Colleges and Universities in New Jersey
P.O. Box 206
Summit 07902
(908) 277-3738
John B. Wilson, president

Institutions censured by the AAUP:
Camden County College,
Rider College

Institution under NCAA sanctions:
Upsala College

FACULTY MEMBERS

Full-time faculty members by rank:
Professor 2,804
Associate professor 2,595
Assistant professor 2,441
Instructor 466
Lecturer 188
No rank 40
Total 8,534

Average pay of full-time professors:
At public 4-year institutions $46,741
At public 2-year institutions $39,293
At private 4-year institutions $46,510
At private 2-year institutions ... n/a
At all institutions $45,136
Men (all institutions) $48,127
Women (all institutions) $38,994

STUDENTS

Enrollment:
Total 314,091
At public 4-year institutions 135,101
At public 2-year institutions 118,443
At private 4-year institutions 56,648
At private 2-year institutions . 3,899
Undergraduate 266,876
First-time freshmen 48,241
Graduate 41,075
Professional 6,140
American Indian 847
Asian 11,196
Black 28,831
Hispanic 17,894
White 232,047
Foreign 11,825

Enrollment highlights:
Women 55.2%
Full-time 49.9%
Minority 20.2%
Foreign 3.9%
10-year change in total
  enrollment .... Up 0.5%

Proportion of enrollment made up of minority students:
At public 4-year institutions . 20.6%
At public 2-year institutions . 21.8%
At private 4-year institutions 16.0%
At private 2-year institutions 23.4%

Degrees awarded:
Associate 9,337
Bachelor's 22,898
Master's 7,024
Doctorate 747
Professional 1,613

Residence of new students: State residents made up 86% of all freshmen enrolled in New Jersey; 58% of all New Jersey residents who were freshmen attended college in their home state.

Test scores: Students averaged 886 on the S.A.T., which was taken by 74% of New Jersey's high-school seniors.

MONEY

Average tuition and fees:
At public 4-year institutions . $2,511
At public 2-year institutions . $1,130
At private 4-year institutions $9,398
At private 2-year institutions $6,748

Expenditures:
Public institutions .. $1,406,490,000
Private institutions ... $714,733,000

State funds for higher-education operating expenses: $1,132,432,000
Two-year change: Up 1%

State spending on student aid:
Need-based: $95,834,000;
  58,754 awards
Non–need-based: $6,246,000;
  5,046 awards
Other: None

Salary of chief executive of largest public 4-year campus:
Francis L. Lawrence, Rutgers University at New Brunswick: $170,000

Total spending on research and development by doctorate-granting universities: $319,797,000
Sources:
Federal government 42.2%
State and local governments . 14.5%
Industry 5.5%
The institution itself 30.1%
Other 7.7%

Federal spending on education and student aid (selected programs):
Vocational and
  adult education $31,763,000
GI Bill $3,769,000
Pell Grants $66,839,000

Total federal spending on college- and university-based research and development: $120,772,000
Selected programs:
Department of Health
  and Human Services $57,291,000
National Science
  Foundation $29,054,000
Department of Defense $14,421,000
Department
  of Agriculture $4,180,000
Department of Energy .. $6,366,000

Largest endowment:
Princeton University $2,527,140,000

Top fund raisers:
Princeton University .. $75,164,000
Rutgers University ... $27,229,000
Drew University $9,253,000

MISCELLANY

- Students with drug and alcohol problems can check into a Rutgers University program that helps them deal with addiction while they attend academic classes.

- Princeton University is the oldest institution of higher education in New Jersey. It was founded in 1746.

NEW MEXICO

SERVING MINORITY college students is of increasing importance to state officials in New Mexico. About 40 per cent of the state's residents are Hispanic—as are the leaders of New Mexico's Senate and House of Representatives.

That proportion is reflected in the kinds of programs being developed by the Commission on Higher Education and in the pressure felt by college

NEW MEXICO
Continued

presidents to make diversity and affirmative action top priorities.

The Commission on Higher Education, for example, has started a program in which the state will provide annual $25,000 stipends to minority students pursuing doctoral degrees. Up to four students will be selected to participate in the program; they will repay the state by teaching a year at New Mexico State University for each year the state provided a stipend.

The commission is exploring a number of avenues to increase the state's college-going rate. For example, high-school students now may enroll in college courses. There is also a continuing effort to improve transfer rates from the state's two-year colleges to its four-year institutions.

Financing of higher education, especially of capital improvements, remains a concern. Gov. Bruce King, a Democrat, signed a budget for fiscal 1992 that gives higher education a 4.2-per-cent increase. But the Legislature did not provide any money for capital improvements.

Higher-education officials and their political allies are debating whether they should try to persuade voters to support a bond measure to finance important projects. In 1990, voters rejected a measure to provide $27.3-million to renovate facilities and construct new buildings at public colleges and universities.

Meanwhile, Richard E. Peck, the University of New Mexico's president, has been working to improve the quality of the institution and to resolve complaints about its affirmative-action policies.

More than any other institution in the state, the University of New Mexico has felt the political impact of the demographic changes. While Mr. Peck, who began his second year in office on July 1, 1991, has made some progress, the institution continues to be criticized by Hispanics for moving too slowly to recruit Hispanic students and faculty members. It also has been criticized by white faculty members for going too far in its zeal to become more pluralistic.

But Mr. Peck is trying to proceed with his goal of making the institution a model of cultural diversity. Among his appointments was that of a Hispanic, Leo M. Romero, as dean of the university's law school.

The Commission on Higher Education, whose members are appointed by the Governor, is the statewide coordinating agency for colleges and universities. The state has 11 governing boards for public institutions.

Only three private, non-profit colleges operate in the state. One is St. John's College in Santa Fe, which is affiliated with St. John's College in Maryland.

DEMOGRAPHICS

Population: 1,515,069   (Rank: 37)

Age distribution:
Up to 17 .... 29.5%
18 to 24 .... 10.0%
25 to 44 .... 32.0%
45 and older 28.5%

Racial and ethnic distribution:
American Indian 8.9%
Asian 0.9%
Black 2.0%
White 75.6%
Other and unknown 12.6%
Hispanic (may be any race) . 38.2%

Educational attainment of adults:
At least 4 years of high school   68.9%
At least 1 to 3 years of college   34.7%
At least 4 years of college ...   17.6%

Per-capita personal income: $14,265

Poverty rate: 21.1%

New high-school graduates in:
1991-92 (estimate) 16,709
2001-02 (estimate) 21,073

New GED diploma recipients: 3,965

High-school dropout rate: 28.1%

POLITICAL LEADERSHIP

Governor: Bruce King (D), term ends 1995

Governor's higher-education aide: Caroline Gaston, Governor's Office, Capitol Building, Santa Fe 87503; (505) 827-3114

U.S. Senators: Jeff Bingaman (D), term ends 1995; Pete V. Domenici (R), term ends 1997

U.S. Representatives:
1 Democrat, 2 Republicans
Bill Richardson (D), Steven Schiff (R), Joe Skeen (R)

Legislature: Senate, 26 Democrats, 16 Republicans; House, 49 Democrats, 21 Republicans

COLLEGES AND UNIVERSITIES

Higher education:
Public 4-year institutions 6
Public 2-year institutions 16
Private 4-year institutions 4
Private 2-year institutions 0
Total 26

Vocational institutions: 39

Statewide coordinating board:
Commission on Higher Education
1068 Cerrillos Road
Santa Fe 87501
(505) 827-7383
Kathleen M. Kies, executive director

Private-college association:
Association of Independent Colleges of New Mexico
650 Granada Street
Santa Fe 87501
(505) 986-1199
Robert E. Rhodes, executive director

Institutions censured by the AAUP: None

Institutions under NCAA sanctions: None

FACULTY MEMBERS

Full-time faculty members by rank:
Professor 551
Associate professor 511
Assistant professor 575
Instructor 177
Lecturer 80
No rank 229
Total 2,123

Average pay of full-time professors:
At public 4-year institutions $37,099
At public 2-year institutions $27,328
At private 4-year institutions $29,226
At private 2-year institutions $21,911
At all institutions $34,661
Men (all institutions) $36,492
Women (all institutions) $30,002

STUDENTS

Enrollment:
Total 81,350

NEW MEXICO
Continued

At public 4-year institutions . 47,591
At public 2-year institutions . 31,768
At private 4-year institutions . 1,991
At private 2-year institutions 0
Undergraduate 70,425
  First-time freshmen 11,378
Graduate 10,310
Professional 615
American Indian 4,546
Asian 929
Black 1,667
Hispanic 20,221
White 50,647
Foreign 1,440

Enrollment highlights:
Women 54.9%
Full-time 54.6%
Minority 35.1%
Foreign 1.8%
10-year change in total
  enrollment .... Up 44.8%

Proportion of enrollment made up of minority students:
At public 4-year institutions . 30.7%
At public 2-year institutions . 41.9%
At private 4-year institutions 33.4%
At private 2-year institutions ... n/a

Degrees awarded:
Associate 1,698
Bachelor's 4,959
Master's 1,868
Doctorate 217
Professional 181

Residence of new students: State residents made up 84% of all freshmen enrolled in New Mexico; 82% of all New Mexico residents who were freshmen attended college in their home state.

Test scores: Students averaged 17.8 on the A.C.T., which was taken by 55% of New Mexico's high-school seniors.

MONEY

Average tuition and fees:
At public 4-year institutions . $1,326
At public 2-year institutions .. $496
At private 4-year institutions $7,335
At private 2-year institutions ... n/a

Expenditures:
Public institutions $456,600,000
Private institutions $16,500,000

State funds for higher-education operating expenses: $349,378,000

Two-year change: Up 18%

State spending on student aid:
Need-based: $7,257,000; 9,156 awards
Non–need-based: $3,990,000;
  2,150 awards
Other: $2,177,000

Salary of chief executive of largest public 4-year campus:
Richard E. Peck, University
  of New Mexico: $138,375

Total spending on research and development by doctorate-granting universities: $151,927,000
Sources:
Federal government 56.4%
State and local governments .. 9.7%
Industry 14.2%
The institution itself 12.8%
Other 6.9%

Federal spending on education and student aid (selected programs):
Vocational and
  adult education $9,171,000
GI Bill $3,605,000

Pell Grants $36,614,000

Total federal spending on college- and university-based research and development: $74,134,000
Selected programs:
Department of Health
  and Human Services . $9,275,000
National Science
  Foundation $6,099,000
Department of Defense $29,578,000
Department
  of Agriculture $2,574,000
Department of Energy .. $4,099,000

Largest endowment:
University
  of New Mexico $57,542,000

Top fund raisers:
University
  of New Mexico $13,681,000
New Mexico Military
  Institute $2,962,000
New Mexico State
  University $2,918,000

MISCELLANY

■ The largest number of American Indians enrolled on the main campus of any university in the country is at the University of New Mexico, where in 1990-91 833 American Indians students made up 3.4 per cent of the total enrollment.

■ The University of New Mexico is the first and only university in the country to offer a bachelor's degree in Flamenco dance.

■ The oldest institution of higher education in the state is the New Mexico State University main campus, founded in 1888.

NEW YORK

THERE'S NOTHING SIMPLE about higher education in New York, or the political and financial issues that bedevil it.

The Empire State has an unusually diverse and sophisticated array of institutions. It has major private research universities like Columbia, Cornell, and New York Universities; private liberal-arts institutions like Colgate University and Vassar and Bard Colleges; and several of the nation's leading institutions for religious training, including the Jewish and Union Theological Seminaries.

It is also home to two mammoth public-university systems. Together they operate 85 campuses, stretching from the gritty streets of the Bronx to the bucolic countryside of Oneonta.

Traditionally the State of New York has shown a willingness to become involved in higher-education affairs, particularly as the provider of student aid to those attending private colleges.

But the state's dire financial condition is now complicating matters for the private institutions and creating havoc for the public colleges. In 1991, New York abolished a well-known merit-scholarship program that had been in place for 78 years, slashed need-based financial aid that benefits both public- and private-college students, and reduced by about a third the operating support it provides to private colleges.

Budgets for the State University of New York, the nation's largest system with 64 campuses, and the City University of New York, the third-largest, were also cut back dramatically. In response, the two systems were forced to increase tuition steeply.

NEW YORK
Continued

The decision to raise tuition was especially controversial at CUNY, which until the mid-1970's charged no tuition at all and still prides itself as the college of opportunity for immigrants and the working class of New York City. The CUNY student body has a substantial number of black, Hispanic, and Caribbean students, many of whom fear the state is withdrawing its historic commitment to public higher education at the very time minority students are enrolling in greater numbers.

The problems are especially acute at CUNY's two-year colleges, since their other source of financing—New York City—is also struggling with giant budget problems.

At the same time, many are wondering whether the cuts in financial aid are a one-time occurrence or a signal of retrenchment by a state that has historically been a national leader in providing financial aid.

On a non-financial front, CUNY has also been drawn into a politically charged debate over the controversial comments of one if its faculty members, Leonard Jeffries, Jr., the chairman of the black-studies department at City College. Jewish groups have accused Mr. Jeffries of anti-Semitism, and several of the state's prominent politicians have accused CUNY of not adequately disciplining him, but Mr. Jeffries's defenders say the criticism reflects racism against a provocative black scholar.

A compromise by the CUNY board, in which Mr. Jeffries was re-approved for a shorter term as chairman than is the norm appears to have satisfied no one in the conflict.

At SUNY, which tends to serve more students from middle-class families, the Board of Trustees for the first time adopted a tuition policy, which calls for small but regular increases in future years.

The budget troubles of the public colleges illustrate political contradictions in the leadership of Gov. Mario M. Cuomo. The Governor, a Democrat serving his third term, has long said he would like to make the public colleges free, but he has never proposed budgets that would allow them to be. In 1991 his proposed budgets would have cut higher education further, if the Legislature—often more responsive to lobbyists than to Mr. Cuomo—had not stepped in to restore some money.

Well-organized and politically active faculty unions and student groups play a major role in the lobbying that accompanies higher-education budget making. The private-college lobby is large and equally aggressive.

Higher education in New York City also benefits from the state's role as a center of philanthropy and the arts. The New York Public Library is a national center for humanities research, and the city is home to the Ford, Andrew W. Mellon, and Rockefeller Foundations and to the Carnegie Corporation of New York.

The state also began the truth-in-testing movement, with a law that requires the producers of standardized tests to make public their questions and answers after the tests have been administered. While the law has been challenged as a threat to federal copyright privileges, the disclosure rules remain in effect.

Cornell, a private university that operates four SUNY units, is the state's land-grant institution. Separate boards of trustees govern SUNY and CUNY. Both systems include community colleges, comprehensive colleges, and professional schools. The systems also include research institutions; one of them, SUNY-Buffalo, was named to the select ranks of the Association of American Universities in 1989. Five other institutions in New York, all of them private, already were members.

DEMOGRAPHICS

Population: 17,990,455 (Rank: 2)

Age distribution:
Up to 17	23.7%
18 to 24	10.9%
25 to 44	32.6%
45 and older	32.8%

Racial and ethnic distribution:
American Indian	0.3%
Asian	3.9%
Black	15.9%
White	74.4%
Other and unknown	5.5%
Hispanic (may be any race)	12.3%

Educational attainment of adults:
At least 4 years of high school	66.3%
At least 1 to 3 years of college	32.2%
At least 4 years of college	17.9%

Per-capita personal income: $22,086

Poverty rate: 13.4%

New high-school graduates in:
1991-92 (estimate)	158,845
2001-02 (estimate)	176,249

New GED diploma recipients: 35,727

High-school dropout rate: 37.7%

POLITICAL LEADERSHIP

Governor: Mario M. Cuomo (D), term ends 1995

Governor's higher-education aide: Daniel Kinley, State Capitol, Executive Chamber, Room 242, Albany 12224; (518) 474-3321

U.S. Senators: Alfonse M. D'Amato (R), term ends 1993; Daniel Patrick Moynihan (D), term ends 1995

U.S. Representatives:
21 Democrats, 13 Republicans
Gary L. Ackerman (D), Sherwood L. Boehlert (R), Thomas J. Downey (D), Eliot L. Engel (D), Hamilton Fish, Jr. (R), Floyd H. Flake (D), Benjamin A. Gilman (R), Bill Green (R), George J. Hochbrueckner (D), Frank Horton (R), Amo Houghton (R), John J. LaFalce (D), Norman F. Lent (R), Nita M. Lowey (D), Thomas J. Manton (D), David O'B. Martin (R), Raymond J. McGrath (R), Matthew F. McHugh (D), Michael R. McNulty (D), Susan Molinari (R), Robert J. Mrazek (D), Henry J. Nowak (D), Major R. Owens (D), Bill Paxon (R), Charles B. Rangel (D), James H. Scheuer (D), Charles E. Schumer (D), José E. Serrano (D), Louise McIntosh Slaughter (D), Stephen J. Solarz (D), Gerald B. H. Solomon (R), Edolphus Towns (D), James T. Walsh (R), Ted Weiss (D)

Legislature: Senate, 26 Democrats, 35 Republicans; House, 93 Democrats, 54 Republicans, 3 vacancies

COLLEGES AND UNIVERSITIES

Higher education:
Public 4-year institutions	42
Public 2-year institutions	48
Private 4-year institutions	186
Private 2-year institutions	50
Total	326

Vocational institutions: 356

NEW YORK
Continued

Statewide coordinating board:
New York State Education
 Department
Cultural Education Center
Room 5B28
Albany 12230
(518) 474-5851
Donald J. Nolan, deputy commissioner for higher and continuing education

Private-college association:
Commission on Independent Colleges and Universities in New York
17 Elk Street
P.O. Box 7289
Albany 12224
(518) 436-4781
C. Mark Lawton, president

Institutions censured by the AAUP:
New York University,
State University of New York,
Yeshiva University

Institutions under NCAA sanctions:
Adelphi University, State University of New York College at Plattsburgh

FACULTY MEMBERS

Full-time faculty members by rank:
Professor 12,637
Associate professor 10,268
Assistant professor 9,540
Instructor 2,019
Lecturer 1,175
No rank 376
Total 36,015

Average pay of full-time professors:
At public 4-year institutions $49,452
At public 2-year institutions $41,741
At private 4-year institutions $42,631
At private 2-year institutions $25,709
At all institutions $44,557
Men (all institutions) $47,258
Women (all institutions) $38,535

STUDENTS

Enrollment:
Total 1,018,130
At public 4-year institutions 358,538
At public 2-year institutions 242,049
At private 4-year institutions 394,521
At private 2-year institutions 23,022
Undergraduate 828,344
 First-time freshmen 162,398
Graduate 163,025
Professional 26,761
American Indian 3,619
Asian 44,043
Black 111,000
Hispanic 70,739
White 742,572
Foreign 35,438

Enrollment highlights:
Women 55.4%
Full-time 61.9%
Minority 23.6%
Foreign 3.5%
10-year change in total
 enrollment .... Up 5.5%

Proportion of enrollment made up of minority students:
At public 4-year institutions . 29.2%
At public 2-year institutions . 24.3%
At private 4-year institutions 17.0%
At private 2-year institutions 37.1%

Degrees awarded:
Associate 45,465
Bachelor's 87,719
Master's 34,442
Doctorate 3,579
Professional 7,046

Residence of new students: State residents made up 64% of all freshmen enrolled in New York; 80% of all New York residents who were freshmen attended college in their home state.

Test scores: Students averaged 881 on the S.A.T., which was taken by 75% of New York's high-school seniors.

MONEY

Average tuition and fees:
At public 4-year institutions . $1,460
At public 2-year institutions . $1,412
At private 4-year institutions $9,517
At private 2-year institutions $5,544

Expenditures:
Public institutions .. $3,802,602,000
Private institutions . $5,594,159,000

State funds for higher-education operating expenses: $2,760,719,000

Two-year change: Down 13%

State spending on student aid:
Need-based: $408,000,000; 330,630 awards
Non–need-based: $30,739,000; 65,620 awards
Other: $385,000

Salary of chief executive of largest public 4-year campus:
William R. Greiner, State University of New York at Buffalo: $134,000

Total spending on research and development by doctorate-granting universities: $1,410,700,000
Sources:
Federal government 65.0%
State and local governments .. 5.4%
Industry 5.5%
The institution itself 12.6%
Other 11.5%

Federal spending on education and student aid (selected programs):
Vocational and
 adult education $81,216,000
GI Bill $11,469,000
Pell Grants $372,653,000

Total federal spending on college- and university-based research and development: $843,497,000
Selected programs:
Department of Health
 and Human Services $551,594,000
National Science
 Foundation $127,480,000
Department of Defense $65,415,000
Department
 of Agriculture $10,399,000
Department of Energy . $44,324,000

Largest endowment:
Columbia University $1,494,938,000

Top fund raisers:
Cornell University ... $161,338,000
Columbia University . $123,225,000
New York University .. $74,676,000

MISCELLANY

■ As part of a consent decree with the U.S. Justice Department, Columbia and Cornell Universities, along with the other Ivy League institutions, agreed in 1991 to stop setting financial-aid policies with other institutions and to stop comparing their student-aid packages with other institutions'.

■ Molloy College has established a unique program to help Soviet émigrés get their nursing licenses.

■ The oldest higher-education institution in New York is Columbia University, founded in 1754.

NORTH CAROLINA

To understand higher education in North Carolina, it helps to consider the economic transformations that have taken place in the state.

Higher education has been instrumental in helping to diversify the state's economy, long dominated by agriculture and manufacturing. This is particularly true of the institutions that define the "Research Triangle": the University of North Carolina at Chapel Hill and Duke and North Carolina State Universities. The triangle draws heavily on the universities' expertise and has brought many high-technology organizations to the region. Those companies, in turn, promote cutting-edge research at the universities.

In recent years, the relationship between business and higher education has been especially visible in the 58-campus community-college system. Known for their aggressive role in providing literacy training to adults, the colleges have become leaders in the movement to provide basic-skills training at people's workplaces. Today the state has more than 700 sites where "work-place literacy" courses are offered, including many textile mills which are becoming more mechanized and require trained workers to operate complicated equipment.

Community-college leaders also have been key players in the state's efforts to train workers for the growing service industry and for specialized fields such as tool manufacturing and horse breeding. Lawmakers have responded generously to the colleges' push for more money to upgrade academic programs, raise faculty pay, and recruit more minority students—even in 1991, when the state faced a major deficit.

While providing money for special community-college programs, the state has been forced to cut spending for general operations and has called on institutions to raise their tuition to accommodate substantial enrollment growth. In the 1990-91 academic year, both the community colleges and the University of North Carolina system were forced to make midyear budget cuts because of the state's financial problems.

Although North Carolina raised its sales tax to 6 per cent, from 5 per cent, and increased tobacco and liquor levies, most of the new revenue went toward closing the deficit.

Raising tuition is an especially sensitive issue in North Carolina, where fees for attending public colleges are among the lowest in the country. Members of the General Assembly take seriously the requirement in the state Constitution that it is their responsibility to make higher education free of expense "as far as practicable." Attempts to tamper with that philosophy are strongly opposed by the politically powerful university system.

Gov. James G. Martin, a Republican, learned that lesson in 1991, when he proposed allowing individual campuses more authority to set tuition policies. The plan was rejected, in part because of concerns that it would favor Chapel Hill and North Carolina State's campuses, which have a lot of students, while hurting small, rural campuses and historically black institutions whose students often come from needy families. The state has five public historically black institutions.

The General Assembly did agree to let the university system designate an as-yet-unspecified number of "special responsibility campuses." Those institutions would be given greater authority in how they spend their money, and would be authorized to carry over into the next budget year any money they don't spend. The measure was introduced at the behest of officials at Chapel Hill, whose pre-eminent standing in the system is sometimes resented by other campuses.

Duke is the best-known private university in North Carolina. The state is also home to many religiously affiliated institutions, such as Wake Forest and Campbell Universities, and seven private, traditionally black institutions, including Johnson C. Smith and Shaw Universities.

The University of North Carolina is governed by a single board, although each campus has its own advisory board. The community colleges are locally controlled, but are coordinated by a statewide board.

DEMOGRAPHICS

Population: 6,628,637 (Rank: 10)

Age distribution:
Up to 17 .... 24.2%
18 to 24 .... 11.8%
25 to 44 .... 32.5%
45 and older 31.5%

Racial and ethnic distribution:
American Indian 1.2%
Asian 0.8%
Black 22.0%
White 75.6%
Other and unknown 0.5%
Hispanic (may be any race) .. 1.2%

Educational attainment of adults:
At least 4 years of high school 54.8%
At least 1 to 3 years of college 27.0%
At least 4 years of college ... 13.2%

Per-capita personal income: $16,293

Poverty rate: 12.6%

New high-school graduates in:
1991-92 (estimate) 63,676
2001-02 (estimate) 64,837

New GED diploma recipients: 11,981

High-school dropout rate: 33.3%

POLITICAL LEADERSHIP

Governor: James G. Martin (R), term ends 1993

Governor's higher-education aide: Jackie Jenkins, 116 West Jones Street, Raleigh 27603; (919) 733-5811

U.S. Senators: Jesse Helms (R), term ends 1997; Terry Sanford (D), term ends 1993

U.S. Representatives:
7 Democrats, 4 Republicans
Cass Ballenger (R), Howard Coble (R), W.G. (Bill) Hefner (D), Walter B. Jones (D), H. Martin Lancaster (D), J. Alex McMillan (R), Stephen L. Neal (D), David E. Price (D), Charlie Rose (D), Charles H. Taylor (R), Tim Valentine (D)

General Assembly: Senate, 36 Democrats, 14 Republicans; House, 82 Democrats, 37 Republicans, 1 Independent

COLLEGES AND UNIVERSITIES

Higher education:
Public 4-year institutions 16
Public 2-year institutions 58
Private 4-year institutions 37
Private 2-year institutions 15
Total 126

NORTH CAROLINA
Continued

Vocational institutions: 72

Statewide coordinating boards:
University of North Carolina
General Administration
P.O. Box 2688
Chapel Hill 27515
(919) 962-6981
C. D. Spangler, president

State Department of Community
 Colleges
200 West Jones Street
Raleigh 27603
(919) 733-7051
Robert W. Scott, president

Private-college association:
North Carolina Association
 of Independent Colleges
 and Universities
879A Washington Street
Raleigh 27605
(919) 832-5817
John T. Henley, president

Institutions censured by the AAUP:
Southeastern Baptist Theological Seminary, Wingate College

Institutions under NCAA sanctions:
None

FACULTY MEMBERS

Full-time faculty members by rank:
Professor 2,604
Associate professor 2,423
Assistant professor 2,367
Instructor 357
Lecturer 548
No rank 1,328
Total 9,627

Average pay of full-time professors:
At public 4-year institutions $40,473
At public 2-year institutions $24,915
At private 4-year institutions $34,592
At private 2-year institutions $17,948
At all institutions $37,207
Men (all institutions) $40,187
Women (all institutions) $31,326

STUDENTS

Enrollment:
Total 345,401
At public 4-year institutions 144,413
At public 2-year institutions 132,649
At private 4-year institutions 63,205
At private 2-year institutions . 5,134
Undergraduate 307,980
 First-time freshmen 66,320
Graduate 30,622
Professional 6,799
American Indian 2,620
Asian 4,353
Black 58,267
Hispanic 2,249
White 260,563
Foreign 4,469

Enrollment highlights:
Women 56.0%
Full-time 63.4%
Minority 20.6%
Foreign 1.3%
10-year change in total
 enrollment .... Up 28.4%

Proportion of enrollment made up of minority students:
At public 4-year institutions . 21.1%
At public 2-year institutions . 20.1%
At private 4-year institutions 19.3%
At private 2-year institutions 31.0%

Degrees awarded:
Associate 9,894
Bachelor's 26,981

Master's 5,872
Doctorate 724
Professional 1,632

Residence of new students: State residents made up 81% of all freshmen enrolled in North Carolina; 94% of all North Carolina residents who were freshmen attended college in their home state.

Test scores: Students averaged 844 on the S.A.T., which was taken by 57% of North Carolina's high-school seniors.

MONEY

Average tuition and fees:
At public 4-year institutions . $1,015
At public 2-year institutions .. $288
At private 4-year institutions $7,373
At private 2-year institutions $4,880

Expenditures:
Public institutions .. $1,799,173,000
Private institutions ... $837,291,000

State funds for higher-education operating expenses: $1,445,790,000
Two-year change: Down 1%

State spending on student aid:
Need-based: $3,714,000; 2,660 awards
Non–need-based: $24,566,000; 26,248 awards
Other: $30,145,000

Salary of chief executive of largest public 4-year campus:
Larry K. Monteith, North Carolina State University: $117,130

Total spending on research and development by doctorate-granting universities: $441,860,000
Sources:
Federal government 62.6%
State and local governments . 14.7%
Industry 9.8%
The institution itself 9.2%
Other 3.6%

Federal spending on education and student aid (selected programs):
Vocational and
  adult education $38,765,000
GI Bill $9,484,000
Pell Grants $71,865,000

Total federal spending on college- and university-based research and development: $287,838,000
Selected programs:
Department of Health
  and Human Services $198,890,000
National Science
  Foundation $29,036,000
Department of Defense $19,267,000
Department
  of Agriculture $11,539,000
Department of Energy .. $6,398,000

Largest endowment:
Duke University $472,923,000

Top fund raisers:
Duke University $108,011,000
University of North Carolina
  at Chapel Hill $54,228,000
North Carolina State
  University $26,400,000

MISCELLANY

■ Salem College, a women's institution founded in 1772, named its first female president in 1991: Julianne Still Thrift. Ms. Thrift had been executive vice-president of the National Association of Independent Colleges and Universities.

■ The oldest institution of higher education in North Carolina is Salem College, a Moravian institution founded in 1772.

NORTH DAKOTA

Gov. GEORGE A. SINNER, a Democrat who was once president of the state's Board of Higher Education, is favorably disposed toward giving North Dakota's colleges and universities more money.

In 1990, he had to slash spending on higher education because the state's economy had been weakened by declines in agriculture and the energy industry. But in 1991, increases in energy prices brought new revenues to the state, and—true to their word—the Governor and Legislative Assembly poured needed dollars into the North Dakota University System.

The system's appropriation was increased by 13 per cent—$34-million—for the 1991-93 biennium. System employees, whose salaries had been frozen in 1990, were given increases of 4 to 6 per cent. Tuition will be frozen at the public two-year colleges through fall 1992. Tuition increases at the four-year institutions are capped at 3 per cent for fall 1991 and frozen for fall 1992.

The financial windfall followed a period of sometimes-controversial streamlining at the university system. In 1989, voters repealed two tax increases and rejected a third, leaving the university system no choice but to sharpen the focus of campus missions, eliminate duplicative programs, and cap or reduce enrollments at the state's four largest institutions.

No campuses were closed, however. The 11 public colleges and universities, which are widely scattered around the state, have become vital to the economies of their communities, and it is unlikely that political leaders would risk the outrage that would greet the closing of a campus. As part of the reorganization, the North Dakota Board of Higher Education, the governing board for public colleges, decided that long-term solutions would require more centralized control of the institutions.

For instance, the state is trying to find low-cost and efficient ways to increase access to higher education for residents of the sparsely populated state. The University of North Dakota is developing a telecommunications network to broadcast courses to various regions. In 1991 it started offering its first graduate program over the North Dakota Interactive Video Network. Students in Bismarck and Grand Forks can pursue a master's degree in business administration over the network.

The board made the Commissioner of Higher Education the chancellor of the North Dakota University System. The president of the University of North Dakota filled the position on an interim basis after the former commissioner left. Eventually, Douglas Treadway, a former president of Southwest State University in Minnesota, was named the system's chancellor.

DEMOGRAPHICS

Population: 638,800   (Rank: 47)

Age distribution:
Up to 17 .... 27.5%
18 to 24 .... 10.6%
25 to 44 .... 30.4%
45 and older 31.5%

Racial and ethnic distribution:
American Indian 4.1%
Asian 0.5%
Black 0.6%
White 94.6%

Other and unknown 0.3%
Hispanic (may be any race) .. 0.7%

Educational attainment of adults:
At least 4 years of high school 66.4%
At least 1 to 3 years of college 35.1%
At least 4 years of college ... 14.8%

Per-capita personal income: $15,215

Poverty rate: 12.5%

New high-school graduates in:
1991-92 (estimate) 7,669
2001-02 (estimate) 8,181

New GED diploma recipients: 795

High-school dropout rate: 11.7%

POLITICAL LEADERSHIP

Governor: George A. Sinner (D), term ends 1992

Governor's higher-education aide:
Carol Siegert, Governor's Office, 600 East Boulevard, Bismarck 58505; (701) 224-2200

U.S. Senators: Quentin N. Burdick (D), term ends 1995; Kent Conrad (D), term ends 1993

U.S. Representative:
1 Democrat
Byron L. Dorgan (D)

Legislative Assembly: Senate, 27 Democrats, 26 Republicans; House, 48 Democrats, 58 Republicans

COLLEGES AND UNIVERSITIES

Higher education:
Public 4-year institutions 6
Public 2-year institutions 9
Private 4-year institutions 4
Private 2-year institutions 1
Total 20

Vocational institutions: 21

Statewide coordinating board:
North Dakota University System
600 East Boulevard Avenue
State Capitol Building, 10th Floor
Bismarck 58505
(701) 224-2960
Douglas Treadway, chancellor

Private-college association:
North Dakota Independent
  College Fund
Box 6082
Jamestown College
Jamestown 58401
(701) 252-3467
Robert L. Richardson,
executive director

Institutions censured by the AAUP:
None

Institutions under NCAA sanctions:
None

FACULTY MEMBERS

Full-time faculty members by rank:
Professor 266
Associate professor 324
Assistant professor 398
Instructor 140
Lecturer 37
No rank 201
Total 1,366

Average pay of full-time professors:
At public 4-year institutions $32,768
At public 2-year institutions $27,642
At private 4-year institutions $24,897
At private 2-year institutions $32,177
At all institutions $30,907
Men (all institutions) $32,627

NORTH DAKOTA
Continued

Women (all institutions) $26,695

STUDENTS

Enrollment:
Total 40,350
At public 4-year institutions . 29,718
At public 2-year institutions .. 7,783
At private 4-year institutions . 2,672
At private 2-year institutions .. 177
Undergraduate 36,334
   First-time freshmen 8,558
Graduate 2,871
Professional 1,145
American Indian 1,486
Asian 212
Black 215
Hispanic 137
White 35,231
Foreign 1,012

Enrollment highlights:
Women 48.5%
Full-time 80.3%
Minority 5.5%
Foreign 2.6%
10-year change in total
   enrollment .... Up 26.5%

Proportion of enrollment made up of minority students:
At public 4-year institutions .. 3.0%
At public 2-year institutions . 14.0%
At private 4-year institutions . 6.2%
At private 2-year institutions ... n/a

Degrees awarded:
Associate 1,797
Bachelor's 4,287
Master's 579
Doctorate 61
Professional 115

Residence of new students: State residents made up 71% of all freshmen enrolled in North Dakota; 84% of all North Dakota residents who were freshmen attended college in their home state.

Test scores: Students averaged 18.7 on the A.C.T., which was taken by 66% of North Dakota's high-school seniors.

MONEY

Average tuition and fees:
At public 4-year institutions . $1,604
At public 2-year institutions . $1,286
At private 4-year institutions $5,149
At private 2-year institutions $2,100

Expenditures:
Public institutions $288,214,000
Private institutions $18,853,000

State funds for higher-education operating expenses: $145,535,000
Two-year change: Up 12%

State spending on student aid:
Need-based: $1,200,000; 2,000 awards
Non–need-based: $292,000;
   number of awards n/a
Other: None

Salary of chief executive of largest public 4-year campus:
Thomas J. Clifford, University
   of North Dakota: $105,000

Total spending on research and development by doctorate-granting universities: $29,966,000
Sources:
Federal government 69.5%
State and local governments .. 3.5%
Industry 9.5%
The institution itself 13.4%
Other 4.1%

Federal spending on education and student aid (selected programs):
Vocational and
  adult education $6,382,000
GI Bill $2,054,000
Pell Grants $23,799,000

Total federal spending on college- and university-based research and development: $11,715,000
Selected programs:
Department of Health
  and Human Services . $1,900,000
National Science
  Foundation $467,000
Department of Defense ... $303,000
Department
  of Agriculture $5,404,000
Department of Energy .. $1,950,000

Largest endowment:
University of North Dakota
  Foundation $16,767,000

Top fund raisers:
University
  of North Dakota $5,155,000
Jamestown College $4,520,000

MISCELLANY

■ Nearly 30 per cent of the state's college students are 24 years or older. On two University of North Dakota branch campuses, Lake Region and Williston—almost half of the students are not of traditional college age.

■ The oldest institution of higher education in North Dakota is the University of North Dakota in Grand Forks, founded in 1883.

OHIO

Ohio's public-college officials were battered from all directions in 1991.

The General Assembly accepted a recommendation from a legislative research office that Ohio's Eminent Scholars program be dropped for the 1991-93 biennium.

The Ohio Technical and Community College Association, as well as a former president of a two-year college, are under investigation by state and federal officials for allegedly funneling public money to state legislators.

Finally, there is the 1991-93 biennial budget, which is about $18-million short of meeting the needs of public colleges as determined by state financing formulas. The General Assembly produced a budget that guaranteed every institution would have at least as much money as it did in fiscal 1991.

That solution would have prevented the state's major research institutions, such as the Ohio State University and the University of Cincinnati, from ending up with less state support in fiscal 1992 than they had in fiscal 1991. But it also would have shortchanged most two-year institutions and a few four-year institutions that had had increases in enrollments.

Republican Gov. George V. Voinovich rejected the legislature's plan and restored the state's original financing formula. Now, seven universities, including Ohio State, are at the low end of the budget seesaw. But state lawmakers eliminated a $12-million grant program for part-time students throughout the state and used the money to restore some of the funds that were cut from the universities' appropriation.

The adoption of the budget does not end the debate on financing for higher education. The Governor has appointed a committee to determine if there is a more efficient way to run Ohio's

OHIO
Continued

public colleges and universities.

Legislators will also review the Eminent Scholars program. Governor Voinovich and the Legislative Office of Education Oversight both recommended temporarily discontinuing support for it. The office said the program had been much more expensive than planned. It also noted that all 22 people who hold the special chairs are men: 17 are white, one is black, and four are Asian.

Adding to Ohio's trials, the Federal Bureau of Investigation, the U.S. Department of Education, and the State Auditor's Office have been reviewing records at the Ohio Technical and Community College Association and Southern State Community College. After George R. McCormick became president of Southern State in January 1989, he began hearing rumors that his predecessor, Lewis C. Miller, had mismanaged funds and used public money to make campaign contributions. For a year, Mr. McCormick tried to get state officials to investigate the complaints. Finally he contacted the FBI.

Since November 1990, the bureau's agents have been sorting through documents relating to a "special-activity fund" that the association maintained. The investigation spread to other institutions when it was discovered that presidents of other community colleges had made political contributions from institutional funds. Several of the presidents publicly apologized and repaid the money. Mr. Miller has denied any wrongdoing.

The governance of higher education in Ohio is highly decentralized. Each institution has its own governing board. Some institutions operate branch campuses as well. The Board of Regents serves as the statewide coordinating agency.

Ohio is known for its many huge campuses. Ohio State enrolls more than 50,000 students, and the University of Cincinnati more than 30,000.

In addition to the state's well-known public institutions, Ohio has many small, private, liberal-arts colleges, like the College of Wooster, Denison University, Kenyon College, and Oberlin College, which has one of the country's outstanding music schools. Ohio is also known for a major private research institution: Case Western Reserve University. Case Western received an $8-million grant from the Kelvin and Eleanor Smith Foundation to help finance construction of its "library of the future." The facility, to be completed in 1994, will be linked with CWRUNET, the nation's first campus network based entirely on optical fibers.

DEMOGRAPHICS

Population: 10,847,115   (Rank: 7)

Age distribution:
Up to 17 .... 25.8%
18 to 24 .... 10.5%
25 to 44 .... 31.4%
45 and older 32.3%

Racial and ethnic distribution:
American Indian 0.2%
Asian 0.8%
Black 10.6%
White 87.8%
Other and unknown 0.5%
Hispanic (may be any race) .. 1.3%

Educational attainment of adults:
At least 4 years of high school 67.0%

At least 1 to 3 years of college 26.5%
At least 4 years of college ... 13.7%

Per-capita personal income: $17,564

Poverty rate: 11.5%

New high-school graduates in:
1991-92 (estimate) 121,401
2001-02 (estimate) 120,681

New GED diploma recipients: 17,281

High-school dropout rate: 20.4%

POLITICAL LEADERSHIP

Governor: George V. Voinovich (R), term ends 1995

Governor's higher-education aide:
Jean R. Droste, 77 South High Street, 30th Floor, Columbus 43215; (614) 644-0793

U.S. Senators: John Glenn (D), term ends 1993; Howard M. Metzenbaum (D), term ends 1995

U.S. Representatives:
11 Democrats, 10 Republicans
Douglas Applegate (D), John A. Boehner (R), Dennis E. Eckart (D), Edward F. Feighan (D), Paul E. Gillmor (R), Willis D. Gradison, Jr. (R), Tony P. Hall (D), David L. Hobson (R), Marcy Kaptur (D), John R. Kasich (R), Charles J. Luken (D), Bob McEwen (R), Clarence E. Miller (R), Mary Rose Oakar (D), Michael G. Oxley (R), Donald J. Pease (D), Ralph Regula (R), Thomas C. Sawyer (D), Louis Stokes (D), James A. Traficant, Jr. (D), Chalmers P. Wylie (R)

General Assembly: Senate, 12 Democrats, 21 Republicans; House, 61 Democrats, 38 Republicans

COLLEGES AND UNIVERSITIES

Higher education:
Public 4-year institutions 25
Public 2-year institutions 36
Private 4-year institutions 65
Private 2-year institutions 26
Total 152

Vocational institutions: 310

Statewide coordinating board:
Ohio Board of Regents
30 East Broad Street
3600 State Office Tower
Columbus 43266
(614) 466-6000
Elaine H. Hairston, chancellor

Private-college association:
Association of Independent Colleges and Universities of Ohio
17 South High Street, Suite 1020
Columbus 43215
(614) 228-2196
Larry H. Christman, president

Institutions censured by the AAUP:
None

Institution under NCAA sanctions:
Miami University

FACULTY MEMBERS

Full-time faculty members by rank:
Professor 4,545
Associate professor 4,432
Assistant professor 4,358
Instructor 1,052
Lecturer 71
No rank 774
Total 15,232

Average pay of full-time professors:
At public 4-year institutions $44,721
At public 2-year institutions $33,091

OHIO
Continued

At private 4-year institutions $34,799
At private 2-year institutions $20,775
At all institutions $40,141
Men (all institutions) $42,939
Women (all institutions) $33,475

STUDENTS

Enrollment:
Total 550,729
At public 4-year institutions 284,356
At public 2-year institutions 127,717
At private 4-year institutions 108,132
At private 2-year institutions 30,524
Undergraduate 478,698
First-time freshmen 108,393
Graduate 60,189
Professional 11,842
American Indian 1,272
Asian 6,140
Black 38,130
Hispanic 4,552
White 478,222
Foreign 13,421

Enrollment highlights:
Women 51.8%
Full-time 60.1%
Minority 9.5%
Foreign 2.5%
10-year change in total
 enrollment .... Up 19.0%

Proportion of enrollment made up of minority students:
At public 4-year institutions .. 8.5%
At public 2-year institutions . 11.9%
At private 4-year institutions 10.5%
At private 2-year institutions . 5.6%

Degrees awarded:
Associate 18,827
Bachelor's 45,141
Master's 12,791
Doctorate 1,652
Professional 3,225

Residence of new students: State residents made up 86% of all freshmen enrolled in Ohio; 87% of all Ohio residents who were freshmen attended college in their home state.

Test scores: Students averaged 19.1 on the A.C.T., which was taken by 52% of Ohio's high-school seniors.

MONEY

Average tuition and fees:
At public 4-year institutions . $2,432
At public 2-year institutions . $1,636
At private 4-year institutions $8,019
At private 2-year institutions $5,690

Expenditures:
Public institutions .. $2,718,408,000
Private institutions ... $980,801,000

State funds for higher-education operating expenses: $1,460,068,000
Two-year change: Up 2%

State spending on student aid:
Need-based: $52,770,000;
 73,000 awards
Non–need-based: $27,271,000;
 44,319 awards
Other: None

Salary of chief executive of largest public 4-year campus:
E. Gordon Gee, Ohio State University main campus: $160,425

Total spending on research and development by doctorate-granting universities: $457,189,000
Sources:
Federal government 57.0%

State and local governments . 10.1%
Industry 8.2%
The institution itself 13.5%
Other 11.2%

Federal spending on education and student aid (selected programs):
Vocational and
   adult education $56,926,000
GI Bill $14,413,000
Pell Grants $189,475,000

Total federal spending on college- and university-based research and development: $238,131,000
Selected programs:
Department of Health
   and Human Services $129,434,000
National Science
   Foundation $26,002,000
Department of Defense $35,312,000
Department
   of Agriculture $8,045,000
Department of Energy .. $5,267,000

Largest endowment:
Case Western Reserve
   University $421,820,000

Top fund raisers:
Ohio State University . $63,273,000
Case Western Reserve
   University $40,772,000
University of Cincinnati $27,421,000

MISCELLANY

■ The Internal Revenue Service told the Ohio State University in 1991 that it must pay taxes on the revenues it receives from companies that advertise on its scoreboard. The ruling is believed to be the first of its kind.

■ The University of Cincinnati produced a coloring book called "Imagine Yourself in College" and gave it to local elementary-school children. Most of the students in the Cincinnati Public Schools come from low-income black or Appalachian backgrounds.

■ The oldest higher-education institution in the state is Ohio University, founded in 1804.

OKLAHOMA

IN AN EFFORT to improve the quality of higher education in the Sooner State, the Oklahoma State Regents for Higher Education has set new standards for students, public institutions, and itself.

With the support of the leadership of the state's 17 public colleges and universities, the state coordinating board adopted a plan to raise gradually the admission requirements for four-year institutions.

By fall 1992, students who want to attend the University of Oklahoma or Oklahoma State University must rank in the top third of their graduating classes. They also must have a grade-point average equal to that of the upper third of Oklahoma's graduating high-school seniors or score in the top third on a national achievement test.

Previously, students could have gained admission by ranking in the upper half of their classes, or with a grade-point average of 3.0.

Convincing lawmakers in this populist state that the more stringent admission standards were needed was not easy for higher-education officials. But the chancellor of the coordinating board cited studies that showed that 35 to 40 per cent of the freshmen at the two research universities dropped out after their first year. By raising admission standards, the state

OKLAHOMA
Continued

would improve the odds that students would be academically successful, the chancellor said.

Oklahoma lawmakers gave higher education a 7.9-per-cent budget increase for fiscal 1992. Even so, money is still a perennial concern, and campus officials have decided to adopt a new budget formula under which certain programs would win new appropriations.

Under the new allocation formula, institutions must rank their programs. Programs with lower priority would receive little or no increase, and some of those with lowest priority would be dropped.

College presidents support the change in the formula because they say higher education's traditional practice of spreading resources thinner and thinner across the whole range of programs is hurting the quality of their institutions.

In July 1991, university and college board members started taking courses in higher-education issues, financing, and management as part of the Regents Education Program. Under the program, which was passed by the Legislature in 1990 and endorsed by the state regents, members of college and university governing boards are required to complete 15 hours of training within two years of taking office.

The regents will probably find an ally in Gov. David Walters, a businessman and former administrator at the University of Oklahoma. Mr. Walters, a Democrat, was elected in 1990. He has supported efforts to raise faculty salaries and to increase financing of scholarships and university research projects.

Oklahoma also has been struggling to attract more minority students to higher education, and black legislators frequently complain that the state's only predominantly black public institution, Langston University, does not receive enough money.

Most private colleges in Oklahoma are church-related. The best known is Oral Roberts University.

DEMOGRAPHICS

Population: 3,145,585 (Rank: 28)

Age distribution:
Up to 17 .... 26.6%
18 to 24 .... 10.2%
25 to 44 .... 30.6%
45 and older 32.6%

Racial and ethnic distribution:
American Indian 8.0%
Asian 1.1%
Black 7.4%
White 82.1%
Other and unknown 1.3%
Hispanic (may be any race) .. 2.7%

Educational attainment of adults:
At least 4 years of high school 66.0%
At least 1 to 3 years of college 31.2%
At least 4 years of college ... 15.1%

Per-capita personal income: $15,457

Poverty rate: 15.9%

New high-school graduates in:
1991-92 (estimate) 33,668
2001-02 (estimate) 41,828

New GED diploma recipients: 5,527

High-school dropout rate: 28.3%

POLITICAL LEADERSHIP

Governor: David Walters (D), term ends 1995

Governor's higher-education aide:
Sandy Garrett, 2500 North Lincoln Boulevard, Suite 121, Oklahoma City 73105; (405) 521-4886

U.S. Senators: David L. Boren (D), term ends 1997; Don Nickles (R), term ends 1993

U.S. Representatives:
4 Democrats, 2 Republicans
Bill K. Brewster (D), Mickey Edwards (R), Glenn English (D), James M. Inhofe (R), Dave McCurdy (D), Mike Synar (D)

Legislature: Senate, 37 Democrats, 11 Republicans; House, 68 Democrats, 32 Republicans, 1 vacancy

COLLEGES AND UNIVERSITIES

Higher education:
Public 4-year institutions 14
Public 2-year institutions 14
Private 4-year institutions 13
Private 2-year institutions 6
Total 47

Vocational institutions: 90

Statewide coordinating board:
Oklahoma State Regents
  for Higher Education
500 Education Building
State Capitol Complex
Oklahoma City 73105
(405) 524-9100
Hans Brisch, chancellor

Private-college association:
Oklahoma Association of
  Independent Colleges and
  Universities
114 East Sheridan, Suite 101
Oklahoma City 73104
(405) 235-0587
James A. Reid, president

Institutions censured by the AAUP:
Central State University,
Southern Nazarene University

Institution under NCAA sanctions:
Oklahoma State University

FACULTY MEMBERS

Full-time faculty members by rank:
Professor 1,003
Associate professor 904
Assistant professor 1,141
Instructor 423
Lecturer 141
No rank 851
Total 4,463

Average pay of full-time professors:
At public 4-year institutions $35,665
At public 2-year institutions $29,554
At private 4-year institutions $36,182
At private 2-year institutions ... n/a
At all institutions $34,508
Men (all institutions) $36,412
Women (all institutions) $30,371

STUDENTS

Enrollment:
Total 175,855
At public 4-year institutions . 94,688
At public 2-year institutions . 56,722
At private 4-year institutions 18,497
At private 2-year institutions . 5,948
Undergraduate 151,543
  First-time freshmen 30,031
Graduate 20,810
Professional 3,502
American Indian 8,014
Asian 2,787
Black 11,777
Hispanic 2,534
White 145,486
Foreign 5,709

OKLAHOMA
Continued

Enrollment highlights:
Women 53.6%
Full-time 57.2%
Minority 14.7%
Foreign 3.2%
10-year change in total
    enrollment .... Up 15.2%

Proportion of enrollment made up of minority students:
At public 4-year institutions . 14.5%
At public 2-year institutions . 14.1%
At private 4-year institutions   13.2%
At private 2-year institutions   27.9%

Degrees awarded:
Associate 6,172
Bachelor's 13,617
Master's 4,112
Doctorate 358
Professional 950

Residence of new students: State residents made up 91% of all freshmen enrolled in Oklahoma; 90% of all Oklahoma residents who were freshmen attended college in their home state.

Test scores: Students averaged 17.7 on the A.C.T., which was taken by 57% of Oklahoma's high-school seniors.

MONEY

Average tuition and fees:
At public 4-year institutions . $1,309
At public 2-year institutions .. $840
At private 4-year institutions $5,133
At private 2-year institutions $5,382

Expenditures:
Public institutions $844,829,000
Private institutions ... $178,905,000

State funds for higher-education operating expenses: $542,277,000
Two-year change: Up 20%

State spending on student aid:
Need-based: $13,177,000;
    16,026 awards
Non–need-based: $3,201,000;
    976 awards
Other: $18,746,000

Salary of chief executive of largest public 4-year campus:
Richard L. Van Horn, University of Oklahoma at Norman: $142,880 from state plus $10,702 from private sources

Total spending on research and development by doctorate-granting universities: $130,650,000
Sources:
Federal government 28.3%
State and local governments .. 5.9%
Industry 5.3%
The institution itself 53.9%
Other 6.7%

Federal spending on education and student aid (selected programs):
Vocational and
    adult education $18,612,000
GI Bill $5,589,000
Pell Grants $80,169,000

Total federal spending on college- and university-based research and development: $30,968,000
Selected programs:
Department of Health
    and Human Services $10,466,000
National Science
    Foundation $5,532,000
Department of Defense . $4,296,000

Department
 of Agriculture $6,452,000
Department of Energy .. $2,645,000

Largest endowment:
University of Tulsa ... $309,769,000

Top fund raisers:
University of Oklahoma $23,967,000
University of Tulsa $6,524,000
Oklahoma Christian
 College $3,613,000

MISCELLANY

- Historically black Langston University and the city in which it is located are both named for John Mercer Langston, a 19th-century black leader who served as vice-president of Howard University, as president of Virginia State College for Negroes (now Virginia State University), and as President Rutherford B. Hayes's resident minister in Haiti.

- The State Regents for Higher Education adopted a rule that requires students at all public colleges to maintain a 2.0 grade-point average to remain in good academic standing.

- The oldest institution of higher education in Oklahoma is Bacone College, founded in 1880.

OREGON

A PROPERTY-TAX REVOLT has shaken Oregon politics, and public higher education is a major casualty.

After the passage in 1990 of a tax-cutting law known as Measure 5, it fell to the state to assume many of the costs for public schools and government services previously financed with local property taxes.

So, even though the state's agriculture- and electronics-based economy is doing well, lawmakers had about 11 per cent less to allocate for 1991-93, and public colleges and universities are feeling the pinch acutely. They responded by cutting enrollments, laying off faculty members, and imposing a steep surcharge on tuition. In 1993, when the full effects of Measure 5 go into effect, the cost of replacing local property-tax funds could be triple that of 1991-93.

There is a glimmer of good financial news for higher education. With strong support from Gov. Barbara Roberts, a Democrat, the Legislative Assembly has begun to put money into programs that will foster cooperation between public and private colleges in the Portland area. Ventures such as shared facilities and joint degree programs are envisioned under the plan.

First to be financed is a new center that will house the joint graduate school of engineering—with advanced courses offered by Portland State University and other public research institutions—and the private Oregon Graduate Institute. Improving opportunities for advanced courses in engineering was a priority for the state's high-technology industry, which has significant political clout.

Private liberal-arts institutions, such as Lewis and Clark and Reed Colleges, would also find ways to share facilities and programs.

The biggest beneficiary of the effort, however, is likely to be Portland State. The institution, long overshadowed by the University of Oregon and Oregon State University, won new backing in the course of the Portland study. It is now being promoted as an

OREGON
Continued

institution that could provide "urban-oriented" research and service to the Portland area.

All public four-year institutions are governed by the Oregon State System of Higher Education.

The Legislative Assembly's decision in 1991 to create a new tracking system for high-school students is also expected to have a big impact on higher education, particularly community colleges. Students would be tested on their mastery of basic skills in the 10th grade and select either a traditional college-preparatory curriculum or a vocational-technical curriculum for their last two years of high school. The voc-tech program envisions two years of postsecondary education in a vocational school or community college.

DEMOGRAPHICS

Population: 2,842,321 (Rank: 29)

Age distribution:
Up to 17 .... 25.5%
18 to 24 .... 9.4%
25 to 44 .... 32.6%
45 and older 32.5%

Racial and ethnic distribution:
American Indian 1.4%
Asian 2.4%
Black 1.6%
White 92.8%
Other and unknown 1.8%
Hispanic (may be any race) .. 4.0%

Educational attainment of adults:
At least 4 years of high school 75.6%
At least 1 to 3 years of college 38.5%
At least 4 years of college ... 17.9%

Per-capita personal income: $17,196

Poverty rate: 10.3%

New high-school graduates in:
1991-92 (estimate) 24,968
2001-02 (estimate) 28,072

New GED diploma recipients: 6,690

High-school dropout rate: 27.0%

POLITICAL LEADERSHIP

Governor: Barbara Roberts (D), term ends 1995

Governor's higher-education aide: Marilynne Keyser, 225 Winter Street, N.E., Salem 97310; (503) 378-2068

U.S. Senators: Mark O. Hatfield (R), term ends 1997; Bob Packwood (R), term ends 1993

U.S. Representatives:
4 Democrats, 1 Republican
Les AuCoin (D), Peter A. DeFazio (D), Michael J. Kopetski (D), Robert F. (Bob) Smith (R), Ron Wyden (D)

Legislative Assembly: Senate, 19 Democrats, 10 Republicans, 1 vacancy; House, 27 Democrats, 32 Republicans, 1 vacancy

COLLEGES AND UNIVERSITIES

Higher education:
Public 4-year institutions 8
Public 2-year institutions 13
Private 4-year institutions 24
Private 2-year institutions 1
Total 46

Vocational institutions: 113

Statewide coordinating board:
Oregon Office of Educational
  Policy and Planning
225 Winter Street, N.E.
Salem 97310
(503) 378-2068
Marilynne Keyser, director

Private-college association:
Oregon Independent
  Colleges Association
7100 Southwest Hampton Street
Suite 222
Portland 97223
(503) 639-4541
Gary K. Andeen, executive director

Institutions censured by the AAUP:
None

Institutions under NCAA sanctions:
None

FACULTY MEMBERS

Full-time faculty members by rank:
Professor	1,085
Associate professor	874
Assistant professor	833
Instructor	189
Lecturer	21
No rank	1,548
Total	4,550

Average pay of full-time professors:
At public 4-year institutions	$35,504
At public 2-year institutions	$32,887
At private 4-year institutions	$34,257
At private 2-year institutions	$24,894
At all institutions	$34,342
Men (all institutions)	$35,884
Women (all institutions)	$30,851

STUDENTS

Enrollment:
Total	161,822
At public 4-year institutions	66,775
At public 2-year institutions	74,536
At private 4-year institutions	20,225
At private 2-year institutions	286
Undergraduate	143,093
First-time freshmen	27,233
Graduate	15,105
Professional	3,624
American Indian	1,540
Asian	6,055
Black	2,013
Hispanic	2,572
White	138,077
Foreign	5,902

Enrollment highlights:
Women	53.1%
Full-time	56.4%
Minority	8.1%
Foreign	3.8%
10-year change in total enrollment	Up 4.7%

Proportion of enrollment made up of minority students:
At public 4-year institutions	8.9%
At public 2-year institutions	7.3%
At private 4-year institutions	8.2%
At private 2-year institutions	7.0%

Degrees awarded:
Associate	4,456
Bachelor's	11,823
Master's	3,120
Doctorate	414
Professional	906

Residence of new students: State residents made up 82% of all freshmen enrolled in Oregon; 92% of all Oregon residents who were freshmen attended college in their home state.

Test scores: Students averaged 922 on the S.A.T., which was taken by 54% of Oregon's high-school seniors.

OREGON
Continued

MONEY

Average tuition and fees:
At public 4-year institutions . $1,738
At public 2-year institutions .. $753
At private 4-year institutions $8,656
At private 2-year institutions $5,250

Expenditures:
Public institutions $880,696,000
Private institutions ... $171,604,000

State funds for higher-education operating expenses: $466,322,000

Two-year change: Up 18%

State spending on student aid:
Need-based: $11,748,000;
 16,095 awards
Non–need-based: None
Other: None

Salary of chief executive of largest public 4-year campus:
Myles Brand, University of Oregon: $110,244

Total spending on research and development by doctorate-granting universities: $171,550,000
Sources:
Federal government 62.6%
State and local governments . 13.2%
Industry 3.7%
The institution itself 11.1%
Other 9.4%

Federal spending on education and student aid (selected programs):
Vocational and
 adult education $13,859,000
GI Bill $4,869,000
Pell Grants $50,767,000

Total federal spending on college- and university-based research and development: $90,171,000
Selected programs:
Department of Health
 and Human Services $38,727,000
National Science
 Foundation $18,314,000
Department of Defense . $8,827,000
Department
 of Agriculture $8,711,000
Department of Energy .. $4,582,000

Largest endowment:
Reed College $89,662,000

Top fund raisers:
Oregon State University $16,197,000
University of Oregon .. $13,589,000
Oregon Health Sciences
 University $12,863,000

MISCELLANY

■ Oregon State University has established a new Center for Analysis of Environmental Change, with financial support from the university, the Environmental Protection Agency, the Department of Agriculture's Forest Service, and Battelle–Pacific Northwest Laboratories.

■ Oregon is the only state to sponsor a sports lottery designed to aid public-college athletics programs. In its first year, little of the Sports Action money actually went to colleges because proceeds were used to underwrite other lottery programs. In 1991 the state changed the program; now all proceeds must be used to finance athletics or financial aid.

■ The oldest higher-education institution in Oregon is Willamette University, founded by Christian missionaries in 1842.

PENNSYLVANIA

PENNSYLVANIA'S college leaders, who have been struggling to develop more enthusiasm among lawmakers for state spending on higher education, learned an important but painful lesson in 1991: Giving a multimillion-dollar retirement package to a college president is most assuredly not the way to a legislator's heart.

Members of the General Assembly were furious when they learned the details of generous benefits that the University of Pittsburgh had arranged for President Wesley Posvar, who retired in July 1991 after 24 years in office.

Within weeks, some were threatening to cut higher-education spending. Others introduced a bill to require salary disclosure at Pitt and the three other "state-related" universities, which receive some financing from the government: Pennsylvania State, Lincoln, and Temple Universities.

College leaders tried to minimize the political fallout by disclosing salary details themselves. But the flap will undoubtedly leave lasting resentment in the legislature and do little to win over Gov. Robert P. Casey, a Democrat whose main education interests have centered on pre-college programs.

It hardly helped that the Pitt flap followed a bitter, month-long faculty strike at Temple—which ended only after the university threatened to cancel classes for the entire fall 1990 semester and a judge ordered professors back to work.

The university and faculty union signed a four-year contract in February 1991, just as state lawmakers began scrambling to close a $3-billion deficit. The outlook for 1991-92 improved in late summer, however, when Governor Casey and the General Assembly resolved their budget impasse by approving more than $2.8-billion in new taxes. College leaders had been among those calling for new taxes, and will now enjoy better-than-expected increases in state financing.

While the deficit preoccupied lawmakers in 1991, they also began investigating new ways to finance higher education. College leaders hope the effort will produce a formula for more support. Their figures show that the state's share of the budgets for state-owned and state-supported institutions dropped to 13 per cent from 19 per cent from 1980 to 1990. College leaders, many of whom are members of an advocacy group called the Pennsylvania Association of Colleges and Universities, say one reason that state support has slipped is that Pennsylvania has not raised taxes since 1984.

Colleges are also quietly hoping the legislature will abolish a two-year-old program initiated by Governor Casey. It rewards institutions with more state money if they keep tuition increases below a specified limit. The colleges think the program is an unstable form of financing because they are asked to give up potential tuition income in exchange for state money that could be vulnerable to cuts.

Reversing a traditionally low college-going rate, enrollments are rising in Pennsylvania, and many institutions face overcrowding. In July 1991, the State System of Higher Education responded with a new plan designed to stabilize enrollments at its 14 four-year colleges.

The two-year-college sector, relatively small given Pennsylvania's size and population, is also feeling the

PENNSYLVANIA
Continued

crunch. Some institutions, including the Harrisburg Area Community College, have responded by establishing new branches in outlying counties. The State Board of Education, which has some say over higher education, has also just approved the creation of a new two-year institution, Erie Technical Institute.

Pennsylvania is also the home of a diverse set of private colleges and universities. Seven of those, including the University of Pennsylvania, the University of the Arts, and the Philadelphia College of Textiles & Science, are "state aided" institutions.

The state has two predominantly black institutions, Lincoln and Cheney Universities, and several prestigious colleges founded by the Society of Friends: Bryn Mawr, Haverford, and Swarthmore Colleges.

DEMOGRAPHICS

Population: 11,881,643   (Rank: 5)

Age distribution:
Up to 17 .... 23.5%
18 to 24 .... 10.3%
25 to 44 .... 30.8%
45 and older 35.4%

Racial and ethnic distribution:
American Indian 0.1%
Asian 1.2%
Black 9.2%
White 88.5%
Other and unknown 1.0%
Hispanic (may be any race) .. 2.0%

Educational attainment of adults:
At least 4 years of high school 64.7%
At least 1 to 3 years of college 24.3%
At least 4 years of college ... 13.6%

Per-capita personal income: $18,686

Poverty rate: 10.6%

New high-school graduates in:
1991-92 (estimate) 119,577
2001-02 (estimate) 125,468

New GED diploma recipients: 17,166

High-school dropout rate: 21.6%

POLITICAL LEADERSHIP

Governor: Robert P. Casey (D), term ends 1995

Governor's higher-education aide: Helen Wise, State Capitol, Room 238, Harrisburg 17120; (717) 787-2500

U.S. Senators: Harris Wofford (D), term ends 1995; Arlen Specter (R), term ends 1993

U.S. Representatives:
12 Democrats, 12 Republicans
Lucien Blackwell (D), Robert A. Borski (D), William F. Clinger, Jr. (R), Lawrence Coughlin (R), William J. Coyne (D), Thomas M. Foglietta (D), Joseph M. Gaydos (D), George W. Gekas (R), William F. Goodling (R), Paul E. Kanjorksi (D), Joe Kolter (D), Peter H. Kostmayer (D), Joseph M. McDade (R), Austin J. Murphy (D), John P. Murtha (D), Thomas J. Ridge (R), Don Ritter (R), Rick Santorum (R), Richard T. Schulze (R), Bud Shuster (R), Robert S. Walker (R), Curt Weldon (R), Gus Yatron (D)

General Assembly: Senate, 24 Democrats, 26 Republicans; House, 107 Democrats, 96 Republicans

COLLEGES AND UNIVERSITIES

Higher education:
Public 4-year institutions 43
Public 2-year institutions 18
Private 4-year institutions 103
Private 2-year institutions 53
Total 217

Vocational institutions: 366

Statewide coordinating board:
State Department of Education
333 Market Street, 12th Floor
Harrisburg 17126
(717) 787-5041
Peter H. Garland, acting commissioner for higher education

Private-college association:
Commission for Independent Colleges and Universities of Pennsylvania
800 North Third Street
Harrisburg 17102
(717) 232-8649
Brian C. Mitchell, president

Institutions censured by the AAUP:
Grove City College, Temple University

Institution under NCAA sanctions:
Robert Morris College

FACULTY MEMBERS

Full-time faculty members by rank:
Professor 6,416
Associate professor 5,967
Assistant professor 6,090
Instructor 1,463
Lecturer 184
No rank 99
Total 20,219

Average pay of full-time professors:
At public 4-year institutions $42,983
At public 2-year institutions $36,545
At private 4-year institutions $40,832
At private 2-year institutions ... n/a
At all institutions $41,177
Men (all institutions) $43,921
Women (all institutions) $34,468

STUDENTS

Enrollment:
Total 610,357
At public 4-year institutions   234,784
At public 2-year institutions   100,317
At private 4-year institutions 214,270
At private 2-year institutions   60,986
Undergraduate 523,380
    First-time freshmen 148,334
Graduate 73,158
Professional 13,819
American Indian 918
Asian 10,583
Black 38,415
Hispanic 6,139
White 504,972
Foreign 12,900

Enrollment highlights:
Women 53.9%
Full-time 64.8%
Minority 10.0%
Foreign 2.2%
10-year change in total
    enrollment .... Up 26.8%

Proportion of enrollment made up of minority students:
At public 4-year institutions .. 9.7%
At public 2-year institutions . 13.0%
At private 4-year institutions . 7.4%
At private 2-year institutions 18.4%

Degrees awarded:
Associate 16,823
Bachelor's 58,890
Master's 14,587
Doctorate 2,027
Professional 3,575

PENNSYLVANIA
Continued

Residence of new students: State residents made up 77% of all freshmen enrolled in Pennsylvania; 82% of all Pennsylvania residents who were freshmen attended college in their home state.

Test scores: Students averaged 876 on the S.A.T., which was taken by 67% of Pennsylvania's high-school seniors.

MONEY

Average tuition and fees:
At public 4-year institutions . $3,210
At public 2-year institutions . $1,419
At private 4-year institutions $9,430
At private 2-year institutions $5,497

Expenditures:
Public institutions . . $2,392,145,000
Private institutions . $3,169,219,000

State funds for higher-education operating expenses: $1,483,233,000

Two-year change: Up 8%

State spending on student aid:
Need-based: $145,057,000;
   122,654 awards
Non–need-based: $519,000;
   201 awards
Other: None

Salary of chief executive of largest public 4-year campus:
Joab Thomas, Pennsylvania State University main campus: $200,004

Total spending on research and development by doctorate-granting universities: $829,518,000

Sources:
Federal government 62.1%
State and local governments . . 3.8%
Industry 11.9%
The institution itself 15.2%
Other 7.0%

Federal spending on education and student aid (selected programs):
Vocational and
   adult education $60,402,000
GI Bill $11,509,000
Pell Grants $192,796,000

Total federal spending on college- and university-based research and development: $484,619,000

Selected programs:
Department of Health
   and Human Services $265,243,000
National Science
   Foundation $62,936,000
Department of Defense $97,075,000
Department
   of Agriculture $9,859,000
Department of Energy . $19,220,000

Largest endowment:
University
   of Pennsylvania $808,409,000

Top fund raisers:
University
   of Pennsylvania $140,045,000
Pennsylvania State
   University $62,433,000
University of Pittsburgh $36,557,000

MISCELLANY

■ Philadelphia is the home of the Middle States Association of Colleges and Schools, a regional accrediting group that has been embroiled in controversy since 1990 over its policy of having accrediting review teams consider colleges' records in recruiting and retaining minority student and faculty members.

- The Moore College of Art and Design is the only college in the world dedicated solely to the education of women in fine arts and design.

- Temple University's doctoral program in black studies—the only one in the nation—awarded its first degree in May 1991. The program takes an Afrocentric approach to the curriculum.

- The University of Pennsylvania, founded in 1740, is the nation's oldest full-fledged university. (Harvard, which dates to 1636, was founded as a college.)

RHODE ISLAND

1991 was a year of difficult choices for Rhode Island's lawmakers and college officials. Gov. Bruce Sundlun, a Democrat, closed 45 banks and credit unions on January 1—his first day in office—because the institutions' private insurer had failed. Since then, he has spent a great deal of his time tussling with federal regulators to resolve the state's banking crisis.

Among those affected were the members of the Brown University Employees' Credit Union, one of several financial institutions that did not qualify for federal insurance after they were closed by the Governor.

Although the credit union is not formally affiliated with the university, Brown offered no-interest loans to all employees and others affected by the closure. The largest bank in the state, Citizens Bank, acquired most of the assets of the credit union after lengthy and complicated negotiations with state and credit-union officials.

When the Governor was not occupied with details of the banking problems, he was busy trying to eliminate a budget deficit.

Tuition at the three public institutions has been increased by about 20 per cent to help compensate for budget cuts. With the increase, students who are Rhode Island residents now pay between 30 per cent and 35 per cent of the actual cost of their education—an increase from 26 per cent. Non-residents are paying the full cost of instruction for the first time. Out-of-state students pay $8,492 a year for tuition at the University of Rhode Island, for example, while residents pay $3,140.

Students are not the only ones who have felt the pinch of the budget shortfall. Faculty and staff unions have agreed to a pay-deferral program that amounts to a 10-per-cent salary cut.

The Rhode Island Children's Crusade for Higher Education continues to have strong bipartisan support from legislators and the new Governor. Despite the state's budget woes, lawmakers allocated $1.5-million for it in 1991. The "early intervention" program established an endowment, financed with public and private funds, to help pay the cost of a college education for needy students who agree in grade school to avoid drugs and meet certain academic requirements.

The Board of Governors for Higher Education is the governing group and the coordinating unit for all public higher education.

Brown and the Rhode Island School of Design, both in Providence, are nationally regarded private institutions.

1991 was also a year of controversy at Brown.

RHODE ISLAND
Continued

In January, administrators expelled a student for shouting anti-black, anti-Semitic, and anti-homosexual remarks in a university courtyard. The student is believed to be the first undergraduate at any institution to be thrown out for violating an anti-harassment code, and his expulsion set off a national debate on the value of such codes.

DEMOGRAPHICS

Population: 1,003,464   (Rank: 43)

Age distribution:
Up to 17	22.5%
18 to 24	12.0%
25 to 44	32.0%
45 and older	33.5%

Racial and ethnic distribution:
American Indian	0.4%
Asian	1.8%
Black	3.9%
White	91.4%
Other and unknown	2.5%
Hispanic (may be any race)	4.6%

Educational attainment of adults:
At least 4 years of high school	61.1%
At least 1 to 3 years of college	28.3%
At least 4 years of college	15.4%

Per-capita personal income: $18,802

Poverty rate: 8.0%

New high-school graduates in:
1991-92 (estimate)	8,702
2001-02 (estimate)	10,020

New GED diploma recipients: 2,455

High-school dropout rate: 30.2%

POLITICAL LEADERSHIP

Governor: Bruce Sundlun (D), term ends 1993

Governor's higher-education aide: Elizabeth Roberts, State House, Room 128, Providence 02903; (401) 277-2080

U.S. Senators: John H. Chafee (R), term ends 1995; Claiborne Pell (D), term ends 1997

U.S. Representatives:
1 Democrat, 1 Republican
Ronald K. Machtley (R), Jack Reed (D)

General Assembly: Senate, 45 Democrats, 5 Republicans; House, 84 Democrats, 16 Republicans

COLLEGES AND UNIVERSITIES

Higher education:
Public 4-year institutions	2
Public 2-year institutions	1
Private 4-year institutions	8
Private 2-year institutions	0
Total	11

Vocational institutions: 28

Statewide coordinating board:
Office of Higher Education
301 Promenade Street
Providence 02908
(401) 277-6560
Americo W. Petrocelli, commissioner of higher education

Private-college association:
Rhode Island Independent
  Higher Education Association
Charles-Orms Building, Suite 120
10 Orms Street

Providence 02904
(401) 272-8270
Robert J. McKenna, president

Institutions censured by the AAUP:
None

Institutions under NCAA sanctions:
None

FACULTY MEMBERS

Full-time faculty members by rank:
Professor	936
Associate professor	587
Assistant professor	553
Instructor	67
Lecturer	39
No rank	87
Total	2,269

Average pay of full-time professors:
At public 4-year institutions	$44,559
At public 2-year institutions	$36,018
At private 4-year institutions	$45,566
At private 2-year institutions	n/a
At all institutions	$43,972
Men (all institutions)	$47,166
Women (all institutions)	$36,767

STUDENTS

Enrollment:
Total	76,503
At public 4-year institutions	25,204
At public 2-year institutions	15,400
At private 4-year institutions	35,899
At private 2-year institutions	0
Undergraduate	66,920
First-time freshmen	13,308
Graduate	9,286
Professional	297
American Indian	218
Asian	1,402
Black	2,185
Hispanic	1,197
White	68,139
Foreign	1,698

Enrollment highlights:
Women	54.8%
Full-time	61.1%
Minority	6.8%
Foreign	2.3%
10-year change in total enrollment	Up 18.7%

Proportion of enrollment made up of minority students:
At public 4-year institutions	5.1%
At public 2-year institutions	9.3%
At private 4-year institutions	6.9%
At private 2-year institutions	n/a

Degrees awarded:
Associate	3,663
Bachelor's	8,493
Master's	1,774
Doctorate	222
Professional	80

Residence of new students: State residents made up 44% of all freshmen enrolled in Rhode Island; 70% of all Rhode Island residents who were freshmen attended college in their home state.

Test scores: Students averaged 880 on the S.A.T., which was taken by 67% of Rhode Island's high-school seniors.

MONEY

Average tuition and fees:
At public 4-year institutions	$2,281
At public 2-year institutions	$1,004
At private 4-year institutions	$10,143
At private 2-year institutions	n/a

Expenditures:
Public institutions	$213,253,000
Private institutions	$315,651,000

RHODE ISLAND
Continued

State funds for higher-education operating expenses: $116,128,000
Two-year change: Down 17%

State spending on student aid:
Need-based: $10,067,000; 9,400 awards
Non–need-based: $123,000; 49 awards
Other: $425,000

Salary of chief executive of largest public 4-year campus:
Robert L. Carothers, University of Rhode Island: $108,000

Total spending on research and development by doctorate-granting universities: $82,634,000
Sources:
Federal government 69.5%
State and local governments .. 6.2%
Industry 5.3%
The institution itself 16.0%
Other 3.0%

Federal spending on education and student aid (selected programs):
Vocational and
   adult education $6,697,000
GI Bill $1,262,000
Pell Grants $13,977,000

Total federal spending on college- and university-based research and development: $49,525,000
Selected programs:
Department of Health
   and Human Services $16,252,000
National Science
   Foundation $14,918,000
Department of Defense $10,142,000
Department
   of Agriculture $1,173,000
Department of Energy .. $2,640,000

Largest endowment:
Brown University $425,750,000

Top fund raisers:
Brown University $42,040,000
University
   of Rhode Island $6,136,000
Providence College $3,763,000

MISCELLANY

- As part of a consent decree with the U.S. Justice Department, Brown University, along with the other Ivy League institutions, agreed in 1991 to stop setting financial-aid policies with other institutions and to stop comparing its students' aid packages with other institutions'.

- The oldest institution of higher education in Rhode Island is Brown University, founded in 1764.

SOUTH CAROLINA

THE UNIVERSITY of South Carolina has a new president—and an opportunity to rebuild its reputation and regain the confidence of legislators and the public.

Taxpayers were angered and key legislators alienated by stories about the free-spending practices of the institution's former president, James B. Holderman.

Mr. Holderman resigned in 1990. But that did not satisfy legislators, who imposed spending restrictions on all institutions including those, such as Clemson University, that had not been accused of inappropriate financial actions. Nor did his resignation end the scandal about his spending habits.

In early 1991 the state Supreme Court ordered the university's Carolina Research and Development Foundation to make its Holderman records public. After foundation officials announced that four years of records had been accidently thrown out in 1988, *The Greenville News*—which along with the Associated Press had sued to gain access to the records, rented a backhoe, went to the local landfill, and dug up piles of the organization's documents.

The unearthed papers contained revelations that led to Mr. Holderman's indictment on two charges: that he had used his position to obtain $25,000 from a law firm in exchange for helping resolve a client's drug case, and that he had failed to pay state income tax on the money. He eventually pleaded guilty to a misdemeanor charge of accepting additional compensation and pleaded no contest to felony charges of evading state income taxes.

He also agreed to cooperate with a federal investigation of U.S. Senator Mark Hatfield, Republican of Oregon, who had received numerous gifts from Mr. Holderman and whose son had attended the university on a scholarship. Investigators want to determine whether there is any connection between those gifts and Mr. Hatfield's support of a $16-million federal grant to the university.

The foundation was fined $227,000 for destroying documents that were the subject of litigation. Its director resigned, but stayed on at the university as a tenured professor of journalism.

In October 1991, the university's new president, John M. Palms, said he intended to begin proceedings to revoke Mr. Holderman's tenure after *The Charlotte Observer* reported that Mr. Holderman had made sexual advances toward four male students while he was president. The students, who worked as interns for Mr. Holderman in the 1980's, told the newspaper that he had made unwanted sexual advances and had given them gifts, including suits and gold chains. Mr. Holderman has denied the allegations.

Mr. Palms has been meeting with legislators, students, and faculty members in an effort to repair the damage to the university's reputation and morale. He has promised to continue many projects that did not receive adequate attention during the height of the Holderman scandal. Mr. Palms has said the quality of teaching and the university's commitment to diversity in student enrollment and faculty staffing will receive special attention.

He will have to achieve those goals, however, without much financial support from the state. Three days before the close of the 1991 legislative session, lawmakers received a report that state revenues were not meeting projections. Lawmakers opted to make across-the-board cuts that left higher education with less money in fiscal 1992 than it had in fiscal 1991.

Now colleges are freezing salaries, increasing class sizes, deferring maintenance, and postponing equipment purchases.

Still, higher-education officials are trying to move forward. The Commission on Higher Education, the state coordinating board, is developing a strategic plan to encourage collaboration between colleges and public schools, to increase the number of residents who attend college, and to provide incentives for improving the quality of programs and instruction.

In 1988 the state started an ambitious program to improve higher edu-

SOUTH CAROLINA
Continued

cation. Called the "Cutting Edge," it included money for new endowed professorships and improved research efforts. Private institutions are eligible for some grants, and needy students at private colleges are eligible for state grants to offset part of their tuition.

Besides the perennial lack of money, higher-education leaders in South Carolina are also concerned about improving the college-going rates of black citizens, who make up a third of the state's population but only about a fifth of the college population. Minority enrollment is even lower at the state's major institutions, the University of South Carolina and Clemson.

DEMOGRAPHICS

Population: 3,486,703   (Rank: 25)

Age distribution:
Up to 17 .... 26.4%
18 to 24 .... 11.7%
25 to 44 .... 32.0%
45 and older 29.9%

Racial and ethnic distribution:
American Indian 0.2%
Asian 0.6%
Black 29.8%
White 69.0%
Other and unknown 0.3%
Hispanic (may be any race) .. 0.9%

Educational attainment of adults:
At least 4 years of high school 53.7%
At least 1 to 3 years of college 26.7%
At least 4 years of college ... 13.4%

Per-capita personal income: $15,151

Poverty rate: 16.2%

New high-school graduates in:
1991-92 (estimate) 36,111
2001-02 (estimate) 37,341

New GED diploma recipients: 5,708

High-school dropout rate: 35.4%

POLITICAL LEADERSHIP

Governor: Carroll A. Campbell, Jr. (R), term ends 1995

Governor's higher-education aide: Janice Trawick, P.O. Box 11369, Columbia 29211; (803) 734-9818

U.S. Senators: Ernest F. Hollings (D), term ends 1993; Strom Thurmond (R), term ends 1997

U.S. Representatives:
4 Democrats, 2 Republicans
Butler Derrick (D), Elizabeth J. Patterson (D), Arthur Ravenel, Jr. (R), Floyd Spence (R), John M. Spratt, Jr. (D), Robin Tallon (D)

General Assembly: Senate, 34 Democrats, 12 Republicans; House, 77 Democrats, 42 Republicans, 1 Independent, 4 vacancies

COLLEGES AND UNIVERSITIES

Higher education:
Public 4-year institutions 12
Public 2-year institutions 21
Private 4-year institutions 20
Private 2-year institutions 11
Total 64

Vocational institutions: 62

Statewide coordinating board:
Commission on Higher Education
1333 Main Street, Suite 300
Columbia 29201

(803) 253-6260
Fred R. Sheheen, commissioner

Private-college association:
South Carolina College Council
P.O. Box 12007
Columbia 29211
(803) 799-7122
Sterling L. Smith, vice-president

Institutions censured by the AAUP:
None

Institutions under NCAA sanctions:
None

FACULTY MEMBERS

Full-time faculty members by rank:
Professor 1,206
Associate professor 1,214
Assistant professor 1,151
Instructor 540
Lecturer 65
No rank 903
Total 5,079

Average pay of full-time professors:
At public 4-year institutions $38,343
At public 2-year institutions $26,117
At private 4-year institutions $29,755
At private 2-year institutions $24,209
At all institutions $34,017
Men (all institutions) $36,795
Women (all institutions) $28,607

STUDENTS

Enrollment:
Total 145,730
At public 4-year institutions . 79,252
At public 2-year institutions . 39,387
At private 4-year institutions 22,490
At private 2-year institutions . 4,601
Undergraduate 125,407
  First-time freshmen 33,752
Graduate 17,892
Professional 2,431
American Indian 236
Asian 1,288
Black 29,247
Hispanic 863
White 113,939
Foreign 2,184

Enrollment highlights:
Women 55.8%
Full-time 67.7%
Minority 21.7%
Foreign 1.5%
10-year change in total
  enrollment .... Up 10.9%

Proportion of enrollment made up of minority students:
At public 4-year institutions . 16.7%
At public 2-year institutions . 24.5%
At private 4-year institutions 30.1%
At private 2-year institutions 39.5%

Degrees awarded:
Associate 4,949
Bachelor's 12,524
Master's 3,269
Doctorate 266
Professional 738

Residence of new students: State residents made up 80% of all freshmen enrolled in South Carolina; 89% of all South Carolina residents who were freshmen attended college in their home state.

Test scores: Students averaged 832 on the S.A.T., which was taken by 58% of South Carolina's high-school seniors.

MONEY

Average tuition and fees:
At public 4-year institutions . $2,162
At public 2-year institutions .. $807

SOUTH CAROLINA
Continued

At private 4-year institutions $5,914
At private 2-year institutions $4,898

Expenditures:
Public institutions $951,848,000
Private institutions ... $196,271,000

State funds for higher-education operating expenses: $634,226,000
Two-year change: Up 4%

State spending on student aid:
Need-based: $18,079,000;
   6,805 awards
Non–need-based: None
Other: $1,368,000

Salary of chief executive of largest public 4-year campus:
John M. Palms, University of South Carolina at Columbia: $135,503 from state plus $25,000 from private donations

Total spending on research and development by doctorate-granting universities: $137,269,000
Sources:
Federal government 33.3%
State and local governments . 12.7%
Industry 9.4%
The institution itself 37.1%
Other 7.6%

Federal spending on education and student aid (selected programs):
Vocational and
   adult education $21,954,000
GI Bill $6,473,000
Pell Grants $49,459,000

Total federal spending on college- and university-based research and development: $38,927,000

Selected programs:
Department of Health
   and Human Services $19,562,000
National Science
   Foundation $6,186,000
Department of Defense . $4,705,000
Department
   of Agriculture $5,590,000
Department of Energy .. $1,513,000

Largest endowment:
Furman University $79,748,000

Top fund raisers:
University of South Carolina
   at Columbia $21,487,000
Clemson University ... $19,956,000
Furman University $10,950,000

MISCELLANY

■ The Citadel, a state-supported military college in Charleston, has instituted a mandatory, random drug-testing program for all incoming students. Under the policy, new students and their parents must sign consent forms that call for cadets to submit to drug tests at the request of campus officials. Those refusing to be tested could be expelled.

■ The oldest higher-education institution in South Carolina is the College of Charleston, founded in 1770.

SOUTH DAKOTA

FARMING HAS BEEN the mainstay of South Dakota's economy for nearly a century, and its influence over higher education is evident in many quarters, from the way the state finances its public colleges to the kind of research that is conducted there.

When they can be, lawmakers are generous to the public colleges, and a recent upswing in prices for such staples as wheat and soybeans resulted in a small windfall for higher education. The money allowed colleges and universities to raise faculty pay, but higher-education leaders say salaries still lag behind those in neighboring states.

Gov. George S. Mickelson, a Republican serving his second term, has been a strong supporter of higher education, particularly as a way to promote economic development. In his first term he helped secure greater autonomy for the South Dakota Board of Regents, the governing board for all of higher education.

He has also supported new taxes to benefit colleges and public schools, but his latest proposal—for a half-cent increase in the sales tax—was defeated in 1991 by the Legislature, which preferred an income tax. South Dakota has no corporate or personal income tax.

The debate ended in a stalemate, but the issue is likely to resurface, particularly after legislators complete a study of higher education's needs.

South Dakota has no state-run community colleges and in many instances depends on its public colleges and universities to provide two-year programs to those who want them. While that approach is economical, it has created some "access" problems, as many potential students live in rural communities and cannot easily commute to college. The state does have some two-year institutions that are controlled by American Indian tribes, local governments, and private entities.

State officials apparently learned lessons from the "bust" years in the 1980's, when declines in agriculture created a budget crisis and drove the state to close a two-year branch of the University of South Dakota. Now, rather than building more campuses, university leaders plan to expand the use of distance learning, employing the technology in the state telecommunications network that is now under development.

With help from Washington, South Dakota's universities are also making strides in expanding their research capacity. Much of the research relates to agriculture, such as studies in "biostress" at South Dakota State University that measure the influence of harsh climates on crops. But the institutions have also been expanding into non-agricultural fields, including materials science.

DEMOGRAPHICS

Population: 696,004   (Rank: 45)

Age distribution:
Up to 17 .... 28.5%
18 to 24 .... 9.8%
25 to 44 .... 29.4%
45 and older 32.3%

Racial and ethnic distribution:
American Indian 7.3%
Asian 0.4%
Black 0.5%
White 91.6%
Other and unknown 0.2%
Hispanic (may be any race) .. 0.8%

Educational attainment of adults:
At least 4 years of high school 67.9%
At least 1 to 3 years of college 31.7%
At least 4 years of college ... 14.0%

Per-capita personal income: $15,797

Poverty rate: 13.6%

SOUTH DAKOTA
Continued

New high-school graduates in:
1991-92 (estimate) 7,659
2001-02 (estimate) 8,849

New GED diploma recipients: 1,075

High-school dropout rate: 20.4%

POLITICAL LEADERSHIP

Governor: George S. Mickelson (R), term ends 1995

Governor's higher-education aide:
James Soyer, 500 East Capitol, Pierre 57501; (605) 773-3661

U.S. Senators: Thomas A. Daschle (D), term ends 1993; Larry Pressler (R), term ends 1997

U.S. Representative:
1 Democrat
Tim Johnson (D)

Legislature: Senate, 17 Democrats, 18 Republicans; House, 25 Democrats, 45 Republicans

COLLEGES AND UNIVERSITIES

Higher education:
Public 4-year institutions 7
Public 2-year institutions 0
Private 4-year institutions 10
Private 2-year institutions 2
Total 19

Vocational institutions: 21

Statewide coordinating board:
Board of Regents
207 East Capitol Avenue
Pierre 57501
(605) 773-3455
Howell Todd, executive director

Private-college association:
South Dakota Association
 of Independent Colleges
P.O. Box 645
Sioux Falls 57101
(605) 331-2927
Betsy Reck, association manager

Institutions censured by the AAUP:
None

Institutions under NCAA sanctions:
None

FACULTY MEMBERS

Full-time faculty members by rank:
Professor 339
Associate professor 237
Assistant professor 361
Instructor 135
Lecturer .... n/a
No rank 159
Total 1,234

Average pay of full-time professors:
At public 4-year institutions $31,351
At public 2-year institutions .... n/a
At private 4-year institutions $24,928
At private 2-year institutions $21,000
At all institutions $29,437
Men (all institutions) $31,378
Women (all institutions) $25,406

STUDENTS

Enrollment:
Total 32,666
At public 4-year institutions . 25,075
At public 2-year institutions 0
At private 4-year institutions . 7,232
At private 2-year institutions .. 359
Undergraduate 28,851

First-time freshmen 6,390
Graduate 3,320
Professional 495
American Indian 1,888
Asian 122
Black 226
Hispanic 69
White 28,526
Foreign 629

Enrollment highlights:
Women 55.2%
Full-time 72.1%
Minority 7.5%
Foreign 2.0%
10-year change in total
 enrollment .... Up 4.4%

Proportion of enrollment made up of minority students:
At public 4-year institutions .. 5.7%
At public 2-year institutions .... n/a
At private 4-year institutions 11.8%
At private 2-year institutions 33.8%

Degrees awarded:
Associate 783
Bachelor's 3,698
Master's 793
Doctorate 48
Professional 130

Residence of new students: State residents made up 72% of all freshmen enrolled in South Dakota; 72% of all South Dakota residents who were freshmen attended college in their home state.

Test scores: Students averaged 19.4 on the A.C.T., which was taken by 66% of South Dakota's high-school seniors.

MONEY

Average tuition and fees:
At public 4-year institutions . $1,718
At public 2-year institutions .... n/a
At private 4-year institutions $6,224
At private 2-year institutions $2,447

Expenditures:
Public institutions $149,092,000
Private institutions $51,675,000

State funds for higher-education operating expenses: $97,273,000
Two-year change: Up 13%

State spending on student aid:
Need-based: $468,000; 1,550 awards
Non–need-based: $90,000; 60 awards
Other: None

Salary of chief executive of largest public 4-year campus:
Robert T. Wagner, South
 Dakota State University: $88,600

Total spending on research and development by doctorate-granting universities: $14,342,000
Sources:
Federal government 47.9%
State and local governments . 40.3%
Industry 2.6%
The institution itself 6.8%
Other 2.3%

Federal spending on education and student aid (selected programs):
Vocational and
 adult education $6,403,000
GI Bill $1,990,000
Pell Grants $20,272,000

Total federal spending on college- and university-based research and development: $6,861,000
Selected programs:
Department of Health
 and Human Services ... $927,000
National Science
 Foundation $2,045,000

SOUTH DAKOTA
Continued

Department of Defense 0
Department
  of Agriculture $2,827,000
Department of Energy $115,000

Largest endowment:
University of
  South Dakota $15,810,000

Top fund raisers:
South Dakota State
  University $4,787,000
Augustana College $2,737,000
University
  of South Dakota $2,670,000

MISCELLANY

- In April 1991, acting for the state's public universities, Governor Mickelson signed an exchange agreement with the University of Warsaw. Faculty members from the University of Warsaw will advise the Governor on trade with Poland and Eastern Europe, while professors from South Dakota will act as the state's representatives in Poland. Students and faculty members will also teach and study abroad as part of the exchange.

- The oldest institution of higher education in South Dakota is the North American Baptist Seminary, founded in 1858.

TENNESSEE

WHEN Ned Ray McWherter was elected to a second term as Governor of Tennessee in 1990, he pledged that he would devote the next four years to improving the quality of the state's schools and colleges—and to increasing financial support for them.

Although he failed in his attempts to pass a state income tax, education officials give him an A for effort and hope he will continue his campaign in 1992.

The General Assembly's rejection of a tax increase, however, left higher education with a $689-million budget for fiscal 1992. That is less money than it received in each of the last three years.

In recent years, public colleges have frozen hiring for vacant positions and deferred equipment purchases. But officials at the Tennessee Higher Education Commission, the state coordinating board, said more stringent measures would be required in 1991. Student grants will be reduced, grants to private colleges will be decreased, salaries will be maintained at present levels, and major new programs will be postponed.

The shortage of state financing will make it particularly difficult for new college presidents to move ahead with their plans. Lamar Alexander, who was the president of the University of Tennessee system until President Bush asked him to become Education Secretary in late 1990, had said he wanted the system to be on a par with the University of Michigan and the University of North Carolina at Chapel Hill.

Now the task of bringing that about falls on the shoulders of the man who was Mr. Alexander's executive vice-president and is now his successor, Joseph E. Johnson.

Mr. Johnson's task has been made more difficult by a series of investigations into business relationships involving Secretary Alexander while he was president of the university. Several individuals who had served under Mr. Alexander while he was Governor of Tennessee had been awarded university contracts without competitive bidding. In addition, the university had spent $65,000 for 14 events at a resort owned in part by Mr. Alexander's wife.

Mr. Alexander has denied any wrongdoing. But questions about his business dealings have prompted some lawmakers to propose tougher conflict-of-interest laws that would apply to university administrators.

James A. Hefner, the new president of Tennessee State University, also faces the challenge of improving his institution's stature. He is beginning by restructuring the administration of the historically black institution. He is also reviewing the institution's academic offerings and has expressed an interest in adding programs in journalism, law, and public policy.

Another historically black institution may undergo changes as well. The president of Meharry Medical College has proposed that the city of Nashville close its aging inner-city hospital, Metropolitan Nashville General, and move its operations to Meharry's hospital.

The plan has been endorsed by Vanderbilt University, the Nashville Chamber of Commerce, local religious leaders, and Health and Human Services Secretary Louis W. Sullivan, who is a former president of the Morehouse School of Medicine. But the board of Metro General has stalled. Civil-rights activists say its failure to act has raised the specter of Tennessee's segregationist history with questions about the quality of white-run versus black-run hospitals and whether white patients would go to a hospital run by a black institution.

Nashville Mayor Phil Bredesen and other city leaders persuaded Metro General's board to give conditional approval to a phased-in merger of the two hospitals. Metro General's board is withholding final approval until it reviews a firm contract. Mayor Bredesen hoped to have a contract prepared by the end of 1991.

The regional and university systems are both coordinated by the Tennessee Higher Education Commission.

Unlike most Southern states, which were covered by a single federal desegregation suit, Tennessee has its own court order, with goals for increasing black enrollment. The state is still trying to meet several of those goals.

Many of the state's black students enroll at historically black colleges, like Tennessee State, a public institution, and Fisk University, which is private.

Several other private institutions are influential in Tennessee, including the University of the South and Vanderbilt.

DEMOGRAPHICS

Population: 4,877,185   (Rank: 17)

Age distribution:
Up to 17 .... 24.9%
18 to 24 .... 10.8%
25 to 44 .... 31.8%
45 and older 32.5%

Racial and ethnic distribution:
American Indian 0.2%
Asian 0.7%
Black 16.0%
White 83.0%
Other and unknown 0.2%
Hispanic (may be any race) .. 0.7%

Educational attainment of adults:
At least 4 years of high school 56.2%

TENNESSEE
Continued

At least 1 to 3 years of college 24.5%
At least 4 years of college ... 12.6%

Per-capita personal income: $15,866

Poverty rate: 17.8%

New high-school graduates in:
1991-92 (estimate) 46,305
2001-02 (estimate) 47,014

New GED diploma recipients: 9,953

High-school dropout rate: 30.7%

POLITICAL LEADERSHIP

Governor: Ned Ray McWherter (D), term ends 1995

Governor's higher-education aide: Billy Stair, G12 State Capitol, Nashville 37243; (615) 741-5098

U.S. Senators: Albert Gore, Jr. (D), term ends 1997; Jim Sasser (D), term ends 1995

U.S. Representatives:
6 Democrats, 3 Republicans
Bob Clement (D), Jim Cooper (D), John J. Duncan, Jr. (R), Harold E. Ford (D), Bart Gordon (D), Marilyn Lloyd (D), James H. (Jimmy) Quillen (R), Don Sundquist (R), John S. Tanner (D)

General Assembly: Senate, 20 Democrats, 13 Republicans; House, 57 Democrats, 42 Republicans

COLLEGES AND UNIVERSITIES

Higher education:
Public 4-year institutions 10
Public 2-year institutions 14
Private 4-year institutions 42
Private 2-year institutions 20
Total 86

Vocational institutions: 127

Statewide coordinating board:
Tennessee Higher
  Education Commission
Parkway Towers, Suite 1900
404 James Robertson Parkway
Nashville 37243
(615) 741-7562
Arliss L. Roaden, executive director

Private-college association:
Tennessee Independent Colleges
  and Universities
611 Commerce Street, Suite 2912
Nashville 37203
(615) 242-6400
Hans Giesecke, president

Institutions censured by the AAUP:
None

Institutions under NCAA sanctions:
Memphis State University, University of Tennessee

FACULTY MEMBERS

Full-time faculty members by rank:
Professor 2,331
Associate professor 1,998
Assistant professor 1,916
Instructor 858
Lecturer 40
No rank 73
Total 7,216

Average pay of full-time professors:
At public 4-year institutions $39,158
At public 2-year institutions $29,094
At private 4-year institutions $34,157
At private 2-year institutions $21,337

At all institutions $36,126
Men (all institutions) $38,984
Women (all institutions) $29,634

STUDENTS
Enrollment:
Total 218,866
At public 4-year institutions 107,780
At public 2-year institutions . 59,276
At private 4-year institutions 45,666
At private 2-year institutions . 6,144
Undergraduate 192,321
   First-time freshmen 37,846
Graduate 21,308
Professional 5,237
American Indian 404
Asian 1,728
Black 28,494
Hispanic 1,166
White 170,510
Foreign 4,104

Enrollment highlights:
Women 54.4%
Full-time 65.7%
Minority 15.7%
Foreign 2.0%
10-year change in total
   enrollment .... Up 9.6%

Proportion of enrollment made up of minority students:
At public 4-year institutions . 14.6%
At public 2-year institutions . 15.6%
At private 4-year institutions 17.5%
At private 2-year institutions 22.9%

Degrees awarded:
Associate 5,605
Bachelor's 17,398
Master's 4,840
Doctorate 582
Professional 1,343

Residence of new students: State residents made up 79% of all freshmen enrolled in Tennessee; 85% of all Tennessee residents who were freshmen attended college in their home state.

Test scores: Students averaged 17.9 on the A.C.T., which was taken by 61% of Tennessee's high-school seniors.

MONEY
Average tuition and fees:
At public 4-year institutions . $1,406
At public 2-year institutions .. $803
At private 4-year institutions $6,530
At private 2-year institutions $3,395

Expenditures:
Public institutions .. $1,081,052,000
Private institutions ... $684,948,000

State funds for higher-education operating expenses: $692,402,000
Two-year change: Down 2%

State spending on student aid:
Need-based: $14,156,000;
   24,000 awards
Non–need-based: $560,000;
   149 awards
Other: $3,286,000

Salary of chief executive of largest public 4-year campus:
John J. Quinn, University of
   Tennessee at Knoxville: $138,375

Total spending on research and development by doctorate-granting universities: $232,121,000
Sources:
Federal government 59.0%
State and local governments . 13.2%
Industry 4.7%
The institution itself 16.8%
Other 6.2%

TENNESSEE
Continued

Federal spending on education and student aid (selected programs):
Vocational and
  adult education $29,411,000
GI Bill $6,414,000
Pell Grants $75,723,000

Total federal spending on college- and university-based research and development: $115,369,000

Selected programs:
Department of Health
  and Human Services $80,489,000
National Science
  Foundation $10,912,000
Department of Defense . $4,370,000
Department
  of Agriculture $6,682,000
Department of Energy .. $5,304,000

Largest endowment:
Vanderbilt University $603,708,000

Top fund raisers:
Vanderbilt University . $43,320,000
University of Tennessee $33,527,000
Rhodes College $8,620,000

MISCELLANY

■ As home of the nation's most extensive collection of network newscasts, Vanderbilt University's Television News Archive worked around the clock to record coverage of the war in the Persian Gulf. Vanderbilt has been taping the evening news broadcasts since 1968.

■ The oldest institutions of higher education in the state are the University of Tennessee at Knoxville and Tusculum College, both founded in 1794.

TEXAS

MANY HIGHER-EDUCATION officials were relieved when Ann W. Richards was elected Governor in 1990.

Her predecessor, Republican William P. Clements, had feuded with college officials over financing and board appointments. In contrast, Ms. Richards, a Democrat and a former State Treasurer, expressed support for public schools and higher education alike. And she promised to increase financial aid for students and support for the state's historically black colleges.

But in 1991 Texas, like many other states, faced a revenue shortfall, and the deficit was a Texas-sized $4.8-billion. Governor Richards called a special session in mid-July to discuss the budget. She also asked Comptroller John Sharp to do an audit of state government and recommend cuts. His report, the Texas Performance Review, left higher-education officials stunned.

He recommended doubling tuition for Texas residents, reducing state appropriations, and replacing state funds with locally generated revenues, such as money from health-care services provided by university medical schools and hospitals.

After much haggling over the proposals, Texas lawmakers approved a state budget that includes $5.7-billion in general revenue for higher education in the 1991-93 biennium. That's higher than the $5.4-billion appropriated for the previous biennium, but $100-million short of what college officials say they need to maintain the current level of services. The state budget also calls for tuition at public colleges and universities to be raised from its current $20 per semester hour to $24 in fall 1992 and to be raised an additional $2 per semester hour each year until it reaches $32 per semester hour in 1996.

In addition to state support, the University of Texas and Texas A&M University Systems receive income from a state trust based on oil revenue. They have invested it wisely: Their endowments are the largest of any public systems in the country.

The residents of South Texas, a predominantly Hispanic region, have long complained that their public colleges do not receive enough money or attention. In recent years, the Legislature has tried to address that issue by merging some of the smaller South Texas college systems into the larger and well-financed University of Texas and Texas A&M systems.

But some higher-education officials fear that budget constraints imposed by the Legislature will make it difficult to finance improvements at the predominantly Hispanic institutions. A lawsuit filed over the state's education of Hispanic college students went to trial in September 1991. After a seven-week trial, a Texas district court jury found that the state's higher-education system was inefficient and failed to provide people living in South Texas with equal access to a "university of the first class."

The jury also found, however, that state officials had not discriminated against the residents of South Texas. The split verdict left both sides claiming victory, and left unresolved the question of what changes, if any, the court might order in the state's higher-education system.

The University of Texas at Austin has been the focus of a debate on "political correctness." At issue was a required freshman English course, "Writing About Difference." Initially, an English-department committee recommended revising the course to emphasize issues relating to race and gender. After critics accused committee members of dictating political correctness and liberal indoctrination, the focus of the course was broadened to include such issues as euthanasia and abortion.

The four-year institutions are governed by 12 boards, and the two-year institutions by 50 boards. Although the institutions retain much control over their day-to-day operations, the Texas Higher Education Coordinating Board is expanding its role in policy making. The coordinating board is studying whether colleges could be run more efficiently and may call for eliminating programs, limiting enrollments, and closing some institutions.

The board is also a leader in the state's effort to improve the success rates for its college students—particularly Hispanics and blacks.

Texas is trying to become a leader in research, and both the University of Texas and Texas A&M claim to be the state's leading research institution. The state vows it will fulfill its pledge of providing $1-billion for the Superconducting Supercollider. That pledge was cited as a key factor in its being selected by the U.S. Department of Energy as the site of the project.

Private colleges and universities are a force in Texas, particularly research institutions such as Rice University and those with religious ties, such as Southern Methodist and Texas Christian Universities.

In September 1990, Baylor University set up an independent governing board, thus removing itself from the direct control of the Baptist General Convention of Texas. The convention has governed Baylor—the world's

TEXAS
Continued

largest Baptist university—since it was founded in 1845. University officials feared that the convention—and therefore the university—would be taken over by conservative Baptists.

DEMOGRAPHICS

Population: 16,986,510   (Rank: 3)

Age distribution:
Up to 17	28.5%
18 to 24	11.1%
25 to 44	33.1%
45 and older	27.3%

Racial and ethnic distribution:
American Indian	0.4%
Asian	1.9%
Black	11.9%
White	75.2%
Other and unknown	10.6%
Hispanic (may be any race)	25.5%

Educational attainment of adults:
At least 4 years of high school	62.6%
At least 1 to 3 years of college	33.8%
At least 4 years of college	16.9%

Per-capita personal income: $16,716

Poverty rate: 17.0%

New high-school graduates in:
1991-92 (estimate)	181,144
2001-02 (estimate)	203,036

New GED diploma recipients: 37,442

High-school dropout rate: 34.7%

POLITICAL LEADERSHIP

Governor: Ann W. Richards (D), term ends 1995

Governor's higher-education aide: Lynn Leverty, Box 12428, Austin 78711; (512) 463-1877

U.S. Senators: Lloyd Bentsen (D), term ends 1995; Phil Gramm (R), term ends 1997

U.S. Representatives:
19 Democrats, 8 Republicans
Michael A. Andrews (D), Bill Archer (R), Richard K. Armey (R), Joe Barton (R), Jack Brooks (D), John Bryant (D), Albert G. Bustamante (D), Jim Chapman (D), Ronald D. Coleman (D), Larry Combest (R), E de la Garza (D), Tom DeLay (R), Chet Edwards (D), Jack Fields (R), Martin Frost (D), Pete Geren (D), Henry B. Gonzalez (D), Ralph M. Hall (D), Sam Johnson (R), Greg Laughlin (D), Solomon P. Ortiz (D), J.J. Pickle (D), Bill Sarpalius (D), Lamar S. Smith (R), Charles W. Stenholm (D), Craig A. Washington (D), Charles Wilson (D)

Legislature: Senate, 22 Democrats, 9 Republicans; House, 93 Democrats, 57 Republicans

COLLEGES AND UNIVERSITIES

Higher education:
Public 4-year institutions	40
Public 2-year institutions	67
Private 4-year institutions	56
Private 2-year institutions	11
Total	174

Vocational institutions: 397

Statewide coordinating board:
Texas Higher Education
  Coordinating Board
P.O. Box 12788
Austin 78711
(512) 483-6100
Kenneth H. Ashworth, commissioner

Private-college association:
Independent Colleges and
 Universities of Texas
P.O. Box 13105
Austin 78711
(512) 472-9522
Carol L. McDonald, president

Institutions censured by the AAUP:
Amarillo College, Blinn College, Frank Phillips College, Houston Baptist University, Southwestern Adventist College, University of Texas of the Permian Basin

Institutions under NCAA sanctions:
Houston Baptist University, Texas A&M University, University of Texas at El Paso

FACULTY MEMBERS

Full-time faculty members by rank:
Professor 5,419
Associate professor 4,640
Assistant professor 4,389
Instructor 1,334
Lecturer 950
No rank 4,359
Total 21,091

Average pay of full-time professors:
At public 4-year institutions $40,233
At public 2-year institutions $32,469
At private 4-year institutions $38,444
At private 2-year institutions $22,529
At all institutions $37,615
Men (all institutions) $40,412
Women (all institutions) $31,876

STUDENTS

Enrollment:
Total 877,859
At public 4-year institutions   410,392
At public 2-year institutions   372,103
At private 4-year institutions   90,771
At private 2-year institutions . 4,593
Undergraduate 766,863
 First-time freshmen 132,051
Graduate 95,487
Professional 15,509
American Indian 2,756
Asian 23,642
Black 75,478
Hispanic 125,778
White 597,400
Foreign 22,138

Enrollment highlights:
Women 53.3%
Full-time 54.1%
Minority 27.6%
Foreign 2.6%
10-year change in total
 enrollment .... Up 29.9%

Proportion of enrollment made up of minority students:
At public 4-year institutions . 25.1%
At public 2-year institutions . 32.0%
At private 4-year institutions   19.8%
At private 2-year institutions   33.5%

Degrees awarded:
Associate 22,595
Bachelor's 56,987
Master's 17,163
Doctorate 2,113
Professional 4,146

Residence of new students: State residents made up 92% of all freshmen enrolled in Texas; 95% of all Texas residents who were freshmen attended college in their home state.

Test scores: Students averaged 874 on the S.A.T., which was taken by 44% of Texas' high-school seniors.

MONEY

Average tuition and fees:
At public 4-year institutions .. $959
At public 2-year institutions .. $455

TEXAS
Continued

At private 4-year institutions $6,047
At private 2-year institutions $5,112

Expenditures:
Public institutions .. $4,375,082,000
Private institutions ... $993,824,000

State funds for higher-education operating expenses: $2,821,810,000

Two-year change: Up 8%

State spending on student aid:
Need-based: $27,318,000; 22,651 awards
Non–need-based: None
Other: $91,050,000

Salary of chief executive of largest public 4-year campus:
William H. Cunningham, University of Texas at Austin: $63,403 from state plus $114,077 from private donations

Total spending on research and development by doctorate-granting universities: $1,123,816,000
Sources:
Federal government 46.5%
State and local governments . 11.6%
Industry 6.9%
The institution itself 22.5%
Other 12.5%

Federal spending on education and student aid (selected programs):
Vocational and
  adult education $89,586,000
GI Bill $23,268,000
Pell Grants $287,782,000

Total federal spending on college- and university-based research and development: $439,820,000

Selected programs:
Department of Health
  and Human Services $255,092,000
National Science
  Foundation $45,251,000
Department of Defense $58,694,000
Department
  of Agriculture $19,235,000
Department of Energy . $25,853,000

Largest endowment:
University of Texas
  System $3,256,192,000

Top fund raisers:
University of Texas
  at Austin $56,704,000
Texas A&M University $50,817,000
University of Texas Anderson
  Cancer Center $37,226,000

MISCELLANY

- A Rice University graduate student in architecture built a 42-square-foot plywood structure to give homeless people more privacy in shelters. Steve Mayman built the "port-a-home" as part of his master's thesis.

- A long-standing dispute between Texas Methodists and Baptists obscures any higher-education institution's clear claim to being the oldest in the state. Southwestern University, a private liberal-arts college affiliated with the United Methodist Church, says it was founded in 1840 as Rutersville College. Baylor University, a private institution affiliated with the Southern Baptist Church, considers that a highly questionable claim and maintains that its 1845 charter from the Republic of Texas Congress makes it the state's oldest college or university.

UTAH

EDUCATION is highly prized in Utah, but the state's politics and demographics place unusual financial pressures on its public colleges and universities. And the University of Utah's embarrassing dalliance with the now-discredited achievement of cold fusion has not helped matters.

The influence of the Church of Jesus Christ of Latter-day Saints is an important factor in higher education—especially at Brigham Young University, a Mormon institution that counts among its alumni many of the state's most prominent political and business figures.

Utah devotes about 70 per cent of all state revenues to education. But because nearly three-quarters of Utah's residents are Mormon and the religion promotes large families, the state has an unusually large number of schoolchildren to educate: 37 per cent of the population is under age 18, compared with the national figure of 26 per cent.

Historically, the fiscally conservative Legislature has been more generous to elementary and secondary schools than to colleges.

The biggest complaint of public higher-education officials is that the Legislature is not financing their institutions adequately to keep up with enrollment growth, or to keep faculty salaries competitive. Enrollment in public higher education has increased 20 per cent since 1985, and the growth is expected to continue.

In 1991, several college and university officials expressed concern about the below-average college-going rate of women in the state—a phenomenon that some say is a product of the Mormons' family-oriented philosophy. The state Board of Regents, the governing and coordinating board for all of higher education, has also recently become concerned with the issue. But so far the board has been cautious about suggesting expensive solutions, such as special scholarships or more state-financed day care, to change the pattern.

The University of Utah is among the institutions that have tried to recruit more women, particularly to mathematics and science—areas of traditional strength in an institution that is known for its work in physics, medicine, and space-related research.

Throughout 1991, the institution took steps to erase the blemish on that scientific reputation. The state shut down the $4.5-million National Cold Fusion Institute, which had been affiliated with the university, after it failed to attract significant sources of outside support. And the university chose as its new president Arthur K. Smith, provost of the University of South Carolina, to replace Chase N. Peterson, who resigned in 1990 after it was learned that an "anonymous" gift to the institute was really money he had authorized to be transferred from other university accounts.

DEMOGRAPHICS

Population: 1,722,850   (Rank: 35)

Age distribution:
Up to 17 .... 36.4%
18 to 24 .... 11.6%
25 to 44 .... 29.0%
45 and older 23.0%

Racial and ethnic distribution:
American Indian 1.4%
Asian 1.9%

UTAH
Continued

Black 0.7%
White 93.8%
Other and unknown 2.2%
Hispanic (may be any race) .. 4.9%

Educational attainment of adults:
At least 4 years of high school 80.0%
At least 1 to 3 years of college 44.1%
At least 4 years of college ... 19.9%

Per-capita personal income: $13,993

Poverty rate: 8.7%

New high-school graduates in:
1991-92 (estimate) 25,369
2001-02 (estimate) 30,977

New GED diploma recipients: 901

High-school dropout rate: 20.6%

POLITICAL LEADERSHIP

Governor: Norman H. Bangerter (R), term ends 1993

Governor's higher-education aide:
Colleen Colton, 210 State Capitol, Salt Lake City 84114; (801) 538-1000

U.S. Senators: Jake Garn (R), term ends 1993; Orrin G. Hatch (R), term ends 1995

U.S. Representatives:
2 Democrats, 1 Republican
James V. Hansen (R), Bill Orton (D), Wayne Owens (D)

Legislature: Senate, 10 Democrats, 19 Republicans; House, 31 Democrats, 44 Republicans

COLLEGES AND UNIVERSITIES

Higher education:
Public 4-year institutions 4
Public 2-year institutions 5
Private 4-year institutions 2
Private 2-year institutions 3
Total 14

Vocational institutions: 40

Statewide coordinating board:
Utah System of Higher Education
355 West North Temple
3 Triad Center, Suite 550
Salt Lake City 84180
(801) 538-5247
Wm. Rolfe Kerr, commissioner of higher education

Private-college association:
None

Institution censured by the AAUP:
Westminster College of Salt Lake City

Institutions under NCAA sanctions:
None

FACULTY MEMBERS

Full-time faculty members by rank:
Professor 1,583
Associate professor 996
Assistant professor 700
Instructor 174
Lecturer 22
No rank 284
Total 3,759

Average pay of full-time professors:
At public 4-year institutions $36,404
At public 2-year institutions $27,109
At private 4-year institutions $43,684
At private 2-year institutions $33,596
At all institutions $38,319

Men (all institutions) $39,738
Women (all institutions) $32,480

STUDENTS

Enrollment:
Total 114,815
At public 4-year institutions . 54,444
At public 2-year institutions . 25,179
At private 4-year institutions 34,164
At private 2-year institutions . 1,028
Undergraduate 104,394
  First-time freshmen 20,374
Graduate 9,191
Professional 1,230
American Indian 1,088
Asian 1,736
Black 619
Hispanic 1,743
White 97,575
Foreign 4,777

Enrollment highlights:
Women 48.4%
Full-time 64.6%
Minority 5.0%
Foreign 4.4%
10-year change in total
  enrollment .... Up 27.0%

Proportion of enrollment made up of minority students:
At public 4-year institutions .. 5.5%
At public 2-year institutions .. 7.7%
At private 4-year institutions . 2.0%
At private 2-year institutions 15.1%

Degrees awarded:
Associate 3,572
Bachelor's 10,682
Master's 2,345
Doctorate 367
Professional 376

Residence of new students: State residents made up 64% of all freshmen enrolled in Utah; 90% of all Utah residents who were freshmen attended college in their home state.

Test scores: Students averaged 18.9 on the A.C.T., which was taken by 67% of Utah's high-school seniors.

MONEY

Average tuition and fees:
At public 4-year institutions . $1,429
At public 2-year institutions . $1,136
At private 4-year institutions $1,975
At private 2-year institutions $2,768

Expenditures:
Public institutions $669,714,000
Private institutions ... $194,649,000

State funds for higher-education operating expenses: $319,561,000
Two-year change: Up 9%

State spending on student aid:
Need-based: $1,001,000; 2,000 awards
Non–need-based: $984,000; 66 awards
Other: $9,501,000

Salary of chief executive of largest public 4-year campus:
Arthur K. Smith, University of Utah: $130,000

Total spending on research and development by doctorate-granting universities: $187,076,000
Sources:
Federal government 67.7%
State and local governments .. 9.1%
Industry 3.9%
The institution itself 15.6%
Other 3.6%

Federal spending on education and student aid (selected programs):
Vocational and
  adult education $9,928,000
GI Bill $3,169,000
Pell Grants $54,196,000

UTAH
Continued

Total federal spending on college- and university-based research and development: $108,117,000

Selected programs:
Department of Health
  and Human Services $45,120,000
National Science
  Foundation $11,862,000
Department of Defense $36,683,000
Department
  of Agriculture $3,178,000
Department of Energy .. $5,419,000

Largest endowment:
University of Utah $64,762,000

Top fund raisers:
University of Utah $46,540,000
Utah State University .. $3,810,000

MISCELLANY

- In 1991 the University of Utah selected Arthur K. Smith as its first non-Mormon president. Mr. Smith, provost of the University of South Carolina, is an Episcopalian.

- The oldest institution of higher education in the state is the University of Utah, founded in 1850.

VERMONT

VERMONT MAY ENJOY a pastoral image, but lately the reality has been less than serene, at least in higher education.

The recession has not spared Vermont, and its public colleges endured several rounds of budget cuts in 1991. In the 1991-92 academic year, they have less state money than they received in the previous year.

Colleges have responded by raising tuition, in some cases dramatically. At the University of Vermont, for example, tuition for state residents increased by nearly 17 per cent in 1991-92.

The rise is particularly touchy for the university—which has been accused of elitism in the past because of its high tuition rates, its heavy enrollment of non-Vermonters, and aggressive attempts to thwart faculty unionization. But the institution has taken deliberate steps in the past two years to smooth its relations with state legislators and officials of its hometown of Burlington.

The university, which is governed by its own board, is unusual in that it was founded as a private college and only began receiving state funds in 1955. It still receives less than 15 per cent of its budget from the state.

The Vermont State Colleges System depends more heavily on state support. The system includes three four-year colleges and two two-year institutions, Vermont Technical College and the Community College of Vermont. The latter does not have a permanent campus and rents space in schools, office buildings, and other facilities. Its part-time faculty members offer courses at 12 "teaching sites" throughout the state.

Recent events at some colleges have led several of them to confront searing questions about race relations and women's issues.

The most-publicized of these took place at the University of Vermont, the state's land-grant institution. In April 1991, about two dozen students took over the office of the then-president, George H. Davis. They were protesting what they said was slow progress in achieving racial diversity. Removed by campus police after more than two weeks, they then erected a "shanty town"—which they call "Diversity University"—on the campus green. University officials let the shanty town remain as an expression of free speech, but it was destroyed by an explosion in November.

The university also appointed a campus committee to recommend ways to promote cultural diversity. Mr. Davis cited the dissension as one reason for his abrupt resignation in October 1991, five days shy of his first anniversary as president. His plans to close the university's projected deficit had also aroused some animosity on the campus.

Timothy Light, the president of Middlebury College, had an equally short tenure. Severely criticized for tactics that he had used in laying off 17 long-time college employees, Mr. Light resigned abruptly in September 1991 after little more than a year in office.

At Johnson State College, Lynn Veach Sadler, the president, resigned in June 1991 after just 17 months in office, out of a "rising sense of moral disgust" with incidents of racism and sexism on her campus.

Vermont has no statewide coordinating board, but many of the duties that would be performed by such a board are handled by the Higher Education Planning Commission. Another overseer of higher education is the Vermont Student Assistance Corporation, which manages financial-aid programs.

State financial aid is available to students at private colleges, a reflection of the long-standing political influence that those institutions enjoy.

About 40 per cent of all Vermont students attend private colleges, and the state is the home of such well-known liberal-arts institutions as Middlebury and Bennington Colleges.

DEMOGRAPHICS

Population: 562,758 (Rank: 49)

Age distribution:
Up to 17 .... 25.4%
18 to 24 .... 11.2%
25 to 44 .... 33.4%
45 and older 30.0%

Racial and ethnic distribution:
American Indian 0.3%
Asian 0.6%
Black 0.3%
White 98.6%
Other and unknown 0.1%
Hispanic (may be any race) .. 0.7%

Educational attainment of adults:
At least 4 years of high school 71.0%
At least 1 to 3 years of college 34.7%
At least 4 years of college ... 19.0%

Per-capita personal income: $17,511

Poverty rate: 9.0%

New high-school graduates in:
1991-92 (estimate) 6,147
2001-02 (estimate) 7,292

New GED diploma recipients: 1,278

High-school dropout rate: 21.3%

POLITICAL LEADERSHIP

Governor: Howard Dean (D), term ends 1993

Governor's higher-education aide: David M. Wilson, Pavilion Office

VERMONT
Continued

Building, 109 State Street, Montpelier 05609; (802) 828-3322

U.S. Senators: James M. Jeffords (R), term ends 1995; Patrick J. Leahy (D), term ends 1993

U.S. Representative:
1 Socialist
Bernard Sanders (Socialist)

General Assembly: Senate, 15 Democrats, 15 Republicans; House, 73 Democrats, 75 Republicans, 2 Independents

COLLEGES AND UNIVERSITIES

Higher education:
Public 4-year institutions 4
Public 2-year institutions 2
Private 4-year institutions 13
Private 2-year institutions 3
Total 22

Vocational institutions: 11

Statewide coordinating board:
Vermont Higher Education
  Planning Commission
109 State Street
Montpelier 05609
(802) 828-2376
Position of executive director vacant

Private-college association:
Association of Vermont
  Independent Colleges
2 Prospect Street
Montpelier 05609
(802) 223-1662
Alan H. Weiss, executive director

Institutions censured by the AAUP:
None

Institutions under NCAA sanctions:
None

FACULTY MEMBERS

Full-time faculty members by rank:
Professor 361
Associate professor 394
Assistant professor 414
Instructor 68
Lecturer 53
No rank 148
Total 1,438

Average pay of full-time professors:
At public 4-year institutions $39,891
At public 2-year institutions $28,138
At private 4-year institutions $34,828
At private 2-year institutions $23,680
At all institutions $36,018
Men (all institutions) $38,472
Women (all institutions) $30,301

STUDENTS

Enrollment:
Total 35,946
At public 4-year institutions . 16,127
At public 2-year institutions .. 4,798
At private 4-year institutions 12,921
At private 2-year institutions . 2,100
Undergraduate 31,510
  First-time freshmen 6,642
Graduate 3,834
Professional 602
American Indian 98
Asian 407
Black 277
Hispanic 234
White 32,953
Foreign 498

Enrollment highlights:
Women 56.7%

Full-time 68.3%
Minority 3.0%
Foreign 1.4%
10-year change in total
 enrollment .... Up 21.6%

Proportion of enrollment made up of minority students:
At public 4-year institutions .. 3.2%
At public 2-year institutions .. 1.3%
At private 4-year institutions . 3.6%
At private 2-year institutions . 1.6%

Degrees awarded:
Associate 1,136
Bachelor's 4,193
Master's 991
Doctorate 49
Professional 85

Residence of new students: State residents made up 43% of all freshmen enrolled in Vermont; 63% of all Vermont residents who were freshmen attended college in their home state.

Test scores: Students averaged 890 on the S.A.T., which was taken by 68% of Vermont's high-school seniors.

MONEY

Average tuition and fees:
At public 4-year institutions . $3,641
At public 2-year institutions . $2,210
At private 4-year institutions $10,928
At private 2-year institutions $5,979

Expenditures:
Public institutions $188,112,000
Private institutions ... $150,689,000

State funds for higher-education operating expenses: $55,742,000

Two-year change: Down 3%

State spending on student aid:
Need-based: $10,965,000;
 11,005 awards
Non–need-based: None
Other: $212,000

Salary of chief executive of largest public 4-year campus:
Thomas P. Salmon (interim),
 University of Vermont: $125,000

Total spending on research and development by doctorate-granting universities: $45,162,000
Sources:
Federal government 67.7%
State and local governments .. 5.3%
Industry 7.7%
The institution itself 14.5%
Other 4.9%

Federal spending on education and student aid (selected programs):
Vocational and
 adult education $6,829,000
GI Bill $511,000
Pell Grants $6,771,000

Total federal spending on college- and university-based research and development: $29,630,000
Selected programs:
Department of Health
 and Human Services $22,753,000
National Science
 Foundation $1,681,000
Department of Defense ... $173,000
Department
 of Agriculture $3,061,000
Department of Energy $314,000

Largest endowment:
Middlebury College .. $227,488,000

Top fund raisers:
University of Vermont . $12,575,000
Middlebury College $9,712,000
Bennington College $2,599,000

VERMONT
Continued

MISCELLANY

■ Marlboro and Champlain Colleges allowed a handful of veterans of the Persian Gulf war to attend the institutions for half the regular tuition price. Administrators said they were offering the discounts to honor the veterans and give them an opportunity to get on with their lives.

■ The oldest institution of higher education in the state is the University of Vermont, founded in 1791.

VIRGINIA

VIRGINIA's higher-education officials, looking beyond the immediate future, plan to continue their efforts to improve the quality of their programs and institutions.

It is an ambitious goal—particularly since state support for higher education was cut by 11 per cent in fiscal 1991 and by an additional 6 per cent for fiscal 1992.

Gov. L. Douglas Wilder, a Democrat, eased his restrictions on tuition increases and allowed institutions to recover part of the loss of state funds. But they still were forced to lay off part-time faculty members and leave hundreds of vacancies unfilled.

Higher-education officials want to see the dollars restored, but they also want more autonomy. The Council of Higher Education issued a report that said that if state support continued to decrease, the state should impose fewer restrictions on how public institutions spend state money and set tuition rates, among other things.

While state officials promise to consider those recommendations, they are also pressing colleges on a variety of fronts. James W. Dyke, Jr., Virginia's Secretary of Education, is more interested in another document produced by the council—a report on faculty productivity. A random survey of 2,800 full-time faculty members persuaded Mr. Dyke that Virginia's faculty members work hard. Even so, he and other higher-education administrators are trying to develop incentives that would encourage faculty members to place more emphasis on teaching.

Governor Wilder, meanwhile, has demanded that colleges prepare policies to fight racism and sexism on campuses. His demand was occasioned by the state's uneven progress in recruiting minority students, particularly at its predominantly white campuses.

Sometimes Mr. Wilder offhandedly drops political bombs, and colleges have experienced the fall-out. After drug raids at three University of Virginia fraternities by law-enforcement officials, Mr. Wilder said a state task force on substance abuse and sexual assaults on college campuses ought to consider mandatory drug testing of students. That suggestion was dropped after an outcry by college officials and civil-rights leaders.

He also has criticized the men only admissions policy at the Virginia Military Institute. He hinted that he might reduce or eliminate state support for the institution if it did not change its policy, but the idea was soon shelved.

Furthermore, a federal judge sided with the institute's policy and ruled that it did not violate federal anti-bias laws. The U.S. Justice Department, which had challenged the policy, plans to appeal.

The institute's loyal alumni are among the most politically influential in the state. They are also generous: The VMI Foundation has the largest endowment per student of any public institution in the nation. Two of the state's other prestigious institutions, the University of Virginia and the College of William and Mary, are among the top 10 institutions in that ranking.

The state Council of Higher Education has some influence with the General Assembly, but the individual Boards of Visitors of the four-year institutions retain considerable power. The State Board for Community Colleges governs two-year institutions, many of which have seen remarkable enrollment increases in recent years.

Historically black institutions include Virginia State and Norfolk State Universities, which are public, and Hampton University, which is private. Other private institutions include the University of Richmond and Liberty University, which is best known for its ties to the evangelist Jerry Falwell.

DEMOGRAPHICS

Population: 6,187,358   (Rank: 12)

Age distribution:
Up to 17 .... 24.3%
18 to 24 .... 11.6%
25 to 44 .... 34.5%
45 and older 29.6%

Racial and ethnic distribution:
American Indian 0.2%
Asian 2.6%
Black 18.8%
White 77.4%
Other and unknown 0.9%
Hispanic (may be any race) .. 2.6%

Educational attainment of adults:
At least 4 years of high school 62.4%
At least 1 to 3 years of college 34.0%
At least 4 years of college ... 19.1%

Per-capita personal income: $19,671

Poverty rate: 10.9%

New high-school graduates in:
1991-92 (estimate) 64,289
2001-02 (estimate) 85,742

New GED diploma recipients: 9,911

High-school dropout rate: 28.4%

POLITICAL LEADERSHIP

Governor: L. Douglas Wilder (D), term ends 1994

Governor's higher-education aide: James W. Dyke, P.O. Box 1475, Richmond 23212; (804) 786-1151

U.S. Senators: Charles S. Robb (D), term ends 1995; John W. Warner (R), term ends 1997

U.S. Representatives:
6 Democrats, 4 Republicans
George Allen (R), Herbert H. Bateman (R), Thomas J. Bliley, Jr. (R), Rick Boucher (D), James Moran (D), Jim Olin (D), L. F. Payne (D), Owen B. Pickett (D), Norman Sisisky (D), Frank R. Wolf (R)

General Assembly: Senate, 22 Democrats, 18 Republicans; House, 57 Democrats, 41 Republicans, 1 Independent, 1 race undecided

COLLEGES AND UNIVERSITIES

Higher education:
Public 4-year institutions 15

VIRGINIA
Continued

Public 2-year institutions 24
Private 4-year institutions 33
Private 2-year institutions 6
Total 78

Vocational institutions: 165

Statewide coordinating board:
State Council of Higher Education
James Monroe Building
101 North 14th Street
Richmond 23219
(804) 225-2600
Gordon K. Davies, director

Private-college association:
Council of Independent Colleges
   in Virginia
P.O. Box 1005
118 East Main Street
Bedford 24523
(703) 586-0606
Robert B. Lambeth, Jr., president

Institutions censured by the AAUP:
Virginia Community College System

Institution under NCAA sanctions:
Hampton University

FACULTY MEMBERS

Full-time faculty members by rank:
Professor 2,988
Associate professor 3,223
Assistant professor 3,009
Instructor 841
Lecturer 94
No rank 33
Total 10,188

Average pay of full-time professors:
At public 4-year institutions $46,232
At public 2-year institutions $34,370
At private 4-year institutions $33,861
At private 2-year institutions $24,068
At all institutions $40,984
Men (all institutions) $43,841
Women (all institutions) $34,570

STUDENTS

Enrollment:
Total 344,284
At public 4-year institutions 158,260
At public 2-year institutions 129,364
At private 4-year institutions 54,389
At private 2-year institutions . 2,271
Undergraduate 297,369
   First-time freshmen 47,098
Graduate 40,818
Professional 6,097
American Indian 738
Asian 9,032
Black 44,164
Hispanic 3,783
White 257,686
Foreign 5,813

Enrollment highlights:
Women 55.6%
Full-time 55.4%
Minority 18.3%
Foreign 1.8%
10-year change in total
   enrollment .... Up 27.2%

Proportion of enrollment made up of minority students:
At public 4-year institutions . 18.1%
At public 2-year institutions . 16.9%
At private 4-year institutions 21.0%
At private 2-year institutions 36.4%

Degrees awarded:
Associate 7,438
Bachelor's 26,028
Master's 6,545
Doctorate 764
Professional 1,695

Residence of new students: State residents made up 68% of all freshmen enrolled in Virginia; 78% of all Virginia residents who were freshmen attended college in their home state.

Test scores: Students averaged 890 on the S.A.T., which was taken by 60% of Virginia's high-school seniors.

MONEY

Average tuition and fees:
At public 4-year institutions . $2,532
At public 2-year institutions .. $813
At private 4-year institutions $7,238
At private 2-year institutions $4,409

Expenditures:
Public institutions .. $1,825,156,000
Private institutions ... $387,455,000

State funds for higher-education operating expenses: $1,030,112,000

Two-year change: Down 5%

State spending on student aid:
Need-based: $7,400,000; 8,304 awards
Non–need-based: $18,114,000; 13,441 awards
Other: None

Salary of chief executive of largest public 4-year campus:
James D. McComas, Virginia Polytechnic Institute and State University: $104,621 from state plus $43,058 from private donations

Total spending on research and development by doctorate-granting universities: $321,547,000
Sources:
Federal government 52.9%
State and local governments . 17.0%
Industry 8.1%
The institution itself 14.5%
Other 7.5%

Federal spending on education and student aid (selected programs):
Vocational and
   adult education $29,378,000
GI Bill $11,050,000
Pell Grants $75,088,000

Total federal spending on college- and university-based research and development: $155,454,000
Selected programs:
Department of Health
   and Human Services $76,621,000
National Science
   Foundation $16,795,000
Department of Defense $15,700,000
Department
   of Agriculture $6,920,000
Department of Energy . $10,506,000

Largest endowment:
University of Virginia $487,007,000

Top fund raisers:
University of Virginia . $51,349,000
Virginia Polytechnic Institute
   and State University $41,222,000
College of William
   and Mary $16,270,000

MISCELLANY

■ In the first action of its kind, federal marshals confiscated three fraternity houses at the University of Virginia in March 1991 following drug raids at the houses. The houses are valued at $890,000. Ten students at the university were indicted on drug-distribution charges following the raids.

■ The oldest institution of higher education in Virginia is the College of William and Mary, founded in 1693.

WASHINGTON

WASHINGTON HAS TAKEN an activist approach to higher education in recent years.

Its efforts to expand college-going opportunities in emerging metropolitan areas, to beef up requirements for teaching certification, and to improve salaries and facilities at existing institutions have created high expectations, and some dissatisfaction.

In particular, state officials are concerned that enrollments at some of the five new branch campuses opened in 1990 have not been as great as expected. Also, some higher-education officials are disappointed that legislators did not give colleges and universities the kinds of increases in state financing in 1991 that they had given in the previous biennium. Although its strong aerospace- and tourism-based economy sheltered the state from the recession, higher education suffered because of competing needs of health care and prisons.

Still, the Legislature and Gov. Booth Gardner, a Democrat, did provide new money to accommodate enrollment growth in the universities, and to add nursing and engineering programs at some of the branch campuses in the hope that such courses would have greater appeal to the adult students who are their target market.

The branches—arms of the University of Washington, and Washington State and Central Washington Universities—are also designed to provide higher-education opportunities to such places as Vancouver, Spokane, and the Puget Sound region, where many minority and part-time students live.

Spurred by Governor Gardner's interest, the universities have been paying greater attention to elementary and secondary education. Higher education was a key player in the state's 1990 reform of teacher preparation, which when phased in will eliminate education as an undergraduate major and require all teachers to obtain a master's degree or lose their certification.

The Higher Education Coordinating Board, which oversees four-year institutions, is also looking into ways colleges can work better with public schools. The schools face pressures as Washington increasingly becomes a destination for many Asian immigrants.

The demand for classes in English as a second language is adding financial strains to the already-burdened community colleges, which historically have provided training in basic skills and literacy in addition to more-traditional courses on the associate-degree level.

The Governor's latest push—to improve the state's work force—has focused even more on two-year institutions. And it has prompted some changes. The most visible of them was the decision to shift responsibility for the state's five vocational-technical institutes from local school boards to the state Board for Community and Technical Colleges.

Adults now make up about 90 per cent of the enrollment in the vocational-technical institutes, and state officials said it made sense to consolidate all adult vocational-education programs under a single agency. The State Board for Community Colleges was renamed as of September 1, 1991 to reflect its expanded role.

Like the community colleges, each technical college will be governed by its own board of trustees.

DEMOGRAPHICS

Population: 4,866,692 (Rank: 18)

Age distribution:
Up to 17 .... 25.9%
18 to 24 .... 10.0%
25 to 44 .... 34.1%
45 and older 30.0%

Racial and ethnic distribution:
American Indian 1.7%
Asian 4.3%
Black 3.1%
White 88.5%
Other and unknown 2.4%
Hispanic (may be any race) .. 4.4%

Educational attainment of adults:
At least 4 years of high school 77.6%
At least 1 to 3 years of college 40.2%
At least 4 years of college ... 19.0%

Per-capita personal income: $18,775

Poverty rate: 9.1%

New high-school graduates in:
1991-92 (estimate) 45,846
2001-02 (estimate) 64,068

New GED diploma recipients: 8,736

High-school dropout rate: 22.9%

POLITICAL LEADERSHIP

Governor: Booth Gardner (D), term ends 1993

Governor's higher-education aide:
Steve Garcia, Insurance Building, Room 100, Olympia 98504; (206) 586-6260

U.S. Senators: Brock Adams (D), term ends 1993; Slade Gorton (R), term ends 1995

U.S. Representatives:
5 Democrats, 3 Republicans
Rod Chandler (R), Norman D. Dicks (D), Thomas S. Foley (D), Jim McDermott (D), John Miller (R), Sid Morrison (R), Al Swift (D), Jolene Unsoeld (D)

Legislature: Senate, 24 Democrats, 25 Republicans; House, 58 Democrats, 40 Republicans

COLLEGES AND UNIVERSITIES

Higher education:
Public 4-year institutions 6
Public 2-year institutions 27
Private 4-year institutions 20
Private 2-year institutions 2
Total 55

Vocational institutions: 143

Statewide coordinating board:
Higher Education Coordinating Board
917 Lakeridge Way, GV-11
Olympia 98504
(206) 753-3241
Ann Daley, executive director

Private-college association:
Washington Friends of
  Higher Education
600 Tower Building
1809 7th Avenue
Seattle 98101
(206) 624-9093
David M. Irwin, president

Institutions censured by the AAUP:
None

Institutions under NCAA sanctions:
None

WASHINGTON
Continued

FACULTY MEMBERS

Full-time faculty members by rank:
Professor 1,762
Associate professor 1,265
Assistant professor 994
Instructor 116
Lecturer 122
No rank 2,497
Total 6,756

Average pay of full-time professors:
At public 4-year institutions $41,097
At public 2-year institutions $31,435
At private 4-year institutions $35,120
At private 2-year institutions ... n/a
At all institutions $36,675
Men (all institutions) $38,517
Women (all institutions) $31,949

STUDENTS

Enrollment:
Total 255,760
At public 4-year institutions . 78,387
At public 2-year institutions 142,975
At private 4-year institutions 32,455
At private 2-year institutions . 1,943
Undergraduate 234,974
   First-time freshmen 66,853
Graduate 17,864
Professional 2,922
American Indian 3,444
Asian 13,492
Black 6,504
Hispanic 4,830
White 219,643
Foreign 5,175

Enrollment highlights:
Women 55.3%
Full-time 57.6%
Minority 11.4%
Foreign 2.0%
10-year change in total
   enrollment .... Down 15.7%

Proportion of enrollment made up of minority students:
At public 4-year institutions . 12.6%
At public 2-year institutions . 11.3%
At private 4-year institutions . 9.3%
At private 2-year institutions . 9.2%

Degrees awarded:
Associate 12,284
Bachelor's 18,118
Master's 4,275
Doctorate 583
Professional 809

Residence of new students: State residents made up 89% of all freshmen enrolled in Washington; 92% of all Washington residents who were freshmen attended college in their home state.

Test scores: Students averaged 913 on the S.A.T., which was taken by 49% of Washington's high-school seniors.

MONEY

Average tuition and fees:
At public 4-year institutions . $1,710
At public 2-year institutions .. $802
At private 4-year institutions $8,096
At private 2-year institutions $7,045

Expenditures:
Public institutions .. $1,399,780,000
Private institutions ... $227,211,000

State funds for higher-education operating expenses: $898,184,000
Two-year change: Up 13%

State spending on student aid:
Need-based: $21,146,000;

22,341 awards
Non–need-based: $32,000; 32 awards
Other: $862,000

**Salary of chief executive
of largest public 4-year campus:**
William P. Gerberding, University
of Washington: $111,696 from state
plus $51,240 from private donations

**Total spending on research and
development by doctorate-granting
universities:** $312,169,000
Sources:
Federal government 73.8%
State and local governments .. 3.0%
Industry 7.9%
The institution itself 12.0%
Other 3.3%

**Federal spending on education
and student aid (selected programs):**
Vocational and
   adult education $21,233,000
GI Bill $10,516,000
Pell Grants $72,746,000

**Total federal spending on college-
and university-based research
and development:** $224,465,000
Selected programs:
Department of Health
   and Human Services $136,499,000
National Science
   Foundation $31,400,000
Department of Defense $28,778,000
Department
   of Agriculture $8,562,000
Department of Energy .. $7,854,000

Largest endowment:
University
   of Washington $170,071,000

Top fund raisers:
University
   of Washington $89,427,000
Washington State
   University $24,975,000

Pacific Lutheran
   University $5,574,000

MISCELLANY

■ Laurel L. Wilkening, provost and vice-president for academic affairs at the University of Washington, was appointed by Vice-President Quayle in 1991 to serve as chairwoman of his Space Policy Advisory Board.

■ The oldest institution of higher education in Washington is Whitman College, founded in 1859.

WEST VIRGINIA

SINCE THE 1989 reorganization of higher education in West Virginia, state officials have been concentrating on how to increase the efficiency and quality of programs and services.

The blueprint for the reorganization was a report by the Carnegie Foundation for the Advancement of Teaching. Most of the recommendations were adopted. But the state is trying alternatives to two of the recommendations: that it eliminate one of its three medical schools and that it create a community-college system.

Gov. Gaston Caperton, a Democrat, proposed consolidating the three schools early in the 1991 legislative session. He eventually abandoned the proposal.

The likely target for closure, the West Virginia School of Osteopathic Medicine, and its political allies have successfully blocked attempts to shut the institution. Supporters of the school argue that it has a better record of providing health care to rural West Virginians than do West Virginia and

WEST VIRGINIA
Continued

Marshall Universities, the other institutions with medical schools.

Instead, lawmakers created a position of vice-chancellor for health sciences to oversee medical education in the University of West Virginia System. The vice-chancellor is expected to develop new ways of coordinating programs at the three medical schools. The progress of those efforts will be measured by a "report card" that legislators are requiring all institutions to submit. In the report card, campus administrators must describe how they spent their state appropriations.

The State College System Board of Directors, which oversees the state's eight four-year institutions and two community colleges, has come up with an alternative to the other remaining Carnegie recommendation. Instead of creating a community-college system, it has set up community-college divisions in the four-year colleges.

The presidents of the four-year colleges had opposed the creation of a two-year-college system because they feared they would lose students—and the state appropriations to serve them.

The state colleges used to be open-admission institutions. But starting in fall 1991, students had to score at least 18 on the mathematics section of the American College Test or the equivalent on the Scholastic Aptitude Test to enroll in college-level mathematics courses.

Otherwise, students have to enroll in a non-credit mathematics course offered by the community-college divisions. Students have to score at least 19 on the language section of the ACT or the equivalent on the SAT to enroll in college-level English courses.

In the last two years, state lawmakers have been able to avoid mid-year budget cuts. Even though higher education in West Virginia has not enjoyed large budget increases, state support has been stable—a circumstance that is welcomed by higher-education officials, who went through a series of mid-year cuts in the 1980's.

The increased coordination by the governing boards is an attempt to reduce the competition between institutions—especially between West Virginia and Marshall—for programs, students, and dollars.

West Virginia University, for example, learned a hard lesson in politics when a brouhaha over its use of student interns to monitor legislation at the State Capitol angered lawmakers and led to the suspension of the program.

Although the lawmakers and boards have placed new demands for quality and efficiency on higher education, they have many deep-rooted problems to overcome. West Virginia is poor and ranks among the lowest in the nation in the number of high-school graduates who go on to college.

Most private higher education in West Virginia consists of religiously affiliated institutions, such as Bethany College.

DEMOGRAPHICS

Population: 1,793,477   (Rank: 34)

Age distribution:
Up to 17 .... 24.7%
18 to 24 .... 10.0%
25 to 44 .... 29.7%
45 and older 35.6%

Racial and ethnic distribution:
American Indian 0.1%
Asian 0.4%
Black 3.1%
White 96.2%
Other and unknown 0.1%
Hispanic (may be any race) .. 0.5%

Educational attainment of adults:
At least 4 years of high school 56.0%
At least 1 to 3 years of college 20.4%
At least 4 years of college ... 10.4%

Per-capita personal income: $13,755

Poverty rate: 17.2%

New high-school graduates in:
1991-92 (estimate) 20,982
2001-02 (estimate) 17,012

New GED diploma recipients: 3,101

High-school dropout rate: 22.7%

POLITICAL LEADERSHIP

Governor: Gaston Caperton (D), term ends 1993

Governor's higher-education aide: position vacant

U.S. Senators: Robert C. Byrd (D), term ends 1995; John D. Rockefeller, IV (D), term ends 1997

U.S. Representatives:
4 Democrats, 0 Republicans
Alan B. Mollohan (D), Nick Joe Rahall, II (D), Harley O. Staggers, Jr. (D), Robert E. Wise, Jr. (D)

Legislature: Senate, 33 Democrats, 1 Republican; House, 74 Democrats, 26 Republicans

COLLEGES AND UNIVERSITIES

Higher education:
Public 4-year institutions 12
Public 2-year institutions 4
Private 4-year institutions 9
Private 2-year institutions 3

Total 28

Vocational institutions: 52

Statewide coordinating boards:
University of West Virginia System
1018 Kanawha Boulevard East
Suite 700
Charleston 25301
(304) 348-4016
Charles W. Manning, chancellor

West Virginia State College System
1018 Kanawha Boulevard East
Suite 700
Charleston 25301
(304) 348-4016
Paul Marion, chancellor

Private-college association:
West Virginia Association
  of Independent Colleges
1106 Security Building
102 Capitol Street
Charleston 25301
(304) 345-5525
Robert F. Prather, president

Institutions censured by the AAUP:
None

Institution under NCAA sanctions:
Marshall University

FACULTY MEMBERS

Full-time faculty members by rank:
Professor 738
Associate professor 689
Assistant professor 720
Instructor 244

WEST VIRGINIA
Continued

Lecturer 53
No rank 0
Total 2,444

Average pay of full-time professors:
At public 4-year institutions $30,975
At public 2-year institutions $24,471
At private 4-year institutions $26,583
At private 2-year institutions $21,295
At all institutions $29,758
Men (all institutions) $31,723
Women (all institutions) ... $25,735

STUDENTS
Enrollment:
Total 82,455
At public 4-year institutions . 62,227
At public 2-year institutions . 10,251
At private 4-year institutions . 7,196
At private 2-year institutions . 2,781
Undergraduate 72,115
  First-time freshmen 18,318
Graduate 8,891
Professional 1,449
American Indian 119
Asian 577
Black 2,876
Hispanic 335
White 75,128
Foreign 1,344

Enrollment highlights:
Women 55.6%
Full-time 67.7%
Minority 4.9%
Foreign 1.7%
10-year change in total
  enrollment .... Up 1.4%

Proportion of enrollment made up of minority students:
At public 4-year institutions .. 5.2%
At public 2-year institutions .. 2.5%
At private 4-year institutions . 5.9%
At private 2-year institutions . 6.3%

Degrees awarded:
Associate 2,640
Bachelor's 7,033
Master's 1,691
Doctorate 112
Professional 315

Residence of new students: State residents made up 71% of all freshmen enrolled in West Virginia; 85% of all West Virginia residents who were freshmen attended college in their home state.

Test scores: Students averaged 17.4 on the A.C.T., which was taken by 52% of West Virginia's high-school seniors.

MONEY
Average tuition and fees:
At public 4-year institutions . $1,591
At public 2-year institutions .. $803
At private 4-year institutions $7,197
At private 2-year institutions $2,554

Expenditures:
Public institutions $376,293,000
Private institutions $73,716,000

State funds for higher-education operating expenses: $277,921,000
Two-year change: Up 10%

State spending on student aid:
Need-based: $5,550,000; 5,632 awards
Non–need-based: None
Other: $7,403,000

Salary of chief executive of largest public 4-year campus:
Neil S. Bucklew, West Virginia University: $104,572

Total spending on research and development by doctorate-granting universities: $46,946,000

Sources:
Federal government	42.0%
State and local governments	2.6%
Industry	21.4%
The institution itself	30.3%
Other	3.7%

Federal spending on education and student aid (selected programs):
Vocational and adult education	$12,095,000
GI Bill	$1,955,000
Pell Grants	$34,050,000

Total federal spending on college- and university-based research and development: $15,092,000

Selected programs:
Department of Health and Human Services	$5,456,000
National Science Foundation	$627,000
Department of Defense	$732,000
Department of Agriculture	$4,122,000
Department of Energy	$1,241,000

Largest endowment:
West Virginia University $64,351,000

Top fund raisers:
West Virginia University	$15,544,000
University of Charleston	$4,306,000
Davis and Elkins College	$3,290,000

MISCELLANY

■ West Virginia State College, once a black land-grant institution, is seeking to have Congress restore that designation.

■ Some dispute exists over the oldest college in West Virginia. Marshall University and West Liberty State College were both founded in 1837. But Bethany College says those two institutions did not become baccalaureate-degree granting institutions until years later. Bethany believes its 1840 charter makes it the oldest institution of higher education in the state.

WISCONSIN

WISCONSIN LAWMAKERS seem to delight in picking on the University of Wisconsin System.

In recent years, university leaders have come under attack for failing to provide enough undergraduate class sections to allow students to graduate on time and for not requiring faculty members to spend more of their time teaching.

The flaps have frequently created controversy but rarely lasting acrimony. That is because lawmakers are well aware of the great pride Wisconsin citizens take in the system, which by virtue of its 32 campuses is highly visible throughout the state. A chief source of the pride is the university's flagship campus in Madison.

The regular flare-ups, however, sometimes obscure the larger political and financial pressures facing the system. In the past, university leaders have complained that the state does not provide them with enough money. But their attempts to compensate, by reducing enrollment and raising tuition, fly in the face of the state's populist traditions.

Kenneth A. Shaw, the chancellor, who left in mid-1991 to assume the presidency of Syracuse University, was among those urging the system to cut its enrollment and payroll unless state financing improves soon. Mr.

WISCONSIN
Continued

Shaw, whose blunt criticism of state financing often angered Gov. Tommy G. Thompson, a Republican, was especially frustrated by the unwillingness of the Governor and Legislature to finance "catch up" pay raises for faculty members.

Enrollment cutbacks and tuition increases are also unpopular notions with the state's active and well-organized student lobby, the United Council of Wisconsin Student Governments. The council has been a strong voice behind many of the university system's efforts to make the campus climate more accommodating to female, minority, and gay students. Student and faculty groups have been particularly active in the nationwide effort to end discrimination against gay students in the Reserve Officers Training Corps.

The Wisconsin Board of Regents is the governing board for the entire system, which includes two-year and four-year institutions. A seat on the 17-member board is a coveted gubernatorial appointment. The state Board of Vocational, Technical, and Adult Education supervises technical colleges.

With the state's heavy dependence on the dairy industry, public spending is affected by the vagaries of milk pricing, and state officials follow prices nearly as closely as budget planners in Wyoming and Alaska track the oil market.

Wisconsin provides no direct support to its private colleges but does maintain a separate financial-aid program for students who attend private institutions, such as Concordia and Marquette Universities.

DEMOGRAPHICS

Population: 4,891,769   (Rank: 16)

Age distribution:
Up to 17 .... 26.4%
18 to 24 .... 10.5%
25 to 44 .... 31.6%
45 and older 31.5%

Racial and ethnic distribution:
American Indian 0.8%
Asian 1.1%
Black 5.0%
White 92.2%
Other and unknown 0.9%
Hispanic (may be any race) .. 1.9%

Educational attainment of adults:
At least 4 years of high school 69.6%
At least 1 to 3 years of college 29.2%
At least 4 years of college ... 14.8%

Per-capita personal income: $17,560

Poverty rate: 8.5%

New high-school graduates in:
1991-92 (estimate) 53,930
2001-02 (estimate) 59,982

New GED diploma recipients: 3,058

High-school dropout rate: 15.1%

POLITICAL LEADERSHIP

Governor: Tommy G. Thompson (R), term ends 1995

Governor's higher-education aide:
Tom Fonfara, State Capitol, P.O. Box 7863, Madison 53707; (608) 266-1212

U.S. Senators: Robert W. Kasten, Jr. (R), term ends 1993; Herb Kohl (D), term ends 1995

U.S. Representatives:
4 Democrats, 5 Republicans
Les Aspin (D), Steve Gunderson (R), Gerald D. Kleczka (D), Scott L. Klug (R), Jim Moody (D), David R. Obey (D), Thomas E. Petri (R), Toby Roth (R), F. James Sensenbrenner, Jr. (R)

Legislature: Senate, 19 Democrats, 14 Republicans; House, 57 Democrats, 40 Republicans, 2 vacancies

COLLEGES AND UNIVERSITIES

Higher education:
Public 4-year institutions	13
Public 2-year institutions	17
Private 4-year institutions	28
Private 2-year institutions	3
Total	61

Vocational institutions: 99

Statewide coordinating board:
University of Wisconsin System
1720 Van Hise Hall
1220 Linden Drive
Madison 53706
(608) 262-2321
Katharine C. Lyall, acting president

Private-college association:
Wisconsin Association of Independent Colleges and Universities
25 West Main Street, Suite 583
Madison 53703
(608) 256-7761
Rolf Wegenke, president

Institutions censured by the AAUP:
Marquette University

Institutions under NCAA sanctions:
None

FACULTY MEMBERS

Full-time faculty members by rank:
Professor	2,737
Associate professor	2,097
Assistant professor	2,077
Instructor	256
Lecturer	244
No rank	2,605
Total	10,016

Average pay of full-time professors:
At public 4-year institutions	$40,920
At public 2-year institutions	$35,501
At private 4-year institutions	$36,133
At private 2-year institutions	n/a
At all institutions	$38,463
Men (all institutions)	$40,411
Women (all institutions)	$33,747

STUDENTS

Enrollment:
Total	290,672
At public 4-year institutions	151,146
At public 2-year institutions	94,822
At private 4-year institutions	43,551
At private 2-year institutions	1,153
Undergraduate	261,620
First-time freshmen	54,348
Graduate	25,463
Professional	3,589
American Indian	1,897
Asian	4,033
Black	9,060
Hispanic	3,497
White	261,147
Foreign	5,593

Enrollment highlights:
Women	54.2%
Full-time	64.5%
Minority	6.6%
Foreign	2.0%
10-year change in total enrollment	Up 13.6%

Proportion of enrollment made up of minority students:
At public 4-year institutions .. 5.4%

WISCONSIN
Continued

At public 2-year institutions .. 7.7%
At private 4-year institutions . 8.2%
At private 2-year institutions 18.6%

Degrees awarded:
Associate 8,658
Bachelor's 25,604
Master's 5,398
Doctorate 771
Professional 1,017

Residence of new students: State residents made up 84% of all freshmen enrolled in Wisconsin; 88% of all Wisconsin residents who were freshmen attended college in their home state.

Test scores: Students averaged 20.1 on the A.C.T., which was taken by 54% of Wisconsin's high-school seniors.

MONEY

Average tuition and fees:
At public 4-year institutions . $1,861
At public 2-year institutions . $1,160
At private 4-year institutions $7,615
At private 2-year institutions $4,001

Expenditures:
Public institutions .. $1,754,395,000
Private institutions ... $373,533,000

State funds for higher-education operating expenses: $863,337,000

Two-year change: Up 9%

State spending on student aid:
Need-based: $42,102,000;
  52,280 awards
Non–need-based: $700,000;
  620 awards
Other: $1,955,000

Salary of chief executive of largest public 4-year campus: Donna E. Shalala, University of Wisconsin at Madison: $114,300

Total spending on research and development by doctorate-granting universities: $363,364,000
Sources:
Federal government 57.5%
State and local governments . 16.3%
Industry 4.7%
The institution itself 13.1%
Other 8.5%

Federal spending on education and student aid (selected programs):
Vocational and
  adult education $25,229,000
GI Bill $6,923,000
Pell Grants $81,790,000

Total federal spending on college- and university-based research and development: $186,093,000
Selected programs:
Department of Health
  and Human Services $106,621,000
National Science
  Foundation $29,927,000
Department of Defense . $9,932,000
Department
  of Agriculture $8,415,000
Department of Energy . $15,143,000

Largest endowment:
University of Wisconsin
  Foundation $127,271,000

Top fund raisers:
University of Wisconsin
  at Madison $124,400,000
Marquette University .. $17,363,000
Beloit College $7,346,000

MISCELLANY

■ Four universities in Wisconsin—far more than in any other state—play host to the summer camps of teams in the National Football League. The four are Saint Norbert College and the Universities of Wisconsin at La Crosse, Platteville, and River Falls.

■ The oldest institution of higher education in Wisconsin is Nashotah House, an Episcopal seminary founded in 1842.

WYOMING

AS ONE WOULD EXPECT from Wyoming's frontier tradition, "big government" is an unpopular notion in the state. As a result, the state's institutions of higher education are often called upon to fill an array of needs beyond traditional college education—be it providing family health care in small towns like Casper or assisting the town of Rock Springs to shore up the coal-mine shafts beneath it.

Such activities have helped to produce a wealth of political and financial support for the University of Wyoming and the state's seven community colleges. With the energy-based economy once again on the upswing, that support has been notably evident in recent years.

In 1990 the Legislature gave the University of Wyoming greater authority in spending its state appropriation. In the 1991 session, lawmakers established the Wyoming Educational Trust Fund and put the first $10-million into its endowment, which they hope will eventually be worth $50-million.

Income from the fund will go for innovative programs at the university, community colleges, and public schools. The Legislature also has given community colleges the go-ahead to formulate proposals for a new tax system to finance the two-year colleges. The proposals will be considered in 1992.

Community-college officials say Gov. Michael Sullivan, a Democrat, has strongly supported their efforts to raise faculty salaries.

The University of Wyoming—which was established in 1886 and predates statehood—also did not escape notice in 1991. Lawmakers approved a bill that ends an open-admissions policy that had been in effect since 1905. University officials say they did not seek the legislation, but favor it because it will force students to come to college better prepared.

Finally, 1991 also saw the creation of a new board to plan and coordinate higher education. The Wyoming Postsecondary Planning and Coordinating Council includes the Governor, legislators, university and community-college leaders, and other top education officials.

Some of the criticism of the university is coming from within. In 1991 it began requiring the Family Practice Centers in Casper and Cheyenne to cover at least some of their costs through patient fees, prompting some clinic officials to accuse university leaders of starving the clinics to death. But university officials say the state should reconsider whether the clinics belong under the auspices of the university or another state agency. The clinics were originally designed to train doctors in family medicine and encourage them to remain in Wyoming, but have evolved into health-care centers for the poor.

DEMOGRAPHICS

Population: 453,588 (Rank: 51)

WYOMING
Continued

Age distribution:
Up to 17 .... 29.9%
18 to 24 .... 9.1%
25 to 44 .... 32.7%
45 and older 28.3%

Racial and ethnic distribution:
American Indian 2.1%
Asian 0.6%
Black 0.8%
White 94.2%
Other and unknown 2.3%
Hispanic (may be any race) .. 5.7%

Educational attainment of adults:
At least 4 years of high school 77.9%
At least 1 to 3 years of college 37.9%
At least 4 years of college ... 17.2%

Per-capita personal income: $16,314

Poverty rate: 10.5%

New high-school graduates in:
1991-92 (estimate) 5,783
2001-02 (estimate) 5,382

New GED diploma recipients: 1,137

High-school dropout rate: 11.7%

POLITICAL LEADERSHIP

Governor: Michael Sullivan (D), term ends 1995

Governor's higher-education aide: Scott Farris, Governor's Office, State Capitol, Cheyenne 82002; (307) 777-7434

U.S. Senators: Alan K. Simpson (R), term ends 1997; Malcolm Wallop (R), term ends 1995

U.S. Representative:
1 Republican
Craig Thomas (R)

Legislature: Senate, 10 Democrats, 20 Republicans; House, 22 Democrats, 42 Republicans

COLLEGES AND UNIVERSITIES

Higher education:
Public 4-year institutions 1
Public 2-year institutions 7
Private 4-year institutions 0
Private 2-year institutions 1
Total 9

Vocational institutions: 14

Statewide coordinating board:
Wyoming Postsecondary Education Planning and Coordinating Council
State Capitol
Cheyenne 82002
(307) 777-7434
Gov. Michael Sullivan, chairman

Private-college association:
None

Institutions censured by the AAUP:
None

Institutions under NCAA sanctions:
None

FACULTY MEMBERS

Full-time faculty members by rank:
Professor 244
Associate professor 158
Assistant professor 177
Instructor 50
Lecturer 45
No rank 316
Total 990

Average pay of full-time professors:
At public 4-year institutions $39,468
At public 2-year institutions $28,961
At private 4-year institutions ... n/a
At private 2-year institutions ... n/a
At all institutions $34,438
Men (all institutions) $36,985
Women (all institutions) $28,495

STUDENTS

Enrollment:
Total 29,159
At public 4-year institutions . 12,335
At public 2-year institutions . 16,218
At private 4-year institutions 0
At private 2-year institutions .. 606
Undergraduate 26,148
  First-time freshmen 5,890
Graduate 2,807
Professional 204
American Indian 376
Asian 82
Black 267
Hispanic 646
White 24,668
Foreign 501

Enrollment highlights:
Women 55.4%
Full-time 56.4%
Minority 5.3%
Foreign 1.9%
10-year change in total
  enrollment .... Up 49.6%

Proportion of enrollment made up of minority students:
At public 4-year institutions .. 4.8%
At public 2-year institutions .. 5.5%
At private 4-year institutions ... n/a
At private 2-year institutions . 6.8%

Degrees awarded:
Associate 1,507
Bachelor's 1,647
Master's 335
Doctorate 73
Professional 57

Residence of new students: State residents made up 77% of all freshmen enrolled in Wyoming; 81% of all Wyoming residents who were freshmen attended college in their home state.

Test scores: Students averaged 19.4 on the A.C.T., which was taken by 60% of Wyoming's high-school seniors.

MONEY

Average tuition and fees:
At public 4-year institutions . $1,003
At public 2-year institutions .. $613
At private 4-year institutions ... n/a
At private 2-year institutions $6,900

Expenditures:
Public institutions $203,307,000
Private institutions .... n/a

State funds for higher-education operating expenses: $124,902,000
Two-year change: Up 8%

State spending on student aid:
Need-based: $241,000; 531 awards
Non–need-based: None
Other: None

Salary of chief executive of largest public 4-year campus:
Terry P. Roark, University
  of Wyoming: $119,940

Total spending on research and development by doctorate-granting universities: $22,831,000
Sources:
Federal government 53.5%
State and local governments .. 9.0%
Industry 8.8%

WYOMING
Continued

The institution itself 27.7%
Other 1.0%

Federal spending on education and student aid (selected programs):
Vocational and
  adult education $6,141,000
GI Bill $859,000
Pell Grants $10,567,000

Total federal spending on college- and university-based research and development: $10,349,000

Selected programs:
Department of Health
  and Human Services . $1,187,000
National Science
  Foundation $4,269,000
Department of Defense . $1,466,000
Department
  of Agriculture $1,743,000
Department of Energy $605,000

Largest endowment:
University of Wyoming $44,312,000

Top fund raiser:
University of Wyoming . $3,751,000

MISCELLANY

■ The Education Commission of the States has picked Wyoming as the first of six states to test a comprehensive program for the simultaneous restructuring of teacher education and the public schools. The University of Wyoming, the Wyoming School-University Partnership, and the state department of education received a $25,000 grant from the commission to get the reform program started.

■ The oldest institution of higher education in the state is the University of Wyoming, founded in 1886.

Sources and Notes

THE STATISTICS IN this Almanac are meant to provide a broad view of higher education in the 50 states and the District of Columbia.

The figures are comparable from state to state, and, in all cases, they were the latest available at press time.

The time covered by the statistics varies from item to item. For example, the racial and ethnic distribution of the adult population of the states was gathered from the decennial census in 1990. However, the federal government has not yet tabulated the 1990 census figures on educational attainment by state, so the most recent figures available at press time were from 1980.

The U.S. Department of Education typically releases statistics from its surveys of colleges and universities one to three years after collecting the data. As a consequence, the latest figures on academic degrees awarded, for example, are from 1988-89.

Many statistics that would be useful to educators and policy makers are not available for every state.

For example, the Education Department does not collect information to show, on a comparable basis across the states, the proportion of high-school students who go on to college, or the proportion of college students who complete their degrees. Some states do collect such information, but those figures are not included in this Almanac because they would not always be comparable.

Because of rounding, figures may not add to 100 per cent. The designation "n/a" indicates that data are not available or not applicable. In some instances, U.S. totals may include data on service schools and outlying areas that are not shown separately.

DEMOGRAPHICS

Population:
SOURCE: Census Bureau
DATE: 1990

Age distribution:
SOURCE: Census Bureau
DATE: 1990

Racial and ethnic distribution:
SOURCE: Census Bureau
DATE: 1990

Educational attainment of adults:
SOURCE: Census Bureau
DATE: 1980
NOTE: Figures cover persons 25 years and older.

Per-capita personal income:
SOURCE: U.S. Department of Commerce
DATE: 1990

Poverty rate:
SOURCE: Census Bureau
NOTE: The state figures represent an average of each state's 1988, 1989, and 1990 poverty rates. Because the figures are based on samples and have relatively large standard errors, the Census Bureau urges users not to rank the states on the basis of the poverty statistics. The U.S. average covers only 1990.

New high-school graduates:
SOURCE: Western Interstate Commission for Higher Education
NOTE: Projections of the number of graduates in 1991-92 and 2001-02 were made in May 1988.

New GED diploma recipients:
SOURCE: American Council on Education
DATE: 1990
NOTE: General Education Development diplomas are high-school equivalency certificates awarded to high-school dropouts who pass the GED test.

High-school dropout rate:
SOURCE: U.S. Department of Education
DATE: 1988
NOTE: The figures cover public schools only, and are calculated by dividing the number of high-school graduates by the ninth-grade enrollment four years earlier. They are adjusted for interstate migration.

POLITICAL LEADERSHIP

Governor:
SOURCE: National Governors' Association

Governor's higher-education aide:
SOURCES: Education Commission of the States; National Governors' Association; *Chronicle of Higher Education* reporting

U.S. Senators:
SOURCE: Secretary of the Senate

U.S. Representatives:
SOURCE: Clerk of the House of Representatives

SOURCES & NOTES
Continued

Legislature:
SOURCE: National Conference of State Legislatures
NOTE: Figures represent the strength of state legislatures as of November 1991.

COLLEGES AND UNIVERSITIES

Higher education:
SOURCE: U.S. Department of Education
DATE: 1989-90

Vocational institutions:
SOURCE: U.S. Department of Education
DATE: 1989-90
NOTE: Figure includes public, private non-profit, and private for-profit non-collegiate institutions that offer post-secondary education.

Statewide coordinating board:
SOURCES: State Higher Education Executive Officers; *Chronicle of Higher Education* reporting
NOTE: These organizations are responsible for planning for public colleges and universities. Some boards also have governing authority. Those that do are indicated in the state narratives.

Private-college association:
SOURCES: National Association of Independent Colleges and Universities; *Chronicle of Higher Education* reporting

Institutions censured by the AAUP:
SOURCE: American Association of University Professors
DATE: Action as of June 1991

NOTE: The AAUP censures institutions when it finds that they have violated its standards of academic freedom and tenure. The standards seek to protect the rights of faculty members to free speech without fear of penalty, and to due process in appointment, promotion, and tenure decisions. The standards are included in the 1940 Statement of Principles of Academic Freedom and Tenure, which was developed by the AAUP and the Association of American Colleges and endorsed by more than 100 other academic organizations. Censure was imposed on administrative officers at all institutions listed except at those noted.

Institutions under NCAA sanctions:
SOURCE: National Collegiate Athletic Association
DATE: Action as of November 1991

FACULTY MEMBERS

Full-time faculty members by rank:
SOURCE: U.S. Department of Education
DATE: 1989-90
NOTE: Figures cover full-time members of the instructional staff on 9- and 10-month contracts only.

Average pay of full-time professors:
SOURCE: U.S. Department of Education
DATE: 1989-90
NOTE: Figures cover full-time members of the instructional staff on 9- and 10-month contracts only.

STUDENTS

Enrollment:
SOURCE: U.S. Department of Education
NOTE: The figures for total enroll-

ment, enrollment by type and control of institution, and enrollment by level are from Fall 1989. Undergraduate enrollment includes first-time freshman enrollment, which is also shown separately. The figures for enrollment by racial and ethnic group, which are compiled every two years, are from Fall 1988. The full definitions of the racial and ethnic categories are as follows: American Indian and Alaskan native; Asian and Pacific Islander; black, non-Hispanic; Hispanic; and white, non-Hispanic. Foreign students are non-resident aliens studying in the United States on a temporary basis.

Enrollment highlights:
SOURCE: U.S. Department
of Education
NOTE: The change in enrollment is from Fall 1979 to Fall 1989. The figures on minority students and foreign students are from Fall 1988. Statistics on full-time students and female students are from Fall 1989. All proportions are based on total enrollment with one exception: The proportion of students who are minority-group members covers only U.S. citizens.

Proportion of enrollment made up of minority students:
SOURCE: U.S. Department
of Education
DATE: Fall 1988

Degrees awarded:
SOURCE: U.S. Department
of Education
DATE: 1988-89

Residence of new students:
SOURCE: U.S. Department
of Education
DATE: Fall 1988
NOTE: The figures cover freshmen only.

Test scores:
SOURCES: U.S. Department
of Education; College Board
DATES: 1989 for A.C.T.; 1991 for S.A.T.
NOTE: The A.C.T. (American College Testing Program's A.C.T. Assessment) is scored on a scale from 1 to 36. The S.A.T.—the College Board's Scholastic Aptitude Test—is scored on a scale from 400 to 1,600. For each state, one score is given, depending on which test was taken by the larger number of students.

MONEY

Average tuition and fees:
SOURCE: U.S. Department
of Education
DATE: 1989-90
NOTE: Figures cover undergraduate charges and are weighted by Fall 1988 full-time-equivalent undergraduate enrollment. The figures for public institutions represent charges to state residents.

Expenditures:
SOURCE: U.S. Department
of Education
DATE: 1985-86

State funds for higher-education operating expenses:
SOURCE: Edward R. Hines, Illinois
State University
DATE: 1991-92
NOTE: Figures include state tax funds appropriated for colleges and universities, for student aid, and for governing and coordinating boards. They do not include funds for capital outlays and money from sources other than state taxes, such as student fees or appropriations from local governments.

SOURCE & NOTES
Continued

State spending on student aid:
SOURCE: National Association of State Scholarship and Grant Programs
DATE: 1990-91
NOTE: "Need-based" aid covers scholarships awarded on the basis of a student's financial situation. "Non-need-based" aid includes scholarships given to reward meritorious students, to encourage students to major in particular disciplines, and to reduce the difference in tuition costs between public and private institutions. The category of "other" aid includes spending for work-study, loan-forgiveness, and loan programs. The statistics cover aid to both undergraduate and graduate students. The figures include most of the money that states spend on student financial aid. However, some states may spend more on programs that are not specifically identified as student-aid programs.

Salary of chief executive of largest public 4-year campus:
SOURCE: *Chronicle of Higher Education* reporting
DATE: 1991-92
NOTE: Institutions were selected on the basis of Fall 1989 enrollment as reported by the U.S. Department of Education.

Total spending on research and development by doctorate-granting universities:
SOURCE: National Science Foundation
DATE: Fiscal year 1990
NOTE: Figures cover spending in science and engineering, and exclude spending in such disciplines as the arts, education, and the humanities.

Federal spending on education and student aid (selected programs):
SOURCE: Census Bureau
DATE: Fiscal year 1990

Total federal spending on college- and university-based research and development:
SOURCE: National Science Foundation
DATE: Fiscal year 1989
NOTE: Figures cover federal obligations, which are funds set aside for payments. Institutions do not always receive them in the year in which they were obligated. Figures include only spending for science and engineering projects, and exclude spending in such disciplines as the arts, education, and the humanities.

Largest endowment:
SOURCES: National Association of College and University Business Officers; *Chronicle of Higher Education* reporting
DATE: As of June 30, 1990

Top fund raisers:
SOURCE: Council for Aid to Education
DATE: 1989-90
NOTE: Figures are based on a survey of 1,056 institutions, which together received about 85 per cent of all private contributions to colleges and universities. Rankings of institutions may be heavily influenced by the timing of fund drives, unusually large gifts, and other factors.

MISCELLANY

SOURCE: *Chronicle of Higher Education* reporting

Enrollment by Race

THE TABLE that follows shows the distribution of enrollment by racial and ethnic group for fall 1988 at more than 3,100 colleges and universities.

The distribution is based on the institution's total enrollment, including full-time and part-time students and undergraduate and graduate students. The total enrollment appears in the last column.

The institutions are listed in alphabetical order by state. Institutions that are part of state systems of higher education appear under the system name.

The figures were compiled by the U.S. Department of Education, which conducts a survey of enrollment by race every two years. The table omits about 250 institutions that did not provide complete information to the Education Department.

Because of rounding, the figures may not add to 100 per cent.

The full definitions of the racial and ethnic groups are as follows: American Indian or Alaskan native; Asian or Pacific Islander; black, non-Hispanic; Hispanic; and white, non-Hispanic. Figures in those groups cover both U.S. citizens and resident aliens. Foreign students include all non-resident aliens who are enrolled in U.S. colleges and universities, regardless of their racial or ethnic backgrounds.

	American Indian	Asian	Black	Hispanic	White	Foreign	Total
ALABAMA							
Alabama A&M U	0.0%	0.3%	75.7%	0.4%	13.2%	10.5%	4,244
Alabama Aviation and Tech C	0.3	1.0	11.9	1.0	85.0	0.8	386
Alabama St U	0.0	0.0	97.1	0.4	1.4	1.0	4,045
Alexander City St JC	0.2	0.2	14.2	0.2	84.7	0.6	1,036
American Inst of Psychotherapy	0.0	0.0	5.3	0.0	94.7	0.0	38
Athens St C	0.5	0.4	5.9	0.4	92.4	0.3	2,115
Auburn U							
Main	0.1	0.5	3.5	0.4	92.5	3.0	20,553
Montgomery	0.1	1.2	15.7	0.2	82.5	0.4	5,580
Bessemer St Tech C	0.0	0.0	25.6	0.1	74.3	0.0	1,659
Birmingham Southern C	0.1	1.5	9.4	0.3	88.2	0.5	1,836
Brewer St JC	0.0	0.0	8.1	0.0	91.9	0.0	743
C A Fredd St Tech C	0.0	0.7	96.1	0.0	3.3	0.0	307
Carver St Tech C	0.0	0.0	95.0	0.0	5.0	0.0	525
Chattahoochee Valley CC	0.2	0.3	26.9	0.9	71.2	0.5	1,572
Chauncey Sparks St Tech C	0.3	0.0	35.1	0.3	64.1	0.3	370
CC of the Air Force	0.1	0.3	17.2	0.3	81.6	0.5	26,354

ALABAMA, cont.

	American Indian	Asian	Black	Hispanic	White	Foreign	Total
Concordia C	0.0%	0.0%	99.7%	0.0%	0.3%	0.0%	343
Douglas MacArthur St Tech C	0.7	0.0	13.3	0.0	85.9	0.0	427
Draughons JC	0.0	0.0	54.5	0.0	45.5	0.0	231
Enterprise St JC	0.2	1.3	10.0	2.1	86.4	0.0	2,020
Faulkner St JC	0.9	0.3	9.1	0.6	88.7	0.4	2,348
Faulkner U	0.1	0.1	25.1	0.2	73.0	1.7	1,967
Gadsden St CC	0.1	0.2	10.7	0.7	81.6	6.7	4,062
G C Wallace St CC Dothan	0.2	0.7	12.6	0.2	86.1	0.2	3,781
G C Wallace St CC Hanceville	0.0	0.1	1.6	0.0	98.2	0.1	3,382
G C Wallace St CC Selma	0.1	0.3	35.1	0.1	64.5	0.0	1,469
Harry M Ayers St Tech C	0.0	0.6	14.0	0.0	85.3	0.0	620
Hobson St Tech C	0.0	0.0	38.3	0.0	61.7	0.0	525
Huntingdon C	0.1	1.4	5.3	0.8	90.4	2.0	866
International Bible C	0.0	2.9	14.3	1.0	79.0	2.9	105
J F Drake St Tech C	0.4	0.3	38.5	0.3	58.6	1.9	694
Jacksonville St U	0.5	0.5	16.6	0.8	79.9	1.7	7,511
Jefferson Davis St JC	0.0	0.1	19.8	0.0	79.7	0.4	896
Jefferson St JC	0.4	0.4	10.3	0.2	87.9	0.8	6,042
John C Calhoun St CC	0.5	0.5	8.7	0.6	89.4	0.2	6,551
John M Patterson St Tech C	0.1	0.6	40.3	0.0	58.9	0.0	672
Judson C	0.0	0.2	4.5	0.2	94.3	0.7	402
Lawson St CC	0.0	0.0	98.9	0.0	1.1	0.0	1,105
Livingston U	0.2	0.3	25.1	0.1	73.4	0.9	1,633
Lurleen B Wallace St JC	0.1	0.0	12.3	0.2	86.2	1.2	1,009
Marion Military Inst	0.0	0.0	10.6	4.1	85.3	0.0	293
Miles C	0.0	0.0	99.7	0.0	0.3	0.0	616
Mobile C	0.2	0.2	14.7	0.0	83.2	1.7	1,054
Muscle Shoals St Tech C	0.0	0.0	15.1	0.0	84.9	0.0	730
N F Nunnelly St Tech C	0.0	0.2	19.8	0.0	80.0	0.0	515
National Ed Ctr National Inst of Tech	0.0	0.0	69.2	0.0	30.8	0.0	52
Northeast Alabama St JC	0.5	0.0	1.0	0.2	98.1	0.2	1,177
Northwest Alabama St JC	0.0	0.0	8.4	0.0	91.5	0.1	1,654
Northwest Alabama St Tech C	0.0	0.2	3.8	0.0	95.5	0.4	446
Oakwood C	0.0	0.0	90.8	0.0	0.0	9.2	1,233
Patrick Henry St JC	0.3	0.0	13.5	0.0	86.2	0.0	761
Reid St Tech C	1.2	0.0	24.2	0.0	74.5	0.0	326
S D Bishop St JC	0.0	0.0	73.1	0.0	25.5	1.4	1,824
Samford U	0.1	0.5	5.7	0.5	93.1	0.0	4,089
Shelton St CC	0.0	3.1	19.0	0.0	77.9	0.0	3,310
Snead St JC	0.1	0.0	0.9	0.1	98.8	0.0	1,399
Southeastern Bible C	0.0	0.0	5.0	0.0	92.8	2.2	139
Southern JC of Business Huntsville	0.0	0.6	43.6	0.0	55.8	0.0	509
Southern Union St JC	0.0	0.2	14.8	0.3	84.5	0.2	2,457
Southwest St Tech C	0.6	0.7	35.9	0.7	62.2	0.0	897
Spring Hill C	0.3	0.9	4.9	2.7	89.4	1.8	1,171
Stillman C	0.0	0.0	98.4	0.0	0.0	1.6	771
Talladega C	0.2	0.0	96.6	1.5	1.7	0.0	528
Trenholm St Tech C	0.0	0.0	75.8	4.0	20.2	0.0	703
Troy St U Main	0.6	0.9	18.1	2.4	77.4	0.6	8,039
Dothan	0.2	0.6	8.1	0.7	90.2	0.3	1,735
Montgomery	0.3	0.9	21.1	2.1	75.6	0.1	1,948
Tuskegee U	0.0	0.0	88.6	0.9	3.4	7.1	3,401
U S Sports Academy	0.0	0.4	2.1	0.8	93.8	2.9	240

	American Indian	Asian	Black	Hispanic	White	Foreign	Total
U of Alabama							
Tuscaloosa	0.2%	2.2%	8.5%	0.7%	86.3%	1.9%	18,510
Birmingham	0.1	1.0	15.8	0.2	79.6	3.2	13,886
Huntsville	0.2	2.5	5.1	0.8	88.3	3.1	7,448
U of Montevallo	0.1	0.1	7.9	0.3	89.6	2.0	2,719
U of North Alabama	0.2	0.2	7.8	0.4	91.1	0.3	5,291
U of South Alabama	0.6	1.3	9.8	0.8	83.4	4.1	10,443
Walker C	0.0	0.2	3.7	0.0	96.0	0.0	827
Walker St Tech C	0.2	0.0	5.6	0.1	94.1	0.0	2,243

ALASKA

	American Indian	Asian	Black	Hispanic	White	Foreign	Total
Alaska Bible C	4.8	0.0	1.2	1.2	85.5	7.2	83
Alaska Pacific U	10.6	2.7	6.4	3.1	74.3	2.8	639
U of Alaska							
Anchorage	4.8	3.5	5.2	2.2	83.7	0.7	13,435
Kenai Peninsula	2.7	0.5	0.5	1.3	94.7	0.2	1,503
Kodiak	7.6	5.4	1.0	2.7	83.3	0.0	628
Matanuska-Susitna	1.7	0.2	0.3	0.8	97.0	0.1	1,164
Fairbanks	10.0	2.8	3.5	1.5	81.8	0.4	6,731
Kuskokwim	59.8	1.7	1.0	1.7	35.9	0.0	301
Northwest	58.1	0.6	0.0	0.0	41.3	0.0	167
Juneau	8.4	2.2	1.9	1.3	85.6	0.6	1,949
Southeast Ketchikan	9.6	1.4	0.3	0.8	87.9	0.0	636
Southeast Sitka	17.0	1.4	0.3	1.1	80.2	0.0	631

ARIZONA

	American Indian	Asian	Black	Hispanic	White	Foreign	Total
American Graduate Sch of International Management	0.1	0.0	0.3	1.2	70.9	27.5	1,083
American Indian Bible C	85.9	1.0	0.0	2.0	11.1	0.0	99
Arizona C of the Bible	2.4	1.6	3.2	4.8	87.2	0.8	125
Arizona St U	1.1	2.8	2.3	5.3	83.8	4.7	43,426
Arizona Western C	1.9	0.7	2.9	36.8	57.4	0.2	4,654
Central Arizona C	5.6	0.8	3.7	17.6	72.3	0.0	5,196
Cochise C	1.1	3.8	4.9	20.8	69.4	0.0	4,756
DeVry Inst of Tech	2.2	5.9	3.1	8.2	79.2	1.4	2,647
Eastern Arizona C	6.6	0.9	2.8	18.1	71.5	0.1	4,619
Frank Lloyd Wright Sch of Architecture	0.0	0.0	0.0	0.0	84.0	16.0	25
Grand Canyon C	2.6	1.2	3.4	6.2	85.4	1.2	1,813
ITT Tech Inst Phoenix	4.6	1.8	7.1	9.1	77.4	0.0	438
ITT Tech Inst Tucson	0.9	0.9	6.9	36.5	54.7	0.0	318
Maricopa County CC Dist							
Gateway CC	3.5	2.0	5.8	12.1	76.1	0.5	5,846
Glendale CC	1.1	2.3	2.3	9.0	84.6	0.7	19,200
Mesa CC	1.7	2.3	2.3	8.1	84.8	0.8	19,627
Phoenix C	2.7	1.9	4.6	13.0	77.5	0.3	13,639
Rio Salado CC	2.0	0.9	3.8	9.1	84.0	0.1	14,223
Scottsdale CC	2.7	1.2	1.2	3.0	91.4	0.5	9,141
South Mountain CC	2.1	1.7	17.6	28.7	49.3	0.6	3,177
Mohave CC	1.9	0.5	0.2	2.5	94.9	0.0	3,523
Northern Arizona U	5.2	0.8	1.4	6.0	83.0	3.6	14,995
Northland Pioneer C	22.8	0.4	0.8	7.4	68.6	0.0	6,481
Ottawa U	0.6	6.9	4.2	8.0	80.3	0.0	1,577
Pima CC	2.1	1.9	3.3	19.6	70.5	2.7	26,810

ARIZONA, cont.	American Indian	Asian	Black	Hispanic	White	Foreign	Total
Pima CC Skill Center	13.4%	1.4%	8.5%	31.7%	45.1%	0.0%	142
Prescott C	5.1	0.3	1.4	2.0	90.5	0.7	294
Southwestern Conservative Baptist Bible C	1.8	0.0	3.0	3.0	91.0	1.2	166
U of Arizona	1.0	2.6	1.6	7.5	80.5	6.7	34,725
Western International U	0.0	8.5	4.8	6.8	57.6	22.3	2,291
Yavapai C	5.7	0.0	0.9	5.1	87.0	1.2	5,717

ARKANSAS

American C	0.4	0.0	0.8	0.4	98.3	0.0	237
Arkansas Baptist C	0.0	0.0	99.6	0.0	0.4	0.0	268
Arkansas C	0.0	1.1	3.3	0.3	95.2	0.1	799
Arkansas St U							
Main	0.3	0.7	9.8	0.2	86.3	2.7	9,026
Beebe	0.8	0.7	6.7	1.2	90.6	0.0	1,823
Arkansas Tech U	0.7	0.3	2.5	0.6	95.3	0.7	3,588
Capital City JC of Business	0.0	0.2	44.2	0.2	55.5	0.0	573
Central Baptist C	0.0	0.5	4.9	0.0	92.3	2.2	183
Crowley's Ridge C	0.0	0.0	1.6	0.0	98.4	0.0	123
East Arkansas CC	0.0	0.2	28.8	0.3	70.7	0.0	1,269
Garland County CC	0.8	0.5	5.7	0.7	92.2	0.1	1,729
Harding U Main	0.1	0.1	1.8	0.8	94.6	2.6	3,155
Henderson St U	0.4	0.2	13.9	0.3	84.6	0.5	3,348
Hendrix C	0.0	0.6	10.6	0.2	84.8	3.8	1,203
John Brown U	1.1	0.6	0.5	0.3	88.0	9.5	874
Mississippi County CC	0.0	1.6	17.8	0.5	80.1	0.1	1,548
National Education Center	0.1	0.1	35.4	0.2	63.6	0.5	838
North Arkansas CC	0.9	0.3	0.1	0.2	98.4	0.0	2,457
Ouachita Baptist U	0.1	0.1	5.8	0.1	92.3	1.6	1,352
Philander Smith C	0.0	2.5	83.7	0.0	0.7	13.1	594
Phillips County CC	0.1	0.4	49.1	0.4	50.0	0.0	1,486
Rich Mountain CC	0.2	0.7	0.0	0.0	99.0	0.0	417
Shorter C	0.0	3.3	80.1	0.0	6.6	9.9	151
Southern Arkansas U							
Main	0.3	0.4	17.4	0.3	81.1	0.6	2,159
El Dorado	0.1	0.3	17.0	0.0	82.5	0.1	736
Tech	0.1	0.4	15.1	0.2	84.2	0.0	830
Southern Baptist C	0.5	0.0	2.0	0.0	96.4	1.0	589
Southern Tech C Little Rock	0.0	0.6	36.6	0.0	62.8	0.0	629
U of Arkansas							
Little Rock	0.3	0.9	10.0	0.7	86.0	2.1	10,064
Medical Sciences	0.2	2.0	7.8	0.3	89.1	0.5	1,327
Pine Bluff	0.0	0.4	82.1	0.1	17.3	0.2	3,333
Fayetteville	0.7	1.4	4.4	0.6	88.9	4.0	13,835
Monticello	0.3	0.2	17.6	0.3	81.5	0.1	1,974
U of Central Arkansas	0.7	0.5	10.8	0.3	86.8	0.8	6,698
U of the Ozarks	0.6	0.3	4.2	0.0	81.3	13.7	795
Westark CC	0.9	2.2	2.9	0.7	93.3	0.2	4,306

CALIFORNIA

Allan Hancock C	2.1	4.3	4.6	14.9	72.5	1.6	7,975
American Academy of Dramatic Arts West	0.7	2.2	5.1	4.3	74.6	13.0	138

	American Indian	Asian	Black	Hispanic	White	Foreign	Total
American Baptist Sem of the West	0.0%	8.9%	11.1%	4.4%	68.9%	6.7%	45
American Conservatory Theatre	0.0	3.4	9.5	3.4	81.6	2.0	147
American Film Inst Center for Advanced Film and Television Studies	0.0	3.5	5.0	5.0	70.0	16.5	200
Antelope Valley C	1.3	3.6	5.8	8.8	79.6	0.8	8,077
Antioch U Los Angeles	0.0	1.4	2.9	2.9	92.8	0.0	415
Antioch U San Francisco	0.4	1.2	5.4	1.7	85.4	5.8	240
Antioch U Santa Barbara	0.0	0.0	3.6	0.7	95.7	0.0	139
Armstrong C	0.0	0.8	3.2	0.0	4.8	91.3	252
Art Center C of Design	0.5	15.4	0.5	5.4	69.1	9.1	1,283
Art Inst of Southern California	0.9	4.3	0.0	5.2	85.3	4.3	116
Azusa Pacific U	0.8	3.3	3.4	5.2	75.0	12.4	2,833
Barstow C	3.4	3.7	10.7	15.3	65.2	1.7	2,233
Bethany Bible C	0.4	2.8	2.8	6.6	86.9	0.6	533
Biola U	0.3	11.4	2.7	4.1	76.7	4.8	2,587
Brooks C	3.7	8.0	10.3	9.1	63.7	5.2	750
Brooks Inst of Photography	0.3	1.9	0.6	4.8	80.5	11.8	626
Butte C	2.9	2.7	1.5	6.0	84.9	1.9	7,928
Cabrillo C	1.0	3.6	1.1	9.8	83.0	1.6	12,075
California Baptist C	0.5	4.8	9.3	6.6	70.6	8.3	666
California C of Arts and Crafts	0.5	9.2	2.6	3.9	74.2	9.5	1,118
California C of Podiatric Medicine	0.5	15.1	2.3	3.2	75.2	3.7	431
Cal Family Study Ctr	0.4	1.6	1.6	3.3	92.2	0.8	243
California Inst of the Arts	0.7	4.0	5.4	3.4	78.0	8.5	850
California Inst of Integral Studies	1.3	4.1	0.6	2.5	89.8	1.6	314
California Inst of Tech	0.1	14.4	0.5	1.7	59.3	24.0	1,841
California Lutheran U	0.5	3.2	2.9	6.0	82.8	4.5	2,749
California Maritime Academy	0.5	4.0	3.5	6.4	82.7	2.9	376
Cal Sch of Professional Psych							
Berkeley	0.0	2.8	3.0	3.4	89.0	1.7	464
Fresno	0.3	1.7	2.8	3.8	88.9	2.4	287
Los Angeles	0.0	4.1	7.5	6.8	79.1	2.6	468
California St U							
Cal Polytechnic St U San Luis Obispo	0.9	8.9	1.6	8.1	79.4	1.0	15,912
Cal St Poly U Pomona	0.8	23.6	3.9	14.5	53.8	3.5	17,905
Bakersfield	0.7	3.9	5.5	14.1	72.9	2.9	4,650
Chico	1.1	1.5	1.7	4.4	88.4	3.0	14,979
Dominguez Hill	0.8	10.1	32.3	11.6	41.3	3.9	7,460
Fresno	1.4	5.2	3.8	16.2	68.1	5.5	17,467
Fullerton	1.0	15.6	2.5	10.5	67.4	2.9	23,376
Hayward	1.3	17.1	9.4	7.1	62.3	2.8	11,757
Long Beach	0.9	18.2	5.4	10.2	62.1	3.2	33,179
Los Angeles	0.6	27.2	10.6	26.4	28.2	7.1	17,960
Northridge	0.7	12.7	5.4	10.1	69.2	2.0	29,401
Sacramento	1.3	9.8	4.4	7.4	74.8	2.2	23,478
San Bernardino	1.4	4.0	6.6	12.6	72.8	2.6	9,154
Stanislaus	1.5	4.7	3.2	10.8	77.1	2.7	4,822
Humboldt St U	2.6	2.2	2.2	4.1	87.9	1.0	6,135
San Diego St U	1.0	9.0	3.5	9.1	75.5	2.0	34,155
San Francisco St U	0.7	26.9	7.4	7.5	51.8	5.7	24,138
San Jose St U	1.0	22.0	4.1	8.8	59.9	4.2	26,450

CALIFORNIA, cont.

	American Indian	Asian	Black	Hispanic	White	Foreign	Total
California St U							
Sonoma St U	1.1%	2.7%	4.0%	5.3%	84.4%	2.3%	6,129
Career Com C of Business	0.0	11.4	43.8	4.6	40.2	0.0	219
Cerritos C	2.2	14.2	6.3	32.0	43.2	2.0	15,886
Chabot C	1.9	14.8	7.5	11.3	62.3	2.2	19,705
Chaffey CC	1.1	4.1	7.6	18.5	66.8	2.0	10,985
Chapman C	0.2	8.2	2.6	5.9	83.1	0.0	2,060
Charles R Drew U	0.0	8.1	52.5	27.3	12.1	0.0	99
Christian Heritage C	0.0	2.3	2.3	4.0	90.0	1.5	399
Church Divinity Sch of the Pacific	0.0	1.9	0.0	0.0	96.2	1.9	104
Citrus C	0.9	6.6	5.6	19.5	63.1	4.3	8,786
City C of San Francisco	0.8	36.9	9.0	11.0	36.5	5.7	24,408
Claremont Graduate Sch	0.4	3.5	3.2	3.7	80.4	8.8	1,664
Claremont McKenna C	0.4	11.1	4.2	6.1	75.1	3.2	856
Coast CC Dist							
Coastline CC	1.1	8.2	1.3	5.2	83.7	0.4	10,950
Golden West C	1.0	14.1	1.2	7.1	74.1	2.5	13,137
Orange Coast C	1.0	11.2	1.4	7.6	76.5	2.3	22,365
Cogswell C	0.4	19.3	1.2	11.5	63.8	3.7	243
C of Marin	1.4	4.4	3.3	3.8	85.0	2.1	9,817
C of Notre Dame	1.0	8.3	4.3	5.2	69.5	11.8	1,052
C of Osteopathic Medicine of the Pacific	0.7	11.8	1.2	5.1	75.9	5.3	432
C of the Canyons	0.7	3.5	1.6	8.5	85.0	0.7	4,815
C of the Desert	1.0	2.2	3.6	16.8	75.9	0.4	7,231
C of the Redwoods	4.8	2.0	1.1	2.2	89.3	0.6	6,147
C of the Sequoias	2.2	3.5	2.3	24.0	67.4	0.5	7,839
C of the Siskiyous	3.0	2.5	2.0	4.0	87.3	1.2	1,851
Columbia C Columbia	1.4	1.0	1.0	3.4	92.7	0.5	2,012
Columbia C Hollywood	0.5	4.7	7.0	6.6	60.1	21.1	213
Compton CC	0.7	1.9	60.1	30.8	4.2	2.4	3,972
Contra Costa CC Sys							
Contra Costa C	0.8	14.3	25.3	13.3	45.1	1.1	6,634
Diablo Valley C	0.7	8.3	2.8	5.7	81.8	0.7	20,255
Los Medanos C	1.2	6.1	6.4	11.8	74.5	0.0	6,367
Crafton Hills C	1.4	2.6	2.9	10.0	82.6	0.7	3,990
Cuesta CC	0.8	3.0	1.5	6.3	87.1	1.4	7,127
Cuyamaca C	1.9	4.9	1.9	9.5	81.0	0.7	3,614
D-Q U	80.0	1.1	0.0	8.3	9.4	1.1	180
DeVry Inst of Tech							
Los Angeles	0.6	18.7	11.6	28.7	38.4	2.0	2,251
Dominican C of San Rafael	0.2	4.5	3.8	4.1	80.2	7.4	665
Dominican Sch of Philosophy and Theology	0.0	11.0	2.2	5.5	73.6	7.7	91
Don Bosco Tech Inst	0.3	17.8	0.9	63.5	17.5	0.0	348
El Camino C	0.9	15.4	19.2	14.2	48.5	1.8	25,789
Fashion Inst of Design and Merchandising Costa Mesa	0.6	5.9	10.0	15.6	67.3	0.6	321
Fashion Inst of Design and Merchandising LA	0.9	6.0	9.8	15.9	66.7	0.7	2,054
Fashion Inst of Design and Merchandising San Diego	0.6	6.0	9.6	15.6	67.7	0.6	167
Fashion Inst of Design and Merchandising SF	0.8	5.8	9.8	16.1	67.0	0.5	634
Fielding Inst	0.3	0.8	3.3	0.8	94.4	0.5	644

	American Indian	Asian	Black	Hispanic	White	Foreign	Total
Foothill De Anza CC Dist							
De Anza C	1.1%	19.6%	3.8%	7.8%	63.6%	4.2%	21,948
Foothill C	1.8	11.1	4.1	5.6	74.0	3.3	12,811
Fresno Pacific C	0.8	1.4	2.0	6.7	86.0	3.1	1,317
Fuller Theological Sem	0.2	10.0	3.9	4.5	69.3	12.0	2,109
Glendale CC	1.1	13.8	1.7	19.2	53.5	10.6	12,072
Golden Gate Baptist Sem	0.3	9.6	4.7	5.7	71.1	8.6	686
Golden Gate U	0.3	10.0	6.4	3.5	73.6	6.2	8,831
Graduate Theological Union	0.0	1.5	0.8	1.0	82.3	14.4	395
Grossmont C	2.0	4.7	2.5	7.7	81.4	1.6	15,357
Hartnell C	2.0	9.4	4.2	28.3	53.9	2.2	6,762
Harvey Mudd C	0.5	17.8	0.7	2.0	77.1	1.8	551
Hebrew Union C California	0.0	0.0	0.0	0.0	100.0	0.0	48
Holy Names C	0.1	4.0	15.2	4.9	60.4	15.3	717
Humphreys C	0.5	6.4	6.6	12.2	74.3	0.0	409
Inst of Transpersonal Psychology	0.0	4.0	1.3	1.3	88.0	5.3	150
International Sch of Theology	0.0	0.0	0.0	1.8	91.1	7.1	56
ITT Tech Inst Buena Park	1.7	19.1	4.4	22.4	51.8	0.4	517
ITT Tech Inst La Mesa	0.9	7.9	9.7	17.9	61.9	1.6	546
ITT Tech Inst Sacramento	0.8	9.7	11.4	15.8	62.3	0.0	36
Jesuit Sch of Theology	0.6	5.6	0.6	4.3	66.7	22.2	162
Kern CC Dist							
Bakersfield C	2.2	3.5	5.0	15.7	72.5	1.2	10,776
Cerro Coso CC	2.3	3.3	4.0	3.6	85.6	1.3	3,673
Porterville C	2.2	3.8	3.1	18.2	70.6	2.1	2,334
Lake Tahoe CC	2.3	3.0	1.2	8.1	83.7	1.8	1,083
Lassen C	6.0	0.9	4.6	4.8	80.8	2.9	2,563
LIFE Bible C	0.8	7.3	4.6	9.7	75.5	2.2	372
Life Chiropractic C West	1.3	4.5	1.3	2.6	87.5	2.8	464
Lincoln U	0.0	4.4	1.8	1.8	26.6	65.3	271
Loma Linda U	0.5	18.2	8.2	9.9	54.2	9.0	4,392
Long Beach City C	1.2	13.9	11.9	10.5	59.2	3.2	18,378
Los Angeles C of Chiropractic	0.2	7.1	1.4	4.8	80.0	6.4	994
Los Angeles CC Dist							
East Los Angeles C	0.5	16.8	3.5	66.0	6.6	6.6	12,447
Los Angeles City C	0.5	21.5	17.4	29.8	20.6	10.1	14,479
Los Angeles Harbor C	0.5	12.7	14.8	23.5	45.9	2.6	8,319
Los Angeles Mission C	0.8	4.5	8.7	42.2	41.0	2.8	4,628
Los Angeles Pierce C	0.7	10.5	3.9	8.9	72.7	3.3	16,970
Los Angeles Southwest C	0.0	0.8	71.3	24.9	1.2	1.7	5,296
LA Trade Tech C	0.5	13.5	31.6	34.9	13.6	5.9	12,030
Los Angeles Valley C	0.6	10.7	6.7	18.2	60.7	3.0	16,457
West Los Angeles C	0.4	7.7	48.7	9.1	30.2	3.9	8,282
Los Rios CC Dist							
American River C	2.3	5.6	5.5	6.2	79.1	1.2	18,716
Cosumnes River C	2.3	7.7	9.8	7.7	71.4	1.1	8,235
Sacramento City C	2.0	13.8	11.9	12.3	55.4	4.5	14,474
Loyola Marymount U	0.2	8.8	3.5	10.2	73.8	3.5	6,479
Marymount C	0.5	7.6	6.7	6.7	64.0	14.4	1,012
Master's C	0.4	2.3	2.1	2.0	91.0	2.1	943
Mendocino C	4.1	1.5	1.2	4.2	87.9	1.0	3,455
Menlo C	0.0	2.7	0.5	1.4	82.1	13.3	592
Mennonite Brethren Biblical Sem	0.0	0.8	0.0	0.8	58.5	39.8	123
Merced C	1.2	2.7	6.2	14.4	66.1	9.4	6,854

THE ALMANAC OF HIGHER EDUCATION • ENROLLMENT BY RACE

CALIFORNIA, cont.

	American Indian	Asian	Black	Hispanic	White	Foreign	Total
Mills C	0.3%	7.2%	6.9%	3.6%	74.2%	7.8%	1,038
Mira Costa C	1.1	4.3	4.6	9.7	79.3	1.0	7,517
Modesto JC	1.0	4.6	1.6	11.9	75.7	5.1	11,300
Monterey Inst of International Studies	0.0	4.4	2.1	4.2	63.8	25.5	525
Mount Saint Mary's C	0.1	11.6	9.0	32.3	46.3	0.8	1,203
Mount San Antonio C	1.0	11.1	7.4	24.9	52.5	3.2	20,563
Mount San Jacinto C	1.5	2.0	3.0	12.2	80.0	1.3	3,978
Napa Valley C	1.0	4.8	3.2	6.9	81.9	2.3	5,715
National U	0.6	6.4	10.7	5.6	74.2	2.4	12,449
New C of California	1.2	2.8	11.9	4.3	77.7	2.2	506
North Orange County CC Dist							
Cypress C	1.9	13.6	2.8	9.6	71.4	0.7	11,917
Fullerton C	1.6	10.0	2.2	14.2	71.7	0.3	17,548
Northrop U	0.1	52.7	5.1	4.2	19.4	18.5	1,190
Occidental C	0.1	11.5	3.1	6.6	74.4	4.3	1,702
Ohlone C	1.0	15.2	3.6	10.4	67.9	1.9	8,130
Otis Art Inst of Parsons Sch of Design	1.9	15.7	5.3	10.8	57.4	9.0	849
Pacific Christian C	0.4	3.7	2.2	3.3	87.4	3.0	539
Pacific Coast C	0.9	5.7	10.1	16.1	66.9	0.3	335
Pacific Coast JC Lemon Grove	0.0	48.1	20.2	14.4	17.3	0.0	104
Pacific Graduate Sch of Psychology	0.4	1.9	1.5	3.1	90.8	2.3	261
Pacific Lutheran Theological Sem	0.8	3.2	1.6	0.0	91.9	2.4	124
Pacific Oaks C	0.6	2.2	6.8	7.1	82.2	1.2	325
Pacific Sch of Religion	0.5	5.6	2.0	0.5	79.6	11.7	196
Pacific Union C	0.3	19.1	3.5	7.5	62.8	6.8	1,636
Palmer C of Chiropractic West	1.4	6.8	0.4	3.1	80.9	7.4	512
Palomar C	1.9	4.6	2.2	8.8	80.5	2.1	16,707
Pasadena City C	0.9	18.9	8.9	19.9	42.8	8.5	19,581
Patten C	0.9	12.2	38.0	17.2	30.8	0.9	221
Pepperdine U	0.7	5.6	4.2	4.5	79.0	6.0	7,146
Peralta CC Dist							
C of Alameda	2.3	14.1	34.9	8.8	36.0	4.0	4,690
Laney C	1.7	17.8	36.5	8.9	30.7	4.4	8,571
Merritt C	1.7	9.0	36.7	12.4	38.2	2.1	4,810
Vista C	1.3	7.6	14.4	8.0	68.0	0.7	3,489
Pitzer C	0.0	6.3	4.0	9.2	73.4	7.2	807
Point Loma Nazarene C	0.4	3.4	2.6	5.0	83.4	5.2	2,165
Pomona C	0.4	10.5	3.3	8.0	73.0	4.7	1,421
Queen of the Holy Rosary C	9.9	11.5	6.6	9.9	56.8	5.3	243
Rancho Santiago C	1.2	14.2	3.2	15.8	59.9	5.7	20,532
Rand Graduate Sch of Policy Studies	0.0	6.7	0.0	0.0	83.3	10.0	60
Rio Hondo C	1.7	7.8	3.9	48.3	34.2	4.0	12,048
Riverside CC	2.1	4.4	9.6	13.5	68.9	1.5	15,683
Saddleback CC Dist							
Irvine Valley C	1.1	10.8	2.2	6.1	76.6	3.2	4,678
Saddleback C	1.4	4.9	1.3	5.5	85.8	1.2	14,527
Saint John's Sem C	0.0	30.6	2.0	33.7	33.7	0.0	98
Saint Joseph's C	0.0	26.3	1.8	10.5	24.6	36.8	57
Saint Mary's C of California	0.2	2.4	4.3	5.0	85.0	3.2	3,420
Saint Patrick's Sem	0.0	21.8	0.0	18.4	49.4	10.3	87
Samuel Merritt C	0.0	14.8	8.1	2.0	73.8	1.3	149

	American Indian	Asian	Black	Hispanic	White	Foreign	Total
San Bernardino Valley C	1.8%	5.0%	13.4%	19.3%	59.2%	1.4%	10,157
San Diego CC Dist							
San Diego City C	1.5	8.9	19.2	15.2	49.2	5.9	13,737
San Diego Mesa C	1.3	9.5	4.2	8.6	73.2	3.2	23,410
San Diego Miramar C	1.7	12.6	4.6	7.0	72.0	2.2	5,378
San Francisco Art Inst	0.1	4.9	2.9	3.3	81.8	7.1	736
San Francisco C of Mortuary Science	0.0	0.0	14.8	6.6	73.8	4.9	61
San Francisco CC Skills Ctr	0.3	13.5	14.9	17.5	52.3	1.6	377
San Francisco Conservatory of Music	1.3	13.7	3.0	4.7	59.7	17.6	233
San Francisco Theol Sem	0.0	3.9	3.8	0.9	71.1	20.4	692
San Joaquin C of Law	0.0	2.8	1.4	7.6	87.5	0.7	144
San Joaquin Delta C	1.7	12.7	4.9	14.5	63.8	2.3	14,792
San Jose Bible C	0.0	12.8	3.7	5.3	71.3	6.9	188
San Jose / Evergreen CC Dist							
Evergreen Valley C	2.1	32.5	6.7	23.7	33.4	1.7	7,430
San Jose City C	2.9	18.6	6.3	22.0	48.7	1.4	8,767
San Mateo County CC Dist							
Cañada C	0.7	5.5	4.7	10.5	72.3	6.4	7,586
C of San Mateo	0.9	13.5	3.5	8.9	70.2	3.1	14,150
Skyline C	0.7	21.4	5.9	15.6	52.9	3.5	7,798
Santa Barbara City C	0.8	3.5	2.2	16.5	74.6	2.4	11,031
Santa Clara U	0.4	16.4	1.4	4.9	72.1	4.7	7,795
Santa Monica C	0.9	10.4	10.1	10.7	59.4	8.4	18,108
Saybrook Inst	0.5	2.6	2.6	0.0	90.2	4.1	194
Sch of Theology at Claremont	0.0	17.8	10.7	2.0	56.9	12.7	197
Scripps C	0.2	8.3	2.1	6.3	80.5	2.6	606
Shasta Bible C	0.0	0.0	0.0	0.0	100.0	0.0	35
Shasta C	3.9	1.5	0.7	3.0	89.8	1.2	8,454
Sierra C	1.9	1.5	0.8	4.0	89.7	2.0	11,637
Simpson C	0.6	19.7	5.6	2.2	69.1	2.8	178
Solano County CC	1.9	13.6	11.6	8.0	64.6	0.3	9,643
Southern California C	1.4	3.3	2.2	8.1	82.2	2.9	930
Southern California C of Optometry	0.3	35.5	0.3	2.9	60.3	0.8	380
Southwestern C	0.7	17.3	5.8	33.5	39.6	3.0	13,010
Southwestern U Sch of Law	0.3	6.8	3.3	6.0	82.5	1.2	1,036
Stanford U	0.7	9.9	5.3	6.3	62.6	15.3	14,386
Starr King Sch for the Ministry	0.0	0.0	0.0	0.0	100.0	0.0	47
State Center CC Dist							
Fresno City C	1.6	6.6	6.4	21.8	60.3	3.3	14,710
Kings River CC	2.5	3.9	2.6	34.2	54.1	2.7	3,078
Taft C	2.5	2.9	10.0	3.0	80.2	1.4	797
Thomas Aquinas C	0.0	2.7	0.7	4.0	80.0	12.7	150
U of California							
Berkeley	1.0	21.7	6.1	9.4	54.6	7.1	30,102
Davis	0.7	19.7	3.5	6.2	65.4	4.5	20,733
Hastings C of Law	0.5	11.6	3.9	6.1	77.9	0.0	1,367
Irvine	0.4	29.8	2.7	8.0	54.2	4.8	14,772
Los Angeles	0.7	19.8	6.4	11.9	54.7	6.4	34,371
Riverside	0.6	20.6	3.5	8.7	62.3	4.3	7,087
San Diego	0.6	17.6	3.0	8.4	65.9	4.4	16,410
San Francisco	0.8	20.1	4.1	6.2	66.3	2.5	3,759
Santa Barbara	1.0	9.9	2.8	8.5	74.9	3.0	17,743
Santa Cruz	0.9	9.5	2.7	7.9	76.8	2.3	8,816

CALIFORNIA, cont.

	American Indian	Asian	Black	Hispanic	White	Foreign	Total
U of Judaism	0.0%	0.7%	0.0%	0.0%	87.0%	12.3%	138
U of La Verne	0.4	4.8	12.0	12.4	66.5	3.9	5,376
U of the Pacific	0.4	13.8	2.6	5.0	73.4	4.8	5,607
U of Redlands	0.6	4.0	5.6	5.3	82.6	1.9	2,924
U of San Diego	0.2	3.0	1.1	5.1	87.8	2.7	5,858
U of San Francisco	0.5	9.0	4.7	6.1	68.2	11.4	7,087
U of West Los Angeles	0.7	5.4	18.5	7.7	57.2	10.6	710
Ventura County CC Dist							
Moorpark C	1.9	4.4	1.6	7.9	83.3	0.9	10,471
Oxnard C	1.9	13.5	6.0	32.8	45.7	0.1	5,542
Ventura C	1.9	4.3	1.9	17.2	74.2	0.4	11,200
Victor Valley C	1.5	3.0	7.1	8.6	79.4	0.5	4,858
West Coast Christian C	2.6	7.2	3.3	30.1	51.0	5.9	153
West Coast U	0.0	11.1	6.9	8.2	62.0	11.8	1,454
West Hills C	1.5	3.7	4.5	23.4	66.8	0.2	2,486
West Valley Mission CC Dist							
Mission C	0.9	32.1	4.7	11.8	48.3	2.1	10,170
West Valley C	0.7	8.5	2.1	7.4	79.5	1.8	12,595
Western St U C of Law							
Orange County	0.8	4.6	4.9	8.3	81.1	0.3	1,164
Western St U C of Law							
San Diego	0.5	3.2	5.8	5.0	85.4	0.0	378
Westminster Theol Sem	0.0	19.8	1.1	1.1	67.0	11.0	91
Westmont C	0.3	1.9	0.6	2.0	94.4	0.7	1,290
Whittier C	0.6	4.9	4.1	12.2	73.5	4.7	1,578
Woodbury U	0.0	8.8	8.8	17.3	44.6	20.6	875
World C West	0.0	0.9	2.7	0.0	84.8	11.6	112
Wright Inst	1.1	2.9	5.7	4.6	83.9	1.7	174

COLORADO

	American Indian	Asian	Black	Hispanic	White	Foreign	Total
Aims CC	1.3	1.1	0.4	13.6	83.7	0.0	7,320
Arapahoe CC	1.4	1.4	1.2	4.9	88.6	2.5	7,040
Bel-Rea Inst of Animal Tech	1.2	0.0	1.2	1.8	95.8	0.0	165
Beth-El C of Nursing	0.0	2.7	2.7	7.0	87.6	0.0	185
Colorado Christian C	0.2	1.6	3.5	2.8	89.6	2.2	492
Colorado C	0.7	2.3	1.6	2.9	88.0	4.5	1,967
Colorado Inst of Art	1.2	3.0	15.2	8.4	71.1	1.1	1,220
Colorado Mountain C	0.7	0.4	0.6	3.4	94.5	0.3	8,957
Colorado Northwestern CC	0.6	0.0	1.0	12.2	86.0	0.2	1,344
Colorado Sch of Mines	0.4	2.5	0.7	3.3	79.0	14.2	2,316
Colorado St U Sys							
Colorado St U	0.6	1.8	1.3	2.8	89.8	3.7	19,201
Fort Lewis C	9.1	0.8	0.6	4.1	84.1	1.4	3,790
U of Southern Colorado	0.7	0.9	2.9	20.7	71.4	3.4	3,970
Colorado Tech C	1.4	1.3	10.5	24.2	62.5	0.0	1,147
CC of Aurora	1.1	3.3	12.4	5.1	77.9	0.2	3,593
CC of Denver	1.6	2.8	10.9	17.8	63.9	3.0	4,111
Denver Inst of Tech	2.0	2.1	4.0	17.0	75.0	0.0	807
Denver Tech C	1.4	1.9	19.6	8.5	68.4	0.3	731
Electronics Tech Inst	0.5	1.4	20.7	16.4	61.0	0.0	213
Front Range CC	0.9	3.0	1.4	8.7	85.3	0.8	5,966
Iliff Sch of Theology	1.2	1.2	7.2	2.0	84.6	3.8	345
ITT Tech Inst	0.7	0.5	5.4	8.1	85.2	0.0	406
Lamar CC	1.2	0.2	1.6	8.3	88.6	0.2	508
Morgan CC	1.4	0.2	0.0	4.4	94.0	0.0	947
Naropa Inst	0.4	0.0	0.4	0.0	92.1	7.1	241

	American Indian	Asian	Black	Hispanic	White	Foreign	Total
National C Colorado Springs	1.4%	0.3%	2.4%	46.1%	49.8%	0.0%	295
National C Denver	3.6	1.4	2.2	41.7	51.1	0.0	139
National C Pueblo	0.7	0.7	0.0	48.5	50.0	0.0	136
National Tech U	0.2	6.6	2.2	1.7	66.2	23.2	1,002
Nazarene Bible C	0.5	1.5	2.9	0.7	93.9	0.5	407
Northeastern JC	0.4	0.3	1.5	3.4	94.5	0.0	1,987
Otero JC	1.2	0.5	2.8	20.3	75.3	0.0	833
Parks JC	0.5	1.1	9.6	20.4	68.4	0.0	945
Pikes Peak CC	1.3	1.7	8.3	7.4	80.8	0.5	5,738
Pueblo CC	1.4	0.3	1.2	29.4	67.5	0.2	2,534
Red Rocks CC	1.0	1.4	1.1	5.5	89.6	1.3	5,173
Regis C	0.2	1.3	2.8	6.1	88.9	0.8	4,085
Saint Thomas Sem	0.0	1.6	0.8	7.4	90.2	0.0	122
St C's in Colorado							
Adams St C	1.2	1.0	2.0	21.4	73.9	0.5	2,499
Mesa St C	0.8	0.4	0.9	4.8	91.2	1.7	4,023
Metropolitan St C	0.4	2.9	4.1	8.7	83.5	0.3	15,733
Western St C	0.4	0.6	1.3	4.0	92.9	0.8	2,431
Trinidad St JC	0.3	0.2	1.3	41.6	53.7	2.9	1,581
U of Colorado							
Boulder	0.5	4.0	1.6	3.9	86.1	3.9	24,065
Colorado Springs	0.4	2.5	2.3	4.2	90.2	0.3	5,809
Denver	0.5	5.0	2.5	4.7	85.9	1.5	10,073
Health Sciences Center	0.4	3.3	1.5	5.0	88.5	1.3	1,547
U of Denver	0.6	1.9	3.1	3.2	83.7	7.5	6,875
U of Northern Colorado	0.4	1.2	1.3	4.9	91.2	1.0	9,813

CONNECTICUT

	American Indian	Asian	Black	Hispanic	White	Foreign	Total
Albertus Magnus C	0.0	0.9	8.7	3.9	83.5	3.0	635
Asnuntuck CC	0.2	1.2	5.8	1.4	90.3	1.3	1,993
Briarwood C	0.0	0.8	7.0	2.0	90.2	0.0	398
Bridgeport Engineering Inst	0.0	2.4	4.9	3.7	88.4	0.6	507
Charter Oak C	0.9	0.2	4.0	2.5	92.5	0.0	810
Connecticut C	0.2	2.1	3.1	1.9	88.3	4.4	1,969
Connecticut St U Sys							
Central Connecticut St U	0.0	1.4	3.2	1.6	93.3	0.3	14,198
Eastern Connecticut St U	0.7	0.4	4.4	2.1	91.3	1.0	4,447
Southern Connecticut St U	0.3	1.2	4.8	1.2	91.1	1.3	12,784
Western Connecticut St U	1.9	1.7	3.3	1.8	90.8	0.5	6,380
Fairfield U	0.0	0.9	1.5	1.4	95.5	0.6	4,878
Greater Hartford CC	0.1	2.9	31.4	13.2	50.2	2.2	2,927
Greater New Haven Tech C	0.4	2.1	9.4	6.6	80.9	0.6	808
Hartford C for Women	0.0	1.2	13.3	6.6	69.5	9.4	256
Hartford Graduate Center	0.2	3.5	1.2	0.9	93.9	0.3	2,457
Hartford Sem	0.0	1.3	13.4	0.7	83.9	0.7	149
Hartford St Tech C	0.0	5.8	8.6	3.0	82.1	0.5	955
Holy Apostles C and Sem	0.0	1.9	1.9	0.0	96.2	0.0	210
Housatonic CC	0.3	1.7	17.2	13.8	65.0	2.1	2,475
Manchester CC	0.3	1.3	5.2	2.5	90.3	0.4	5,989
Mattatuck CC	0.1	0.4	4.9	2.4	91.6	0.5	3,812
Middlesex CC	0.3	0.8	3.2	2.5	92.5	0.6	3,080
Mitchell C	0.0	6.4	5.3	4.7	82.5	1.1	1,137
Mohegan CC	0.4	1.1	4.2	2.1	91.9	0.2	2,819
Northwestern Conn CC	0.1	0.4	1.1	0.3	97.7	0.5	2,346
Norwalk CC	0.1	2.0	14.8	11.4	67.2	4.5	3,338
Norwalk St Tech C	0.3	5.6	15.2	6.7	71.8	0.5	1,101

CONNECTICUT, cont.

	American Indian	Asian	Black	Hispanic	White	Foreign	Total
Paier C of Art	0.0%	0.6%	2.9%	0.0%	95.8%	0.6%	312
Post C	0.0	0.4	7.1	1.6	90.0	1.0	1,654
Quinebaug Valley CC	0.0	0.5	0.5	4.9	94.1	0.0	1,320
Quinnipiac C	0.0	0.2	0.6	0.6	98.3	0.3	2,925
Sacred Heart U	0.1	1.6	5.8	4.4	86.8	1.4	4,305
Saint Alphonsus C	0.0	0.0	16.1	9.7	74.2	0.0	31
Saint Basil's C	0.0	0.0	20.0	0.0	60.0	20.0	5
Saint Joseph C	0.2	0.7	5.9	2.4	90.6	0.1	1,634
South Central CC	0.2	0.8	17.6	7.1	72.6	1.7	3,158
Thames Valley St Tech C	0.3	1.0	2.3	2.9	93.1	0.4	1,021
Trinity C	0.0	4.4	4.2	2.6	86.8	2.0	2,043
Tunxis CC	0.2	0.7	1.8	2.1	94.5	0.7	3,254
U S Coast Guard Academy	0.8	4.1	1.6	2.4	90.0	1.1	892
U of Bridgeport	0.0	2.1	5.1	1.9	82.0	8.9	5,376
U of Connecticut	0.2	3.1	3.5	2.5	88.4	2.3	25,374
U of Conn Health Ctr	0.6	5.3	3.3	3.3	86.0	1.4	508
U of Hartford	0.1	1.7	4.2	1.8	86.6	5.6	7,703
U of New Haven	0.1	1.4	7.0	3.0	84.0	4.5	6,320
Waterbury St Tech C	0.2	1.2	2.8	2.6	93.3	0.0	1,522
Wesleyan U	0.1	4.2	6.7	2.2	84.5	2.2	3,428
Yale U	0.2	6.5	5.2	3.3	74.6	10.3	10,893

DELAWARE

Delaware St C	0.2	0.8	57.5	1.2	40.0	0.4	2,510
Delaware Tech and CC							
Southern	0.6	0.6	14.9	0.6	82.9	0.4	2,479
Stanton-Wilmington	0.3	1.8	13.8	2.0	81.2	1.1	5,127
Terry	0.6	1.4	14.8	1.7	81.2	0.2	1,711
Goldey Beacom C	0.2	2.4	11.5	1.3	84.6	0.1	1,827
U of Delaware	0.1	1.7	4.3	0.6	90.4	2.9	19,818
Wesley C	0.1	0.2	11.3	0.9	87.4	0.0	972
Widener U Sch of Law	0.0	0.8	2.5	0.5	96.3	0.0	1,180
Widener U Delaware	0.1	0.6	5.9	0.3	93.0	0.1	1,154
Wilmington C	0.0	0.5	17.8	1.1	80.4	0.1	1,482

DISTRICT OF COLUMBIA

American U	0.2	3.0	6.3	3.7	74.6	12.2	11,155
Catholic U of America	0.1	2.7	4.5	3.0	82.2	7.4	7,010
Corcoran Sch of Art	0.4	1.4	3.9	5.0	80.6	8.6	279
De Sales Sch of Theology	0.0	4.2	4.2	0.0	91.7	0.0	48
Defense Intelligence C	0.0	1.9	82.2	3.0	5.0	7.9	845
Dominican House of Studies	0.0	0.0	0.0	0.0	95.6	4.4	45
Gallaudet U	0.2	1.6	6.5	3.7	75.0	13.0	2,165
George Washington U	0.3	4.7	5.8	2.3	73.4	13.6	19,232
Georgetown U	0.2	4.5	7.1	4.1	75.8	8.3	11,516
Howard U	0.1	0.8	82.1	0.5	1.4	15.2	11,617
Mount Vernon C	0.0	2.5	12.3	2.9	73.3	8.9	551
Oblate C	0.0	0.0	7.9	13.2	68.4	10.5	38
Southeastern U	0.0	12.2	51.7	0.0	9.1	27.0	801
Strayer C	0.6	3.2	46.8	2.7	19.6	27.1	1,050
Trinity C	0.0	1.2	28.0	1.7	67.3	1.9	1,125
U of the District of Columbia	0.0	2.0	82.1	3.0	5.0	8.0	11,263
Wesley Theological Sem	0.0	2.6	18.9	1.1	75.1	2.3	349

FLORIDA

	American Indian	Asian	Black	Hispanic	White	Foreign	Total
Art Inst of Fort Lauderdale ...	0.3%	0.8%	6.1%	10.0%	80.0%	2.8%	1,893
Baptist Bible Inst	0.0	0.3	2.2	1.1	95.4	1.1	368
Barry U	0.1	1.4	9.2	18.8	63.6	6.9	5,238
Bethune Cookman C	0.0	0.3	94.5	0.4	1.0	3.8	1,860
Brevard CC	0.4	1.4	5.2	2.4	89.2	1.4	12,375
Broward CC	0.7	2.1	9.0	8.0	78.0	2.3	21,682
Caribbean Ctr for Advanced Studies Miami Inst	0.0	1.0	5.4	61.3	29.4	2.9	204
Central Florida CC	0.3	0.8	7.7	2.1	88.9	0.2	3,995
Chipola JC	0.5	0.6	13.2	0.8	84.9	0.0	1,922
Clearwater Christian C	0.3	0.0	1.4	1.1	91.5	5.7	353
C of Boca Raton	0.2	1.2	12.0	9.9	71.6	5.1	1,135
Daytona Beach CC...........	0.1	1.7	9.5	3.5	83.6	1.6	9,365
Eckerd C	0.1	0.9	3.1	2.4	84.4	9.1	1,293
Edison CC	0.2	0.7	2.9	2.9	92.6	0.8	7,249
Edward Waters C	0.0	0.0	85.3	0.0	0.0	14.7	597
Embry-Riddle Aeronautical U	0.5	2.5	5.1	4.0	85.9	2.1	10,766
Flagler Career Inst	0.2	2.5	34.5	46.9	15.9	0.0	441
Flagler C	0.1	0.5	1.4	1.6	95.2	1.2	1,201
Florida Christian C	0.0	0.0	1.6	0.0	98.4	0.0	123
Florida C	1.1	0.5	2.9	0.8	92.4	2.4	380
Florida CC Jacksonville	0.3	3.0	14.2	1.9	80.0	0.6	16,778
Florida Inst of Tech	0.2	1.2	3.1	3.7	77.7	14.0	6,254
Florida Keys CC	0.5	2.1	4.2	8.7	82.7	1.7	1,840
Florida Southern C	0.1	0.3	1.9	0.7	94.8	2.1	2,670
Gulf Coast CC	0.6	1.4	7.3	1.6	86.0	3.1	5,149
Hillsborough CC	0.2	2.0	8.1	9.5	79.4	0.8	15,573
Hobe Sound Bible C	1.0	0.0	0.5	1.0	87.1	10.4	202
Indian River CC	0.1	1.4	3.4	0.6	94.0	0.5	9,483
International Fine Arts C	0.0	3.4	8.5	30.9	33.6	23.5	446
ITT Tech Inst	0.0	1.5	9.4	6.8	79.5	2.8	531
Jacksonville U	0.3	2.3	5.7	4.7	83.3	3.7	2,344
Lake City CC	0.3	0.8	9.3	1.5	88.1	0.0	1,893
Lake-Sumter CC	0.1	1.0	7.7	1.0	89.9	0.2	2,078
Liberty Christian C	0.0	0.4	3.5	0.4	93.7	2.1	284
Manatee CC	0.2	0.7	3.2	0.9	93.4	1.6	7,874
Miami Christian C	0.0	3.6	15.7	28.9	50.0	1.8	166
Miami-Dade CC	0.1	1.6	14.5	53.0	26.3	4.3	43,880
National Education Center Tampa Tech Inst	0.4	2.8	20.1	5.9	70.3	0.5	1,566
New England Inst of Tech Palm Beach	0.9	2.4	14.8	9.8	70.2	1.9	580
North Florida JC	0.2	0.3	28.2	1.1	70.1	0.2	1,220
Nova U	0.3	1.1	13.8	7.8	73.7	3.3	8,759
Okaloosa-Walton JC	0.3	1.3	6.1	1.9	89.8	0.7	5,270
Orlando C	0.1	1.3	20.5	8.0	69.7	0.4	838
Palm Beach Atlantic C	0.3	0.8	6.1	3.2	89.0	0.6	1,139
Palm Beach JC	0.1	0.9	5.8	4.6	83.9	4.8	13,121
Pasco Hernando CC	0.3	1.1	2.4	1.7	94.4	0.1	3,973
Pensacola JC	1.8	3.1	9.6	0.9	84.2	0.3	10,866
Polk CC	0.1	0.8	7.7	1.8	88.3	1.3	5,879
Prospect Hall C	0.0	0.0	38.4	7.9	38.9	14.8	216
Ringling Sch of Art and Design	0.6	1.7	1.9	4.3	89.4	2.1	483
Rollins C	0.4	1.5	3.7	3.7	88.3	2.5	3,738
Saint John Vianney C Sem ...	0.0	0.0	1.6	64.1	29.7	4.7	04

FLORIDA, cont.

	American Indian	Asian	Black	Hispanic	White	Foreign	Total
Saint Johns River CC	0.2%	0.4%	5.6%	1.3%	92.0%	0.5%	2,453
Saint Leo C	1.2	1.5	14.8	3.3	78.6	0.5	5,772
Saint Petersburg JC	0.8	1.6	4.6	1.9	90.4	0.8	18,870
Saint Vincent De Paul Regional Sem	0.0	0.0	0.0	32.3	66.7	1.0	99
Santa Fe CC	0.2	1.6	8.0	4.4	82.6	3.3	9,633
Seminole CC	0.2	2.0	4.6	4.6	87.9	0.7	6,996
South Florida CC	0.2	1.0	14.2	5.6	79.0	0.1	1,308
Southeastern C of the Assemblies of God	0.6	1.0	2.0	3.1	91.0	2.3	1,155
Spurgeon Baptist Bible C	0.0	0.0	0.0	0.0	100.0	0.0	57
St U Sys of Florida							
Florida A&M U	0.0	0.6	85.5	1.3	10.8	1.9	6,396
Florida Atlantic U	0.0	2.7	5.0	5.3	82.9	4.1	11,325
Florida International U	0.1	2.5	8.8	40.1	42.8	5.8	18,128
Florida St U	0.2	0.9	6.3	3.6	86.2	2.9	25,907
U of Central Florida	0.2	2.9	3.8	4.5	86.6	2.0	18,342
U of Florida	0.1	2.8	5.8	5.1	81.6	4.5	33,282
U of North Florida	0.2	2.4	6.5	1.7	88.4	0.8	7,162
U of South Florida	0.1	2.2	3.9	5.2	86.3	2.2	29,912
U of West Florida	0.2	1.7	4.8	1.2	89.7	2.3	7,095
Stetson U	0.3	0.9	1.8	2.1	91.5	3.3	2,974
Tallahassee CC	0.3	0.7	14.8	2.7	79.2	2.2	7,264
Talmudic C of Florida	0.0	0.0	0.0	0.0	100.0	0.0	94
United Electronics Inst of Florida	0.2	1.0	22.9	23.1	49.3	3.4	493
U of Miami	0.1	2.6	5.6	17.7	62.6	11.3	13,828
U of Tampa	0.1	1.0	3.1	4.7	85.6	5.4	2,401
Valencia CC	0.4	2.6	7.1	7.4	80.8	1.6	14,840
Warner Southern C	0.3	0.3	6.9	0.3	89.0	3.3	363
Webber C	0.0	0.8	7.5	2.6	77.4	11.7	265

GEORGIA

	American Indian	Asian	Black	Hispanic	White	Foreign	Total
Abraham Baldwin Agricultural C	0.1	0.1	8.5	0.1	89.8	1.5	1,893
Agnes Scott C	0.4	1.5	7.0	2.1	85.7	3.3	517
Albany St C	0.2	0.1	82.7	0.2	16.8	0.0	2,104
Andrew C	0.0	0.0	14.2	1.7	66.1	18.0	345
Armstrong St C	0.3	1.5	13.6	0.6	82.9	1.1	3,257
Art Inst of Atlanta	0.3	0.6	29.3	1.2	67.4	1.1	1,464
Atlanta Christian C	0.0	4.1	10.1	0.0	81.7	4.1	169
Atlanta C of Art	0.0	4.3	15.7	2.9	76.3	0.8	375
Atlanta Metropolitan C	0.0	0.2	90.9	0.1	1.5	7.3	1,425
Atlanta U	0.0	2.6	78.1	0.8	4.0	14.5	1,023
Augusta C	0.2	1.7	15.5	0.9	81.1	0.5	4,827
Bainbridge C	0.1	0.4	17.1	0.2	82.1	0.0	800
Ben Hill-Irwin Tech Inst	0.0	0.0	44.9	0.0	55.1	0.0	492
Berry C	0.2	0.5	1.8	0.4	96.1	1.0	1,820
Brenau C	0.0	0.4	8.6	0.3	89.8	0.8	1,921
Brewton-Parker C	0.0	1.1	20.4	0.4	78.1	0.0	1,470
Brunswick C	0.2	0.9	17.0	1.3	79.9	0.7	1,338
Chattahoochee Tech Inst	0.1	0.9	8.7	0.6	89.7	0.1	1,708
Clayton St C	0.2	1.1	11.4	1.1	85.7	0.5	3,661
Columbia Theol Sem	0.0	3.9	4.6	0.6	87.4	3.5	541
Columbus C	0.1	2.0	17.5	1.9	77.0	1.4	3,786
Columbus Tech Inst	1.2	1.5	29.7	2.6	64.9	0.0	3,465

	American Indian	Asian	Black	Hispanic	White	Foreign	Total
Coosa Valley Tech Inst	0.1%	0.3%	8.7%	0.2%	90.7%	0.0%	943
Covenant C	0.2	0.2	2.3	0.4	93.8	3.2	533
Crandall JC	0.2	0.8	63.8	0.6	34.7	0.0	643
Dalton C	0.0	0.3	1.7	0.2	97.7	0.1	1,861
Darton C	0.2	0.6	19.8	0.4	78.9	0.2	1,887
Dekalb C	0.2	2.5	17.1	1.3	78.3	0.6	10,566
DeKalb Tech Inst	0.3	1.3	20.9	0.8	76.1	0.6	3,152
DeVry Inst of Tech	0.4	2.7	53.7	1.6	40.3	1.2	3,028
East Georgia C	0.0	0.3	13.9	0.2	85.6	0.0	617
Emmanuel C	0.0	0.0	8.3	0.0	91.7	0.0	336
Emmanuel C Sch of Christian Ministries	0.0	0.0	0.0	0.0	100.0	0.0	30
Emory U	0.1	2.9	6.9	1.4	82.8	5.9	9,285
Floyd JC	0.1	0.8	7.5	0.2	91.4	0.0	1,485
Fort Valley St C	0.1	0.2	92.1	0.2	5.7	1.8	1,915
Gainesville C	0.4	0.6	2.6	0.5	93.5	2.4	2,150
Georgia C	0.2	0.4	15.6	0.5	82.3	1.1	4,522
Georgia Inst of Tech	0.1	5.1	6.1	2.4	79.4	6.9	11,887
Georgia Military C	0.2	2.1	32.6	7.7	56.8	0.5	1,462
Georgia Southern C	0.1	0.5	12.2	0.3	86.2	0.8	9,843
Georgia Southwestern C	0.0	0.1	15.9	0.2	82.4	1.3	2,151
Georgia St U	0.2	2.0	16.4	1.6	76.2	3.6	22,176
Gordon C	0.4	0.6	17.6	0.2	80.8	0.4	1,389
Gupton Jones C of Funeral Services	0.0	0.8	14.8	2.5	80.2	1.6	243
Gwinnett Tech Inst	0.4	3.4	3.0	1.1	92.1	0.0	2,480
Heart of Georgia Tech Inst ...	0.0	0.0	23.2	0.0	76.8	0.0	289
Interdenominational Theol Center	0.0	0.0	88.8	0.4	2.3	8.5	260
Kennesaw St C	0.3	0.7	2.8	1.0	93.8	1.5	8,601
La Grange C	0.1	0.6	7.0	0.1	84.6	7.6	953
Lanier Tech Inst	0.2	4.0	7.0	0.4	87.9	0.4	445
Life C	0.7	0.7	2.3	2.8	91.2	2.4	1,369
Macon C	0.4	0.5	18.7	0.9	79.6	0.0	3,512
Macon Tech Inst	0.7	0.2	42.8	0.4	55.9	0.0	1,013
Massey Business C	0.0	0.0	69.0	1.7	29.0	0.2	465
Meadows JC	0.0	0.0	69.6	2.0	28.5	0.0	358
Medical C of Georgia.........	0.4	2.5	8.9	2.1	82.2	3.9	2,279
Mercer U Main	0.2	1.1	10.9	1.3	86.1	0.5	3,725
Atlanta	0.4	1.4	12.3	1.9	72.3	11.7	2,370
Middle Georgia C	0.3	0.8	14.7	0.5	83.4	0.3	1,464
Morehouse C	0.0	0.0	98.3	0.0	0.0	1.7	2,690
Morehouse Sch of Medicine .	0.7	5.1	76.6	5.1	10.9	1.5	137
Moultrie Area Tech Inst	0.0	0.5	23.4	0.2	75.9	0.0	586
North Georgia C	0.2	0.0	2.1	0.1	97.0	0.5	2,181
Oglethorpe U	0.1	2.6	5.7	1.0	85.8	4.9	1,042
Paine C	0.0	0.2	91.9	0.2	5.1	2.6	606
Phillips C Augusta	0.0	0.0	58.4	0.0	41.6	0.0	586
Phillips C Columbus	0.0	0.0	51.0	1.0	47.9	0.0	574
Pickens Tech Inst	0.0	0.0	0.2	0.0	99.8	0.0	612
Piedmont C	0.0	0.9	6.7	0.0	86.1	6.3	555
Reinhardt C	0.0	0.0	2.7	0.0	95.1	2.2	597
Savannah C of Art and Design	0.0	0.9	6.4	1.6	88.8	2.2	1,397
Savannah St C	0.1	0.2	81.4	0.1	14.2	4.0	1,904
Shorter C	0.0	1.0	5.3	0.0	92.3	1.4	832
South C	0.0	0.2	58.7	0.0	41.1	0.0	579

GEORGIA, cont.

	American Indian	Asian	Black	Hispanic	White	Foreign	Total
South Georgia C	0.6%	0.4%	19.2%	0.4%	77.7%	1.7%	1,010
Southern C of Tech	0.1	2.5	12.8	1.2	80.9	2.4	3,767
Spelman C	0.0	0.0	98.5	0.0	0.0	1.5	1,742
Thomas C	0.0	0.6	13.6	0.3	82.7	2.7	330
Toccoa Falls C	0.0	1.1	0.9	0.4	90.0	7.5	743
Truett McConnell C	0.0	0.0	13.9	0.0	86.1	0.0	1,488
U of Georgia	0.1	1.1	4.7	0.7	89.6	3.8	27,176
Upson Tech Inst	0.4	0.0	31.2	0.4	68.1	0.0	279
Valdosta St C	0.2	0.4	15.0	0.6	83.3	0.5	6,950
Valdosta Tech Inst	0.0	0.4	18.4	0.0	81.2	0.0	799
Watterson Career Centre	0.0	0.0	98.9	0.0	1.1	0.0	183
Waycross C	0.0	0.8	12.6	0.0	86.6	0.0	499
Wesleyan C	0.0	4.3	11.7	2.0	81.6	0.4	512
West Georgia C	0.1	0.4	14.5	0.6	83.9	0.6	6,705
Young Harris C	0.0	0.2	0.0	0.4	99.4	0.0	468

HAWAII

Brigham Young U Hawaii	0.4	18.6	0.4	1.3	39.6	39.8	2,141
Chaminade U of Honolulu	0.3	31.6	6.0	2.6	56.1	3.5	2,537
Hawaii Loa C	2.3	24.2	4.8	4.1	43.2	21.5	484
Hawaii Pacific C	1.0	23.7	8.5	4.0	43.8	19.0	4,560
International C and Graduate Sch of Theology	0.0	32.6	4.3	0.0	41.3	21.7	46
U of Hawaii							
Hilo	0.4	60.8	0.5	1.8	33.6	2.8	3,634
Manoa	0.2	65.5	0.6	0.7	25.6	7.3	18,424
Honolulu CC	0.4	79.7	1.2	1.5	15.1	2.0	4,292
Kapiolani CC	0.3	73.5	0.8	1.4	23.7	0.4	5,467
Kauai CC	0.2	67.3	0.3	2.4	28.8	1.0	1,231
Leeward CC	0.3	69.1	2.2	2.2	25.6	0.7	5,439
Maui CC	0.4	60.0	0.4	1.7	35.2	2.4	1,995
West Oahu C	0.2	55.5	1.8	1.8	40.0	0.6	492
Windward CC	0.4	52.5	1.2	1.4	43.6	1.0	1,555

IDAHO

Boise Bible C	1.5	0.0	1.5	3.0	94.0	0.0	67
C of Southern Idaho	0.6	0.5	0.6	1.9	94.1	2.3	2,775
Idaho St U	1.8	1.5	0.8	1.8	92.4	1.8	7,121
Lewis-Clark St C	2.1	0.2	0.4	0.3	96.0	1.1	2,275
North Idaho C	1.2	0.6	0.5	0.9	95.7	1.1	2,565
Northwest Nazarene C	0.4	1.5	0.9	1.4	94.6	1.1	1,138
Ricks C	0.8	0.9	0.2	0.8	93.2	4.1	7,694
U of Idaho	0.8	1.4	0.8	1.2	91.5	4.4	9,450

ILLINOIS

Alfred Adler Inst of Chicago	0.0	1.4	6.3	3.5	87.3	1.4	142
American Academy of Art	0.4	3.7	5.1	6.8	82.9	1.1	790
American Conservatory of Music	0.0	5.4	10.7	3.6	67.0	13.4	112
American Islamic C	0.0	2.9	32.4	0.0	20.6	44.1	34
Augustana C	0.0	0.5	3.3	0.7	92.5	2.9	2,241
Aurora U	0.4	1.5	11.7	4.3	81.4	0.8	2,066
Barat C	0.0	1.6	0.3	0.3	95.0	2.8	674

	American Indian	Asian	Black	Hispanic	White	Foreign	Total
Belleville Area C	0.7%	1.8%	6.1%	1.1%	90.2%	0.2%	12,511
Bethany Theol Sem	0.0	0.0	2.5	0.8	82.0	14.8	122
Black Hawk C							
East	0.0	0.4	0.9	0.3	97.9	0.5	754
Quad-Cities	0.3	0.8	5.1	3.8	90.0	0.0	5,317
Blackburn C	0.2	0.6	6.7	0.6	89.0	2.9	480
Blessing-Rieman C of Nursing	0.0	0.0	0.9	0.0	99.1	0.0	106
Board of Governors of St C's and U's							
Chicago St U	0.1	1.0	82.8	2.7	12.2	1.3	6,134
Governors St U	0.1	0.8	17.5	1.8	79.3	0.5	5,089
Eastern Illinois U	0.1	0.5	4.6	0.7	93.4	0.7	11,159
Northeastern Illinois U	0.3	8.2	10.7	11.9	68.0	0.9	9,846
Western Illinois U	0.2	0.9	7.9	1.3	86.0	3.6	12,749
Bradley U	0.0	1.7	6.9	1.1	85.0	5.2	5,171
Brisk Rabbinical C	0.0	0.0	0.0	0.0	100.0	0.0	12
Carl Sandburg C	0.4	0.8	5.0	1.8	91.4	0.6	2,826
Catholic Theol Union	0.0	1.6	1.9	1.0	78.1	17.5	315
Chicago C of Osteopathic Medicine	0.5	7.9	1.4	1.9	88.2	0.0	416
Chicago Sch of Professional Psychology	0.0	0.0	2.9	0.0	95.6	1.5	136
Chicago Theol Sem	0.0	7.2	21.0	0.6	71.3	0.0	181
City C's of Chicago							
Chicago City-Wide C	0.5	4.7	45.6	21.4	27.8	0.0	12,994
Richard J Daley C	0.4	2.3	20.5	31.3	45.5	0.0	7,406
Harold Washington C	0.7	10.8	59.5	9.0	20.1	0.0	7,915
Kennedy-King C	0.5	2.0	68.8	22.7	6.0	0.0	8,650
Malcolm X C	0.4	16.6	49.3	26.8	6.9	0.0	9,853
Olive-Harvey C	0.8	1.4	76.0	18.3	3.5	0.0	8,080
Harry S Truman C	1.0	18.3	14.4	40.0	26.3	0.0	12,973
Wilbur Wright C	0.4	8.5	13.7	21.6	55.7	0.0	7,043
C of Automation	0.0	0.0	78.3	8.4	10.8	2.4	83
C of Du Page	0.1	6.1	2.2	3.9	87.6	0.1	26,489
C of Lake County	0.2	2.8	5.8	6.4	84.8	0.0	11,587
C of Saint Francis	0.3	0.8	3.3	1.1	94.3	0.1	4,075
Columbia C	0.7	2.5	26.2	6.8	62.9	0.9	6,062
Concordia C	0.1	1.5	4.2	1.0	92.4	0.8	1,121
Danville Area CC	0.8	1.1	8.6	1.8	87.6	0.1	2,925
De Paul U	0.2	5.3	9.8	4.9	78.3	1.5	14,699
DeVry Inst of Tech Chicago	0.4	11.3	28.3	15.8	41.8	2.3	3,163
DeVry Inst of Tech Lombard	0.2	5.1	7.8	3.7	82.7	0.4	2,370
Dr William Scholl C of Podiatric Medicine	0.2	3.3	6.0	2.3	85.2	3.1	487
Elgin CC	0.1	2.5	2.7	3.9	90.6	0.2	5,780
Elmhurst C	0.1	1.4	2.4	1.1	94.2	0.8	3,135
Eureka C	0.0	0.4	6.8	0.6	91.2	1.0	500
Forest Inst of Professional Psychology	0.4	2.4	2.8	1.2	93.3	0.0	252
Garrett-Evangelical Theol Sem	0.0	5.9	11.5	0.5	72.0	10.1	375
Gem City C	0.0	0.0	2.0	0.0	97.4	0.7	151
Greenville C	0.1	0.8	5.1	4.2	88.9	0.9	745
Harrington Inst of Interior Design	0.0	2.9	4.9	1.2	89.1	1.9	411
Hebrew Theol C	0.0	0.0	0.0	0.0	100.0	0.0	235

ILLINOIS, cont.

	American Indian	Asian	Black	Hispanic	White	Foreign	Total
Highland CC	0.1%	0.7%	3.2%	0.0%	95.9%	0.1%	2,878
Illinois Benedictine C	0.2	1.7	2.4	1.2	94.5	0.0	2,550
Illinois Central C	0.1	1.0	3.8	0.8	94.2	0.1	12,022
Illinois C	0.0	0.5	1.4	0.1	97.4	0.6	842
Illinois C of Optometry	0.0	8.4	2.9	3.4	81.8	3.4	583
Illinois Eastern CC	0.1	0.3	0.2	0.3	99.1	0.1	6,571
Illinois Inst of Tech	0.1	10.7	7.6	3.7	66.4	11.4	6,267
Ill Medical Training Center	0.0	2.1	84.6	6.6	6.8	0.0	487
Illinois Sch of Professional Psychology	0.4	0.4	2.9	1.8	94.0	0.4	448
Illinois St U	0.2	1.2	4.8	0.9	91.6	1.4	22,322
Illinois Tech C	0.0	4.8	67.7	10.2	15.6	1.6	186
Illinois Valley CC	0.2	0.9	2.3	1.1	95.5	0.0	3,850
Illinois Wesleyan U	0.4	1.9	1.8	0.7	92.4	2.8	1,750
ITT Tech Inst	0.0	3.8	5.4	5.9	84.9	0.0	186
John A Logan C	0.2	0.5	4.6	0.4	94.0	0.2	5,183
John Marshall Law Sch	0.0	1.0	5.3	2.7	90.7	0.2	1,273
John Wood CC	0.1	0.7	1.9	0.1	96.8	0.5	2,695
Joliet JC	0.2	1.2	8.3	4.7	85.4	0.2	9,454
Judson C	0.0	0.8	3.3	1.1	94.1	0.8	523
Kankakee CC	0.2	0.8	7.9	0.3	90.7	0.1	3,473
Kaskaskia C	0.4	0.7	5.8	1.1	91.9	0.1	2,806
Keller Graduate Sch of Management	0.0	2.3	5.4	1.3	88.6	2.4	1,120
Kendall C	0.0	0.8	20.6	1.6	74.5	2.6	384
Kishwaukee C	0.4	2.4	4.6	3.2	89.2	0.2	3,113
Knox C	0.2	3.9	4.3	1.3	84.0	6.3	1,024
Lake Forest C	0.0	2.3	5.2	1.2	90.3	0.9	1,149
Lake Forest Graduate Sch of Management	0.0	2.3	2.5	0.8	94.3	0.0	475
Lake Land C	0.5	0.6	3.6	0.6	94.6	0.2	3,952
Lewis and Clark CC	0.3	0.7	4.4	0.4	94.0	0.2	5,012
Lewis U	0.2	1.1	18.7	4.2	75.1	0.6	3,502
Lincoln Christian C and Sem	0.0	0.2	0.6	0.2	98.0	1.0	488
Lincoln Land CC	0.2	0.6	4.2	0.6	94.2	0.2	7,848
Lutheran Sch of Theology	0.0	0.5	4.4	1.5	81.5	12.1	390
MacCormac JC	0.0	0.8	7.3	48.6	41.9	1.4	504
MacMurray C	0.2	0.4	13.9	3.1	82.2	0.2	842
Mallinckrodt C of the North Shore	0.0	3.3	2.6	6.6	69.5	18.0	272
McCormick Theol Sem	0.2	5.9	5.5	8.5	76.3	3.7	544
McHenry County C	0.0	0.5	0.2	1.3	97.9	0.1	3,487
McKendree C	0.2	0.7	14.2	1.4	83.0	0.5	1,012
Meadville / Lombard Theol Sch	0.0	3.1	0.0	0.0	93.8	3.1	32
Mennonite C of Nursing	0.0	0.0	5.9	0.0	94.1	0.0	102
Metropolitan Business C	0.0	1.5	81.6	4.0	12.9	0.0	272
Metropolitan Skill Center	0.0	0.0	97.0	2.0	1.0	0.0	100
Midstate C	0.0	0.2	7.6	1.2	91.0	0.0	420
Midwest C of Engineering	0.0	20.0	0.0	0.0	80.0	0.0	15
Millikin U	0.2	0.7	3.2	0.5	95.3	0.1	1,736
Monmouth C	0.0	5.5	7.4	0.4	86.6	0.0	674
Montay C	0.0	8.2	16.3	16.7	57.1	1.7	233
Moody Bible Inst	0.1	2.0	1.3	0.4	87.0	9.2	1,484
Moraine Valley CC	0.1	0.9	3.9	2.1	92.8	0.2	12,914
Morrison Inst of Tech	0.0	0.0	5.3	3.7	91.1	0.0	246
Morton C	0.2	2.4	0.4	17.6	78.4	0.9	3,625

	American Indian	Asian	Black	Hispanic	White	Foreign	Total
Mundelein C	0.2%	2.0%	17.3%	8.0%	71.7%	0.8%	1,010
National C of Chiropractic	0.4	0.9	1.3	2.4	91.5	3.6	785
National C of Education	0.5	5.6	13.0	6.0	74.9	0.1	4,566
North Central C	0.1	3.0	5.9	1.8	89.0	0.2	2,335
North Park C and Theol Sem	0.7	4.9	5.9	11.2	76.2	1.1	1,218
Northern Baptist Theol Sem	0.0	2.1	15.2	19.4	46.6	16.8	191
Northern Illinois U	0.3	3.0	4.9	2.2	86.8	2.9	24,255
Northwestern U	0.2	7.3	5.8	1.6	78.1	7.0	16,592
Oakton CC	0.2	6.8	2.7	2.2	88.0	0.0	11,596
Olivet Nazarene U	0.2	1.3	4.4	1.0	90.9	2.2	1,823
Parkland C	0.7	2.2	6.6	1.2	88.4	0.9	7,911
Parks C of Saint Louis U	0.1	1.6	4.3	2.9	80.5	10.7	1,105
Prairie St C	0.3	0.9	20.2	4.4	74.2	0.0	4,831
Principia C	0.0	0.3	0.6	0.6	91.9	6.6	654
Quincy C	0.0	0.7	2.6	0.8	95.2	0.7	1,076
Ray C of Design	0.1	6.3	25.8	9.4	55.2	3.1	681
Rend Lake C	0.4	0.3	5.3	0.6	93.4	0.0	3,148
Richland CC	0.1	0.6	9.6	0.3	89.3	0.1	3,743
Robert Morris C	0.3	0.9	42.2	21.1	35.5	0.0	2,313
Rock Valley C	0.2	1.2	3.9	1.7	92.6	0.4	7,703
Rockford C	0.0	1.7	2.1	1.4	94.1	0.8	1,449
Roosevelt U	0.2	2.7	26.5	3.4	60.1	7.0	6,374
Rosary C	0.1	1.3	5.6	4.2	86.8	1.9	1,601
Rush U	0.3	9.8	4.9	2.1	80.3	2.6	1,123
Saint Augustine C	0.0	0.0	0.0	99.7	0.2	0.1	997
Saint Francis Med Ctr C of Nursing	0.0	0.0	3.2	3.2	93.6	0.0	125
Saint Xavier C	0.2	1.2	11.6	3.6	82.9	0.5	2,641
Sangamon St U	0.2	1.0	5.6	0.5	90.2	2.6	3,942
Sauk Valley CC	0.9	0.4	3.2	3.6	91.9	0.0	2,769
Sch of the Art Inst of Chicago	0.1	4.8	5.2	5.4	78.9	5.5	2,147
Seabury-Western Theol Sem	10.0	1.1	3.3	0.0	84.4	1.1	90
Shawnee CC	0.1	0.1	15.2	0.0	84.6	0.0	1,433
Shimer C	0.0	0.0	9.2	3.4	87.4	0.0	87
South Suburban C	1.3	1.0	23.0	3.7	71.0	0.0	8,263
Southeastern Illinois C	0.4	0.4	12.7	1.7	84.7	0.1	2,756
Southern Illinois U							
Carbondale	0.3	1.6	9.4	1.8	80.0	6.9	24,217
Edwardsville	0.2	1.1	11.2	0.8	84.7	2.0	11,352
Spertus C of Judaica	0.0	3.4	31.0	3.4	62.1	0.0	87
Spoon River C	0.1	0.5	1.6	0.2	97.2	0.6	1,723
Springfield C	0.3	0.5	5.5	0.3	92.7	0.8	385
State CC at East Saint Louis	0.1	0.3	97.1	0.0	2.4	0.0	1,184
Telshe Yeshiva Chicago	0.0	0.0	0.0	3.7	92.7	3.7	82
Trinity Christian C	0.0	1.1	9.3	2.0	86.0	1.6	550
Trinity C	0.3	2.2	6.5	1.4	88.6	1.0	630
Trinity Evangelical Divinity Sch	0.0	7.2	3.3	0.8	86.9	1.9	1,132
Triton C	0.3	3.4	14.0	10.6	71.4	0.3	17,691
U of Chicago	0.2	8.3	3.6	2.0	76.3	9.7	10,409
U of Health Sciences Chicago Med Sch	0.1	12.7	4.0	0.9	79.4	2.9	892
U of Illinois							
Chicago	0.2	12.5	9.1	8.5	64.4	5.3	23,986
Urbana-Champaign	0.2	6.8	4.8	2.5	78.7	7.0	38,337
U of Saint Mary of the Lake Mundelein Sem	0.0	2.1	0.7	6.2	89.7	1.4	291

ILLINOIS, cont.

	American Indian	Asian	Black	Hispanic	White	Foreign	Total
VanderCook C of Music	0.0%	0.0%	13.9%	4.9%	79.2%	2.1%	144
Waubonsee CC	0.6	0.7	5.2	14.9	77.1	1.5	5,378
Wheaton C	0.2	3.8	1.0	0.9	91.7	2.4	2,529
William Rainey Harper C	0.1	4.4	1.4	4.3	89.0	0.8	16,121

INDIANA

Ancilla Domini C	0.0	0.2	1.1	0.7	97.8	0.2	456
Anderson U	0.9	0.3	3.5	0.2	94.0	1.0	2,050
Ball St U	0.2	0.6	3.4	0.5	94.2	1.1	18,732
Bethel C	0.2	0.2	2.2	0.4	96.5	0.6	539
Butler U	0.2	1.3	4.4	0.5	93.4	0.2	3,912
Calumet C of Saint Joseph	0.5	0.5	22.9	13.1	63.0	0.1	1,049
Christian Theological Sem	0.4	1.5	8.8	0.8	87.3	1.2	260
Concordia Theological Sem	0.0	1.4	1.4	0.7	96.0	0.5	424
Davenport C South Bend	0.0	0.0	26.5	2.1	71.4	0.0	238
Davenport C Merrillville	0.3	0.3	37.7	5.7	56.1	0.0	369
De Pauw U	0.1	1.0	2.4	0.5	94.7	1.3	2,480
Earlham C	0.2	1.4	3.9	0.6	92.3	1.7	1,249
Fort Wayne Bible C	0.0	0.3	4.0	0.3	94.9	0.5	371
Franklin C of Indiana	0.0	1.1	2.3	0.4	95.9	0.2	812
Goshen Biblical Sem	0.0	0.0	0.0	2.4	85.9	11.8	85
Goshen C	0.3	1.1	2.9	2.8	86.8	6.2	1,073
Grace C	0.5	0.9	0.5	0.7	95.6	1.8	769
Grace Theological Sem	0.3	3.1	2.8	0.9	90.6	2.2	319
Hanover C	0.0	0.0	0.8	0.3	98.0	0.8	1,075
Holy Cross JC	0.0	0.0	6.7	1.2	90.1	1.9	416
Huntington C	0.2	0.0	1.9	0.2	90.1	7.7	574
Indiana Inst of Tech	0.0	0.0	28.0	1.1	47.6	23.3	464
Indiana St U	0.2	0.5	6.9	0.7	86.1	5.5	11,677
Indiana U Sys							
Bloomington	0.1	2.0	3.8	1.3	87.6	5.2	33,776
East	0.1	0.5	3.0	0.4	95.9	0.1	1,628
Kokomo	0.4	0.4	2.3	1.1	95.7	0.2	3,115
Northwest	0.1	0.7	22.4	6.6	70.0	0.2	4,812
Purdue U Indianapolis	0.2	2.0	7.3	0.9	88.8	0.8	24,808
Purdue U Fort Wayne	0.1	0.8	3.1	0.8	94.6	0.5	11,073
South Bend	0.1	0.7	4.2	0.9	93.4	0.6	6,447
Southeast	0.2	0.2	1.7	0.1	97.6	0.2	5,192
Ind Vocational Tech C							
Central Indiana	0.7	0.8	19.1	0.5	78.9	0.0	4,407
Columbus	0.3	0.4	1.3	0.2	97.7	0.0	2,255
Eastcentral	0.1	0.2	5.6	0.5	93.7	0.0	1,646
Kokomo	0.6	0.3	3.5	0.6	94.9	0.0	2,197
Lafayette	0.5	0.5	1.7	0.3	97.0	0.0	1,783
North Central	0.6	0.7	6.7	1.3	90.7	0.0	2,445
Northeast	0.1	0.5	3.9	0.8	94.7	0.0	2,895
Northwest	0.3	0.3	30.0	4.7	64.6	0.0	2,816
Southeast	0.1	0.1	0.4	0.0	99.3	0.0	750
Southcentral	0.3	0.1	2.7	0.1	96.8	0.0	1,455
Southwest	0.3	0.6	4.3	0.1	94.5	0.0	2,011
Wabash Valley	0.5	0.7	3.7	0.3	94.8	0.0	1,935
Whitewater	0.8	0.2	5.6	0.2	93.1	0.0	854
Indiana Wesleyan U	0.1	0.3	5.8	1.2	91.8	0.7	2,019
International Business C	0.0	0.4	3.9	1.1	94.7	0.0	567
Interstate Tech Inst	0.0	0.0	15.2	0.0	83.7	1.1	92
ITT Tech Inst Fort Wayne	0.1	0.7	15.7	2.0	81.5	0.0	1,034

	American Indian	Asian	Black	Hispanic	White	Foreign	Total
ITT Tech Inst Indianapolis	0.2%	0.6%	8.7%	1.1%	89.5%	0.0%	1,236
ITT Tech Inst Evansville	0.0	0.2	6.3	0.4	93.1	0.0	448
Lockyear C Indianapolis	0.0	0.4	62.6	0.4	36.6	0.0	257
Lockyear C Evansville	0.9	0.3	13.8	0.0	85.1	0.0	348
Manchester C	0.2	0.6	1.8	1.2	93.9	2.3	1,028
Marian C	0.0	0.0	12.8	0.7	84.0	2.4	1,215
Martin Center C	0.0	0.0	78.7	0.9	20.1	0.3	328
Mennonite Biblical Sem	0.0	0.0	0.0	0.0	71.1	28.9	76
Mid American C of							
Funeral Service	1.0	0.0	12.1	0.0	86.9	0.0	99
Oakland City C	0.0	1.0	0.6	0.0	98.4	0.0	627
Purdue U							
Main	0.3	2.4	3.1	1.3	87.0	5.8	36,517
Calumet	0.2	1.1	8.4	7.0	83.3	0.1	7,393
North Central	0.2	0.4	2.8	0.9	95.6	0.0	3,065
Rose-Hulman Inst of Tech	0.4	3.1	0.6	0.4	95.5	0.0	1,424
Saint Francis C	0.2	1.0	4.3	1.1	93.0	0.3	960
Saint Joseph's C	0.1	0.3	4.4	1.5	92.8	0.9	1,003
Saint Mary-of-the-Woods C ...	0.3	0.9	2.3	1.2	94.1	1.2	910
Saint Mary's C	0.0	1.1	0.3	1.8	95.5	1.3	1,782
Saint Meinrad C	0.0	2.3	0.8	3.1	87.7	6.2	130
Saint Meinrad Sch of Theol ..	0.0	3.1	3.9	3.1	89.0	0.8	127
Taylor U	0.1	0.6	0.8	0.4	96.9	1.3	1,635
Tri-State U	0.0	1.2	1.8	0.9	82.0	14.2	1,037
U of Evansville	0.1	0.7	2.5	0.2	92.6	3.9	3,379
U of Indianapolis	0.3	0.7	5.5	0.6	91.3	1.5	3,274
U of Notre Dame	0.4	2.0	3.3	3.8	87.2	3.4	9,335
U of Southern Indiana	0.4	0.5	2.4	0.3	95.7	0.7	5,264
Valparaiso U	0.2	0.7	1.7	1.0	95.3	1.1	3,890
Vincennes U							
Main	0.1	0.3	7.3	2.0	88.3	2.0	7,556
Jasper	0.0	0.3	0.4	0.0	99.2	0.1	729
Wabash C	0.0	2.1	3.0	1.1	91.7	2.1	872

IOWA

American Inst of Business	0.1	0.9	0.8	0.3	97.9	0.0	1,120
Briar Cliff C	0.2	0.4	0.7	0.8	97.0	0.9	1,090
Buena Vista C	0.1	0.4	0.3	0.2	98.9	0.0	2,721
Central U of Iowa	0.0	0.9	0.9	0.5	95.4	2.4	1,507
Clarke C	0.0	0.0	1.6	0.2	97.5	0.7	830
Coe C	0.0	0.6	1.6	0.5	86.6	10.8	1,242
Cornell C	0.4	2.0	3.0	1.8	90.6	2.2	1,129
Des Moines Area CC	0.3	2.4	3.4	0.8	92.7	0.4	9,861
Divine Word C	0.0	56.1	0.0	1.5	28.8	13.6	66
Dordt C	0.0	2.2	0.4	0.1	85.0	12.3	987
Drake U	0.1	0.9	2.7	0.7	93.3	2.3	6,618
Emmaus Bible C	0.0	1.0	2.9	6.3	82.0	7.8	205
Faith Baptist Bible C and Sem	0.3	1.6	0.3	0.7	97.1	0.0	307
Graceland C	0.4	0.7	3.1	0.4	92.7	2.8	1,622
Grand View C	0.1	2.1	3.4	1.4	89.8	3.1	1,359
Grinnell C	0.1	3.0	4.3	0.8	85.5	6.3	1,302
Hawkeye Inst of Tech	0.3	0.2	3.4	0.2	95.9	0.1	1,885
Indian Hills CC	0.3	0.5	0.9	0.4	97.9	0.0	2,588
Iowa Central CC	0.1	1.0	2.3	0.2	96.4	0.0	2,036
Iowa Lakes CC	0.2	0.6	0.6	0.2	98.4	0.1	1,787
Iowa St U	0.1	1.3	2.1	0.9	87.7	7.9	20,475

IOWA, cont.

	American Indian	Asian	Black	Hispanic	White	Foreign	Total
Iowa Valley CC Dist							
Ellsworth CC	0.0%	0.3%	8.0%	0.0%	91.7%	0.0%	959
Marshalltown CC	2.6	1.1	0.6	0.1	94.8	0.9	1,229
Iowa Wesleyan C	0.1	0.6	2.1	0.0	94.7	2.5	679
Iowa Western CC	0.2	0.7	1.7	0.7	96.5	0.2	2,604
Kirkwood CC	0.1	0.9	1.3	0.9	96.0	0.7	7,053
Lincoln Tech Inst	0.0	0.7	4.2	2.1	93.0	0.0	143
Loras C	0.0	0.7	1.7	0.0	97.6	0.0	1,933
Luther C	0.0	2.5	1.2	0.2	93.0	3.0	2,160
Maharishi International U	0.6	2.4	1.2	0.9	58.8	36.1	782
Marycrest C	0.1	0.1	2.3	2.9	93.7	0.8	2,002
Morningside C	2.0	0.5	2.0	0.2	95.3	0.0	1,229
Mount Mercy C	0.3	0.4	1.2	0.4	97.0	0.6	1,568
Mount Saint Clare C	0.0	0.3	8.2	0.6	89.3	1.6	317
North Iowa Area CC	0.0	0.4	2.3	1.1	96.1	0.0	2,510
Northeast Iowa Tech Inst	0.1	0.2	0.1	0.2	99.5	0.0	1,153
Northwest Iowa Tech C	0.0	0.9	0.0	0.0	99.1	0.0	528
Northwestern C	0.1	0.3	0.7	0.1	95.4	3.3	965
Palmer C of Chiropractic	0.6	0.7	0.4	0.7	87.5	10.1	1,622
Saint Ambrose U	0.3	0.8	3.2	2.4	92.9	0.4	2,110
Scott CC	0.5	0.6	3.3	1.5	93.6	0.6	5,374
Simpson C	0.1	0.5	1.0	0.2	98.1	0.2	1,710
Southeastern CC	0.1	0.7	2.4	0.8	95.9	0.0	2,341
Southwestern CC	0.0	0.2	1.2	0.1	97.8	0.7	907
U of Dubuque	0.5	0.8	5.1	0.6	86.3	6.8	1,187
U of Iowa	0.4	2.2	2.2	1.3	87.6	6.5	30,001
U of Northern Iowa	0.1	0.5	1.3	0.4	96.4	1.2	12,396
U of Osteopathic Medicine and Health Sciences	0.1	5.4	3.7	3.0	85.3	2.5	1,150
Upper Iowa U	0.2	0.7	6.3	1.0	91.5	0.2	1,725
Vennard C	0.0	0.7	0.0	0.7	95.8	2.8	144
Waldorf C	0.0	0.6	2.3	0.2	94.0	3.0	529
Wartburg C	0.1	0.1	1.5	0.2	93.9	4.3	1,358
Wartburg Theological Sem	0.0	0.9	0.5	0.9	91.0	6.6	211
Western Iowa Tech CC	4.9	1.5	1.5	1.1	90.8	0.1	1,576
Westmar C	0.0	0.4	4.6	1.0	93.7	0.4	505
William Penn C	0.1	0.6	2.7	0.3	95.4	0.9	675

KANSAS

	American Indian	Asian	Black	Hispanic	White	Foreign	Total
Allen County CC	1.4	0.6	2.7	0.8	94.2	0.3	1,267
Baker U	0.1	0.5	3.1	0.6	93.9	1.8	873
Barton County CC	0.4	0.5	5.0	1.4	92.7	0.1	3,531
Benedictine C	0.4	0.5	3.1	3.3	90.9	1.8	735
Bethany C	0.3	0.3	3.2	1.4	92.4	2.4	715
Bethel C	0.2	1.1	5.6	1.1	87.2	4.8	623
Butler County CC	1.2	2.0	6.2	2.3	87.0	1.4	4,048
Central Baptist Theological Sem	2.1	0.7	25.5	1.4	69.5	0.7	141
Central C	0.8	1.5	12.5	5.3	79.6	0.4	265
Cloud County CC	0.4	0.6	1.8	0.9	96.2	0.1	2,128
Coffeyville CC	0.2	0.9	8.0	0.7	87.1	3.0	1,938
Colby CC	0.1	0.2	0.6	1.0	97.8	0.2	1,624
Cowley County CC	2.1	0.5	3.3	2.1	92.0	0.0	2,191
Dodge City CC	0.1	0.7	1.9	4.2	92.9	0.2	2,213
Donnelly C	0.9	4.9	51.7	7.9	16.2	18.4	445
Emporia St U	0.3	0.2	2.3	1.1	93.9	2.1	5,763

	American Indian	Asian	Black	Hispanic	White	Foreign	Total
Fort Hays St U	0.6%	1.2%	1.3%	1.0%	95.9%	0.0%	5,005
Fort Scott CC	0.9	0.4	3.7	0.3	94.7	0.1	1,379
Friends Bible C	1.0	1.0	1.0	3.8	89.4	3.8	104
Friends U	0.3	0.7	4.6	1.3	90.0	3.3	1,185
Garden City CC	0.6	2.8	5.4	9.3	81.6	0.4	1,117
Haskell Indian JC	100.0	0.0	0.0	0.0	0.0	0.0	842
Hesston C	0.4	1.5	2.9	1.7	86.2	7.3	521
Highland CC	1.6	0.2	3.3	0.9	94.0	0.0	1,861
Hutchinson CC	0.7	0.5	3.8	2.1	92.0	0.9	3,456
Independence CC	0.6	0.5	5.4	1.2	92.3	0.1	1,471
Johnson County CC	0.4	1.8	2.6	1.7	93.2	0.3	11,161
Kansas City C and Bible Sch	0.0	2.2	11.1	4.4	82.2	0.0	90
Kansas City Kansas CC	0.6	1.3	18.3	3.6	76.1	0.0	4,167
Kansas C of Tech	0.1	0.5	1.2	1.1	96.9	0.1	737
Kansas Newman C	1.0	0.9	4.8	5.5	85.7	2.2	691
Kansas St U	0.3	0.9	2.9	1.8	88.0	6.1	19,301
Kansas Wesleyan	0.8	0.2	14.6	3.8	79.3	1.3	474
Labette CC	2.4	0.4	3.9	1.1	91.6	0.7	2,667
Marymount C	0.0	0.8	3.7	1.7	93.3	0.6	653
McPherson C	0.4	1.0	4.6	2.1	88.8	3.1	482
MidAmerica Nazarene C	0.4	1.0	1.6	1.3	91.7	3.9	1,112
National C	1.6	0.0	81.1	1.6	15.6	0.0	122
Neosho County CC	1.0	0.3	2.3	1.9	94.2	0.3	1,180
Ottawa U	1.5	0.8	7.3	2.9	79.1	8.4	521
Pittsburg St U	0.7	0.8	1.2	0.7	93.4	3.2	5,637
Pratt CC	0.1	0.0	3.2	1.5	94.9	0.3	984
Saint Mary C	3.4	1.0	24.9	5.2	63.7	1.9	1,066
Saint Mary of the Plains C	0.3	0.0	2.7	4.4	90.4	2.2	930
Seward County CC	0.7	1.2	2.2	3.4	92.5	0.1	1,370
Southwestern C	0.6	0.8	10.9	2.6	84.2	1.1	663
Tabor C	0.6	0.6	3.2	1.1	92.4	2.1	476
U of Kansas							
Main	0.6	1.6	2.6	1.4	86.9	7.0	26,020
Medical Center	0.4	4.7	1.8	2.4	89.6	1.2	2,383
Washburn U of Topeka	0.9	1.1	4.9	3.4	88.9	0.8	6,586
Wichita St U	0.9	3.4	4.7	2.2	84.0	4.7	16,673

KENTUCKY

Alice Lloyd C	0.0	0.0	0.0	0.0	100.0	0.0	507
Asbury C	0.2	0.7	0.8	1.2	95.6	1.4	988
Asbury Theological Sem	0.3	0.6	0.6	0.4	92.9	5.3	717
Bellarmine C	0.0	0.1	1.6	0.2	97.6	0.4	3,343
Berea C	0.1	0.7	8.6	0.3	84.7	5.6	1,527
Brescia C	0.0	0.0	2.0	0.2	97.1	0.8	666
Campbellsville C	0.1	0.7	5.3	0.0	92.8	1.1	732
Centre C	0.0	1.4	1.2	0.0	96.9	0.6	860
Clear Creek Baptist Bible C	0.0	0.0	0.6	1.2	98.2	0.0	168
Cumberland C	0.1	0.1	5.6	0.3	90.4	3.5	1,904
Eastern Kentucky U	0.1	0.3	5.9	0.2	92.4	1.0	13,635
Georgetown C	0.1	0.2	2.7	0.3	96.1	0.5	1,471
Inst of Electronic Tech	0.0	0.0	9.4	0.0	89.7	0.9	224
Kentucky Christian C	0.0	0.2	0.9	0.0	98.7	0.2	548
Kentucky St U	0.1	0.3	41.6	0.3	56.4	1.3	2,218
Kentucky Wesleyan C	0.0	0.4	4.3	0.0	94.4	0.9	765
Lees C	0.0	1.9	7.2	0.0	91.0	0.0	432
Lexington Theol Sem	0.0	0.0	5.5	0.0	92.2	2.3	128

THE ALMANAC OF HIGHER EDUCATION • ENROLLMENT BY RACE

KENTUCKY, cont.

	American Indian	Asian	Black	Hispanic	White	Foreign	Total
Lindsey Wilson C	0.0%	0.0%	4.2%	0.0%	95.3%	0.5%	1,059
Louisville Tech Inst	0.0	0.2	6.9	0.8	92.1	0.0	505
Mid-Continent Baptist Bible C	0.0	0.0	2.0	0.0	95.1	2.9	102
Midway C	0.0	0.0	2.0	0.5	93.7	3.8	396
Morehead St U	0.0	0.1	3.2	0.1	95.7	0.9	7,360
Murray St U	0.3	0.4	5.0	0.3	92.7	1.4	7,593
National Education Center Kentucky C of Tech	0.2	0.2	14.7	0.2	84.4	0.2	475
Northern Kentucky U	0.1	0.2	1.4	0.1	97.5	0.7	9,490
Owensboro JC of Business	0.0	0.0	5.0	0.0	95.0	0.0	318
Pikeville C	0.0	0.0	0.9	0.0	99.0	0.1	915
RETS Electronic Inst	1.4	0.1	10.3	0.1	88.0	0.1	740
Saint Catharine C	0.0	0.0	10.2	0.0	86.1	3.8	266
Spalding U	0.1	0.6	8.7	0.1	90.6	0.0	1,196
Sue Bennett C	0.0	0.4	1.5	0.2	97.8	0.2	551
Sullivan JC of Business	0.1	0.1	15.0	0.4	83.6	0.9	1,989
Thomas More C	0.4	0.2	1.8	0.3	97.1	0.3	1,097
Transylvania U	0.0	0.1	0.9	0.3	97.4	1.3	1,041
Union C	0.0	0.5	4.7	0.3	94.3	0.3	1,048
U of Kentucky	0.4	1.1	3.2	0.7	93.1	1.6	22,230
Ashland CC	0.7	0.3	0.8	0.2	98.0	0.0	2,609
Elizabethtown CC	0.7	1.1	6.0	1.4	90.7	0.1	2,710
Hazard CC	1.3	1.0	1.1	0.0	96.6	0.0	1,038
Henderson CC	0.0	0.3	4.4	0.2	95.0	0.0	1,239
Hopkinsville CC	0.6	1.6	13.7	2.9	81.2	0.0	1,741
Jefferson CC	0.4	0.6	12.7	0.3	85.7	0.3	8,197
Lexington CC	0.9	0.7	6.1	0.6	91.6	0.1	3,401
Madisonville CC	0.9	0.4	3.7	0.1	94.8	0.1	1,819
Maysville CC	0.2	0.1	2.0	0.1	97.6	0.0	870
Paducah CC	0.4	0.2	3.8	0.2	95.3	0.2	2,437
Prestonsburg CC	0.7	0.2	0.5	0.3	98.2	0.1	2,085
Somerset CC	1.3	0.5	0.5	0.1	97.5	0.1	1,583
Southeast CC	0.3	0.4	1.5	0.1	97.6	0.0	1,601
U of Louisville	0.3	1.8	8.4	0.9	87.1	1.6	21,313
Western Kentucky U	0.2	0.3	5.8	0.2	92.5	1.0	14,056

LOUISIANA

Bossier Parish CC	0.0	0.6	11.1	1.6	86.7	0.0	2,221
Centenary C of Louisiana	0.3	0.5	6.3	0.5	91.4	1.1	1,110
Delgado CC	1.0	2.6	30.9	5.3	58.4	1.8	7,315
Dillard U	0.0	0.1	98.9	0.0	0.1	0.9	1,400
Grambling St U	0.0	0.1	94.1	0.1	3.8	1.9	6,003
Louisiana C	1.3	1.0	4.6	0.6	91.2	1.3	985
Louisiana St U Sys Louisiana St U and A&M C	0.3	2.1	7.1	1.5	84.4	4.6	27,348
Alexandria	0.5	0.6	9.7	0.7	88.5	0.0	2,203
Eunice	0.3	0.2	13.6	0.5	85.2	0.2	1,723
Medical Center	0.2	4.2	8.4	2.5	82.2	2.4	2,415
Shreveport	0.6	1.4	8.5	0.7	88.7	0.2	4,499
U of New Orleans	0.2	2.5	15.2	4.7	75.3	2.0	16,076
Louisiana Tech U	0.2	0.8	12.3	0.9	83.1	2.7	10,044
Loyola U	0.4	1.9	11.6	5.7	77.9	2.5	4,961
McNeese St U	0.6	0.5	13.6	0.8	83.1	1.5	7,378
New Orleans Baptist Theological Sem	0.1	0.4	3.4	4.8	90.7	0.4	1,351
Nicholls St U	0.5	0.1	11.4	1.3	86.3	0.4	7,159

	American Indian	Asian	Black	Hispanic	White	Foreign	Total
Northeast Louisiana U	0.6%	1.0%	14.7%	0.2%	80.6%	2.9%	10,498
Northwest St U	1.1	1.3	20.4	2.2	74.4	0.6	6,455
Notre Dame Sem	0.0	24.2	4.2	3.2	68.4	0.0	95
Our Lady of Holy Cross C	0.8	1.5	26.2	2.5	68.8	0.2	848
Phillips JC	0.2	1.7	24.0	7.6	66.2	0.3	1,099
Saint Bernard Parish CC	0.7	1.0	2.1	2.7	93.6	0.0	828
Saint Joseph Sem C	0.0	9.6	2.6	6.1	81.6	0.0	114
Southeastern Louisiana U	0.3	0.5	6.6	0.7	91.0	0.9	8,520
Southern Tech C Lafayette	0.0	1.0	35.1	2.8	55.6	5.6	502
Southern Tech C Monroe	0.0	0.0	47.5	0.0	52.1	0.4	259
Southern U and A&M C Sys							
Baton Rouge	0.0	0.2	92.5	0.4	3.5	3.5	8,968
New Orleans	0.1	0.5	89.8	0.4	6.5	2.7	3,434
Shreveport	0.0	0.2	90.2	0.2	9.5	0.0	1,229
Tulane U	0.2	3.3	7.1	3.6	80.3	5.5	10,778
U of Southwestern Louisiana	0.2	1.2	16.4	0.7	74.8	6.7	15,033
Xavier U	0.1	0.4	90.5	0.5	4.9	3.5	2,528

MAINE

	American Indian	Asian	Black	Hispanic	White	Foreign	Total
Andover C	0.0	0.6	1.1	0.4	97.8	0.0	464
Bangor Theological Sem	0.0	0.0	0.0	0.0	99.0	1.0	104
Bates C	0.1	2.4	2.1	1.0	92.0	2.5	1,557
Beal C	0.0	0.4	0.0	0.0	98.6	1.1	279
Bowdoin C	0.1	2.5	2.9	1.7	91.2	1.5	1,426
Casco Bay C	0.0	0.0	0.4	0.0	99.6	0.0	253
Central Maine Medical							
Center Sch of Nursing	0.0	0.0	0.0	0.0	100.0	0.0	74
Central Maine Tech C	0.1	0.3	0.3	0.0	99.2	0.0	906
Colby C	0.1	1.3	1.2	0.8	94.6	2.0	1,736
C of the Atlantic	0.0	0.0	0.5	0.0	97.0	2.5	197
Husson C	0.6	0.8	1.3	0.4	95.6	1.3	1,789
Kennebec Valley Tech C	0.0	0.0	0.0	0.0	100.0	0.0	977
Maine Maritime Academy	0.6	1.2	1.2	0.6	89.2	7.3	507
Northern Maine Tech C	3.1	0.1	0.4	0.0	96.4	0.0	828
Portland Sch of Art	0.0	1.0	0.0	0.7	98.0	0.3	300
Saint Joseph's C	0.2	0.5	0.7	0.3	97.7	0.5	572
Southern Maine Tech C	0.4	0.7	0.1	0.3	98.5	0.0	1,907
Thomas C	0.0	0.0	0.1	0.2	99.2	0.5	1,013
Unity C	0.5	0.3	0.5	0.0	97.7	1.0	395
U of Maine Sys							
U of Maine	0.9	0.6	0.5	0.3	97.5	0.3	10,967
Augusta	0.0	0.1	0.1	0.0	99.7	0.1	3,853
Farmington	0.0	0.1	0.0	0.1	99.9	0.0	1,931
Fort Kent	0.3	0.0	0.8	0.2	98.7	0.0	620
Machias	2.8	0.0	0.5	0.1	94.9	1.6	851
Presque Isle	1.0	0.7	2.0	0.7	93.6	1.9	1,398
U of Southern Maine	0.4	0.1	0.0	0.1	99.4	0.0	10,071
U of New England	0.1	1.2	1.5	0.2	96.6	0.4	1,071
Westbrook C	0.0	0.9	1.0	0.4	97.0	0.6	677

MARYLAND

	American Indian	Asian	Black	Hispanic	White	Foreign	Total
Allegany CC	0.1	0.2	2.0	0.1	97.6	0.0	2,220
Anne Arundel CC	0.4	1.4	7.8	1.2	88.8	0.4	11,664
Baltimore Hebrew U	0.0	0.0	0.0	0.0	100.0	0.0	231

MARYLAND, cont.

	American Indian	Asian	Black	Hispanic	White	Foreign	Total
Baltimore International Culinary C	0.3%	2.7%	18.4%	3.6%	75.0%	0.0%	332
Capitol C	0.1	11.7	15.6	2.3	66.6	3.7	778
Catonsville CC	0.2	2.1	14.0	0.7	82.7	0.3	11,444
Cecil CC	0.7	0.6	3.5	0.3	94.5	0.3	1,447
Charles County CC	0.4	0.9	8.2	0.9	89.5	0.1	4,966
Chesapeake C	0.0	0.4	11.1	0.3	88.2	0.0	2,247
C of Notre Dame of Maryland	0.0	0.9	13.4	1.9	82.5	1.4	2,461
Columbia Union C	0.1	6.3	33.5	4.3	55.8	0.0	1,096
CC of Baltimore	0.6	1.3	71.0	1.0	24.1	2.0	4,487
Dundalk CC	0.4	1.4	10.8	0.7	86.7	0.0	3,206
Eastern Christian C	0.0	0.0	8.1	0.0	89.2	2.7	37
Essex CC	0.4	1.4	6.5	0.7	91.0	0.0	10,218
Frederick CC	0.2	0.8	3.4	0.8	93.9	0.9	3,470
Garrett CC	0.0	0.0	1.6	0.3	98.0	0.0	612
Goucher C	0.2	4.5	4.3	2.7	86.9	1.4	974
Hagerstown Business C	0.0	0.0	1.3	0.0	98.7	0.0	463
Hagerstown JC	0.4	0.5	6.4	0.8	92.0	0.0	2,641
Harford CC	0.6	1.5	6.5	0.8	90.6	0.0	4,454
Hood C	0.1	2.2	5.5	3.2	86.8	2.2	1,859
Howard CC	0.2	3.2	13.1	1.1	81.8	0.5	3,925
Johns Hopkins U	0.2	5.9	4.7	1.4	80.8	7.0	12,647
Loyola C	0.1	2.0	3.1	1.1	92.6	1.1	5,821
Maryland C of Art and Design	1.2	3.7	20.0	5.0	70.0	0.0	80
Maryland Inst C of Art	0.4	3.5	6.5	2.1	85.0	2.5	1,285
Montgomery C							
Germantown	0.4	4.3	5.8	2.3	86.8	0.5	3,124
Rockville	0.4	9.8	9.0	5.8	72.3	2.8	14,113
Takoma Park	0.3	8.2	33.9	5.6	47.9	4.1	4,328
Morgan St U	0.2	0.4	91.7	0.4	3.0	4.4	4,066
Mount Saint Mary's C	0.1	0.4	3.4	0.7	95.4	0.1	1,783
Ner Israel Rabbinical C	0.0	0.0	0.0	0.0	95.2	4.8	352
Peabody Inst of Johns Hopkins U	0.0	4.8	4.5	1.3	73.7	15.8	463
Prince Georges CC	0.4	4.1	44.1	2.0	48.4	1.0	13,443
Saint John's C	0.0	2.1	1.9	1.1	93.4	1.5	467
Saint Mary's C of Maryland	0.3	1.5	5.6	1.8	90.5	0.4	1,585
Saint Mary's Sem and U	0.0	0.0	1.7	0.0	98.0	0.3	297
Sojourner-Douglass C	0.0	0.0	98.3	0.0	1.7	0.0	353
Uniformed Services U of the Health Sciences	0.3	7.7	2.7	1.8	84.8	2.7	943
U S Naval Academy	0.6	4.5	5.5	5.4	83.3	0.7	4,557
U of Maryland Sys							
Baltimore	0.3	6.7	10.6	1.7	78.1	2.7	4,563
Baltimore County	0.2	7.2	12.0	1.2	77.2	2.3	9,868
C Park	0.2	7.4	8.6	2.4	75.1	6.3	36,681
Eastern Shore	0.3	1.2	71.4	0.7	21.4	5.1	1,559
U C	0.6	6.3	18.3	2.9	71.6	0.4	14,263
Bowie St U	0.2	1.9	64.0	0.5	32.2	1.1	3,325
Coppin St C	0.3	2.0	90.0	0.1	4.7	2.9	2,246
Frostburg St U	0.2	0.6	6.5	0.6	92.0	0.1	4,525
Salisbury St U	0.1	0.8	6.8	0.4	91.6	0.4	5,260
Towson St U	0.2	1.7	8.2	0.9	87.5	1.4	15,169
U of Baltimore	0.2	1.6	14.5	0.9	80.9	1.9	5,228
Villa Julie C	0.0	0.8	15.9	0.6	82.7	0.0	1,271
Washington Bible C	0.0	9.6	24.9	1.6	54.9	8.9	437
Washington C	0.0	0.9	1.2	0.9	95.2	1.7	988

	American Indian	Asian	Black	Hispanic	White	Foreign	Total
Washington Theological Union	0.0%	1.4%	1.8%	3.9%	92.9%	0.0%	280
Western Maryland C	0.0	0.8	2.2	0.6	95.2	1.1	2,002
Wor-Wic Tech CC	0.0	0.2	20.8	0.4	78.6	0.0	1,032

MASSACHUSETTS

	American Indian	Asian	Black	Hispanic	White	Foreign	Total
American International C	0.0	1.1	9.3	1.7	84.3	3.7	1,869
Amherst C	0.2	6.8	5.3	4.4	81.0	2.3	1,592
Andover Newton Theological Sch	0.0	0.2	4.8	2.1	88.6	4.3	421
Anna Maria C	0.0	0.4	1.9	0.9	94.1	2.7	1,180
Aquinas JC							
Milton	0.0	0.0	1.4	0.8	97.8	0.0	359
Newton	0.0	0.0	0.4	0.0	99.6	0.0	262
Arthur D Little Management Education Inst	0.0	0.0	0.0	1.9	5.8	92.3	52
Assumption C	0.1	0.1	1.1	2.1	96.0	0.6	2,904
Atlantic Union C	0.1	0.3	18.4	12.6	52.8	15.8	795
Babson C	0.1	0.8	0.8	1.5	91.7	5.0	2,971
Bay Path JC	0.5	1.2	2.8	2.8	92.6	0.2	579
Bay St JC of Business	0.0	0.5	7.0	2.4	89.4	0.8	631
Becker JC							
Leicester	0.0	4.0	1.5	1.5	90.9	2.1	529
Worcester	0.0	0.1	3.2	0.3	95.4	0.9	965
Bentley C	0.2	1.9	1.5	2.2	90.9	3.3	7,151
Berklee C of Music	0.1	1.6	4.7	3.1	68.7	21.8	2,830
Boston Architectural Center	1.8	2.1	1.8	2.3	92.0	0.0	661
Boston C	0.2	4.7	3.2	4.2	84.4	3.3	14,594
Boston Conservatory	0.0	0.7	3.2	2.3	89.0	4.8	435
Boston U	0.2	6.4	3.0	2.7	75.2	12.6	28,555
Bradford C	0.5	0.5	3.5	2.3	86.0	7.2	428
Brandeis U	0.0	4.0	3.0	1.9	82.2	9.0	3,755
Cambridge C	0.4	0.6	20.1	5.7	72.7	0.4	472
Catherine Laboure C	0.0	1.0	14.9	1.0	83.1	0.0	302
Central New England C of Tech	0.2	2.0	0.5	0.5	96.1	0.7	562
Clark U	0.2	2.7	2.1	2.2	83.2	9.6	3,350
C of the Holy Cross	0.0	0.8	3.6	1.9	93.5	0.2	2,647
C of Our Lady of the Elms	0.0	1.3	3.8	3.4	91.0	0.6	1,065
Conway Sch of Landscape Design	0.0	0.0	0.0	0.0	100.0	0.0	17
Curry C	0.1	0.2	3.1	1.3	94.2	1.2	1,270
Dean JC	0.0	0.4	0.4	0.3	98.3	0.7	2,538
Eastern Nazarene C	0.3	1.0	6.0	3.8	86.5	2.3	979
Emerson C	0.2	1.0	3.0	1.6	91.9	2.2	2,668
Emmanuel C	0.1	1.0	7.5	3.9	83.6	3.9	977
Endicott C	0.2	0.4	1.1	1.3	90.3	6.8	843
Episcopal Divinity Sch	0.8	1.7	2.5	2.5	81.7	10.8	120
Fisher C	0.4	1.0	7.5	1.7	88.5	0.9	2,115
Forsyth Sch of Dental Hygienists	0.0	5.1	1.7	0.8	91.5	0.8	118
Franklin Inst of Boston	0.2	7.1	10.7	4.2	77.0	0.9	553
Gordon C	0.2	1.2	2.2	0.7	93.7	2.1	1,184
Gordon-Conwell Theol Sem	0.0	2.6	17.3	9.1	68.1	2.9	717
Hampshire C	0.1	2.1	2.6	1.7	88.2	5.3	1,282
Harvard U	0.4	6.1	4.9	3.7	75.0	0.8	24,194

MASS., cont.

	American Indian	Asian	Black	Hispanic	White	Foreign	Total
Hebrew C	0.0%	0.0%	0.0%	0.0%	88.5%	11.5%	78
Hellenic C-Holy Cross Greek Orthodox Sch of Theology	0.0	0.8	0.0	0.0	81.1	18.2	132
Lasell JC	0.0	1.4	1.6	2.3	89.8	5.0	441
Lesley C	0.2	1.0	3.0	1.9	92.1	1.7	4,460
Marian Court JC	0.0	0.6	1.8	3.0	94.5	0.0	165
Mass Bd of Regents Sys							
Southeastern Mass U	0.2	1.3	1.9	0.8	94.0	1.8	7,589
U of Lowell	0.2	4.7	1.9	1.2	88.4	3.6	14,493
U of Mass Amherst	0.3	2.1	3.1	2.8	85.0	6.7	27,918
U of Mass Boston	0.4	4.4	8.6	2.9	81.0	2.7	13,666
U of Mass Medical Sch Worcester	0.7	5.6	2.9	2.7	88.2	0.0	449
Bridgewater St C	0.2	0.5	1.4	0.6	97.2	0.2	8,962
Fitchburg St C	0.0	1.0	2.5	1.0	95.3	0.1	6,224
Framingham St C	0.3	0.7	1.8	1.0	95.8	0.5	6,677
Massachusetts C of Art	0.3	2.4	2.3	1.5	90.7	2.7	2,371
Mass Maritime Acad	0.2	0.7	2.7	6.6	89.9	0.0	602
North Adams St C	0.0	0.3	2.3	0.6	96.5	0.3	2,743
Salem St C	0.4	0.7	2.5	1.3	94.4	0.7	9,565
Westfield St C	0.3	0.4	2.2	1.1	95.9	0.1	5,106
Worcester St C	0.5	0.7	1.4	1.1	95.1	1.2	6,435
Berkshire CC	0.2	0.5	0.6	0.4	96.5	1.8	3,158
Bristol CC	0.7	1.1	2.7	1.0	93.7	0.8	4,699
Bunker Hill CC	0.4	11.6	13.9	6.8	62.3	4.9	6,456
Cape Cod CC	0.4	0.2	0.8	0.9	97.5	0.1	4,991
Greenfield CC	0.0	0.9	1.0	1.3	95.9	0.9	2,231
Holyoke CC	0.5	0.3	2.3	5.1	91.2	0.5	5,283
Massachusetts Bay CC	0.2	1.8	5.6	2.2	87.8	2.3	4,125
Massasoit CC	0.3	1.1	4.6	1.0	92.8	0.3	6,591
Middlesex CC	0.6	3.8	1.3	3.1	91.0	0.2	6,469
Mount Wachusett CC	0.2	0.2	1.4	1.8	95.8	0.5	3,793
North Shore CC	0.2	2.1	4.9	4.8	87.1	0.9	5,810
Northern Essex CC	0.5	1.4	0.3	11.6	85.6	0.6	6,349
Quinsigamond CC	0.5	1.7	3.2	5.7	88.8	0.2	4,411
Roxbury CC	0.2	7.1	62.8	12.3	17.1	0.5	2,467
Springfield Tech CC	0.2	0.8	9.8	6.3	82.3	0.6	5,941
Mass C of Pharmacy & Allied Health Sciences	0.9	6.9	3.7	5.5	70.4	12.6	1,073
MGH Inst of Health Professions	0.0	3.6	1.0	0.0	94.9	0.5	197
Mass Inst of Tech	0.3	9.7	3.5	3.7	62.0	20.9	9,500
Massachusetts Sch of Professional Psychology	0.0	0.0	1.2	0.0	97.6	1.2	169
Merrimack C	0.2	1.7	1.5	1.4	92.3	2.9	3,483
Montserrat C of Art	0.0	0.9	2.3	0.0	96.7	0.0	215
Mount Holyoke C	0.2	4.8	4.2	1.9	81.6	7.2	1,987
Mount Ida C	1.0	1.4	6.4	2.5	79.6	9.0	1,537
New England C of Optometry	0.0	6.4	3.5	4.8	77.6	7.7	375
New England Conservatory of Music	0.4	2.9	2.4	4.0	69.0	21.3	755
New England Inst of Applied Arts and Sciences	0.0	0.0	2.0	0.0	96.9	1.0	98
New England Sch of Law	0.1	0.5	1.4	1.4	96.6	0.0	1,192
Newbury C	0.0	3.4	20.3	18.7	54.9	2.8	3,385
Nichols C	0.0	0.4	0.4	0.4	98.2	0.6	1,489
Northeastern U	0.5	3.7	5.6	1.7	85.1	3.4	32,385

	American Indian	Asian	Black	Hispanic	White	Foreign	Total
Pine Manor C	0.0%	2.6%	2.2%	4.5%	79.1%	11.6%	646
Quincy JC	0.3	1.9	4.9	0.8	88.3	3.8	2,644
Radcliffe C	0.3	12.2	9.6	5.4	66.7	5.8	2,691
Regis C	0.2	0.5	1.0	4.5	89.3	4.6	1,005
Saint Hyacinth C and Sem	0.0	0.0	3.3	0.0	90.0	6.7	30
Saint John's Sem	0.0	6.0	1.3	3.3	84.1	5.3	151
Sch of the Museum of Fine Arts Boston	0.1	3.2	0.9	0.9	91.7	3.2	1,371
Simmons C	0.1	1.6	2.9	1.6	90.2	3.6	2,878
Simon's Rock of Bard C	0.0	6.3	6.3	2.5	81.9	2.9	315
Smith C	0.2	7.0	3.2	2.0	80.7	6.9	3,039
Springfield C	0.0	0.1	2.4	0.7	94.6	2.2	3,204
Stonehill C	0.0	0.2	0.4	0.3	98.6	0.4	3,054
Suffolk U	0.1	1.7	3.6	1.3	89.2	4.1	5,390
Tufts U	0.1	5.9	2.9	2.4	80.3	8.4	8,013
Wellesley C	0.3	14.6	6.1	3.8	71.3	4.0	2,237
Wentworth Inst of Tech	0.2	4.1	6.1	2.0	81.4	6.2	3,861
Western New England C	0.2	0.7	2.7	1.3	93.8	1.3	5,182
Weston Sch of Theology	0.0	0.0	0.0	0.0	90.3	9.7	186
Wheaton C	0.2	1.7	3.1	1.6	87.5	5.9	1,161
Wheelock C	0.4	0.6	7.4	2.6	88.1	0.8	1,648
Williams C	0.0	6.6	6.6	3.5	79.9	3.4	2,076
Worcester Polytechnic Inst	0.0	3.5	0.5	0.6	86.5	8.8	3,767
Worcester JC	0.2	1.5	1.2	1.1	94.9	1.0	1,325

MICHIGAN

Adrian C	0.6	1.1	3.5	1.3	91.7	1.9	1,229
Albion C	0.0	1.7	2.4	0.2	94.9	0.8	1,652
Alma C	0.1	0.4	1.2	0.7	97.2	0.4	1,198
Alpena CC	0.1	0.4	2.4	0.5	96.5	0.2	2,281
Andrews U	0.6	5.4	15.1	6.4	57.2	15.4	2,858
Aquinas C	0.3	1.0	4.1	1.1	92.7	0.8	2,532
Baker C Owosso	0.7	0.4	0.4	1.4	97.0	0.0	900
Baker C Flint	0.6	1.3	13.5	0.6	84.1	0.0	2,654
Bay De Noc CC	2.6	0.0	0.0	0.2	97.1	0.0	2,171
Calvin C	0.1	0.9	1.0	0.4	89.1	8.4	4,448
Calvin Theological Sem	1.3	7.1	1.3	3.4	56.7	30.3	238
Center for Creative Studies C of Art and Design	0.2	1.4	6.4	1.1	89.2	1.7	1,114
Center for Humanistic Studies	1.4	0.0	5.6	0.0	93.0	0.0	71
Central Michigan U	0.5	0.4	2.1	0.8	95.1	1.1	19,024
Charles S Mott CC	1.2	0.4	14.3	1.9	82.1	0.1	10,516
Cleary C	0.2	1.9	5.3	2.1	89.9	0.6	1,003
Concordia C	0.2	0.9	6.9	0.0	90.6	1.3	533
Cranbrook Academy of Art	0.0	2.2	1.5	0.0	91.0	5.2	134
Davenport C Grand Rapids	0.3	0.3	3.9	0.7	94.8	0.0	3,232
Davenport C Kalamazoo	0.3	0.6	9.5	0.8	88.8	0.0	1,009
Davenport C Lansing	0.7	2.6	13.4	15.0	68.3	0.0	1,287
Delta C	0.3	0.5	5.7	3.1	90.3	0.1	9,651
Detroit C of Business Dearborn	0.4	0.6	45.8	3.0	50.1	0.2	2,331
Detroit C of Business Madison Heights	0.0	0.3	30.3	0.6	68.7	0.0	630
Detroit C of Business Flint	0.0	0.1	47.5	0.1	52.3	0.0	1,100
Detroit C of Law	0.3	1.4	11.3	0.8	85.2	1.0	711
Eastern Michigan U	0.3	1.1	6.8	1.3	86.5	4.0	23,060

MICHIGAN, cont.

	American Indian	Asian	Black	Hispanic	White	Foreign	Total
Ferris St U	0.4%	0.5%	3.9%	0.7%	93.1%	1.5%	11,762
GMI Engineering and Management Inst	0.3	5.0	5.5	1.3	79.9	8.0	3,068
Glen Oaks CC	0.2	0.4	1.3	0.4	97.5	0.1	1,370
Gogebic CC	1.7	0.3	0.6	0.0	97.5	0.0	1,178
Grace Bible C	1.5	0.0	2.3	3.1	89.3	3.8	131
Grand Rapids Baptist C and Sem	0.1	0.2	1.3	0.2	97.1	1.1	929
Grand Rapids JC	0.9	1.3	6.4	1.6	89.6	0.2	10,634
Grand Valley St U	0.3	0.8	2.9	1.1	94.7	0.3	9,768
Great Lakes Bible C	0.0	0.8	0.0	0.0	99.2	0.0	123
Great Lakes JC of Business	0.3	0.3	12.6	4.8	81.9	0.0	1,756
Henry Ford CC	0.5	1.4	13.3	2.1	82.6	0.1	15,791
Highland Park CC	1.6	0.0	98.2	0.0	0.2	0.0	2,342
Hillsdale C	0.0	0.0	1.1	0.0	97.4	1.5	1,071
Hope C	0.4	0.9	0.9	1.0	94.4	2.5	2,781
Jackson CC	0.6	0.7	11.3	1.5	85.6	0.2	5,782
Jordan C	0.4	0.2	58.3	0.7	40.3	0.0	2,271
Kalamazoo C	0.2	4.7	1.8	0.7	87.8	4.9	1,255
Kalamazoo Valley CC	1.0	0.8	7.4	1.2	88.2	1.5	9,161
Kellogg CC	0.4	0.8	6.7	1.0	90.1	1.0	4,478
Kendall C of Art and Design	0.7	0.7	2.7	2.0	91.8	2.2	744
Kirtland CC	0.6	0.2	5.1	0.4	93.6	0.0	1,146
Lake Michigan C	0.7	0.9	12.7	0.9	84.7	0.2	3,020
Lake Superior St U	4.8	0.3	1.3	0.4	70.9	22.3	3,155
Lansing CC	0.7	1.5	6.2	2.3	88.4	0.9	21,470
Lawrence Tech U	0.6	1.7	7.3	1.3	86.8	2.3	5,443
Lewis C of Business	0.0	0.0	99.0	0.0	1.0	0.0	291
Macomb CC	0.4	1.0	1.5	0.6	96.3	0.3	31,462
Madonna C	0.4	0.6	7.6	1.5	88.1	1.8	3,950
Marygrove C	0.4	0.0	70.7	0.5	26.6	1.8	1,205
Mercy C of Detroit	0.2	1.3	37.5	1.3	59.4	0.4	2,362
Michigan Christian C	0.4	0.8	19.2	1.9	74.1	3.8	266
Michigan St U	0.3	1.8	6.1	1.4	85.3	5.1	44,480
Michigan Tech U	0.5	1.4	0.6	0.5	92.2	4.8	6,502
Mid Michigan CC	0.6	0.2	0.4	0.5	97.4	0.8	1,910
Monroe County CC	0.2	0.4	1.1	0.8	97.2	0.2	3,083
Montcalm CC	0.7	0.6	10.0	2.4	86.3	0.0	1,918
Muskegon C	0.1	0.1	8.0	1.6	90.2	0.0	1,741
Muskegon CC	2.9	0.3	7.4	1.8	87.5	0.1	4,941
Nazareth C	0.0	1.0	5.6	1.2	92.2	0.0	730
Northern Michigan U	1.6	0.4	2.2	0.6	94.7	0.5	8,185
Northwestern Michigan C	1.9	0.4	0.3	0.5	96.9	0.1	4,307
Northwood Inst	0.7	0.2	7.4	0.0	76.6	15.1	1,809
Oakland CC	0.5	1.4	9.5	1.5	86.7	0.3	26,854
Oakland U	0.2	1.9	5.2	1.0	90.9	0.9	12,254
Olivet C	0.0	0.6	9.1	0.8	89.5	0.0	783
Reformed Bible C	1.1	3.7	0.0	2.1	61.7	31.4	188
Sacred Heart Major Sem	0.0	0.0	9.1	4.6	86.3	0.0	197
Saginaw Valley St U	0.5	0.7	5.5	2.7	90.1	0.6	5,850
Saint Clair County CC	0.2	0.1	1.5	1.2	96.3	0.7	4,064
Saint Mary's C	0.4	5.8	3.9	1.5	85.7	2.7	259
Schoolcraft C	0.2	0.9	3.5	0.6	94.2	0.6	8,499
Siena Heights C	0.1	0.5	6.5	4.0	87.6	1.3	1,667
Southwestern Michigan C	0.7	0.5	6.3	1.0	89.3	2.2	2,492
Spring Arbor C	0.2	0.7	14.4	0.8	82.3	1.7	1,319
Thomas M Cooley Law Sch	0.0	1.4	3.7	3.0	91.2	0.6	1,254

	American Indian	Asian	Black	Hispanic	White	Foreign	Total
U of Detroit	0.4%	1.8%	18.3%	1.1%	73.1%	5.3%	6,021
U of Michigan							
Ann Arbor	0.4	5.8	5.8	2.3	78.8	6.9	36,001
Dearborn	0.6	3.3	5.7	1.9	88.1	0.5	7,494
Flint	1.0	1.1	8.3	1.2	88.4	0.0	6,310
Walsh C of Accountancy and Business Admin	0.3	1.7	4.3	0.5	92.9	0.3	2,663
Washtenaw CC	0.9	2.8	11.4	1.2	83.4	0.3	9,523
Wayne County CC	0.8	1.2	64.7	2.1	29.6	1.6	12,098
Wayne St U	0.6	3.5	21.9	1.6	67.8	4.6	30,751
West Shore CC	0.7	0.3	1.1	1.1	96.8	0.0	1,186
Western Michigan U	0.3	0.6	4.6	0.7	90.1	3.7	24,861
Western Theological Sem	0.0	0.7	1.4	0.7	91.4	5.7	140
William Tyndale C	0.2	1.2	30.4	0.5	67.2	0.5	418
Yeshiva Gedolah Rabbinical C	0.0	0.0	0.0	0.0	100.0	0.0	43

MINNESOTA

	American Indian	Asian	Black	Hispanic	White	Foreign	Total
Alexandria Tech Inst	0.7	0.2	0.0	0.3	98.8	0.1	1,674
Augsburg C	1.7	1.9	3.3	0.4	89.9	2.7	2,506
Bethany Lutheran C	0.3	0.3	2.2	0.0	95.5	1.6	312
Bethel C	0.2	0.7	0.8	0.2	98.1	0.0	1,800
Bethel Theological Sem	0.4	2.8	3.0	0.6	90.0	3.2	501
Carleton C	0.4	5.6	3.3	2.5	87.5	0.7	1,897
C of Saint Benedict	0.1	1.1	0.2	0.6	96.8	1.3	1,961
C of Saint Catherine	0.6	1.2	0.9	1.3	93.4	2.5	2,727
C of Saint Catherine Saint Mary's campus	1.1	0.6	6.3	0.7	90.9	0.4	536
C of Saint Scholastica	1.9	0.4	0.3	0.2	96.6	0.6	1,849
C of Saint Teresa	0.4	0.8	0.8	2.0	96.0	0.0	249
C of Saint Thomas	0.3	1.2	1.0	0.5	96.3	0.8	8,810
Concordia C Moorhead	0.7	0.8	0.2	0.3	95.2	2.8	2,880
Concordia C Saint Paul	0.3	4.2	3.2	0.0	91.5	0.8	1,133
Dakota County Tech Inst	0.2	1.3	0.4	0.4	97.8	0.0	1,613
Dr Martin Luther C	0.4	0.0	1.3	0.0	98.2	0.0	447
Gustavus Adolphus C	0.1	0.3	1.2	0.1	96.5	1.8	2,451
Hamline U	0.1	1.8	2.1	0.6	94.2	1.3	2,223
Luther Northwestern Theological Sem	0.4	1.4	1.2	0.6	94.5	1.9	724
Macalester C	0.9	2.2	3.2	1.5	84.1	8.1	1,847
Mayo Foundation							
Grad Sch of Medicine	0.4	3.7	2.4	1.4	75.2	16.9	1,105
Medical Sch	1.9	7.0	1.3	1.9	87.9	0.0	157
Medical Inst of Minnesota	0.8	5.0	3.7	1.7	88.7	0.0	240
Minneapolis C of Art and Design	0.7	2.8	2.1	1.3	92.1	1.0	713
Minnesota Bible C	0.0	2.2	0.0	0.0	94.4	3.3	90
Minnesota CC Sys							
Anoka-Ramsey CC	0.6	0.5	0.3	0.3	98.3	0.1	5,844
Arrowhead CC Region							
Hibbing CC	1.3	0.0	0.4	0.0	98.3	0.0	1,345
Itasca CC	7.8	0.0	0.8	0.1	91.2	0.2	1,245
Mesabi CC	4.5	0.1	1.2	0.1	93.8	0.3	1,481
Rainy River CC	15.2	0.2	0.7	0.2	82.7	1.1	613
Vermilion CC	1.6	0.2	0.3	0.5	97.4	0.0	576
Austin CC	0.1	0.3	0.3	0.2	98.2	0.9	1,106

MINNESOTA, cont.

	American Indian	Asian	Black	Hispanic	White	Foreign	Total
Minnesota CC Sys							
Brainerd CC	2.6%	0.5%	0.5%	0.1%	96.0%	0.3%	1,526
Fergus Falls CC	0.2	0.0	0.4	0.1	99.0	0.4	1,090
Inver Hills CC	0.1	1.1	1.5	0.6	96.6	0.1	4,853
Lakewood CC	0.2	2.3	0.7	0.7	96.0	0.1	5,277
Minneapolis CC	2.7	2.6	13.5	1.2	75.5	4.5	3,266
Normandale CC	0.1	1.4	0.7	0.2	96.9	0.6	8,560
North Hennepin CC	0.3	0.4	1.1	0.4	96.1	1.7	5,498
Northland CC	7.4	0.1	0.9	0.3	91.4	0.0	1,033
Rochester CC	0.4	2.2	0.6	0.4	95.8	0.6	3,839
Willmar CC	0.3	0.3	0.2	0.8	98.4	0.1	1,325
Worthington CC	0.5	1.1	1.1	0.2	96.4	0.8	854
National C at Saint Paul	1.5	12.3	4.5	6.3	68.8	6.6	333
National Education Center							
Brown Inst	1.3	5.2	4.1	1.0	87.7	0.7	1,655
North Central Bible C	0.5	1.0	2.6	1.0	92.6	2.4	1,146
Northwestern C	0.2	0.6	1.6	0.4	96.4	0.7	973
Northwestern C of							
Chiropractic	0.0	0.7	0.2	0.9	93.3	4.9	569
Oak Hills Bible C	0.0	0.0	0.0	0.8	99.2	0.0	129
Pillsbury Baptist Bible C	0.5	0.0	1.3	1.8	94.9	1.5	391
Rasmussen Business C	0.2	0.0	1.4	0.5	97.7	0.2	427
Saint John's U	0.3	1.0	0.8	0.7	95.1	2.2	1,998
Saint Mary's C	0.8	0.8	1.1	0.7	95.2	1.4	1,938
Saint Olaf C	0.2	1.8	0.5	0.4	95.5	1.6	3,118
Saint Paul Bible C	0.2	7.4	0.4	0.2	91.1	0.8	526
Saint Paul Tech Inst	1.4	1.1	1.2	0.7	95.1	0.5	1,678
Sch of the Associated Arts	0.7	1.5	1.5	0.0	96.3	0.0	134
St U Sys							
Bemidji St U	3.8	0.0	0.3	0.3	94.6	0.9	4,996
Mankato St U	0.2	1.0	0.7	0.4	95.9	1.9	15,944
Metropolitan St U	0.7	0.9	3.3	0.9	94.2	0.0	5,799
Moorhead St U	0.6	0.6	0.3	0.3	97.1	1.2	8,103
Saint Cloud St U	0.3	0.7	0.7	0.3	97.3	0.7	16,252
Southwest St U	0.1	0.2	1.3	0.0	97.4	1.0	2,475
Winona St U	0.5	0.9	0.6	0.4	95.1	2.5	7,079
U of Minnesota							
Crookston	0.5	0.2	0.2	1.0	97.4	0.7	1,221
Duluth	1.0	0.7	0.7	0.3	96.2	1.2	9,523
Morris	2.0	1.7	2.0	1.0	92.9	0.5	2,178
Twin Cities	0.5	3.0	1.6	1.0	90.0	4.1	61,556
Waseca	0.1	0.2	0.2	0.0	99.1	0.4	1,169
United Theological Sem							
of the Twin Cities	1.0	1.4	1.4	1.0	93.7	1.4	207
William Mitchell C of Law	0.6	1.2	2.2	1.2	94.8	0.0	1,089

MISSISSIPPI

Alcorn St U	0.0	0.4	91.6	0.2	7.8	0.0	2,757
Belhaven C	0.1	0.3	7.1	1.0	88.2	3.3	693
Blue Mountain C	0.0	0.3	7.5	0.3	91.6	0.3	332
Clarke C	0.0	0.0	22.4	0.0	77.6	0.0	116
Coahoma CC	0.0	0.0	98.6	1.4	0.0	0.0	1,407
Copiah-Lincoln CC	0.4	0.4	25.2	0.4	73.6	0.1	1,382
Delta St U	0.1	0.5	19.5	0.1	79.8	0.0	3,672
East Central JC	2.7	0.0	5.7	0.0	91.6	0.0	3,624
East Mississippi CC	0.1	0.1	36.5	0.1	63.2	0.0	896

	American Indian	Asian	Black	Hispanic	White	Foreign	Total
Hinds CC Raymond	0.1%	0.4%	35.3%	0.2%	63.9%	0.2%	8,228
Holmes JC	0.0	0.1	19.9	0.1	79.7	0.2	1,827
Itawamba CC	0.0	0.1	16.1	0.0	83.6	0.2	2,633
Jackson St U	0.1	0.4	93.0	0.1	3.5	2.9	6,777
Jones County JC	0.3	0.1	18.5	0.2	80.9	0.0	3,252
Mary Holmes C	0.0	0.0	99.2	0.0	0.2	0.6	519
Meridian CC	1.5	0.8	25.3	0.6	71.6	0.1	2,844
Millsaps C	0.0	1.8	4.8	0.6	91.9	0.8	1,445
Mississippi C	0.1	0.5	11.8	0.4	86.9	0.3	3,540
Mississippi Delta JC	0.1	0.4	41.9	0.2	57.5	0.0	1,712
Mississippi Gulf Coast JC	0.8	1.0	13.7	0.9	82.7	0.9	8,393
Mississippi St U	0.2	1.2	11.1	0.2	82.8	4.5	12,407
Mississippi U for Women	0.3	0.3	17.8	0.2	81.3	0.0	2,063
Mississippi Valley St U	0.0	0.0	99.3	0.0	0.7	0.0	1,756
Northeast Mississippi JC	0.0	0.1	11.2	0.0	88.7	0.0	2,735
Northwest Mississippi JC	0.0	0.1	24.2	0.1	75.6	0.0	3,619
Pearl River JC	0.2	0.1	16.1	0.1	83.5	0.0	2,336
Phillips JC Gulfport	0.0	0.5	21.6	0.1	77.7	0.0	772
Phillips JC Jackson	0.1	0.0	43.4	0.0	56.4	0.0	677
Prentiss Normal and Industrial Inst	0.0	0.0	100.0	0.0	0.0	0.0	47
Reformed Theological Sem	0.3	1.1	0.8	0.6	86.0	11.3	363
Rust C	0.0	0.0	96.1	0.0	2.8	1.1	925
Southeastern Baptist C	0.0	0.0	5.1	0.0	94.9	0.0	79
Southwest Mississippi JC	0.0	0.0	20.9	0.0	79.1	0.0	1,353
Tougaloo C	0.0	0.0	99.7	0.0	0.3	0.0	794
U of Mississippi Main	0.1	0.5	6.6	0.2	87.6	5.1	9,927
U of Mississippi Medical Ctr	0.1	2.0	10.8	0.5	83.5	3.1	1,404
U of Southern Mississippi	0.3	0.7	13.4	0.4	83.2	2.1	12,581
Wesley Biblical Sem	0.0	0.0	10.7	0.0	83.9	5.4	56
Wesley C	1.8	0.0	5.4	0.0	92.9	0.0	56
William Carey C	0.2	0.2	18.7	0.6	79.1	1.2	1,931
Wood JC	0.0	0.0	10.5	0.0	88.3	1.2	486

MISSOURI

Aquinas Inst of Theology	0.0	0.0	0.9	0.9	98.1	0.0	107
Assemblies of God Theol Sem	0.3	1.3	1.7	2.7	91.6	2.3	298
Avila C	0.7	1.5	8.5	2.0	87.4	0.0	1,585
Baptist Bible C	0.1	0.4	0.4	0.8	97.3	1.0	781
Calvary Bible C	0.0	1.6	4.7	0.6	90.5	2.5	317
Central Bible C	0.9	2.0	1.1	2.4	92.7	0.8	881
Central Christian C of the Bible	0.0	0.0	1.2	0.0	96.4	2.4	83
Central Methodist C	0.0	0.1	7.5	0.4	89.4	2.5	710
Central Missouri St U	0.0	0.4	7.5	0.3	88.8	2.9	10,104
Cleveland Chiropractic C	0.3	1.3	1.0	2.3	90.3	4.9	308
Columbia C	1.5	1.7	13.7	2.3	79.9	0.8	3,566
Conception Sem C	0.0	2.6	0.0	6.4	88.5	2.6	78
Concordia Sem	0.0	0.8	0.6	0.0	95.3	3.2	493
Cottey C	0.3	0.9	0.6	1.7	91.4	5.1	350
Covenant Theological Sem	0.0	3.3	3.3	0.0	88.9	4.6	153
Crowder C	1.1	0.3	0.9	0.3	97.2	0.1	1,487
Culver-Stockton C	0.0	0.9	5.0	0.0	94.1	0.0	1,032
DeVry Inst of Tech	0.5	4.2	9.8	1.1	83.9	0.7	1,692
Drury C	0.4	0.3	2.4	0.4	95.8	0.7	3,158

MISSOURI, cont.

	American Indian	Asian	Black	Hispanic	White	Foreign	Total
East Central C	0.2%	0.0%	0.3%	0.1%	99.3%	0.1%	2,509
Eden Theological Sem	0.0	3.0	5.6	0.0	89.4	2.0	198
Evangel C	0.4	0.4	3.4	1.2	94.4	0.3	1,564
Fontbonne C	0.0	1.2	10.6	0.4	82.0	5.8	1,036
Forest Inst of Professional Psychology	1.3	2.5	2.5	1.3	91.1	1.3	79
Hannibal-La Grange C	0.4	0.3	1.3	0.3	97.4	0.4	763
Harris-Stowe St C	0.2	0.2	78.3	0.4	20.2	0.8	1,725
ITT Tech Inst	0.0	0.2	21.2	0.0	78.6	0.0	617
Jefferson C	0.2	0.4	0.6	0.3	98.4	0.1	3,294
Kemper Military Sch and C	1.0	5.8	28.8	2.6	60.2	1.6	191
Kenrick-Glennon Sem	0.0	1.5	1.5	0.0	97.1	0.0	68
Kirksville C of Osteopathic Medicine	0.8	4.5	0.2	3.4	90.6	0.6	531
Lincoln U	0.5	0.4	26.8	0.2	69.5	2.7	2,743
Lindenwood C	0.1	1.4	11.0	0.5	86.7	0.3	1,771
Logan C of Chiropractic	0.3	1.1	1.9	0.4	92.3	4.0	699
Maryville C	0.2	0.6	3.2	0.6	92.8	2.6	2,934
Metropolitan CC Sys							
Longview CC	0.2	0.6	5.4	0.8	92.8	0.2	7,684
Maple Woods CC	0.3	0.6	0.8	1.0	97.2	0.1	3,848
Penn Valley CC	0.4	2.4	34.8	3.1	55.9	3.5	5,481
Mineral Area C	0.0	0.2	0.3	0.0	99.5	0.0	2,205
Missouri Baptist C	0.4	1.2	14.0	0.5	79.9	4.1	849
Missouri Southern St C	1.2	0.5	0.9	0.5	96.7	0.1	5,404
Missouri Valley C	1.3	1.6	26.1	2.2	68.4	0.3	1,175
Missouri Western St C	1.8	0.4	3.0	0.6	94.2	0.0	4,083
Moberly Area JC	0.4	0.3	9.5	0.5	88.0	1.3	1,317
National Education Ctr Kansas City	2.8	0.6	42.5	4.4	48.6	1.1	181
Nazarene Theological Sem	0.7	1.2	2.2	1.5	85.8	8.6	409
North Central Missouri C	0.3	0.3	1.5	0.0	98.0	0.0	737
Northeast Missouri St U	0.0	0.2	3.1	0.2	93.8	2.5	6,419
Northwest Missouri St U	1.0	0.1	2.4	0.3	93.7	2.5	5,306
Ozark Christian C	0.0	0.0	0.6	1.4	96.3	1.8	514
Platt JC	1.5	1.1	4.6	1.5	91.2	0.0	262
Research C of Nursing	0.0	0.9	3.6	0.9	94.6	0.0	112
Rockhurst C	0.1	1.9	7.5	2.0	87.6	1.0	3,125
Saint Louis Christian C	0.0	0.0	2.5	0.0	89.8	7.6	118
Saint Louis C of Pharmacy	0.0	2.6	3.2	0.3	92.7	1.2	772
Saint Louis CC	0.1	0.8	15.0	0.8	83.2	0.2	30,291
Saint Louis Conservatory of Music	0.0	4.4	2.6	3.5	67.5	21.9	114
Saint Louis U	0.2	3.7	6.0	1.6	85.2	3.3	12,935
Saint Paul Sch of Theology	0.0	0.8	5.1	0.4	92.0	1.7	237
Sch of the Ozarks	0.0	0.3	1.7	0.1	95.6	2.4	1,310
Southeast Missouri St U	0.1	0.3	7.6	0.2	88.9	2.9	8,778
Southwest Baptist U	0.3	2.6	3.5	0.4	93.2	0.1	1,834
Southwest Missouri St U	0.2	0.9	1.4	0.5	96.4	0.6	17,006
State Fair CC	0.3	0.2	3.0	0.7	95.7	0.0	1,750
Stephens C	0.2	0.8	3.7	0.7	94.7	0.0	1,256
TAD Tech Inst	0.0	5.1	8.6	1.7	84.6	0.0	175
Tarkio C	0.0	0.4	13.7	7.5	78.0	0.3	2,063
Three Rivers CC	0.0	0.2	2.1	0.1	97.6	0.0	1,776
U of Missouri							
Columbia	0.3	1.3	3.4	0.8	88.5	5.7	23,568
Kansas City	0.6	3.1	6.7	1.8	84.3	3.6	11,628

	American Indian	Asian	Black	Hispanic	White	Foreign	Total
Rolla	0.4%	4.8%	2.4%	0.9%	85.4%	6.2%	5,724
Saint Louis	0.2	2.2	9.5	0.8	86.9	0.4	13,932
Washington U	0.1	5.6	4.5	1.5	82.0	6.4	11,498
Webster U	0.4	1.2	11.7	2.9	82.6	1.3	8,120
Wentworth Military Academy and JC	0.5	0.5	4.4	1.1	92.1	1.4	366
Westminster C	0.4	0.7	1.9	0.1	96.7	0.1	689
William Jewell C	0.2	0.3	1.5	0.1	97.9	0.1	1,984
William Woods C	0.1	0.0	0.4	0.1	99.3	0.0	760

MONTANA

Blackfeet CC	91.9	0.0	0.3	0.0	7.7	0.0	297
Carroll C	0.6	0.8	0.3	0.2	96.1	2.0	1,413
C of Great Falls	5.0	0.8	2.4	1.7	88.2	1.9	1,187
Dawson CC	4.0	0.0	0.6	0.4	94.5	0.6	531
Dull Knife Memorial C	84.9	0.0	0.6	0.0	14.5	0.0	179
Flathead Valley CC	2.2	0.6	0.0	1.5	95.4	0.3	1,900
Fort Peck CC	84.6	0.0	0.0	0.4	15.0	0.0	234
Miles CC	3.5	0.0	0.0	0.3	95.3	0.8	593
Montana U Sys							
Eastern Montana C	5.0	0.4	0.3	1.2	92.9	0.2	3,992
Montana C of Mineral Science and Tech	0.4	0.2	0.3	0.8	92.8	5.5	1,818
Montana St U	2.0	0.4	0.3	0.6	94.7	2.1	10,024
Northern Montana C	8.8	0.3	0.4	0.4	89.3	0.8	1,593
U of Montana	2.3	0.3	0.5	0.7	93.2	3.0	8,879
Western Montana C	0.7	0.4	0.2	0.5	98.3	0.0	1,097
Rocky Mountain C	1.4	1.0	0.6	2.4	91.1	3.5	705
Salish Kootenai CC	68.5	0.0	0.0	0.0	31.5	0.0	704

NEBRASKA

Bellevue C	1.5	0.5	5.4	2.0	90.0	0.5	1,862
Bishop Clarkson C	0.0	0.4	2.3	0.7	96.6	0.0	565
Central Tech CC Area	0.3	0.3	0.2	0.7	98.5	0.0	9,676
Chadron St C	0.2	0.7	0.3	0.2	98.6	0.0	2,450
C of Saint Mary	0.3	0.4	4.0	1.1	94.1	0.2	1,133
Concordia Teachers C	0.1	0.1	1.3	0.3	96.8	1.4	779
Creighton U	0.3	4.3	2.5	2.6	87.4	3.0	5,958
Dana C	0.6	1.2	5.6	0.6	89.1	2.8	496
Doane C	0.2	0.0	2.4	0.5	93.4	3.5	935
Gateway Electronics Inst	0.0	0.0	1.6	0.5	97.9	0.0	188
Grace C of the Bible	1.9	1.5	2.2	0.4	90.0	4.1	269
Hastings C	0.2	0.5	4.6	1.0	93.4	0.3	935
Kearney St C	0.1	0.2	0.2	0.6	97.9	0.9	9,094
McCook CC	0.1	0.2	0.8	0.9	97.6	0.4	922
Metropolitan CC	2.4	1.8	11.1	2.2	82.5	0.0	6,629
Mid Plains CC	0.2	0.1	0.2	1.5	98.0	0.0	1,983
Midland Lutheran C	0.4	0.7	4.3	1.1	92.7	0.8	910
Nebraska Christian C	0.0	0.0	0.0	0.7	98.6	0.7	148
Neb C of Tech Agriculture	0.0	0.0	0.0	0.0	100.0	0.0	208
Nebraska Methodist C of Nursing and Allied Health	0.0	0.4	3.8	0.8	94.1	0.8	238
Nebraska Wesleyan U	0.2	0.8	1.0	0.6	96.8	0.7	1,527
Northeast CC	0.3	0.1	0.2	0.2	99.2	0.0	2,687
Peru St C	0.3	0.2	3.6	0.4	95.1	0.3	1,441

	American Indian	Asian	Black	Hispanic	White	Foreign	Total
NEBRASKA, cont.							
Southeast CC							
Beatrice	0.0%	0.4%	1.4%	0.0%	98.1%	0.2%	569
Lincoln	0.4	0.9	1.3	0.9	96.3	0.2	4,409
Milford	0.1	0.2	0.1	0.2	98.9	0.5	883
Union C	0.8	0.8	2.1	2.9	84.9	8.5	615
U of Nebraska							
Lincoln	0.2	0.7	1.6	0.9	92.4	4.1	23,985
Medical Center	0.4	2.6	2.3	1.6	90.6	2.5	2,278
Omaha	0.2	1.0	4.1	1.4	92.2	1.1	14,985
Wayne St C	0.3	0.2	1.3	0.2	97.6	0.4	2,874
Western Nebraska CC	1.0	0.0	0.4	4.2	94.2	0.2	2,508
York C	1.8	0.0	3.3	1.1	91.3	2.5	276
NEVADA							
Sierra Nevada C	0.0	0.0	0.0	0.0	96.9	3.1	161
U of Nevada Sys							
Las Vegas	0.5	3.6	5.5	5.0	84.1	1.2	14,673
Reno	1.1	2.5	1.9	2.5	88.5	3.6	10,506
Clark County CC	1.3	3.9	9.6	6.8	78.4	0.0	10,519
Northern Nevada CC	5.6	1.3	0.4	6.6	86.2	0.0	1,596
Truckee Meadows CC	2.1	3.4	1.4	4.0	87.9	1.3	9,006
Western Nevada CC	2.7	3.0	4.5	6.0	83.4	0.5	2,346
NEW HAMPSHIRE							
Antioch New England Graduate Sch	0.0	0.0	1.1	0.5	96.7	1.7	645
Castle JC	0.0	0.0	0.0	1.4	97.9	0.7	146
Colby-Sawyer C	0.0	0.4	0.7	0.0	98.7	0.2	446
Daniel Webster C	0.1	0.6	1.4	0.6	96.0	1.2	1,088
Dartmouth C	1.7	5.3	5.6	2.3	78.7	6.3	4,777
Franklin Pierce C	0.1	0.6	2.2	1.5	95.1	0.5	3,568
Franklin Pierce Law Center	0.9	0.9	0.6	0.3	97.4	0.0	341
Magdalen C	0.0	0.0	0.0	0.0	98.1	1.9	52
New England C	0.1	0.0	0.3	0.0	97.2	2.5	1,128
New Hampshire C	0.0	1.2	1.0	4.6	89.1	4.1	6,308
NH Tech C Berlin	0.2	0.0	0.0	0.0	99.8	0.0	496
NH Tech C Claremont	0.0	0.0	0.0	0.0	100.0	0.0	460
NH Tech C Laconia	0.9	0.2	0.4	1.1	97.4	0.0	539
NH Tech C Manchester	0.0	0.3	0.0	0.0	99.7	0.0	1,190
NH Tech C Nashua	0.6	1.1	1.2	0.8	96.3	0.0	1,045
NH Tech C Stratham	1.6	0.9	0.6	0.6	96.0	0.2	849
New Hampshire Tech Inst	0.0	0.2	0.5	0.0	99.2	0.0	2,098
Notre Dame C	0.5	0.1	0.0	0.4	98.9	0.1	842
Rivier C	0.2	1.4	0.9	1.5	94.4	1.4	2,427
Saint Anselm C	0.1	0.1	0.1	0.2	99.2	0.5	1,934
U Sys of New Hampshire							
U of New Hampshire	0.2	0.5	0.3	0.5	97.2	1.2	12,984
Plymouth St C	0.3	0.5	0.3	0.3	98.3	0.3	3,936
Sch For Lifelong Learning	0.3	0.4	0.9	1.1	97.0	0.3	1,592
U of NH Manchester	0.6	0.4	0.4	0.5	98.0	0.1	1,564
White Pines C	0.0	0.0	0.0	0.0	87.5	12.5	48
NEW JERSEY							
Assumption C for Sisters	0.0	40.7	0.0	0.0	59.3	0.0	27

	American Indian	Asian	Black	Hispanic	White	Foreign	Total
Atlantic CC	0.5%	2.5%	10.0%	3.3%	82.1%	1.6%	4,303
Bergen CC	0.1	4.8	4.2	7.5	79.5	3.8	10,923
Berkeley Sch C of Business	0.0	0.1	9.4	11.4	79.1	0.0	731
Beth Medrash Govoha	0.0	0.0	0.0	0.9	93.6	5.4	1,161
Bloomfield C	0.1	2.1	36.8	6.9	53.4	0.7	1,484
Brookdale CC	0.1	2.9	6.1	2.4	88.2	0.3	10,633
Burlington County C	0.3	2.0	14.3	2.3	80.3	0.8	6,252
Caldwell C	0.0	1.8	10.1	3.1	83.1	2.0	945
Camden County C	0.1	2.4	11.6	2.2	83.7	0.1	9,358
Centenary C	0.0	1.1	9.5	2.8	83.4	3.3	613
C of Saint Elizabeth	0.1	2.7	7.5	6.9	80.5	2.3	1,039
County C of Morris	0.2	3.2	2.5	3.0	89.2	1.9	8,401
Cumberland County C	1.3	0.1	10.7	7.2	79.1	1.5	2,246
Don Bosco C	0.0	17.1	0.0	7.3	75.6	0.0	41
Drew U	0.2	2.9	5.8	2.2	83.4	5.5	2,346
Essex County C	0.2	1.6	55.2	17.2	20.0	5.7	5,664
Fairleigh Dickinson U							
Main	0.8	4.6	6.7	4.2	77.4	6.3	4,972
Edward Williams C	0.1	3.9	14.9	8.2	70.8	2.1	1,549
Madison	0.2	2.4	6.6	1.2	89.0	0.7	3,709
Rutherford	0.2	2.5	6.7	4.1	80.7	5.9	2,447
Felician C	0.2	4.2	7.3	5.7	80.5	2.3	619
Georgian Court C	0.1	0.6	2.9	2.5	93.6	0.3	2,054
Glassboro St C	0.5	1.2	8.2	2.5	86.0	1.7	9,495
Gloucester County C	0.1	0.6	7.0	1.0	87.5	3.8	3,672
Hudson County CC	0.6	10.0	14.5	46.6	23.9	4.4	2,736
Jersey City St C	0.1	5.2	13.7	14.9	52.8	13.3	7,482
Katharine Gibbs Sch	0.3	1.5	18.3	10.7	69.1	0.0	327
Kean C of New Jersey	0.1	2.6	12.3	9.0	74.3	1.7	12,404
Mercer County CC	0.3	2.2	12.9	4.2	78.5	1.9	8,643
Middlesex County C	0.8	7.5	7.3	7.4	75.7	1.2	11,220
Monmouth C	0.1	2.3	3.8	1.9	87.2	4.7	4,430
Montclair St C	0.7	1.9	7.3	7.9	80.4	1.8	12,657
New Brunswick Theol Sem	0.0	7.4	31.9	5.2	53.3	2.2	135
Northeastern Bible C	0.5	2.6	13.8	5.6	74.4	3.1	195
Ocean County C	0.8	0.9	2.2	1.7	94.3	0.0	6,214
Passaic County CC	0.1	5.2	20.9	45.3	23.3	5.1	2,837
Princeton Theological Sem	0.1	5.7	7.4	1.2	77.1	8.5	767
Princeton U	0.2	6.4	4.7	3.2	70.5	15.0	6,338
Ramapo C of New Jersey	0.1	1.5	7.6	2.6	85.6	2.7	4,046
Raritan Valley CC	0.5	3.7	3.2	2.0	90.6	0.0	4,841
Rider C	0.7	0.8	4.6	3.2	89.4	1.3	5,415
Rutgers U							
Camden	0.4	2.7	8.7	2.7	85.1	0.4	5,187
New Brunswick	0.1	7.3	7.6	4.9	74.6	5.4	32,901
Newark	0.1	6.9	18.0	9.2	61.5	4.3	9,694
Saint Peter's C	0.1	5.7	7.0	13.0	72.6	1.6	3,346
Salem CC	0.4	1.2	13.6	3.2	81.6	0.0	1,202
Seton Hall U	0.1	2.1	7.3	4.6	84.6	1.3	9,284
Stevens Inst of Tech	0.2	12.1	3.3	5.1	52.6	26.7	2,859
Stockton St C	0.4	1.4	10.7	2.5	84.5	0.6	5,287
Sussex Co CC Commission	0.0	0.1	0.2	0.4	99.3	0.0	1,759
Thomas A Edison St C	0.5	0.8	8.3	2.9	83.6	4.0	6,842
Trenton St C	0.2	1.7	8.4	2.8	86.0	0.8	7,416
Union County C	0.0	1.1	15.7	5.7	64.0	13.4	8,741
U of Medicine and Dentistry of New Jersey	0.1	7.8	7.4	4.9	72.6	7.2	2,901

NEW JERSEY, cont.

	American Indian	Asian	Black	Hispanic	White	Foreign	Total
Upsala C							
Main	0.0%	2.3%	36.9%	4.8%	54.4%	1.6%	1,093
Wirths	0.0	1.2	0.3	0.6	97.9	0.0	329
Warren Co CC Commission	0.1	0.1	1.2	0.5	96.7	1.4	999
Westminster Choir C	0.3	3.7	8.6	2.6	82.7	2.0	347
William Paterson C	0.2	1.2	5.8	4.8	87.3	0.7	9,222

NEW MEXICO

	American Indian	Asian	Black	Hispanic	White	Foreign	Total
Albuquerque Tech-Voc Inst	8.5	1.6	3.4	35.1	51.3	0.0	7,778
C of Santa Fe	10.1	0.9	3.9	28.2	56.8	0.2	1,289
C of the Southwest	0.0	1.0	1.9	13.8	79.0	4.3	210
Eastern New Mexico U							
Main	1.3	1.0	4.7	15.4	75.5	2.0	3,765
Roswell	1.1	0.1	1.7	24.8	72.3	0.1	1,595
Clovis	0.9	1.3	6.1	13.0	77.8	0.9	2,806
Inst of American Indian and Alaska Native Culture and Arts Development	94.1	0.0	0.0	0.0	5.9	0.0	119
National C Albuquerque	5.5	2.4	1.6	48.8	41.7	0.0	127
New Mexico Highlands U	3.7	0.3	2.3	70.8	22.0	0.8	2,017
NM Inst of Mining and Tech	3.0	1.6	0.3	9.7	74.0	11.4	1,222
New Mexico JC	0.6	0.3	4.4	12.5	81.5	0.7	2,513
New Mexico Military Inst	0.7	5.1	5.6	16.0	69.3	3.3	449
New Mexico St U							
Main	2.1	0.5	1.4	24.0	68.6	3.4	14,279
Alamogordo	2.9	1.5	4.6	15.2	75.8	0.0	1,680
Carlsbad	1.2	0.7	0.6	19.7	77.7	0.0	964
Dona Ana	2.9	0.3	1.9	42.1	51.4	1.5	1,366
Grants	16.9	0.4	0.2	28.0	54.4	0.0	485
Northern New Mexico CC	10.0	0.6	0.4	73.0	16.1	0.0	1,445
Saint John's C	0.2	1.4	0.9	2.1	95.1	0.2	430
San Juan C	27.5	0.2	0.1	10.1	61.6	0.4	2,851
Santa Fe CC	1.7	0.6	0.5	49.0	48.1	0.2	2,351
U of New Mexico							
Main	3.2	2.0	1.6	21.3	69.6	2.4	24,433
Gallup	68.8	0.5	0.6	8.3	21.7	0.1	1,610
Los Alamos	1.5	1.7	0.4	18.2	76.6	1.5	920
Valencia	2.0	0.1	0.7	49.7	47.6	0.0	1,066
Western New Mexico U	1.9	0.5	2.1	38.2	56.0	1.4	1,680

NEW YORK

	American Indian	Asian	Black	Hispanic	White	Foreign	Total
Adelphi U	0.1	2.3	8.6	3.8	85.0	0.3	9,068
Albany Business C	0.3	0.6	26.6	0.3	70.3	2.0	357
Albany C of Pharmacy	0.3	3.8	1.5	1.1	91.6	1.7	653
Albany Law Sch	0.3	2.1	3.8	1.6	91.6	0.7	765
Albany Medical C	0.0	13.6	2.1	2.2	80.3	1.7	631
Alfred U	0.2	1.2	3.5	1.4	92.2	1.6	1,736
American Academy of Dramatic Arts	0.5	0.0	3.5	4.0	76.7	15.3	202
American Acad McAllister Inst of Funeral Service	0.0	0.0	28.6	10.7	60.7	0.0	112
Bank Street C of Education	0.3	1.6	8.1	9.4	80.6	0.0	639
Bard C	0.0	1.5	3.2	2.6	90.2	2.5	929

	American Indian	Asian	Black	Hispanic	White	Foreign	Total
Barnard C	0.0%	16.2%	3.4%	3.3%	74.1%	2.8%	2,192
Berkeley Sch of Long Island	0.0	1.5	17.0	7.3	73.3	1.0	206
Berkeley Sch of Westchester	0.0	1.2	10.2	7.2	81.3	0.0	566
Beth Jacob Hebrew Teachers C	0.0	0.0	0.0	0.0	100.0	0.0	539
Bramson ORT Tech Inst	0.0	0.0	1.1	0.8	98.1	0.0	471
Briarcliffe Sch	0.4	0.4	12.8	13.6	68.8	4.0	522
Brooklyn Law Sch	0.0	3.2	3.9	5.2	87.3	0.4	1,335
Bryant & Stratton Business Inst	0.5	0.6	12.7	4.7	81.5	0.1	3,256
Bryant & Stratton Business Inst main	0.6	0.4	16.3	0.6	82.2	0.0	1,795
Canisius C	0.2	0.6	5.3	1.2	92.0	0.7	4,514
Cathedral C of the Immaculate Conception	0.0	5.9	0.0	11.8	82.4	0.0	17
Cazenovia C	0.2	0.7	3.4	0.5	94.6	0.5	914
Central Yeshiva Tomchei Tmimim Lubavitz	0.0	0.0	0.0	0.0	52.9	47.1	448
Christ the King Sem	0.0	0.0	0.0	0.0	100.0	0.0	99
City U of New York							
Bernard Baruch C	0.4	19.0	17.7	13.5	46.1	3.3	16,463
Borough of Manhattan CC	0.1	7.0	54.1	29.5	7.4	1.9	12,651
Bronx CC	0.8	4.2	48.4	42.3	2.7	1.7	5,725
Brooklyn C	0.1	9.5	18.8	12.6	56.7	2.3	15,933
City C	0.4	12.4	32.0	22.7	25.1	7.5	12,778
C of Staten Island	0.7	4.2	8.2	5.7	77.3	3.8	10,678
Graduate Sch and U Center	0.5	5.7	13.2	8.2	68.4	4.1	4,139
Hostos CC	0.1	1.0	12.1	83.4	1.6	1.8	4,024
Hunter C	0.5	8.1	19.0	16.6	52.5	3.3	20,755
John Jay C of Criminal Justice	0.3	2.3	35.3	27.6	33.7	0.8	7,308
Kingsborough CC	0.3	4.6	22.3	10.6	61.5	0.7	12,817
La Guardia CC	0.4	10.8	33.1	42.0	13.6	0.0	8,994
Lehman C	7.4	4.9	24.7	26.4	35.6	1.0	9,494
Medgar Evers C	0.3	0.6	91.0	3.7	0.3	4.2	2,431
New York City Tech C	0.1	7.9	55.7	21.4	12.8	2.1	10,324
Queens C	0.2	9.1	10.6	10.6	65.0	4.5	16,944
Queensborough CC	0.6	10.1	20.8	15.2	53.2	0.0	11,644
Sch of Law Queens C	0.4	5.3	13.7	8.2	68.6	3.8	452
York C	0.3	6.2	60.0	15.7	7.1	10.6	4,832
Clarkson U	0.2	1.0	0.4	0.4	89.1	8.9	3,602
Cochran Sch of Nursing	0.0	3.5	39.5	12.8	44.2	0.0	86
Colgate Rochester-Bexley Hall-Crozer Divinity Sch	1.0	2.5	14.6	1.0	79.9	1.0	199
Colgate U	0.2	5.5	3.7	2.1	85.1	3.4	2,750
C for Human Services	1.4	0.4	71.1	18.3	8.7	0.0	703
C of Aeronautics	0.4	10.9	26.2	30.0	29.4	3.1	1,255
C of Insurance	0.0	7.7	11.8	7.0	69.4	4.1	712
C of Mount Saint Vincent	0.0	4.3	7.0	8.7	78.6	1.4	1,007
C of New Rochelle	0.1	0.8	45.5	8.9	44.4	0.2	4,491
C of Saint Rose	0.1	0.2	1.4	0.2	97.1	0.9	3,231
Columbia U	0.1	8.7	4.2	3.2	78.3	5.4	17,296
Columbia U Teachers C	0.1	3.4	10.8	5.4	69.5	10.8	4,143
Concordia C	0.6	2.3	11.2	2.7	73.2	10.1	526
Cooper Union	0.0	23.9	4.1	3.5	62.0	6.5	1,001
Cornell U Endowed C's	0.3	10.8	3.7	3.7	70.3	11.2	11,525
Cornell U Medical Center	0.0	9.4	6.8	5.2	68.4	10.1	572
Culinary Inst of America	0.1	0.4	1.1	0.8	96.2	1 5	1,835

NEW YORK, cont.

	American Indian	Asian	Black	Hispanic	White	Foreign	Total
Daemen C	0.4%	1.3%	15.3%	3.4%	79.4%	0.1%	1,630
Dominican C of Blauvelt	0.0	1.3	5.1	3.5	90.1	0.0	1,443
Dowling C	0.0	0.9	2.3	1.8	94.8	0.3	3,977
D'Youville C	0.8	0.7	9.9	3.8	79.5	5.4	1,061
Edna McConnell Clark Sch of Nursing	0.0	2.1	64.9	10.3	22.7	0.0	97
Elizabeth Seton C	0.7	2.3	42.8	14.9	39.0	0.2	979
Elmira C	0.2	1.1	1.6	0.6	96.6	0.0	1,880
Five Towns C	0.0	0.0	17.1	6.7	75.3	0.9	461
Fordham U	0.1	1.7	3.5	5.1	87.2	2.4	13,036
Friends World C	0.0	3.1	6.2	2.6	79.9	8.2	194
Hamilton C	0.1	2.7	2.4	2.0	88.7	4.1	1,643
Hartwick C	0.0	0.8	0.7	0.6	96.8	1.2	1,543
Helene Fuld Sch of Nursing	0.0	1.2	82.6	4.1	12.2	0.0	172
Hilbert C	0.6	0.0	4.6	0.9	93.7	0.2	653
Hobart and William Smith C's	0.3	0.6	3.4	1.2	93.0	1.6	1,964
Hofstra U	0.2	2.1	5.5	2.8	88.3	1.0	12,329
Holy Trinity Orthodox Sem	0.0	0.0	0.0	2.9	47.1	50.0	34
Houghton C	0.3	1.4	2.0	0.6	91.3	4.3	1,181
Inst of Design and Construction	0.0	4.1	31.7	9.9	53.1	1.2	243
Iona C	0.2	1.1	5.1	3.7	89.4	0.5	5,987
Ithaca C	0.1	0.5	2.1	1.2	95.1	1.0	6,105
Jamestown Business C	0.3	0.3	1.6	0.6	97.1	0.0	309
Jewish Theological Sem of America	0.0	0.0	0.2	0.0	96.4	3.4	494
Juilliard Sch	0.0	12.0	4.1	3.5	53.7	26.8	1,084
Katharine Gibbs Sch Melville	0.0	0.0	4.9	1.4	93.7	0.0	347
Katharine Gibbs Sch New York City	0.0	1.5	22.1	21.9	52.8	1.7	411
Keuka C	0.5	0.5	7.7	2.3	88.8	0.2	596
King's C	0.0	3.8	6.0	3.4	84.0	2.8	501
Kol Yaakov Torah Center	0.0	0.0	0.0	0.0	100.0	0.0	39
Laboratory Inst of Merchandising	0.0	3.1	7.7	8.7	79.5	1.0	195
Le Moyne C	0.2	0.8	2.4	0.6	95.8	0.2	2,270
Long Island C Hospital Sch of Nursing	0.0	1.4	57.2	6.5	34.8	0.0	138
Long Island U							
Administration	0.5	0.8	4.5	3.0	91.0	0.2	1,003
Brooklyn	0.3	6.2	42.6	12.6	34.7	3.7	5,960
C W Post	0.1	1.5	6.8	3.2	81.4	7.0	8,947
Rockland	0.0	0.6	5.0	2.1	92.1	0.2	483
Southampton C	0.9	0.8	6.0	2.8	87.9	1.7	1,262
Machzikei Hadath Rabbinical C	0.0	0.0	0.0	0.0	100.0	0.0	119
Manhattan Sch of Music	0.0	6.5	4.0	2.6	62.5	24.4	774
Manhattanville C	0.1	2.3	4.1	4.9	81.6	7.0	1,518
Mannes C of Music	0.2	11.9	5.8	4.7	69.4	8.0	536
Maria C	0.0	0.6	4.6	1.1	93.3	0.3	927
Maria Regina C	0.0	10.0	0.0	0.0	90.0	0.0	10
Marist C	0.2	0.6	8.2	5.4	85.1	0.5	4,545
Maryknoll Sch of Theology	0.0	0.0	0.0	2.5	78.7	18.8	80
Marymount C	0.0	1.6	13.0	9.5	74.2	1.7	1,248
Marymount Manhattan C	0.2	2.7	14.6	9.9	70.0	2.6	1,277
Mater Dei C	15.4	0.6	3.0	1.7	79.0	0.2	525
Medaille C	0.5	0.2	31.1	3.9	64.4	0.0	1,053

	American Indian	Asian	Black	Hispanic	White	Foreign	Total
Mesivta Eastern Parkway Rabbinical Sem	0.0%	0.0%	0.0%	0.0%	100.0%	0.0%	55
Mesivta Torah Vodaath Rabbinical Sem	0.0	0.0	0.0	0.0	100.0	0.0	435
Mirrer Yeshiva Central Inst	0.0	0.0	0.0	0.0	100.0	0.0	235
Molloy C	0.4	0.9	7.9	3.3	87.3	0.3	1,384
Monroe Business Inst main	0.7	0.4	44.9	51.0	3.0	0.0	2,101
Mount Saint Mary C	0.1	0.4	8.2	3.2	86.1	2.0	1,226
Mount Sinai Sch of Medicine	0.0	11.4	3.9	6.7	77.8	0.2	492
Nazareth C of Rochester	0.3	0.4	2.8	0.9	95.2	0.4	2,935
New Sch for Social Research	0.4	5.6	7.0	5.3	69.8	11.8	6,381
New York Chiropractic C	0.1	0.9	1.6	4.2	92.6	0.5	758
New York C of Podiatric Medicine	0.0	3.1	12.8	4.7	78.8	0.6	486
New York Inst of Tech							
Main	0.1	2.7	5.0	3.1	75.2	14.0	7,566
Central Islip	0.1	0.4	7.4	2.0	79.7	10.4	2,057
Metro	0.1	4.0	13.8	9.7	32.4	40.2	2,952
New York Law Sch	0.1	3.6	4.1	3.9	88.0	0.3	1,246
New York Medical C	0.1	9.9	9.6	3.9	75.7	0.8	1,248
New York Sch of Interior Design	0.0	8.9	8.2	19.9	58.9	4.1	637
New York Theological Sem	0.0	19.2	40.1	14.5	25.2	0.9	317
New York U	0.2	10.5	5.5	5.6	70.7	7.5	30,750
Niagara U	0.4	0.5	5.5	0.6	80.4	12.7	3,048
Nyack C	0.1	12.7	5.3	4.8	73.8	3.4	861
Ohr Somayach Insts	0.0	0.0	0.0	0.0	100.0	0.0	51
Olean Business Inst	1.3	0.0	1.3	1.3	96.1	0.0	154
Pace U							
New York	0.6	8.9	15.1	10.6	55.2	9.7	9,780
Pleasantville-Briarcliff	0.6	1.5	3.7	4.1	88.0	2.2	4,342
White Plains	0.8	4.3	5.3	3.3	84.6	1.7	4,254
Paul Smith's C of Arts and Sciences	0.1	0.0	1.4	0.4	93.4	4.8	813
Phillip Beth Israel Sch of Nursing	0.0	6.3	48.3	8.0	35.8	1.7	176
Plaza Business Inst	0.0	12.0	30.4	28.2	29.0	0.4	493
Polytechnic U	0.0	27.4	4.9	4.5	53.2	10.0	4,219
Pratt Inst	0.0	9.2	11.3	7.4	60.0	12.0	3,639
Rabbi Isaac Elchanan Theological Sem	0.0	0.0	0.0	0.0	97.2	2.8	319
Rabbinical C Bobover Yeshiva B'nei Zion	0.0	0.0	0.0	0.0	100.0	0.0	293
Rabbinical Sem M'kor Chaim	0.0	0.0	0.0	0.0	100.0	0.0	112
Rabbinical Sem of America	0.0	0.0	0.0	0.0	100.0	0.0	203
Rensselaer Polytechnic Inst	0.2	8.0	2.3	2.8	76.8	9.9	6,706
Roberts Wesleyan C	0.9	0.4	5.7	2.7	82.4	7.9	820
Rochester Business Inst	0.4	0.0	32.8	1.7	65.1	0.0	241
Rochester Inst of Tech	0.3	2.4	3.1	1.4	90.1	2.6	12,346
Rockefeller U	0.0	3.4	0.9	0.9	54.7	40.2	117
Russell Sage C main	0.2	0.8	5.8	1.8	90.7	0.6	4,165
Saint Bernard's Inst	0.0	0.0	1.0	4.0	95.0	0.0	100
Saint Bonaventure U	0.4	0.4	0.9	0.6	97.2	0.5	2,853
Saint Elizabeth Hospital Sch of Nursing	0.0	0.0	2.2	0.0	97.8	0.0	136
Saint Francis C	0.4	1.6	22.9	10.4	61.1	3.7	1,929
Saint John Fisher C	0.2	0.7	3.5	1.2	93.8	0.6	2,359

NEW YORK, cont.

	American Indian	Asian	Black	Hispanic	White	Foreign	Total
Saint John's U	0.1%	5.3%	7.2%	6.7%	76.2%	4.5%	19,143
Saint Joseph's C							
Main	0.0	7.9	37.3	7.6	47.2	0.0	794
Suffolk	0.0	0.1	3.7	6.2	90.0	0.0	1,766
Saint Joseph's Sem & C	0.0	0.0	1.2	2.7	94.6	1.5	259
Saint Lawrence U	1.2	0.4	2.7	0.4	92.2	3.3	2,232
Saint Thomas Aquinas C	0.0	0.9	2.7	2.8	93.3	0.2	2,038
Sarah Lawrence C	0.0	3.4	5.2	2.7	88.1	0.7	1,202
Sch of Visual Arts	0.1	4.2	7.0	4.8	81.2	2.8	4,832
Sem of the Immaculate Conception	0.5	0.0	0.5	2.2	96.2	0.5	185
Siena C	0.0	1.2	1.3	1.3	96.0	0.2	3,481
Skidmore C	0.0	2.0	5.0	2.4	89.1	1.5	2,595
St U of New York							
Albany	0.1	3.0	6.5	4.0	82.2	4.2	16,561
Binghamton	0.1	5.2	4.6	3.6	82.9	3.6	12,588
Buffalo	0.5	4.3	5.6	2.3	80.5	6.8	28,005
Stony Brook	0.2	10.3	6.9	4.9	69.4	8.3	16,728
Empire St C	0.3	0.8	8.2	5.1	85.1	0.5	6,495
C at Brockport	0.2	0.8	6.2	1.5	90.5	0.8	8,840
C at Buffalo	0.5	0.6	7.6	2.0	88.2	1.1	12,721
C at Cortland	0.2	0.4	1.5	1.1	96.4	0.5	7,261
C at Fredonia	0.3	0.3	2.1	1.2	95.8	0.3	4,994
C at Geneseo	0.2	0.7	1.3	1.0	96.7	0.1	5,321
C at New Paltz	0.3	2.0	7.8	4.9	83.2	1.9	8,093
C at Old Westbury	0.2	4.7	27.2	8.7	56.9	2.2	3,923
C at Oneonta	0.1	0.8	1.8	1.7	94.4	1.1	6,017
C at Oswego	0.2	1.1	2.5	1.4	94.6	0.2	8,672
C at Plattsburgh	0.3	0.7	2.2	1.3	94.4	1.1	6,594
C at Potsdam	0.6	0.6	1.0	0.6	96.4	0.8	4,310
C at Purchase	0.1	1.4	4.1	2.8	90.2	1.3	4,143
Health Science Center Brooklyn	0.2	6.5	27.6	2.9	59.0	3.7	1,681
Health Science Center Syracuse	0.2	5.1	6.6	2.0	82.7	3.3	979
C of Optometry	0.0	12.5	3.0	4.1	74.9	5.5	271
C of Ag & Tech Cobleskill	0.0	0.2	3.7	1.8	94.0	0.3	2,729
C of Ag & Tech Morrisville	0.3	0.6	4.7	1.3	92.9	0.2	3,362
C of Tech Alfred	0.8	0.7	2.3	0.7	95.2	0.4	3,775
C of Tech Canton	0.6	0.4	2.3	0.5	95.9	0.3	2,326
C of Tech Delhi	0.2	1.0	4.7	2.0	92.0	0.1	2,453
C of Tech Farmingdale	0.1	2.1	9.3	4.7	83.6	0.2	10,802
C of Tech Utica-Rome	0.2	1.0	3.1	0.6	93.6	1.6	2,620
C of Environmental Science and Forestry	0.4	0.7	1.1	1.4	87.0	9.4	1,398
Maritime C	0.1	6.3	2.3	3.9	76.4	11.0	828
Fashion Inst of Tech	0.0	10.4	18.0	9.7	59.5	2.4	11,944
C of Ceramics Alfred U	0.6	1.3	1.4	1.3	90.0	5.5	869
C of Ag and Life Sciences Cornell U	0.3	5.1	1.9	2.2	79.2	11.3	4,221
C of Human Ecology Cornell U	0.3	8.5	4.8	3.3	77.7	5.4	1,471
C of Veterinary Medicine Cornell U	1.7	2.1	1.7	4.3	78.9	11.4	421
Sch of Industrial and Labor Relations Cornell U	0.8	2.0	12.0	5.2	78.5	1.5	2,043
Adirondack CC	0.2	0.3	0.6	0.5	98.2	0.2	3,096

	American Indian	Asian	Black	Hispanic	White	Foreign	Total
Broome CC	0.1%	0.9%	1.2%	0.4%	95.9%	1.5%	5,815
Cayuga County CC	0.1	0.1	2.0	0.8	96.8	0.1	2,683
Clinton CC	0.2	1.2	8.8	3.6	86.0	0.2	1,812
Columbia-Greene CC	0.6	0.4	4.2	2.0	92.8	0.0	1,613
CC of the Finger Lakes	0.3	0.1	1.1	0.4	98.1	0.0	3,355
Corning CC	0.3	0.3	1.9	0.7	96.8	0.0	3,229
Dutchess CC	0.4	1.9	7.7	2.9	86.8	0.4	6,417
Erie CC City	0.9	0.6	26.0	4.9	67.6	0.1	3,089
Erie CC North	0.3	0.8	4.3	0.4	92.7	1.5	6,062
Erie CC South	0.4	0.3	0.8	0.4	98.1	0.0	3,418
Fulton-Montgomery CC	0.5	0.3	2.2	1.5	94.1	1.4	1,843
Genesee CC	0.2	0.1	1.0	0.1	98.5	0.1	2,955
Herkimer County CC	0.0	0.2	1.5	0.1	98.1	0.1	2,219
Hudson Valley CC	0.2	0.5	2.7	0.5	95.7	0.4	8,596
Jamestown CC	0.9	0.2	1.5	0.6	96.7	0.1	4,038
Jefferson CC	0.3	1.4	6.3	2.2	89.8	0.0	2,194
Monroe CC	0.4	2.0	8.2	2.4	86.6	0.4	12,768
Mohawk Valley CC	0.3	0.8	4.6	1.4	92.1	0.7	6,147
Nassau CC	0.4	1.6	9.2	4.2	83.2	1.5	20,130
Niagara County CC	1.6	0.4	4.0	0.4	93.3	0.3	4,693
North Country CC	0.5	0.2	3.4	1.4	94.0	0.5	1,520
Onondaga CC	1.5	1.0	5.8	1.1	89.8	0.8	7,173
Orange County CC	0.1	0.8	3.5	3.6	91.4	0.5	4,826
Rockland CC	0.5	3.9	10.4	5.2	76.9	3.2	7,644
Schenectady County CC	0.2	0.5	2.2	0.8	96.3	0.0	3,026
Suffolk County CC Eastern	0.2	0.5	3.1	1.5	94.7	0.0	2,031
Suffolk County CC Selden	0.2	1.1	1.7	2.5	94.6	0.0	11,267
Suffolk County CC Western	0.3	0.7	6.3	6.3	86.4	0.0	4,317
Sullivan County CC	0.1	0.6	14.8	4.8	79.6	0.1	1,889
Tompkins-Cortland CC	0.3	1.1	2.6	0.8	94.8	0.3	2,595
Ulster County CC	0.1	0.9	6.1	3.2	89.6	0.1	2,816
Westchester CC	0.3	3.1	12.7	7.2	75.6	1.1	8,241
Stenotype Academy	0.0	1.0	28.8	16.3	50.9	2.9	583
Syracuse U	0.2	2.2	4.7	1.6	84.4	7.0	22,086
Utica C	0.1	0.6	5.0	1.7	91.1	1.4	2,523
Taylor Business Inst	0.0	3.7	49.3	39.0	8.0	0.0	536
Tech Career Insts	0.0	34.0	27.0	18.1	15.6	5.3	1,910
Tobe-Coburn Sch of Fashion Careers	0.0	2.8	10.5	18.0	68.4	0.3	399
Trocaire C	0.5	0.6	5.4	1.0	92.1	0.4	826
Union C	0.0	3.5	2.1	1.8	90.5	2.0	2,980
U S Merchant Marine Acad	0.2	3.8	1.4	2.4	90.2	2.0	851
U S Military Academy	0.7	4.0	7.3	4.2	83.8	0.0	4,310
U of Rochester	0.1	5.0	4.2	1.9	80.0	8.9	9,195
U of the St of NY Regents C Degrees	0.5	5.7	13.2	8.2	68.3	4.1	16,480
Utica Sch of Commerce	0.0	0.0	3.0	0.0	97.0	0.0	502
Vassar C	0.1	5.8	7.5	3.4	80.1	3.1	2,395
Villa Maria C Buffalo	0.0	0.0	7.1	0.4	91.9	0.7	567
Wadhams Hall Sem and C	0.0	0.0	0.0	0.0	100.0	0.0	62
Wagner C	0.1	1.0	8.3	2.5	75.9	12.3	1,767
Wells C	0.2	1.2	3.2	1.0	93.6	0.7	408
Westchester Business Inst	0.0	0.0	28.4	24.5	47.0	0.0	897
Wood Sch	0.2	2.0	18.3	46.3	33.2	0.0	404
Yeshiva Gedolah Bais Yisroel	0.0	0.0	0.0	0.0	84.8	15.2	46
Yeshiva Derech Chaim	0.0	0.0	0.0	0.0	100.0	0.0	130
Yeshiva Karlin Stolin	0.0	0.0	0.0	0.0	94.9	5.1	79
Yeshiva U	0.0	1.5	2.8	1.9	89.5	4.1	4,543

NORTH CAROLINA

	American Indian	Asian	Black	Hispanic	White	Foreign	Total
Alamance CC	0.3%	0.3%	16.5%	0.3%	82.6%	0.0%	3,096
Anson CC	0.1	0.1	24.0	0.3	75.5	0.0	797
Asheville Buncombe Tech CC	0.3	0.6	5.2	0.3	93.3	0.3	3,050
Atlantic Christian C	0.1	0.5	9.4	0.5	88.4	1.1	1,382
Barber-Scotia C	0.0	0.0	98.8	0.0	0.2	0.9	422
Beaufort County CC	0.1	0.4	20.9	0.4	78.2	0.0	1,202
Belmont Abbey C	0.6	2.1	3.9	1.5	89.6	2.3	1,052
Bennett C	0.0	0.0	97.6	0.0	0.3	2.1	615
Bladen CC	1.4	0.2	34.7	0.6	63.1	0.0	510
Blue Ridge CC	0.1	0.4	3.4	0.5	95.0	0.5	1,168
Brevard C	0.4	0.1	5.8	0.6	88.0	4.9	668
Brookstone C of Business	0.0	0.0	48.7	0.0	51.3	0.0	156
Brunswick CC	0.3	0.3	18.7	0.3	80.4	0.0	621
Caldwell CC and Tech Inst	0.0	0.4	3.8	0.2	95.6	0.0	2,553
Campbell U	0.7	14.3	6.9	1.2	75.6	1.3	4,375
Cape Fear CC	0.5	0.2	13.3	0.7	85.2	0.1	2,480
Carteret CC	0.4	0.4	7.6	0.5	91.0	0.0	1,344
Catawba C	0.3	0.1	9.4	0.3	89.4	0.5	1,030
Catawba Valley CC	0.2	0.6	5.8	0.6	92.8	0.0	2,641
Cecils C	0.0	0.0	6.9	0.0	93.1	0.0	189
Central Carolina CC	1.0	0.5	21.0	0.6	76.9	0.1	2,424
Central Piedmont CC	0.3	2.3	15.6	0.6	79.4	1.8	16,442
Chowan C	0.4	0.8	29.7	0.7	64.9	3.5	973
Cleveland CC	0.1	1.1	17.8	0.5	80.6	0.0	1,425
Coastal Carolina CC	0.4	1.8	15.4	4.1	78.1	0.2	3,404
C of the Albemarle	0.1	0.6	17.3	0.6	81.3	0.0	1,603
Craven CC	0.3	0.9	18.7	2.5	77.5	0.1	2,108
Davidson C	0.3	4.5	4.0	0.8	90.4	0.0	1,395
Davidson County CC	0.2	0.5	7.6	0.2	91.4	0.1	2,212
Duke U	0.2	3.4	4.4	2.0	83.9	6.1	10,689
Durham Tech CC	0.3	2.1	35.3	0.7	61.0	0.5	4,430
East Coast Bible C	0.0	0.8	7.1	1.6	90.5	0.0	252
Edgecombe CC	0.5	0.3	47.1	0.0	51.8	0.3	1,341
Elon C	0.2	0.3	4.8	0.3	93.8	0.7	3,314
Fayetteville Tech CC	1.8	2.1	28.9	3.2	63.9	0.1	6,043
Forsyth Tech C	0.2	0.7	19.8	0.4	78.8	0.0	4,422
Gardner-Webb C	0.1	0.4	10.7	0.4	87.7	0.7	2,139
Gaston C	0.1	0.6	9.4	0.3	89.5	0.1	3,300
Greensboro C	0.3	0.4	12.2	0.6	84.8	1.7	967
Guilford C	0.5	0.8	5.6	0.6	89.2	3.3	1,755
Guilford Tech CC	0.7	1.2	17.6	0.6	79.6	0.4	6,232
Halifax CC	1.1	0.4	37.6	0.3	60.5	0.0	983
Haywood CC	0.9	0.1	0.7	0.5	97.8	0.1	1,026
High Point C	0.1	0.4	6.0	0.6	91.1	1.9	1,930
Isothermal CC	0.2	0.3	7.9	0.1	91.6	0.0	1,554
James Sprunt CC	0.6	0.1	24.8	0.4	74.0	0.1	846
John Wesley C	1.8	0.0	8.8	0.0	89.5	0.0	57
Johnson C Smith U	0.0	0.0	99.6	0.0	0.1	0.3	1,197
Johnston CC	0.2	0.1	16.8	0.4	82.2	0.1	2,030
Lees-McRae C	0.0	0.4	10.7	0.1	87.5	1.3	787
Lenoir CC	0.2	0.2	28.8	0.5	70.2	0.1	2,178
Lenoir-Rhyne C	0.1	0.4	4.4	0.4	94.5	0.1	1,596
Livingstone C	0.0	0.0	97.3	0.0	0.4	2.3	558
Louisburg C	0.1	0.1	8.3	0.0	91.0	0.4	904
Mars Hill C	0.4	0.1	5.0	0.1	93.4	1.0	1,345
Martin CC	0.2	0.3	38.3	0.5	60.8	0.0	655
Mayland CC	0.3	0.0	3.2	0.3	96.1	0.1	775

	American Indian	Asian	Black	Hispanic	White	Foreign	Total
McDowell Tech CC	0.2%	0.3%	3.5%	0.3%	95.5%	0.2%	600
Meredith C	0.3	0.6	2.6	0.5	94.7	1.4	2,124
Methodist C	0.9	1.9	13.0	4.1	79.5	0.7	1,501
Mitchell CC	0.1	0.3	10.8	0.2	88.6	0.1	1,392
Montgomery CC	3.1	0.0	24.6	0.2	72.1	0.0	524
Montreat-Anderson C	0.3	0.0	5.7	0.0	87.8	6.2	386
Mount Olive C	0.0	0.8	15.6	1.3	82.2	0.0	997
Nash CC	1.6	0.3	22.3	0.2	75.5	0.0	1,501
North Carolina Wesleyan C	0.7	0.1	17.4	0.6	80.2	0.9	1,513
Pamlico CC	0.0	0.0	23.7	0.6	75.6	0.0	160
Peace C	0.4	1.1	0.4	0.4	97.5	0.2	530
Pfeiffer C	0.2	0.5	8.6	0.9	88.6	1.3	875
Piedmont Bible C	0.0	0.4	3.1	0.0	94.7	1.8	227
Piedmont CC	0.4	0.3	41.4	0.6	57.3	0.0	990
Pitt CC	0.4	0.4	22.9	0.2	75.9	0.2	3,247
Queens C	0.3	0.1	6.0	0.4	91.3	1.9	1,373
Randolph CC	0.2	0.3	4.3	0.2	94.7	0.2	1,267
Richmond CC	3.5	0.2	26.7	0.7	68.8	0.2	936
Roanoke Bible C	0.0	0.0	4.6	0.0	94.4	0.9	108
Roanoke-Chowan CC	0.8	0.2	50.8	0.5	47.8	0.0	634
Robeson CC	32.3	0.2	23.8	0.3	43.3	0.0	1,345
Rockingham CC	0.0	0.2	14.8	0.1	84.8	0.1	1,576
Rowan-Cabarrus CC	0.2	0.5	11.9	0.2	87.1	0.1	2,606
Rutledge C Durham	0.0	0.0	92.0	0.0	8.0	0.0	224
Rutledge C Fayetteville	0.3	0.9	74.2	2.9	21.7	0.0	341
Rutledge C Raleigh	0.5	0.5	92.1	0.5	6.5	0.0	214
Rutledge C Winston-Salem	0.0	0.0	72.1	0.9	26.6	0.4	233
Saint Andrews Presbyterian C	0.2	1.2	7.6	0.4	86.4	4.1	802
Saint Augustine's C	0.0	0.3	96.5	0.1	0.3	2.7	1,788
Saint Mary's C	0.0	0.3	0.7	0.7	95.0	3.3	303
Salem C	0.0	0.9	3.3	0.6	94.3	1.0	819
Sampson CC	1.8	0.5	24.4	0.5	72.8	0.1	848
Sandhills CC	2.5	0.4	14.1	0.4	82.6	0.1	1,961
Shaw U	0.0	0.0	90.6	0.1	9.3	0.0	1,507
Southeastern Baptist Theol Sem	0.1	1.0	2.4	0.0	94.6	1.8	819
Southeastern CC	4.5	0.4	16.1	0.2	78.9	0.0	1,376
Southwestern CC	9.5	0.1	1.8	0.2	88.5	0.0	1,249
Stanly CC	0.2	0.4	11.3	0.3	87.6	0.1	1,338
Surry CC	0.1	0.1	5.3	0.3	94.2	0.0	2,768
Tri-County CC	1.4	0.0	0.8	0.5	97.3	0.0	867
U of North Carolina							
Asheville	0.1	0.6	3.5	0.8	94.2	0.8	3,124
Chapel Hill	0.6	1.9	7.8	0.7	86.3	2.7	23,626
Charlotte	0.3	1.9	9.7	0.7	84.9	2.5	13,181
Greensboro	0.3	0.9	9.7	0.6	87.0	1.4	11,477
Wilmington	0.3	0.8	7.3	0.3	91.1	0.2	6,953
Appalachian St U	0.2	0.4	4.5	0.3	94.2	0.3	11,548
East Carolina U	0.5	0.7	10.4	0.6	87.2	0.6	16,501
Elizabeth City St U	0.1	0.1	81.5	0.2	17.6	0.4	1,641
Fayetteville St U	0.8	0.8	70.0	1.2	27.1	0.1	2,726
North Carolina A&T St U	0.2	0.4	83.8	0.2	12.8	2.6	6,297
North Carolina Central U	0.4	0.8	82.6	0.5	15.5	0.2	5,182
NC Sch of the Arts	0.2	0.2	11.1	2.9	82.7	2.9	515
North Carolina St U	0.3	2.4	9.3	0.8	83.1	4.1	25,725
Pembroke St U	23.4	1.0	12.1	0.3	63.2	0.1	2,835
Western Carolina U	1.5	0.5	4.7	0.2	91.8	1.4	6,162

N.C., cont.

	American Indian	Asian	Black	Hispanic	White	Foreign	Total
U of North Carolina Winston-Salem St U	0.2%	0.3%	84.6%	0.1%	14.7%	0.0%	2,532
Vance-Granville CC	1.2	0.4	37.2	0.3	60.9	0.1	1,900
Wake Forest U	0.1	1.4	4.3	0.4	92.9	0.9	5,337
Wake Tech CC	0.3	2.1	17.2	0.5	78.8	1.1	5,405
Warren Wilson C	0.2	1.7	2.7	0.8	87.4	7.3	523
Wayne CC	0.1	0.9	21.7	0.6	76.5	0.1	2,166
Western Piedmont CC	0.3	0.5	4.8	0.3	94.1	0.1	2,290
Wilkes CC	0.1	0.1	4.6	0.1	95.0	0.1	1,765
Wilson Tech CC	0.2	0.0	30.6	0.9	68.3	0.0	1,439
Wingate C	0.0	0.2	6.4	0.5	92.0	0.9	1,709

NORTH DAKOTA

	American Indian	Asian	Black	Hispanic	White	Foreign	Total
Fort Bethold CC	83.2	0.0	0.0	0.8	16.0	0.0	125
Jamestown C	2.1	0.5	0.9	0.6	93.3	2.5	796
Little Hoop CC	100.0	0.0	0.0	0.0	0.0	0.0	120
ND St Bd of Higher Ed Sys U of North Dakota							
Main	2.3	0.7	0.3	0.5	93.6	2.6	11,824
Lake Region	2.7	0.7	4.3	1.2	90.6	0.5	923
Williston	7.3	0.2	0.0	0.3	92.0	0.2	586
North Dakota St U Main	0.6	0.7	0.3	0.2	94.8	3.5	9,536
Dickinson St U	0.8	0.1	0.3	0.4	97.6	0.9	1,417
Mayville St U	0.8	0.5	1.3	0.1	92.5	4.8	755
Minot St U	2.0	0.3	1.3	0.6	89.5	6.3	3,246
ND St C of Science	1.9	0.7	0.5	0.1	96.1	0.7	2,385
ND St U Bottineau	5.1	0.2	1.4	0.0	87.3	5.9	489
Valley City St U	0.6	0.1	0.8	0.5	96.2	1.8	1,154
Bismarck St C	2.5	0.1	0.1	0.1	96.8	0.4	2,492
Standing Rock CC	93.1	0.0	0.0	0.0	6.9	0.0	262
Trinity Bible C	1.6	0.0	2.5	1.1	92.8	2.0	445
Turtle Mountain CC	93.2	0.0	0.0	0.0	6.8	0.0	309
U of Mary	6.0	1.1	0.1	0.4	91.5	0.9	1,418

OHIO

	American Indian	Asian	Black	Hispanic	White	Foreign	Total
Air Force Inst of Tech	0.1	1.4	4.9	0.7	87.8	5.2	737
Antioch C	0.4	0.4	8.5	1.4	85.7	3.7	566
Antioch Sch for Adult and Experiential Learning	1.3	0.7	9.1	2.4	86.1	0.4	453
Art Academy of Cincinnati	0.0	0.4	5.8	0.0	93.3	0.4	223
Antonelli Inst of Art and Photography	0.0	0.8	19.5	1.6	78.0	0.0	123
Ashland U	0.0	0.2	8.5	0.3	88.5	2.4	4,053
Athenaeum of Ohio	0.0	0.7	1.0	0.0	98.3	0.0	294
Baldwin-Wallace C	0.1	1.2	5.5	0.5	91.8	0.9	4,563
Belmont Tech C	0.0	0.3	1.7	0.1	97.9	0.0	1,901
Bluffton C	0.0	0.5	4.4	0.0	91.8	3.3	608
Borromeo C of Ohio	0.0	0.0	1.8	3.6	94.6	0.0	56
Bowling Green St U							
Main	0.1	0.6	3.5	0.8	93.5	1.5	18,345
Firelands C	0.1	0.1	1.7	0.8	97.3	0.0	1,206
Bradford Sch	0.0	0.5	5.1	0.0	94.5	0.0	217
Capital U	0.0	0.4	8.0	0.3	90.2	1.0	3,016
Career Com C of Business	0.0	0.0	59.9	0.0	40.1	0.0	187

	American Indian	Asian	Black	Hispanic	White	Foreign	Total
Case Western Reserve U	0.2%	5.0%	4.7%	1.0%	76.8%	12.4%	8,333
Cedarville C	0.0	0.3	0.7	0.5	97.4	1.0	1,879
Central Ohio Tech C	0.3	0.4	2.0	0.2	96.8	0.2	1,446
Chatfield C	0.0	1.7	0.0	0.0	98.3	0.0	115
Cincinnati C of Mortuary Science	0.0	0.0	4.1	0.0	95.9	0.0	122
Cincinnati Metropolitan C	0.0	0.3	43.9	0.0	55.8	0.0	351
Cincinnati Tech C	0.5	0.7	16.3	0.4	82.1	0.0	4,404
Circleville Bible C	0.0	0.6	5.6	0.0	93.8	0.0	161
Clark St CC	0.3	0.6	8.1	0.1	90.5	0.2	2,154
Cleveland Inst of Art	0.0	2.1	5.5	1.4	89.7	1.4	513
Cleveland Inst of Music	0.0	2.2	2.6	1.7	81.5	12.0	416
Cleveland St U	0.7	0.5	10.0	1.0	84.2	3.6	17,346
C of Mount Saint Joseph	0.0	0.2	4.5	0.2	93.3	1.8	2,209
C of Wooster	0.1	0.7	4.7	0.3	87.6	6.5	1,895
Columbus C of Art and Design	0.3	1.9	5.5	1.9	88.8	1.5	1,557
Columbus St CC	0.4	1.3	15.8	1.1	80.6	0.8	9,520
Cuyahoga CC	0.5	1.4	23.6	1.4	71.9	1.2	22,010
Davis C	0.0	3.0	10.0	1.5	85.0	0.5	400
Defiance C	0.1	0.1	3.3	1.6	93.0	1.9	1,026
Denison U	0.0	0.8	4.3	0.5	93.4	1.0	2,133
DeVry Inst of Tech	0.0	1.9	13.3	0.8	83.1	0.9	3,013
Dyke C	0.0	1.4	46.9	1.3	50.3	0.1	1,334
Edison St CC	0.3	1.0	1.7	0.1	96.7	0.1	2,574
ETI Tech C	0.0	1.7	41.0	3.2	54.0	0.0	692
Franciscan U of Steubenville	0.0	0.4	1.3	3.1	92.6	2.6	1,369
Franklin U	0.2	1.2	12.5	0.5	84.5	1.1	4,280
Hebrew Union C-Jewish Inst of Religion	2.5	0.0	0.0	0.0	91.6	5.9	119
Heidelberg C	0.3	1.4	3.3	1.2	92.3	1.6	1,178
Hiram C	0.0	0.9	4.0	0.6	94.4	0.1	1,220
Hocking Tech C	0.1	0.3	6.1	0.4	92.0	1.1	4,108
ITT Tech Inst	0.0	0.0	13.3	1.3	85.4	0.0	624
ITT Tech Inst Stanley campus	0.0	0.5	11.0	0.3	87.8	0.3	617
Jefferson Tech C	0.0	0.0	4.2	0.0	95.7	0.1	1,410
John Carroll U	0.1	0.8	2.5	0.6	95.3	0.6	4,081
Kent St U							
Main	0.1	0.8	5.0	0.5	91.3	2.3	22,753
Ashtabula	0.2	0.2	0.8	0.7	97.8	0.2	868
East Liverpool	0.2	0.0	1.8	0.2	97.8	0.0	546
Geauga	0.0	0.0	0.2	0.4	99.4	0.0	471
Salem	0.0	0.0	1.3	0.1	98.6	0.0	791
Stark	0.1	0.2	2.9	0.1	96.6	0.1	1,811
Trumbull	0.2	0.4	4.7	0.5	94.1	0.1	1,681
Tuscarawas	0.0	0.2	1.0	0.0	98.6	0.1	955
Kenyon C	0.0	1.8	1.3	1.2	93.8	1.9	1,588
Kettering C of Medical Arts	0.8	1.0	4.5	0.7	93.0	0.0	597
Lake Erie C	0.1	0.6	2.6	1.0	95.6	0.0	685
Lakeland CC	0.2	0.6	2.0	0.3	96.9	0.0	7,840
Lima Tech C	0.2	0.5	6.1	0.6	92.3	0.3	1,945
Lorain County CC	0.2	0.2	4.6	3.7	91.0	0.2	5,963
Lourdes C	0.4	0.1	4.9	0.9	93.5	0.1	773
Malone C	0.1	0.2	4.0	0.1	95.0	0.6	1,318
Marietta C	0.0	0.4	1.3	0.1	96.8	1.5	1,339
Marion Tech C	0.2	0.7	5.7	0.3	92.9	0.1	1,350
Medical C of Ohio	0.0	6.2	5.7	1.6	79.5	7.0	757
Miami-Jacobs JC of Business	0.0	0.4	31.0	0.2	68.4	0.0	548

THE ALMANAC OF HIGHER EDUCATION • ENROLLMENT BY RACE

OHIO, cont.

	American Indian	Asian	Black	Hispanic	White	Foreign	Total
Miami U							
Hamilton	0.1%	0.7%	2.7%	0.1%	96.3%	0.0%	2,154
Middletown	0.1	0.3	2.3	0.3	96.7	0.4	1,904
Oxford	0.1	1.2	2.3	0.4	94.8	1.3	16,027
Mount Union C	0.0	0.6	5.6	0.7	89.6	3.6	1,294
Mount Vernon Nazarene C	0.0	0.2	0.5	0.4	98.4	0.6	1,087
Muskingum Area Tech C	0.5	0.1	2.3	0.2	96.9	0.0	1,944
Muskingum C	0.3	0.9	1.3	0.2	96.1	1.2	1,142
North Central Tech C	0.3	0.3	2.6	0.6	96.2	0.0	1,828
Northeastern Ohio U's C of Medicine	0.3	20.5	1.1	1.8	76.3	0.0	380
Northwest Tech C	0.1	0.1	0.3	2.6	96.9	0.0	1,869
Northwestern Business C-Tech Center	0.0	0.2	3.1	0.7	96.1	0.0	1,221
Notre Dame C	0.3	0.8	26.0	4.0	67.2	1.7	749
Oberlin C	0.1	7.2	8.8	2.6	78.4	2.8	2,876
Ohio C of Podiatric Medicine	0.2	3.8	15.3	4.2	75.0	1.4	424
Ohio Dominican C	0.0	0.6	10.5	3.2	78.4	7.3	1,331
Ohio Northern U	0.1	1.1	2.6	0.6	93.9	1.7	2,537
Ohio St U							
Main	0.2	2.5	4.7	1.2	85.9	5.5	53,661
Agricultural Tech Inst	0.3	0.1	4.1	0.0	94.8	0.6	677
Lima	0.0	0.2	2.2	0.5	97.1	0.0	1,276
Mansfield	0.4	0.4	2.0	0.5	96.8	0.0	1,276
Marion	0.4	0.4	4.5	0.1	94.6	0.0	1,134
Newark	0.1	0.3	1.7	0.1	97.7	0.0	1,503
Ohio U							
Main	0.3	0.3	4.7	0.6	87.2	6.9	17,836
Belmont	0.3	0.0	0.6	0.3	97.0	1.9	1,090
Chillicothe	0.1	0.0	1.2	0.1	98.0	0.5	1,468
Ironton	0.2	0.0	1.2	0.0	98.5	0.1	1,303
Lancaster	0.4	0.1	1.9	0.2	97.2	0.2	1,809
Zanesville	0.1	0.2	1.7	0.1	97.8	0.2	1,261
Ohio Wesleyan U	0.1	1.0	3.3	0.5	90.1	5.0	1,773
Otterbein C	0.0	0.4	1.9	0.2	95.3	2.2	2,177
Owens Tech C	0.3	0.3	7.0	2.4	89.8	0.2	6,014
Pontifical C Josephinum	0.0	5.0	2.2	7.7	79.6	5.5	181
Saint Mary Sem	0.0	1.4	0.0	0.0	98.6	0.0	72
Shawnee St U	0.6	0.1	5.3	0.3	93.5	0.1	2,967
Sinclair CC	0.4	1.4	12.7	0.8	84.5	0.2	16,632
Southern Ohio C	0.0	0.7	29.8	0.0	69.5	0.0	574
Southern St CC	0.2	0.0	0.3	0.2	99.2	0.2	1,317
Stark Tech C	0.4	0.2	4.7	0.4	94.4	0.0	3,275
Tiffin U	0.0	0.0	9.4	0.8	87.6	2.2	777
U of Akron							
Main	0.4	0.9	7.6	0.4	87.5	3.2	27,818
Wayne C	0.8	0.5	0.9	0.4	97.1	0.2	1,220
U of Cincinnati							
Main	0.3	2.3	9.3	0.7	84.3	3.1	31,432
Clermont C	1.0	0.6	0.8	0.0	97.7	0.0	1,251
Raymond Walters C	0.6	1.4	7.2	0.5	89.6	0.5	3,725
U of Dayton	0.1	1.1	4.1	1.2	91.7	1.8	11,121
U of Findlay	0.5	0.5	15.4	3.3	79.1	1.3	1,686
U of Rio Grande	0.2	0.2	2.1	0.1	95.8	1.8	1,884
U of Toledo	0.5	0.8	6.1	1.4	83.8	7.5	22,806
Urbana U	0.3	1.3	28.9	0.0	69.0	0.5	765
Ursuline C	0.0	0.8	10.2	1.1	86.9	1.0	1,298

	American Indian	Asian	Black	Hispanic	White	Foreign	Total
Virginia Marti C of Fashion and Art	0.0%	0.4%	29.8%	2.1%	67.2%	0.4%	238
Walsh C	0.0	0.0	5.2	2.5	89.5	2.7	1,297
Washington Tech C	0.5	0.1	0.9	0.2	98.3	0.0	1,716
West Side Inst of Tech	0.0	0.5	19.4	1.1	79.0	0.0	372
Wilberforce U	0.0	0.0	99.7	0.0	0.1	0.1	767
Wilmington C	0.0	0.0	18.3	0.1	79.6	1.9	1,473
Wittenberg U	0.0	0.8	3.5	0.7	92.7	2.4	2,273
Wright St U							
Main	0.1	1.7	5.0	0.6	90.6	2.0	16,149
Lake	0.2	0.5	0.0	0.5	98.7	0.1	828
Xavier U	0.2	1.5	6.9	1.7	87.9	1.8	6,412
Youngstown St U	0.1	0.4	7.0	0.7	90.2	1.5	14,710

OKLAHOMA

	American Indian	Asian	Black	Hispanic	White	Foreign	Total
Bacone C	46.9	0.2	12.5	0.2	40.2	0.0	463
Bartlesville Wesleyan C	3.0	0.9	1.2	1.2	85.5	8.2	427
Cameron U	3.6	2.3	14.6	4.0	75.1	0.4	5,777
Carl Albert JC	12.6	0.2	2.4	1.5	83.3	0.0	1,479
Central St U	1.8	1.5	7.5	1.2	82.7	5.2	14,269
Connors St C	7.1	0.2	8.7	0.5	83.5	0.0	1,740
Dickinson Business Sch	2.0	0.3	30.7	1.1	65.9	0.0	745
East Central U	7.6	0.4	3.0	0.8	88.0	0.2	4,244
Eastern Oklahoma St C	10.9	0.2	6.2	0.5	82.1	0.2	1,772
El Reno JC	2.6	1.1	5.5	1.4	88.0	1.4	1,328
Flaming Rainbow U	50.8	0.0	2.5	0.8	45.9	0.0	122
Hillsdale Free Will Baptist C	4.3	0.9	7.8	0.0	87.0	0.0	115
Langston U	1.5	1.2	54.2	1.0	39.6	2.5	2,308
Mid-America Bible C	2.6	0.0	9.8	0.4	86.0	1.3	235
Murray St C	7.0	0.3	3.6	0.9	88.2	0.0	1,401
National Education Ctr- Spartan Sch of Aeronautics	4.1	2.7	5.9	3.5	80.0	3.8	2,293
Northeastern Okla A&M C	14.0	0.2	7.1	0.2	77.0	1.5	2,469
Northeastern St U	16.1	0.2	4.3	0.7	77.9	0.9	8,742
Northern Oklahoma C	6.3	0.5	1.8	1.1	89.8	0.5	1,897
Northwestern Oklahoma St U	1.8	0.1	2.5	1.0	94.2	0.5	1,751
Oklahoma Baptist U	3.2	1.0	6.5	0.5	87.5	1.2	1,847
Oklahoma Christian C	0.9	2.0	4.6	0.9	91.1	0.4	1,617
Oklahoma City CC	2.6	2.9	5.0	1.6	87.0	1.0	8,511
Oklahoma City U	3.0	3.0	5.0	1.9	69.1	18.0	2,957
Oklahoma JC	0.2	1.3	37.7	1.4	59.2	0.2	559
Oklahoma JC of Business and Tech	4.8	1.0	20.9	1.6	71.4	0.3	2,103
Oklahoma Mission Baptist C	1.2	2.4	10.8	0.0	85.6	0.0	167
Oklahoma St U							
Main	2.7	1.2	2.7	0.9	85.4	7.1	21,258
Okmulgee	2.4	3.6	6.4	1.5	85.5	0.7	3,290
C of Osteopathic Medicine	4.5	1.9	4.1	2.6	86.2	0.7	269
Oral Roberts U	0.7	2.2	13.4	4.0	74.5	5.2	4,148
Oklahoma Panhandle St U	0.4	0.4	3.9	5.9	89.4	0.1	1,140
Phillips U	0.7	0.2	4.1	1.0	83.2	10.7	942
Rogers St C	9.9	0.8	1.6	0.7	82.7	4.4	3,055
Rose St C	2.9	2.6	14.0	2.4	77.3	0.8	9,460
Saint Gregory's C	2.7	2.0	6.0	5.3	79.4	4.7	301
Seminole JC	10.2	0.3	4.7	0.7	82.9	1.1	1,486
Southeastern Oklahoma St U	25.3	2.9	3.6	0.9	66.3	1.0	3,563

OKLAHOMA, cont.

	American Indian	Asian	Black	Hispanic	White	Foreign	Total
Southern Nazarene U	0.8%	0.4%	4.5%	0.9%	87.2%	6.2%	1,393
Southwestern C of Christian Ministries	0.8	6.7	2.5	0.8	89.2	0.0	120
Southwestern Oklahoma St U	2.8	1.3	2.7	1.3	91.4	0.6	5,309
Tulsa JC	2.2	1.1	5.1	0.9	90.6	0.0	16,778
U of Oklahoma							
Health Sciences Center	4.2	4.2	4.7	1.4	83.0	2.5	2,459
Norman	2.4	2.3	4.4	1.4	84.0	5.5	22,224
U of Science and Arts of Oklahoma	7.2	0.9	4.5	1.0	84.4	2.0	1,374
U of Tulsa	2.2	1.8	3.1	1.1	83.1	8.8	4,344
Western Oklahoma St C	1.8	1.3	7.8	5.0	84.1	0.0	2,056

OREGON

	American Indian	Asian	Black	Hispanic	White	Foreign	Total
Bassist C	0.5	3.4	1.4	1.0	88.9	4.8	208
Blue Mountain CC	2.0	0.8	0.5	2.4	94.3	0.0	1,617
Central Oregon CC	1.6	0.4	0.1	0.7	96.0	1.2	2,314
Chemeketa CC	1.4	2.2	0.7	2.1	93.5	0.1	8,726
Clackamas CC	0.5	3.0	0.8	3.9	90.8	0.8	5,456
Clatsop CC	2.4	2.7	0.1	1.6	93.2	0.0	821
Columbia Christian C	0.0	2.9	3.2	0.7	91.1	2.1	280
Concordia C	0.4	4.9	4.2	0.9	74.0	15.6	450
Eugene Bible C	0.0	0.0	0.8	4.1	91.0	4.1	122
George Fox C	0.1	1.7	0.7	1.8	94.0	1.7	828
ITT Tech Inst	0.8	2.3	1.7	1.5	93.6	0.2	660
Lane CC	2.0	2.2	1.0	1.4	90.9	2.5	7,254
Lewis and Clark C	0.8	4.5	1.2	1.3	85.9	6.3	3,225
Linfield C	0.7	4.6	0.8	0.7	87.7	5.5	2,035
Linn-Benton CC	0.6	0.9	0.4	0.6	96.6	0.9	5,492
Marylhurst C for Lifelong Learning	1.0	1.0	1.4	0.8	95.6	0.2	1,005
Mount Angel Sem	0.0	6.7	0.0	4.8	79.0	9.5	105
Mount Hood CC	0.8	2.8	1.6	1.3	93.3	0.2	7,885
Multnomah Sch of the Bible	0.7	2.8	1.4	1.1	90.8	3.1	710
Northwest Christian C	0.5	1.8	0.5	1.4	90.8	5.0	218
Oregon Graduate Center	0.0	11.4	0.0	0.0	61.2	27.3	245
Oregon Polytechnic Inst	0.3	2.7	2.1	1.8	92.5	0.6	332
Oregon St Sys of Higher Ed							
Eastern Oregon St C	1.4	2.8	0.8	1.5	89.3	4.2	2,224
Oregon Health Science U	0.6	7.5	0.8	1.2	87.3	2.6	1,288
Oregon Inst of Tech	1.9	3.2	1.8	1.4	89.9	1.8	2,987
Oregon St U	1.4	5.2	1.0	1.3	81.2	9.8	16,042
Portland St U	0.9	5.8	1.8	1.5	85.5	4.6	17,316
Southern Oregon St C	1.3	1.3	0.5	1.5	93.9	1.5	5,164
U of Oregon	0.8	4.4	1.2	1.5	84.5	7.6	18,840
Western Oregon St C	0.7	0.9	0.5	5.5	89.6	2.8	4,571
Pacific Northwest C of Art	1.5	3.4	0.5	1.5	89.7	3.4	203
Pacific U	1.4	12.8	1.5	2.0	79.3	3.1	1,364
Portland CC	0.6	5.9	2.6	1.7	88.0	1.2	20,904
Reed C	0.2	6.1	1.4	1.9	89.0	1.5	1,286
Rogue CC	1.2	0.7	0.1	0.0	97.4	0.5	2,460
Southwestern Oregon CC	1.6	1.0	0.7	1.1	95.1	0.5	2,570
Treasure Valley CC	0.6	2.2	0.9	3.5	89.4	3.4	1,268
Umpqua CC	1.1	0.6	0.9	0.9	96.4	0.1	1,408
U of Portland	0.5	5.3	1.1	1.4	79.1	12.5	2,367
Warner Pacific C	0.6	2.5	2.5	0.6	90.1	3.7	354

	American Indian	Asian	Black	Hispanic	White	Foreign	Total
Western Baptist C	0.6%	1.5%	1.8%	0.9%	95.1%	0.0%	328
Western Conservative Baptist Sem	0.0	0.5	0.0	0.0	93.1	6.4	423
Western Evangelical Sem	0.0	0.8	2.5	0.0	80.2	16.5	121
Western Sts Chiropractic C	0.5	1.8	0.3	2.3	87.2	8.0	399
Willamette U	0.6	4.2	0.9	1.7	89.9	2.7	2,089

PENNSYLVANIA

	American Indian	Asian	Black	Hispanic	White	Foreign	Total
Academy of the New Church	0.0	0.0	0.0	0.6	74.7	24.7	158
Albright C	0.1	1.9	1.7	0.7	93.9	1.7	1,892
Allegheny C	0.1	1.4	3.3	1.1	91.3	2.8	1,997
Allentown C of Saint Francis De Sales	0.1	0.1	0.3	0.6	98.8	0.1	1,679
Alvernia C	0.2	0.4	1.3	1.6	96.1	0.4	1,060
American C	0.0	0.0	0.0	0.0	100.0	0.0	437
Annenberg Research Inst	0.0	8.3	0.0	0.0	91.7	0.0	12
Antioch C Philadelphia	0.3	0.0	76.1	3.8	19.8	0.0	343
Baptist Bible C of Pa	0.2	0.5	1.3	0.7	96.9	0.5	613
Beaver C	0.0	1.7	7.4	1.0	89.0	0.7	2,197
Berean Inst	0.0	1.6	95.8	1.6	0.0	1.0	192
Biblical Theological Sem	0.0	6.6	1.1	0.0	87.9	4.4	182
Bryn Mawr C	0.2	8.2	3.7	2.2	79.3	6.4	1,847
Bucknell U	0.1	1.2	2.0	0.9	93.3	2.5	3,412
Bucks County CC	0.1	1.1	1.3	0.7	96.8	0.0	10,028
Butler County CC	0.0	0.2	0.8	0.3	98.8	0.0	2,488
Cabrini C	0.0	0.6	2.2	0.4	96.8	0.0	1,262
Carlow C	0.8	0.6	14.4	0.4	82.5	1.1	962
Carnegie Mellon U	0.1	2.2	2.2	0.2	83.5	11.8	6,993
Cedar Crest C	0.2	0.4	0.5	1.2	97.4	0.4	1,039
Center for Degree Studies	0.2	0.6	18.9	1.8	78.1	0.4	17,738
Central Pennsylvania Business Sch	0.1	0.7	1.6	0.9	96.6	0.1	696
Chatham C	0.0	1.2	8.3	0.7	87.9	1.9	686
Chestnut Hill C	0.0	2.1	6.7	2.4	88.4	0.3	1,191
C Misericordia	0.0	0.0	0.6	0.0	98.9	0.5	1,232
CC of Allegheny County	0.3	0.8	10.8	0.3	87.5	0.3	18,211
CC of Beaver County	0.0	0.0	4.9	0.0	95.1	0.0	2,603
CC of Philadelphia	0.4	5.3	38.8	4.1	51.4	0.0	14,215
Curtis Inst of Music	0.0	6.1	2.5	3.1	57.1	31.3	163
Dean Inst of Tech	0.0	0.0	13.9	0.8	85.2	0.0	122
Delaware County CC	0.1	1.0	4.0	0.4	94.4	0.0	8,273
Delaware Valley C	0.0	0.0	2.6	0.0	97.4	0.0	1,654
Dickinson C	0.0	2.3	0.7	0.9	94.8	1.3	2,041
Dickinson Sch of Law	0.0	1.2	1.3	0.7	95.0	1.8	596
Drexel U	0.2	5.5	4.4	1.0	83.6	5.3	12,263
Du Bois Business C	0.0	0.7	0.0	0.0	99.3	0.0	278
Duquesne U	1.0	1.4	3.3	1.0	92.9	0.4	6,366
Eastern Baptist Theol Sem	0.0	2.8	27.4	2.0	64.7	3.1	351
Eastern C	0.1	1.2	6.8	1.5	84.1	6.3	1,155
Elizabethtown C	0.0	0.8	0.7	0.2	97.9	0.4	1,788
Erie Business Center	0.0	0.0	4.8	0.0	95.2	0.0	248
Evangelical Sch of Theology	0.0	4.8	0.0	0.0	95.2	0.0	62
Faith Theological Sem	0.0	43.4	0.0	1.9	5.7	49.1	53
Franklin and Marshall C	0.0	3.0	2.8	1.2	90.7	2.2	2,410
Gannon U	0.2	1.0	1.8	0.3	94.9	1.7	3,687
Geneva C	0.2	1.1	4.7	0.2	93.1	0.7	1,234

PA., cont.

	American Indian	Asian	Black	Hispanic	White	Foreign	Total
Gettysburg C	0.0%	0.9%	1.7%	0.6%	95.2%	1.5%	2,022
Gratz C	0.0	0.0	11.5	0.0	86.1	2.4	582
Grove City C	0.0	2.2	0.2	0.8	96.7	0.0	2,152
Gwynedd-Mercy C	0.2	1.4	3.0	0.4	92.9	2.2	1,795
Hahnemann U	0.3	6.0	12.8	1.9	77.5	1.6	2,042
Harcum JC	0.0	1.7	7.3	1.4	85.0	4.5	762
Harrisburg Area CC	0.1	2.0	5.1	1.0	91.5	0.3	6,686
Haverford C	0.0	6.9	4.8	3.7	84.6	0.0	1,105
Holy Family C	0.1	0.7	1.3	1.0	95.3	1.6	1,657
Hussian Sch of Art	0.0	0.0	7.3	2.2	90.4	0.0	178
Immaculata C	0.0	0.8	3.1	3.2	91.3	1.6	2,095
Johnson Tech Inst	0.0	0.2	0.0	0.0	99.5	0.2	440
Juniata C	0.0	0.8	0.7	0.0	96.0	2.5	1,137
Keystone JC	0.1	0.2	2.7	0.3	95.7	1.0	1,245
King's C	0.0	0.2	0.2	0.5	98.8	0.3	2,304
La Roche C	0.0	0.6	1.6	0.6	97.0	0.1	1,852
La Salle U	0.0	0.4	5.3	0.6	93.7	0.0	6,364
Lackawanna JC	0.2	0.3	1.6	0.3	97.7	0.0	1,192
Lafayette C	0.0	2.0	3.0	0.9	90.9	3.1	2,352
Lancaster Bible C	0.0	0.8	1.8	1.1	94.2	2.1	380
Lancaster Theological Sem	0.0	0.5	8.9	0.5	87.9	2.3	214
Lebanon Valley C	0.2	1.0	0.5	0.5	97.6	0.2	1,274
Lehigh County CC	0.0	1.6	1.1	1.8	95.2	0.3	3,487
Lehigh U	0.0	3.1	1.5	1.4	86.1	7.8	6,569
Lincoln Tech Inst	0.0	0.9	1.3	1.2	95.8	0.9	687
Lincoln U	0.0	0.5	90.5	1.4	7.1	0.6	1,251
Lutheran Theological Sem at Gettysburg	0.0	0.4	2.2	0.7	95.9	0.7	270
Lutheran Theological Sem at Philadelphia	0.0	1.8	22.3	1.8	73.3	0.7	273
Luzerne County CC	0.1	1.1	1.2	0.4	97.2	0.1	5,688
Lycoming C	0.0	1.2	0.7	0.5	97.5	0.1	1,150
Manor JC	0.3	1.1	9.2	2.2	86.7	0.5	368
Mary Immaculate Sem	0.0	0.0	0.0	2.7	97.3	0.0	37
Marywood C	0.1	0.2	0.3	0.7	97.9	0.9	3,006
McCarrie Schs of Health Sciences & Tech	0.0	0.0	61.1	13.0	25.9	0.0	54
Medical C of Pennsylvania	0.2	9.7	5.4	1.1	81.4	2.2	554
Median Sch of Allied Health Careers	0.0	0.0	16.3	0.0	83.7	0.0	252
Mercyhurst C	0.2	0.4	4.1	0.2	95.1	0.0	2,018
Messiah C	0.1	1.4	2.0	1.0	93.8	1.8	2,184
Montgomery County CC	0.5	2.8	4.5	0.9	91.3	0.0	7,170
Moore C of Art and Design	0.1	2.9	6.7	1.3	86.1	2.8	685
Moravian C	0.1	0.7	0.7	0.3	98.2	0.0	1,804
Mount Aloysius JC	0.0	0.2	1.2	0.2	98.0	0.4	943
Muhlenberg C	0.0	1.9	0.6	0.8	96.0	0.7	2,084
Neumann C	0.1	1.1	6.1	0.7	91.7	0.4	1,139
Northampton County Area CC	0.2	1.0	1.7	2.5	94.1	0.4	4,712
Northeastern Christian JC	0.6	0.0	22.9	1.7	65.4	9.5	179
Peirce JC	0.3	1.4	40.7	2.5	54.3	0.8	1,197
Pennsylvania C of Optometry	0.2	4.1	5.4	2.1	87.5	0.8	634
Pennsylvania C of Podiatric Medicine	0.2	4.6	6.2	2.1	84.4	2.5	437
Pennsylvania C of Tech	0.1	0.3	1.2	0.2	98.2	0.0	3,700
Pennsylvania Inst of Tech	0.0	1.7	19.7	0.3	78.1	0.3	360

	American Indian	Asian	Black	Hispanic	White	Foreign	Total
Pennsylvania St U							
Main	0.2%	2.1%	3.9%	1.4%	87.8%	4.7%	37,269
Allentown	0.0	3.2	0.6	1.4	94.5	0.3	781
Altoona	0.2	1.2	3.7	0.7	94.0	0.2	2,604
Beaver	0.1	0.9	4.7	0.8	93.4	0.1	1,104
Berks	0.0	1.6	0.3	1.0	97.1	0.0	1,440
Delaware	0.1	2.5	6.4	1.0	90.1	0.0	1,861
Du Bois	0.5	0.4	0.3	0.2	98.3	0.2	957
Erie-Behrend C	0.1	1.3	3.7	0.7	94.0	0.1	2,830
Fayette	0.0	0.3	2.7	0.4	96.4	0.1	894
Great Valley	0.9	6.8	4.2	0.8	87.2	0.1	886
Harrisburg-Capital C	0.1	2.2	3.7	0.8	92.4	0.8	3,144
Hazleton	0.2	1.9	2.0	2.4	93.4	0.1	1,276
Hershey Medical C	0.3	3.4	4.0	0.9	87.7	3.7	698
McKeesport	0.1	1.4	9.0	0.1	89.3	0.1	1,463
Mont Alto	0.3	2.6	4.5	0.9	91.4	0.2	970
New Kensington	0.1	0.6	1.8	0.1	97.4	0.1	1,428
Ogontz	0.1	3.1	5.9	1.1	89.8	0.1	3,502
Schuylkill	0.0	1.8	1.1	0.7	96.4	0.0	1,122
Shenango Valley	0.1	0.4	2.9	0.1	96.6	0.0	1,078
Wilkes-Barre	0.1	0.9	1.0	0.4	97.4	0.1	980
Worthington-Scranton	0.2	0.6	0.2	0.7	98.3	0.0	1,321
York	0.2	2.8	2.3	0.9	93.8	0.0	1,662
Philadelphia C of Bible	0.7	1.4	5.7	2.7	86.1	3.4	584
Philadelphia C of Osteopathic Medicine	0.0	2.0	2.8	1.2	93.8	0.1	808
Philadelphia C of Pharmacy and Science	0.0	8.9	2.1	0.6	86.0	2.6	1,603
Philadelphia C of Textiles and Science	0.0	2.1	8.3	0.5	84.5	4.6	3,417
Pinebrook JC	0.0	2.7	14.2	0.0	73.6	9.5	148
Pittsburgh Inst of Aeronautics	0.1	0.1	2.1	0.1	97.6	0.0	878
Pittsburgh Theological Sem	0.0	1.3	5.8	0.3	92.5	0.0	308
Point Park C	0.0	1.1	8.0	0.7	86.1	4.1	2,820
Reading Area CC	0.4	1.3	6.9	5.3	85.7	0.4	1,640
Reformed Presbyterian Theol Sem	0.0	0.0	38.7	0.0	58.7	2.5	80
RETS Electronic Sch	0.3	0.9	14.4	1.1	83.0	0.3	348
Robert Morris C	0.2	0.3	4.4	0.2	94.2	0.6	5,500
Rosemont C	0.0	1.1	2.9	1.4	94.3	0.3	648
Saint Charles Borromeo Sem	0.0	1.7	3.1	2.6	92.6	0.0	351
Saint Francis C	0.0	0.3	1.6	0.2	98.0	0.0	1,791
Saint Joseph's U	0.0	1.3	5.9	1.9	87.7	3.2	5,787
Saint Vincent C	0.1	0.3	1.2	1.0	96.6	0.7	1,205
Saint Vincent Sem	0.0	0.0	0.0	0.0	100.0	0.0	55
Seton Hill C	0.1	0.6	3.3	4.8	90.0	1.1	870
Spring Garden C	0.1	2.8	10.9	1.3	83.6	1.2	1,545
St Sys of Higher Education							
Bloomsburg U of Pa	0.1	0.5	2.3	0.6	95.8	0.7	6,804
California U of Pa	0.2	0.7	3.9	0.4	94.1	0.7	6,313
Cheyney U of Pa	0.1	0.1	92.5	0.4	3.9	3.1	1,361
Clarion U of Pa	0.1	0.2	2.2	0.1	94.9	2.4	6,601
East Stroudsburg U of Pa	0.1	0.7	2.6	1.1	94.0	1.6	4,910
Edinboro U of Pa	0.2	0.4	3.5	0.3	94.3	1.3	7,001
Indiana U of Pa	0.1	0.5	4.0	0.4	92.6	2.4	13,650
Kutztown U of Pa	0.1	0.6	3.0	0.9	94.5	0.9	7,167
Lock Haven U of Pa	0.2	0.3	3.0	0.3	94.3	1.9	3,012

PA., cont.

	American Indian	Asian	Black	Hispanic	White	Foreign	Total
St Sys of Higher Education							
Mansfield U of Pa	0.1%	0.1%	2.9%	0.3%	95.8%	0.9%	2,980
Millersville U of Pa	0.2	1.5	4.7	1.3	92.0	0.4	7,389
Shippensburg U of Pa	0.1	0.7	3.1	0.4	94.7	1.0	6,352
Slippery Rock U of Pa	0.3	0.3	3.1	0.4	94.2	1.8	7,360
West Chester U of Pa	0.1	1.1	6.0	0.7	90.8	1.3	11,475
Susquehanna U	0.1	0.5	0.4	0.5	97.8	0.8	1,697
Swarthmore C	0.3	4.6	6.7	1.7	81.6	5.1	1,356
Temple U	0.3	3.9	14.2	2.1	76.0	3.5	32,139
Thiel C	0.0	0.2	5.6	0.0	93.0	1.2	917
Thomas Jefferson U	0.5	6.1	7.1	1.7	83.1	1.5	2,112
Trinity Episcopal Sch for Ministry	0.0	0.0	2.6	0.9	92.2	4.3	116
United Wesleyan C	0.0	0.0	6.6	1.3	76.3	15.8	152
U of the Arts	0.6	2.7	7.8	1.7	82.7	4.5	1,396
U of Pennsylvania	0.2	5.6	5.2	2.2	74.7	12.1	22,169
U of Pittsburgh							
Main	0.1	1.9	8.2	0.8	84.1	4.9	28,524
Bradford	0.2	0.9	2.9	0.5	95.4	0.0	954
Greensburg	0.0	0.6	0.6	0.1	98.7	0.0	1,452
Johnstown	0.0	0.4	1.4	0.2	98.0	0.1	3,270
Titusville	0.0	0.8	0.5	0.3	98.5	0.0	394
U of Scranton	0.1	0.6	0.2	0.4	98.0	0.6	4,929
Ursinus C	0.2	1.0	1.1	0.5	96.7	0.4	2,286
Valley Forge Christian C	0.2	3.8	3.6	1.8	89.7	1.0	506
Valley Forge Military JC	0.0	1.0	4.1	2.6	87.8	4.6	196
Villa Maria C	0.0	1.0	2.3	0.0	96.8	0.0	708
Villanova U	0.1	1.6	2.2	0.7	95.0	0.4	12,054
Washington and Jefferson C	0.1	1.3	1.7	0.6	96.0	0.4	1,390
Watterson Career Center	0.0	0.0	89.0	9.9	1.1	0.0	91
Watterson Sch of Business and Tech	0.0	0.0	72.1	26.2	1.6	0.0	305
Waynesburg C	0.0	0.4	5.1	0.0	92.6	1.9	990
Westminster C	0.0	0.1	0.5	0.0	99.2	0.1	1,475
Westminster Theol Sem	0.2	18.1	3.9	1.0	66.0	10.7	485
Westmoreland County CC	0.1	0.3	1.4	0.0	98.2	0.0	4,570
Widener U	0.2	1.1	7.5	0.6	90.3	0.3	6,173
Wilkes C	0.0	0.9	0.3	0.2	98.0	0.6	3,626
Wilson C	0.0	0.0	0.9	0.4	97.4	1.3	702
York C of Pennsylvania	0.0	0.9	1.7	0.5	96.8	0.1	4,873

RHODE ISLAND

	American Indian	Asian	Black	Hispanic	White	Foreign	Total
Brown U	0.1	7.6	6.0	2.7	76.8	6.8	7,612
Bryant C	0.0	0.5	0.7	1.0	96.9	0.9	5,658
CC of Rhode Island	0.7	1.7	4.2	2.7	90.4	0.3	14,715
Johnson & Wales U	0.3	1.0	6.0	1.6	88.3	2.9	7,210
New England Inst of Tech	0.1	0.6	1.5	0.3	97.3	0.3	1,770
Providence C	0.0	0.4	1.0	0.6	97.4	0.6	5,750
Rhode Island C	0.2	1.0	1.9	1.4	95.0	0.6	8,431
Rhode Island Sch of Design	0.1	2.9	2.5	1.1	83.5	9.8	1,943
Roger Williams C	0.3	0.7	0.5	0.7	95.8	2.1	3,655
Salve Regina the Newport C	0.2	0.3	0.5	0.4	97.2	1.4	2,252
U of Rhode Island	0.3	1.6	2.0	1.4	91.5	3.1	15,843

SOUTH CAROLINA

	American Indian	Asian	Black	Hispanic	White	Foreign	Total
Aiken Tech C	0.7%	0.9%	28.4%	0.7%	69.1%	0.2%	1,485
Anderson C	0.0	0.2	9.8	0.3	87.8	2.0	1,045
Baptist C at Charleston	0.2	0.8	20.6	0.8	77.7	0.0	1,926
Benedict C	0.0	0.0	98.5	0.0	0.0	1.5	1,448
Bob Jones U	0.0	0.5	29.6	0.4	68.6	0.9	4,384
Career Com C of Business	0.0	0.0	88.0	0.0	12.0	0.0	92
Central Wesleyan C	0.0	0.6	8.8	0.0	89.5	1.0	679
Chesterfield-Marlboro Tech C	1.2	0.3	24.2	0.1	74.1	0.0	731
Citadel Military C of SC	0.2	0.5	7.8	0.3	90.5	0.7	3,628
Claflin C	0.0	0.0	99.1	0.0	0.5	0.4	742
Clemson U	0.1	0.6	5.3	0.5	89.5	3.9	14,794
Clinton JC	0.0	0.0	100.0	0.0	0.0	0.0	88
Coker C	0.4	0.4	25.8	1.1	71.1	1.2	814
C of Charleston	0.2	1.5	6.5	0.5	89.7	1.7	6,205
Columbia Bible C and Sem	0.0	2.0	2.6	1.8	85.8	7.8	929
Columbia C	0.2	1.1	20.5	0.6	77.4	0.2	1,213
Columbia JC of Business	0.0	0.0	86.9	0.2	12.6	0.2	427
Converse C	0.1	0.4	3.2	0.5	95.4	0.4	1,251
Denmark Tech C	0.0	0.0	98.6	0.0	1.4	0.0	699
Erskine C and Sem	0.1	0.3	7.0	0.6	90.4	1.6	674
Florence Darlington Tech C	0.1	0.2	25.5	0.3	73.9	0.1	1,875
Francis Marion C	0.2	0.6	14.2	0.2	84.5	0.3	3,929
Furman U	0.0	0.8	3.8	0.3	95.0	0.0	3,205
Greenville Tech C	0.1	0.9	12.5	0.6	85.7	0.2	6,135
Horry-Georgetown Tech C	0.2	1.0	16.0	0.5	82.2	0.1	1,661
Johnson & Wales U Charleston	1.0	1.0	14.3	0.8	82.8	0.0	495
Lander C	0.1	0.4	16.1	0.3	81.8	1.4	2,461
Limestone C	0.0	0.1	17.7	0.5	81.1	0.5	921
Lutheran Theol Southern Sem	0.0	0.0	6.9	0.0	93.1	0.0	160
Medical U of South Carolina	0.2	2.8	7.0	0.6	88.4	1.0	2,118
Midlands Tech C	0.3	0.7	28.5	1.2	69.2	0.0	6,082
Morris C	0.0	0.0	100.0	0.0	0.0	0.0	774
Newberry C	0.4	0.4	16.8	0.3	81.8	0.3	686
Nielsen Electronics Inst	0.0	2.6	60.7	0.0	36.7	0.0	229
North Greenville C	0.4	0.6	33.3	0.4	65.0	0.4	532
Orangeburg-Calhoun Tech C	0.2	0.4	42.3	0.3	56.5	0.3	1,149
Piedmont Tech C	0.0	0.2	28.3	0.2	71.3	0.0	1,745
Presbyterian C	0.0	0.2	4.1	0.2	95.0	0.5	1,108
Rutledge C Charleston	0.0	2.2	49.3	2.5	45.9	0.0	357
Rutledge C Spartanburg	0.0	0.0	44.4	0.0	55.6	0.0	135
Sherman C of Straight Chiropractic	0.0	1.6	4.1	0.0	81.1	13.1	122
South Carolina St C	0.1	0.4	91.8	0.0	7.5	0.2	4,399
Spartanburg Methodist C	0.0	0.5	20.5	0.3	78.5	0.2	976
Spartanburg Tech C	0.2	1.4	13.3	0.2	84.8	0.1	1,725
Sumter Area Tech C	0.1	0.8	37.4	1.2	60.4	0.1	1,564
Tech C of the Lowcountry	2.0	0.6	34.7	1.1	60.8	0.7	950
Tri-County Tech C	0.1	0.3	9.0	0.8	89.1	0.7	2,327
Trident Tech C	0.3	2.6	18.2	1.0	77.6	0.4	5,594
U of South Carolina Columbia	0.1	1.3	12.4	0.8	82.2	3.3	26,435
Aiken	0.0	0.5	14.6	0.8	83.8	0.3	2,532
Beaufort	0.5	1.3	13.6	2.5	81.6	0.0	1,010

S.C., cont.

	American Indian	Asian	Black	Hispanic	White	Foreign	Total
U of South Carolina							
Coastal Carolina	0.2%	0.7%	7.9%	0.5%	89.6%	1.1%	4,135
Lancaster	0.1	0.4	13.6	0.0	85.7	0.2	1,004
Salkehatchie	0.3	0.6	26.6	0.0	72.1	0.3	628
Spartanburg	0.0	1.0	8.7	0.4	89.0	0.8	3,265
Sumter	0.1	1.2	15.8	1.1	81.7	0.2	1,440
Union	0.3	0.0	16.9	0.3	82.5	0.0	343
Williamsburg Tech C	0.0	0.0	35.8	0.2	63.9	0.0	402
Winthrop C	0.1	0.4	14.8	0.7	81.6	2.4	5,351
Wofford C	0.1	1.0	6.4	0.5	91.6	0.4	1,118

SOUTH DAKOTA

Augustana C	0.3	0.4	0.7	0.1	94.9	3.5	2,048
Dakota Wesleyan U	8.8	0.3	0.7	0.0	89.4	0.7	667
Huron U	14.9	0.0	10.1	0.8	71.4	2.7	483
Kilian CC	1.3	0.0	0.8	0.0	97.9	0.0	237
Mount Marty C	1.5	0.5	0.5	0.1	97.3	0.1	850
National C	5.1	0.5	4.7	2.7	86.2	0.8	918
National C Sioux Falls	2.8	0.8	1.7	1.4	93.2	0.0	355
North American Baptist Sem	0.0	1.6	0.0	0.0	94.3	4.1	123
Oglala Lakota C	90.5	0.0	0.0	0.0	9.5	0.0	897
Presentation C	14.1	0.6	0.0	0.3	84.5	0.6	354
Sinte Gleska C	74.5	0.0	0.0	0.0	25.5	0.0	502
Sioux Falls C	0.8	0.8	0.6	0.1	97.4	0.3	880
SD St Bd of Regents Sys							
U of South Dakota	1.7	0.5	0.7	0.1	96.5	0.6	6,759
South Dakota St U	0.7	0.3	0.2	0.1	95.8	2.9	7,735
Black Hills St U	1.6	0.2	0.7	0.4	97.1	0.1	2,282
Dakota St C	0.4	0.6	1.2	0.2	97.3	0.4	1,111
Northern St U	2.5	0.2	0.1	0.0	97.1	0.1	3,066
Sisseton-Wahpeton CC	85.5	0.0	0.0	0.0	14.5	0.0	145
SD Sch of Mines and Tech	1.4	0.7	0.5	0.2	85.2	12.1	2,048

TENNESSEE

American Baptist C	0.0	0.0	86.5	0.5	0.0	13.0	185
Aquinas JC	0.5	1.4	5.2	1.6	89.3	2.0	440
Belmont C	0.1	0.5	3.0	0.3	92.8	3.3	2,580
Bethel C	0.0	0.0	6.5	0.0	92.1	1.3	596
Bristol U	0.0	0.0	13.0	1.0	85.5	0.5	193
Career Com C of Business	0.4	0.0	21.9	0.7	76.3	0.7	274
Carson-Newman C	0.3	0.2	3.6	0.4	94.9	0.7	1,999
Christian Brothers C	0.3	1.6	19.5	0.8	75.4	2.4	1,798
Church of God Sch of Theol	0.5	1.0	3.4	3.4	72.4	19.2	203
Cooper Inst	0.0	0.0	30.4	0.0	69.6	0.0	79
Crichton C	0.0	0.3	35.0	0.3	63.4	1.0	314
Cumberland U	0.0	1.1	7.4	0.3	90.6	0.6	651
David Lipscomb U	0.1	0.3	2.6	0.2	96.2	0.6	2,320
Draughons JC Bristol	0.0	0.0	4.1	0.0	95.9	0.0	197
Draughons JC Johnson City	0.0	0.3	3.0	0.0	96.7	0.0	300
Draughons JC Kingsport	0.0	0.6	3.7	0.0	95.1	0.6	164
Draughons JC Knoxville	0.2	0.0	19.0	0.4	79.6	0.9	568
Draughons JC Memphis	0.0	0.0	78.6	0.0	21.4	0.0	388
Draughons JC Nashville	0.0	0.6	30.1	10.0	59.4	0.0	512
Emmanuel Sch of Religion	0.0	0.6	1.3	0.6	92.3	5.1	156

	American Indian	Asian	Black	Hispanic	White	Foreign	Total
Fisk U	0.0%	0.0%	98.1%	0.0%	0.1%	1.8%	774
Free Will Baptist Bible C	0.7	0.0	0.3	0.7	96.5	1.7	286
Freed-Hardeman C	0.1	0.5	5.7	0.1	90.7	2.9	1,144
Harding U Grad Sch of Religion	0.0	0.0	3.7	0.0	90.7	5.6	162
Hiwassee C	0.0	0.0	6.8	0.0	89.2	3.9	584
Johnson Bible C	0.0	0.2	0.7	0.9	95.6	2.6	430
King C	0.0	1.9	0.9	4.3	91.2	1.9	588
Knoxville Business C	0.0	2.0	20.0	0.0	78.0	0.0	250
Knoxville C	0.2	0.0	98.9	0.0	0.3	0.7	1,310
Lambuth C	0.0	0.3	13.5	0.1	82.3	3.7	747
Lane C	0.0	0.0	99.6	0.0	0.0	0.4	541
Lee C	0.5	0.7	2.0	3.1	89.8	4.0	1,535
Lemoyne-Owen C	0.0	0.0	98.1	0.0	0.3	1.6	1,130
Lincoln Memorial U	0.0	0.1	1.5	0.1	86.5	11.8	1,582
Martin Methodist C	0.3	0.0	9.7	1.2	80.6	8.2	330
Maryville C	0.1	0.4	3.8	0.9	90.6	4.2	787
McKenzie C	0.0	0.0	29.1	1.3	69.6	0.0	237
Memphis C of Art	0.0	1.2	14.6	1.2	82.3	0.8	254
Memphis Theological Sem	0.0	0.7	24.5	0.0	74.8	0.0	143
Mid-America Baptist Theol Sem	0.0	0.2	1.4	0.0	95.7	2.7	414
Milligan C	0.0	0.8	1.8	1.4	95.4	0.6	658
Rhodes C	0.0	1.6	4.5	0.5	92.6	0.8	1,346
Rutledge C Memphis	0.0	0.0	92.9	0.0	6.5	0.6	170
Southern C of Optometry	0.8	2.1	3.9	1.8	91.4	0.0	382
Southern C of Seventh-Day Adventists	0.4	2.3	7.5	4.9	82.9	2.1	1,443
St U and CC Sys of Tenn							
Austin Peay St U	0.3	1.3	15.4	2.5	80.0	0.5	5,177
East Tennessee St U	0.3	0.5	2.6	0.4	95.3	0.9	10,983
Memphis St U	0.2	0.5	16.8	0.3	78.7	3.4	20,267
Middle Tennessee St U	0.2	0.3	8.1	0.4	88.8	2.2	13,174
Tennessee St U	0.2	3.3	62.8	0.4	33.4	0.0	7,352
Tennessee Tech U	0.1	0.8	3.2	0.5	92.9	2.6	7,901
Chattanooga St Tech CC	0.3	0.7	10.7	0.4	87.9	0.1	7,365
Cleveland St CC	0.3	0.3	5.0	0.8	93.4	0.2	2,977
Columbia St CC	0.3	0.2	8.1	0.2	89.5	1.8	2,665
Dyersburg St CC	0.3	0.2	12.0	0.2	87.3	0.0	1,742
Jackson St CC	0.0	0.1	12.8	0.1	86.9	0.0	2,774
Motlow St CC	0.1	0.4	5.4	0.4	93.7	0.0	2,396
Nashville St Tech Inst	0.1	1.4	12.1	0.7	85.6	0.1	5,358
Pellissippi St Tech CC	0.3	1.0	3.9	0.3	93.8	0.8	2,981
Roane St CC	0.2	0.5	2.9	0.2	96.1	0.1	3,868
Shelby St CC	0.2	0.5	56.8	0.3	42.3	0.0	3,822
St Tech Inst Memphis	0.2	0.9	30.7	0.5	67.5	0.1	7,398
Tri-Cities St Tech Inst	0.1	0.3	1.1	0.0	98.4	0.0	1,667
Volunteer St CC	0.3	0.4	4.9	0.5	93.9	0.1	3,473
Walters St CC	0.8	0.2	2.6	0.2	96.1	0.2	3,332
Tennessee Temple U	0.1	0.6	3.3	1.6	93.3	1.0	1,406
Tennessee Wesleyan C	0.3	0.5	6.5	0.2	87.7	4.8	600
Tomlinson C	0.0	0.3	6.6	3.7	81.7	7.6	301
Trevecca Nazarene C	0.1	0.3	20.5	0.2	78.4	0.5	1,977
Tusculum C	0.0	0.0	9.3	0.2	89.4	1.0	953
Union U	0.0	0.0	7.1	0.0	92.1	0.7	2,031
U of Tennessee Chattanooga	0.3	1.2	10.1	0.0	85.5	2.1	7,526

TENNESSEE, cont.

	American Indian	Asian	Black	Hispanic	White	Foreign	Total
U of Tennessee							
Knoxville	0.2%	1.0%	4.5%	0.4%	90.8%	3.1%	24,985
Martin	0.1	0.5	13.0	0.2	82.5	3.7	4,653
Memphis	0.2	3.7	6.3	0.6	86.5	2.7	1,773
U of the South	0.1	0.3	1.0	0.4	96.2	2.0	1,171
Vanderbilt U	0.1	2.0	3.9	0.7	87.3	5.9	8,960
William Jennings Bryan C	0.0	0.2	5.6	0.4	89.6	4.3	517

TEXAS

	American Indian	Asian	Black	Hispanic	White	Foreign	Total
Abilene Christian U	0.1	1.6	4.0	2.0	91.6	0.8	4,181
Alamo CC Dist							
Palo Alto C	0.7	0.7	5.9	55.1	37.2	0.5	3,386
St Philip's C	0.4	1.6	24.5	37.2	35.6	0.6	5,867
San Antonio C	0.4	1.5	5.7	42.9	48.9	0.6	21,593
Amarillo C	0.6	2.4	2.9	9.6	84.0	0.5	5,395
Amber U	0.7	0.9	19.5	4.0	71.9	2.9	1,233
American Tech U	0.8	1.2	20.4	8.3	67.6	1.7	593
Angelina C	0.7	0.3	12.6	2.1	84.2	0.0	2,962
Angelo St U	0.3	0.8	4.5	11.8	80.8	1.8	6,334
Art Inst of Houston	0.3	2.2	13.6	18.8	65.0	0.0	987
Austin C	0.5	3.3	2.9	3.7	88.7	0.9	1,269
Austin CC	0.4	3.3	6.6	14.9	74.1	0.7	21,418
Austin Presbyterian Theol Sem	0.4	1.2	2.5	3.3	90.5	2.1	241
Baptist Missionary Association Theol Sem	0.0	0.9	16.7	0.0	81.5	0.9	108
Bauder Fashion C	0.0	0.7	1.4	6.3	90.2	1.4	441
Baylor C of Dentistry	0.0	10.0	3.2	5.8	78.4	2.6	468
Baylor C of Medicine	0.1	11.0	1.1	5.2	73.0	9.6	937
Baylor U	0.3	2.4	2.1	2.5	91.0	1.6	11,789
Bee County C	0.4	0.7	2.6	52.7	43.6	0.0	2,550
Blinn C	0.3	0.7	7.0	6.8	82.8	2.4	5,889
Brazosport C	0.3	0.9	7.0	10.8	80.8	0.3	3,550
Central Texas C	0.5	2.9	20.8	9.0	65.8	1.0	6,079
Cisco JC	0.2	0.7	6.6	6.3	86.2	0.0	1,972
Clarendon C	0.3	0.0	5.0	4.1	90.5	0.0	916
C of the Mainland	0.6	1.2	14.8	9.0	73.3	1.2	3,458
Collin County CC	0.3	1.8	2.1	3.2	92.4	0.2	7,153
Concordia Lutheran C	0.4	0.6	5.1	7.9	86.0	0.0	507
Cooke County C	0.6	0.7	3.2	2.8	90.8	1.9	2,968
Criswell C	0.3	2.9	7.3	6.0	78.9	4.7	383
Dallas Baptist U	0.3	2.9	22.0	4.1	66.8	3.8	2,018
Dallas Christian C	1.0	1.0	6.0	4.0	86.0	2.0	100
Dallas County CC Dist							
Brookhaven C	0.4	5.8	7.5	7.0	78.2	1.1	7,929
Cedar Valley C	0.5	0.8	39.2	5.2	54.1	0.1	3,083
Eastfield C	0.8	4.4	8.6	7.8	77.9	0.5	9,396
El Centro C	0.5	2.4	44.8	9.3	41.4	1.6	5,761
Mountain View C	0.7	3.7	20.5	14.0	60.7	0.4	5,967
North Lake C	0.5	4.9	7.6	7.5	78.9	0.7	6,126
Richland C	0.4	6.0	7.5	5.4	79.8	0.9	13,101
Dallas Theological Sem	0.2	5.5	5.5	1.0	79.3	8.7	1,244
Del Mar C	0.4	0.9	3.1	47.5	48.0	0.2	9,972
DeVry Inst of Tech	0.6	5.6	21.2	14.9	55.8	1.9	2,354
East Texas Baptist U	0.5	0.9	7.3	1.1	88.8	1.5	809
East Texas St U	0.6	0.7	9.3	2.6	82.8	4.0	7,315

	American Indian	Asian	Black	Hispanic	White	Foreign	Total
East Texas St U Texarkana ...	0.5%	0.2%	9.6%	0.7%	88.5%	0.5%	1,286
El Paso County CC	0.5	0.8	4.5	71.5	21.9	0.8	14,820
Episcopal Theological Sem of the Southwest	0.0	0.0	1.4	4.3	88.6	5.7	70
Frank Phillips C	0.9	0.1	3.2	5.5	89.8	0.4	965
Galveston C	0.1	2.6	19.6	16.0	60.9	0.7	2,215
Grayson County C	0.9	0.7	5.2	1.6	91.6	0.0	4,003
Hardin-Simmons U	0.3	0.5	2.6	5.9	89.7	1.0	1,928
Hill C	0.1	0.2	7.1	6.1	86.3	0.3	1,534
Houston Baptist U	0.2	9.8	9.0	8.3	69.4	3.3	2,429
Houston CC	0.2	7.5	20.2	13.0	58.2	0.8	30,236
Houston Graduate Sch of Theology	0.0	11.1	21.5	5.6	59.0	2.8	144
Howard County JC Dist	0.2	0.9	6.2	18.5	73.8	0.3	1,645
Howard Payne U	0.2	0.2	6.5	6.7	86.1	0.2	1,247
Huston-Tillotson C	0.0	1.2	70.6	2.2	3.2	22.9	506
Incarnate Word C	0.4	1.1	7.3	39.4	49.0	2.9	2,240
Inst for Christian Studies	0.0	1.4	5.5	5.5	84.9	2.7	73
ITT Tech Inst	0.0	6.5	16.3	27.1	50.2	0.0	658
Jacksonville C	0.0	0.4	8.3	0.8	71.8	18.8	266
Jarvis Christian C	0.0	0.0	99.4	0.0	0.6	0.0	538
Kilgore C	0.2	0.3	11.7	1.1	86.5	0.1	4,289
Lamar U							
Main	0.3	1.8	17.0	2.5	75.4	3.0	11,809
Orange	0.6	0.5	9.6	2.2	87.0	0.0	1,110
Port Arthur	0.3	2.5	27.5	4.8	64.6	0.3	1,707
Laredo JC	0.0	0.4	0.2	89.6	6.2	3.7	4,891
Le Tourneau C	0.3	0.5	0.9	0.9	91.6	5.7	749
Lee C	0.4	0.5	16.1	11.3	71.3	0.3	5,163
Lon Morris C	0.0	0.0	13.2	4.4	74.2	8.2	341
Lubbock Christian U	0.2	0.8	3.6	3.8	86.9	4.7	1,073
McLennan CC	0.1	0.8	13.4	6.5	79.0	0.2	5,411
McMurry C	0.7	0.7	8.3	7.4	81.2	1.8	1,683
Midland C	0.2	1.3	4.8	13.5	79.5	0.8	3,680
Midwestern St U	0.5	2.4	4.5	4.3	86.5	1.8	5,149
Miss Wade's Fashion Merchandising C	0.5	2.7	27.3	12.3	56.2	1.0	406
Navarro C	0.0	3.3	17.4	4.3	74.8	0.2	2,310
North Harris County C Dist ...	0.6	3.1	5.4	7.9	82.5	0.4	13,302
Northeast Texas CC	0.4	0.4	7.5	1.0	90.7	0.0	1,673
Northwood Inst	0.0	0.0	10.1	10.6	78.3	0.9	217
Odessa C	0.5	1.2	5.5	19.2	73.4	0.1	4,625
Our Lady of the Lake U	0.4	0.6	7.7	45.0	45.1	1.2	2,245
Panola C	0.0	0.1	14.6	1.0	84.3	0.1	1,454
Paris JC	1.0	0.4	10.2	0.9	84.9	2.6	2,221
Parker C of Chiropractic	0.5	2.0	2.0	3.3	92.1	0.0	393
Paul Quinn C	0.0	0.0	95.7	0.4	3.1	0.8	517
Ranger JC	0.5	0.2	32.1	9.1	57.8	0.3	635
Rice U	0.1	4.8	3.2	3.6	78.3	10.0	4,202
Saint Edward's U	0.2	1.3	5.5	20.5	65.1	7.4	2,823
Saint Mary's U	0.3	2.1	5.0	38.5	53.1	1.1	3,654
Sam Houston St U	0.3	0.5	8.8	4.7	84.2	1.5	11,561
San Jacinto C Sys							
Central	0.3	2.1	4.3	10.4	76.9	6.0	9,180
North	0.4	2.6	12.3	13.2	69.7	1.8	3,442
South	0.2	5.2	6.0	10.5	76.1	2.1	4,681
Schreiner C	0.2	1.0	3.3	11.3	82.4	1.8	602

TEXAS, cont.

	American Indian	Asian	Black	Hispanic	White	Foreign	Total
South Plains C	0.4%	0.8%	6.5%	17.8%	73.8%	0.7%	4,394
Southern Methodist U	0.2	3.5	3.1	3.6	85.8	3.9	8,944
Southwest Texas JC	0.3	0.6	1.2	59.1	38.2	0.7	2,450
Southwest Texas St U	0.3	0.8	4.6	12.7	80.7	1.0	20,505
Southwestern Adventist C	1.0	1.8	6.5	12.6	71.1	7.0	771
Southwestern Assemblies of God C	0.8	0.5	1.9	8.3	87.7	0.7	731
Southwestern Christian C	0.0	0.0	87.3	0.0	1.5	11.3	275
Southwestern U	0.1	2.7	2.6	6.3	86.6	1.6	1,171
Stephen F Austin St U	0.2	0.7	4.7	2.4	91.7	0.3	12,574
Sul Ross St U	0.1	0.1	4.1	36.7	57.5	1.5	2,236
Tarrant County JC Dist	0.4	2.4	8.4	6.7	81.9	0.2	25,946
Temple JC	0.2	0.9	9.5	9.1	79.6	0.6	2,383
Texarkana C	0.1	0.3	9.7	0.5	89.3	0.1	3,755
Texas A&M U Sys							
Corpus Christi St U	0.4	0.8	1.9	30.1	66.4	0.4	4,045
Laredo St U	0.1	0.4	1.1	80.8	12.0	5.7	1,076
Prairie View A&M U	0.1	0.8	83.1	1.2	8.8	6.0	5,640
Tarleton St U	0.2	0.2	2.2	2.5	94.5	0.4	5,667
Texas A&I U	0.2	1.5	3.5	55.5	36.1	3.2	5,614
Texas A&M U Main	0.2	2.3	2.7	6.8	83.2	4.7	39,163
Texas A&M U Galveston	0.3	1.5	0.9	4.9	91.0	1.5	742
Texas Chiropractic C	0.0	2.6	1.3	5.1	90.0	1.0	390
Texas Christian U	0.2	1.1	3.7	2.7	89.4	2.9	6,993
Texas C	0.0	1.0	87.1	0.0	0.2	11.7	410
Texas C of Osteopathic Med	0.5	7.7	1.3	6.1	84.4	0.0	391
Texas Lutheran C	0.2	1.5	4.9	10.2	82.0	1.1	1,319
Texas Southern U	0.2	1.1	77.5	3.9	3.5	13.9	8,666
Texas Southmost JC	0.2	0.2	0.1	85.6	12.1	1.8	5,526
Texas St Tech Inst Sys							
Amarillo	0.7	2.7	5.0	11.4	80.2	0.0	858
Harlingen	0.1	0.2	0.6	82.2	16.4	0.5	2,623
Waco	0.3	0.7	10.7	9.0	78.3	0.9	4,022
Sweetwater	0.1	1.6	4.9	17.9	75.4	0.0	748
Texas Tech U							
Main	0.2	0.7	2.4	6.8	85.9	3.9	24,605
Health Science Center	0.4	4.6	1.9	8.2	82.2	2.7	826
Texas Woman's U	0.4	1.1	13.7	6.1	74.2	4.4	8,898
Trinity U	0.5	4.0	1.3	8.1	83.9	2.2	2,412
Trinity Valley CC	0.4	0.4	14.9	4.9	78.6	0.7	4,276
Tyler JC	0.4	0.2	13.6	1.3	83.4	1.1	7,820
U of Dallas	0.6	3.9	3.1	4.4	77.3	10.6	2,649
U of Houston							
Clear Lake	0.2	4.0	4.5	6.1	83.6	1.6	7,196
Downtown	0.2	11.3	24.4	18.7	41.8	3.7	7,409
U Park	0.4	8.3	7.2	7.8	70.1	6.2	30,372
Victoria	0.6	0.7	2.5	9.5	86.8	0.0	1,059
U of Saint Thomas	0.2	5.8	4.7	12.9	68.2	8.2	1,646
U of Texas Sys							
Arlington	0.4	6.9	6.8	4.8	76.2	4.8	23,383
Austin	0.2	5.3	3.6	9.9	74.3	6.8	50,106
Dallas	0.3	5.9	4.4	3.1	82.1	4.3	7,667
El Paso	0.3	1.1	3.1	55.3	35.5	4.8	10,491
Tyler	0.6	0.4	6.7	0.9	90.2	1.2	3,859

	American Indian	Asian	Black	Hispanic	White	Foreign	Total
Health Science Center Houston	0.3%	10.1%	7.5%	9.3%	68.4%	4.3%	2,837
Health Science Center San Antonio	0.2	6.9	3.2	16.0	71.9	1.8	2,219
Medical Branch Galveston	0.6	9.1	6.7	9.6	71.3	2.7	1,705
Permian Basin	0.1	0.5	1.9	8.0	89.0	0.5	2,132
Pan American U	0.2	0.5	0.9	81.6	16.5	0.4	11,204
Pan American U Brownsville	0.2	0.0	1.3	74.2	24.1	0.3	1,516
San Antonio	0.2	2.6	3.4	26.7	66.3	0.8	13,134
SW Medical Ctr Dallas	0.1	6.4	3.2	6.8	79.7	3.8	1,458
U of North Texas	0.3	1.3	6.4	3.6	83.2	5.1	24,498
Vernon Regional JC	0.7	2.0	8.2	6.7	82.5	0.1	1,729
Victoria C	0.4	0.5	3.1	18.6	77.2	0.2	3,229
Wayland Baptist U	0.1	0.4	3.5	5.4	89.1	1.4	1,755
Weatherford C	2.1	0.1	3.2	0.5	91.5	2.5	2,040
West Texas St U	0.4	0.9	2.9	6.6	86.8	2.6	5,756
Western Texas C	0.1	0.1	4.2	9.2	86.0	0.3	966
Wharton County JC	0.1	0.6	10.6	15.9	72.3	0.4	2,553
Wiley C	0.0	0.0	97.0	0.3	0.3	2.4	369

UTAH

Stevens Henager C	1.4	0.5	4.2	3.8	90.1	0.0	212
Utah Higher Education Sys							
U of Utah	0.5	2.6	0.6	2.4	87.1	6.8	23,756
Utah St U	0.8	1.3	0.5	0.7	89.0	7.8	13,777
Southern Utah St C	3.0	0.6	0.6	0.7	94.6	0.5	2,952
Weber St C	0.5	2.0	1.1	2.0	92.9	1.3	12,146
C of Eastern Utah	10.5	0.0	0.8	4.6	84.1	0.0	2,210
Dixie C	1.6	1.0	1.0	1.0	94.8	0.6	2,166
Salt Lake CC	1.2	3.3	0.5	4.0	90.9	0.1	9,048
Snow C	1.2	1.7	0.9	0.8	87.6	7.8	1,544
Utah Valley CC	1.6	1.3	0.1	1.8	92.9	2.3	6,833
Westminster C of Salt Lake City	0.3	1.6	1.4	3.9	90.8	2.0	1,854

VERMONT

Bennington C	0.2	2.1	2.1	1.5	87.6	6.5	613
Burlington C	0.0	0.5	3.0	0.0	95.9	0.5	197
Champlain C	0.3	0.5	0.7	0.0	97.9	0.5	2,029
C of Saint Joseph	1.2	0.7	1.2	0.7	95.9	0.5	434
Goddard C	1.4	0.8	1.6	0.9	92.8	2.5	1,005
Green Mountain C	0.0	0.2	0.9	0.2	96.0	2.6	529
Landmark C	0.0	0.0	0.0	0.0	95.7	4.3	23
Marlboro C	0.0	0.4	0.8	0.8	94.6	3.3	240
Norwich U	0.6	1.5	2.2	1.9	91.8	2.0	2,488
Saint Michael's C	0.0	0.1	0.7	0.2	96.3	2.6	2,231
Sch for International Training	0.4	1.7	0.8	1.5	86.9	8.6	521
Southern Vermont C	0.2	0.8	1.3	0.8	95.9	1.1	635
Sterling C	0.0	0.0	1.5	0.0	96.9	1.5	65
Trinity C	0.2	0.5	0.3	0.4	98.7	0.0	1,043
U of Vermont	0.2	2.3	0.6	0.9	94.8	1.2	11,287
Vermont St C's Sys							
Castleton St C	0.1	0.3	0.4	0.3	98.7	0.2	1,803

VERMONT, cont.

	American Indian	Asian	Black	Hispanic	White	Foreign	Total
Vermont St C's Sys							
CC of Vermont	0.5%	0.3%	0.1%	0.2%	97.1%	1.7%	3,465
Johnson St C	0.2	0.2	0.1	0.3	98.3	1.0	1,547
Lyndon St C	0.0	0.1	0.3	0.2	99.1	0.4	1,125
Vermont Tech C	0.0	0.7	0.4	0.4	98.2	0.3	740

VIRGINIA

	American Indian	Asian	Black	Hispanic	White	Foreign	Total
Averett C	0.1	1.8	11.9	0.9	81.3	4.0	982
Bluefield C	0.0	1.6	4.4	0.0	92.1	1.9	366
Bridgewater C	0.1	1.1	2.4	0.5	94.7	1.2	973
Christendom C	0.0	0.0	0.0	1.3	93.7	5.0	159
Christopher Newport C	0.4	1.4	10.7	0.9	86.3	0.3	4,647
C of William and Mary	0.1	2.4	5.9	0.9	87.7	3.1	7,372
Richard Bland C	0.6	2.0	18.3	1.7	76.8	0.6	1,015
Community Hospital of Roanoke Valley C of Health Sciences	0.0	0.0	11.6	0.0	88.4	0.0	181
Commonwealth C	0.0	0.5	66.3	0.0	32.2	1.0	202
Commonwealth C Hampton	0.0	1.9	64.3	0.0	33.9	0.0	322
Commonwealth C Virginia Beach	0.0	0.8	14.3	4.4	80.5	0.0	502
Eastern Mennonite C	0.0	0.6	2.0	0.8	91.5	5.1	1,049
Eastern Va Medical Sch of the Medical C of Hampton Roads	0.0	9.6	6.7	1.3	82.4	0.0	448
Emory and Henry C	0.0	0.4	2.5	0.0	97.1	0.0	788
Ferrum C	0.4	0.6	6.8	1.2	90.1	0.9	1,206
George Mason U	0.4	6.5	4.8	2.6	82.4	3.4	18,965
Hampden-Sydney C	0.1	0.5	1.6	0.5	97.2	0.0	937
Hampton U	0.1	0.2	91.3	0.1	6.0	2.3	5,305
Hollins C	0.0	0.2	2.0	0.4	96.6	0.8	1,063
Inst of Textile Tech	0.0	0.0	2.9	2.9	94.3	0.0	35
James Madison U	0.1	1.5	7.8	1.2	89.1	0.3	10,906
Liberty U	0.1	0.2	4.4	0.5	93.6	1.2	10,902
Longwood C	0.2	1.5	8.7	0.4	88.8	0.4	3,042
Lynchburg C	0.1	0.5	4.9	0.3	91.9	2.2	2,447
Mary Baldwin C	0.2	0.8	3.4	0.8	92.9	1.9	1,186
Mary Washington C	0.1	1.3	3.4	1.0	93.3	0.9	3,427
Marymount U	0.2	4.3	7.2	3.3	78.1	7.0	2,977
Norfolk St U	0.2	0.4	84.6	0.3	12.7	1.8	8,123
Old Dominion U	0.5	3.0	9.8	1.2	82.9	2.7	16,364
Presbyterian Sch of Christian Education	0.0	3.8	3.8	0.0	74.5	17.9	106
Protestant Episcopal Theol Sem in Va	0.0	0.0	3.2	0.5	93.1	3.2	218
Radford U	0.3	1.2	3.1	0.9	92.9	1.7	8,764
Randolph-Macon C	0.0	1.2	1.9	0.4	95.3	1.3	1,117
Randolph-Macon Woman's C	0.1	0.8	2.5	1.1	92.2	3.2	746
Roanoke C	0.2	0.8	1.5	0.2	97.1	0.3	1,594
Saint Paul's C	0.0	0.0	97.3	0.0	1.6	1.1	555
Shenandoah C and Conservatory of Music	0.1	2.7	7.5	0.5	89.2	0.0	1,007
Southern Sem C	0.3	0.3	1.0	0.7	94.7	3.0	302
Sweet Briar C	0.0	0.2	4.5	0.7	90.2	4.3	553
Union Theological Sem in Va	0.0	2.7	2.2	0.5	88.7	5.9	186
U of Richmond	0.2	0.9	3.3	0.6	94.5	0.4	4,948

	American Indian	Asian	Black	Hispanic	White	Foreign	Total
U of Virginia							
Main	0.0%	3.7%	7.6%	0.6%	85.3%	2.8%	20,802
Clinch Valley	0.1	0.3	1.2	0.4	97.8	0.2	1,688
Virginia Commonwealth U	0.4	2.7	13.1	1.0	81.6	1.2	20,645
Virginia CC Sys							
Blue Ridge CC	0.2	0.5	2.9	0.3	96.1	0.0	2,483
Central Virginia CC	0.1	0.3	13.1	0.1	86.3	0.0	3,721
Dabney S Lancaster CC	0.1	0.1	5.4	0.2	94.3	0.0	1,277
Danville CC	0.2	0.1	19.7	0.2	79.8	0.0	2,680
Eastern Shore CC	0.2	0.4	19.5	0.4	79.4	0.0	456
Germanna CC	0.3	0.4	7.6	0.8	90.7	0.2	2,250
J Sargeant Reynolds CC	0.5	1.6	23.4	0.5	73.7	0.3	9,747
John Tyler CC	0.1	1.1	19.1	0.9	78.1	0.7	4,243
Lord Fairfax CC	0.2	0.4	2.7	0.2	96.5	0.0	2,473
Mountain Empire CC	0.0	0.1	1.4	0.0	98.4	0.0	2,350
New River CC	0.1	0.4	4.0	0.2	95.1	0.2	3,044
Northern Virginia CC	0.4	7.7	8.0	3.9	78.0	2.0	31,896
Patrick Henry CC	0.3	0.3	13.1	0.1	86.2	0.0	1,726
Paul D Camp CC	0.1	0.5	29.8	0.3	68.9	0.3	966
Piedmont Virginia CC	0.1	1.0	8.6	0.5	89.4	0.3	4,053
Rappahannock CC	0.6	0.1	17.4	0.3	81.6	0.1	1,559
Southside Virginia CC	0.2	0.3	34.1	0.4	64.9	0.1	2,416
Southwest Virginia CC	0.0	0.1	1.1	0.0	98.7	0.0	4,082
Thomas Nelson CC	0.4	2.1	22.2	1.2	73.9	0.2	6,640
Tidewater CC	0.3	4.9	12.3	1.3	80.1	1.1	16,557
Virginia Highlands CC	0.1	0.1	2.6	0.1	97.2	0.0	1,975
Virginia Western CC	0.1	0.8	7.5	0.2	91.3	0.1	6,755
Wytheville CC	0.2	0.1	3.2	0.0	96.5	0.1	1,843
Virginia Intermont C	0.0	1.1	3.1	0.9	90.9	4.0	450
Virginia Military Inst	0.1	3.0	6.6	1.6	87.0	1.8	1,285
Virginia Polytechnic Inst and St U	0.1	4.2	3.6	0.9	85.5	5.7	24,280
Virginia St U	0.1	0.4	88.4	0.2	10.3	0.6	3,855
Virginia Union U	0.2	0.0	98.5	0.2	0.8	0.4	1,248
Virginia Wesleyan C	0.4	1.4	5.0	0.9	91.2	1.1	1,261
Washington and Lee U	0.1	1.1	3.1	0.5	94.8	0.4	1,971
WASHINGTON							
Antioch C Seattle	1.3	0.3	1.9	0.3	93.6	2.7	376
Art Inst of Seattle	0.3	3.2	3.1	3.0	89.4	0.9	1,269
Bellevue CC	0.3	4.4	1.0	0.8	93.3	0.2	9,138
Big Bend CC	0.8	1.7	0.4	6.3	83.1	7.7	1,843
Central Washington U	1.2	2.8	1.6	2.7	90.3	1.3	7,109
Centralia C	1.7	0.8	3.9	1.5	92.0	0.1	3,372
Clark C	1.3	2.9	1.0	1.2	93.5	0.1	7,460
Cogswell C North	0.0	8.1	1.0	1.4	89.5	0.0	210
Columbia Basin C	0.6	2.2	0.4	2.2	94.6	0.0	5,186
Cornish C of the Arts	1.0	2.3	2.5	2.7	89.1	2.5	521
Edmonds CC	1.4	3.3	2.9	1.9	90.4	0.1	7,059
Everett CC	1.9	3.2	0.8	1.2	92.8	0.2	6,636
Evergreen St C	1.6	3.3	3.6	1.9	88.5	1.2	3,165
Gonzaga U	1.0	3.6	0.6	2.1	88.8	3.7	3,592
Grays Harbor C	3.5	0.8	0.4	0.7	94.4	0.3	2,132
Green River CC	1.2	2.3	1.1	1.3	94.1	0.0	5,421
Griffin C	0.1	4.7	8.3	2.5	79.6	4.8	1,756
Heritage C	23.0	4.0	2.1	17.2	52.2	1.6	379

WASHINGTON, cont.

	American Indian	Asian	Black	Hispanic	White	Foreign	Total
Highline CC	1.3%	6.7%	2.9%	2.1%	86.0%	0.9%	7,368
Lower Columbia C	0.7	1.0	0.2	0.8	97.2	0.0	3,163
Lutheran Bible Inst of Seattle	0.0	2.9	2.2	0.0	91.2	3.7	136
Olympic C	1.6	4.8	2.9	2.0	88.7	0.1	5,601
Pacific Lutheran U	0.6	2.9	1.4	1.1	87.6	6.3	3,970
Peninsula C	3.6	1.5	1.2	1.8	90.7	1.2	2,669
Pierce C	1.5	5.4	9.1	3.3	80.3	0.5	7,715
Puget Sound Christian C	0.0	2.3	2.3	1.1	93.2	1.1	88
Saint Martin's C	0.6	5.2	5.7	2.6	82.8	3.2	1,200
Seattle CC Dist							
North Seattle CC	0.9	10.7	2.6	2.0	83.7	0.1	6,485
Seattle Central CC	2.0	16.7	12.4	2.3	66.5	0.1	5,886
South Seattle CC	2.1	13.3	5.7	2.0	76.6	0.2	5,335
Seattle Pacific U	0.8	2.9	0.9	0.8	89.0	5.6	3,356
Shoreline CC	0.9	7.8	0.9	1.3	88.7	0.4	6,485
Skagit Valley C	1.6	2.4	0.7	2.4	92.8	0.1	5,092
South Puget Sound CC	1.7	4.2	1.0	1.9	91.3	0.0	3,655
Tacoma CC	1.5	6.1	7.3	2.0	83.0	0.0	4,503
U of Puget Sound	0.6	4.5	1.3	1.2	91.8	0.7	4,234
U of Washington	1.0	12.6	3.1	2.1	76.5	4.8	33,460
Walla Walla C	0.5	2.8	1.8	3.4	85.4	6.2	1,428
Walla Walla CC	1.5	1.1	7.5	3.7	85.8	0.3	4,093
Washington St CC Dist							
Spokane CC	1.9	2.2	0.7	1.2	93.9	0.1	6,242
Spokane Falls CC	2.2	2.4	1.5	2.2	91.4	0.3	10,345
Washington St U	0.8	3.8	1.8	1.2	86.2	6.1	16,405
Wenatchee Valley C	6.2	1.1	1.0	1.8	89.8	0.1	2,147
Western Washington U	0.9	2.6	1.0	1.2	93.1	1.2	9,837
Whatcom CC	2.1	1.7	0.6	1.2	94.2	0.2	2,252
Whitman C	0.1	5.8	0.7	1.4	89.7	2.3	1,284
Whitworth C	0.4	2.6	0.9	0.8	92.6	2.8	1,840
Yakima Valley CC	4.0	1.5	1.5	7.3	85.6	0.1	3,750

WEST VIRGINIA

	American Indian	Asian	Black	Hispanic	White	Foreign	Total
Alderson Broaddus C	0.0	1.0	3.7	0.5	91.6	3.2	728
Appalachian Bible C	0.0	2.7	2.2	1.1	93.4	0.5	182
Beckley C	0.0	0.5	5.7	0.3	93.5	0.0	1,605
Davis & Elkins C	1.6	2.4	2.3	1.4	90.2	2.0	789
Huntington JC of Business	0.0	0.2	6.0	0.2	93.5	0.0	448
Ohio Valley C	0.0	0.0	4.5	0.0	93.2	2.3	221
Parkersburg CC	0.1	0.2	0.3	0.1	98.7	0.5	3,219
Salem-Teikyo U							
Main	0.2	0.9	12.2	3.9	79.3	3.5	564
Clarksburg	0.0	0.0	6.6	0.0	93.4	0.0	166
U of Charleston	0.4	0.5	3.3	0.7	92.9	2.2	1,528
U of West Virginia Sys							
Marshall U	0.2	0.6	3.0	0.4	94.9	0.9	12,350
C of Graduate Studies	0.1	0.7	3.4	0.4	94.9	0.6	2,596
West Virginia U	0.1	1.5	2.6	0.5	91.2	4.2	18,746
Potomac St C	0.1	0.3	5.1	0.1	94.4	0.1	1,081
West Virginia Sch of							
Osteopathic Medicine	0.4	3.0	2.2	1.7	91.8	0.9	232
West Virginia St C Sys							
Bluefield St C	0.1	0.1	8.5	0.1	90.5	0.7	2,487
Concord C	0.2	0.9	4.2	0.1	94.6	0.0	2,450

	American Indian	Asian	Black	Hispanic	White	Foreign	Total
West Virginia St C Sys							
Fairmont St C	0.2%	0.2%	2.0%	0.4%	97.2%	0.0%	5,758
Glenville St C	0.0	0.2	1.7	0.0	96.7	1.3	2,205
Shepherd C	0.3	0.1	2.4	0.4	96.7	0.0	4,010
West Liberty St C	0.1	0.2	2.0	0.3	96.9	0.5	2,435
West Virginia Inst of Tech	0.2	0.5	6.3	1.2	87.1	4.7	2,955
West Virginia St C	0.1	0.5	11.8	0.4	87.0	0.2	4,509
Southern West Virginia CC	0.1	0.1	1.9	0.1	97.8	0.0	2,688
West Virginia Northern CC	0.0	0.2	2.9	0.3	96.1	0.5	2,660
West Virginia Wesleyan C	0.3	0.9	3.7	0.6	92.3	2.2	1,484
Wheeling Jesuit C	0.2	1.1	0.9	0.2	95.0	2.6	1,206

WISCONSIN

	American Indian	Asian	Black	Hispanic	White	Foreign	Total
Alverno C	0.5	0.8	11.5	3.2	83.9	0.2	2,191
Bellin C of Nursing	3.5	0.0	0.0	0.0	96.5	0.0	143
Beloit C	0.1	2.9	2.2	1.1	88.9	4.7	1,203
Blackhawk Tech C	0.2	0.6	2.2	0.6	96.4	0.0	1,738
Cardinal Stritch C	0.2	1.1	5.9	0.8	92.0	0.0	3,044
Carroll C	0.4	0.7	2.2	1.3	94.9	0.5	2,202
Carthage C	0.1	0.5	4.7	1.4	93.1	0.3	1,842
Chippewa Valley Tech C	0.6	0.6	0.0	0.1	98.6	0.0	3,407
Concordia U	2.9	0.9	5.3	0.3	89.0	1.6	1,175
Edgewood C	0.1	0.8	0.6	0.4	95.0	3.2	1,076
Fox Valley Tech C	0.8	1.3	0.3	0.8	96.7	0.0	3,906
Gateway Tech C	0.7	1.0	5.3	1.6	90.9	0.6	8,153
Inst of Paper Science and Tech	0.0	0.0	0.0	0.0	91.2	8.8	68
Lakeland C	0.2	0.7	5.1	1.1	92.2	0.7	1,535
Lakeshore Tech C	0.3	1.3	0.0	0.2	98.2	0.0	2,352
Lawrence U	0.2	1.5	1.9	0.2	93.4	2.8	1,231
Madison Area Tech C	0.4	0.8	1.9	1.0	95.5	0.4	10,611
Madison Business C	0.0	0.0	0.0	0.0	99.5	0.5	374
Maranatha Baptist Bible C	0.2	2.2	1.7	2.0	93.4	0.4	458
Marian C of Fond Du Lac	0.3	0.7	2.5	0.7	95.6	0.1	869
Marquette U	0.3	3.5	2.9	2.9	86.1	4.2	12,142
Medical C of Wisconsin	0.2	12.6	1.5	3.2	80.8	1.6	849
Mid-State Tech C	0.4	0.5	0.1	0.4	98.5	0.1	2,219
Milwaukee Area Tech C	0.7	1.8	17.7	2.8	76.9	0.1	19,693
Milwaukee Inst of Art and Design	0.6	1.5	2.1	1.1	94.2	0.4	466
Milwaukee Sch of Engineering	0.2	2.3	2.0	1.2	93.2	1.0	2,808
Moraine Park Tech C	0.4	0.9	0.2	0.4	98.1	0.0	4,921
Mount Mary C	0.4	0.7	3.4	1.2	92.8	1.5	1,367
Mount Senario C	14.4	1.9	2.8	1.1	78.7	1.1	1,701
Nashotah House	0.0	0.0	5.4	3.6	83.9	7.1	56
Nicolet Area Tech C	3.1	0.5	0.6	0.3	95.5	0.0	1,311
North Central Voc-Tech Adult Ed Dist	0.9	0.9	0.1	0.2	97.3	0.5	3,489
Northeast Wisconsin Tech C	1.7	1.1	0.1	0.3	96.8	0.0	5,558
Northland C	9.1	1.2	1.4	2.2	84.4	1.7	647
Northwestern C	0.0	0.0	0.0	0.0	100.0	0.0	202
Ripon C	0.2	1.3	0.7	0.9	93.8	3.0	857
Sacred Heart Sch of Theology	0.8	0.8	0.0	4.6	86.2	7.7	130
Saint Norbert C	0.8	0.3	0.4	0.5	97.7	0.3	1,827
Silver Lake C	0.1	0.6	0.0	0.4	98.6	0.3	790

	American Indian	Asian	Black	Hispanic	White	Foreign	Total
WISCONSIN, cont.							
Stratton C	1.5%	0.5%	27.6%	5.3%	65.1%	0.0%	601
U of Wisconsin							
Madison	0.4	2.6	1.7	1.5	87.4	6.4	43,364
Eau Claire	0.3	0.6	0.4	0.3	96.8	1.6	11,038
Green Bay	1.7	0.5	0.7	0.4	95.4	1.2	5,221
La Crosse	0.3	0.7	0.7	0.4	97.1	0.8	9,242
Oshkosh	0.5	1.1	1.2	0.6	95.7	0.9	11,209
Milwaukee	0.7	1.7	5.9	2.2	86.5	2.9	25,212
Parkside	0.2	1.2	3.2	2.5	92.3	0.5	5,172
Platteville	0.3	0.7	0.6	0.4	97.0	1.0	5,334
River Falls	0.3	0.6	1.0	0.4	96.8	0.9	5,544
Stevens Point	0.9	0.7	0.6	0.4	95.4	2.1	9,318
Stout	0.4	1.4	0.9	0.6	95.1	1.5	7,597
Superior	1.6	0.9	1.4	0.4	94.2	1.6	2,437
Whitewater	0.2	0.7	2.4	1.0	94.8	1.0	10,458
Centers	0.4	0.7	1.1	0.8	96.3	0.6	11,184
Viterbo C	0.5	0.8	1.2	0.4	97.2	0.0	1,060
Waukesha County Tech C	0.2	0.3	0.2	1.1	98.0	0.1	4,424
Western Wisconsin Tech C	0.3	1.1	0.1	0.2	98.3	0.0	3,452
Wisconsin Indianhead Tech C	3.0	0.3	0.3	0.3	96.2	0.0	3,157
Wisconsin Lutheran C	0.0	0.0	1.8	0.4	96.4	1.3	224
WYOMING							
Casper C	0.5	0.2	0.8	1.2	97.1	0.2	3,471
Central Wyoming C	10.8	0.2	0.6	1.7	86.3	0.4	1,406
Eastern Wyoming C	0.8	0.1	1.0	2.1	96.0	0.0	1,362
Laramie County CC	0.8	0.6	2.7	4.3	91.6	0.0	3,676
Northwest C	0.3	0.0	0.3	1.7	96.5	1.2	1,739
Sheridan C	0.7	0.2	0.5	0.7	97.4	0.6	1,980
U of Wyoming	1.3	0.2	0.8	2.2	91.2	4.2	10,773
Western Wyoming CC	0.6	0.9	0.9	5.0	92.6	0.1	1,504
Wyoming Tech Inst	0.3	0.6	0.5	5.4	93.2	0.0	629

The Chronicle of Higher Education

EDITOR Corbin Gwaltney

MANAGING EDITOR Malcolm G. Scully **ASSOCIATE EDITOR** Edward R. Weidlein

ASSOCIATE MANAGING EDITORS Cheryl M. Fields (Point of View & Opinion), Paul Desruisseaux (International), Scott Jaschik (National)
NEWS EDITOR Robin Wilson
SENIOR EDITORS Rose Engelland (Photography), Jean Evangelauf (Statistics), Catherine J. Hosley (Editorial Operations), Douglas Lederman (Athletics), Kim A. McDonald (Scholarship), Liz McMillen (Business & Philanthropy), Carolyn J. Mooney (Personal & Professional), Peter H. Stafford (Art Director), Edith U. Taylor (Gazette), Beverly T. Watkins (Information Technology)
SENIOR WRITERS Lawrence Biemiller, Ellen K. Coughlin, Robert L. Jacobson
ASSOCIATE SENIOR EDITOR Gail Lewin (Section 2)
COPY EDITOR Brian Manning
ASSISTANT EDITORS Nina C. Ayoub, Debra E. Blum, Goldie Blumenstyk, Mary Crystal Cage, Michele N-K Collison, Colleen Cordes, Thomas J. DeLoughry, Susan Dodge, Courtney Leatherman, Denise K. Magner, Julie L. Nicklin, Frances H. Oxholm, Chris Raymond, Jean Rosenblatt, Lora Thompson, David L. Wheeler, David L. Wilson
ASSISTANT ART DIRECTOR Ellen Verdon
EDITORIAL ASSISTANTS Stephen Burd, Michael R. Snyder, Esther S. Washington, Anne Millar Wiebe
ART ASSISTANT Carl T. Benson
STUDENT ASSISTANTS Michael M. Brown, Jaemin Kim, Hope Anne Nathan, Robert R. Schmidt, Jr., Sara Sklaroff

PRODUCTION AND COMPUTER DIRECTOR Gerard A. Lindgren
MANAGERS Cynthia J. Kennedy, Steve Smith
ASSISTANT PRODUCTION MANAGER Timothy A. Steele
PRODUCTION ASSOCIATES Pamela Barton, Brenda Hulme, Carol E. King, Pegeen McGlathery, David N. Miller, Charles E. Short, E. Day Wilkes

EDITORIAL AND BUSINESS OFFICES 1255 Twenty-Third Street, N.W., Washington, D.C. 20037, (202) 466-1000